The Holy Spirit and Higher Education

The Holy Spirit and Higher Education

Renewing the Christian University

Amos Yong & Dale M. Coulter

BAYLOR UNIVERSITY PRESS

Front cover and book design by Kasey McBeath, cover layout by *the*BookDesigners
Cover images: Unsplash/Nathan Dumlao, Thaï Ch. Hamelin

The Library of Congress has cataloged this book under ISBN 978-1-4813-1814-3.

Library of Congress Control Number: 2023932228

Dedicated to

Our children (Dale's):
Anna "Bella" Isabella Coulter, Sophia Grace Coulter, and Christian Michael Coulter

and grandchildren (Amos'):
Serenity Joy Yong, Valor Amoz Yong, Rio Joseph Yong, Kairo Ricardo Yong,
Isabel Sage Simonson, and Xander Cole Simonson

to whom the future of higher education belongs

Contents

II | What Difference *Can* the Holy Spirit Make?
Constructive Reenvisioning

Preface and Acknowledgments

Unexpected disruptions—intrainstitutional issues, institutional traditions, and other life circumstances—have resulted in this project dating back over a decade to the summer of 2011, when we were colleagues at the School of Divinity at Regent University. Although both of us were then teaching graduate-level seminarians, this was in a university context with a half dozen other schools, and both of us had taught at the undergraduate level for years before converging at Regent (Amos from 1999–2005 at Bethel University in St. Paul, Minnesota, and Dale from 1999–2007 at Lee University in Cleveland, Tennessee). Upon comparing notes and after conversation, we dreamt up this joint project, with Dale crafting the historical narrative (what turned out to be part 1 of this book) and Amos the constructive vision (part 2). Having both also been lifelong participants in pentecostal churches and denominations (Amos with the Assemblies of God and International Church of the Foursquare Gospel, and Dale with the Church of God, Cleveland, Tennessee), we initially were motivated to see how we might contribute to and advance the then emerging literature on pentecostal institutions of higher education. However, especially given our own ecumenically inclined theological horizons, we quickly also wondered how our pentecostally inspired perspective might revitalize the Christian higher educational endeavor more broadly. Our long histories and experiences of schools in the Council of Christian Colleges and Universities network also encouraged us to write for this wider audience.

As the vagaries of life have kept us from completing this book sooner than we would have liked, over the last decade, both of us have incurred many debts:

- Our former dean, Michael Palmer, for allowing Amos to work from a distance at Biola University in the spring of 2012 and for giving Dale a course release in 2012–2013 to work on the book;

- Gregg Ten Elshof, Steve Porter, and Tom Crisp at Biola University's Center for Christian Thought (CCT) for their inviting Amos to be one of four external fellows at the CCT inaugural semester in the spring of 2012, from out of which he wrote (and they published) "The Holy Spirit and the Christian University: The Renewal of Evangelical Higher Education," in *Christian Scholarship in the Twenty-First Century: Prospects and Perils*, edited by Thomas M. Crisp, Steve L. Porter, and Gregg A. Ten Elshof (Grand Rapids: Eerdmans, 2014), 163–80 (gratitude to Eerdmans for allowing adaptation of a few sections for the introductory chapter of the present volume);

- CCT staff Todd Vasquez and Rachel Dee, (then) graduate assistant Evan Rosa, and other spring 2012 fellows—Jonathan Anderson, Liz Hall, Natasha Duquette, and Brad Christerson from Biola, and Dariusz Bryćko (now Erskine Theological Seminary), George Hunsinger (Princeton Seminary), and Craig Slane (Simpson University), as external fellows—whose work and conversational input facilitated Amos' fellowship and research on his part of the book;

- Individuals at various institutions and organizations for giving us the opportunity to share about the project and its ideas with others engaged with the task of Christian higher education and thereby develop them before committing to writing:
  - Jared Wielfaert at Lee University, Cleveland, Tennessee (April 8, 2011), for inviting Dale to speak at the Colloquium on Christianity and Culture on "*Studia Humanitatis*: Pentecostalism, the Liberal Arts, and Christian Humanism";
  - Jamie Huff and Jeff Hittenberger at Vanguard University, Costa Mesa, California (February 7, 2012), for inviting Amos' talk "What Difference Does the Holy Spirit Make at a Christian University? The Renewal of Christian Higher Education in the 21st Century";
  - Martin Mittelstadt at Evangel University, Springfield, Missouri (November 1, 2012), for inviting Amos' lecture "Pentecostals and Christian Higher Education: New Wine for the 21st Century";
  - Ulrik Josefsson at the Academy for Leadership and Theology, Stockholm, Sweden (January 9, 2013), for inviting Amos' exhortation "The Pastoral Vocation, Spirit-Empowerment and the Life of the Mind";
  - Andrew Picard and colleagues from Carey Baptist College and Laidlaw Centre for Church Leadership, Auckland, New Zealand (July 4, 2013), for welcoming Amos' seminar on "Pentecostal Leadership, Spirit-Empowerment and the Life of the Mind";
  - Dan Hedges and Tammy Dunahoo at Foursquare National Education Symposium, Life Pacific College, San Dimas, California (March 2, 2016), for inviting Amos' keynote, "The Life in the Spirit and the Life of the Mind: Luke 10:25-29," which was later transcribed and published as chapter 12 in Amos' *The Kerygmatic Spirit: Apostolic Preaching in the 21st Century*, edited by Josh Samuel, commentary and afterword by Tony Richie (Eugene: Cascade, 2018).
  - Shane Clifton at Alphacrucis College, Parramatta, Australia (August 17–18, 2017), for inviting Amos' series of lectures "Finding the Holy Spirit at a Christian University: Renewing Christian Higher Education";

- Fr. Bryan Wandel, curator of the Nickel City Forum, Buffalo, New York (March 1, 2018), for inviting Amos to speak on "Charismatic Spirituality and the Life of the Mind: An Alternative Model of the Intellectual Life?";
- L. William (Bill) Oliverio at SUM Bible College and Seminary, El Dorado Hills, California (April 16–17, 2019), for inviting Amos to a discussion on "Christian Higher Education and Theological Education after Pentecost";
- Eric Lopez at Life Pacific University, San Dimas, California (January 16, 2020), for inviting Amos to speak on "Theology and Education in Pentecostal Communities," at their Bi-Annual Master of Arts in Theological Studies Lectures, and who, along with his colleagues Michael Salmeier and Doretha O'Quinn, also provided responses to the presentation;
- Jennifer Wasmuth at the Institute for Ecumenical Research, Strasbourg (July 7, 2021), for inviting Dale to speak at their summer seminar on the "Primacy of Spirituality: Pentecostalism, Ecumenism, and Mysticism," which gave him the opportunity to tease out ideas on Pentecostalism, mysticism, and populism.

- Amos' graduate assistants, Vince Le (Regent University) and Hoon Jung (Fuller Theological Seminary), for helping with the research and other matters, and Fuller Seminary School of Mission & Theology student office assistant Mike Shetler for help with the volume indexing;
- Amos' former graduate student Daniel Topf, for reading the manuscript and providing me feedback on its various parts (congratulations, Daniel, for finishing your own PhD Intercultural Studies thesis under my supervision and publishing that before this book: *Pentecostal Higher Education: History, Current Practices, and Future Prospects*, in Palgrave/Springer's Christianity and Renewal—Interdisciplinary Studies series [2021]);
- Dale's graduate assistant, Bob Smith (Regent University), for assistance with the initial research on ancient education in Hellenism;
- Feedback provided to Dale from Daniel Castello of Duke Divinity School, Hans Boersma of Nashotah House Theological Seminary, and Mark Hutchinson of Alphacrucis College;
- Shirley Mullen, Perry Glanzer, and William Kay, for reading the version of the manuscript that led to its penultimate form, and providing pages of very helpful critical and constructive feedback that helped strengthen the work variously.

There are undoubtedly others we should have acknowledged; the above provides only some preliminary indication of the debts we have incurred over the years in the formulation of this book.

Thanks to the wonderful staff at Baylor University Press for their enthusiasm about this book and professional handling of the copyediting and production process. David Aycock and Cade Jarrell and the Press team have been extremely patient, not to mention a joy to work with, and John Morris was a copyeditor extraordinaire to whom we are grateful.

Our spouses, Esther Coulter and Alma Yong, have lived with this book as long as we have. Their patience across the long arc of this book is real and has been sustaining for us at every turn, not least the institutional transitions both our families undertook at different points during the time of writing this book. Their love, prayers, and support have carried us through the twists and turns of the academic vocation that we write about here. You, the reader, should realize that this book you hold in your hands is as much to their credit as it is to us.

But we take full responsibility for any errors of fact or interpretation in the following pages; none of those named above are to be faulted for the shortcomings of this book.

Unless otherwise noted, all scriptural quotations will be from the New Revised Standard Version of the Bible, all rights reserved.

1

Introduction

The Spirit Says Go! Toward a Pentecost-Theology
of Christian Higher Education

This is a long book, but its basic message is very simple: Christian higher education can be revitalized in the present conflicted time similar to how Christian formation has been effectuated in the past, through attentiveness to the triune God's redemptive work, especially via the person and work of the Holy Spirit. Being centered on the formation of the person, education concerns the cultivation of a *habitus* that shapes and orients the individual toward the proper ends for human flourishing. In Christian terms, education is about being Christ-shaped and Spirit-infused. Christ is the pattern, while the Spirit is the transforming presence driving the educational process. This introductory chapter will describe the genesis of the basic theological idea, specify and clarify its Pentecost-related character, and then map the two parts of the argument.

1.1 WHAT DIFFERENCE DOES THE HOLY SPIRIT MAKE? A PENTECOSTAL SPRINGBOARD

Both of us come from and have been affiliated with and ministered in classical pentecostal churches[1]—the Church of God (Cleveland, Tennessee), the Assemblies of God, and the International Church of the Foursquare Gospel, more specifically—our entire lives. As such, our scholarly work has been motivated by our bringing pentecostal-related questions and perspectives to bear on a range of historical and theological issues. Having also, between us, taught at three different universities in North America, all member schools of the Council of Christian Colleges and Universities (CCCU), we have been thinking theologically about Christian higher education for the length of this tenure stretching back over two decades. Our pentecostal background and experience have led us to ask the question that is hinted at in the title of this book: what difference can or should the Holy Spirit make in a Christian university?

---

[1] Throughout this book we do not capitalize *pentecostal* when used adjectivally, but do when referring to proper names or used as nouns; for this practice, and for discussion of *classical Pentecostalism* as describing the group of churches or denominations with roots in the Azusa Street revival at the beginning of the twentieth century, see Amos Yong, *The Spirit Poured Out on All Flesh: Pentecostalism and the Possibility of Global Theology* (Grand Rapids: Baker Academic, 2005), 14–18.

At first blush, this might seem an odd question. Yet it is only two steps removed from the overall oddity in our present age of thinking theologically about higher education to begin with. Early in the final decade of the preceding century, the appearance of *The Search for God at Harvard* caught the attention of onlookers precisely because it was presumed that God belonged only, if anywhere, in private spaces, and surely not since the deity had been excised (some might say *exorcised*!) from the university during the modern era.[2] To be sure, this was a personalized account of a year-long sojourn through Harvard Divinity School, and it may well have been that the divinity faculty, more scholars of the world's religions than (confessional) theologians, would have been embarrassed that God was to be found in its hallways. Yet the author, an Orthodox Jew, found spiritual renewal and revitalization, not just intellectual stimulation and discovery. So much so that the publication a few years later of another volume, *Finding God at Harvard*, was no longer surprising.[3] And if God could be encountered at Harvard, then why not at other, even secularized, universities, colleges, and places of higher learning?[4] That the God phenomenon was more prevalent at the turn of the century may have been due to the efforts of Christians to prompt inquiry for and attentiveness to the divine manifestation, but regardless of why, deity was no longer perceived as absent from these spaces of serious scholarly inquiry.

Now for those who teach, administer, or work in specifically Christian colleges and universities—our primary audience—not only is it presumed that God is present in these spaces but his Son, Jesus Christ, is pervasively active through the Spirit. Many evangelically oriented institutions of higher education, especially those affiliated with (or seeking formal ties to) the CCCU, are explicitly committed to advancing "the cause of *Christ-centered higher education* and to help our institutions transform lives by faithfully relating scholarship and service to biblical truth."[5] On the one hand, Christian colleges and universities have been growing, providing a faith-filled option for believing families to send their children.[6] On the other hand, there has been a perennial temptation of

---

[2]   Ari L. Goldman, *The Search for God at Harvard* (New York: Ballantine Books, 1992). For more on the secularization of the university, see, e.g., Russell Kirk, *Decadence and Renewal in the Higher Learning: An Episodic History of American University and College since 1953* (South Bend, Ind.: Gateway, 1978); Page Smith, *Killing the Spirit: Higher Education in America* (New York: Viking, 1990); George M. Marsden, *The Soul of the American University Revisited: From Protestant to Postsecular* (New York: Oxford University Press, 2021); Jeffrey Hart, *Smiling through the Cultural Catastrophe: Toward the Revival of Higher Education* (New Haven: Yale University Press, 2001); Melanie M. Morey and John J. Piderit, S.J., *Catholic Higher Education: A Culture in Crisis* (Oxford: Oxford University Press, 2006); and C. John Sommerville, *The Decline of the Secular University* (Oxford: Oxford University Press, 2006).

[3]   See Kelly Monroe, ed., *Finding God at Harvard: Spiritual Journeys of Christian Thinkers* (Grand Rapids: Zondervan, 1996).

[4]   Kelly Monroe Kullberg, *Finding God beyond Harvard: The Quest for Veritas* (Downers Grove: IVP, 2009), and Trent Sheppard, *God on Campus: Sacred Causes and Global Effects* (Downers Grove: IVP, 2009).

[5]   This is the stated mission of the CCCU; see http://www.cccu.org/about (emphasis added); see also David L. McKenna, *Christ-Centered Higher Education: Memory, Meaning, and Momentum for the Twenty-First Century* (Eugene: Cascade, 2012), and Duane Litfin, *Conceiving a Christian College* (Grand Rapids: Eerdmans, 2004), chs. 3–4.

[6]   See William C. Ringenberg, *The Christian College: A History of Protestant Higher Education in America*, 2nd ed. (Grand Rapids: Baker Academic, 2006), esp. chs. 6–7; Naomi Schaefer Riley, *God on the Quad: How Religious Colleges and the Missionary Generation Are Changing America* (Chicago: Ivan R. Dee, 2006); and Samuel Schuman, *Seeing the Light: Religious Colleges in Twenty-First-Century America* (Baltimore:

secularization even for these institutions, even as more recently demographic trends indicate lesser demand in the midterm future.[7] Hence leading Christian educational theorists have been calling for a recommitment to the theological underpinnings of Christian formation, including reemphasizing the import of a Christ-animated approach in Christian colleges and universities.[8] For these educators, the answer to the question about whether God makes a difference for Christian higher education is both *yes* and that this happens specifically through Jesus Christ.[9]

As pentecostal believers, theologians, and Christian higher educators, including with experience in universities friendly to pentecostal-charismatic constituencies as well as formally affiliated with classical pentecostal denominations, of course we agree that God *in Christ* makes a difference, otherwise there is no point in having specifically Christian options in the higher educational realm. To the degree that pentecostal churches have founded Bible institutes and these have become colleges over time and, more recently, have also evolved into universities,[10] these schools and institutions have grown into membership with the CCCU and embrace its basic tenets, including its Christ-centeredness and biblical commitments. It is surely the case that the quest for regional accreditation has led many in these pentecostal-charismatic colleges and universities to follow the lead of others with longer histories in this network of institutions. The point is that in many important respects, CCCU member schools are more alike than not, seeking to provide a higher educational alternative to the secular university and in that respect, guided by specifically Christian commitments, including fundamental theological notions such as those related to devotion to Christ and pursuit of discipleship in his way.

Yet if all Christian colleges and universities were exactly alike, why attend one affiliated with pentecostal churches or charismatic movements? This relates to the question that prominent Christian higher educational theorists have asked in this way: "Is there really Baptist, Catholic, or Quaker teaching," or are there unique contributions of particular theological traditions in the Christian higher educational enterprise?[11] While the initial question is more pedagogically focused, the broader query remains: what difference

---

Johns Hopkins University Press, 2010). For reflections on the successes experienced, see Samuel Joeckel and Thomas Chesnes, eds., *The Christian College Phenomenon: Inside America's Fastest Growing Institutions of Higher Learning* (Abilene: Abilene Christian University Press, 2012).

[7] On the former front, see James Tunstead Burtchaell, *The Dying of the Light: The Disengagement of Colleges and Universities from Their Christian Churches* (Grand Rapids: Eerdmans, 1998); on the latter, see Nathan D. Grawe, *Demographics and the Demand for Higher Education* (Baltimore: Johns Hopkins University Press, 2018).

[8] E.g., Perry L. Glanzer, Nathan F. Alleman, and Todd C. Ream, *Restoring the Soul of the University: Unifying Christian Higher Education in a Fragmented Age* (Downers Grove: IVP Academic, 2017); for more on a "Christ-animating" approach, see Perry L. Glanzer, Theodore F. Cockle, Elijah G. Jeong, and Britney N. Graber, *Christ-Enlivened Student Affairs: A Guide to Christian Thinking and Practice in the Field* (Abilene: Abilene Christian University Press, 2020), 226–27.

[9] Here riffing off Glanzer et al., *Christ-Enlivened Student Affairs*, question in the title of their ch. 3, "Does God Make a Difference for Student Affairs?"

[10] As told by Daniel Topf, *Pentecostal Higher Education: History, Current Practices, and Future Prospects*, Christianity and Renewal—Interdisciplinary Studies (New York: Palgrave Macmillan, 2021), esp. ch. 2.

[11] These questions derive from the title and subtitle, respectively, of Perry L. Glanzer and Nathan F. Alleman, *The Outrageous Idea of Christian Teaching* (Oxford: Oxford University Press, 2019), ch. 5.

does pentecostal experience and spirituality make for the Christian college or university? Coming from our pentecostal background, we'd like to be able to respond affirmatively regarding a pentecostal contribution.

Our initial reply finds encouragement from the fact that pentecostal spirituality has been generative for thinking more deeply about the person and work of the Holy Spirit in the Christian life as it unfolds in the world. This has led, over the last two decades, to developments in various theological directions, as well as in pentecostal epistemology, hermeneutics, and educational praxis, in most cases with the Spirit's role centrally understood and articulated.[12] What if we gathered up such considerations and applied them consistently to what we do as college and university educators? How might such a pentecostal perspective illuminate the work of the Spirit in and across the higher educational endeavor? What might be understood afresh, highlighted or accentuated, or perhaps even innovated from out of such an exploration?

1.2 RENEWING THE CHRISTIAN UNIVERSITY: A PENTECOST-PROPOSAL

Having started down this road, however, we soon realized that we were actually considering a more radical proposal, one that went back to the roots of the Christian faith. Rather than simply presenting a set of contemporary pentecostal perspectives for this task, we were convinced that ours was a proposal fundamentally informed by the day of Pentecost event as narrated in the book of Acts. We will provide readings of Acts chapter 2 and its surrounding material throughout this book, but here we want to lay out some basic reasons why we have pivoted to this Pentecost (rather than pentecostal) approach.

First, a pentecostal philosophy of higher education would surely be apologetic in nature, in effect providing an extended argumentation responding to this specific version of the previously asked question: "Is there really a pentecostal form of teaching or education?" At one level, there may be good reasons to undertake such an apologetic, not least since Mark Noll's thesis regarding the so-called "scandal of the evangelical mind" laid the blame at least in part on pentecostal churches and their legacies.[13] Pentecostalism's perceived anti-intellectualism has been widely recognized, not least by those within the movement, and that is not the least of its acknowledged sins that would undercut its higher educational efforts.[14] If pentecostal churches and communities were to have viable colleges and universities, such a response would need to be made to name the impediments

---

[12] E.g., James K. A. Smith, *Thinking in Tongues: Pentecostal Contributions to Christian Philosophy*, Pentecostal Manifestos (Grand Rapids: Eerdmans, 2010); Lee Roy Martin, ed., *Pentecostal Hermeneutics: A Reader* (Leiden: Brill, 2013); and Cheryl Bridges Johns, *Pentecostal Formation: A Pedagogy among the Oppressed*, Journal of Pentecostal Theology Supplement Series 2 (Sheffield: Sheffield Academic Press, 1993).

[13] Mark A. Noll, *The Scandal of the Evangelical Mind* (Grand Rapids: Eerdmans, 1995).

[14] Pentecostal scholars who have been able to grapple directly with some of the weaknesses in the movement include Rick M. Nañez, *Full Gospel, Fractured Minds: A Call to Use God's Gift of the Intellect* (Grand Rapids: Zondervan Academic, 2010), and David J. Courey, *What Has Wittenberg to Do with Azusa? Luther's Theology of the Cross and Pentecostal Triumphalism* (New York: T&T Clark, 2015); see also the critical perspective of Ben Witherington III, *The Problem with Evangelical Theology: Testing the Exegetical Foundations of Calvinism, Dispensationalism, Wesleyanism, and Pentecostalism*, rev. ed. (Waco: Baylor University Press, 2015).

and suggest alternative construals to move the discussion forward. Yet although we grant the need for some kind of apologetic—which we take up also at some length vis-à-vis Noll and others in particular in chapter 4 below—we have also come to see that merely answering the questions posed by others cannot get us far enough and that the generating of creativity can only happen when a more forward-looking rather than defensive posture is adopted. A pentecostal approach may respond to important criticisms, but a Pentecost-vision is essential for a more constructive account.

This leads to a second realization: the pentecostal movement that emerged in the early twentieth century did not promote itself, but the person and work of the Holy Spirit for the renewal of all the churches. The point in those years was not to develop something called *Pentecostalism* but to witness to the wondrous work of God in Christ by the power of the Holy Spirit. Hence and similarly, while there is merit in articulating more clearly a baptistic, Quaker, or other ecclesially informed philosophy of teaching or of higher education—and we engage with some of these educational visions in chapter 5 below—their value can be understood as a kind of educational charism that benefits not only their denominationally affiliated colleges and universities but also other Christian institutions and programs of study. As those in the Reformed tradition who have led the way in faith-and-learning-integration conversations in the CCCU have realized, the insights from any theological tradition should be adopted because such views and related practices serve well students and learners across denominations and churches. As the strengths of any ecclesial tradition compensate for its blind spots, so also the contributions of each benefits others. In short, the goal of formulating any pentecostal philosophy of higher education cannot be limited to utility only within its own schools; instead, the value of a pentecostal perspective is in the long run confirmed by its reception among those in other ecclesial spaces.

Third, as already intimated, there are specifically biblical and theological reasons why a pentecostal perspective points beyond the modern pentecostal movement, and this has to do with the historical revelation of the triune God's redemptive work in Christ by the Spirit. Jesus Christ of Nazareth is who he is and does what he does as the Messiah, the one anointed by the divine breath, and then as the ascended Son of Man he pours out of this same Spirit on the world. Incarnation, including crucifixion, resurrection, and ascension, is therefore also pneumatically accomplished and then interwoven with Pentecost, when the messianic power is made available to all to bear messianic witness. Pentecost thus funds not only Pentecostalism but the church because it returns the church to the trinitarian ground of its existence. Alternatively put, Pentecost belongs not to any one group of believers, nor to Pentecostalism as a whole, but to the body of Christ and the people of God as the temple of the divine Spirit. In other words, the depths and riches of pentecostal spirituality are not copyrighted by any denomination or movement but carried by the work of the Spirit of Pentecost, and hence any pentecostal proposal can be and is robust only insofar as it lives into the full promise of that Day when the Spirit was poured out on all flesh (Acts 2:17).[15] A full-fledged reconsideration of Pentecost therefore

---

[15]   Thus, Yong's recent work has emphasized not the pentecostal perspective (without denying such) but the theologic or the day of Pentecost frame, e.g., *Mission after Pentecost: The Witness of the Spirit from Genesis to Revelation*, Mission in Global Community (Grand Rapids: Baker Academic, 2019).

brings creation to fulfillment via incarnation and opens up to a truly trinitarical vision, one that not only presumes and develops the second article—Christology—but also neither neglects nor overlooks attention to the third article: pneumatology. Pneumatology detached from christology undermines the understanding of the Spirit and Son as the two hands of the Father, even as patrology and christology with an underdeveloped pneumatology remain binitarian rather than authentically trinitarian.[16]

We realized the interrelatedness of these theological principles in our previous work on the Holy Spirit and the affections.[17] Given the embodied character of pentecostal spirituality, we sought to further explore, not just theologically but also historically, the work of the Holy Spirit poured out upon, resident within, and active through human flesh. Embodiedness is one reason why we prosecute a case for the cultivation of a *habitus* that integrates the whole human person. On the one hand, our historical inquiry led us back through the Christian tradition and enabled us to observe pneumatic and charismatic manifestations of the Spirit's work long before the modern pentecostal movement came about; on the other hand, our pneumatological inquiry, opened up quickly in trinitarian directions, led us to consider the Spirit's work in incarnation and Pentecost as the culmination of the divine plan to redeem not just soulish creatures but human persons in the materiality and affectivity of their being. The historical and soteriological provided complementary insights into the convergence of pneumatological and trinitarian loci. What emerged was a richer ecumenical and trinitarian understanding of God's mission to save the world, but this involved explicit pneumatological articulation and development as observed across Christian traditions. Put another way: the work of the Spirit was essential yet especially crucial in illuminating the redemption of the diversity of Creation and the reorientation of the many toward the divine.

It is for this reason that while we neither reject nor attempt to minimize our pentecostal background and experience, we offer the following as a Pentecost (rather than pentecostal) perspective. It may be obvious why two pentecostal scholars would ask what difference the Holy Spirit makes in a Christian university, but we hope that it would be not only interesting but also perhaps imperative that all Christians at work in higher educational contexts would want to explore this question with us and the way it led us back to the trinitarian ground of the faith. The lack of emphasis on the work of the Spirit in other traditions results, we believe, in an inadequate trinitarian vision for Christian faith and learning, one that this volume seeks to redress.

1.3   THESES AND ARGUMENT: WHAT THE BOOK IS AND ISN'T ABOUT

We argue the following primary and secondary theses in the pages to come. Primarily, we proffer that our pentecostal perspective and Pentecost reconsideration is distinctively

---

[16] For more on the logic of third-article approaches, see Yong, *Spirit-Word-Community: Theological Hermeneutics in Trinitarian Perspective*, New Critical Thinking in Religion, Theology and Biblical Studies (Burlington: Ashgate, 2002; repr., Eugene: Wipf and Stock, 2006); also Yong, "The Pneumatological Imagination: The Logic of Pentecostal Theology," in *The Routledge Handbook of Pentecostal Theology*, ed. Wolfgang Vondey (New York: Routledge, 2020), 152–62.

[17] See Dale M. Coulter and Amos Yong, eds., *The Spirit, the Affections, and the Christian Tradition* (Notre Dame: University of Notre Dame Press, 2016).

positioned to reclaim a lost legacy of Christian philosophy of higher education grounded in the work of the early church, persisting through the Middle Ages and further developed in Pietist circles, even if obscured otherwise during the early modern era. This legacy offers a perspective on Christian higher education that restores a proper role for the Holy Spirit in guiding us into all dimensions of our truth-seeking via deployment of the various tools of learning that God has provided for us. It also addresses the whole person—the cognitive, affective, and bodily dimensions that we metaphorically call the head, heart, and hands—while correcting the modernist conception of rationality, which divides reason from the emotions and desires. In doing so, it seeks to empower the work of education with the global and pluralistic context (not unlike that of the Hellenized Roman Empire in the first-century Mediterranean world) of the contemporary church's participation in the mission of God, which bears witness to and with the world. Such a vision must be drawn forward by a trinitarian view of the "end" of education: that we would be formed into the image of Christ under the guidance of the Holy Spirit for service in the coming reign of God.

Secondarily, we argue that too much of the narrative of American religious history in the late nineteenth and twentieth centuries has been shaped by the preoccupation with the fundamentalist-modernist debate, and this has occluded also the possible contributions of pentecostal movements in a variety of arenas, not least in the area of Christian higher education. This historiography of North American religious history, particularly within evangelicalism, has resulted in an elevation of the Reformed tradition, with its emphasis on doctrine, propositional revelation, and the cognitive dimension in general. It has also produced an understanding of "anti-intellectualism" that is not sufficiently distinguished from "antirationalism" or "anticonversionism," with pejorative connotations for especially Pietist traditions, including pentecostal and charismatic movements. This argument flows from our contention that contemporary pentecostal movements are distinct from and collaborators with the broader evangelical traditions, each with distinctive charisms for Christian higher education, especially when considering both as interwoven movements in international and transnational (not just North American) contexts. We prosecute these primary and secondary theses not step by step but via the overarching historical retrieval in part 1, and then a constructive philosophical and theological proposal in part 2.

Using this paradigm as a lens, we have explored the history of education in Christianity. While we make it clear that this has led us to affirm a robust trinitarianism in which education must be Christ-patterned and Spirit-infused, we have attempted to explore that trinitarian approach by arguing for the cultivation of a *habitus* by the individual that is invested in moral formation, open to transcendence, and engaged in mission (chapter 2). By *habitus* we mean a new disposition that integrates head, heart, and hands into a way of being and living in the world fundamentally Christ-patterned and Spirit-infused.[18] It is in cultivating such a *habitus* that we discover how Christians articulated a genuine humanism. Drawing

---

[18]   What is signaled in the triadic title of Rick Ostrander, *Head, Heart, and Hand: John Brown University and Modern Evangelical Higher Education* (Fayetteville: University of Arkansas Press, 2003), does not play any major material, formal, or theoretical role in what is otherwise a rather straightforward—even if very interesting—historical narrative about this evangelical university.

on a trinitarian framework, we weave the triad of moral formation, openness to transcendence, and engagement in mission into the triad of head, heart, and hands to show how the former gave rise to the integral humanism represented by the latter.

Moral formation speaks to the sanctifying work of the Spirit con-forming the person to Christ, and openness to transcendence relates to the Spirit's charismatic presence, which ecstatically transports the believer into the presence of Christ. To be caught up into the presence of Christ was both charismatic and eschatological insofar as the vision of Christ the wisdom of God was also a vision of the end and thus the purpose of the kingdom. For this reason, cultivating a *habitus* invested in moral formation and open to encounters with the transcendent God translated into an engagement in mission.

This process unfolded as the believer participated in the story of God, which early Christians placed in opposition to becoming Hellenized in accordance with the dominant customs that defined citizenship in the empire. While ancient education prepared the child for mission in the city by holding out the model of the sage, early Christianity countered with its own cosmopolitan vision of the saint whose mission unfolds as extending divine *philanthropia* through the reign of God. What early Christianity saw as a piety and teaching that exemplified and embodied God's own love for humanity, medieval, Renaissance, and Reformation Christians interpreted as an integral humanism (medieval) that was both literary (Renaissance) and biblical (Reformation). By allowing Christians to hold together pneumatology and Christology, the story of God became the narrative context within which the integral humanism bound up in the *habitus* was given shape.

We continue to prosecute our case for this *habitus* by arguing that the modern period became concerned with the relationship between the formation of the person and the formation of culture, in part because of the need to create a united people for the success of fledgling democracies (chapter 3). Moral formation continued under the guise of self-cultivation expressed through the German term *Bildung*. Religion continued to function in this new framework as a kind of spirituality devoid of confessional content yet still open to encounters with transcendence, primarily within nature. This spirituality centered on the scholar as hero (the modern sage) and mission become, once again, life in the city. Secularization was first about the sacralization of culture as rational intuitionism, divine immanence, and social progressivism formed the heart of the educational enterprise for the new research university. We summarize the triad of intuitionism, immanence, and progressivism as the Romantic sensibility, a heuristic description designed to show how these emphases formed part of the social imaginary of the nineteenth century. Grounded in the intuitive grasp of the self and the infinite, moral formation opened the scholar up to encounters with the divine that drove the scientific enterprise and the cultural formation that flowed from this enterprise in the form of the preservation of Western civilization.

Holiness and pentecostal adherents participated in the triad of intuitionism, immanence, and progressivism, although they wed it to populism and the transformation of folk cultures rather than the creation of a new liberal high culture (chapters 3 and 4). Pneumatology replaced the focus on the divine within nature while the sanctifying and charismatic operations of the Spirit grounded rational intuitionism and social progressivism. Spirit-enlightened minds meant a fusion of discursive and nondiscursive (intuitive) modes of rationality; Spirit-led hands concerned a progressive populism that gravitated toward more utilitarian models of education such as the normal school or the multipurpose college; and Spirit-infused hearts underscored the ordering of the affections in the context of narratives like spiritual biographies as located within the broad history of salvation.

This highly selective interpretation of Christian tradition remains firmly focused on the central claim that education concerns the formation of a *habitus* that embodies the integral humanism Christians sought to develop. Head, heart, and hands become our shorthand for this integral humanism in part 2, although we continue to insist that the cultivation of a *habitus* invested in moral formation, open to transcendence, and engaged in mission is how this unfolds on a practical level. Our attempt to answer what difference the Spirit makes leads us to the conclusion that the story of God supplies the narrative context within which the *habitus* becomes a new disposition that is Christ-shaped and Spirit-infused. This is the Pentecost-model we offer to our readers.

The argument of the chapters in part 2 will adapt the triadic Pietist structure of heads-hearts-hands to present a vision for understanding the mutuality of intellectual life and life in the Spirit (chapter 5), to comprehend Christian teaching and learning as a kind of pedagogy-of-the-heart through which human persons are transformed by the Spirit (chapter 6), and to envision Christian higher education as inviting participation in the mission of God to redeem the world in Christ by the power of the Spirit (chapter 7). While our movements in these chapters will be from the scholarly and academic pursuit of knowledge and truth through a holistic pattern of inquiry that involves invested bodies and impassioned affections in the hopes of heralding the shalom and justice of the reign of God for a broken world, the argument must be understood as reiterative. Heads, hearts, and hands are interwoven and reciprocally informing, and there is no sense in which one precedes the other in terms of logical priority. One might have constructed the argument in reverse, for instance, starting with the telos of Christian higher education driven by Christian witness to the coming divine reign, and moving then to formational and pedagogical strategies, culminating with considerations about the disciplines of knowledge, and such reframing would provide differentiated emphases although not necessarily contrary outcomes.[19] So while our Pentecost-vision can be entered from along any of these trajectories, we have opted as a heuristic strategy to move from content through pedagogy to mission, all the while inviting our readers to be alert to how entering the conversation from another direction can also shift emphases, spark new connections, and prompt different applications.

We should also be clear about what we are not attempting to do. First, part 1 of this book should not be read as if it were either a history of Christian formation or higher education or even a history of higher education in the modern Pentecost-movement. As we stated, ours is a selective theological and pneumatological account, one inspired by pentecostal sensibilities to be sure, and in that respect highlighting neglected historical elements for the purposes of commending a Pentecost-vision for Christian higher education. Further, our historical work does not seek to adjudicate the contested historiographic issues surfaced, much less to resolve them. Instead, we attempt to remap

---

[19]   In fact, this process of beginning missionally and then moving through pedagogy to scholarship is what structures the argument in Yong, *Renewing the Church by the Spirit: Theological Education after Pentecost*, Theological Education between the Times (Grand Rapids: Eerdmans, 2020), esp. part 3.

some historical developments when refracted not only through pentecostal lenses but also theological orientation (around the third article of the Creed related to the work of the Holy Spirit, for instance) in order to retrieve neglected themes for constructive pedagogical and higher educational purposes. Additionally, we realize that ours may seem like a Eurocentric account, no matter how historically selective. On the one hand, even if such may be expected since many if not most of the schools within the orbit of the CCCU that is our primary audience are situated within the narrative arc of the first part of this book, we have both resisted the older perspective on the history of Christianity viewing Hellenism as a fundamentally Western, meaning Greek- and Latin-based, tradition, in part because individuals we survey in especially the second chapter were of multiethnic and migratory contexts or of North African origination even if they all wrote and spoke in Greek and Latin (which is no different than a contemporary African writing and speaking in English), and attempted to include, if only by way of gestured references, Syriac Christianity in the school of Nisibis, Ethiopianism, and pentecostal universities in Ghana in our historical account. On the other hand, we also take up at the end of this book the question of what would happen if we were to engage with the educational philosophies of other cultures not as marginal or incidental but as central to the Christian higher educational enterprise. Future works in this vein ought to foreground Asian, African, or Latin American contexts and incorporate literatures in the relevant primary languages beyond what most individual scholars, ourselves included, can.[20] If a more global approach were attempted, then what emerges in part 1 would tell a much more expansive story, and then also reshape our creativity and imagination in what is part 2 later.

Last but not least, then, about what this book does not attempt: the second part of the volume stays at a fairly high theological—and pneumatological or Pentecost—level, rather than descending into prescription about what to implement in three, four, or five concrete curricular, cocurricular, administrative, or other steps. So those who are bemoaning the future of the university in general or of Christian higher education more specifically amid their many disruptions may be disappointed that we cannot just invite the Holy Spirit to fix or solve all of our problems.[21] Even if not oblivious to these disruptions, we are convinced that attending to the pneumatic and Pentecost imagination, what we do here in this book, is the fundamental and necessary theological step to holding established structures and models light enough so that they can be abandoned as necessary and alternative approaches developed in place. Simultaneously, rather than coming along as if the new pentecostal kids on the higher educational block now had answers to the perennial questions in this space, one might say that much of what we propose is

---

[20] And then there are indigenous traditions, not least across the Americas, that also have their own story to tell; a part 1 oriented around those histories would have to build on many of the primary sources called attention to by Oscar García-Johnson, *Spirit Outside the Gate: Decolonial Pneumatologies of the American Global South* (Downers Grove: IVP Academic, 2019).

[21] A good summary of the overarching challenges confronting contemporary higher education can be found in Arthur Levine and Scott van Pelt, *The Great Upheaval: Higher Education's Past, Present, and Uncertain Future* (Baltimore: Johns Hopkins University Press, 2021), even as indicators for helpful next steps can be found in works such as Joseph E. Aoun, *Robot-Proof: Higher Education in the Age of Artificial Intelligence* (Cambridge, Mass.: MIT Press, 2018), and Bryan Alexander, *Academia Next: The Futures of Higher Education* (Baltimore: Johns Hopkins University Press, 2020).

not new but theologically undergirded reappropriations from past insights and present realizations. Indeed, our primary desire has been to engage in something of a pneumatological *ressourcement* rather than a novel theory attuned to contemporary sensibilities.

Many who work in CCCU circles may recognize what is being suggested as already in place in their institutions, although we hope that they see the theological underpinnings laid more fully bare in the pages to come. There is a sense in which we have begun with what we are already seeing on the Christian higher educational ground and seek here to clarify their theological foundations, so that there is a dialectical conversation between the historical and current practice of Christian formation and our Pentecost theological commitments in an effort to better name what we believe the Holy Spirit is already doing and to renew our personal and collective efforts so that we can even more deeply experience the Spirit's work.[22] In short, even in cases when our constructive proposals involve disciplinary, pedagogical, and broader initiatives currently well underway across the CCCU, the hope is that we will find new inspiration for recognizing the impulses of the Holy Spirit and be renewed in our capacities to participate in that work for the sake of God's desire to save the world.

---

[22] A parallel dialectical approach between the practice of higher education and pneumatology, albeit one focused on religious education more broadly, is Bert Roebben and Siebren Miedema, "The Wind Blows Where It Wishes . . . (John 3:8): Towards a Pneumatological Religious Education," presented at "Theology and Religious Education: Relational, Practical, and Interfaith Dimensions," the annual meeting of the Religious Education Association, Dallas, Texas, November 22–24, 2009, https://old.religiouseducation.net/proceedings/2009_papers.html.

Part I

What Difference *Has* the Holy Spirit Made?

Historical Lessons

2

Revisiting Ancient *Didaskalia*

Patristic Foundations, Medieval Renewal, and Renaissance/Reformation Expansion

When the fifth-century North African writer Martianus Capella set out to compose a work celebrating the liberal arts, he intentionally framed his discussion in terms of an allegorical marriage between Philology and Mercury.[1] Modeling his tale on the story of Psyche and Cupid in Apuleius' *The Golden Ass*, Capella rehearses a union between human wisdom or learning (Philology) and divine eloquence (Mercury) that is grounded upon their mutual passion for one another. He has Virtue extol Philology's worth as one who has tamed the savagery of Psyche (the soul) by beautifying her and, indeed, contributing to Psyche's own immortality.[2] Philology is also patroness of prophecy because she penetrates the secrets of knowledge.[3] These qualities of learning so attract Mercury that he showers Philology with the seven liberal arts as his betrothal gifts, who become her handmaidens in the ongoing quest for wisdom and understanding. At the same time, as any college freshman quickly discovers, learning has no benefit to others without eloquence, the capacity to communicate in clear and effective ways that capture the heart and cause the imagination to take flight. Mercury's and Philology's passion emerges from their need for one another.

Capella has not only given us a description of learning as capable of beautifying the soul and extracting wisdom from the cosmos, he also places his allegory in a decidedly religious context. The marriage between Philology and Mercury cannot occur until Philology ascends into the realm of the gods through a kind of apotheosis. She must be granted the gift of immortality like the gods themselves. Yet this munificent bestowal comes only at the end of an arduous journey into the heavens. By opening the person up to the divine, learning transforms human wisdom so that it approximates the gods. Philology is the patroness of prophecy after all. As her handmaids, the seven liberal arts, which include the *trivium* (grammar, rhetoric, and dialectic) and *quadrivium* (arithmetic, geometry, astronomy, and music), are a *via*, a path or road that leads into the heavens.

---

[1] Martianus Capella, *De nuptiis Philologiae et Mercurii*, ed. James Willis, Bibliotheca Scriptorum Graecorum et Romanorum Tevbneriana (Leipzig: Teubner, 1983); *Martianus Capella and the Seven Liberal Arts*, vol. 2: *The Marriage of Philology and Mercury*, trans. William H. Stahl and Richard Johnson with E. L. Burge (New York: Columbia University Press, 1977).

[2] Capella, *De nuptiis* 1.23 (Willis, 11; Stahl and Johnson, 14).

[3] Capella, *De nuptiis* 1.22–23 (Willis, 10–11; Stahl and Johnson, 14).

Through the allegory of a marriage, Capella places the liberal arts into the familiar context of ancient philosophy's twin concerns for moral formation and openness to transcendence as critical dimensions of human flourishing. The liberal arts serve as handmaids in this journey from earth to the heavens. Early Christian writers like Augustine would assimilate these emphases by reframing the journey to heaven in terms of a pilgrimage to one's true homeland through Incarnate Wisdom and the Uncreated Charity.[4] While retaining the concerns for moral formation and openness to transcendence, the common cultural framework of viewing learning as a journey enabled Augustine to place moral formation and openness to transcendence in the context of ongoing conversion to Christ punctuated by encounters with the Spirit. Moreover, along with other early Christian thinkers, he came to view openness to transcendence within an eschatological framework. The journey into the heavens became an encounter with Incarnate Wisdom through the Spirit and the *telos* of human existence. This encounter opened up the path to human flourishing consummated in the eschaton. As source and goal of human existence, Christ became the pattern and the Spirit the transforming presence. The ancient vision of the liberal arts and philosophy as facilitating moral formation through an openness to transcendence so eloquently depicted by Capella was recast in view of the sanctifying, charismatic, and eschatological dimensions of Christianity.

In this chapter, we argue that what emerged from the debate among Christian thinkers about the role of philosophy and the liberal arts is an educational framework centered on the cultivation of a *habitus* that fused together two elements: (1) moral formation with Christian conversion; (2) openness to transcendence with the Christian understanding of encounter as a charismatic and eschatological event.[5] The use of "framework" is intentional since there were multiple models that fit such a framework. What we mean by *habitus* is a reorientation of the self through the cultivation of a habitual disposition invested in moral formation and open to transcendence. This reorientation binds together head, heart, and hands.

What distinguished the Christian view of learning from its Hellenistic counterpart was the story of the triune God and a descent/ascent motif that replaced philosophy as the means to encounter the divine. It was still the case that education facilitated a journey into the heavens, even if its role was minimized as handmaid to God's actions in history and the individual person. Cultivating a *habitus* was a formative process advancing a way of being in the world that contributed to human flourishing rather than a conceptual scheme about the world. From this perspective, learning emphasizes "salutary teaching" (*hygiainousē didaskalia*) (1 Tim 1:10; 2 Tim 4:3), which includes more than communicating a system of beliefs.[6]

---

4   Augustine, *On Christian Teaching* 1; see *Saint Augustine: Teaching Christianity*, trans. and notes by Edmund Hill, O.P. (New York: New City Press, 1996), 106–28.

5   In a work such as this one, the argument must of necessity be selective. It is hoped, however, that such selectivity works in continuity with the broader historical contexts surveyed below.

6   See Ronald H. Nash, *Faith and Reason: Searching for a Rational Faith* (Grand Rapids: Zondervan, 1988), 24. We agree with James K. A. Smith that there should be a moratorium on worldview thinking. See James K. A. Smith, *Desiring the Kingdom: Worship, Worldview, and Cultural Formation* (Grand Rapids: Baker, 2009), 63–74; James K. A. Smith, "From Christian Scholarship to Christian Education," *Christian Scholar's Review* 39.2 (2010): 229–32; and James K. A. Smith, "Worldview, Sphere Sovereignty, and

Christians understood the purpose of learning and education to facilitate the journey to one's homeland through the cultivation of the human person, whose moral formation and openness to transcendence advanced human flourishing and mission in the world. They arrived at this conclusion through the story of God, in which this journey was Christ-patterned and Spirit-infused. Moral formation concerned the sanctifying work, while encounters with transcendence related to the charismatic dimension and its relationship to ecstasy. The liberal arts provided tools that aided moral formation and promoted human flourishing, thereby contributing to the renewal of the human person in the image of God. This is the heart of Christian humanism.

To make this argument, the chapter begins (§2.1) with an analysis of ancient philosophy before turning to its assimilation by early Christian thinkers. This sets the stage for the cultivation of two new models of learning, medieval scholasticism and Renaissance humanism (and its Reformation manifestation), which will be explored in the final two sections (§2.2–2.3). While the models of learning shift, the basic framework of cultivating a *habitus* remains consistent.

2.1 ANCIENT PHILOSOPHY, THE LIBERAL ARTS, AND THE CULTIVATION OF A *HABITUS*

Martianus Capella's depiction of the marriage of learning and eloquence confirms Pierre Hadot's claim that ancient philosophy concerned the cultivation of a *habitus* or way of being in the world.[7] Drawing on the ancient connection between tilling the soil for planting and tending the soul, Cicero opined that "philosophy is the cultivation of the soul" because through it the person learns to remove corrupting habits and beliefs formed from family and society.[8] Learning required leaving behind social customs as part of tilling the soil within which a new way of being could take root. This was the process of formation behind ancient *paideia*, which Cicero understood as the studies of a free male.[9] Through a set of practices that Hadot refers to as "spiritual exercises" (*askēses/exercitationes*), ancient philosophers sought to inculcate the wisdom they discovered from learning as a mechanism of transformation on the personal and societal levels. Although different philosophical schools engaged in different sets of practices, this asceticism (*askēsis*) had self-mastery as its aim by discovering the true self obscured through attachments to objects of emotion and desire. For Philo of Alexandria (ca. 20 BC–50 AD), one must become a "practitioner" (*askētēs*) of wisdom and knowledge by actively seeking to control the self (*enkrateia*), engaging in meditation (*meletē*), and employing a host of other mental

---

Desiring the Kingdom: A Guide for (Perplexed) Reformed Folk," *Pro Rege* 39.4 (2011): 15–24, at 17—to whose work we will return in §6.1.1 below.

   [7]   Pierre Hadot, *Philosophy as a Way of Life: Spiritual Exercises from Socrates to Foucault*, ed. Arnold I. Davidson, trans. Michael Chase (Oxford: Blackwell, 1995), 264–76; Pierre Hadot, *What Is Ancient Philosophy?* trans. Michael Chase (Cambridge, Mass.: Belknap Press, 2002), 172–233.

   [8]   Cicero, *Tusculan Disputations* 1.4.13; also *Tusculan Disputations* 3.1.2–3.

   [9]   Cicero, *On the Orator* III.31.125–32.128; *On Moral Ends* III.17.57; *Tusculan Disputations* II.2.6. When Cicero wishes to describe a good education, he generally says *liberalis educatio, liberalis doctrina, liberaliter eruditi*, by which he means teaching that befits a free male and is therefore among the upper classes of Roman society.

exercises designed to train the mind and restore balance to the soul.[10] As the author of *De liberis educandis* makes clear, the learner cannot cultivate a *habitus* apart from practice (*askēsis*).[11] These points underscore Martha Nussbaum's claim that ancient philosophy concerned a therapy of desire designed to heal the soul, which occurred through engaging in a set of practices that comprised a new way of living in the world.[12]

In this brief section on ancient philosophy and the liberal arts, we survey a select group of thinkers from the first century BC to the early fourth century AD in order to set the immediate backdrop to early Christian ideas about learning. The point of this survey is to suggest a common set of ideas among these literary accounts concerning the basic aims and overarching structure of education: to prepare the individual for civic duty (§2.1.1); to facilitate a journey of moral formation and humanization (§2.1.2); and to cultivate an openness to transcendence (§2.1.3).

2.1.1 Education as Preparation for Civic Duty (Mission in the *Polis*)

Civic duty flowed from the kind of cosmopolitanism that such an educational journey was intended to facilitate. In the world of the early Roman Empire, Hellenism became intertwined with imperial politics as part of a concerted effort to civilize conquered groups by forming a Roman identity over against local identities. Yet, even in the late Roman Republic, philosophy and education were in the service of the state, as Cicero points out in *De res publica* by arguing that "true humans are those who have been educated in the truly human arts" and then claiming that such education in philosophy cultivates skills that make one useful to the state.[13] Plutarch makes a similar point by linking *paideia* and *philosophia* together repeatedly in his *Lives*.[14] The moral qualities necessary for Plutarch's hero stem from the habituation of the passions that produces *philanthropia*, a genuine concern for humanity. Greek *paideia* "cultures" the person, making such habituation possible.[15]

Cosmopolitanism, with its subtext of cultural identity, represented the pragmatic application of the cosmic consciousness cultivated by the idealized philosophical sage, who sought to become "conscious of being a part of the world, and plunged himself into the totality of the cosmos."[16] Epictetus opens his discourse on duties by reminding the student, "You are a citizen of the world (*politēs tou kosmou*) . . . for you are capable of understanding

---

[10] Philo of Alexandria, *Who Is the Heir of Divine Things* 253–54, trans. F. H. Colson and G. H. Whitaker, vol. 4: *Works of Philo*, Loeb Classical Library (Cambridge, Mass.: Harvard University Press, 1968), 412–13; Philo of Alexandria, *On Mating with the Preliminary Studies* 24–34, vol. 4: *Works of Philo*, Loeb Classical Library, 470–75. Philo produces a somewhat standard list of what Hadot calls "philosophical therapeutics." See Hadot, *Philosophy as a Way of Life*, 84–86. *Enkrateia* (Latin, *continentia*) is of Stoic provenance and usually appears as a subcategory of temperance (*sōphrosynē*; Latin, *temperentia*).

[11] Pseudo-Plutarch, *On the Education of Children* (*De liberis educandis*) 2.4, in *Plutarch's Moralia*, vol. 1, trans. Frank Cole Babbit (Cambridge, Mass.: Harvard University Press, 1969), 8–9.

[12] Martha C. Nussbaum, *The Therapy of Desire: Theory and Practice in Hellenistic Ethics*, with a new introduction (Princeton: Princeton University Press, 1994), 13–47.

[13] Cicero, *On the Commonwealth* 1.29–33.

[14] Plutarch, *Agesilaus* 27.4, in which he describes the ambassador to Sparta Epaminondas as a man esteemed for "learning and philosophy" (*paideia kai philosophia*). See also *Cato the Elder* 23.1–2, in which Plutarch derides Cato for mocking philosophy and Greek learning. It's clear that *paideia* is closely associated with philosophy and being Hellenized culturally.

[15] See Tim Duff, *Plutarch's Lives: Exploring Virtue and Vice* (Oxford: Oxford University Press, 1999), 76–78.

[16] Hadot, *Philosophy as a Way of Life*, 32.

the divine administration and of calculating what follows from it."[17] Philosophy and learning helped the person discern a particular place in relation to the whole. In this way, ancient writers could fuse Roman and Greek intellectual traditions into a broader cultural matrix that allowed even someone from the hinterlands of Asia Minor to feel a sense of connection to Rome in the early days of empire. As Peter Brown has noted, "education gave the child to the city, not the school."[18] The moral grooming that occurred in the forum sustained the upper classes, who could propagate the city's interests in the context of empire. For ancient writers, learning involved traversing a path fraught with difficulty to awaken the self to another way of living in the world that healed the soul, promoted its flourishing, and connected it to cultural ideals and transcendent realities.

By facilitating moral formation and an openness to transcendence, this inculcated *habitus* aimed for civic duty in the context of a journey through an educational "system" to arrive at philosophy and oratory, wisdom and eloquence. It may be better, as Teresa Morgan proposes, to see this system as less a curricular model of education with a specific set of texts than a core model with a relatively stable center beyond which students could go as they moved from lower to higher levels.[19] One of the major purposes of this system was to enable a child to move from childhood to adulthood. This is the underlying rationale of the *De liberis educandis*, a manual produced by someone associated with Plutarch's literary circle. Martin Bloomer rightly notes that the pseudonymous work may be better titled *Child to Citizen Transformation* since that is its primary aim.[20] In the case of the *De liberis educandis*, the child arrives at adulthood through a process of cultivation that blossoms with philosophy, "the fount of education."[21] For the writer, philosophy appears in the broadest sense of the way of life the educator seeks to inculcate in the child. Formation concerns the shaping of a child through a set of social and moral practices that produce the *habitus* of a citizen.

At the lower levels was the *enkyklios paideia*, a phrase referring to a program of common instruction into which a student was fully immersed.[22] It was not, as in the French encyclopedists' project, an attempt to transmit all knowledge within a rational order. Quintilian (ca. 35–100 AD), who taught prominent Romans such as Pliny the Younger, translated the Greek phrase as "circle of teaching" (*orbis doctrinae*), which reveals an intention to envelop the student in the arts through a program of teaching.[23] Quintilian's translation picks up on the meaning of *enkyklios* as "circular," which fills out the other meanings of "complete, common, or ordinary" to point toward a system that surrounds the student.[24]

---

[17] Epictetus, *The Discourses* 2.10.

[18] Peter Brown, "Late Antiquity," in *A History of Private Life: From Pagan Rome to Byzantium*, vol. 1, ed. Paul Veyne (Cambridge, Mass.: Harvard University Press, 1987), 240.

[19] Teresa Morgan, *Literate Education in the Hellenistic and Roman Worlds* (Cambridge: Cambridge University Press, 1998), 67–73.

[20] W. Martin Bloomer, *The School of Rome: Latin Studies and the Origins of Liberal Education* (Berkeley: University of California Press, 2011), 59.

[21] Pseudo-Plutarch, *On the Education of Children* 7.10D, in *Plutarch's Moralia*, vol. 1, 34–35.

[22] Henri I. Marrou, *A History of Education in Antiquity*, trans. George Lamb (Madison: University of Wisconsin Press, 1956), 176–77; Morgan, *Literate Education*, 33–39.

[23] Quintilian, *The Orator's Education* 1.10.1, trans. H. E. Butler, Loeb Classical Library (Cambridge, Mass.: Harvard University Press, 1980), 158–61.

[24] Morgan, *Literate Education*, 33.

Likening it to Abraham's concubine Hagar, Philo viewed this system as intermediate instruction that functioned as a handmaid to the pursuit of wisdom and virtue.[25] The handmaid supplies the womb from which the children of wisdom and virtue spring. Pseudo-Plutarch employs *paideia* as a synonym for *agogēs* (education, training, instruction) to speak generically about the education of the child while reserving *enkyklia paideumata* for what Seneca called *liberalia studia* and Cicero called the *artes liberales*. These descriptions pointed toward a grouping of arts that could include geometry, music, grammar, rhetoric, dialectic, astronomy, arithmetic, medicine, and architecture, if one takes into consideration Varro's list of nine *disciplinae*.[26]

It is most likely that by the beginning of the first century AD a core of seven arts emerged, helped along in the Latin West by Varro's lost *Disciplinarum libri*.[27] At this point, we must register an important qualification: virtually all of the literary accounts of ancient education come from persons occupying the upper crust of Roman society with some accounts, such as Quintilian's, reflecting education in Rome for future emperors, senators, and governors of the empire.[28] Education was an elite enterprise although there was some stratification that allowed for those in the provinces, in particular, to move into more prominent positions. Taken together, these diverse accounts point toward a programmatic journey, beginning around seven years of age with basic lessons in grammar and reading, designed to produce a citizen who embodied the cultural ideals of the Greco-Roman world and who was placed on the path of human flourishing.[29] The *habitus* that facilitated moral formation and encounters with transcendent wisdom had as its aim a citizen who could help the empire. Education combined human flourishing with mission in the *polis*.

2.1.2 Education as Facilitating Moral Formation and Humanization

Since learning combined a process of inculturation with a humanism, *paideia* came to mean culture as well as training or education. One finds this most clearly in Aulus Gellius

---

[25] Philo, *On Mating with the Preliminary Studies*, trans. F. H. Colson and G. H. Whitaker, Loeb Classical Library 4 (Cambridge, Mass.: Harvard University Press, 1958), 458–551, utilizes a number of different phrases to refer to what Marrou called "general studies" or what other Latin writers referred to as the "liberal arts" or "liberal studies." These are *mesē paideia*, *mesē enkyklios*, *enkyklios paideia*, *enkyklia propaideumata*, and *enkyklios mousikē*. While in classical Greece *mousikē* referred to the Muses and thus the arts over which they presided (poetry, dance, play writing), Philo sees it as synonymous with the "preliminary instruction" provided by the liberal arts.

[26] See Pseudo-Plutarch, *On the Education of Children* 10, Loeb, 32–33; Cicero, *On the Orator* 3.32, Loeb, 98–101; Marrou, *History of Education*, 177; Morgan, *Literate Education*, 35–36. On Varro, see Shanzer, "Augustine's Disciplines," in *Augustine and the Disciplines*, 98–103.

[27] So Marrou, *History of Education*, 177. On the debate as to whether the seven liberal arts emerged from Varro or Neoplatonic literary circles, see I. Hadot, *Arts libéraux et philosophie dans la pensée antique*, 2nd ed. (Paris: Vrin, 2005).

[28] From late Roman Republic authors like Varro of Reatus and Cicero to early Empire authors like Seneca, Quintilian, Philo of Alexandria, and Plutarch, it is hard to find a writer who does not reflect a wealthy status. The slave turned philosopher Epictetus stands out as an exception to the more general trend. Nevertheless, there are variations between Philo and Plutarch, who represent ethnic positions in the broader empire, and Varro, Cicero, Seneca, and Quintilian, who operate in Rome even if, like Quintilian, they originated in the provinces.

[29] Quintilian, *The Orator's Education* I.1.15–17, Loeb, 26–27; Marrou, *History of Education*, 142.

(ca. 125–180), who connects *paideia* with *humanitas*.[30] Those who pursue learning and instruction are thoroughly humanized (*maxime humanissimi*) or "cultured." Education in the liberal arts is a human endeavor that aims to fulfill human potential and advance human flourishing. To establish the connection of *humanitas* to *paideia*, Gellius mistakenly distances the former from *philanthrōpia*, a term he takes to mean kindness and benevolence.[31] Even with his appreciation for Plutarch, Gellius missed the connection Plutarch had made between *philanthrōpia* and culture. As Hubert Martin notes, civilization, Hellenism, and *philanthrōpia* are inseparable in Plutarch's thought.[32] Humanism invariably meant exercising a devotion to human life, which framed Plutarch's understanding of *philanthrōpia*.[33] In his *Life of Philopoemen*, Plutarch credits Aratus (d. ca. 213 BC) with bringing a "Hellenic and humane form of government" (*Hellēnikēn kai philanthōpon politeian*) to the Peloponnesian region of Achaea.[34] When Philopoemen took over after Aratus' death, he continued the effort by fusing philosophy with statecraft in good Platonic fashion. One can see in Plutarch the connection between virtues such as *philanthrōpia*, civilization, and learning through philosophy. Like Gellius, Plutarch saw learning as a humanizing process that could not be separated from advancing Hellenic culture and civilization.

Central to learning as a humanizing process was the role of philosophy in extracting wisdom to bring therapy to the soul. In his *Hortensius* Cicero had followed Aristotle in composing an exhortation to philosophy as part of a larger program designed to introduce it to a Roman audience. Although the *Hortensius* is no longer extant, one can glimpse Cicero's perspective from his other works, in which he described philosophy as the "mother of arts" and the art that deals with life in general.[35] In a flight of rhetorical panache, he wonders, "What else is [philosophy] if not, as Plato said, a gift, or, as I say, the invention of the gods? It first taught us about worship of the gods, next the human justice that resides in human social bonds, and then moderation and magnanimity. It is philosophy that has dispelled darkness from the eyes of the mind so that we might see all things above and below, first, last, and in between."[36] Cicero thought that the Greek philosophical schools embodied the desire to extract wisdom from the cosmos, and his desire was to fuse it with a Roman concern for the praxis of civic life. The three schools he interacted with most in his writings (Epicureans, Stoics, and Peripatetics) wrote on a wide array of subjects, including the role of language, constructing arguments, the natural world, political and moral life, and agriculture. As he makes clear in *De divinatione*, his own literary project was an effort to cover the vast terrain of learning for the

---

[30]   Aulus Gellius, *Attic Nights* XIII.17.1, Loeb, 456–57; Marrou, *History of Education*, 98–99.

[31]   See L. Holford-Strevens, *Aulus Gellius: An Antonine Scholar and His Achievement* (Oxford: Oxford University Press, 2003), 177, 248–49.

[32]   Hubert Martin Jr., "The Concept of *Philanthropia* in Plutarch's Lives," *American Journal of Philology* 82.2 (1961): 167.

[33]   On this point, see José Ribeiro Ferreira, "La douce caresse de la *philanthropia*," in *Philosophy in Society: Virtues and Values in Plutarch*, ed. José Ribeiro Ferreira, Luc van der Stockt, and Maria do Céu Fialho (Coimbra-Leuven: University of Coimbra Press, 2008), 99–106.

[34]   Plutarch, *Life of Philopoemen* 8.1, Loeb, 275. See also Plutarch, *Life of Pyrrhus* 1.3, Loeb, 347. Martin, "Concept of *Philanthropia*," 167, provides these citations.

[35]   Cicero, *Tusculan Disputations* I.26.64; *On Moral Ends* III.2.4.

[36]   Cicero, *Tusculan Disputations* I.26.64.

sake of his fellow Romans.[37] Such a cosmopolitan vision unfolded within a love for the wisdom laced through all of life.

This love for wisdom aimed at healing the soul. Cicero's own position is difficult to pin down, yet it is clear that he accepted the Stoic idea that the problem with human beings was improper beliefs and bad behavior.[38] Such beliefs and behavior came from "warped habits" (*depravatio consuetudinum*) and false opinions largely derived from an uncritical acceptance of socialization into the larger culture.[39] While human nature had within it all of the seeds of virtue and the potential for flourishing, Cicero suggests that "we quickly extinguished with evil behavior and twisted belief the small flicker of light she gave to us."[40] He goes on to relate that without philosophy the soul cannot be healed and there will be no end to its misery.

The therapeutic enterprise Cicero envisions occurred within overlapping matrices. The first was philosophical discourses, which informed and supported the way of life. Whether in the form of meditations, dialogues, or some other genre, the point was to orient one's choices toward a particular end alongside a concrete set of practices that enabled pursuit of this end.[41] Learning was crucial here precisely as it informed the art of living. The point of pursuing wisdom was to become a sage who participated in human flourishing through virtue and other goods. As Philo pointed out, "the course of studies precedes virtue for the former is the path that carries one to the latter."[42] In their role as preliminary studies, the arts provided an aid to growth in virtue by opening up the wisdom of creation. Through mental practices like meditation that cultivated this *habitus* of learning, the person was slowly healed as the passions were redirected and humanized at the same time. There could be no separation between learning and moral formation.

2.1.3 Education as Cultivating an Openness to Transcendence

There was an overtly religious dimension to the pursuit of learning. Learning involved an ascent or a return to the self, nature, and the divine governance of the world expressed in nature. Despite his attempt to separate philosophy from liberal studies, Seneca expressed a common sentiment that liberal studies prepares the soul for the cultivation of virtue and virtue results from the love of wisdom found in philosophy itself.[43] Philosophy pursues *sapientia*, which is not only "the perfect good of the human mind," but also the "knowledge

---

[37]   Cicero, *On Divination* II.1–2.2.7. He describes the works he composed as "ways of the best arts" (*optimarum artium vias*), listing them in a particular philosophical order (logic, ethics, physics). Thus, philosophy is shorthand for the entire edifice of learning. The order is as follows: *Hortensius, Academics, On Moral Ends, Tusculan Disputations, On the Nature of the Gods, On Divination, On the Commonwealth, On Consolation, On Old Age, Cato, On Oratory, Brutus, The Orator*. He acknowledges that he had been unable to write works covering the entire range of philosophy.

[38]   On this point, see Margaret R. Graver, *Stoicism and Emotion* (Chicago: University of Chicago Press, 2007), 158–71.

[39]   Cicero, *On the Laws* I.28–46; *Tusculan Disputations* III.1–7.

[40]   Cicero, *Tusculan Disputations* III.1.2.

[41]   Hadot, *Philosophy as a Way of Life*, 49–70; Hadot, *What Is Philosophy?* 159, 175–79.

[42]   Philo, *On Mating with the Preliminary Studies* 3.10.

[43]   Seneca, *Epistle 88*, in *Ad Lucilium epistulae morales*, trans. Richard M. Gummere, vol. 5, Loeb Classical Library (Cambridge, Mass.: Harvard University Press, 1970), 360, 361.

of things divine and human."[44] While the latter definition most likely stems from Cicero, it is also found in a number of ancient texts and reflects early Stoicism.[45] The person who pursues wisdom begins to perceive eternal reason and the divine in the cosmos so that the entire universe becomes "the temple of the gods." From this high perch of worship for the divine and fellowship with humanity, philosophy contains all of the virtues, including religion, piety, and justice. Philosophy forms the capstone of a journey into the heights of wisdom with the liberal arts cultivating the soul in preparation for this journey. This is crucial to see because, as we will note in the next chapter, the Enlightenment marked a return to philosophy as the capstone of the university, which facilitated secularization.

The connection between learning and religion stemmed from the view of the soul as divine. The maxim "Know thyself" pointed to an examination of the nature of the soul in relationship to the whole. Hence, "the one who knows himself, first will perceive that he possesses something divine and will think that his own intellectual capacity within himself is a sort of consecrated image of the divine."[46] Reflecting this approach, the *Distichs of Cato* begin with the aphorism "If our rational soul is divine, as the poems declare, you should especially cultivate it with a pure mind."[47] Distichs were moral maxims in the form of imperatives that guided learners. Composed in the second or third century AD, the *Distichs* became a standard text in the Middle Ages that introduced students to the educational enterprise. As Bloomer makes clear, the distichs offered an initial moral orientation for the young student as they were spoken and copied.[48] This moral orientation pointed in a decidedly religious direction. From the outset, the student imbibed a view of education as cultivating the immortal soul destined for the gods. The soul was designed for transcendence.

Education as a journey was combined with the notion of ascent and return. To discover wisdom involved a mental ascent through the visible world to the divine, which is how a philosopher became the sage. This ascent marked both a return back to the origin and meaning of existence and a movement toward happiness as the *telos* of human life. It represented a teleology grounded in a return to human origins and a deeper understanding of human nature as an expression of wisdom. Moral formation through cognitive and behavioral practices facilitated the mental ascent and the arrival at happiness since to train the soul was to overcome the passions.

One can see this in Philo's two treatises *On the Preliminary Studies* and *Who Is the Heir?* Taken together, they set forth a path from the visible to the invisible. This path opens up as the mind produces offspring with the wives of the patriarchs, all of whom are subsumed under Abraham's (the mind) mating first with Hagar (the liberal arts) and

[44]   Seneca, *Epistle 89*, in *Ad Lucilium epistulae morales*, trans. Richard M. Gummere, vol. 5, Loeb Classical Library (Cambridge, Mass.: Harvard University Press, 1970), 380, 381.

[45]   Cicero, *On Duties* 2.5; Philo, *On Mating with the Preliminary Studies* 14.79; 4 Maccabees 1:16; Sextus Empiricus, *Against the Physicists* 1.13. For the Stoic origins, see René Brouwer, *The Stoic Sage: The Early Stoics on Wisdom, Sagehood and Socrates* (Cambridge, Mass.: Cambridge University Press, 2014), 9–18.

[46]   Cicero, *On the Laws* 1.58.

[47]   *Distichs of Cato* 1.1. See *The Distichs of Cato: A Famous Medieval Textbook*, trans. Wayland Johnson Chase (Madison: University of Wisconsin Press, 1922), 16. My own translation follows closely the translation given by Bloomer in *School of Rome*, 142.

[48]   Bloomer, *School of Rome*, 139–69.

then with Sarah (wisdom and virtue). The movement is from slavery to the sensible world (Egypt) through the struggle with passions and vices (Canaan) to wisdom and virtue (the promised land). Symbolized by Moses, who is prophet and sage, the heir of divine things is the person who finally comes to possess the divine as the mind soars into the heights of wisdom and perceives the archetypal ideas that are "the patterns (*paradeigmata*) of visible and sensible things."[49] The practice of meditation laid the foundation for this ascent. By becoming a lover of learning (*philomathēs*), the soul purifies itself of ignorance and passions so that it might engage in the contemplative vision (*theōrias*) that returns the pilgrim home.[50] There is clearly a Platonic trajectory in Philo's depiction of the ascent.

His intertwining of Hebrew prophet and Hellenistic sage prompts Philo to infuse ecstatic encounters into the journey as the divine descends and meets the soul in its upward ascent. Whereas in *On the Preliminary Studies* Philo describes a continuous movement between learning and philosophy, or acquiring knowledge and ascending through this knowledge to wisdom and virtue, in *Who Is the Heir?* he explores how ecstatic encounters are a feature of the journey to wisdom. He describes these potential encounters with a variety of terms such as "divine possession" (*entheos katokōchē*), "frenzy" (*mania*), "divine indwelling" (*enthuousiasmos*), and "divine infilling" (*theophorētos*).[51] Utilizing terms of geography and migration, Philo wraps ecstatic states in the mind's exodus and return as the divine Spirit enters and recedes. This fusion of prophetic ecstasy and ascent enables him to bring together the Hellenistic emphasis on education as cultivating an openness to transcendence with the Hebrew understanding of prophetic inspiration. The concrete practices of ancient learning open up the possibility of ecstatic encounter.

Speaking of specific experiences while writing philosophy, Philo states, "I have approached my work empty and have suddenly become full, the ideas falling in a shower from above and being sown invisibly, so that I have been filled with corybantic frenzy under the influence of divine possession, and have not known anything, not my location, those present, myself, or what I was saying or writing. For I obtained language, ideas, an enjoyment of light, keenest vision, crystalline distinctness of objects, such as might be received through the eyes as the result of clearest shewing."[52] This autobiographical comment modifies his description of a state of ecstasy in terms of the mind being evicted or surrounded by darkness.[53] Rather than a suspension of mental activity, ecstasy involves an alternate conscious state in which there is a loss of awareness of the self and the external world as a mental vision of ideas unfolds in transparent clarity within the mind.

The practices of meditation and study give rise to ecstatic encounter as the mind takes flight. With the thoughts rapidly moving (*mania*) in a kind of dance around mental projections of the visible world, the mind enters a "sober intoxication" (*methē nēphalios*), becoming a frenzied festival of thoughts as it is seized with Platonic passion for such beauty.[54] Love, beauty, and wisdom swirl around in the mind, dislocating discursive

---

[49] Philo, *Who Is the Heir of Divine Things* 57.280.
[50] Philo, *Who Is the Heir of Divine Things* 55.271–74.
[51] For a close examination of Philo on ecstasy, see John R. Levison, "Inspiration and the Divine Spirit in the Writings of Philo Judaeus," *Journal for the Study of Judaism* 26.3 (1995): 272–323. It's clear that Philo is drawing on Plato's *Phaedrus*.
[52] Philo, *On the Migration of Abraham* 1.34–35.
[53] Philo, *Who Is the Heir of Divine Things* 264.
[54] Philo, *On the Creation of the World* 69–71.

reasoning as a vision emerges that includes the shadow of a divine other. This comports with the terms he employs for ecstasy, in which the divine "colonizes" the mind through an in-breathing and indwelling from which insight and creativity emerge.[55] Transcendence through ecstatic vision marks the path to becoming a citizen of the cosmos. This event marked a moment of crisis in an otherwise arduous process.

Philo was not the only ancient thinker to incorporate ecstasy into his understanding of learning as ascent to wisdom and encounter with transcendence. For all of his hatred of Christianity, Porphyry, the student of the third-century philosopher Plotinus, argued for a relationship between practices like abstinence, philosophical discourses, and encounters with transcendence.[56] Plotinian ecstasy emerges in the pursuit of the good and the forms of the good. It is the moment when "the soul, receiving into itself an outflow from [the Good], is moved and dances wildly and is all stung with longing and becomes love."[57] This is all part of the path of learning through "spiritual exercises in which the soul sculpts herself: that is, she purifies and simplifies herself, rises up to the plane of pure thought and finally transcends herself in ecstasy."[58]

We see here a trend to understand all exercises of learning in terms of ascetical practices that inculcate virtue and open up to ecstatic encounter. Through self-denial and learning, one cultivated a *habitus* that opened the mind to ecstatic encounters. Fueled by erotic passion, these encounters in turn brought a deeper consciousness of the world. As Groethuysen notes, "the sage never ceases to have the whole constantly present to his mind, never forgets the world, thinks and acts in relation to the cosmos."[59] Self-consciousness and cosmic consciousness require transcendence.

The soul's link to the divine grounded the formation of a cosmic consciousness. Citing the kinship between God and humans, Epictetus asserted that humans should see themselves as citizens of the world first and foremost.[60] The exemplar Epictetus has in mind is Socrates, who transcended his own citizenship in Athens. Cicero clarifies Epictetus' point when he notes that philosophy acquires wisdom by which the soul comes to know itself as a divine image destined for the happy life. There comes a moment at the end of the ascent of learning in which bodily pleasure has been conquered and virtue acquired. Cicero describes it in this way:

> For when the mind, having attained knowledge and perceived the virtues, has abandoned obedience to and indulgence of the body, and conquered pleasure like it was some shameful stain, and escaped every fear of death and pain; when the mind has entered an association of love with its own, recognized all of those joined to it by nature

---

[55] See Ruth Padel, "Women: Model for Possession by Greek Daemons," in *Images of Women in Antiquity*, ed. Averil Cameron and Amélie Kuhrt (London: Routledge, 1983), 18n20. Padel points to the common word group that would include *katoikizō* (I occupy, colonize). The point is that the divine occupies or sets up residence temporarily.

[56] Hadot, *What Is Philosophy?* 157–68.

[57] Plotinus, *Ennead* VI.7.22, Loeb, 154–57.

[58] Pierre Hadot, *Plotinus or the Simplicity of Vision*, 22.

[59] Bernhard Groethuysen, *Philosophische Anthropologie* (Munich, 1931), as cited in Hadot, *Philosophy as a Way of Life*, 251; and idem, *What Is Philosophy?* 229.

[60] Epictetus, *Discourses* 1.9. Epictetus employs several terms to describe the relationship between God and humans: *suggeneias, koinoneō, sunanastrophē*. Each term intensifies the connection from familial kinship to fellowship to intimate exchange.

as its own, taken up the worship of the gods and true religion, and sharpened both the gaze of the eyes and the intelligence to choose good things and reject their opposite—a virtue known as prudence from the capacity to perceive what is coming—then what can be said or thought to be more happy than this?[61]

Having obtained the pinnacle of learning, the person becomes a sage who can apply the knowledge of "first things" to life through prudence.

There is a sense in which this corresponds to a vision of the whole as it comes before the mind, coupled with the ability to perceive the good and direct one's action accordingly. *Sapientia* resides in grasping the whole, while *prudentia* is its application to the particularities of life in a kind of foresight (*providentia*). We see here the difference between mental vision (*theoria*) and the inculcation and application of this vision through concrete practices (*praxis*) that underscores the distinction between wisdom and prudence. The purpose of education for citizenship and empire has been transcended in the flight back to the realm of the divine. This is what it means to know oneself and to possess the happy life. Moreover, the acquisition of wisdom leads to a connection to the cosmos from which the mind "realizes that it is not enclosed about at a particular location by human walls, but is a citizen of the entire world as though of a single city."[62] In the *Tusculan Disputations*, Cicero describes this in terms of the true meaning of exile as a continuous voyage through life because the sage knows that he belongs "to the world" rather than any particular homeland (*patria*).[63] Apart from encounters with transcendent wisdom, the soul never achieves the kind of cosmopolitan vision that opens up the entire world.

Ancient education cultivated a program of study with the liberal arts as handmaids on the journey to wisdom. It may be best to see philosophy as unfolding through the entire journey and yet also forming the pinnacle. Calling for the cultivation of a *habitus* that ingrained practices in relationship to a set of ends (a way of life), philosophy marks both the process of formation and the completion of the soul's beautification, which is how it can be both the journey itself and the capstone. The primary aims of forming this *habitus* through ascetical practices were moral formation of the intellect and the will (virtue) and openness to transcendence (vision). This was how ancient education held together civic duty and humanization, with the former pointing toward a proximate end and the latter a more ultimate end that stemmed from becoming a sage, a citizen of the world.

In the midst of this pursuit, insights could emerge from ecstatic encounters with wisdom as the soul danced around the ideas that flowed from the good and became enraptured by them. Because the soul was immortal, it was designed for flight into the heavens, which occurred as the person took on the *habitus* through the program of studies. The process of formation could open up to the momentary ecstatic crisis of encounter with wisdom through vision of the archetypes that governed the whole. Education not only gave the child to the city; it opened the child to the entire cosmos by helping the child cultivate virtue and enter into a kind of association with all that is. In this important sense, moral formation and encounters with transcendence facilitated comprehensive mission

---

[61] Cicero, *On the Laws* 1.60.
[62] Cicero, *On the Laws* 1.61.
[63] Cicero, *Tusculan Disputations* 5.37.107.

in the *polis*, although much of the time this was taken as being a good Roman citizen who promoted Hellenistic culture and values.

2.2 EARLY CHRISTIANITY, THE STORY OF GOD, AND THE FRAMEWORK FOR LEARNING

While there were differences between early Christianity and Hellenism's approach to learning, lines of continuity were drawn in the first century that bridged the two. Early Christians entertained Hellenistic cultural motifs by drawing on the prominent role of teaching common to the Roman and Jewish worlds and fusing it with the importance of piety because of its close association with Jewish ideas about justice/righteousness. Prominent in Luke and the Pastoral Epistles, the connection between piety and righteousness became an important way early Christians understood the *habitus* resulting from learning. Moreover, early Christians understood the need for the person to be cured and centered this healing upon the reordering of passions and desires. In one of his earliest letters, Paul described the problem of sin in terms of "the flesh with its passions and desires" (*tēn sarka . . . sun tois pathēmasin kai tais epithymiais*) (Gal 5:24). The use of passion (*pathos*) and desire (*epithymia*) to describe slavery to worldly things through the disease of sin resonated with Hellenistic ideas about education and moral formation.[64]

While these examples show a degree of continuity between Christianity and Hellenism, Christians interpreted the human condition through a new cosmic framework grounded in their understanding of God and God's actions in time and space. We identify this narrative as the story of God to illustrate how it took on a trinitarian frame and to underline it as a metanarrative that Christians embraced. In the second century it was identified as the rule of faith or canon of truth, but it expanded into an entire Christian vision of history that began with God and creation and concluded in the consummation of all things (the economy of salvation). Education still concerned narrative catechesis for citizenship, with the story of God replacing Homer and other cultural narratives. The child was no longer for the earthly city but the city of God.

In the Christian story of God, cosmic wisdom and its cosmopolitan outlook were connected to union with Christ effected by the Spirit. On the one hand, the Son fully expressed cosmic wisdom as Word and Image. To be a lover of wisdom was, ultimately, to be a lover of the Son. On the other hand, the incarnation marked the entrance of cosmic wisdom into human history. To be united and conformed to Christ meant both perceiving the wisdom of God (faith) and moving toward a greater vision of this wisdom (understanding). As ancient philosophers had argued, perceiving wisdom (vision) meant embodying wisdom (virtue), but Christians saw this as both seeing the wisdom of the Son of God as Logos and enacting this wisdom through the Spirit's activity in love and gifts. So important was this point that Gregory of Nazianzus coined *theosis* (deification) to argue for the prior *kenosis* (humanization) of the Son, without which the journey from

---

[64] See also Rom 1:24–32; 6:12; 7:5; Eph 2:3; 4:22; Col 3:5; 1 Thess 4:5; 1 Tim 6:9; 2 Tim 3:6; Titus 3:6; Jas 1:14–15; 1 Pet 1:4; 4:2–3; 2 Pet 2:18; 1 John 2:16–17; Jude 1:16, 18.

virtue and wisdom to God became impossible.[65] The journey that the liberal arts aided was a movement from the initial vision of faith and union through regeneration to a deeper understanding and likeness culminating in the beatific vision.

The Spirit made such a movement possible. Poured out on the day of Pentecost, the Spirit of wisdom and revelation birthed Christ in the soul and conformed the believer to Christ through a process of formation. The starting point of the ascent to God was the incarnation and the descent of the Spirit in the economy of salvation. While formation of the soul remained central to early Christians, they merged formation into ongoing conversion into the image of Christ through the Spirit. Ultimately, the *habitus* Christians were after was the Christ-patterned soul.

Over the course of Christianity's first five hundred years, early Christians located discussions of the liberal arts and learning in the context of a salutary teaching and piety that situated learners into the story of God and God's new humanity. Christian cosmopolitanism replaced the sage with the saint who began to see the story of the cosmos as the story of God. This approach understood the turn toward the good (*conversio*) within a broader story of God's descent into the world (the *oikonomia* or economy of God) in order to form and heal humans. The Christian understanding of God as triune reinforced the story about God's actions in creation, thereby filling out the new cosmic narrative for education and learning. Being conformed to Christ through the Spirit marked the ascent, which meant that learning, teaching, and piety formed part of God's gracious extension of salvation to all.

The divine plan had a pedagogical purpose, and this broader teleology became the means by which the goals of therapy, flourishing, and cosmic citizenship could be assimilated into a Christian understanding of education. Such an approach allowed early Christian writers to retain a role for the liberal arts in the formation of virtue as a preliminary set of practices designed to cultivate virtue and unlock wisdom. As Origen advised Gregory, "I have desired that with all of the power of your good nature you would apply yourself, ultimately, to Christianity. I have, for this reason, prayed that you would accept effectively those things from the philosophy of the Greeks that can serve as a general course of studies (*enkyklia mathēmata*) or an introduction (*propaideumata*)."[66] The whole edifice of learning continued to assist the person in the quest to be conformed to wisdom. Such an approach was how early Christians fused moral formation with conversion and openness to transcendence with a Christian understanding of encounter as an eschatological and charismatic event. The result was Christian mission in the world as the Christian became a citizen of the city of God.

Against the preceding backdrop, this second section focuses the discussion of education among early Christians upon three areas to show how they assimilated the view of education as a *habitus* invested in moral formation and openness to transcendence. Early

---

[65] See Donald F. Winslow, *The Dynamics of Salvation: A Study in Gregory of Nazianzus* (Cambridge, Mass.: Philadelphia Patristic Foundation, 1979), 95–97; Christopher A. Beeley, *Gregory of Nazianzus on the Trinity and the Knowledge of God: In Your Light We Shall See Light* (New York: Oxford University Press, 2008), 115–51.

[66] Origen, *Ep. ad Greg.* With slight modification, translation taken from Joseph W. Trigg, *Origen*, The Early Church Fathers (London: Routledge, 1998), 211. *Euphuia* could be rendered "innate capacity" or "good nature." It is in reference to the natural goodness humans possess at creation.

Christians viewed learning and education in terms of participation in the story of God's descent into history (§2.2.1) that was conveyed through salutary teaching (§2.2.2) for the purposes of cultivating genuine piety in the soul and enabling the soul to encounter God (§2.2.3). This piety was the expression of the *habitus* or new way of life Christians sought.

2.2.1 Education as Participation in the Story of God

Early Christians framed their understanding of history in terms of the outworking of the divine plan in time. The temporal framework for the story of God stemmed from the way first-century Christians understood the coming of Christ as a divine plan that unfolded in the midst of the succession of "ages." As Paul asserted, the Christ event revealed God's "plan for the fullness of time" (*oikonomian tou plērōmatos tōn kairōn*) (Eph 1:9–10). Not only did this phrase underscore a climactic moment in history: it connected this moment to the providential administration of time. While *oikonomia* retained the basic meaning of domestic or political management by a steward (*oikonomos*), it could be applied to the management of the cosmos through its arrangement or the literary structure of a text.[67] The continuity among these nuances was design: the assigning of a particular shape, order, or structure to a household, city, or piece of literature.

Luke-Acts utilizes a similar approach through a narrative catechesis that taught early Christians how the plan of God unfolded in the subplots of Christ (Luke) and the Spirit (Acts). The literary arrangement in Luke's narrative gestures toward a divine architect arranging time into a particular story. For Luke-Acts, "conversion is not so much an acquiescence to a particular set of faith claims as it is participation in the unfolding of a particular story."[68]

This understanding of history led to a contrast in the Pastoral Epistles between "myths" and "God's architectural arrangement" (*oikonomia theou*) (1 Tim 1:4; Titus 1:14). In the Pastoral Epistles, the distinction between two different narrative accounts of origins and identity became the basis for two distinct types of teaching, with only "salutary teaching" facilitating the healing of the soul.[69] As the inspired record of God's story, Scripture conveys the wisdom that cures, thereby remaining beneficial "for teaching" (*pros didaskalian*) and "for training in righteousness" (*pros paideian tēn en dikaiosunē*) (2 Tim 3:16).

Not only did the idea of a plan offer a replacement story of origins and identity to early Christians, it pointed toward a structure to time itself. As God's household (*oikos*) and God's story, creation unfolded through a series of plots that culminated in the coming of Christ who

---

[67] John H. Reumann, *Stewardship and the Economy of God* (Grand Rapids: Eerdmans, 1992; repr. Eugene: Wipf and Stock, 2014), 11–38; Giorgio Agamben, *The Kingdom and the Glory: For a Theological Genealogy of Economy and Government*, trans. Lorenzo Chiesa (Stanford: Stanford University Press, 2011), 1–67. The Latin equivalents of *oikonomia* (*dispositio/dispensatio*) also referred to the structure or order (*taxis*) of a text. See Aristotle, *On Rhetoric* 3.13; Quintilian, *Institutio oratoria* 7.1. What for Aristotle is the *taxis* or *oikonomia* of an argument becomes its *dispositio* in Quintilian. Both are speaking of the orderly arrangement.

[68] Joel B. Green, *Conversion in Luke-Acts: Divine Action, Human Cognition, and the People of God* (Grand Rapids: Baker Academic, 2015), 87.

[69] The term *mythos* can mean a fable or a cosmic story that signaled cultural and religious identity as well as origins. Plutarch moved between both meanings of the term. For our interpretation of *mythos* in the PE, see Korinna Zamfir, *Men and Women in the Household of God: A Contextual Approach to the Roles and Ministries in the Pastoral Epistles* (Göttingen: Vandenhoeck & Ruprecht, 2013), 173.

summarized those plots and the Spirit who drove history toward its telos.[70] In the second century Irenaeus of Lyons claimed that the Word "was made the steward (*dispensator*) of the Father's grace for the benefit of humanity for whose sake he made these dispensations (*dispositiones*), showing God to humanity and displaying humanity to God."[71] Every "dispensation" in the story of God was a subplot within an overarching narrative that unfolded through the stewardship of the Son and the Spirit. The triune God was the architect of time.[72]

The ascent from visible to invisible realities occurred through participation in and deeper understanding of the story of God. While Clement of Alexandria described this structure to his pagan audience as the poetic song of wisdom incarnate, Irenaeus of Lyons utilized it to demonstrate the veracity of apostolic preaching.[73] Origen's *On First Principles*, however, offered the first systematic interpretation of this story as a movement between theology proper (vision of God) and economy (plan of God in time) through an exposition of apostolic teaching supplemented by the teaching of the church.[74] In the Latin West, Augustine reframed the story of God in terms of two societies, each bound together by its loves.[75] Augustine's predecessor Lactantius grounded his *Divine Institutes* in a universal Christian history that situated the history of Rome within the epic panorama of God's providence.[76] These patristic writers illustrate how early Christians operated out of a shared commitment to a teleological structure to history that served as a framework by which insights from philosophy and the liberal arts could be adjudicated. The entire approach to theology in the early church was historical and catechetical. Both were informed by the basic narrative framework found in the rule of faith passed along through episcopal teaching. Education was first and foremost about entering into a story that now defined the person.

The idea that God had orchestrated time and history according to a particular structure became the basic way to understand Christian identity. The Pauline emphasis on a divine in-breaking of the age to come into this present age was adapted to the distinction between the heavenly and the earthly and the permanent and the transient. The story of God's dramatic involvement in time became the basis for what Denise Buell has called "ethnic reasoning." Over against the cosmopolitanism of Hellenistic education, early Christians saw this story as forming a new ethnicity and a Christian identity that they then argued was the most authentic form of *humanitas*.[77]

[70] On the meaning of *oikonomia* in Ephesians 1:10, see Stephen E. Fowl, *Ephesians: A Commentary* (Louisville: Westminster John Knox, 2012), 46; Andrew T. Lincoln, *Ephesians*, Word Biblical Commentary 42 (Grand Rapids: Zondervan, 1990), 31–32; Ernest Best, *Ephesians* (London: T&T Clark, 1998), 138.

[71] *Against Heresies* 4.20.7.

[72] The phrase is taken from Eric Osborn, *Irenaeus of Lyons* (Cambridge: Cambridge University Press, 2001), 74. While Osborn uses it of Irenaeus, it applies equally well to the first century.

[73] Clement of Alexandria, *Exhortation to the Greeks*; Ireneaus of Lyons, *Against Heresies*; Irenaeus of Lyons, *Demonstration of the Apostolic Preaching*.

[74] See the introduction by John Behr in *Origen: On First Principles*, vol. 1 (Oxford: Oxford University Press, 2017), xv–lxxxix.

[75] Augustine, *City of God* 19.24.

[76] See Oliver Nicholson, "*Civitas Quae Adhuc Sustentat Omnia*: Lactantius and the City of Rome," in *The Limits of Ancient Christianity: Essays on Late Antique Thought and Culture in Honor of R. A. Markus*, ed. William E. Klingshirn and Mark Vessey (Ann Arbor: University of Michigan Press, 1999), 7–24.

[77] Denise K. Buell, *Why This Race: Ethnic Reasoning in Early Christianity* (New York: Columbia University Press, 2005); and Judith Lieu, *Neither Jew nor Greek? Constructing Early Christian Identity* (New York: T&T Clark, 2005).

One can see this in *The Epistle to Diognetus*, in which the author declares that Christians live in their own countries as aliens because "every foreign land is their homeland and every homeland is foreign" (Diog. 5:5). For this reason, Christians are to the cosmos what the soul is to the body. They are spread throughout the whole and yet their piety remains invisible (Diog. 6:1–4). Whereas Hellenistic educational ideals employed *paideia* and *humanitas* to forge a cultural fabric that gave rise to a common identity across the empire, Christian writers understood *humanitas* through the Christian story that defined them as a new *ethnos* of people who were also translocal.[78] The saint replaced the sage as the one who saw the vision of the heavenly city after having been caught up ecstatically into the presence of Christ through the Spirit.

The theological wrestling over how to integrate learning and education into Christianity largely took place over concerns about the story of God becoming distorted in light of other cosmic stories. Tertullian's questioning of Athenian philosophy comes in the context of citing the Pastoral Epistle's rejection of myths and fables. It is no mistake that Tertullian refers to philosophy as "the subject matter of the wisdom belonging to this *saeculum*." His primary concern was to resist efforts by gnostic Christians to rewrite the story of God by appealing to other cosmic narratives about human life.[79] To do so was to engage in sophistry. In his *On Idolatry*, he quotes Paul, "Where is the sage, where the school master (*litterator*), where the disputer of this age (*conquisitor huius aevi*)? Has not God made foolish the wisdom of this *saeculum*?" (1 Cor 1:20, authors' translation) in order to launch into a discussion of elementary instruction through the schoolmaster (*ludimagister*). There is clearly an overlap for Tertullian between *saeculum*, *mundus*, and *aevum*. The *saeculum* is the present [evil] age embodied in the world, which he links to Hellenism and empire.[80] While recognizing that "worldly studies" (*saecularia studia*) serve as a necessary preliminary education to the divine, he rails against the fact that the task of the schoolmaster was to inculcate Hellenism into the child. Education was bound up with the cultural realities of citizenship in the empire.

The primary problem with Hellenistic learning is that it gives the child to the city. Even so, Tertullian recognizes that "literature is a tool for all of life."[81] As scholars have noted, despite his criticism of Athens, Tertullian still employed Stoic ideas and utilized his training in rhetoric to clarify and defend the Christian faith.[82] He was a philosopher in the

---

[78] See Judith Perkins, *Roman Imperial Identities in the Early Christian Era* (New York: Routledge, 2009), 26; and Greg Woolf states, "Roman rule is presented as providing the conditions for human beings to realize their potential fully, by becoming civilized, and so truly human." Greg Woolf, *Becoming Roman: The Origins of Provincial Civilization in Gaul* (Cambridge: Cambridge University Press, 1998), 57.

[79] Tertullian, *Prescription against Heretics* 7.

[80] Tertullian, *On Idolatry* 9–10. See also Tertullian, *To the Martyrs* 2–3, in which he uses *saeculum* and *mundum* interchangeably, but then also refers to a "citizenship in the heavens [that] is glory into the ages of the ages" (*politia in caelis, gloria in saecula saeculorum*). Tertullian is most likely taking both phrases from Paul's reference in Philippians to "citizenship in the heavens" (*to politeuma en ouranois*) (3:20) and "glory for ever and ever" (*doxa eis tous aiōnas tōn aiōnōn*) (4:20).

[81] Tertullian, *On Idolatry* 10. The chapter begins with the elementary instruction received under the schoolmaster and moves to all liberal arts, which he incapsulates by weaving together *littera*, *litteratura*, and *secularia studia*.

[82] On debate over Tertullian and philosophy, see David E. Whilhite, *Tertullian the African* (Berlin: De Gruyter, 2007), 19–23; Eric Osborn, *Tertullian: First Theologian of the West* (Cambridge: Cambridge University Press, 1997), 27–47.

ancient sense of a person pursuing wisdom through a particular way of life. The question was whether the Christian capitulated to Hellenism and the present age or the new way of life in Christ. For Tertullian, the *regula fidei* summarized this way of life within a narrative (the story of God) that could not be broken apart.

He makes a similar point in *Against Praxeas* when he claims that the rule of faith demonstrates that the one God "under this arrangement" (*sub hac dispensatione*) has a Son and a Spirit.[83] Revealing his education in rhetoric, Tertullian shows the reader that he knows full well *dispensatio* means *oikonomia*. He proceeds to argue from the orderly arrangement of the divine plan in history to an internal structure that governs triune existence. He warns his opponents that those "overthrowing the structure and arrangement (*dispositionem et dispensationem*)" of God will end up destroying the divine monarchy itself.[84] Christian thinkers primarily rooted in Hellenism's *mythos* fail to see the connection between an order to time and an internal order to God's own life. The rule of faith implicitly reveals this very connection. As two competing narratives of identity, Athens and Jerusalem could not be reconciled. It would be wrong to conclude, however, that insights from philosophy could not still illuminate the Christian story. Learning and education came to mean cultivating deeper insights into the story of God as a means of participating in it.

Tertullian's criticisms were simply a more strident form of the basic Christian critique of Hellenism. One of the challenges of Hellenistic *paideia* was its attempt to create a cultural identity: *humanitas* became *Romanitas*. Early Christian writers expressed deep concern over the way Hellenism habituated individuals away from piety and toward idolatry and immorality in the context of creating a new cultural identity. In his appeal to Antoninus Pius, Justin Martyr hoped that the emperor would aim for the kind of "piety and philosophy" that seeks to live in light of the truth rather than custom.[85] Referring to the effects of custom, Justin claimed that "we were brought up in coarse habits and wicked education."[86] Clement of Alexandria saw the common opinions arising from the poetic myths that grounded Hellenism as perpetuating "wicked custom," which, like a deadly drug, enslaves and turns individuals into raving lunatics. His primary aim in his *Protrepticus* was "to prove to you that it was from madness and from this thrice miserable custom that hatred of piety sprang."[87]

Writing at the beginning of the fourth century, Lactantius assured his audience that "men of the highest genius have bordered upon truth and almost touched it, except that custom (*consuetudo*), smeared with warped opinions (*pravis opinionibus*), has twisted and seized them."[88] Even though writing after Christianity had gained control of the mechanisms of political and social power, Basil of Caesarea still warned young men to read the poets in light of the Christian concern to prepare for the life to come that

---

[83] Tertullian, *Against Praxeas* 2.
[84] Tertullian, *Against Praxeas* 4.
[85] Justin Martyr, *First Apology* 12. There is a close connection between custom, culture, and character in the term *ethos*, which Aristotle had employed in his *Art of Rhetoric* to describe a set of arguments that appealed to the character of a person.
[86] Justin Martyr, *First Apology* 61.
[87] Clement of Alexandria, *Exhortation to the Greeks* 10 (Loeb, 197).
[88] Lactantius, *Divine Institutes* 1.5.

Scripture declares through its mysteries. Hellenistic learning is only useful if the student becomes like a bee who discriminates among flowers and knows how to extract the right nectar that facilitates the healing of the soul through virtue.[89] These Christian writers shared a concern for the way in which Hellenistic literature propagated an ethos (a culture that constructed a character) that contributed to the warping of human desire and the ignorance of the mind.

Christian writers recast learning and education through the story of God. This is the case not simply for those writing in Latin or Greek, but even for Syriac writers attempting to offer a rationale for the school of Nisibis. In his *The Cause of the Foundation of the Schools*, Barhadbeshabbā explained the purpose of learning by appealing to a basic narrative that begins with the condescension of grace, moves to God, angels, and humans, and concludes with a history that divides humanity into schools of thought from Adam to the school of Nisibis. The speech combines history and catechesis under the framework of the story of God to show students how to integrate pagan schools and learning into their journey at Nisibis. The story of God was a unifying narrative that equated *humanitas* with God's *philanthropia* to create and restore humanity. It grounded this *humanitas* in God's own orderly arrangement of time, which itself reflected a deeper structure to God's own life. Education emerges from this trinitarian vision of life.

2.2.2 Salutary Teaching: Christic Meditation

Reflecting back on the first several decades of the movement, both Paul and Luke viewed teaching as central to Christianity's mission, no doubt due to Jesus' role as teacher and the Spirit's pentecostal outpouring of inspired speech and charismatic gifting.[90] The Gospel of Matthew described Jesus' teaching through a rabbinic prism, while Luke and John treated it more in terms of its Hellenistic milieu. Following the meal, the symposium offered a time of drink and conversation allowing for philosophical discussion. Plutarch justified philosophical talk with good wine because philosophy concerned how one should live.[91] These times of "table talk" became the place to disseminate philosophical ideas in popular form, which may be one reason why Luke and John place the Last Supper into the context of the symposium. Philosophy as a way of life easily merged into the new "way" that Christ became for his disciples. Such "table talk" found a receptive womb in the house church as shared meals, worship, and teaching—reinforced by the presence of the risen Lord, the teacher in the midst of the gathering—became the mechanisms of discipleship. These early Christian portraits of Jesus explain the prominent role of *didaskalia* within Christian communities and its salutary aim.

Salutary teaching concerned the articulation of the story of God in the context of the educational enterprise. The numerous "faithful sayings" laced throughout the Pastoral Epistles established a narrative framework for the proclamation that "God's grace has appeared, bringing salvation to all humanity, educating (*paideuousa*) us so that, denying

---

[89]   Basil of Caesarea, "Letter to the Young on Pagan Literature" 2–4 (Loeb, 381–91).

[90]   Note the role of teachers in Luke-Acts and Ephesians. We assume Pauline influence if not authorship of Ephesians and Lukan authorship of Luke-Acts. Moreover, both Luke-Acts and Ephesians offer a take on the first three decades of Christianity (roughly 30 AD–60 AD).

[91]   Plutarch, *Table Talk*, Question 1, Loeb, 9.

impiety and worldly desires, we should live soberly, justly, and piously in this present age" (Titus 2:11–12, authors' translation). The Pastoral Epistles frame their instruction in terms of two contrasting forms of teaching (*didaskalia*), the first of which is a "divergent teaching" (*heterodidaskalein*) that contributes to the soul's sickness, while the second is a salutary teaching (*hygiainousē didaskalia*) that contributes to human flourishing. Christian views of education centered around the meaning of teaching that advanced flourishing over against teaching that increasingly warped human desire thereby worsening the soul's sickness. This meant that teaching must occur within the borders of the new narrative of identity that the story of God embodied.

To be salutary, however, this teaching must participate in the role of Christ as teacher. The teaching of Christ did not simply refer to his earthly ministry but also involved the way in which the Son was the Logos who ordered creation and continued to speak through it. Ultimately, to call Christ teacher referred to the harmony between the Word in creation and redemption. Within the story of God, the Word never ceased to teach humanity. This view of the Word allowed Christian writers to redescribe the origin of the arts in terms of Christ's revelatory work as the wisdom that governed life and to see that an encounter with wisdom was an encounter with Christ. Augustine describes his discovery of Cicero's *Hortensius* while undergoing the course of studies in Carthage as causing him to yearn for wisdom. He later interpreted this enkindled love for wisdom through a transcendent encounter as a love for Christ, the wisdom of God.[92] Salutary teaching had the cosmic Christ who unified creation and redemption as its ground.

Grounded in the Word's universal activity, salutary teaching referred to human flourishing through the healing of the soul and its participation in Christ. In describing his conversion to Christianity, Justin Martyr recounts his journey through Hellenistic educational ideals, which culminated in his learning under a Platonist. As a result of his learning, he found that "the perception of immaterial things quite overpowered me, and the contemplation of ideas furnished my mind with wings, so that in a little while I supposed that I had become wise; and such was my stupidity, I expected immediately to look upon God, for this is the end of Plato's philosophy."[93] Through Platonism Justin concluded that flourishing (*eudaimonia*) was the result of the knowledge and wisdom that comes from a vision of being and truth. Human reasoning must be a deeper reflection of the rational principle governing creation. He also followed Platonism in concluding that there was a kinship (*suggeneia*) between the soul and God. This affinity had to be acted upon through *eros*, which cultivated virtue as crucial to the vision of God.[94] While the quest for moral formation and encounters with transcendence came from his philosophical journey, Justin concluded that philosophy could not make good on its promises to heal the soul through an ascent into the heavens.

This philosophical position laid the groundwork for his turn to see the Word as the embodiment of the wisdom already present within creation. In his second apology

---

[92] Augustine, *Confessions* 3.4.7–8.

[93] Justin Martyr, *Dialogue with Trypho* 2. *Saint Justin Martyr: The First Apology, The Second Apology, Dialogue with Trypho, Exhortation to the Greeks, Discourse to the Greeks, The Monarchy or Rule of God*, trans. Thomas B. Falls, The Fathers of the Church 6 (Washington, DC: Catholic University of America Press, 1948), 149–51.

[94] Justin Martyr, *Dialogue with Trypho* 4 (Falls, 153–56).

Justin argued that every human participated in the Word through their own rationality.[95] There was a christological pattern to human existence evinced in the rational structures of the soul. Yet this "seed" of divine rationality was only the potential to imitate God by reasoning. Justin states, "The seed and imitation of something, given in terms of a capacity, is one thing while the thing itself, the participation and imitation of which occurs according to His grace, is another."[96] The capacity had to be cultivated in the right way.

Justin argued this could only come through conscious recognition that the pattern of human rationality was the Word who had become flesh. Such a recognition came through a divine act of grace. The similarity between Platonic philosophy and Christian theology was due to the same Word speaking either through creation or through redemption. Justin used the same argument in his dialogue with Trypho to claim that the Word spoke in the Old Testament through theophanies.[97] By taking this approach, he laid the groundwork for how Christians would appropriate philosophical insights.

Because of the role of the Son in creation, Clement of Alexandria claimed that the Word was the teacher who gave philosophy to the Greeks.[98] Clement saw the Son as "the Father's most ancient Word and his Wisdom. He is most properly called the Teacher of the beings fashioned by him."[99] Even more than Justin, Clement argued that the Word was the unity behind sacred and secular learning. Any insights from philosophy were themselves a partial glimpse of the Word's continuous discourse within creation. Greek philosophy primed the soul for true wisdom by purging it of falsehoods in preparation for faith. Clement thought of philosophy as a covenant given to the Greeks to enable them to climb up "to the philosophy which is according to Christ."[100]

Clement reveals how Christians fused moral formation with conversion to Christ. As John Behr notes, Clement understands the economy (story of God) from the perspective of *paideia* so that the pattern of the Word in exhorting, training, and teaching is the ground of human advancement.[101] The ascent to God was through Christ "the foundation and superstructure" by moving from faith to knowledge and then to love, which assimilated the person to God's character. The ground of true gnosis is the wisdom found in the Son, which unfolds through the story of God from prophets to apostles, and this wisdom, when known and embodied, culminates in "the unending and unchangeable habit of contemplative vision."[102] This was more than mere moral formation. It was a full realization of human rationality and personal identity through a reshaping of the structures of the soul to the pattern in Christ. The *habitus* resulting from formation to the Word through

---

[95] Justin Martyr, *Second Apology* 13. *St. Justin Martyr: The First and Second Apologies*, trans. Leslie William Barnard (New York: Paulist, 1997), 83–84.

[96] Justin Martyr, *Second Apology* 13 (Barnard, 84). I have altered the translation.

[97] See Justin Martyr, *Dialogue with Trypho* 55–61 (Falls, 230–45).

[98] Clement of Alexandria, *Stromata* 7.2. Alexander Roberts and James Donaldson, eds., *Ante-Nicene Christian Library*, vol. 12.2, *Writings of Clement of Alexandria* (Edinburgh: T&T Clark, 1869), 410 (hereafter ANCL).

[99] Clement of Alexandria, *Stromata* 7.2 (ANCL, vol. 12.2, 411).

[100] Clement of Alexandria, *Stromata* 6.8 (ANCL, vol. 12.2, 340–41).

[101] John Behr, *Asceticism and Anthropology in Irenaeus and Clement* (Oxford: Oxford University Press, 2000), 133.

[102] Clement of Alexandria, *Stromata* 6.7 (ANCL, vol. 12.2, 339).

ongoing encounters leads to the final stability of the vision of the end.[103] Philosophy and the liberal arts could never supply the apotheosis that pagan writers had claimed. The only path to healing was through assimilation to the Word, which was how Clement integrated philosophy into Christian teaching so that it became salutary.

By the early fourth century, this basic approach of grounding moral formation and the encounter with transcendence in the cosmic Christ became part of the Christian understanding of *paideia*. Echoing Justin and Clement, Origen set the tone by claiming that "all who are rational are partakers of the Word of God, that is, of Reason, and through this, like certain seeds implanted within them, they bear wisdom and justice, which is Christ."[104] One can see this approach fully in Athanasius, whom Gregory of Nazianzus later recalled as having been primarily trained in religious customs and instructions with a brief excursion into the cycle of studies related to philosophy.[105]

Athanasius' early two-volume work (*Against the Greeks* and *On the Incarnation of the Word*) bears out Gregory's claim as Athanasius engages and incorporates philosophical ideas in order to communicate the "teaching of Christ" (*tēs christou didaskalias*).[106] The treatises represent a deep reworking of Christian tradition that formed the primary basis for Athanasius' education in Alexandria. Like Clement, Athanasius grounded *humanitas* in the *philanthrōpia* of the Word who created and then re-created humanity. The divine purpose in creation and salvation was an outworking of the divine *philanthrōpia* expressed in and through the Word, which formed the fundamental pattern for humanness. He repeatedly refers to the event of the incarnation as the embodiment of divine *philanthrōpia* because it underscores the salutary teaching of the Word in creation and salvation.[107] All forms of learning begin with the "humanizing" movement of the Word, the embodiment of the divine "love-for-humanity." This sets the tone for how the Word educates humanity.

---

[103] Clement of Alexandria, *Stromata* 6.8 (ANCL, vol. 12.2, 339–44). See also Norman Russell, *The Doctrine of Deification in the Greek Patristic Tradition* (Oxford: Oxford University Press, 2004), 121–40.

[104] Origen, *On First Principles* 1.3.6 (Behr, 75); translation modified.

[105] Gregory of Nazianzus, *Oration* 21. Philip Schaff and Henry Wace, eds., *A Select Library of Nicene and Post-Nicene Fathers of the Christian Church*, vol. 12: *Cyril of Jerusalem and Gregory Nazianzen* (New York: Christian Literature Society, 1894), 269–80 (hereafter NPNF). Gregory employs the term *enkyklios*, suggesting Athanasius had some exposure to the cycle of studies that formed the basis for Hellenistic education, although Gregory also indicates that it was limited. On Athanasius' education, see Timothy D. Barnes, *Athanasius and Constantine: Theology and Politics in the Constantinian Empire* (Cambridge, Mass.: Harvard University Press, 1993), 10–15; Gerald J. Donker, *The Text of the Apostolos in Athanasius of Alexandria* (Atlanta: Society of Biblical Literature, 2011), 10–14.

[106] Athanasius, *Against the Greeks* 1 (NPNF, vol. 4, 4). Athanasius also refers to this teaching as divinely inspired (*entheos didaskalia*). See *On the Incarnation of the Word* 3 (NPNF, vol. 4, 37–38).

[107] Note the following: *Against the Greeks* 41 (NPNF, vol. 4, 26): "But the God of all is by nature good and beyond beauty, and for this reason is also a lover of humanity (*philanthrōpos*). For one who is good would not envy anyone, which is why he does not withhold existence out of envy but desires that all exist so that he might express his love for humanity (*philanthrōpeuesthai*)"; *On the Incarnation of the Word* 1 (NPNF, vol. 4, 36): "being by nature incorporeal and Word from the beginning, yet, in accordance with his own Father's goodness and love for humanity (*philanthrōpian*), he appeared to us in a human body for our salvation"; *On the Incarnation of the Word* 4 (NPNF, vol. 4, 38): "we must speak of human origins so that you may know that we were the cause of his coming and that our transgression called forth the Word's love for humanity (*philanthrōpian*)." See Khaled Anatolios, *Athanasius: The Coherence of His Thought* (London: Routledge, 2004), 40–56.

Athanasius presents the Word as teacher in three ways to argue for a Christian vision of moral formation and encountering transcendence. Drawing on the language of types and shadows in Hebrews, he begins with the basic claim that humanity was given a share in the Word because human rationality functioned as a kind of "shadow" (*skias*) of the Word.[108] In Athanasius' words, God "constituted humanity to contemplate (*theōrētēn*) and understand being through likeness to him, giving [humanity] a conception and knowledge of its own eternity."[109] By virtue of the rational structure of human existence, humanity already possessed the capacity for contemplative vision of the wisdom behind creation. Under the tutelage of the Word, human freedom could ascend beyond the natural capacity for corruption and death endemic to creatureliness. The ascent to God began in the *capax dei* found in the image of God.

Second, the rationality of human existence found its counter in the rational structure of creation. Athanasius sees the Word as a kind of regulative principle "moving all things in creation" as one who is "distinct in being" and yet always present in energizing activity and power.[110] Because of the Word's presence within the cosmos, "creation through its order and harmony like written letters shouts out the signs of its lord and maker."[111] This is an early formulation of the idea that all of creation is a book whose structure mimics the internal structure of the mind, the divine arrangement of history in the story of God, and the internal structure to God's own life.

The fall for Athanasius was a turning away from the inherent connection to the Word and the contemplative vision this connection offered. Humans could no longer hear the divine discourse of the Word within creation. Without such a grounding in the stability of the Word, humanity turned back toward the nothingness out of which it had been created, resulting in the loss of bodily integrity and psychological integrity (corruption and death). The emergence of the passions as disordered desires concretizes the loss of psychological integrity summarized by the term corruption. The only path of return was through the same Word becoming flesh to lead humanity out of ignorance and corruption once again. The incarnation represents the third and final mode through which the Word teaches and heals humanity by displaying in human nature the same divine power and activity through miracles and wonders that he displayed in creation itself.

Athanasius fills out the story of God by focusing on the threefold activity of the Word—as the *imago Dei* in human beings, as the rational structures of creation, and in incarnation—who remains distinct from creation and yet deeply woven into it. This threefold activity means that the structures of life are themselves a replication of the patterns in the Word. In these early works, Athanasius has reframed the goal of philosophical ascent christologically. The Word heals the soul and enables contemplative vision by assimilating humanity to his own person. Hence the famous Athanasian paraphrase of Irenaeus that "he became human in order that we might be formed into the divine (*theopoiēthōmen*)."[112]

---

[108] *On the Incarnation of the Word* 3 (NPNF, vol. 4, 37–38).
[109] Athanasius, *Against the Greeks* 2 (NPNF, vol. 4, 5).
[110] Athanasius, *On the Incarnation of the Word* 17 (NPNF, vol. 4, 45).
[111] Athanasius, *Against the Greeks* 34 (NPNF, vol. 4, 22).
[112] Athanasius, *On the Incarnation of the Word* 54 (NPNF, vol. 4, 65–66). We have taken the term *theopoieō* in the sense of being given form or shape to since Athanasius has a basic idea of the Word as the divine artist giving shape to creation by regulating it.

Salutary teaching was defined christologically because the Word was the health and well-being of the soul. Christ was the *skopos* of the book of creation and the book of Scripture. This approach allowed for early Christian thinkers to place moral formation and the cultivation of virtue within a framework of conversion in which the soul was healed through the threefold work of the Word. The quest for wisdom was a search for the structures of humanity and creation that revealed the cosmic Christ. Moreover, to encounter wisdom was to encounter Christ as the teacher both within the soul and within the cosmos. Such a view set the tone for the early Augustine's focus on Christ as the inward teacher who illuminated the mind and made the ascent to truth possible.[113] The liberal arts retained the basic function of meditative tools that they had in a philosopher like Epictetus, but they were not related to creating a sage who had a cosmic vision of the world. Instead, they concerned the creation of a saint in whom contemplative vision, ecstatic embrace, and prophetic insight coalesced. Yet this move into sainthood required the holiness commensurate with piety, which meant to be infused by the Spirit.

2.2.3 Cultivating Genuine Piety: Infused with the Spirit

One of the central aims of education was to facilitate social cohesion through the cultivation of a cosmopolitan identity that transcended local cultures within the empire. The terms that most embodied this goal were *eusebeia/theosebeia/pietas*. In many respects, piety symbolized in a single term the kind of *habitus* that education in the service of empire sought to cultivate. As Robert Wilken makes clear, piety became a relational term designating the bonds between family, custom, and the traditions of the empire.[114] It exemplified an internal disposition of devotion and a set of external relations bound up in the display of honor. Piety symbolized the bonds created in the reciprocity found in Hellenistic ideas of benefaction. On the Greek side of the empire, piety (*eusebeia/theosebeia*) functioned as a term for religion insofar as it expressed the honor reciprocated to the benefaction of ancestral customs and traditions over against superstition. The combination of inward disposition and outward relational bonds provided the basic framework that fused together moral formation and openness to transcendence with the narrative rationality of the Christian message. This fusion continued against the backdrop of a common cultural framework, which was prevalent in the late antique society of the Roman Empire.

As an internal reality, piety pointed toward a sanctity that cured the soul of the disease of disordered desire or the passions. Clement frames his discussion of the gnostic Christian in terms of a conversation with philosophers, hoping that they will draw upon their own training (*paideia*) to see the point that "the Gnostic alone is holy and pious."[115] This piety unfolds in terms of service given back to God as the soul's continuous pursuit of God in ceaseless love (*agapē*). It continues in the service to neighbor through medical art and philosophy as well as deeds that contribute to

---

[113] See Augustine, *The Teacher*. Augustine, *Against the Academicians and The Teacher*, translated with introduction and notes by Philip King (Indianapolis: Hackett, 1995), 94–146.

[114] Robert Louis Wilken, *The Christians as the Romans Saw Them*, 2nd ed. (New Haven: Yale University Press, 2003), 54–62.

[115] Clement of Alexandria, *Stromata* 7.1 (ANCL, vol. 12.2, 406–9).

human flourishing. Grace concerned the lavish gifts of God, which were reciprocated in the bond of piety.

Through all of this, Clement sees piety as a "habit (*hexis*) that preserves what is fitting to God," thereby making the person a lover of God (*theophilēs*). By cultivating piety through knowledge and holiness, the Gnostic is already "being assimilated" to God.[116] Citing the prophecy in Joel 2, Clement argues that the divine mind does not come through some effluence as the philosophers had claimed, but through the Spirit.[117] He goes on to say that "the beauty of the soul becomes a temple of the Holy Spirit when it acquires the disposition in assimilation to the gospel."[118] Such assimilation means being cured of the passions, which are disordered movements in the soul so that "through the habit or disposition of the soul endued with virtue" the pious and holy believer has "transcended the entire life of passion."[119] The work of philosophy to heal the soul has been taken up in the work of the Word and the Spirit to demonstrate that Christian perfection entails the cultivation of the internal disposition of holiness or piety that opens up the person for mission.

The Christian integration of the Hellenistic education became centered upon the argument over the nature of genuine piety. For Lactantius, the fundamental purpose to human existence revolved around piety. He states, "If humanity was wise, its purpose would be clear: humanity (*humanitas*) is its unique property. What is humanity, however, if not justice (*iustitia*) and what is justice if not piety (*pietas*)? Now, piety is nothing else than knowledge of God our procreator. For this reason, the highest good of humanity consists in religion alone (*in sola religione*)."[120] The problem is that philosophers have failed to understand the proper connection between religion and wisdom as two essential features of what it means to be human. Humanism is itself an outworking of justice and piety stemming from the pursuit of wisdom and religion.

Gregory of Nyssa makes similar claims in his discussion of Moses' ascent up the mountain to contemplative vision. He likens the education he received to placing Moses in the basket so that he might float on top of the water to Pharoah's daughter, who, as an Egyptian, symbolizes "foreign philosophy."[121] Philosophy is a kind of barren wisdom that cannot give birth to the knowledge of God because truth is the "sure apprehension of genuine being" and "participation in genuine being." Gregory defines "genuine being" in terms of the triune God, which means in relation to the revelation of the Word and the Spirit.

What is required is a person like Moses who knows how to slay anything that is foreign to piety (*eusebeia*). The problem ultimately is not the knowledge generated by education, but knowing how to take the wealth from the Egyptians and use it to beautify the mystery of faith. While Gregory acknowledges that the cycle of studies through moral and natural

---

[116] Clement of Alexandria, *Stromata* 7.1 (ANCL, vol. 12.2, 406–9).

[117] Clement of Alexandria, *Stromata* 5.12 (ANCL, vol. 12.2, 267–270); *Stromata* 6.15 (ANCL, vol. 12.2, 326–28).

[118] Clement of Alexandria, *Stromata* 7.11 (ANCL, vol. 12.2, 449–54).

[119] Clement of Alexandria, *Stromata* 7.11 (ANCL, vol. 12.2, 449–54). Clement employs *hexis* and *diathesis* as synonyms.

[120] Lactantius, *Divine Institutes* 3.9.19–10.1. *Lactantius: Divine Institutes*, trans. Anthony Bowen and Peter Garnsey (Liverpool: Liverpool University Press, 2003), 204–5.

[121] Gregory of Nyssa, *Life of Moses* 2.7–14. *Gregory of Nyssa: The Life of Moses*, trans. Abraham J. Malherbe, Classics of Western Spirituality (New York: Paulist, 1978), 56–58.

philosophy, geometry, and other disciplines contributes to the soul's beautification through virtue, this only leads to genuine piety when this learning is dedicated to the church and to God. Gregory sees his older brother Basil of Caesarea as embodying this idea.

In the fourth century, the debate around cultivating piety raged between polemics, with other Christians like the Eunomians who denied the Son was God, and pagans like the emperor Julian who decreed that Christians could no longer teach in the schools because they failed to maintain the cultural ethos necessary to propagate Hellenism. Central to this debate over the meaning of genuine piety was the role of *philanthropia* as both a divine quality and a human practice. Julian wanted Hellenistic learning and culture to embody *philanthropia*, to the point that he scolded his fellow pagans that they had not engaged in acts of kindness toward their fellow human beings as Christians had done even though *philanthropia* was itself connected to the gods.[122] Basil of Caesarea, Gregory of Nazianzus, and Gregory of Nyssa engaged Julian on this point of the relationship between *philanthropia*, piety, and service to the empire.

When Gregory of Nazianzus praised Basil of Caesarea for cultivating true philosophy, he pointed toward "the storehouse of piety" Basil had created through his construction of "Basileias," a series of buildings that together served as a hospice for the sick and the poor.[123] The concept of *philanthropia* became a way for the Cappadocians to fuse together Hellenistic learning with Christian love in the service of piety. Gregory of Nyssa framed his *Catechetical Oration* around the "mystery of piety." He then claimed that because *philanthropia* was "the characteristic property of the divine nature" God became flesh. Gregory states, "The goodness of [his purpose] would have profited nothing had wisdom not made love for humanity active."[124] In his work on the Spirit, Basil of Caesarea would relate *philanthropia* to the work of the Son and the Spirit in the economy of salvation because they express divine benefaction through the gifts they bestow, which, in turn, create the holiness commensurate with piety.[125]

Over the course of two decades, the Cappadocians delivered sermons that sought to apply *philanthropia* to matters of helping the poor through generosity of giving and engaging in civic duty. This was life in the city of God and, in Gregory of Nyssa's view, part of the path to healing the passions. Under the Cappadocians, philosophy, education, and learning meant cultivating an interior holiness through the love of the Spirit, which embodied God's own "humanizing" movement (*philanthropia*). As Basil put it, genuine piety meant following the way of Christ through the Spirit, which is the

---

[122] On this point, see Glanville Downey, "Philanthropia in Religion and Statecraft in the Fourth Century after Christ," *Historia* 4.2/3 (1955): 199–208; Brian E. Dailey, 1998 NAPS Presidential Address, "Building a New City: The Cappadocian Fathers and the Rhetoric of Philosophy," *Journal of Early Christian Studies* 7.3 (1999): 431–61.

[123] Gregory of Nazianzus, *Oration* 43.63. *Funeral Orations by St. Gregory Nazianzen and St. Ambrose*, trans. Leo P. McCauley, S.J., John J. Sullivan, C.S. Sp., Martin R. P. McGuire, and Roy J. Defferari, The Fathers of the Church (Washington, DC: Catholic University of America Press, 1953), 80. See Daley, "Building a New City," 432.

[124] Gregory of Nyssa, *Catechetical Oration* prologue; 15.2; 20.4. Gregory of Nyssa, *Catechetical Discourse: A Handbook for Catechists*, trans. Ignatius Green, Popular Patristics Series (New York: St. Vladimir's Seminary Press, 2019), 60, 96, 107.

[125] Basil of Caesarea, *On the Holy Spirit* 19.50. *On the Holy Spirit: Basil of Caesarea*, trans. and intro. Stephen Hildebrand (New York: St. Vladimir's Seminary Press, 2011), 86–87.

"orderly and sequential progress toward perfection through works of righteousness and through the illumination of knowledge, as we stretch ever onward and extend ourselves toward what remains until we arrive at a happy end, the contemplation of God that the Lord grants through himself to those who believe in him."[126] One can see how Basil has reframed true philosophy in terms of the *habitus* of piety, which keeps moving toward perfection and the final end. Such piety necessarily involved the internal disposition of holiness and its external manifestation of humanness (*philanthropia*). Moral formation was Christocentric mimesis through the Spirit's forming Christ within by reordering of the affective center of the person. To talk about education as the cultivation of a *habitus* places the dispositions and practices associated with learning in the broader context of the Christian understanding of salvation as divine therapy for the disease of sin. In this way, Christians forged links between moral formation and conversion as the Spirit's internal renewal of the image of God grounded upon the image of Christ.

The relationship between piety, holiness, and the ascent to God found its greatest exponent in Augustine. Augustine's interaction with the liberal arts moves from attempting to develop a program of learning around them to a modified approach bordering on rejection. In his Cassiciacum writings (386–87 AD), shortly after his conversion, he embraced the view that the liberal arts could move the person from the visible world to the invisible world through a process of moral formation. This move perpetuated the ancient idea that the liberal arts in relation to philosophy served the project of moral development and opened the person up to transcendence in a way that produced human flourishing. Placing Christian conversion in the context of an ascent to God through virtue, he claimed that the happy life entailed the possession of "that which always endures and cannot be snatched away through any severe misfortune."[127]

In this early phase, the liberal arts helped the person cultivate a habit of turning away from sensory things and focusing the mind on the self by enabling the person to sift the crowd of daily opinions on the path to truth.[128] In this way, they helped to combat depraved customs and the habits emerging from them. Although scholars have noted a shift in Augustine's attitude toward the liberal arts in the *Confessions* and *On Christian Teaching*, the ascent to God from the material to the immaterial through authority and reason remained fundamental to his program.[129] When Augustine began *On the Trinity* in 400, he framed his musings in terms of a journey from faith to sight or a movement to contemplation and enjoyment of the triune God.[130] Like Odysseus, the student must sail out of the harbor and find the way back home.[131] For these sailors,

---

[126] Basil of Caesarea, *On the Holy Spirit* 8.19 (Hildebrand, 48–50).

[127] Augustine, *On the Happy Life* 11. *Saint Augustine: The Happy Life, Answer to Skeptics, Divine Providence and the Problem of Evil, Soliloquies*, ed. Ludwig Schopp, The Fathers of the Church (Washington, DC: Catholic University of America Press, 1948), 58.

[128] Augustine, *On Order* 1.1.3 (Schopp, 239–40).

[129] See the essays in Karla Pollmann and Mark Vessey, eds., *Augustine and the Disciplines: From Cassiciacum to Confessions* (Oxford: Oxford University Press, 2005); and Kim Paffenroth and Kevin L. Hughes, *Augustine and Liberal Education* (Burlington: Ashgate, 2000).

[130] Augustine, *On the Trinity* 1.3.14–21.

[131] Augustine, *On the Happy Life* 1.2–3 (Schopp, 43–45).

philosophy has become a beacon pointing the way home, and yet initial successes at studying philosophy can lead them astray.

As he began to think more deeply about the Christian life, Augustine substituted Christology and pneumatology as the beginning and end of the ascent. To love wisdom was ultimately to be moved by the Spirit toward Wisdom. This modification did not mean that Augustine rejected ancient *paideia*; rather, he recognized that philosophy could not supply the kind of therapy that the soul ultimately needed in order to flourish, nor could it lead one to the triune God. As he explained to Lawrence, *sapientia* corresponds to *pietas* because genuine piety is worship of the God who alone grounds all existence.[132] Despite his battles with Pelagian views of the salvation, he retained the basic Ciceronian impulse that the human inability to ascend to God remained bound up with depraved social customs that had formed into bad habits. Part of the role of teaching and learning, especially for the Christian, was to cooperate with the Spirit to purify the mind, whose "sharpness was weakened by the habit of living under the shadow of the flesh."[133]

Learning presupposed a prior disposition and inculcated a basic *habitus* invested in the ascent to God, which culminated in the beatific vision. To this goal of learning, Augustine adapted the ancient ideal of piety as the foundational *habitus* that the Spirit births and that fuels the ascent if it is properly cultivated. One must always move through particular goods and truths to goodness and truth. Only the Spirit's outpouring of divine love could liberate human affectivity and desire to make this movement, thereby producing the piety that took humans on an ecstatic flight into a vision of God. Augustine repeatedly asserted that the soul changes over time through its affections.[134] As a fundamental appetite, love (*amor*) drives the affections, shaping them in various ways that either further warp or make the will upright. Love can become charity or cupidity depending on its direction and its proper moderation. Learning had to be a pneumatic enterprise as the person cooperated with the Spirit to move continuously through the goods of creation to God as the ultimate good. It was not to ignore temporal and created realities but to rightly relate to them by recognizing that the goodness and veracity of life is always derivative and participatory from the eternal ground of all things.

At one point, Augustine claims that those who love, know love in the act of loving and already have God intimately present within.[135] This is in part because the Spirit fills all things by his "witnessing and ordering presence."[136] Augustine's association of the Spirit with love means that humans are from the outset Christ-shaped and Spirit-infused, with the Spirit being present in the movement of *amor*. Learning always involves a journey into God through the nature of creation and humanity. By increasing knowledge of creation in light of God, one learns how to use material realities and enjoy one's fellow human beings

---

[132] Augustine, *Enchiridion* prologue.2. Augustine offers the same point to Julian of Eclanum when he applauds Julian for placing the good of human existence in virtue but failing to see "the virtue of true piety, for God has said to man: 'Behold, piety is wisdom'" (Job 28:28). See Augustine, *Opus imperfectum contra Julianum* 3.21.48.

[133] Augustine, *On Christian Teaching* 1.9.21.

[134] Augustine, *On True Religion* 10.18; Augustine, *On the Trinity* 8.7.11.

[135] Augustine, *On the Trinity* 8.4.9–8.5.12.

[136] Augustine, *Miscellany of Questions in Response to Simplician* 2.1.5.

as part of the community of being in which the journey is undertaken. At any point, however, the individual might become fixated through cupidity on this or that aspect of creation, which is why the Spirit's love is always necessary to transform love into charity. In light of christology and pneumatology, the liberal arts and philosophy could no longer be viewed as the primary and secondary mechanisms of the transformation and elevation of the human person.

Augustine represents a deeper step to Christianizing the liberal arts by bringing them up into a trinitarian understanding of ascent. Interpreting Augustine's project in terms of *On the Trinity* offers one way to view the relationship of *On Christian Teaching* to his early treatises.[137] Rather than rejecting philosophy and the liberal arts, Augustine placed them within a hierarchy of authorities with Scripture and the fathers at the top. This is clear in his *Against Julian*, where in the first book he registers his preference for the fathers over the philosophers, while in the fourth book he returns to Cicero's *Hortensius* to denounce Julian as not understanding the great philosophers on the soul and virtue in relation to the pleasure of the body. Situating philosophy and the liberal arts in their preparatory role, Augustine retained their role in the quest for truth as preliminary studies, which are surpassed by Scripture and the fathers. Cicero's quest to be a "citizen of the whole world" (*civis totius mundi*) who sees the world as a "single city" (*una urbs*) becomes Augustine's desire to perceive with keen intellectual vision the most glorious city of God, a pilgrim through this world by faith, yet destined to receive the final security of his eternal home.[138] Unpacking Augustine's pneumatological and christological poles reveals how he can hold a positive yet limited view of secular learning. The Spirit alone can produce the eternal form of the Word in the soul, and yet there is a pneumatological ground to all human existence found in the deep connection to love itself. The Spirit is always bearing witness by ordering love in fundamental ways, especially in and through the affections. Such an approach sets the stage for the medieval understanding of education and learning.

2.3   THE LIBERAL ARTS AND ENCOUNTER IN PERIODS OF REBIRTH

In two previous sections, we established a model of education centered on the cultivation of a *habitus*. This *habitus* emerges from moral formation and encounters with transcendence while facilitating mission in the world. These elements constitute the common framework between Hellenistic and Patristic approaches to education. We also argued that early Christians altered the framework within which moral formation and encounters with transcendence emerge. They substituted the story of God for the myths that grounded the civic identity of Roman citizenship, and this altered the mission from civic duties to Christian service. This trinitarian ground allowed early Christians to critique the purpose of education as forming a child for the city, even the cosmic city (cosmopolitanism), by substituting the saint for the sage.

---

[137] This is to follow Lewis Ayres' lead in *Augustine and the Trinity* (Cambridge: Cambridge University Press, 2010), 121–41.

[138] Cicero, *On the Laws* 1.61; Augustine, *On the City of God* preface; 23.1.

We also argued that the story of God allowed early Christians to fuse together Christology and pneumatology. The Jesus of the Scriptures was the Word in creation and thus the pattern for humanity. Restoration of the image of God required conforming to the pattern of Christ already present in the soul, albeit diseased and corrupted. This meant that moral formation concerned salutary teaching that drew upon the Word in creation and salvation to form and shape the human person. At the same time, piety (holiness) became shorthand for the formation of the *habitus* by the Spirit in and through love. The soul becomes a temple of the Spirit through the Spirit's sanctifying and charismatic operations, which form the person and open him or her up to transcendence. This shaping happens in the affections, which constitute the center of the human person. Moreover, piety was rooted in the concreted expression of divine *philanthropia*, which embodied true humanness. The Spirit enabled humans to take on a *habitus* that reflected God's "love for humanity" and thus a genuine humanism.

In this section, we turn to medieval scholasticism and the humanism driving the Renaissance and Reformation. While we recognize that covering such a long period will necessarily require us to be highly selective, we extend our argument by showing that the basic framework of a *habitus* continued. Key to our analysis is the claim that medieval scholasticism advanced an integral humanism.[139] The overarching purpose of this integral humanism was to form the whole person by showing how all knowledge contributed to the restoration of the image and the final end of the beatific vision. The broader concern of scholasticism was to place the liberal arts in a framework of moral transformation (sanctifying) and revelatory encounters (charismatic) to bring about personal and societal renewal (mission). The purpose of building great "cathedrals of the heart" was the unity of truth, goodness, and beauty in service of the integrity of the person and participation in that final unity who is Father, Son, and Holy Spirit.[140]

When we turn to the Renaissance and Reformation, we will show how literary and biblical humanism also emphasized an integral humanism. Renaissance humanism developed through the confluence of a number of historical and cultural factors. The outbreak of the Black Death and the Babylonian captivity of the papacy in Avignon combined with French and Byzantine scholarship to stimulate a generation of Italian thinkers. Emerging from these factors was a renewed focus on the liberal arts. By the end of the fourteenth century and the beginning of the fifteenth, this renewed focus was encapsulated in the phrase *studia humanitatis*, which "came to stand for a clearly defined cycle of scholarly disciplines, namely grammar, rhetoric, history, poetry, and moral philosophy."[141] As a new

---

[139] Jean Leclercq, O.S.B., *The Love of Learning and the Desire for God: A Study of Monastic Culture* (New York: Fordham University Press, 1982), 140. While we take the phrase from Leclercq, we also note that Jacques Maritain argued for an integral humanism in his *Humanism intégral: Problèmes temporels et spirituels d'une nouvelle chrétienté* (Paris: Ferdinand Auber, 1936).

[140] Our use of "cathedrals of the heart" is a play on Étienne Gilson's famous claim that medieval scholastics built cathedrals of the mind. See Étienne Gilson, *Christianity and Philosophy*, trans. Ralph MacDonald (London: Sheed and Ward, 1939), 114.

[141] Paul Oskar Kristeller, *Renaissance Thought: The Classic, Scholastic, and Humanist Strains* (New York: Harper, 1961), 9–10. See also idem, *Renaissance Thought: Papers on Humanism and the Arts* (New York: Harper, 1965), 1–19.

approach to learning, Renaissance humanism combined the liberal arts with an emphasis on moral philosophy and history.[142] This new approach ultimately represented a concern for the literary legacy of antiquity, which we interpret as a literary humanism.[143]

Even though Renaissance humanists saw their educational model as different from scholasticism, we argue that one can find similar themes that allow for the continued understanding of an integral humanism, grounded in the pursuit of ancient texts and an emphasis on human freedom and history. Due to their emphasis on Scripture, Protestant Reformers saw this humanism as "biblical" because it centered on the reading of scriptural texts and understood them as the locus of encounter and faith.

Our examination of medieval, Renaissance, and Reformation thinkers centers on the development of three humanisms: integral, literary, and biblical. The first part of this section examines the Abbey of St. Victor to argue that medieval thinkers reinvigorated the liberal arts around an integral humanism that wove together a developmental understanding of human nature with an ascent through creation to the Creator (§2.3.1). The second part turns to select thinkers from the Renaissance in order to show how Renaissance thinkers grounded human dignity in an emphasis on freedom, moral formation, and transcendence (§2.3.2). The final part attempts to show what happens to the liberal arts in the biblical humanism that the Protestant Reformers tried to develop (§2.3.3).

2.3.1 Scholasticism and the Abbey of St. Victor: An Integral Humanism

Scholasticism emerged initially in Paris at the dawn of the twelfth century. The Abbey of St. Victor provides an important example of the kind of trajectory we wish to describe because those associated with the abbey forged a comprehensive understanding of human learning in the service of the Gregorian reforms that were sweeping Europe.[144] The most important thinker at the abbey was Hugh of St. Victor. Over the course of twenty-five years (1115–1140), he developed a comprehensive program of reading and meditation grounded in the fundamental dignity of the human person. At the center of that program was a commitment to Christ as the pattern and agent of creation and salvation and the Spirit as the perfecter who operated within the structures of the world and the human person. The "journey of the mind" to God occurred through a comprehensive investigation of the books of creation and Scripture grounded upon Christ and the Spirit.

At its most basic level, the image of God underscored the mind's capacity to mirror God and creation simultaneously. What grounded this capacity was not only the mind's having been patterned upon divine Wisdom but also its possessing a natural aptitude to

---

[142] See Erika Rummel, *The Confessionalization of Humanism in Germany* (Oxford: Oxford University Press, 2000), 10.

[143] Nicholas Mann, "The Origins of Humanism," in *The Cambridge Companion to Renaissance Humanism*, ed. Jill Kraye (Cambridge: Cambridge University Press, 2004), 2.

[144] On the relationship between St. Victor and the rise of the university, see Stephen C. Ferruolo, *The Origins of the University and Their Critics, 1100–1215* (Stanford: Stanford University Press, 1985), 27–44; Olaf Pedersen, *The First Universities: "Studium Generale" and the Origins of University Education in Europe*, trans. Richard North (Cambridge: Cambridge University Press, 1997), 92–154; R. W. Southern, *Scholastic Humanism and the Unification of Europe*, vol. 2: *The Heroic Age*, notes and additions by Benedicta Ward and Leslie Smith (Oxford: Blackwell, 2001), 56–66; Perry L. Glanzer, Nathan F. Alleman, and Todd C. Ream, *Restoring the Soul of the University: Unifying Christian Higher Education in a Fragmented Age* (Downers Grove: IVP Academic, 2017), 17–38.

reason by virtue of its participation in the patterns of created things. The production of knowledge was an analogical process that began with the person's linguistic capacity to find correspondences between the interior world of self and the exterior world. In Hugh's words, "Having been stamped with the likeness of all things, the mind is called all things in that it receives its composition from all things and contains them, not completely, but in terms of a power and a capacity."[145] The mind could imaginatively construct mental words and images of created things because the structure of its mental architecture reflected and participated in the deep patterns behind all living things.

For Hugh, these deep patterns were nothing less than the divine ideas that formed the basis for what he described as the machine of the world. Central to the divine ideas were power, wisdom, and goodness, which Hugh saw as the primordial causes for all things. Hugh also discerned a trinitarian pattern with power being particular to the Father, wisdom to the Son, and goodness to the Spirit. The triune God created by power, disposed by wisdom, and willed by goodness. As the fount of divinity, the Father pours out his own Wisdom, who becomes the living pattern arranging all things by the Father's Goodness, who moves all things to perfection. To participate in the divine ideas was to have a share in power, wisdom, and goodness. This meant that humanity participated both in the Spirit through the goodness expressed in desire for the good and in the Son through the mind's rational structure and capacity to assimilate wisdom.

Love was the expression of goodness that oriented humanity toward the wisdom in creation. The mind built up a thick account of the external world because the person constantly participated in creation through love. Hugh referred to this early stage of learning as "thinking" (*cogitatio*). Driven by love, the mind roamed aimlessly over the landscape of texts and the external world constructing image after image or word after word. This movement meant that humans were bound up with the concreteness and particularity of creation. The basic impulse of love oriented them toward this created good or that truth without understanding how all fit into a whole that revealed the final good of God himself. Unless humans learned to organize and control the internal world of the self, their love would be ever absorbing creation and yet never fully grasping its teleology and thus how it should be utilized in the service of human life.

Each person had to move beyond mere "thinking" to the craft of meditation in order to learn to read correctly God's two great books of creation and Scripture. Individuals had to shape thought and desire. Drawing on Pentecost, Hugh saw the Spirit as the artisan who illuminated the mind with the light of knowledge and inflamed the will with the passion of desire.[146] Hugh's program stemmed from Christ as the wisdom toward which God had oriented humanity and the Spirit as the artist who formed and shaped knowledge and desire. He centered this program in the *Didascalicon* on reading and meditation. Reading concerned the assimilation and interpretation of texts as the

---

[145] Hugh of St. Victor, *Didascalicon* 1.1. *Didascalicon de studio legendi: A Critical Text*, ed. C. H. Buttimer (Washington, DC: Catholic University of America Press, 1939), 5–6; translation is my own. For a complete English translation, see Franklin Harkins and Frans van Liere, eds., *Interpretation of Scripture: Theory*, Victorine Texts in Translation 3 (Turnhout: Brepols, 2012), 80–201.

[146] Hugh of St. Victor, *On the Sacraments of the Christian Faith*, trans. Roy J. Deferrari, repr. (Eugene: Wipf and Stock, 2007), 1.6.17 (106); 2.2.1 (253–54).

received wisdom of the ancients. while meditation took flight from those texts into the world of the self and the cosmos.

Hugh also had a developmental understanding of human persons that informed his thought. While God created humans with being and life, the divine plan was to form and shape human existence in such a way as to become beautiful. Human development entailed a process of beautification in which forming human persons corresponded to sculpting a work of art.[147] This further underscored the importance of the Spirit as the artist who shaped human thought and affection. Like ancient Christian writers and philosophers, Hugh saw moral formation as the beautification of the soul.

By using the liberal arts to read God's language again, each person engaged in the artistic reshaping of the soul. Like Athanasius, Hugh understood creation to be the language of God, albeit encoded in the individual being of each thing. Scripture was another book that helped unlock the book of creation. This process invariably meant building up a thick body of knowledge, which Hugh thought required a mnemonic device. While the liberal arts were crucial to investigating creation and the language humans used to describe it, they required an aid to memory. Hugh proposed Noah's ark as a kind of master symbol that each person could use to shape the mind. The mind became a storehouse of knowledge by building an internal ark that held together everything one learned. Human integrity concerned achieving a unity in the self by participating in creation and using creation as a means to become like God. Reflected in Scripture and creation, divine beauty became internalized as one began to utilize the symbolic and mnemonic potential of the ark to reshape the soul. Flourishing as a human being concerned perfecting human potential by shaping one's life in a way that leads to the integration of the human person. Integrity is wholeness, shalom on the level of the person, and wholeness evinces beauty. To become beautiful is to flourish and to flourish is to be beautiful.

God invited humans to participate in this project of forming their lives. The liberal arts were tools that humans used to participate in the Spirit's sculpting of human existence. For example, the *trivium* of grammar, rhetoric, and dialectic deals with human language as the vehicle by which humans describe the world they inhabit. Yet, for Hugh, the *trivium* was not simply a way or path to grapple with human language as a mechanism of getting at the truth, it was also a means of organizing and shaping one's inner thought life. To begin to understand the relationships between terms in human language (the domain of grammar and logic/dialectic) and to begin to know how to formulate and harness the power of human language (the domain of dialectic and rhetoric) is to begin to take ownership of one's own thought life. The shaping and organizing of human language in the mind is part of moral formation. It is sculpting the mind's natural capacity for language in such a way as to make the mind a more effective vehicle in the discovery and promotion of truth. The liberal arts provide tools by which humans can become co-artists with God in the shaping of their own lives.

Another important idea that informed Hugh's thought concerned how the fallen nature of human life created obstacles to the project of moral formation. In good Augustinian

---

[147] Boyd Taylor Coolman, *The Theology of Hugh of St. Victor: An Interpretation* (Cambridge: Cambridge University Press, 2010), 15–21, 43–45.

fashion, Hugh understood ignorance, vice, and weakness as the marks of fallen life.[148] Ignorance and vice relate to a condition of the soul and weakness to a condition of the body. As a result of sin, the soul's emotions and desires remain disordered, creating and reinforcing ignorance, which the weakness and infirmity of the body only accentuates. Bodily movements like hunger and thirst intersect with psychological movements like the affections, which in turn reinforce ignorance. Humans are caught up in their own disordered cravings, desires, and emotions stemming from a weakened body that, in turn, obscures the truth. This further reinforces the work of the Spirit as the artisan who turns disordered desire into virtue by enabling each person to order and moderate emotion and desire. Virtue is the result of habituation that directs emotion and desire to their appropriate ends and brings balance to them.

To show how the liberal arts offer tools to overcome a fallen human condition, Hugh expanded his categories by drawing on a different classification of learning ultimately stemming from Aristotle. He suggested that one could divide the curriculum of the liberal arts into the theoretical, practical, and mechanical arts.[149] By virtue of their connection to *theoria*, the theoretical arts aid the individual in the discovery of truth and the construction of truthful vision of uncreated and created reality. The practical arts (politics, ethics, etc.) aid individuals in the development of virtue, while the mechanical arts (farming, medicine, theater, etc.) strengthen the body. Moreover, as humans learn these arts they begin to love their neighbors. Consequently, there is a social dimension that continues the process of moral formation because in learning about medicine and its purpose an individual becomes able to help a neighbor. The purpose of education in the arts was to investigate every good of creation and to learn every truth about those goods. This was the basis for scientific advancement. Yet the very investigation of individual goods or particular truths could short-circuit the journey to God because love might fixate on particularity or get mired in the concreteness of life. The movement must always be from the particular to the universal or from the visible to the invisible. While the liberal arts fuel the formation of the self and aid in mission, the Spirit sanctifies human love by helping students move through the goods of creation to God as the final good. As humans become properly related to the goods of creation, they are in a better position to use each art to work toward restoration from sin on a social level. When placed in a pneumatological framework, the liberal arts served the self and humanity.

The liberal arts not only were tools to aid in moral formation, they also expanded the mind's capacities. Extending Hugh's thought, Richard of St. Victor described the learning process as a *dilatatio mentis*, an expansion of the imaginative capacities of the mind to develop a richer picture of the self, the world, and the divine.[150] First, the mind expands its capacities to think by sculpting interior thoughts through the study of language. These mental skills sharpen the intellect so that it can perceive the truth more clearly, and thus there is an expansion of the mind's capacity to think. Second, the mind expands its

---

[148] Hugh of St. Victor, *Didascalicon* 6.14 (Buttimer, 130–32).

[149] Hugh of St. Victor, *Didascalicon* 2.1 (Buttimer, 23–25); 6.14 (Buttimer, 130–32).

[150] Richard of St. Victor, *On the Mystical Ark* 5.1–3; M.-A. Aris, *Contemplatio: Philosophische Studien zum Traktat Benjamin Maior des Richard von St. Victor* (Frankfurt: Josef Knecht, 1996), 123–27. See Dale M. Coulter, *Per Visibilia ad Invisibilia: Theological Method in Richard of St. Victor (d. 1173)*, Bibliotheca Victorina IX (Turnhout: Brepols, 2006).

capacities by investigating individual goods and learning the truth about every aspect of creation, which it retains in memory.

Richard uses the ancient Israelite artist Bezalel because Bezalel constructed the ark of the covenant according to the divine pattern. This symbolism fuses the Spirit as artisan with the need to sculpt one's life. Like Bezalel, humans can create a structure for the mind, a storehouse of memory that can be filled with images and ideas. Building an internal ark of the covenant concerns structuring the mind to receive and retrieve information. System-building, whether theological or otherwise, is more about shaping the mind and preparing it for a larger vision of the whole of creation in God. It involves constructing a cathedral in the heart by conforming the affections to wisdom, which can give birth to creative insights through "invention."[151] Hugh and Richard used "master symbols" as a way to shape the architecture of the mind. The mind is its own repository, which means that sculpting it by using a device to aid memory and focus the thoughts merely enhances the mind's capacity. The figure of Bezalel points to another way, in which humans become co-artists with the Spirit in the sculpting of their interior life by expanding its imaginative capacity.

This trajectory reveals a concern to synthesize the intellectual and moral lives around the notion of an enlarged vision that comes through reading and meditating upon God's two great books of creation and Scripture. Such an investment in the study of particularity makes possible the ecstasy of contemplative vision as the free flight of the mind having been elevated above particularity through the comprehensive vision it beholds in wonder. The sanctifying work of the Spirit in artistic formation of the self opens up the possibility for a flight into transcendence.

Following Augustine, Richard understood the final move into this contemplative vision as a disengagement of the mind (*alienatio mentis*) from the self and creation in its free flight. Such a disengagement occurs when the mind is rapt in wonder to the point that it loses conscious awareness, as though a barrier has been erected that closes off everything but the vision itself. Called the cloud of unknowing by other authors, this barrier symbolizes the way the affections have been seized in erotic delight at the vision of God so as to cause the person to forget everything else. This is the combination of the prophetic and charismatic within the ascent to God.

Enlargement of mind cannot simply mean passive reception of data to expand the memory, but must also include the development of an analytical, distributive, and harmonizing process. It is no mistake that Hugh and Richard conceived of such a process as unfolding in the context of contemplative vision, in which the individual experiences creative insight or *revelatio* precisely as the mind becomes enlarged. Meditation opened up contemplation or moral formation prepared one for the ecstatic flight into transcendence. Through meditation the individual focused on the goods of creation while contemplation concerned the sudden elevation of the mind to see how each good fit together into a more comprehensive whole. One could then move from whole to part or part to whole.

The emphasis on the role of the liberal arts at St. Victor set the tone for the numerous schools that grew up around Paris, each of which was centered upon a *magister* who took

---

[151] Mary Carruthers, *The Craft of Thought: Meditation, Rhetoric, and the Making of Images, 400–1200* (Cambridge: Cambridge University Press, 1998), 221–76.

in pupils. It was in this context of multiple masters that the 1215 statutes Robert of Courson issued as papal legate formally recognized the university as a corporate entity.[152] The term *universitas* in its medieval designation meant a corporation and thus pointed toward "masters" who formed an association (*collegium*). Due to the challenges of economic survival and urban life, the masters borrowed from other guilds and formed a "corporation" that eventually came to be called a *studium generalia* or a place where "general studies" could be pursued. While the earliest medieval universities were created by masters, princes and popes went on to found a number of universities. Still, these universities were entirely faculty-driven as students entered the tutelage of a master. Of the first universities (Paris, Oxford, and Bologna), the Parisian-Oxford model became the standard for much of northern Europe and Britain.

Scholasticism was a model for education that informed the particular organizational structure of the medieval university. The basic division was into lower and higher studies, with the liberal arts framing the lower studies for a bachelor's and law, medicine, and theology forming the three areas of higher studies where one would become a master. The idea was to move from a study of the particularity of creation to a vision of the whole, which is why theology was a kind of queen in which all goods were seen as participating in the goodness of God. One can see in this division between lower and higher a basic commitment to the patristic idea that the liberal arts were preparatory in the ascent to God. Over time, the study of language as key to argumentation and advancement meant that the *trivium* became crucial, especially logic. Eventually, Aristotle's logical works dominated the *trivium* and his works on physics, metaphysics, and natural philosophy. The dominance of Aristotle and dialectic helps explain the developments in logic in the fourteenth century and their use to fuel the emergence of William of Ockham and Duns Scotus, who began to apply the new logic to theological problems. This dominance in logic set the tone for the reaction of Renaissance humanists to the scholastic project, even if scholasticism remained focused on bringing all learning to the service of the beatific vision.

2.3.2 Renaissance and the *Studia humanitatis*: A Literary Humanism

When one turns to the Italian Renaissance and its outworking in northern Europe, one finds a similar concern among certain thinkers to develop an educational model that places the liberal arts in the context of moral formation and opens the individual up to transcendence. It is possible to plot out a trajectory that maintains the connections between the liberal arts, the moral life, and transcendence. Rather than exploring one or two humanists, our intention is to trace out this trajectory through a number of thinkers.

The connection between the liberal arts and moral formation centered upon the way both promoted human flourishing. In a letter written in 1402 to the young son of Francesco Carrara, the governor of Padua, Pier Paolo Vergerio the Elder, explains that "we call those studies liberal which are worthy of a free (*liber*) man; those studies by which we attain and practice virtue and wisdom; that education which calls forth, trains, and develops those

---

[152] On the structure of medieval universities, see the still useful account by Hastings Rashdall, *The Universities of Europe in the Middle Ages*, 2 vols. (Oxford: Clarendon Press, 1895); Gordon Leff, *Paris and Oxford Universities in the Thirteenth and Fourteenth Centuries: An Institutional and Intellectual History* (New York: John Wiley, 1968); Alan B. Cobban, *The Medieval English Universities: Oxford and Cambridge to c. 1500* (Berkeley: University of California Press, 1988); Ian P. Wei, *Intellectual Culture in Medieval Paris: Theologians and the University, c. 1100–1330* (Cambridge: Cambridge University Press, 2012).

highest gifts of body and of mind which ennoble men, and which are rightly judged to rank next in dignity to virtue only."[153] There is an implicit connection between human freedom, which is the ground of human dignity, and the pursuit of truth. Since the liberal arts open up the pursuit of truth in all areas of knowledge, they aid moral formation. This is why history and moral philosophy rank first and second in Vergerio's list of arts to be studied. History offers insights from the wisdom of past generations, which informs philosophical discourse of how to achieve the good life and thus to flourish.

The relationship between truth, freedom, and moral formation is also present in Coluccio Salutati's defense of the liberal arts. Focusing on the *trivium* as a path or way to human flourishing, Salutati argues that all the liberal arts have as their aim inquiry into the truth.[154] As a path to moral transformation, however, the *trivium* should not be confused with the end, which would equate learning with salvation itself rather than something that facilitates salvation. To speak of the liberal arts as offering a path in relationship to the purpose or end of human life enabled thinkers like Salutati to understand human dignity as more than the endowment of freedom itself. In relationship to the project of human flourishing, human freedom entails conformity to the truth as an intrinsic part of moral formation, and the liberal arts liberate human freedom. Honoring human dignity involves leading humans toward their final end.

During the quattrocento, the emphasis on human dignity prompted a turn toward the connection between the liberal arts, moral formation, and transcendence as the ultimate purpose of human freedom. This is particularly the case at the Florentine Academy with its recovery and emphasis on Plato's works and their Neoplatonic interpreters. Pico della Mirandola points out the connection in terms of the liberal arts promoting friendship and peace with God.

> This is that peace which God makes on his heights and which the angels descending to earth announced to men of good will, that by this peace the men themselves ascending into heaven might become angels. Let us desire this peace for our friends, for our age.... Let us desire it for our soul, that through this peace she may become the house of God; that after she has, through morals and dialectics, cast off her meanness and has adorned herself with manifold philosophy as with a princely garment, and has crowned with garlands of theology the summits of the gates, the King of Glory may descend, and, coming with the Father, may make his residence in her.[155]

For Pico, peace means eschatological reconciliation with God as a result of harmonizing one's interior life so that the internal war among thoughts, emotions, and desires comes to an end. Moral philosophy, dialectic, and natural philosophy tame the manifold discord (*multiplex discordia*) and tumults of reason (*turbas rationis*).[156] Internal peace and

---

[153] *De ingenuis moribus et liberalibus adolescentiae studiis* 3, in William H. Woodward, *Vittorino da Feltre and Other Humanist Educators* (Cambridge: Cambridge University Press, 1897), 102.

[154] Coluccio Salutati, *Letter in Defense of Liberal Studies*, in *The Italian Renaissance*, ed. Werger L. Gundersheimer (Englewood Cliffs, N.J.: Prentice-Hall, 1965), 15, 21, 24.

[155] Pico della Mirandola, *Oratio de hominis dignitate*, ed. Eugenio Garin, Edizioni Studio Tesi (Pordenone: Studio Tesi, 1994), 25; *On the Dignity of Man*, trans. Charles Glenn Wallis, Paul J. W. Miller, and Douglas Carmichael (Indianapolis: Hackett, 1998), 12.

[156] Pico della Mirandola, *Oratio de hominis dignitate* (Garin, 22; Wallis, Miller, and Carmichael, 10–11).

peace with God both concern forms of friendship, that is, a holistic way of relating to the self and to God. Moreover, this peace and friendship emerge with the beautification of the soul, her putting on a princely garment. The purpose of such beautification that the liberals arts help realize is encounter with the living Christ, who descends upon the soul thus beautified. If the liberal arts aid beautification, they do so in part by opening up the individual toward encounter, which facilitates peace and friendship. We can begin to see here how self-knowledge through moral transformation leads to knowledge of God.

Marsilio Ficino, following Nicholas of Cusa, would develop this thought more than most humanist thinkers in his *Platonic Theology* and *On Christian Religion*. Ficino borrowed from scholasticism the idea that humans are fundamentally oriented toward the good by virtue of a natural appetite.[157] All humans possess this natural appetite for God and thus find themselves inclined toward goodness, truth, and beauty. By design, humans are drawn toward transcendence.

Ficino's thought echoes his Florentine predecessor, Dante, who in the first canto of *Paradiso* has Beatrice declare,

> All things created have an order
> in themselves, and this begets the form
> that lets the universe resemble God.
>
> Here the higher creatures see the imprint
> of the eternal Worth, the end
> for which that pattern was itself set forth.
>
> In that order, all natures have their bent
> according to their different destinies,
> whether nearer to their source or farther from it.
>
> They move, therefore, toward different harbors
> upon the vastness of the sea of being,
> each imbued with an instinct that impels it on its course.[158]

Beatrice goes on to liken this internal ordering to providence's bow, which launches creatures, as arrows, toward the heavenly realms. Arrows thus launched, however, can still deviate from their intended course, especially when false pleasures attract persons to temporal realities and pull them back down toward earth. By sculpting the human person through the liberal arts, we hone human freedom so that this internal arrow hits its mark.

There is another dimension to transcendence. For Ficino, to begin to move toward that to which one is naturally inclined is to open oneself up to encounter with God as part of the

---

[157] Paul Kristeller, *The Philosophy of Marsilio Ficino*, trans. Virginia Conant (Gloucester, Mass.: Peter Smith, 1964), 171–205. Ficino uses a variety of expressions, e.g., a natural instinct (*naturae instinctus*), a natural motion grounded in a certain disposition of the soul's nature (*naturalis motus . . . propter quandam naturae suae affectionem*), a natural appetite (*appetitus naturalis*). See Ficino, *De Christiana religione* 2 (*Opera*, 1, 2); *Theologia Platonica* 2.6 (*Opera*, 2, 99), 14.1 (*Opera*, 2, 305–6); *In Philebum Platonis* 1.2 (*Opera*, 2, 1208–9). Marsilius Ficinus, *Opera omnia*, 2 vols., 2nd ed. (Basel, 1576), repr. (Turin: Bottega d'Erasmo, 1962).

[158] Dante, *Paradiso* 1.103–14, trans. Robert Hollander and Jean Hollander (New York: Anchor, 2007), 9.

journey, not simply its final end. This is because the liberal arts can elevate the mind and orient it back toward its true home. Rehabilitating Plato's understanding of poetry as involving a kind of divine madness or ecstatic inspiration, Ficino indicates that, as part of his own study, he moves from theology to music and poetry since the true poet composes in the context of an encounter with the divine.[159] Artistic activity is connected to encounter, prompted by the openness to transcendence, which in turn fuels the journey upward. Poetry, music, and theology, each in its own way, evoke a visionary encounter with God. What connects these various forms is the way in which love, beauty, and rapture lead to embrace and encounter. The liberal arts form part of the way toward such an encounter because they help transform the person into the truth and thus into God, who is the Truth.

In a sense, with Ficino we have come full circle to Martianus Capella. Ficino sees a connection between poetry and prophecy in and through ecstatic inspiration, the divine madness that drives each of them. Rather than the finale of a divine/human drama of transformation, encounter can occur as the narrative unfolds to enliven its progression and help the arrow hit its final mark. This may be why Ficino writes in his preface to a translation of the Psalter that the soul receives liberation through intercourse with God.[160] It is the gift of charity from the Holy Spirit that joins humans to the Seraphim by igniting them with a flame that liberates them from earth and propels them, like Paul, into the third heaven.[161] Throughout late antiquity, the Middle Ages, and the Renaissance, David was viewed as both poet and prophet, and the Psalms as poetry and prophecy that described and elicited encounters with God.

There is also a continuity between the madness of encounter that generates poetry and prophecy and the madness at the end of all things. Erasmus had signaled such a connection at the end of his *Encomium moriae*, where Folly proclaims,

> He who loves vehemently no longer lives in himself but in what he loves, and his joy is in proportion to his withdrawal from self and his preoccupation with what is outside himself. When the soul meditates on traveling without the use of its limbs, this is certainly insanity (*furorem*). . . . The more perfect the love (*porro quo amor est absolutior*), the greater the madness (*hoc furor est major*). Therefore what is this future life of heaven . . . ? It consists in the first place of an absorption of the body by the spirit . . . then the spirit will be in a marvelous manner absorbed by the Highest Mind [and] in this way the entire man (*totus homo*) will be outside of himself (*extra se*), and his happiness will be due to no other fact than that, so placed, he will share in the Highest Good which draws all to Itself (*omnia in se rapiente*).[162]

The completion of the journey is nothing less than the full ecstatic, loving embrace between bride and bridegroom, to which all other encounters point. It is the culmination

---

[159] Marsilio Ficino, Letter 7: *De divino furore, The Letters of Marsilio Ficino*, vol. 1 (London: Shepheard-Walwyn, 1975), 42–48. Cf. Plato, *Phaedrus* 244–45a. Plato consistently employs the Greek terms *mania* and *katokōchē*. The latter implies possession in the sense of inspired and the former a kind of inspired frenzy. Ficino may be following Cicero by rendering *mania* as *furor* (frenzy, madness). Cf. Cicero, *Tusculan Disputations* 3.5.11.

[160] See Kristeller, *Philosophy of Marsilio Ficino*, 316.

[161] Ficino, *In epistolas Pauli* prologue (*Opera*, 1, 415).

[162] John Dolan, *The Essential Erasmus* (New York: Penguin, 1964), 172.

of the kind of beautification that the liberal arts help bring about in their liberating the person to embrace God unencumbered by slavery to the world. As Levison notes in his recent work on the Spirit, New Testament writers like Luke invoke images of ecstasy with their appeals to a fiery, intoxicating encounter in which tongues express the full movement outside the self.[163] It is a sobering ecstasy because intoxication by the Spirit sobers the individual toward the world, which makes a clearer vision of life possible, and in this way anticipates the beatific vision at the end as the frivolity and play of a divine dance.[164] The intoxicating ecstasy that gives rise to poetry and prophecy is but a glimpse of that final ecstatic embrace.

2.3.3 Early Reformation *Paideia*: A Biblical Humanism

The relationship between *studia humanitatis*, encounter, and a text that Ficino had connected to the Psalms becomes apparent in thinkers like Jacques Lefèvre d'Etaples (1455–1536), who borrowed heavily from Ficino and Pico, fusing their thought with medieval mysticism to create a new approach to the study of Scripture.[165] Lefèvre was part of a groundswell of humanists who sought to apply the lessons of philology to the study of Scripture as part of the program *ad fontes*. His desire to fuse together ideas of encountering transcendence with the use of language in the study and recovery of texts would lead him, in his introduction to the Psalms, to postulate an understanding of the literal sense as involving "the intention of the prophet and the Holy Spirit speaking in him."[166] This more prophetic interpretation of the literal sense over against a strictly historical approach allowed Lefèvre to interpret the Psalter christologically. To grasp the prophetic sense required an encounter with the Spirit on the part of the interpreter. One must be given eyes to see through the Spirit's illumination, which elevates the mind and leads to a vision of faith.[167]

What Lefèvre had accomplished was to articulate a double meaning to the literal sense (historical and prophetic) that corresponded to what Hugh and Richard of St. Victor had called meditation and contemplation.[168] Contemplative vision was to see

---

[163] John R. Levison, *Filled with the Spirit* (Grand Rapids: Eerdmans, 2009), 317–47.

[164] Note that C. S. Lewis described the life of heaven in terms of dance and game, a blend of boundless freedom and order in self-abandonment, or, as he put it, "joy is the serious business of heaven." See *The Joyful Christian: 127 Readings from C. S. Lewis* (New York: Macmillan, 1977), 227–28.

[165] On Jacques Lefèvre d'Etaples, see Philip Edgcumbe Hughes, *Lefèvre: Pioneer of Ecclesiastical Renewal in France* (Grand Rapids: Eerdmans, 1984); Guy Bedouelle, "Jacques Lefèvre d'Etaples (c. 1460–1536)," in *The Reformation Theologians: An Introduction to Theology in the Early Modern Period*, ed. Carter Lindberg (Oxford: Blackwells, 2002), 19–33; Guy Bedouelle, "Attacks on the Biblical Humanism of Jacques Lefèvre d'Etaples," in *Biblical Humanism and Scholasticism in the Age of Erasmus*, ed. Erika Rummel (Leiden: Brill, 2008), 117–42.

[166] Jacques Lefèvre d'Etaples, *Epistle 66: Et videor mihi alium videre sensum, qui scilicet est intentionis prophetae et spiritus sancti in eo loquentis, et hunc litteralem appello, sed qui cum spiritu coincidit*, in *The Prefatory Epistles of Jacques Lefèvre d'Etaples and Related Texts*, ed. Eugene F. Rice (New York: Columbia University Press, 1972). For English translation, see Heiko Oberman, *Forerunners of the Reformation: The Shape of Late Medieval Thought Illustrated by Key Documents* (Philadelphia: Fortress, 1981), 297–301.

[167] Lefèvre d'Etaples, *Prefatory Epistles*. Lefèvre utilizes *illuminatio* for the gift of illumination and *attollo sursum* to indicate an elevation on high or a broad vision as though looking at the whole.

[168] Lefèvre was deeply influenced by Richard of St. Victor's writings and published an edition of Richard's *De Trinitate* with commentary in 1510. See *Egregrii patris et calri theologi Richardi quondam*

the whole spread out and thus discover a kind of intertextual harmony, which was, in fact, what many medieval interpreters had understood by allegory. For Lefèvre, one can only access this more contemplative interpretation of the prophetic significance of the text through an elevation by the Spirit, which is precisely what Richard of St. Victor had understood to be necessary for contemplation. Within this biblical humanism, the text of Scripture became the primary launching pad for the elevation of the mind that came to be defined as saving faith.

Lefèvre's understanding of interpretation helped to set the tone for the later emphasis among early Protestant Reformers on the written and preached word as places of encounter out of which faith emerges. One of the earliest Protestant slogans, *sola fide*, was originally intended to underscore the clarity of vision in the midst of the sobering ecstasy of encounter. Martin Luther, whose approach to the Psalms was influenced by Lefèvre, developed his understanding of faith in concert with ideas associated with ecstasy. He interpreted the Vulgate rendering of Psalm 116:11 ("I said in my ecstasy, 'Every man is a liar'") to be a reference to the exercise of faith. Luther states, "This is the ecstasy in which [David] is elevated by faith beyond himself so that he might see future goods."[169] In the interlinear gloss on this text, Luther interpreted ecstasy (*excessus*) to mean the "sense of faith" (*sensus fidei*) as opposed to the literal sense, a *raptus mentis* that brings clear cognition of faith, and an *alienatio mentis* or *pavor mentis* that unfolds in persecution.[170] These three meanings of ecstasy share the idea of a mental ascent that brings an alternative vision as the mind is detached from all below it. Faith is an ecstatic ascent from the text on the basis of a trembling or internal anxiety (Luther's *Anfechtungen*) when one stands naked before the living God. Hence, Luther declared that what makes a true theologian is rapture and ecstasy.[171]

The early Luther combined Lefèvre's biblical humanism with his disdain for Aristotelean philosophy by recentering ecstatic flight away from the liberal arts and toward the text of Scripture. He further defined faith in terms of this ascent in which *fiducia* (trust) was an affective movement out of the self and into Christ. In his Galatians commentary, Luther stated that "faith and hope are distinct affections (*fides et spes distincti affectus sunt*)."[172] Regeneration involved the Spirit giving "new and pious affections, such as fear of God, trust, and hope," which is how Luther interpreted the Pauline notion of putting on Christ.[173] Faith or *fiducia* is the "form of Christ" in the soul, but this form comes as the Spirit shapes the will's various affections into Christ.

---

deuoti coenobitae sancti Victoris juxta muros parisienses de superdiuina Trinitate theologicum opus (Paris: Estienne, 1510).

[169] *D. Martin Luthers Werke*, Kritische Gesamtausgabe 4 (Weimar: Hermann Böhlaus Nachfolger, 1886), 273 (hereafter WA): *Iste est excessus, quo per fidem levatur super se, ut videat futura bona*.

[170] WA 4, 265. See Heiko Oberman, *The Dawn of the Reformation: Essays in Late Medieval and Early Reformation Thought* (Grand Rapids: Eerdmans, 1992), 150, who quotes this passage as part of his larger discussion of Luther and mysticism.

[171] WA 3, 372.

[172] WA 40/1, 28; *Luther's Works*, vol. 27, ed. J. Pelikan (St. Louis: Concordia, 1964), 24.

[173] WA 40: 540–42; LW 26: 352–53: *Exurgit enim in baptisatis, praeter hoc quod regenerantur & renovantur per Spiritum sanctum ad caelestem iustitiam et vitam aeternam in baptismo, etiam nova lux et flamma, oriuntur novi et pii affectus, timor, fiducia Dei, spes, &c. oritur nova voluntas, hoc tum est proprie, vere et Evangelice Christum induere.*

The shift to faith as an ecstatic and affective movement allowed the Reformers to capitalize on the distinction between affectivity and virtue in order to develop their biblical humanism. Melanchthon followed Luther in grounding faith in *fiducia*, which he described as an affective movement occurring in the heart. To be righteous by faith correlated to trust in the vision of seeing Christ mediating at the right hand of the Father and thus that one's sins are forgiven and one is accepted as righteous.[174] Melanchthon understood virtue to be a habit inclining the will, whereas affections were interior movements in the heart.[175] The move to faith as affective ascent in ecstasy became part of a larger project to consign virtue to civic righteousness or justice, which enabled Melanchthon to integrate philosophy into the curriculum through the distinction between law and gospel.

As an ardent humanist, Melanchthon was much more open to philosophy and the liberal arts than Luther had been. Yet he embraced Luther's clear distinction between law and gospel, applying the former to philosophy. As he states, "The Gospel is not a philosophy or a law, but it is the forgiveness of sins and the promise of reconciliation and eternal life for the sake of Christ, and human reason by itself cannot apprehend any of these things."[176] The ascent to God was only through the gospel and the study of Scripture, in which faith encountered the living God through the promises.

The liberal arts functioned in three ways within this new framework of biblical humanism. First, the Reformers embraced wholeheartedly the study of language and textual criticism as flowing from the *trivium*. In one speech, Melanchthon proclaimed that the study of languages was the most agreeable part of philosophy because it inculcated eloquence and argument while also supplying important tools to understand Scripture and prevent false interpretations on the basis of a failure to know the parts of speech. Second, moral philosophy, history, and the study of literature and poetry were necessary for political life and public virtue. For this reason, Melanchthon could argue that "scholars are necessary for the conservation of piety, religion, civil order, and also for the administration of the state." In another lecture, he summoned the powers of language to argue that students must study Homer because through his poetic genius one could be "initiated into these sacred rites of the Muses, or admitted to this sanctuary of humanity and virtue."[177] Melanchthon saw Homer as crucial for the kind of public virtue necessary to advance a civic humanism.

What becomes clear is that the Reformers retained the idea of education in support of moral formation, but saw this moral formation in relationship to public virtue and civic humanism rather than Christian righteousness and biblical humanism. Law and gospel were not the same, and neither were philosophy and theology, although they functioned along parallel tracks, with the former being crucial for political life and the latter for the life of the soul. One can see here the beginnings of what would become a chasm between social justice or civic virtue and internal justice or Christian righteousness. Encounters with transcendence were relegated to the ascent of faith from encountering Christ in the gospel.

---

[174] Philip Melanchthon, *Loci communes* (Basel, 1546), *On the Term Faith*.

[175] See Melanchthon, *Elements and Exposition of the Doctrine of Ethics*. He defines virtue and the affections.

[176] Philip Melanchthon, "On the Distinction Between the Gospel and Philosophy," in *Orations on Philosophy and Education*, ed. Sachiko Kusukawa (Cambridge: Cambridge University Press, 1999), 24.

[177] Philip Melanchthon, "Preface to Homer," in *Orations on Philosophy and Education*, 53.

Under the Reformed emphasis on divine election, the bifurcation between public virtue and Christian righteousness became even more pronounced. John Calvin's vision of
education in Geneva was advanced along these lines. The liberal arts remained important
handmaids in the service of the study of Scripture by those already regenerate and for the
regulation of Christian political life. The pursuit of philosophy served as a propaedeutic
to politics and a prophylactic against social sin. Calvin was theoretically committed to
the idea that all truth was God's truth, but he worried about the wrong use of philosophy,
which is why he repudiated the Dionysian corpus, saying, "Farewell, then, to that Platonic
philosophy of seeking access to God through angels, and of worshiping them with intent
to render God more approachable to us."[178] The liberal arts could never be part of a path
to God or a means to encounter transcendence and thus facilitate the creation of the righteousness that only faith could bring.

One can see an important connection between Renaissance humanism and the Reformation through the emphasis on moral transformation, interpretation, and encounter. Yet, this common interest diverged in terms of whether the liberal arts could be
part of the formation of an internal righteousness and thus the path to a vision of
God. The biblical humanism of the Reformers postulated that genuine piety before
God required Christian righteousness, which is how Calvin began his *Institutes*. This
was not the public piety that Aristotle espoused. It was a different way to argue for
theology as the queen of all the liberal arts and thus integrate them into an educational
curriculum.

Renaissance thinkers reinvigorated the liberal arts as a program of studies by arguing for their connection to moral transformation and human freedom. The liberal arts
liberate human freedom by aiding persons in their pursuit of the truth about the world,
the self, and God. Since the liberal arts aim at truth, they form part of the journey into
the truth, a journey that requires the individual to be conformed or changed so that she
now lives "in the truth." In addition, the liberal arts promote the dignity of the human
person by facilitating encounters with transcendence. Beautification of the soul leads to
the indwelling of God because the soul becomes more and more like the one to whom it
ascends. The ascent to God is really a becoming like God, which fulfills the person's natural appetite for truth, beauty, and goodness.

The liberal arts also do not simply aid a journey that culminates in final union with
God, they facilitate ongoing encounters with transcendence now. By orienting the mind
back toward its home, the liberal arts create space for the divine to intersect with the
human. This is nowhere more apparent than poetry and prophecy, in which the person
is caught up in the madness of ecstasy and speaks the language of heaven. As Christian
poetry and prophecy, the Psalms offer to the interpreter a place to encounter God, and,
in the midst of such an encounter, "spiritual" interpretation becomes possible because the
gift of the Spirit brings the gift of faith. The liberal arts supply the tools for the act of interpretation, but the final movement of this act concerns a fusion of horizons as the Spirit
meets the person through the written word and the preached word.

---

[178] John Calvin, *Institutes* 1.14.12; John T. McNeill, ed., *Calvin: Institutes of the Christian Religion*, vol. 1,
trans. Ford Lewis Battles (Philadelphia: Westminster, 1960), 172.

Among the many debates within ancient, medieval, and early modern Christianity, there was an ongoing dialogue and concerted effort to synthesize Christian claims about God, salvation, and the human person with an ancient understanding of the liberal arts and philosophy as facilitating a *habitus*, a way of being in the world open to the divine and invested in moral transformation. More specifically, it was the intersection between moral transformation and Christian conversion on the one hand, and the confluence of openness to transcendence and the Christian understanding of encounter, with its eschatological and charismatic impulses, on the other hand, that provided the fertile terrain for a fusion of Christian and Hellenistic approaches to learning and the liberal arts as part of a shared cultural frame of reference.

Forging this intersection did not mean that Christian writers were uncritical of learning as a formalized process that utilized Hellenistic resources and privileged the culturally elite among society. They understood Cicero's connection between *paideia* and the liberal education or teaching of a freeman. The process of assimilating ancient *paideia* into an emerging Christian religious milieu could not have occurred without the sometimes deep suspicion expressed by Christian critics, from Clement of Alexandria's qualified approval to Augustine's initial acceptance and then seeming rejection of liberal studies and Hugh of St. Victor's rehabilitation in early scholasticism. Much of this debate centered on the relationship between the descent/ascent of the Son and the Spirit's recapitulation of that process in the human person to achieve salvation over against the claim within Hellenistic thought that the path to apotheosis was through learning and philosophy. The liberal arts could no longer be handmaids to philosophy as the primary vehicle by which the soul formed itself morally and encountered transcendence through wisdom. Instead, all of secular learning became a handmaid to an understanding of salvation and human flourishing grounded upon the Son's role as wisdom incarnate and the Spirit's dispensing of the gifts of wisdom and understanding. It was out of this debate over the utility of philosophy and the liberal arts, sometimes occurring even in the same thinker, that late antique, medieval, and early modern thinkers forged connections between revelatory encounters, moral formation, and the liberal arts.

At the same time, moral formation occurs best in an atmosphere that cultivates an openness to the other through an openness to transcendence, which is to say that it occurs best in a tradition of inquiry that cultivates these practices and the goods inherent to them. The eschatological impulse within Christianity allowed Christian thinkers to exploit the connection between a vision of God, a vision of the end, and a comprehensive Christian mission in the *polis*. A Christian humanism that seeks to cultivate the human person will understand learning to necessitate ongoing revelatory encounters with transcendent reality as part of a process of moral and intellectual formation. In addition to providing for moral and intellectual formation, the liberal arts open the person to encounters with transcendence by accessing the wisdom laced throughout creation that places the person in touch with the self, the world, and the divine. This means that central to education is a crisis-process dialectic in which formation occurs alongside of encounter to cultivate a *habitus*.

Ancient, medieval, Renaissance, and Reformation thinkers saw the liberal arts as important tools in the promotion of a Christian humanism. Their importance resides in the way the liberal arts aided in the development of the Christian *habitus* or way of living in the world by offering a set of practices that altered patterns of thinking and open the individual up to neighbor and God. While the liberal arts do not establish shalom—the wholeness of relations with the God, the world, and the self—they could help to facilitate its actualization. In this sense, then, they advance Christian humanism.

Education is fundamentally about a journey that advances human flourishing through a way of being in the world formed in a crisis-process dialectic. Even in ancient philosophy it was always the case that human flourishing had a religious dimension because of a basic commitment that humans were designed for transcendence. Christians merely adapted and modified this concern to form humans by helping students ascend into the heights of wisdom and then return to the world to impact the *polis*.

3

(Re)constructing the University

Modernity and the Quest for Alternative Paradigms

The nineteenth and twentieth centuries witnessed a transition from the world of old Europe, with its aristocratic stranglehold on power and colonial domination, to the New World espousal of republican values and indigenous control. Central to these broadscale upheavals was the emergence of modernity as a cultural system, although this occurred slowly over the course of the long nineteenth century from the French and American revolutions to the First World War (1776–1914).[1] Industrialization, urbanization, and capitalism fueled efforts to construct alternative cultural programs and to make sense of history in the wake of revolutions and Napoleonic schemes. Developed in part from regional pockets of Enlightenment thought (German, Scottish, English, and French), the purpose of such cultural programs was to forge a common bond among the people since democracies invested sovereignty in the governed. These historical processes culminated in the Gilded Age and Progressive Era (c. 1870–1920, America) and the Belle Époque (1889–1919, Europe). While the previous chapter covered a larger period of time to establish the basic thesis of constructing a *habitus* invested in moral formation, open to transcendence, and engaged in mission, the current chapter focuses on dawn of the nineteenth century up to beginning of the Progressive Era (1890) as the context within which American models of higher education took shape along with their holiness and pentecostal counterparts.

Before one can explore learning and education within the holiness and pentecostal movements (1880–1980), it is necessary to see those movements as flowing from the broad historical streams that fed modernity and the various educational models to which they gave rise. There are three central claims this chapter makes. First (§3.1), over the course of the nineteenth century, a new set of concerns entered the social imaginary, which we will call the Romantic sensibility. In our account, Romantic sensibility is not the same as Romanticism but refers to a broader set of emphases impacting approaches to education. We employ the phrase as a heuristic device to identify three emphases—rational intuitionism,

---

[1] The idea of a long nineteenth century comes from the British social historian Eric Hobsbawm, who develops it in his now-classic trilogy *The Age of Revolution 1789–1848* (1962); *The Age of Capital 1848–1875* (1975); *The Age of Empire 1875–1914* (1987). This was followed by his *The Age of Extremes: The Short Twentieth Century, 1914–1991* (1994).

divine immanence, and social progressivism—and argue that these emphases functioned alongside of the Common Sense philosophy stemming from Thomas Reid (1710–1796) and Dugald Stewart (1753–1828), among others, and the Baconian evidentialism associated with it.[2] The historiography of American evangelicalism, in particular, and Protestantism, in general, has argued for the strong influence of "evidential Christianity" as residing behind the orthodox rationalism of the nineteenth century and a dominant force in evangelicalism.[3] Orthodox rationalism resulted from the combination of Scottish Common Sense and Baconian inductive reasoning. Evidential Christianity is not the entire story, however; rather, the common characteristics we described as the Romantic sensibility better situate the understanding of education among evangelicals in the holiness and pentecostal movements.

Second, education in the nineteenth century was largely concerned with the relationship between the formation of the person and the formation of a culture in order to secure fledgling democracies. The second section (§3.2) focuses on this modern project of forming a humanism through the fusion of intuitive knowledge with participatory encounter and the need for a liberal culture to cultivate the self. The cultivation of virtue as part of the late antique, medieval, and Renaissance approaches to education was placed in the service of creating a *demos* united by a common cultural framework rather than a monarch or aristocracy. This is how the *habitus* of moral formation continued as part of the educational enterprise. Religion retained a role in this new endeavor, but only as it was evacuated of confessional content in favor of a spirituality that facilitated persons who were moral and cultured, which was the basic meaning of being "civilized." The quest for an encounter with transcendence was transmuted into a spirituality centered on the scholar as hero (the modern sage) who experienced the divine within nature. We see this most fully in the way the German concept of *Bildung* entered Anglo-American intellectual life. The rise of the research university and its utilitarian counter in state normal schools, institutes, and the multipurpose college occurs in the context of this project. The secularization of society resulted from a return to the ancient idea of the sage and the sacralization of culture. Mission became life in the *polis* once again.

The final section (§3.3) turns to examine evangelical approaches to education. We argue that evangelical approaches to learning and education must be understood within these broad parameters, which reveal modernity's emergence and the birth of secularization. While drawing on the emphases found in the Romantic sensibility, evangelicals sought to train the laity and therefore gravitated toward multipurpose colleges, normal schools, and institutes as paradigms for their Bible schools. Moreover, the focus on

---

[2]   With his inductive science, Francis Bacon was the "patron saint of evidential Christianity" in American Protestantism. See E. Brooks Holifield, *Theology in America: Christian Thought from the Age of the Puritans to the Civil War* (New Haven: Yale University Press, 2003), 174–75.

[3]   For more on the influence of Common Sense philosophy and evidentialism, see Holifield, *Theology in America*, 5–8; Theodore D. Bozeman, *Protestants in an Age of Science: The Baconian Ideal and Antebellum American Religious Thought* (Chapel Hill: University of North Carolina Press, 1977); George Marsden, *Fundamentalism and American Culture*, 2nd ed. (New York: Oxford University Press, 2006), 14–17; Mark Noll, *The Princeton Theology, 1812–1921: Scripture, Science, and Theological Method from Archibald Alexander to Benjamin Breckinridge Warfield* (Grand Rapids: Baker, 1983); Mark Noll, "Common Sense Traditions and American Evangelical Thought," *American Quarterly* 37.2 (1985): 216–38. See also Kenneth Richard Walters, *Why Tongues? The Initial Evidence Doctrine in North American Pentecostal Churches* (Dorset: Deo, 2016), 8–33.

intuitionism and divine immanence fit well the emerging pneumatology of the holiness movement, which supplied the theological and experiential rationale for adopting more utilitarian models. In the evangelical world of the Progressive Era, the Romantic sensibility vied with evidential Christianity for dominance, especially as it became wedded to a Wesleyanism already espousing a pneumatological approach to Christian perfection fueled with concerns for personal and social holiness. The debates over what models of education best suited the American experiment must be viewed in light of these three claims. Within the context of these claims, education continued to focus on cultivating a *habitus* in moral formation, open to transcendence, and invested in mission.

3.1 A NEW SOCIAL IMAGINARY: THE ROMANTIC SENSIBILITY AND LIBERAL CULTURE

Prior to Darwin's publication of *The Origin of Species* (1859) and possibly having an important impact on Darwin himself, one can detect a gradual shift in an effort to come to terms with the effects of what Hobsbawm called the age of revolution.[4] Our use of Romantic sensibility captures a set of emphases that formed part of this gradual shift. First, while absorbing features of British Romanticism and German idealism, these emphases came about through a complex set of interlocking trends that coalesced around a desire to form a more democratized political order. Second, these emphases shaped in new ways the philosophy of Common Sense, which had dominated American life at least through 1830.[5] Refracted through French, English, and Scottish thinkers, German idealism merged with the evangelical thrust toward a more pietistic and mystical form of Christianity to ground an emerging Protestant pluralism in spiritualities that combined virtue with various types of encounter.

At the dawn of the Progressive Era (1890), one can detect a fracturing in the Romantic sensibility fostered in large part by ideologies imported from eastern European immigration, a privileging of God at work in natural and historical processes to the exclusion of interventionist accounts, and an effort to deal with the conflicts over labor, the role of women, and the new reality of Jim Crow. The subsequent bifurcation in Protestantism after 1870 into Wesleyan, Keswick, and higher critical wings was driven in part by the fragmentation of the emphases comprising the Romantic sensibility. Common Sense philosophy and Baconian evidentialism remained most influential within Presbyterianism by providing an epistemological foundation for the orthodox rationalism advanced at Old Princeton.[6]

---

[4] For the debate about the extent of the influence of *Naturphilosophie* from German idealism on Darwin, see Robert J. Richards, *The Romantic Conception of Life: Science and Philosophy in the Age of Goethe* (Chicago: University of Chicago Press, 2002); Michael Ruse, "The Romantic Conception of Robert J. Richards," *Journal of the History of Biology* 37.1 (2004): 3–23.

[5] So George M. Marsden, *The Soul of the American University Revisited: From Protestant to Postsecular* (New York: Oxford University Press, 2021), 82–84. Marsden sees common sense philosophy as dominating the American landscape by 1830, but then being challenged by German influences from the 1850s onward. We see this challenge as occurring in the 1830s already in dissenting forms of Protestantism on both sides of the Atlantic.

[6] On this point, see James H. Moorhead, *Princeton Seminary in American Religion and Culture* (Grand Rapids: Eerdmans, 2012); Noll, *Princeton Theology, 1812–1921*; Kim Riddlebarger, *The Lion of Princeton: B. B. Warfield as Apologist and Theologian* (Bellingham: Lexham, 2015).

Following Charles Taylor, we employ "social imaginary" to identify the way in which persons understand their identity as part of a larger social dynamic. To claim that the Romantic sensibility was part of the social imaginary is to identify the way in which individuals *imagine* their social existence, their relationship with their fellow human beings, their own expectations for their lives and society, and the deeper normative ideas and images that ground their expectations.[7] A social imaginary is not a worldview in the sense of a set of intellectual commitments that can be fully identified. One can, however, get at features of the social imaginary and shifts in the social imaginary without an exhaustive explanation that is ultimately reductionistic. This is what we hope to do in utilizing the phrase "Romantic sensibility."

In this first section we hope to establish the common emphases of what we are calling the Romantic sensibility. They are a form of rational intuitionism, an emphasis on divine immanence, and a social progressivism that used culture to bring about moral formation. To make this argument, we begin with the claim that Dugald Stewart developed Common Sense philosophy in the direction of a rational intuitionism (§3.1.1). We then turn to Samuel Taylor Coleridge's participatory understanding of the truth through his own version of rational intuitionism and the symbolic use of language (§3.1.2). Broadly speaking, intuitionism involves a position that there are certain rational or moral judgments that must be known immediately or nonreferentially through a direct perception. There are multiple sources related to the emergence of intuitionism in the late eighteenth and nineteenth centuries, including Locke's notion of intuition, the moral sense theory of Frances Hutcheson, Goethe's notion of intuition in relation to creativity, Coleridge's intuitive rationality, and Reid and Stewart's properly basic belief. Rather than describe all of them as Scottish Common Sense, we view them as a common emphasis on intuitive knowledge and hence part of the Romantic sensibility.[8]

While Common Sense philosophy gave support to Francis Bacon's evidentialism, the focus on intuition could be extracted and brought into conversation with other thinkers like Coleridge through the insight that intuition was an immediate perception born of a connection between disparate ideas in the mind. This is exactly what Stewart's development of Reid's philosophy allowed to happen, and it set the stage for the fusion of Scottish philosophy with German idealism. By the middle of the nineteenth century, the major debate in moral philosophy was between forms of intuitionism and utilitarianism.[9] Moreover, intuitive knowledge fit well with a second emphasis on divine immanence through a connection between the natural and the supernatural. The development of intuitive knowledge in Stewart and Coleridge and the emphasis on divine immanence fertilized the soil for an elite liberal culture that would morally shape citizens and produce moral progress in society (§3.1.3).

---

[7] Charles Taylor, *Modern Social Imaginaries* (Durham: Duke University Press, 2004), 23–32; Charles Taylor, *A Secular Age* (Cambridge, Mass.: Belknap, 2007), 159–211.

[8] Noll, "Common Sense Traditions and American Evangelical Thought," 216–38; Mark Noll, *America's God: From Jonathan Edwards to Abraham Lincoln* (New York: Oxford University Press, 2002), 247–48, 318, 350, 357.

[9] J. B. Schneewind, *Essays on the History of Moral Philosophy* (Oxford: Oxford University Press, 2010), 42–62.

3.1.1 Common Sense, Dugald Stewart, and Intuitive Truth

Dugald Stewart (1751–1828) is almost unknown outside of scholarly circles concerned with Scottish Common Sense philosophy. As professor of moral philosophy at Edinburgh, he sought to distill Thomas Reid's Common Sense approach to a new generation as a defense against philosophical skepticism, the political radicalism emerging from the French Revolution, and a greater tolerance for the science of the mind.[10] The fountainhead of Scottish Common Sense philosophy, Thomas Reid (1710–1796) had argued that certain propositional ideas (the principles of common sense) emerge from the constitution of the human person and must be taken for granted as foundational assumptions upon which are based any concerns or actions.[11]

By "common" Reid did not mean the basic moral intuitions of the *hoi polloi* that Thomas Payne would later draw upon in his 1776 pamphlet *Common Sense*.[12] Stewart would lament the choice of "common sense" to describe this philosophical position precisely because of the confusion with the more popular notion of moral intuitions among ordinary folk. Instead, Scottish Common Sense combined Bacon's inductive method of moving from observation to larger accounts through empirical evidence (evidentialism) with the claim that there were instincts in human nature that gave rise to self-evident principles. During his efforts to expand and popularize Reidian common sense, Stewart counted men such as the novelist Sir Walter Scott (1771–1832) and the historian and essayist Thomas Carlyle (1795–1881), about whom we will say more later, among his students. After Stewart's death, Carlyle wrote to his brother about a potential professorship in London and the desperation to fill the post with the words "No wonder they are: Dugald Stewart is dead, and British Philosophy with him."[13]

In his efforts to distinguish the technical meaning of common sense from its more popular meaning, Stewart increasingly referred to the mind's arrival at simple ideas like personal identity as an intuitive truth or judgment.[14] He expanded John Locke's notion of intuitive knowledge from involving the mind's immediate perception of an agreement or disagreement between two ideas (a circle is not a triangle) to a class of ideas unrelated to

---

[10]   Charles Bradford Bow, "Dugald Stewart and the Legacy of Common Sense in the Scottish Enlightenment," in *Common Sense in the Scottish Enlightenment*, ed. Charles Bradford Bow (Oxford: Oxford University Press, 2018), 200–208.

[11]   See Thomas Reid, *Inquiry into the Human Mind on the Principles of Common Sense* (Edinburgh: Stirling & Slade, 1819), 59. Reid published the work in 1764. This was followed by *Essays on the Intellectual Powers of Man* (1785) and *Essays on the Active Powers of Man* (1788). On Reid and Scottish Common Sense, see Alexander Broadie, *A History of Scottish Philosophy* (Edinburgh: Edinburgh University Press, 2009), 235–300; Douglas McDermid, *The Rise and Fall of Scottish Common Sense Realism* (Oxford: Oxford University Press, 2018); Terence Cuneo and René van Woudenberg, eds., *The Cambridge Companion to Thomas Reid* (Cambridge: Cambridge University Press, 2004).

[12]   On Thomas Paine's notion that "common sense will tell us," see Jack Fruchtman Jr., "Nature and Revolution in Paine's *Common Sense*," *History of Political Thought* 10.3 (1989): 421–38; idem, *Thomas Paine: Apostle of Freedom* (New York: Four Walls / Eight Windows, 1994).

[13]   Thomas Carlyle, "Letter 36: To Dr. Carlyle, Munich," in *Letters of Thomas Carlyle, 1826–1836*, ed. Charles Eliot Norton (London: Macmillan, 1889), 121.

[14]   This began at least as early as 1802 in his *Account of the Life and Writings of Thomas Reid*. For an overview of Stewart, see Gordon MacIntyre, *Dugald Stewart: The Pride and Ornament of Scotland* (Brighton: Sussex Academic, 2003).

sensation or discursive reflection.[15] These simple ideas were not placed in the mind fully formed as though they were its furniture.[16] Instead, simple ideas were "fundamental laws of belief," a description Stewart preferred to Reid's "principles of common sense," and thus part of the structure of human rationality.[17]

They were so distinct from ideas generated through discursive reasoning and sensory impressions that Stewart called them transcendental or metaphysical truths that formed "the original stamina of human reason."[18] Because these ideas came from the mind's architecture, they formed properly basic beliefs. One did not need (and really could not formulate) a rational argument to demonstrate them. Stewart referred to them as the necessary "conditions" that form human rationality even if one perceives them in the act of perception.[19] Any sort of discursive argument for these beliefs, like one's own existence, presupposed those very beliefs. Following Reid, Stewart grounded realism in an intuitive act of perception from which basic beliefs about the self and the external world emerged, and yet these very beliefs were themselves elements of rationality so that all discursive thinking assumed them.

The moment an impression from an external source produces a sensation "we learn two facts at once,—the existence of the sensation, and our own existence as sentient beings;—in other words, the very first exercise of consciousness necessarily implies a belief, not only of the present existence of what is felt, but of the present existence of *that* which feels and thinks: or (to employ plainer language) the present existence of that being which I denote by the words *I* and *myself*" (author's emphasis).[20] The intuitive recognition of an association between these two ideas—one from external sensory data and the other from the structure of the mind itself—explained how sensation provided the *occasion* for the emergence of the belief in personal identity and yet still differentiated it from any belief formed by impressions from the senses. These two beliefs were temporally simultaneous and associated with one another, but belief in personal identity was prior in the order of nature because it was part of the mind's constitution. Reid's "principles of common sense" turned out to be transcendental truths grasped in the context of an intuitive perception.

Stewart expanded the notion of intuition as the immediate perception of a connection between two ideas to include the processing of reasoning itself. There are some persons, he concluded, whether through natural ability or habituation, who could see the connection between diverse ideas immediately without the need for an extended chain of argumentation. Stewart saw the swiftness of finding connections between diverse ideas or different kinds of arguments as a species of intuitive knowledge (what Hugh and Richard of St. Victor saw as pneumatically induced contemplation). What connects these different

---

[15]   John Locke, *Essay Concerning Human Understanding* (London: Tegg and Son, 1836), 392.

[16]   Dugald Stewart, *Philosophical Essays*, The Works of Dugald Stewart 4 (Cambridge: Hilliard and Brown, 1829), 72–73.

[17]   Bow, "Dugald Stewart and the Legacy of Common Sense," 204.

[18]   Dugald Stewart, *Elements of the Philosophy of the Human Mind*, vol. 2, The Works of Dugald Stewart 3 (Edinburgh: Thomas Constable, 1854), 44; idem, *The Philosophy of the Active and Moral Powers of the Mind*, Works of Dugald Stewart, vol. 7 (Cambridge: Hilliard and Brown, 1829), 178.

[19]   Stewart, *Elements of the Philosophy of the Human Mind*, 47.

[20]   Stewart, *Elements of the Philosophy of the Human Mind*, 41.

usages of intuition is the immediacy of the perception even when that perception occurs through a mental process quickened by natural ability or habituation.

For Stewart, intuitive knowledge concerned an immediate connection the mind perceived. By describing the mental act of perception as an intuitive judgment of a simple idea *occasioned* by sensation, Stewart had defended an intuitive form of rationality that implied a participation in the external world as the context of its emergence.[21] In this way, he built on Reid's idea that there were rational "instincts" built into human rationality that one's participation in creation brought to the fore. Such an approach offered a framework that resonates with how early Christians understood the teaching of the Word in creation (§2.2.2).

3.1.2 Samuel Taylor Coleridge and Participating in the Truth

During the same decade that Stewart was defending Reid's position as an alternative to Lockean epistemology, Coleridge was working out his thoughts on the relationship between the reason and the understanding over against what he described as "mechanico-corpuscular philosophy," a pejorative description of William Paley's evidentialism and Berkeleyan idealism.[22] To combat these alternatives, Coleridge insisted on viewing human reason as a distinct mental operation involving a contemplative and intuitive grasp rather than reflective and discursive activity.

Coleridge differentiated between understanding and reason as two faculties in the soul. Because the understanding was "the faculty according to sense," it inhabited the empirical realities of the sensory world and thus, on its own, could never behold the heavens. The understanding individuates, breaks down and assesses, and trades in the multiplicity of things. The inductive reasoning grounded in empirical observation of fact that Bacon championed bears its fruit at this level, which is its proper sphere. Despite efforts by his predecessors to elucidate empirical realities, Coleridge remained convinced that the understanding could not track fully the relationship between parts and the larger whole and so move beyond proximate ends.[23] He insisted that this was the problem with William Paley's (1743–1805) use of evidentialism as part of his argument for a creator. It sought to climb the ladder to the divine through discursive analysis of the natural world and arrived at a "Fate . . . not a Moral Creator and Governor."[24]

The reason (*nous* or spirit) represented that higher part of human intelligence. As the *capax dei*, it was an "irradiative power" in which the mind beheld and participated in truths above sense.[25] The discursive work of the understanding could be taken up into

---

[21] It is beyond the scope of the present inquiry to examine the impact of the philosophy of Sir William Hamilton as a translator of Scottish Common Sense. For Hamilton's extension of intuitionism, see Gordon Graham, "A Reexamination of Sir William Hamilton's Philosophy," in *Scottish Philosophy in the Nineteenth and Twentieth Centuries*, ed. Gordon Graham (Oxford: Oxford University Press, 2015), 47–66.
[22] Samuel Taylor Coleridge, *Aids to Reflection: In the Formation of a Manly Character on the Several Grounds of Prudence, Morality, and Religion* (London: William Pickering, 1836), 393.
[23] Samuel Taylor Coleridge, *The Friend: A Series of Essays* (London: George Bell and Sons, 1875), 340.
[24] Coleridge, *Aids to Reflection*, 398–99. William Paley published *Evidences of Christianity* in 1794 and then his immensely popular *Natural Theology* in 1802. See William Paley, *Evidences of Christianity* (New York: S. King, 1824); William Paley, *Natural Theology* (Boston: Gould, Kendall and Lincoln, 1837).
[25] Samuel Taylor Coleridge, "Essay on Faith," in *The Literary Remains of Samuel Taylor Coleridge*, ed. Henry Nelson, vol. 3 (London: William Pickering, 1838), 431–34; idem, *Aids to Reflection*, 206–25.

reason's service as part of a broader and higher vision, but not the converse. Through its intuitive grasp of the truth, reason offered a certainty that Coleridge described as truths having evidence in themselves, the necessary convictions that ground everything. Coleridge brought Baconian induction into a larger framework that relegated it to discursive analysis of the objects comprising the visible world.

In Coleridgean discourse, intuition took several forms all of which converged on an immediate and simultaneous beholding of the whole. This intuitive act was analogous to the way the mind organized sensory impressions into a whole vision.[26] In this respect, his views paralleled Stewart's even when he utilized different sources to construct them. Coleridge's claims about intuition privileged immediacy over the mediation of knowledge through reflective activity. Unlike an impression in wax, this insight emerges through the mind's active roaming over the fields of imagination. In a plagiaristic gloss of the German philosopher Friedrich Schelling, Coleridge referred to a primary intuition of the self-conscious spirit in the act of thinking.[27] As part of its interior vision of impressions, the mind beholds itself as object of knowledge and thinking subject simultaneously. This knowledge of the self occurs through an immediate perception resulting from the entire act of thinking. It emerges from the whole conscious self in act rather than any particular moment of cogitation. Because active thought required agency, Coleridge combined will and reason, concluding that together they constituted the mental activity of the self-conscious spirit.

Coleridge extended the interior vision of the whole conscious self to an immediate beholding of an entire field of external vision at once, connecting it still further to the imagination. As an individual looked upon a forest, the mind organized this data into an interior vision of the imagination, which allowed the mind to view the whole while also zooming in on this tree or that leaf. Such a view closely resembled the twelfth-century understanding of contemplation as an ecstatic beholding of the whole over against meditation's focus on particular lines of argumentation (see §2.3.1). The common sources were Platonism and mysticism.[28]

Humans by nature possess a "high spiritual instinct . . . impelling us to seek unity by harmonious adjustment."[29] This instinct compels humans to move toward unity, the integration of all things and their participation in this whole. To see the whole and the harmonious interplay of its parts required an imaginative reconstruction that combined the "many circumstances into one moment of thought to produce that ultimate end of human Thought, and human Feeling."[30] It is only through an act of the imagination in concert with wonder that the whole appears as one visionary insight, which is why Coleridge held that reason was concerned with ultimate ends rather than the proximate ends of discursive analysis.

---

[26] Coleridge, *Aids to Reflection*, 225; idem, *Bibliographia Literaria, or Biographical Sketches of My Literary Life and Opinions* (New York: Leavitt, 1834), 146.

[27] On the relationship between Coleridge and Schelling, see Giles Whiteley, *Schelling's Reception in Nineteenth-Century British Literature* (London: Palgrave Macmillan, 2018), 50–56; Alexander M. Schlutz, *Mind's World: Imagination and Subjectivity from Descartes to Romanticism* (Seattle: University of Washington Press, 2009), 214–54.

[28] See Peter Cheyne, *Coleridge's Contemplative Philosophy* (Oxford: Oxford University Press, 2020), 125–225; idem, ed., *Coleridge and Contemplation* (Oxford: Oxford University Press, 2017), 171–92, 211–20.

[29] Coleridge, *Bibliographia Literaria*, 217.

[30] Henry Nelson Coleridge, ed., *The Literary Remains of Samuel Taylor Coleridge* (London: William Pickering, 1836), 56.

The total act of the conscious self is an act of the imagination, which reflects God's own eternal creative act and thus unites the person to God.[31] Humans experience two visions of the world corresponding to diverse mental operations, one of which relates to a reflective mode of discourse and the other to an intuitive mode of discourse, one dealing with the material and the other with the spiritual. While both types of vision yield truth, the latter produces an immediate awareness of the whole. This flash of intuition is part of the movement toward unity that brings ultimate ends before the mind. It is Coleridge's version of Anselm of Canterbury's *excitatio mentis*—that of which a greater cannot be conceived—a movement into transcendence that glimpses the perfect being who stands behind and within the whole. Like Anselm, Coleridge had been describing a kind of ecstatic event that mirrored the final beatific vision.

To describe how this vision unfolds, Coleridge fused a symbolist mentality with his understanding of reason. He states, "In looking at the objects of Nature while I am thinking, as at yonder moon dim-glimmering thro' the dewy window-pane, I seem rather to be seeking, as it were *asking*, a symbolical language for something within me that already and forever exists, than observing any thing new."[32] The particular (in this case Coleridge's view of the moon) becomes a window, a symbolic opening onto the universal through an imaginative movement of the human spirit that is the essence of Coleridgean intuition.

Stewart and Coleridge exemplify a widening philosophical perspective that fused intuition with knowledge as participatory encounter. Intuition pointed toward an expansive vision of the imagination to behold the whole, a swiftness of mental movement, and an awareness of a belief instantly apparent yet exceeding the boundaries of reflective analysis. The division of knowledge into direct and immediate (intuitive) and indirect and mediate (discursive) was subsequently employed by holiness thinkers such as Methodist Daniel Steele or by New England Congregationalists such as Horace Bushnell. Moreover, Coleridge made specific religious connections in the form of a spirituality in which Christianity became a lived reality rather than a confessional system. It was a vision of life grounded upon theological truths not asserted in the form of confessional dogmas.

This perspective on Christianity merged easily with the growing influence of Christian mystical writers and spiritualists in the Anglo-American context. A case in point is the influence of Emanuel Swedenborg's thought on Henry James Sr. (1811–1882), father of William James (1842–1910) and the novelist Henry James (1843–1916). Swedenborg offered James the elder a theological vision of a divine humanity achieved by the push toward a utopian future, which he found in the Frenchman Charles Fourier's socialist vision.[33] It was through socialism that humanity could overcome its fundamental selfishness and turn toward a society of love that mimicked the spiritual reality underneath the physical universe. Henry James Sr. represents a growing connection between viewing the natural and the supernatural as an organic union that informed political union

---

[31] See Jonathan Wordsworth, "The Infinite I AM: Coleridge and the Ascent of Being," in *Coleridge's Imagination: Essays in Memory of Pete Laver*, ed. R. Gravil, L. Newlyn, and N. Roe (Cambridge: Cambridge University Press, 1985), 33.

[32] Samuel Taylor Coleridge, *Notebooks*, vol. 2: 1804–1808, ed. K. Coburn (1961), as cited in Nicholas Reid, *Coleridge, Form and Symbol, or The Ascertaining Vision* (Burlington: Ashgate, 2006), 1.

[33] Henry James, *The Secret of Swedenborg: Being an Elucidation of His Doctrine of the Divine Natural* (Boston: Fields, Osgood, 1869).

in democratic societies. Christian mystics and spiritualists offered new arteries through which the emphases on intuitive knowledge and immanent encounter continued to flow into more parts of the nineteenth century.

3.1.3 Liberal Culture and Cultivating the Human

By the second half of the nineteenth century the emphasis on intuitive knowledge through transcendent encounter was coalescing around a literati who sought to facilitate a "liberal culture."[34] The push toward a cultural consensus through a Protestant nonsectarianism formed an important component in the rise of the modern research university and its secularization.[35] This is not to deny the role of nationalization in Europe and America but to place the movement toward national identity and state control in the broader context of the creation of culture.[36] In some respects, the desire to create a liberal culture represented a conservative reaction to the concerted effort by entrepreneurs to take over higher education through their appointment to governing boards. Between 1860 and 1900, there was a large increase in the numbers of businessmen, bankers, and lawyers on institutional boards, which further eroded the role of scholars in shaping university life.

Professionalization seemed to link education to economic ends rather than the pursuit of knowledge and the development of the person. Slowly an alliance of literati emerged to fight against the corporate liberalism that would "secularize" the academy in the name of private enterprise.[37] By the 1950s the battle between entrepreneurs and academics had turned into an alliance to transform culture as the former through foundations and other entities poured millions of dollars into higher education. Just after the Civil War, however, the battle was just beginning on whether education should be oriented more to intellectual formation for moral ends or practical formation for professional ends. This was a battle between two sets of elites.

By the onset of the Gilded Age, many American intellectuals had embraced Matthew Arnold's (1822–1888) conclusion that in a democracy culture must replace monarchy and aristocracy as the unifying center of national life since "nations are not truly great solely because the individuals composing them are numerous, free, and active; but they are great when these members, this freedom, and this activity are employed in the service of an ideal higher than that of an ordinary man, taken by himself."[38] A graduate of Oxford,

---

[34] Laurence R. Veysey, *The Emergence of the American University* (Chicago: University of Chicago Press, 1965), 180–251.

[35] See George M. Marsden, *The Soul of the American University Revisited*; idem, *The Outrageous Idea of Christian Scholarship* (New York: Oxford University Press, 1997), 14–15; and Gertrude Himmelfarb, "The Christian University: A Call to Counterrevolution," *First Things* 59 (January 1996): 16–19, who notes that the quest to create a culture lay behind secularization.

[36] Perry L. Glanzer, Nathan F. Alleman, and Todd C. Ream, *Restoring the Soul of the University: Unifying Christian Higher Education in a Fragmented Age* (Downers Grove: IVP Academic, 2017), 57–95.

[37] On this point, see Peter Dobkin Hall, *The Organization of American Culture, 1700–1900: Private Institutions, Elites, and the Origins of American Nationality* (New York: New York University Press, 1982); Peter Dobkin Hall, "Noah Porter Writ Large? Reflections on the Modernization of American Education and Its Critics, 1866–1916," in *The American College in the Nineteenth Century*, ed. Roger L. Geiger (Nashville: Vanderbilt University Press, 2000), 196–220.

[38] Matthew Arnold, "Democracy," in *Culture and Anarchy and Other Writings*, ed. S. Collini (Cambridge: Cambridge University Press, 1993), 14. The essay was originally published in 1861 as part of Arnold's report on education in France.

Arnold rose to prominence as a social critic in the 1860s for his writings on democracy, education, and culture partly because of his translation of German ideas into English idioms and partly for his argument of a common culture between the Old World and the New that could ground democracy and unite the two. Arnold's writings on culture remained a dominant force among the elite in Britain and America at least through T. S. Eliot and Lionel Trilling in the 1950s.[39]

With Arnold's help, the connection between democracy and culture in turn fueled the "sacralization of culture." Art and literature became conveyors of the divine alongside of the rise of a European pantheon of intellectuals and artists. The rise of the modern research university was part of larger cultural project to develop and disseminate a common religious-cultural vision by northern Protestant denominations (the de facto religious establishment) in response to the onset of modernity.

Taking a cue from Matthew Arnold's attempt to anglicize *Bildung* (self-cultivation/formation) as a commitment to culture, advocates of liberal culture came to see it as a vehicle for the transformation of society. Arnold understood culture as having its origin in the love of perfection and thus involving the study of perfection through scientific passion for pure knowledge and moral and social passion for doing good.[40] Alongside Arnold, John Stuart Mill used *Bildung* to humanize Jeremy Bentham's more quantitative approach to utilitarianism making culture and self-formation central to his preference for the higher pleasures of aesthetic and moral sensibilities. Arnold and Mill offered a way to move back toward the liberal arts in order to facilitate the formation of the student as the central role of education.

One of the issues between the development of *Bildung* and its transmission into Anglo-American settings was the relationship between self-cultivation and society at large. How could individual autonomy in the process of self-creation/spiritual development come together with culture? How could self-determination fit with socialization?[41] The connection was to see aesthetics as the spiritual path of self-cultivation and the driving force of culture. While we explore *Bildung* and the research university more carefully in the next section, it is crucial to understand how the advocates of liberal culture thought of culture as a vehicle to change society with education central to it.

Laurence Veysey's analysis of the emphasis on liberal culture in the American university reveals a potpourri of ideas associated with advocating culture as the primary aim of education. At its core, it was a turn to the study of literature for its content, not simply its form or structure, the introduction of fine arts as part of the exploration of beauty, and the importance of philosophy.[42] Through their alliance against an overemphasis on research and professionalism in the university, the advocates of liberal culture sought to continue the vision of civilizing human beings through a renewed emphasis on liberal

[39] On the importance of Arnold, see John Henry Raleigh, *Matthew Arnold and American Culture* (Berkeley: University of California Press, 1957); Lionel Trilling, *Matthew Arnold*, 2nd ed. (New York: Columbia University Press, 1949); James Walter Caufield, *Overcoming Matthew Arnold: Ethics in Culture and Criticism* (Burlington: Ashgate, 2012); Nicholas Murray, *A Life of Matthew Arnold* (New York: St. Martin's, 1997).

[40] Matthew Arnold, *Culture and Anarchy*, 58–59.

[41] Jesse Raber, *Progressivism's Aesthetic Education: The Bildungsroman and the American School, 1890–1920* (London: Palgrave Macmillan, 2018), 5–7.

[42] Veysey, *Emergence of the American University*, 183.

arts and the humanities and the use of the novel to form persons. This was essentially a return to Hellenistic models of education with philosophy and rhetoric at the top rather than theology.

One of the principal architects of this perspective was Charles Eliot Norton, who was hired in 1874 to teach art and literature by his cousin, Harvard president Charles W. Eliot. If James Turner is correct, Norton is to be credited with viewing the idea of "Western civilization" as a pedagogical strategy rather than a historical reality to provide a unifying center to education and a common moral purpose.[43] As Linda Dowling noted, after the Civil War "Norton and other liberals of his generation recognized in Mill's idea of culture both a conclusive answer to the emergent new Southern myth of the 'Lost Cause' and a counterweight to the recrudescence of Northern 'barbarism.'"[44] Southern advocates of the Lost Cause reframed the war in terms of a battle between distinct cultures and traditions in a way that idealized the South and portrayed Confederates as noble actors who fought valiantly against northern aggression.[45] In the words of Edward Pollard, a member of the editorial board of the *Richmond Examiner*, "there may not be a political South. Yet there may be a social and intellectual South."[46]

One purpose of Western civilization as a grand narrative with a Western canon was to replace the planter class of the southern aristocracy with a new nobility. Norton desired to form his students morally through the use of art and literature, which exposed them to the great ideas and moral dilemmas of the human condition. Although an agnostic in the mold of Thomas Huxley, he retained a sense of the connection between beauty and goodness since the beautiful in life embodied humanity's highest ideals. Norton strove to develop an approach that would see Jesus as part of a pantheon of heroes and the Bible as a literary masterpiece alongside other works in a Western canon. The point was to recreate the ideal world of Christianity in order to reinforce moral virtue without having to resolve the question of God or the immortality of the soul. Norton represented the secular side of the Romantic sensibility, which retained a vague notion of religion and encounter with transcendent beauty, truth, and goodness without postulating the existence of God.

Cultivation of the self depended upon arousing the imagination to sympathy with others through intellectual converse with the great figures and artists from the past. Norton's communion with the saints was a communion with the greatest minds.[47] By putting individuals in touch with the past, he sought to cultivate and civilize in the hope that eventually a "cultured" humanity would achieve moral harmony. Ironically, it was Norton's program of Western civilization, with its emphasis on the fine arts as a means to cultivate the human, that many American evangelical institutions adopted when they moved from

---

[43] James Turner, *The Liberal Education of Charles Eliot Norton* (Baltimore: John Hopkins University Press, 1999), 368–92.

[44] Linda Dowling, *Charles Eliot Norton: The Art of Reform in Nineteenth-Century America* (Hanover: University Press of New England, 2007), 91.

[45] On the Lost Cause, see Gary W. Gallagher and Alan T. Nolan, eds., *The Myth of the Lost Cause and Civil War History* (Bloomington: Indiana University Press, 2010).

[46] Edward A. Pollard, *The Lost Cause: A New Southern History of the War of the Confederates*, rev. ed. (New York: E. B. Treat, 1867), 752.

[47] Charles Eliot Norton, *History of Ancient Art*, ed. H. F. Brown and W. H. Wiggin Jr. (Boston: Alfred Mudge and Son, 1891), 1–11.

Bible schools to four-year liberal arts colleges. This is no doubt in part because Norton retained a spirituality in his approach that viewed the encounter with beauty in religious terms. In addition, Western civilization offered a new national narrative that could be rooted in a more remote past as a counter to the Lost Cause myth. The narrative of Western civilization was an encounter with a history and a set of ideals that transcended the individual and unified the nation.

While Norton cultivated a pedagogical strategy for a liberal culture, literary realists like William Dean Howells and Henry James extended these aims into the broad swath of middlebrow America through their novels and guardianship of elite magazines (the *Atlantic Monthly, Harpers Weekly*, among others). Literary realists retained notions of creativity, the imagination, and morality espoused by German and British writers of Romantic literature, but sought to distance themselves from the use of ideal types to convey moral lessons. The difference, as Howells put it, was literary realism's emphasis that "fidelity to experience and probability of motive are essential conditions of a great imaginative literature."[48] It was a conscious awareness of a universal human condition through an encounter with others.

This difference belied a shared outlook of the artist as visionary genius with a heroic sensitivity to all of life and an imaginative capacity to reconstruct all experience into a narrative form. In this sense, literary realism retained Thomas Carlyle's notion of the hero who experiences revelatory encounters amidst life in the march toward perfection, connecting it to the artist rather than a literary figure at the center of a narrative. Literary realists attempted to offer a genuine picture of life, an entire vision of human consciousness as it struggled with the vagaries and vicissitudes of existence.

From Willa Cather's portraits of western migration and life on the plains to Theodore Dreiser's and Kate Chopin's depictions of the struggles of women in urban centers (*Sister Carrie*) or enclaves of a regional culture (*The Awakening*), these writers wrestled with the human quest for meaning and identity. This was the moral scope of the novel, and it required of the artist "an immense sensibility, a kind of huge spider-web of the finest silken threads suspended in the chamber of consciousness, and catching every airborne particle in its tissue. It is the very atmosphere of the mind; and when the mind is imaginative—much more when it happens to be that of a man of genius—it takes to itself the faintest hints of life, it converts the very pulses of the air into revelations."[49] As Howells put it, a realist "feels in every nerve the equality of things and the unity of men; his soul is exalted, not by vain shows and shadows and ideals, but by realities, in which alone the truth lives."[50] This was a new humanism still suffused with a vague religiosity or spirituality that saw transcendence as solidarity with humanity and the greatest minds of human history.

Although the group of individuals who sought to cultivate a liberal culture remained small, they held important positions from which they attempted to shape a nation. From William Dean Howells, who saw to publication the works of Gilded Age writers,

---

[48] William Dean Howells, *Criticism and Fiction* (New York: Harper and Brothers, 1891), 15.

[49] Henry James, "The Art of Fiction," in *Henry James: The Future of the Novel*, ed. L. Edel (New York: Vintage, 1956), 12.

[50] Howells, *Criticism and Fiction*, 16.

to Charles Eliot Norton and the articulation of Western civilization, these individuals pushed for a national consensus around philosophy, literature, and the fine arts grounded upon a "religion of humanity."[51] They were the very center of the high-culture manifestation of the intuitionism, focus on immanence, and progressivism that defined the Romantic sensibility.

Woodrow Wilson's ascendance to the presidency in 1912 represented a high point in the effort to forge a common vision centered on culture that embraced religion and pluralism. Wilson had successfully installed this vision during his presidency at Princeton University, and his assuming the highest position in the land was a realization of the aspirations of this high-culture movement.[52] Some historians have found connections between Wilson's progressivism and the social gospel movement, but the deeper concordance resides in the impulses of the Romantic sensibility within the social imaginary, with its emphasis on the hero's intuitive encounter with transcendence, from which a cosmopolitan vision of life—a liberal cultural—emerges.[53] The push toward perfection in the progressivist vision was a religious-cultural understanding of life for Woodrow Wilson at the beginning of the twentieth century no less than for Henry Tappan in the middle of the nineteenth. This connects Walter Rauschenbusch's Jesus, whose sensitivity to life absorbs all of the world's evils on the cross, with William Dean Howells' vision of the artist and Henry Tappan's understanding of the scholar. Yet Wilson's own beliefs in the continued inferiority of African Americans and his distaste for Reconstruction reveal how racism could find the soil of this new emphasis on liberal culture hospitable and nurturing. Just as it had for the Germans, the use of *Bildung* to develop a notion of liberal culture around a new narrative of Western civilization reinforced national identity in a way that allowed racism to remain.

3.2   EDUCATION AND FORMING THE SELF: RESEARCH, UTILITY, AND TRAINING

Historians of higher education in America have routinely pointed out the importance of the German university as a model. With the founding of the University of Berlin (1810) by the Prussian state, as Thomas Howard notes, "*the modern university* first appeared on the historical stage" (emphasis orig.).[54] While the figure of Wilhelm von Humboldt

---

[51]   Marsden, *Soul of the American University Revisited*, 151–62; James Turner, "Secularization and Sacralization: Speculations on Some Religious Origins of the Secular Humanities Curriculum, 1850–1900," in *The Secularization of the Academy*, ed. G. M. Marsden and B. J. Longfield (New York: Oxford University Press, 1992), 74–106.

[52]   On the relationship between Wilson's academic career and his presidency, see Ronald J. Pestritto, *Woodrow Wilson and the Roots of Modern Liberalism* (Lanham: Rowman and Littlefield, 2005); Veysey, *Emergence of American University*, 241–44.

[53]   See Pestritto, *Woodrow Wilson and the Roots of Modern Liberalism*, 41–43; C. Howard Hopkins and Ronald C. White Jr., *The Social Gospel: Religion and Reform in Changing America* (Philadelphia: Temple University Press, 1976), 179–89.

[54]   Thomas Albert Howard, *Protestant Theology and the Making of the Modern German University* (Oxford: Oxford University Press, 2006), 4. See also William Clark, *Academic Charisma and the Origins of the Research University* (Chicago: University of Chicago Press, 2008); Glanzer, Alleman, and Ream, *Restoring the Soul of the University*, 65–69. While it is beyond the scope of our current analysis, it's important to note that the roots of the University of Berlin reside in the universities of Halle (founded 1694) and Göttingen (founded 1737).

(1767–1835) stands as the key representative of the foundation of the University of Berlin, it was a group of individuals who together set forth the key ideas of a new model of education. Over the course of two decades, Friedrich Schleiermacher (1768–1834), Johann G. Fichte (1762–1814), and Friedrich W. J. Schelling (1775–1854) developed their ideas in relation to the formation of a new university in the Prussian capital. Of the four, only Schleiermacher was a theologian; the remaining were philosophers. Humboldt summarized their ideas in the basic claim that the new university would pursue *Wissenschaft* in the service of *Bildung*.

As we noted in the previous section, the German notion of *Bildung* offered fertile soil for the concept of liberal culture advanced by American literati in the postbellum period. Stemming from the German *Bild* ("picture/image") and *bilden* (to form/represent), the term *Bildung* came into use through late medieval Rhineland mysticism, particularly Meister Eckhart, who exploited the connection to *imago* and *formatio* (*reformatio/transformatio*) to describe a process of formation centered on the Plotinian image of sculpting a statue out of marble.[55] Eckhart utilized the flexibility in the German language to describe a process of letting go of false images that deform (*entbilden*), viewing the soul in light of eternity (*überbilden*), and the Word in the soul (*erbilden*).[56] The point is a dynamic process in which God pours out divine goodness through the birth of the Son in the soul and the person cooperates to form the self through detachment and letting go. The ultimate aim of this process is final union and, in some sense, full identification with God.

Education becomes a process of sculpting the self as God descends and the soul ascends by being formed into God. His use of the Dionysian corpus and borrowing from Neoplatonism prompted Eckhart to think in the same terms as Bonaventure's *On the Reduction of the Arts to Theology*. The *reductio* was a leading back to God grounded in the Latin deployment of *reducere* to translate the Dionysian use of material symbols to "uplift" the soul.[57] Eckhart utilized the metaphor of light being poured into the soul because divine goodness flowed in and spilled over as part of the soul's formation. In this sense, *transformatio* was also a *transfiguratio*. As Hedley suggests, in Eckhart this was an *educere*, that is, a leading out through the formation of the self.[58]

The deep Christian use of *Bildung* entered German theological thought through the Rhineland mystics and strongly influenced German Pietism, from which it came, to thinkers like Goethe and the circle of German philosophers and theologians who influenced Humboldt. Under men like Goethe and Humboldt, a kind of secularization of *Bildung* occurred, so that it came to underscore the autonomy of the individual in the dynamic development of the self. Humboldt thought that the goal of humanity was "the highest

---

[55] For Eckhart and the use of *Bild/Bildung*, see Douglas Hedley, "Bild, Bildung, and the 'Romance of the Soul': Reflections upon the Image of Meister Eckhart," *Educational Philosophy and Theory* 50.6–7 (2018): 614–20; Jennifer A. Herdt, *Forming Humanity: Redeeming the German Bildung Tradition* (Chicago: University of Chicago Press, 2019), 42–47; Mauritius Wilde, *Das neue Bild vom Gottesbild: Bild und Theologie bei Meister Eckhart* (Freiburg/Schweiz: Univ.-Verl., 2000), 159–60; Richard Woods, *Meister Eckhart: Master of Mystics* (London: Continuum, 2011), 137–40.

[56] Hedley, "Bild, Bildung," 616.

[57] Paul Rorem, "Dionysian Uplifting (Anagogy) in Bonaventure's 'Reductio,'" *Franciscan Studies* 70 (2021): 183–88.

[58] Hedley, "Bild, Bildung," 616.

and most proportionate development [*Bildung*] of all his powers into a whole."[59] Since this development was dynamic and moving from within, one could translate *Bildung* as self-cultivation, self-education, or self-formation. Goethe's work built this emphasis into the genre of the *Bildungsroman* (the apprenticeship novel) in which the novel utilized a hero who consciously sought self-cultivation and enlightenment.[60] The autonomy of the self was established. The base ingredient of individualism and authenticity was set.

There was also a transcendent quality grounded in the connection to humanity. The full realization of the self occurs through an engagement with others and the world, which itself is a kind of ecstatic movement, albeit evacuated of connection to the divine. Art and philosophy replaced theology in Humboldt's thought as the means of self-cultivation. There is a deeply aesthetic dimension as art and philosophy put the person in touch with beauty in the process of sculpting the self. Moral formation through education is an aesthetic movement in the community of scholars who pursue *Wissenschaft*.

As the counter to self-formation (*Bildung*), *Wissenschaft* retained within it the dual meaning of *scientia* as both knowledge and science. In this sense, it also implied scholarly inquiry. Humboldt reframed the purpose of the university entirely around the production of knowledge for its own sake through scientific study. Philosophy was moved from lower studies in the liberal arts to higher studies as theology was dethroned. The professor became a researcher (*Wissenschaftler*). In this context, scholars must be free from confessional constraints as they seek to advance reason and contribute to human progress through the pursuit of knowledge as an end. Moreover, this pursuit was not primarily about the assimilation of the past so much as the experimentation and elaboration of new knowledge. The professor was a producer of knowledge. The modern university must privilege academic freedom in terms of self-formation and pure research in its production of knowledge.

The movement of these ideas into an Anglo-American context was much more haphazard and complex than simply copying the University of Berlin. Reflecting back on university education during the Progressive Era, William Carpenter, who was then professor of Germanic languages at Columbia, but who would serve as provost, quipped that "our universities, however, neither are, nor should be, German universities . . . for our needs, as determined by our particular social life and institutions, are not those of Germany."[61] German concepts had to be translated into Anglo-American idioms, which occurred through a number of thinkers over the course of the nineteenth century. First, there were a set of thinkers who mediated the basic ideas in *Bildung* in relation to the pursuit of knowledge. The primary French interpreter was Victor Cousin (1792–1867), and the primary English interpreters were Samuel Taylor Coleridge (1772–1834), Thomas Carlyle (1795–1881), John Stuart Mill (1806–1873), and Matthew Arnold (1822–1888). Second, there were founders of universities in America that attempted to imitate Berlin. The key players were Daniel Coit Gilman at Johns Hopkins, Charles William Eliot at Harvard, William Rainey Harper at Chicago, and Henry Philip Tappan at Michigan.

---

[59] Wilhelm von Humboldt, *The Sphere and Duties of Government*, trans. Joseph Coulthard (London: John Chapman, 1854), 11.

[60] Gisela Argyle, *Germany as Model and Monster: Allusions in English Fiction, 1830s–1930s* (Montreal: McGill-Queen's University Press, 2002), 12–27.

[61] William Carpenter, "A Plea for a Rational Terminology," *Educational Review* 34.3 (1907): 259–71, at 270.

The ideas of Henry Tappan help set the context for the connection between the formation of the research university and the transmission of German ideas. Tappan drew from British interpreters of *Bildung* like Thomas Carlyle to forge a nonsectarian vision of the university as a place of research invested in the formation of the self and of culture through the scholar as hero. This was not initially a secularized version of moral formation, but, rather, a fusion of a common spirituality (a sort of Protestant pluralism) into the formation of the person and the encounter with transcendence as part of the production of knowledge. Still, the mission was the production of knowledge for the sake of the country. Arising from the same spring, Tappan's vision easily flowed into the liberal culture of the literati.

The vision of a research university that drew upon German models was introduced alongside of other developments in American higher education. While older liberal arts colleges had been modeled on Oxford and Cambridge, there were a new set of schools that aimed at educating the masses rather than elites who governed society. The rise of technical institutes and state normal schools represented the flourishing of more utilitarian models that stood in tension with the research university. This more utilitarian approach became an important feature of the American landscape and served as more of a model for evangelicalism in the late nineteenth century.

The connections between Tappan's adaptation of German ideas and the holiness and pentecostal movements may be found in the social imaginary both inhabited in the late nineteenth century. The emphases embedded in what we have called the Romantic sensibility were shaped into a high-church movement, a high-culture movement, and a populist movement. It is within the latter that adherents of holiness ideas found themselves, although there was crossover between high culture and populism through persons like Harriet Beecher Stowe and Thomas Upham.

This second section to the chapter argues the following: first, German ideas, anglicized by British and American writers, fueled the rationale behind the modern research university as an elite institution for the elite producers of culture (§3.2.1); second, utilitarian models in the form of state normal schools and the multipurpose college took shape alongside of the research university, and it's from these models that evangelical, holiness, and pentecostal adherents drew (§3.2.2); and third, the emphases of the Romantic sensibility unfolded in three distinct movements that infused it into more elite and more populist forms (§3.2.3).

3.2.1 *Bildung*, Spirituality, and the Research University

One of the central architects of the university as facilitating cultural transformation was Henry Tappan. Tappan fused together religion and the liberal arts under the broad canopy of *Bildung*, albeit refracted through the prism of its French and English interpreters and assimilated to midwestern realities.[62] As chancellor of the University of Michigan in

---

[62] The importance of Tappan is not in whether his ideas were uniformly implemented (they were not), but in the way they exemplify and inspire a movement that adapted German ideas even if in a haphazard manner. For more, see James Turner and Paul Bernard, "The German Model and the Graduate School: The University of Michigan and the Origin Myth of the American University," in Geiger, *American College in the Nineteenth Century*, 221–41.

1855, Tappan reminded the members of its literary societies that the men of the classical period were heroic figures:

> Each formed himself by individual effort, under the inspirations of his own genius, availing himself of the knowledges which were accessible, studying the examples which were presented, seizing the occasions which were offered, moulding language, and developing forms of beauty with an originality which could belong only to a period when the human mind, awakening to a consciousness of its powers under the great eye of nature, instead of finding authorities in the past, was driven in upon itself and created authorities for the future, and like a discoverer in regions untrodden before, wandered freely abroad in joyful expectation of wonders of truth and beauty.[63]

Tappan made it clear that the universities of the medieval period likewise emerged spontaneously through the efforts of great individuals, the end of whose association was the advancement of knowledge. This view buttressed one of Tappan's central contentions that the university was a voluntary association preceding the state that sprang forth like Athena from "'many-sided' men, who . . . are smit with the love of all knowledges and spiritual accomplishments, and so co-work together for the great purpose of building up human souls after a true and noble ideal."[64]

At the pinnacle of this process stood the German university, which combined scholastic organization with a classical sense of the free man whose mind is unencumbered by authorities. The twofold purpose had remained the same: to pursue knowledge and to create and advance culture. This was Tappan's bourgeois notion of *Bildung* with its commitment to self-cultivation and to the cultivation of civilized society by men of real genius. As Turner and Bernard note, Tappan's loyalty was to the liberal arts paradigm because "the culmination of education was the integrative culture that [Tappan] associated with 'the highest learning.'"[65] Personal development contributed to the larger whole of social development, which maintained the movement between the particular and the universal, the *humanitas* and *civitas* essential to *Bildung*.

Tappan's depiction of university scholars as men of real genius who become the shapers of culture drew from Thomas Carlyle's understanding of history as moved by great men. Carlyle's vision of heroic figures as "the modellers, patterns, and in a wide sense, creators, of whatsoever the general mass of men contrived to do or to attain," with a possible Emersonian flourish, forms an underground stream throughout Tappan's discourse.[66] Where Carlyle preserved the domain of the heroic for a more select group, Ralph Waldo Emerson had attempted to democratize it by describing its traits as self-trust and "an obedience

---

[63] Henry P. Tappan, *The Progress of Educational Development: A Discourse* (Ann Arbor: Advertiser Power Presses, 1855), 6.

[64] Henry P. Tappan, *University Education* (New York: George Putnam, 1851), 18.

[65] See Paul Bernard and James Turner, "The Prussian Road to University? German Models and The University of Michigan, 1837–c. 1895," in *Intellectual History and Academic Culture at the University of Michigan: Fresh Explorations*, ed. Margaret A. Lourie (Ann Arbor: Horace H. Rackham School of Graduate Studies, 1989), 15.

[66] Thomas Carlyle, *On Heroes, Hero-Worship, and the Heroic in History* (London: Chapman and Hall, 1840); Ralph Waldo Emerson, "Heroism," in *Essays* (Boston: James Monroe, 1841), 201–18. William Kay explores the emergence of liberal education in England in "Liberal Education: A Renewed Role within Religious Education," *Journal of Beliefs and Values* 32.2 (2011): 185–93.

to a secret impulse of an individual's character."[67] Yet Emerson's effort to adapt Carlyle's thought to the American context by focusing on heroic traits rather than persons did not fit the new paradigm of scholarship.

Under Carlyle's influence, scholars became heroic men who forged a Promethean existence in which they extracted the secrets of the gods through their own creativity before descending from the realms of knowledge to bring their gifts to humanity. Without the freedom to cultivate their own creative genius, such heroic figures would wither and die. Goethe had composed lyrical odes to Prometheus and infused *Faust* with Promethean virtue as part of the apprenticeship novel. Through his views of creativity as an intuitive act by which the artist creates on analogy with the divine, Goethe retained a notion of divine/human interaction even as his pantheism collapsed divine transcendence into an immanent frame.[68] Nevertheless, one finds the figure of Prometheus woven into German and British Romanticism as a symbol of autonomous human creativity and protest. Lord Byron and Percy Shelley composed odes to Prometheus, with Shelley, in the preface to *Prometheus Unbound*, asserting a theory of the artist as both mirroring and reconfiguring the world in his own consciousness.[69] This is how Romanticism assimilated the notion of self-cultivation and self-formation. Few Romantics heeded Mary Shelley's warning that heroic creativity and autonomy could destroy life as easily as give it.[70] This was the tradition upon which Tappan drew for his conception of the scholar as an autonomous genius at once encountering the divine in the world, creating new forms of knowledge, and imparting them to humanity.[71]

Writing in the 1850s, Tappan was transmitting into the American context his own understanding of education as the formation of the human person or as self-cultivation (*Bildung*). The German tradition of *Bildung* was laden with Platonic ideas lending onto-logical weight to the process of formation. The development of the soul involved an evolving perfection whereby it received and recovered its true form. By the late eighteenth century Goethe associated *Bildung* with biological metaphors to illustrate cultivating the latent potential in humanity, which occurred through the struggle of the hero to develop fully all of his powers.[72] This is the meaning that Wilhelm von Humboldt adapted in describing the process of education and the role of the Prussian university. John Stuart Mill encountered Humboldt's expression in the English translation of *The Sphere and Duties of Government*, which he quoted in his *On Liberty*. Describing Humboldt as a savant and politician, Mill agreed with his claim that the "immutable dictates of reason"

[67]   Emerson, "Heroism," 206.

[68]   Nicholas Saul, "Goethe the Writer and Literary History," in *The Cambridge Companion to Goethe*, ed. Lesley Sharpe (Cambridge: Cambridge University Press, 2002), 26.

[69]   Percy Bysshe Shelley, *Prometheus Unbound: A Lyrical Drama in Four Acts*, ed. G. Lowes Dickinson (London: J. M. Dent, 1898), xiv–xv.

[70]   Mary Shelley, *Frankenstein: or, The Modern Prometheus*, 2 vols. (London: G. and W. B. Whittaker, 1823).

[71]   One can detect this view of history in Daniel Boorstin's trilogy on the heroic. See his *The Discoverers: A History of Man's Search to Know His World and Himself* (New York: Vintage, 1983); idem, *The Creators: A History of Heroes of the Imagination* (New York: Vintage, 1993); idem, *The Seekers: The Story of Man's Continuing Quest To Understand His World* (New York: Vintage, 1998); and, of course, Joseph Campbell's approach to world religions and mythmaking.

[72]   Argyle, *Germany as Model and Monster*, 12–27.

led one to conclude the end of human existence in terms of the harmonious development of human powers, which required complete freedom and individuality.[73] In this sense, self-cultivation was also self-culture. To become cultured required autonomy, freedom, and the right set of circumstances.

In Germany, the cultivation of the individual (*Bildung*) went together with the cultivation of society (*Kultur*). The former pointed toward the development of the interior life as the proper domain of the artist/scholar, while the latter pointed toward its integration into the larger whole of society. This was the purpose of science (*Wissenschaft*) in its early idealist conception as "a devout faith in the mind's duty and capacity to enquire into and represent the basic essence of things, and through such activities to improve human character (*Bildung*)."[74] *Wissenschaft* was in the service of the *Kulturstaat* in Germany by minimizing confessionalism and maximizing a scholarly vocation to cultivate humanity and society.

Thomas Carlyle translated it into the English context as "the great law of culture," which involved each person becoming "all that he was created capable of being."[75] The scholar's pursuit of the moral life was the pursuit of personal culture and the harmonization of human powers as an internal condition. Such is the concept of *Bildung* Tappan introduced into his understanding of the American university, and it became the basis for sacralizing academic freedom as well as Mill's assertion of individuality and autonomy as necessary to well-being.

The university was the wellspring of culture through the scholars who, buoyed by amply supplied institutional supports, advanced knowledge as part of their project in self-formation and the formation of others. It was a trickle-down theory of education. Trickle-down pronouncements were common to the Progressive Era, being easily aligned with a notion of democracy as the diffusion of knowledge throughout society.[76] To find a nonsectarian unifying vision for the university's intellectual life, Tappan fused self-cultivation with French and Scottish philosophy. Drawing on Victor Cousin's attempt to synthesize German idealism with the philosophy of Reid and Stewart, Tappan argued that human reason contained innate ideas of the true, the beautiful, and the good.[77] Being embedded in human nature, these ideas take the form of capacities that generate the desire to know expressed through curiosity thereby making knowledge of the transcendentals possible. They are brought forth and developed as humans reflect upon sensory data from the world. Since the entire universe is a reflection of the divine ideas, knowledge of the transcendentals occurs through a kind of union between the human person and the cosmos.

---

[73] John Stuart Mill, *On Liberty*, 2nd ed. (London: John W. Parker and Son, 1859), 103.

[74] Howard, *Protestant Theology*, 28.

[75] Thomas Carlyle, "Jean Paul Friedrich Richter (1827)," in *Critical and Miscellaneous Essays in Five Volumes*, vol. 1 (New York: Charles Scribner's Sons, 1900), 19.

[76] See Veysey, *Emergence of the American University*, 64.

[77] Cousin had borrowed from Reid and Stewart and German idealists to chart a path between the idealism of George Berkley and the empiricism of Locke. Tappan follows him in this respect. See Victor Cousin, *Course of the History of Modern Philosophy*, trans. O. W. Wight, vol. 1 (New York: Appleton, 1852); and Henry P. Tappan, *Elements of Logic, Together with an Introductory View of Philosophy in General and a Preliminary View of the Reason* (New York: Appleton, 1856).

Tappan also incorporated insights from Coleridge when he identified this as the reason's intuitive grasp of the infinite, a grasp flowing from an encounter with transcendence. The beginning of knowledge involves "a period of spontaneous communication between the soul and nature, springing up from the relation between the ideas within and their embodiment without. A voice from without calls to the soul within, and the soul joyfully answers back."[78] Although Tappan's language would not echo Thomas Carlyle's bald identification of this movement as a leap "into the promised land, where *Palingenesia*, in all senses, may be considered as beginning,"[79] he still claimed it as a "time of awakening" in the soul that initiated the process of self-cultivation. Protestant notions of regeneration morphed into the soul's awakening to the divine in the process of self-cultivation. Enlightenment, autonomy, and individuality were really bastardized interpretations of the cultivation of the human that transmuted the divine into nature and the common connection to humanity.

What Tappan pushed toward would take a long time to realize in American higher education. There were several reasons for this. For starters, Tappan aimed his vision at those who saw the fusion of democracy and culture. Even with all of the effort to build educational institutions, by 1900 it was still the case that only 4 percent of the American population was enrolled in institutions of higher education.[80] The percentage of those attending elite research institutions and their graduate programs was even less. Robert Mark Wenley, who served as head of the University of Michigan's philosophy department, would later claim that "the universities tend to become the prey of the *bourgeoisie*." In the quest to turn out successful professionals and experts, universities had created "an immense number of identical spools, all fitted to find place in a huge, undifferentiated *bourgeois* stratum."[81] What Wenley meant was the emerging entrepreneurial class that Charles Eliot Norton and others had resisted, but his comments also strike at the heart of this elite project.

Second, the multiple streams influencing American higher education created confusion between the definition of a university, a college, and an institute or school. William Carpenter tried to differentiate between them by defining a college as a liberal arts institution granting bachelor degrees, a university as a postgraduate institution engaged in scientific research and granting graduate and doctoral degrees, and a school or institute as a vocational institution that trained persons for professions like business or teaching.[82] Recognizing that the university was a new educational model only emerging in the 1870s, Carpenter concluded that the university exists for the few while colleges and schools serve the many. It would take the better part of a century and two world wars before Tappan's ideal was fully established.

---

[78]   Tappan, *Elements of Logic*, 55.

[79]   Thomas Carlyle, *Sartor Resartus: The Life and Opinions of Herr Teufelsdröckh*, 3.8 (London: Chapman and Hall, 1831), 203.

[80]   Truman Commission Report, "Higher Education for American Democracy, 1947," in *American Higher Education Transformed, 1940–2005: Documenting the National Discourse*, ed. Wilson Smith and Thomas Bender (Baltimore: Johns Hopkins University Press, 2008), 86.

[81]   R. M. Wenley, "Can We Stem the Tide?" *Educational Review* 34 (1907): 242–43. See also Veysey, *Emergence of the American University*, 190–91, who cites Wenley.

[82]   Carpenter, "Plea for a Rational Terminology."

3.2.2 Liberal Arts, State Normal Schools, and Utilitarian Models of Education

Tappan's vision privileged the liberal arts and graduate-level education where scholars did their best work. This vision came face to face with the pragmatic spirit of America and the drive toward industrialization to exert pressure on colleges to relate to "real-world" conditions. As Alexis de Tocqueville had observed two decades earlier, democratic societies push their citizens away from the leisure required for meditation and toward the earthy and practical dimensions of life. He saw this as particularly the case in America and even prescribed that "in democratic times, individual interest, as well as the security of the state, insists that the education of the masses should be scientific, commercial, and industrial rather than literary."[83] Emerging in antebellum American, this more utilitarian paradigm at times competed with the older liberal arts ideal of the classical college, although by the end of the century it had been incorporated into many institutions, giving rise to an elective system, agriculture and mechanical arts, and the multipurpose college.[84] The liberal arts served the end of inculturating individuals as citizens, while agricultural, mechanical, and even scientific disciplines served more utilitarian ends of the economy and technological advancement. While Tappan's University of Michigan aspired to embody a research approach that would end with the University of Chicago, Ezra Cornell's university attempted to maintain a more utilitarian aim.

From across the Atlantic, Matthew Arnold criticized Cornell's approach as a form of provincialism in its linking of culture with the production of technological aptitude.[85] At Harvard, Charles W. Eliot inaugurated his presidency by saying that ideally poetry, philosophy, and science converged on the material well-being of humanity, meaning that they all served the utilitarian aim.[86] The utilitarian approach appealed to a more technologically oriented society, fueling what Neil Postman would later call a technocracy that eventually viewed culture as a technopoly and culminating in a view of the scholar as expert.[87] Cornell and Harvard became places that sought to combine the liberal arts with utilitarian aims. Fusing economic and education interests, this approach led to the creation of a multiuniversity, fragmented into electives and specialized domains.[88] It drove

---

[83]   Alexis De Tocqueville, *Democracy in America: And Two Essays on America*, trans. Gerald E. Bevan (New York: Penguin, 2003), 524–52.

[84]   Many analyses of the transition in higher education in the nineteenth century discuss the tensions between a "utilitarian" ideal and a "liberal arts" ideal. For starters, see Bernard and Turner, "Prussian Road to University?"; Roger L. Geiger, "The Era of Multipurpose Colleges in American Higher Education, 1850–1890," in Geiger, *American College in the Nineteenth Century*, 127–52; idem, "The Rise and Fall of Useful Knowledge: Higher Education for Science, Agriculture, and the Mechanical Arts, 1850–1875," in Geiger, *American College in the Nineteenth Century*, 153–68.

[85]   Arnold, *Culture and Anarchy and Other Writings*, 200.

[86]   Charles W. Eliot, *Educational Reform: Essays and Addresses* (New York: Century, 1905), 1–2.

[87]   Neil Postman, *Technopoly: The Surrender of Culture to Technology* (New York: Vintage, 1992), 40–55. Postman sees the transition from technocracy to technopoly as happening during the Progressive Era. In England the emergence of the civic universities (so-called red brick) occurred during the same era in the industrialized cities of the Midlands and the North. These were initially engineering universities committed to the utilitarian model.

[88]   Glanzer, Alleman, and Ream, *Restoring the Soul of the University*, 96–109.

increasing specialization instead of facilitating an integration of knowledge that fit the older approach and resonated with the *Bildung* of German idealism.

How colleges assimilated these two basic paradigms depended in part on the complementary forces of regionalism and denominationalism.[89] Most schools of higher education experienced the regional and denominational tensions between a utilitarian mode that trained laity for practical ends and a classical mode that cultivated souls for more ultimate ends. One can even see this debate refracted through the famous exchange between W. E. B. Du Bois and Booker T. Washington. Being trained at Harvard and the University of Berlin, Du Bois argued in favor of *Bildung* and the humanities, whereas Washington espoused moral uplift through technical training. By the time Washington established Tuskegee Institute in Alabama (1881), he was bucking a growing trend among Black colleges to move toward the liberal arts in the service of Black culture and life.

A similar divide occurred within evangelical Protestantism in the late nineteenth century. The small but growing body of Protestant seminaries had embraced the professionalization of scholarship, seeing the field of biblical and historical studies as "classical fields" or disciplines.[90] Whether they recognized it or not, such professionalization was driven in part by the idea of the scholar as hero who engaged in self-cultivation and then formed a culture. In the case of Protestant scholars, the culture was both the church and society. As we noted, *Bildung* was behind Rauschenbusch's vision of Jesus as the cosmopolitan hero who became a sage fully in touch with himself and the world around him. This rehabilitation of the Hellenistic sage found in writers like Epictetus drove the second and third quests for a historical Jesus, from the religious genius who resembled an existentialist to the countercultural sage.[91] For Rauschenbusch, the role of the hero translated into the biblical category of the prophetic in which the consciousness of the kingdom of God is brought to bear on social evil.[92] The Bible school movement began from a more pragmatic set of aims that sought training in a basic knowledge of the English Bible with teaching, hygiene, and other basic skills. Still, some within the Bible school movement attempted to combine the classical (intense study of Scripture through acquisition of original languages) with the utilitarian (techniques that prepared laity for mission).[93]

---

[89] Roger L. Geiger, "Introduction: New Themes in the History of Nineteenth-Century Colleges," in Geiger, *American College in the Nineteenth Century*, 23–24.

[90] Glenn T. Miller, *Piety and Profession: American Protestant Theological Education, 1870–1970* (Grand Rapids: Eerdmans, 2007), 61–62.

[91] On Jesus the Sage as one of the most common designations, see Sarah E. Rollens and Anthony Le Donne, "The Historical Jesus," in *The Cambridge Companion to the New Testament*, ed. Patrick Gray (Cambridge: Cambridge University Press, 2021), 50–72.

[92] Walter Rauschenbusch, *A Theology for the Social Gospel* (New York: Macmillan, 1917), 42. "The social gospel is above all things practical. It needs religious ideas which will release energy for heroic opposition against organized evil and for the building of a righteous social life."

[93] See "Missionary Training Schools," *Missionary Review of the World* 3.13 (1890): 300–302, which seems to position Bible schools between the utilitarian and classic models. The review was edited by A. T. Pierson and J. M. Sherwood, who were leaders in the Higher Life wing of the holiness movement.

Out of this tension between utilitarian and research approaches came the multipurpose university. Oberlin Collegiate Institute became a prototype of this new approach, combining the education of ministers with a teaching college when it opened in 1833.[94] Part of its reforming zeal, the focus on training teachers occurred six years before the first normal school opened its doors.[95] Oberlin also retained a desire to reach all classes in keeping with its revivalist and perfectionist approaches to theology, which meant not only admitting women and African Americans but also establishing a preparatory school that could elevate those at lower levels of learning. Oberlin exemplified colleges built on the frontier, which retained a focus on the liberal arts while adding other programs, such as teaching and music, that had more pragmatic ends suited to the region.

Alongside the multipurpose college was the emergence of the state normal school. Beginning in the 1840s, state normal schools came about to train teachers for elementary education at a time when the lines were blurred between various forms of secondary education.[96] Inspired by the French philosopher Victor Cousin's report on German education, the normal school offered a basic curriculum required to teach a number of subjects in preparation to serve common schools. Working-class men and women (largely women) from different ethnic backgrounds could attend classes at a time when most women and African Americans were shut out of colleges and universities.

During the height of their popularity (1870–1900), normal schools expanded course offerings to include courses in grammar and rhetoric alongside of science, mathematics, and history. One can see in these offerings a kind of expansion of the *trivium* and *quadrivium* along with Renaissance humanism's insistence on history. To these more "academic" courses were added practical training courses in civics, bookkeeping, and other life skills. The goal was to produce generalists rather than experts. Under the weight of the turn toward a liberal culture, some normal schools tried to move toward studies in literature and Latin as a way of giving their students social capital. They also tightened admissions standards by requiring a high school degree. This placed normal schools on a trajectory that led to their incorporation into state college systems and their final movement into regional colleges and universities during the 1950s and 1960s. It is often forgotten how many American regional universities such as UCLA began as state normal schools. State normal schools became another model of education, especially for the masses.

Utilitarian approaches diverged on how society was to be transformed. Some, like Charles Eliot, followed Tappan's top-down approach and combined it with a proliferation of electives, while normal schools, Bible institutes, and the multipurpose college focused on training the average citizen. Even among those evangelicals who embraced classical studies and founded liberal arts universities, there was still a strong populist sense that society must be changed at the level of the *hoi polloi*, which required an army of lay volunteers spreading throughout every sector. Oberlin illustrates how holiness and revivalism

---

[94] J. H. Fairchild, *Oberlin: Its Origin, Progress, and Results* (Oberlin: Shankland and Harmon, 1860), 4. See also J. Brent Morris, *Oberlin, Hotbed of Abolitionism: College, Community, and the Fight for Freedom and Equality in America* (Chapel Hill: University of North Carolina Press, 2014).

[95] Donald W. Dayton with Douglas M. Strong, *Rediscovering an Evangelical Heritage: A Tradition and Trajectory of Integrating Piety and Justice*, 2nd ed. (Grand Rapids: Baker, 2014), 85–93.

[96] Christine A. Ogren, *The American State Normal School: An Instrument of Great Good* (New York: Palgrave Macmillan, 2005), 1–52.

could serve an educational program that sought to facilitate reform in soul and society. What connected these divergent approaches was a sensibility that understood moral transformation as requiring regular encounters with the divine.

3.2.3 Transitions and Connections: Diffusing the Romantic Sensibility

The previous examination of the emergence of the research university loosely modeled on German ideals of science and self-cultivation helps to see one way the Romantic sensibility unfolded in the nineteenth century. The union between intuitionism and an encounter with transcendence grounded in an emphasis on divine immanence, on the one hand, and a progressivism that generates social transformation through moral persuasion, on the other hand, shaped the social imaginary of the Gilded Age and Progressive Era. Yet these emphases took shape in different ways depending on the social and intellectual milieu they influenced. One can detect at least three overlapping movements that drew insights from this social imaginary: a high-church movement (Oxford Movement, Orestes Brownson, John Williamson Nevin, Philip Schaff, and Johann Adam Möhler), a high-culture movement (Thomas Carlyle, Matthew Arnold, Henry Tappan, and Henry James), and a populist movement (Edward Irving, Asa Mahan, Phoebe Palmer, and Thomas Upham). While Protestantism intersected with all three movements, Protestant thinkers who formed the center of what Gary Dorrien has called the liberal tradition of theology operated within high culture and sought to adapt Christianity to its use of a liberal culture as a civilizing influence on society.[97] Revivalists in the holiness and later pentecostal movements remained more populist, which is borne out by the educational institutions they sought to cultivate. Before we can explore those connections fully in the next section, we return briefly to a point we made earlier that these movements emerged from the same womb and possess similar traits. The differences account for their social and institutional expression and how the major emphases of the Romantic sensibility fit within their intellectual framework.

The vision of a university as the place where heroic figures encountered transcendence to form the souls of both the person and the society appealed to Tappan's New School Presbyterian sensibilities. Such a "spirituality" of learning allowed him to expunge sectarianism in the name of Protestant pluralism while at the same time maintaining the centrality of Christianity and its notion of encountering God. As the locus of divine ideas, creation became the intersection between the person and the transcendentals from which the arts and sciences sprang forth. Tappan's approach to education exemplifies a broader movement among the British and American intelligentsia from 1820 to 1860 to construct an alternative philosophical model around a form of intuitive rationality with a focus on encountering transcendence in the natural order. It is not so much that Tappan set in motion certain forces as that he embodied a move to reshape the American classical college inspired by German idealism as filtered through French, English, and Scottish thinkers.

In this model nature was suffused with the presence of the divine, which connected all living things and fueled their progressive development. It was a kind of sacramentalist view of nature that mirrored the twelfth-century symbolist mentality, in which a Peter Abelard could employ the Platonic idea of a world soul to explain the Spirit's

---

[97] Gary Dorrien, *The Making of American Liberal Theology: Imagining Progressive Religion, 1805–1900* (Louisville: Westminster John Knox, 2001), xiii–xxv.

presence in creation. An alternative to deism's insistence on a separation between God and the world, this *Naturphilosophie* took various forms from pantheism to an evangelical commitment to the Spirit in creation.

The construction of this alternative was haphazard and multilateral although unified in charting a course between the Scylla of Lockean empiricism and German idealism and the Charybdis of evidential Christianity. Intuitive rationality and encountering the divine in nature were features of Romanticism that seeped into New England intellectuals like Emerson and Orestes Brownson, who became the John Henry Newman of nineteenth-century American Catholicism. The counterpart to Emerson and Brownson in Britain was the Oxford Movement and Thomas Carlyle and Matthew Arnold. If Emerson represented one end of the continuum and Brownson the other end in America, the same could be said of Arnold and Carlyle compared to the Oxford Movement.

Its primary literary stream in the Anglo-American context was no doubt Carlyle's "natural supernaturalism," first articulated in *Sartor Resartus* (1833–1834) and adapted to America by Emerson's *Nature* (1836). It is also no mistake that both Carlyle and Emerson embraced forms of intuitionism. This perspective allowed agnostics enamored with science like Thomas Huxley and John Tyndall to hold to a mysterious presence within nature, a wonder experienced by the naturalist leading to a religion of nature.

When Thomas Carlyle delivered his triumphant inaugural address as rector of the University of Edinburgh on April 2, 1866, he was flanked by Thomas Huxley and John Tyndall.[98] Tyndall was an Irish-born physicist and outdoor enthusiast who became a public intellectual impacting the development of science. Along with Huxley, he was a member of the Metaphysical Society, which was formed in 1869 and at the first planning meeting of which Huxley proposed the term *agnostic*. Both Huxley and Tyndall had been shaped by Carlyle's work, with Huxley admitting that Carlyle helped him to find a version of religion shorn of theology.[99] By embedding the divine in nature and wedding it to self-cultivation, Carlyle's natural supernaturalism allowed for science to unfold according to natural laws and empirical investigation, while an avid lover of nature like Tyndall could still experience a sense of wonder and awe when climbing a mountain. Both Huxley and Tyndall pushed forward a scientific naturalism that would come to define a more secularized approach to scientific research. Carlyle's translation of German ideas became the midwife to a view of nature as a self-contained system of laws with nothing beyond it.

Late nineteenth-century thinkers retained an emphasis on the supernatural largely by espousing an immanence in which the divine worked within nature or was identified with nature. These points form the milieu for the holiness and pentecostal movements, accounting at least for part of the emphasis on the immanent work of the Spirit in relation

---

[98] See Ursula DeYoung, *A Vision of Modern Science: John Tyndall and the Role of the Scientist in Victorian Culture* (New York: Palgrave Macmillan, 2011), 59–88; Paul White, *Thomas Huxley: Making the "Man of Science"* (Cambridge: Cambridge University Press, 2003), 94–97; Roland Jackson, *The Ascent of John Tyndall: Victorian Scientist, Mountaineer, and Public Intellectual* (Oxford: Oxford University Press, 2018); Matthew Stanley, *Huxley's Church and Maxwell's Demon: From Theistic Science to Naturalistic Science* (Chicago: University of Chicago Press, 2015).

[99] Jackson, *Ascent of John Tyndall*, 56.

to a Wesleyan understanding of prevenient grace and the emerging connection between Pentecost and perfection.

One can detect this shared milieu on immanence, immediacy, and intuitionism in Horace Bushnell (1802–1876), Asa Mahan (1799–1889), and Daniel Steele (1824–1914). Although he never occupied an academic post, Bushnell takes center stage in Dorrien's account of liberal Christianity as both "the theological father of mainstream American liberal Protestantism" and "America's greatest nineteenth-century theologian."[100] He drew upon Coleridge, French quietism, and his own spiritual experiences to argue that the supernatural is immanent, acting within nature through multiple expressions of divine power while remaining distinct.[101] On this basis, Bushnell criticized the idea of development, which he called "the rational gospel of self-culture," expressed through *Bildung* because it assumed human nature could develop on its own rather than in and through regenerative grace or the process of new creation.[102] At the same time that Bushnell was arguing for an immediate and personal knowledge of God deeper than discursive thought, Asa Mahan claimed that all inward convictions produced by the Spirit were intuitive and thus direct and immediate perceptions of divine truth, and Daniel Steele used the philosophy of William Hamilton (1788–1856) to argue that what John Wesley meant by the Spirit's witness was a form of intuitive knowledge.[103]

The emphases of the Romantic sensibility also help explain how holiness leaders could support education through building Bible schools and colleges while espousing a kind of anti-intellectualism. The anti-intellectual cast of evangelical revivalism was not a rejection of rational intuitionism nor an encounter with transcendence or the progressive effort to create a new culture that went along with it. It was not, ultimately, a rejection of the same emphases upon which Henry Tappan (1805–1881), Horace Bushnell, and others drew for their visions. Rather, it represents a more populist version of the Romantic sensibility, grounded in an immediate awareness of the Spirit's presence and power in the life of a person. Whereas Tappan and Bushnell were more committed to cultivating a liberal high culture shaped by the emerging research ethos of professional schools and Protestant seminaries, most members of the holiness movement in the late nineteenth century sought to train laity for vocational ends in a way that shaped the clash of subcultures in the industrialized world of the Gilded Age. It was an on-the-ground form of Protestant pluralism flowing from a common set of spiritual experiences that facilitated moral transformation and deepening union with God.

In its more populist mode, the commitment to rational intuitionism and moments of crisis through divine intervention facilitated an antagonism toward any view of education that rejected encounters with transcendence and toward any view of education as

---

[100] Dorrien, *Making of American Liberal Theology*, 111.

[101] Horace Bushnell, *Nature and the Supernatural, as Together Constituting One System of God*, 4th ed. (New York: Charles Scribner, 1859), 36–63. See also Dorrien, *Making of American Liberal Theology*, 157–63.

[102] Bushnell, *Nature and the Supernatural*, 220–49.

[103] See Horace Bushnell, "The Immediate Knowledge of God," in *Sermons on Living Subjects* (New York: Charles Scribner's Sons, 1887), 114–28; Asa Mahan, *The Baptism of the Holy Ghost* (New York: George Hughes and Co., 1870), 200–6; Daniel Steele, *Love Enthroned: Essays on Evangelical Perfection* (New York: Phillips and Hunt, 1880), 214–226. Bushnell's sermon was first published in 1872, while Mahan's lectures were published in 1870 and Steele published his work in 1875.

being inherently inhumane that restricted efforts to "save" humanity to heroic figures who forged new cultural programs. Anti-intellectualism, in the former, took the shape of resistance to a perceived anticonversionism, whereas in the latter it was a war against the cultural moralism of the emerging bourgeoisie. Within the evangelical ethos of the holiness movement, conversion meant ongoing dramatic encounters, and thus Bushnell's efforts to minimize such encounters in favor of Christian nurture or any educational program that excluded a dramatic in-breaking in a moment of crisis from human formation were resisted. Moreover, it went together with an anti-embourgeoisement that equated formation through liturgical processes as advancing an urban religiosity ultimately capitulating to culture rather than transforming it.

These two dimensions went together. To be anticonversionist was to be antimoralistic insofar as holiness leaders thought that the genuinely human could only be achieved in and through a concrete and dramatic encounter with transcendent love. Education may help to facilitate and explain such an encounter, but to remove encounter would mean sowing the seeds of its own destruction. It may be better to label the holiness ethos not as fomenting an anti-intellectualism so much as a form of what Richard Hofstadter called "anti-rationalism," by which he meant a philosophical position found in writers like Ralph Waldo Emerson, William Blake, and William James.[104] The holiness movement became a rival tradition alongside of evidential Christianity and the research climate and liberal high culture that connected Protestant theologians like Horace Bushnell with agnostics like Charles Eliot Norton.

Nor is it the case that one can foist distinctions between holiness and pentecostal thinkers and other groups exemplifying the Romantic sensibility based on class or formal education, as some historians have done previously.[105] Men like Henry Tappan and William Dean Howells (1837–1920) no doubt viewed themselves as at the vanguard of a cultural elite whose task was to bequeath to America a distinct cultural identity while fostering a cosmopolitan vision of life through engagement with European thinkers. Yet theologians who wrote popular theology for the movement, like Daniel Steele or Thomas Upham, also penned more sophisticated works for those inhabiting the high-culture expression. These thinkers still plied their thoughts from the same social imaginary, even if they took it in another direction. The difference is that by the beginning of the Progressive Era cultural elites came to view themselves as heroic figures whose task it was to shape a nation in partnership with the financiers of high culture (e.g., John D. Rockefeller and Andrew Carnegie), whereas holiness and pentecostal adherents saw themselves as a populist movement among the laity that transformed regional cultures.

The shared outlook of rational intuitionism, encounters with transcendence, and a progressivism that transformed culture through moral persuasion (holiness or self-cultivation) was torn asunder under the weight of philosophical and historical developments during the Gilded Age and Progressive Era. In its own way, the holiness and pentecostal movements participated in the Romantic sensibility, which sought to cultivate a

---

[104] Richard Hofstadter, *Anti-intellectualism in American Life* (New York: Vintage, 1963), 8–9.

[105] Hofstadter, *Anti-intellectualism in American Life*; Robert Mapes Anderson, *Vision of the Disinherited: The Making of American Pentecostalism* (Peabody: Hendrickson, 1979). It should come as no surprise that in the late 1960s Anderson wrote the dissertation that would become *Vision of the Disinherited* while studying at Columbia, where Hofstadter taught until his premature death in 1970.

model of education open to the divine and invested in moral transformation for the sake of cultural transformation. The privileging in American religious historiography of the slow fracturing of northern Protestantism, culminating in the fundamentalist-modernist controversy, has obscured this broad connection.

3.3 ENCOUNTERING THE SPIRIT AND TRAINING FOR MISSION: HOLINESS AND RELATED STIRRINGS

In keeping with the major thesis of part 1, we have thus far attempted to show that there was a continued emphasis on moral formation, encounters with transcendence, and engagement in mission. The first two sections of this chapter argued that a set of emphases we have called the Romantic sensibility formed the backdrop in the nineteenth century to the development of higher education in America and its continuing emphasis on moral formation and encounter with transcendence. The cultivation of a liberal (high) culture became the dominant vehicle by which elites sought to engage in civic mission to form the larger populace. Infused with a spirituality shorn of confessional and denominational guardrails, culture as a literary and artistic enterprise was in the service of democracy. Universities and colleges were to be the drivers of culture. This return to ancient philosophical ideas of education meant a sacralization of culture that led to its secularization.

In contradistinction, what drove the institutions of the holiness movement was a populism centered in utilitarian aims. Moral formation was about sanctification, while encounters with transcendence came through crisis experiences worked out in the context of revivalism. Advocates of holiness wrapped both emphases in a pneumatology in which the Spirit shaped the affections and facilitated the encounters with transcendent love, which then fueled mission. This set the tone for populist missions that sought to remake society from the ground up.

The headwaters of the holiness movement emerged from the events of the 1830s, leading to a publishing program by Charles Finney, Asa Mahan, Thomas Upham, and Phoebe Palmer in the 1840s, which, in turn, gave rise to a movement. Phoebe Palmer and her husband Walter formed one center that initially included the Congregationalist Thomas Upham and the New School Presbyterian William Boardman (who would publish in 1858 *The Higher Christian Life*).[106] Upham represented another center of activity with his connections to Calvin Stowe and Harriet Beecher Stowe. The Stowes had been part of Lane Seminary in Cincinnati and the guiding hand of Lyman Beecher before moving to Maine and Bowdoin College. Finally, Charles Finney and Asa Mahan represented a third center branching out from Oberlin College. As the holiness movement entered its second phase (1860–1890), a series of overlapping relational networks that spanned England and America had developed. By 1875 many of these figures who were prominent in the first phase had either passed away or ceased to exercise a formative influence on the direction of the movement.[107] Nevertheless, not only did they set the agenda for many of the key ideas that would later be implemented during the Gilded Age, they shaped the leaders who advanced those ideas.

---

[106] William E. Boardman, *The Higher Christian Life* (Boston: Henry Hoyt, 1858).
[107] Between 1872 and 1875, Thomas Upham, Phoebe Palmer, and Charles Finney passed away.

The argument for this final section moves through the following claims: from how holiness leaders drew from the emphases of the Romantic sensibility, which connected to their understanding of head and heart through intuitionism and sanctification via a pneumatological grounding (§3.3.1), through how holiness leaders adopted more utilitarian models of education as the primary vehicles through which personal formation in holiness occurred (§3.3.2), to how holiness leaders focused their mission among the people as social transformation through revivalism (§3.3.3). The final two parts of this section focus more on hands both in terms of training for mission and social transformation.

3.3.1 Convergences: Knowledge, the Spirit, and Encounter

The holiness movement reached its apogee during a period of generational transition. The decade of the 1870s saw leading holiness figures among a loose coalition of revivalists from the 1830s and 1840s begin to pass away and a new group of leaders emerge. What held this coalition together was a progressive populism that wedded holiness, experiential religion, and social transformation. At its broadest, holiness in antebellum America encompassed three overlapping relational networks first centered in the Northeast and then in the Midwest. One could describe these three networks as Oberlin perfectionism, Methodist revivalism, and New School Presbyterianism, with Congregationalists and Baptists moving between all three wings. From these overlapping relational networks, the Higher Life and Wesleyan branches of the holiness movement emerged in the 1870s beginning in the Northeast and Midwest and moving to the South.[108] As such, the holiness movement followed the development of American higher education from Northeast to Midwest and then to the southern states.

Emerging between 1830 and 1860, many of the ideas central to the holiness message coalesced at the beginning of the Gilded Age and became radicalized during the Progressive Era. Intuitive knowledge, encounters with the divine, and perfectionism, all grounded in a turn to pneumatology, were important areas of convergence with the Romantic sensibility. These areas set the basic parameters for learning and education. To confirm this judgment we will look at three holiness thinkers—Thomas Upham, Phoebe Palmer, and Asa Mahan—who sought to fuse together personal transformation with social transformation through populist movements rather than a literary and scholarly movement.

As Timothy Smith and Melvin Dieter have noted, popular romanticism in America provided an important background to understanding the optimism of the holiness movement found in Palmer and Upham.[109] One might add that the Wesleyan endorsement of a graced human existence provided a hospitable ground within which popular romanticism could flourish. There was no pure state of nature without grace in terms of the Spirit's presence as love leading each person. Rooted in the power of the Spirit,

---

[108] Randall Stephens, *The Fire Spreads: Holiness and Pentecostalism in the American South* (Cambridge, Mass.: Harvard University Press, 2008), 1–55.

[109] Timothy L. Smith, *Revivalism and Social Reform in Mid-Nineteenth-Century America* (Nashville: Abingdon, 1957), 143; Melvin Dieter, *The Holiness Revival of the Nineteenth Century* (Metuchen: Scarecrow, 1980), 5.

the Wesleyan vision of optimistic grace fueled a revivalist vision for personal and social transformation.[110]

After Upham experienced entire sanctification under Palmer's guidance in 1837, he developed a theology of holiness that combined what he had learned from Scottish Common Sense philosophy with his wide-ranging exploration of the Christian mystical tradition. His publication of a biography of Madame Guyon in 1846 combined commentary with Guyon's own words to argue that sanctification involved a deeper spiritual work and brought about moral and spiritual union through which the soul came to rest in God and move out toward others.[111] Although he never embraced transcendentalism, there was a kinship between the combination of mysticism and holiness revivalism in Upham and Emerson's thought. Upham's understanding of the Spirit's abiding presence through his operations closely resembled the notion of communion with the oversoul.[112] This kinship was a result of the Romantic sensibility and the close alliance between perfectionism, encounters with the divine, and the immanent work of the Spirit.

Despite her misgivings about the quietism that Thomas Upham had embraced, Phoebe Palmer's theology was a form of practical mysticism.[113] Her "shorter way" to entire sanctification began with the active consecration of the entire self to God as an act of simple faith that God would embrace the sacrifice. This consecration involved seeing Christ as the altar upon which the soul's powers would be consumed. For Palmer, the experience of sanctification or entire consecration followed the act of faith, in which "her very existence seemed lost and swallowed up in God; and she seemed plunged as it were, into an immeasurable ocean of love, light and power."[114] The baptism of fire from Pentecost became the counter to the consecrating act of dedicating the soul's powers upon the altar of Christ's own sacrifice. Entire consecration led to a moment of transformed ecstasy in which the person experienced divine love in union with God.

What made Palmer's mysticism "practical" was the democratizing effect she saw in the experience of Christian perfection. Fusing her theology of consecration with John Fletcher's connection between Pentecost and Christian perfection, Palmer further suggested that entire sanctification was a baptism of fiery love in which the Spirit enveloped and empowered the person so that she became a prophetic emissary of God.[115] Consecration and faith would eventually bring about the sanctifying experience of Spirit baptism. Thus,

---

[110] Henry H. Knight III, *Anticipating Heaven Below: Optimism of Grace from Wesley to the Pentecostals* (Eugene: Cascade, 2014).

[111] Thomas Upham, *Life and Religious Opinions and Experiences of Madame de la Mothe Guyon*, vol. 1 (New York: Harper and Brothers, 1847), 191–207; 38–400.

[112] Smith, *Revivalism and Social Reform*, 142–44; Thomas Upham, *Principles of the Interior or Hidden Life*, 2nd ed. (Boston: Wait, Pierce, 1844), 361–78.

[113] So Thomas Oden, ed., *Selected Writings of Phoebe Palmer* (New York: Paulist, 1988), ix. For a full defense of Palmer's theology as mystical, see Elaine Heath, *Naked Faith: The Mystical Theology of Phoebe Palmer* (Eugene: Pickwick, 2009).

[114] Phoebe Palmer, *The Way of Holiness* (New York: Piercy and Reed, 1843), 36. In his biography of Catherine of Genoa, written just two years later, Thomas Upham would utilize Palmer's terminology of entire consecration, altar, and union to describe Catherine's mystical experiences. The act of consecration involved not only prayer but service to others, from which ecstatic union with God would emerge. See Thomas Upham, *Life of Madame Catherine Adorna*, 3rd ed. (New York: Harper and Brothers, 1858).

[115] Phoebe Palmer, *The Promise of the Father* (Boston: H. V. Degen, 1859).

the pentecostal promise of the Father was a particular function of a new dispensation of the Spirit and it compelled men and women to become prophetic agents of Christ. On this basis, Palmer argued that women must be allowed to teach and preach, which mean that they must be trained in educational institutions. In Palmer's mature theology, the baptism of the Spirit and fiery love empowered the person for prophetic activity. The encounter from such a confluence of the Spirit and the soul was ecstatic union that reordered the affections and opened up internal perceptions of God more clearly. Upham had described this new clarity of mental vision in terms of possessing an "intuitive perception."[116]

Palmer's popularization of John Fletcher's idea of a dispensation of the Spirit and connection between the day of Pentecost and Christian perfection was part of a pneumatological turn that impacted other holiness advocates. Through his lectures on the baptism in the Spirit at Adrian College in the 1860s, Asa Mahan argued that Spirit baptism marked a distinct unfolding of the Spirit in the stages of the Christian life. Drawing an analogy with the impact of great human minds upon an individual, Mahan suggested that Spirit baptism quickens mental powers so that "thought is expanded, emotion deepened, and activity energized."[117] Carlyle's notion of the hero was democratized through the Spirit's operation in the heart. The assurance that flows from the mind's expansion was a species of divine illumination, which Mahan defined as "direct and inward beholding of divine truth."[118] The work of the Spirit in the mind became for Mahan what the communion with human minds in the form of heroes was for Charles Eliot Norton. Just like reading great books, the Spirit gave wings so that the mind could take flight and begin to forge connections among ideas.

Mahan understood divine illumination to be a form of intuitive knowledge involving the direct perception of an object. Behind this claim was his course in mental philosophy, which was developed in conversation with Coleridge, Cousin, and Kant, "to whom I feel most indebted as a philosopher."[119] Knowledge unfolds through reason, consciousness, and sense as the three primary intuitive functions of the intelligence.[120] Consciousness and sense involve perception of phenomena, either within the mind (consciousness) or external to it (sense), whereas reason perceives truths logically prior to such phenomena. While Mahan saw these functions as occurring simultaneously in the mind, under the influence of Coleridge and Cousin, he thought reason was primary. As a function of the structure of the mind, reason was the intellect's direct and immediate perception of truths such as goodness, truth, and beauty and thus placed the person in communion with the divine. Consciousness and sense offered the forms of life to the mind, from which it discovered more fundamental and absolute truths as being logically antecedent. Particular forms of beauty revealed the idea of the beautiful as logically prior to such forms and existing within the mind. Following Coleridge, Mahan saw the function of understanding as discursive and reason as intuitive. Divine illumination was a form of intuitive knowledge

---

[116] Thomas Upham, *Life of Madame Catherine Adorna*, 163.

[117] Mahan, *Baptism of the Holy Ghost*, 52.

[118] Mahan, *Baptism of the Holy Ghost*, 200–3. See also idem, *Out of Darkness into Light* (Boston: Willard Tract Repository, 1876), 7–8, in which he differentiates between belief, which is related to probabilities, and absolute knowledge, which is certain. The latter is intuitive.

[119] Asa Mahan, *A System of Intellectual Philosophy*, rev. and enlarged (New York: A. S. Barnes, 1855), v.

[120] Mahan, *System of Intellectual Philosophy*, 38–107.

by which the soul peered into divine realities, which became immediately apparent and absolute. He simply demurred when Coleridge and Cousin suggested a closer connection to the divine that smacked of pantheism. In its place, Mahan postulated the role of the Spirit through divine illumination so that the "evidence" came from an encounter that placed the mind in touch with eternal verities rather than from inductive reasoning.

The overlapping networks of the holiness movement allowed for the spread of ideas that converged with the Romantic sensibility. By the close of the Gilded Age, Asa Mahan, Daniel Steele, and the Wesleyan Methodist evangelist George Watson (1845–1924) were all describing the knowledge accompanying baptism of the Spirit in terms of some form of intuition, which they understood to be direct and immediate. Since this knowledge came through a unitive encounter with the Spirit, all three holiness thinkers privileged intuition as enabling humans to perceive the invisible world of the divine and the promises of God.

In popular discourse, the terminology sometimes mattered less than the encounter. Martin Wells Knapp (1853–1901) recognized that persons grabbed for familiar vocabulary; here he quotes from John Allen Wood's *Perfect Love*:

> *The fact that they were in the land doubtless affected each person in a different way. . .*
>
>> One person realizes principally a marked increase of faith, and calls it the *"rest of faith."* Another is conscious of a deep, sweet resting in Christ, and he calls it *"resting in God."* Another is permeated with a sense of the divine presence, and filled with ecstatic rapture, and he calls it the *"fullness of God."* Another feels his heart subdued, melted, refined, and filled with God, and he calls it *"holiness."* Another realizes principally a river of sweet, holy love flowing through the soul, and he calls it *"perfect love."* Another is prostrated under the power of the refining, sin-killing Spirit, and he calls it *"the baptism of the Holy Ghost"*; and another realizes principally a heaven of sweetness in complete submission to God, and he calls it *"entire sanctification"*; while another may feel clearly and strongly conscious of complete conformity to all of the will of God, and calls it *"Christian perfection"*;
>
> or, as sometimes is the case, these different feelings may so blend and intertwine that he will rejoice in the consciousness of a mighty, soul-satisfying change, without stopping to name it. He *knows*, and *knows* that he *knows*, that his will is sweetly lost in his Heavenly Father's.[121]

One finds vocabulary familiar to Upham, Mahan, Finney, and Palmer encased by common Wesleyan terms. A Methodist minister turned radical holiness, Knapp's description also demonstrates how this illumination by intuition informed what Donald Dayton called the "subjectivizing hermeneutic" of the holiness movement. The allegorizing of Scripture meant that historical narratives such as the exodus became a locus of personal history and exegesis in the believer. This was a recovering of the symbolic meaning of Scripture behind the letter.[122] The operations of the Spirit in the soul opened the person

---

[121] Martin Wells Knapp, *Out of Egypt into Canaan: Lessons in Spiritual Geography*, 10th ed. (Boston: McDonald, Gill; Albion, Mich.: Revivalist Publishing, 1889), 111–12, quoting John Allen Wood, *Perfect Love; Or, Plain Things For Those Who Need Them, Concerning the Doctrine, Experience, Profession, and Practice of Christian Holiness* (London: Elliot Stock, 1874), 57 (emphasis orig.). On Knapp, see William Kostlevy, *Holy Jumpers: Evangelicals and Radicals in Progressive Era America* (New York: Oxford University Press, 2010); Wallace Thornton Jr., *When the Fire Fell: Martin Wells Knapp's Vision of Pentecost and the Beginnings of God's Bible School* (Cincinnati, Ohio: Emeth, 2014).

[122] Donald Dayton, *Theological Roots of Pentecostalism* (Peabody: Hendrickson, 1987), 23.

up to transcendence, forming Christ in the soul and giving rise to revelation in the form of intuitive knowledge that then unlocked the Scriptures. Connecting these spiritual experiences to Pentecost and Wesley's idea of Christian perfection had a democratizing effect that fueled the populist reform these thinkers sought to implement. Taken together, these ideas pointed advocates of holiness toward utilitarian models of education through which an army of sanctified saints could be trained and unleashed.

3.3.2 Training for Mission and Moral Formation

In the holiness movement, education was first and foremost a utilitarian enterprise with the aim of maintaining denominational distinctions and training generations of laity and ministers to engage in ministry and service. This explains partly why the majority of new institutions in the Gilded Age remained denominational, although this began to change in the 1880s.[123] Of the 415 colleges and universities in existence by 1890, only 99 did not have formal ties to a church body. This number does not include normal schools, schools of agriculture and mechanical arts, or professional schools of law and theology. In addition, the activist ethos of the holiness movement flowed from a commitment to social reform, which required a more pragmatic approach to education.[124]

Founded by A. B. Simpson (1843–1919), A. J. Gordon (1836–1895), and D. L. Moody (1837–1899), the earliest missionary training institutes focused on raising up more lay workers who could reach the working-class poor in America and establish missionary bases in foreign lands. Before these institutes in the 1880s, Methodists were already founding training institutes for women and men as well as colleges in keeping with their denominational push. By 1890 Methodism accounted for seventy-four colleges and universities among its various branches.[125] Many of the prominent leaders of the Wesleyan wing of the holiness movement had attended Methodist colleges or institutes. When they began to open their own schools, they followed either the institute model or the multipurpose college model. This meant that alongside early holiness colleges like Asbury College in Wilmore, Kentucky, across the river in Cincinnati one could find God's Bible School. Henry Clay Morrison, who became president of Asbury in 1910, had attended Vanderbilt for one year, while the founder of God's Bible School, Martin Wells Knapp, left Albion College in Michigan two years before his graduation. The common feature of these various forms of education was a commitment to maximizing lay participation for the sake of missions through some form of vocational training in keeping with the emerging holiness theology. In short, whether through establishing liberal arts colleges like Texas Holiness University (later merged into what would become Southern Nazarene University) or Bible schools like Moody Bible Institute, virtually all advocates of holiness opted for a more utilitarian model of education rather than the emerging research university.

---

[123] See Geiger, "Era of Multipurpose Colleges."

[124] This commitment has been well documented. See Smith, *Revivalism and Social Reform*, 135–238; Dayton and Strong, *Rediscovering an Evangelical Heritage*; Douglas M. Strong, *Perfectionist Politics: Abolitionism and the Religious Tensions of American Democracy* (Syracuse: Syracuse University Press, 1999).

[125] John Marshall Barker, *Colleges in America* (Cleveland: Cleveland Printing and Publishing, 1894), 45–67; Geiger, "Era of Multipurpose Colleges."

While the first missionary training schools may have found their inspiration in England and Europe, their basic ethos resonated with trends closer to home.[126] The final three decades of the nineteenth century represented the heyday of the state normal school, which focused on the nontraditional student. S. Y. Gillian's claim that the state normal school was "a school of the people existing for and representing the masses and not the classes" found its counter in statements by Moody, Simpson, and Gordon that they prepared workers for the working class.[127] In the earliest issues of *The Word, the Work, and the World*, Simpson indicated the need for "lay missionary colleges" along the lines of H. Grattan Guinness' East London Institute for Home and Foreign Mission. Standing between high school and college, these institutes served the "non-professional Christian worker" whose circumstances prevented attendance of a college or seminary.[128] In calling for a new missionary movement, Simpson wanted it to be filled with common lay persons, "humble men and women . . . who come from the plow and work shop and store with very ordinary education" and who then receive a specific kind of missionary training.[129]

As Brereton indicates, Bible schools most closely resembled normal schools on a number of levels.[130] Like state normal schools, Bible schools were coeducational, with some institutes being founded by women.[131] Emma Dryer, who did the most work to found Moody's Training School of the Chicago Evangelization Society (later Moody Bible Institute), had taught at Illinois State Normal University.[132] Most state normal schools offered a single course of study that could take between two or three years, which corresponded to the typical two-year program at Bible institutes. Normal schools and Bible schools also had a flexibility that allowed students to enter at different stages of educational preparedness, even those who had not completed high school. Thus, they appealed to students with little education and from more working-class backgrounds. Students graduated with certificates, not bachelor's degrees, that allowed them to engage in some form of teaching, which both types of institutions aimed to produce.

There was also an overlap in curriculum, not simply in courses on teaching methods, but also in basic introductions to medical science and music. While Moody may have been correct that the point was to "have the workers trained in everything that will give

---

[126] See Virginia Lieson Brereton, *Training God's Army: The American Bible School, 1880–1940* (Bloomington: Indiana University Press, 1990), 55–60.

[127] *Semi-Centennial History of the Illinois State Normal University, 1857–1907* (Normal: Illinois Normal State University, 1907), 202, as cited by Ogren, *American State Normal School*, 55.

[128] "Lay Missionary Colleges," *The Word, the Work, and the World* 1.3 (1882): 118. Simpson published the first edition of the magazine in January 1882. Simpson's fourfold gospel was an important influence on early Pentecostalism. See Charles Nienkirchen, *A. B. Simpson and the Pentecostal Movement: A Study in Continuity, Crisis, and Change* (Eugene: Wipf and Stock, 2010); Bernie A. Van De Walle, *The Heart of the Gospel: A. B. Simpson, the Fourfold Gospel, and the Late Nineteenth-Century Evangelical Theology* (Eugene: Pickwick, 2009).

[129] "A New Missionary Movement," *The Word, the Work, and the World* 1.1 (1882): 33.

[130] Brereton, *Training God's Army*, 156–58. See also Larry J. McKinney, *Equipping for Service: A Historical Account of the Bible College Movement in North America* (Fayetteville: Accrediting Association of Bible Colleges, 1997).

[131] On the role of women in Bible schools, see Abraham Ruelas, *Women and the Landscape of American Higher Education: Wesleyan Holiness and Pentecostal Founders* (Eugene: Pickwick, 2010).

[132] Nina Bissett, *Woman of Nobility: The Story of Sophronia Emeline Cobb Dryer* (Eugene: Resource, 2016).

them access practically to the souls of people, especially the neglected classes," this meant that students needed a basic knowledge in a number of subjects.[133] In 1890 the *Missionary Review of the World* reported that A. J. Gordon's Boston Training Institute had contracted a professor of pathology from the local dentist college to offer lectures on "medical and simple surgical lay treatment."[134] Given that the percentage of those attending any institute of learning beyond high school was less than one percent of the total population and just over one percent of fifteen- to nineteen-year-olds, one can understand the push to train the nontraditional student and thus maximize lay participation in the cause of reform.[135]

Alongside of Bible institutes, Congregationalists and Wesleyans founded a number of colleges that adopted a multipurpose model. This was the case for Wheaton College (1848, but refounded as Wheaton in 1861), Asbury College (founded 1890), and Texas Holiness University (founded 1899). As the first president of Texas Holiness University, A. M. Hills consciously modeled the university on his alma mater, Oberlin College.[136] Music and business programs, among other kinds of vocational training, buffered a liberal arts curriculum and an emphasis on holiness theology. He had attended Yale after Oberlin and became good friends with R. A. Torrey, although he split with Torrey over issues surrounding the Wesleyan view of Christian perfection. Before his death, Hills would be part of four holiness colleges that maintained the multipurpose model. He ended his career as a Nazarene writing one of the first systematic theologies for the fledgling denomination. Hills maintained the postmillennial position his entire life, fighting against most of the doctrines that came to define fundamentalism, including premillennial eschatology, penal substitutionary atonement, and the mechanical dictation theories of inspiration found among inerrantists.

In a report on Wheaton, then-president Jonathan Blanchard noted that they held to "the American or 'classical' college course, modified and made pliant to the popular necessities, and sound and enlightened progress."[137] Blanchard had been drawn to the Oberlin vision of perfection of soul and society at least since his days at Lane Seminary in 1837 and noted that the early Wheaton was coed, with most students being involved in manual labor.[138] Given that most of these colleges were planted as part of midwestern expansion, they served as monasteries in the wilderness, training up local laity who could work to build the town and keep it grounded upon solid Christian principles. This followed the model first established at Oberlin, which initially involved a covenant for the town built

---

[133] "Mr. Moody's Training School," 69.

[134] "Missionary Training Schools," *Missionary Review of the World* 13 (1890): 301.

[135] As of the 1890 census, the total population of the United States was just over 62.6 million, with 6.5 million fifteen- to nineteen-year-olds. The total number of those in higher education programs was just under 98,000, with 34,814 in normal schools and 78,920 in commercial colleges. See *Report of the Population of the United States: Eleventh Census, 1890* (Washington, DC: Government Printing Office, 1895), xi; Geiger, "Era of Multipurpose Colleges," 130, table 1.

[136] See C. J. Branstetter, *Purity, Power, and Pentecostal Light: The Revivalist Doctrine and Means of Aaron Merritt Hills* (Eugene: Pickwick, 2012), 6–51.

[137] "Wheaton College," in *Reports Made to the General Assembly of Illinois, January 4, 1869*, vol. 2 (Springfield: Illinois Journal Printing Office, 1869), 227 (745).

[138] Blanchard delivered the commencement address at Oberlin in 1839. For two views of Blanchard in relation to the holiness movement and evangelicalism, see George M. Marsden, *Fundamentalism and American Culture*, 27–32; Dayton, *Rediscovering an Evangelical Heritage*, 53–60.

around the college. For Blanchard, Wheaton being for Christ meant a multipurpose college that exemplified the reform spirit of the early holiness movement. While the primary aim of education was moral formation, its secondary aims involved transformation of society by training up laity who could help establish Christ's rule. What remained consistent for Blanchard even after he joined Moody in the Keswick wing of the movement was the emphasis on social reform. Education remained in the service of this reform.

The concern in Methodism that preparation for the ministry remain grounded primarily in Christian experience only intensified in the holiness movement between 1880 and 1900. At Garrett Biblical Institute, Charles Bradley spoke for many when he asserted that "Methodism is true to the Scriptures and to history in asserting that the Christian ministry is not necessarily a learned profession, that the only absolutely essential, special preparation for it is wrought in the heart by the Spirit of God, that preaching not based on Christian experience is worse than 'sounding brass or a clanging cymbal.'"[139] Bradley was trying to mount a defense for why students should study Greek and Hebrew, yet he knew that Garrett had originated from camp meetings in 1855 due to the generous donation of Eliza Garrett.[140] A person no less renowned than Phoebe Palmer had toured the school in 1869 and then led a three-week revival in 1876, two years after women began taking classes. At the conclusion of her tour, Palmer called Garrett a school of the prophets, praying that it become known "for the reception of the full baptism of the Holy Ghost, on the part of all who, in coming time, shall be trained within these walls for the holy ministry."[141] It was during the revival in 1876 that a young Frances Willard professed entire sanctification.

John Wesley Hughes started Asbury College because he wanted to remain true to Christian experience in good Methodist fashion. In response to one college president who chided him for promoting the fanaticism of radical holiness in a college setting, Hughes stated, "We will endeavor, as a faculty, to do all in our power to lead our students to the Bible experiences of regeneration and entire sanctification and to live daily a consecrated, holy life with warm hearts and cool heads."[142] Central to Hughes' conception of Asbury was the Bible and Christian experience, with all other curriculum orbiting around them. The problem, as he saw it, was that many Methodist schools had abandoned the experience of entire sanctification and thus forsaken encounters with the Spirit in favor of a process of intellectual formation. Holiness meant moral formation through the Spirit's sanctifying touch. Nevertheless, the school followed the general direction of the multipurpose college in placing music and other programs alongside the liberal arts in an effort to reach the undereducated. Hughes proudly talked about the first graduate, who came from the farm and went on to write nationally on sex education.[143] Under Hughes and its later president Henry Clay Morrison, Asbury College

---

[139] Charles F. Bradley, "The Greek New Testament and the Methodist Ministry," in *Inaugural Addresses* (Evanston, Ill.: Garrett Biblical Institute, 1885), 28.

[140] See Ruelas, *Women and the Landscape of American Higher Education*, 3–7.

[141] Richard Wheatley, *The Life and Letters of Phoebe Palmer* (New York: W. C. Palmer Jr., 1876), 451.

[142] John Wesley Hughes, *Autobiography: Founder of Asbury and Kingswood Colleges* (Louisville: Pentecostal Publishing, 1923), 105.

[143] T. W. Shannon, "Ethics of the Unmarried," in *Nature's Secrets Revealed: Scientific Knowledge of the Laws of Sex Life and Heredity; Or Eugenics: Vital Information for the Married and Marriageable of All Ages* (Marietta, Ohio: S. A. Mullikin, 1916).

came to embody the holiness college as attempting to combine spiritual experience and education as part of the learning process.

Men and women who became part of the holiness movement in the beginning of the Progressive Era gravitated toward educational models that combined holiness of life, encounters with the divine, and social reform in the context of vocational training. When searching for paradigms to organize their understanding of what a college should be, they instinctively drew from the emerging multipurpose college and the state normal school. These efforts to reach out to the undereducated in regional contexts appealed to the holiness drive to maximize lay participation. Moral formation was placed in the context of the practical training behind the utilitarian approach to education. In addition, there was a concern especially within Wesleyan holiness circles to wed Bible study to spiritual experiences. Education had to be punctuated with encounters with transcendence through the Spirit. Following Mahan, Finney, and Palmer, this utilitarian model was intended to alter the social landscape by bringing Christ to bear on all of life. Caught up into the presence of Christ by the Spirit, individuals had their minds expanded and hearts inflamed. This approach was less about bringing the kingdom of God than about unleashing the power of Pentecost so that holiness would renew the churches and unite the people. It was, in the end, a kind of social reform aimed at reviving the regional folk cultures of America and bringing unity in the face of immigration from continental Europe and industrialization.

3.3.3 Holiness and Reforming the Churches and the Nation

While the advocates for liberal culture represented an elite group who attempted to transform America from the top down, those within the holiness movement remained connected to the regional cultures they inhabited. This is not to say that they did not try to facilitate social reform across the American or British landscape, but they did so through populist movements. The basis for institutions, colleges, and new organizations came from the need for a structure to facilitate ongoing training that drew upon and facilitated internal spiritual renewal. Ultimately, they agreed with Alexis de Tocqueville that education had to have a democratizing effect, which represented another reason why those within the holiness movement rejected the notion of the scholar as hero who led cultural reform.

Even among national members of the movement like Frances Willard, one is hard pressed to find a connection between self-cultivation and culture that could be found among literary realists and those at elite colleges and universities. Instead, there was a connection between internal moral formation through spiritual encounters and the transformation of society. Expressing this position, A. B. Simpson noted that "two schools of thought divide the minds of men, the one is evolution, the other is the supernatural. . . . The whole character of the gospel is opposed to this. It is not a development; it is not the improvement of moral and social conditions through culture. It is a revolution rather than an evolution."[144] In making this claim, Simpson was not reacting to Darwinism so much as German idealism's understanding of the evolutionary progress

---

[144] A. B. Simpson, *Isaiah*, The Christ in the Bible Commentary (Harrisburg: Christian Publications, 1930), 92.

of soul and society through time. Yet one can see how a late nineteenth-century thinker might easily promote evolution and cultural development through self-cultivation. In Simpson's view, new creation entailed an upheaval in human existence rather than the gradual self-improvement of *Bildung*. His view of providence echoed the holiness emphasis on change through dramatic intervention rather than the slow, steady hand of God, who gradually and surely realized his plan. Changing society required a change in the human heart.

Central to notions of reform was the connection between personal holiness and social holiness. The former concerned a personal encounter with divine love and the latter its overflow into the world. On the holiness view, if personal transformation through the crises of ongoing conversion was not preserved, social reform would fail. In her 1883 address on the relationship between the Salvation Army and the state, Catherine Booth intoned that social reformers mistakenly assumed moral reform came through the intellect. "You must reform man by his SOUL!" she declared.[145] Booth also wedded this point to an entire social program that she subsequently outlined. Her desire was to stake out a middle terrain between those who taught an "only believe gospel" in the churches and those who focused on the material benefits of humans.[146] For Booth, the difference resided in the emphasis the Salvation Army placed upon "aggressive Christianity," by which she meant the apostolic witness after Pentecost.[147] Because Booth followed Upham, Palmer, and Mahan in seeing Pentecost and union with God as effected by the sanctifying power of the Spirit, she could at once talk about the civilizing impact of the Salvation Army on society and claim that this did not come through intellect or culturing individuals. While denying the need for a liberal culture, Booth's nonconformist Wesleyan revivalism utilized "with great success all of the elements of applied romanticism—the rhetoric, the melodrama, the music, the evocative ritual and symbolism."[148] The overriding concern for spiritual renewal and the interventionist account of supernaturalism underneath it became the basis for the holiness support of many causes.

The holiness movement garnered the largest numbers in keeping with the desire for populist reform. One of the most well-known women of the late nineteenth century, Frances Willard became president of the largest organization of women, the Woman's Christian Temperance Union (WCTU), in 1879, and held that office until her death in 1898. An ardent Methodist, Willard experienced entire sanctification under the preaching of Phoebe Palmer, although in light of the debates within Methodism over Palmer's approach she would later question it. Given her wide range of connections, including being a speaker at D. L. Moody's conferences, Willard has been claimed as both a liberal Methodist who embraced feminism and an evangelical member of the holiness

---

[145] Catherine Booth, *The Salvation Army in Relation to the Church and State* (London: John Snow, 1890), 11.

[146] Booth, *Salvation Army in Relation*, 39–41.

[147] Catherine Booth, *Papers on Aggressive Christianity* (London: S. W. Partridge, 1880). See in particular her sermon on "The Holy Ghost" at the end of the volume.

[148] G. Kitson Clark, *The Making of Victorian England* (New York: Atheneum, 1967), 189, as cited in Andrew Mark Eason, *Women in God's Army: Gender and Equality in the Early Salvation Army* (Waterloo, Ont.: Wilfrid Laurier University Press, 2003), 19.

movement.[149] Bizzell's position is probably closest in describing Willard as being in the tradition of Methodist women preachers influenced by Phoebe Palmer's middle-class Methodist ethos, which also claimed the likes of Hannah Whitall Smith and Thomas Upham.[150] Willard was praised by A. J. Gordon, who included her on the list of "special contributors" for *Watchword* in 1880. In many respects, she was the American counterpart to Catherine Booth, a person who could easily move between the language of social reform and the language of Christian conversion and revival. Although at one point a college president, she saw her leadership of the WCTU as the best way to impact nations and change societies.

For Willard, the United States and the British Empire were forms of Christian civilization that needed to "raise the standard of the law to that of Christian morals."[151] Not only did Willard follow Palmer and Booth in arguing for women to preach on the basis of Pentecost, she saw the WCTU as a manifestation of the Acts outpouring, saying that "the inspiration of prayer was the foundation of the Women's Temperance Crusade; it was God's Pentecost in the homes of the people."[152] By cradling the "trinity" of prohibition, women's liberation through suffrage, and labor's uplift in Pentecost, Willard claimed that the ultimate goal was "the regnancy of Christ, not in form, but in fact."[153] On this basis, she extended the category of holiness to include wholeness and thus broadened salvation so that it encompassed bringing the kingdom to bear on all of society. The fusion of holiness rhetoric with social activism represented the continued democratization of Pentecost among the laity, particularly an army of women evangelists and reformers. This was the populism of the holiness movement at high tide.

The concern for populist reform through revival also bridged into other areas. In the Wesleyan wing, entire sanctification was part of a continuous process of growth in grace. This was how holiness thinkers maintained Wesley's idea of a "perfecting perfection." Yet, the reordering of affections in the experience of divine love associated with the pentecostal outpouring was supposed to bring unity to the churches and to society. In his introduction to A. J. Gordon's book on the Spirit, F. B. Meyer longed for the completion of the age of the Spirit, when Pentecost would spread to the ends of the earth, noting that

---

[149] Ruth Bordin's biography attempts to create distance between Willard and the holiness movement in order to portray her more as a political reformer. See her *Frances Willard: A Biography* (Chapel Hill: University of North Carolina Press, 1986). Nevertheless, most accounts place Willard firmly within the holiness movement. It should be remembered that in the 1880s and 1890s the holiness wing could accommodate a variety of views, including Hannah Whitall Smith's universalism. See Nancy Hardesty, *Women Called to Witness: Evangelical Feminism in the Nineteenth Century*, 2nd ed. (Knoxville: University of Tennessee Press, 1999), 1–12.

[150] Patricia Bizzell, "Frances Willard, Phoebe Palmer, and the Ethos of the Methodist Woman Preacher," *Rhetoric Society Quarterly* 36.4 (2006): 377–98; see also Christopher H. Evans, *Do Everything: The Biography of Frances Willard* (New York: Oxford University Press, 2022), who shows connections between Palmer and Willard.

[151] Frances Willard, *Do Everything: A Handbook for the World's White Ribboners* (Chicago: Woman's Temperance Publishing Association, 1895), 23–24.

[152] Frances Willard, *Do Everything*, 21; idem, *Women in the Pulpit* (Boston: D. Lothrop, 1888), 36, 44, 149. Willard repeatedly used the image of Pentecost to describe the movement, even calling December 23, 1873, as "the women's Temperance Pentecost" (*Do Everything*, 8, 168).

[153] Willard, *Do Everything*, 173.

even now "there is a widespread recognition of the unity of all who believe, together with an increasing desire to magnify the points of agreement and minimize those of divergence."[154] The holiness evangelist W. B. Godbey went further in claiming that entire sanctification rooted out all prejudice, sectarianism, and self-will because divine love flowed in and compelled love for neighbor.[155] There was within the broad holiness movement a nonsectarian spirituality centered on holiness and the Spirit. Even though in reality life was much more complicated, holiness advocates continued to espouse that holiness achieved unity among diverse peoples regardless of creed, race, or nationality. The spirituality connected to holiness replaced church and culture as the common medium that could facilitate unity within societies.

The initial criticisms of evolution among holiness adherents flowed from a concern for unity among the races through holiness and a concern to preserve the need for a divine in-breaking. First, the evolutionary view of history and progress was viewed as discounting the need for revivalist experience. With its collapse of the divine into nature, Carlyle's natural supernaturalism, as it worked out in Bushnell's view of Christian nurture, denied revival experiences. A. M. Hills had Bushnell in his sights when he said that "a prominent official of a great church . . . took the position that children did not need conversion. . . . He made religion to be an evolution and education. He discounted religious experience, and by assertion and illustration made religion to consist merely in taking hold and performing Christian work."[156]

Second, Darwinism was at times employed to reinforce racial distinctions and thus could be used to buttress racist rhetoric. Darwin himself had acknowledged a kind of hierarchy among the races, which made the move from Darwinism to social Darwinism easy for many thinkers.[157] One could see this in the case of the geologist Alexander Winchell's short book *Adamites and Preadamites*, in which he suggested that African Americans were preadamite and therefore did not descend from Adam like the white race. This led Winchell to conclude that the biological conditions of African Americans made them inferior. Winchell was a Methodist who taught at Vanderbilt, but was let go by the board in 1878 for espousing Darwinism, which made him a martyr for science in Andrew Dickson White's *A History of the Warfare of Science with Theology in Christendom*.

While little was mentioned of the racism in Winchell's work at Vanderbilt, his views were picked up by Charles Carroll, who used them to argue that African Americans were not in the image of God but mere beasts and thus rightly subject to control.[158] In response,

---

[154] A. J. Gordon, *The Ministry of the Spirit* (Chicago: Fleming H. Revel, 1894), xiv.

[155] W. B. Godbey, *Autobiography of W. B. Godbey* (Cincinnati: God's Revivalist Office, 1909), 135; idem, *Patriotism and Politics* (Cincinnati: God's Revivalist Office, 1911).

[156] A. M. Hills, *The Secret of Spiritual Power* (Kansas City: Beacon Hill, 1952), 73. The book was written against the Keswick understanding of higher life, which Hills found at Moody Bible Institute when he was invited by Torrey to speak. While Hills regretted having to take on Torrey and F. B. Meyer, he nevertheless felt the need to defend the Wesleyan view. As a former Congregationalist, Hills was intimately familiar with Bushnell and had positive things to say as well (see Branstetter, *Purity, Power, and Pentecostal Light*, 198–233).

[157] See Carl N. Degler, *In Search of Human Nature: The Decline and Revival of Darwinism in American Social Thought* (Oxford: Oxford University Press, 1991), 3–31.

[158] Charles Carroll, *The Negro a Beast* (St. Louis: American Book and Bible House, 1900).

William G. Schell, editor of *The Gospel Trumpet*, wrote a refutation of Carroll's position.[159] Schnell was a member of the Church of God movement, stemming from the work of Daniel Warner. Schnell noted that although Carroll blasted away at Darwinian evolution, his arguments came "from evolution sources" like Alexander Winchell, Ernst Haeckel, and Thomas Huxley. Embedding holiness rhetoric in democratic sensibilities, Schnell argued that Christ destroyed distinctions between Jew and Gentile, instituting a common equality in his church. Likewise "Christianity destroys the distinctions that existed between various classes of the human family" so that "equality is a prominent doctrine of the New Testament."[160]

Schnell was no doubt drawing on holiness experiences such as that of George Watson, who had claimed that his experience of entire sanctification in 1876 removed the hatred he had felt when serving as a Confederate soldier. Godbey went even further, claiming that Ohio and other free states represented political sanctification.[161] In the popular holiness mind, Winchell and Carroll were cut from the same cloth, with both espousing racism and using Darwinist ideas to support their beliefs.

The concern for an instantaneous in-breaking also governed the adoption of the premillennial position by some holiness thinkers. Shortly after he embraced the doctrine, George Watson drew the parallel between entire sanctification as a divine in-breaking and premillennialism. For Watson, spiritual growth was a perpetual process destined to go on even among the saints, whereas entire sanctification was a purgative experience of cleansing. "Purification is a complete, finished work, (so long as retained) but growth is never finished in this life, and so far as we know, all holy creatures will progress forever in love, knowledge and power."[162] His revivalism remained fueled with perfectionist hopes and the Wesleyan optimism of grace, yet it was grounded in an interventionist account, for "however much the cause of Christ may wax stronger, yet the Millennium will not come gradually, but there will be a great crisis, with an instantaneous overthrow of the opposite governments, and the instantaneous over enthronement of the Heir of David over the world, and then follows the matchless growth and marvelous prosperity of the millennial kingdom."[163] Watson retained the perfecting perfection punctuated by encounters with transcendence, whether those were on the personal level or the historical. The disease of sin would be eradicated through the sanctifying presence of the Spirit, who inaugurated the Christ-filled life and laid the foundation for perpetual growth.

The long nineteenth century proved to be a time of great ferment as fledgling democracies sought to establish themselves. A central question was how to unite the people of any democracy since sovereignty was invested in them. The French and American Revolutions showed how violent the turn to democratic values could be, which heightened the need to find a solution. To answer this question, many thinkers drew on what

---

[159] William Schnell, *Is the Negro a Beast? A Reply to Charles Carroll's Book* (Moundsville, W.Va.: Gospel Trumpet, 1901).

[160] Schell, *Is the Negro a Beast?* 153–54.

[161] See Stephens, *Fire Spreads*, 78–80.

[162] George Watson, *White Robes: Or, Garments of Salvation and Spiritual Feasts* (Cincinnati: God's Revivalist, 1883), 85.

[163] George Watson, *Bridehood Saints: Treating of the Saints Who Are the "Selection from the Selection," Those Saints Who Are to Make Up the Bride of Christ*, repr. (Noblesville: Newby Book Room, 1972), 138–48.

we have described as the Romantic sensibility. This sensibility was a fusion of divine immanence, rational intuitionism, and progressive reform of society. It became the common social imaginary that connected those in the holiness movement to those in the high culture movement.

The Romantic sensibility meant that education involved moral formation through encounters with transcendence, by which the mind was expanded to embrace the world. For the advocates of high culture, this primarily occurred in scholars and men and women of literary qualities who embodied the heroic. They became one with the great minds of history and so entered into a communion that placed them in touch with the divine. As they sought to cultivate their own lives (*Bildung*), they came to embody Promethean freedom, which positioned them to impact the larger culture. Carlyle's natural supernaturalism forged the common links that allowed the purveyors of high culture to maintain a religion of nature approximating the Protestant nonsectarianism that Tappan thought was necessary to build a university. Grounded in the emerging research culture of the university guild, this top-down approach meant that the literati were responsible for uniting the people by building a culture of Western civilization that would supply the moral framework necessary for democracy to flourish.

Those within the holiness movement drank from the same wells of the Romantic sensibility even while adapting them to Wesleyan notions of holiness and perfection. The turn to pneumatology during the 1830s solidified a movement that embraced immanence through the Spirit's work in revivalism and Pentecost. For men like Upham and Mahan, it was the encounter with the Spirit in sanctification that facilitated a deeper union and expanded the mind. Thus, approaches to education had to retain encounters with transcendence, without which moral and intellectual formation would not be possible. Through intuitive knowledge the Spirit placed the individual in touch with eternal verities that conformed the gospel and opened up beauty, truth, and goodness. This communion was not with great minds but with the triune God through the work of the Spirit.

Democracy succeeded on the holiness view by training the laity who populated the new towns and urban centers being constructed in the industrial revolution. Education had to serve utilitarian ends if it was going to be a force for social transformation. This is why the multipurpose college and the state normal school became the most viable models. Yet there was still a desire to infuse education with spiritual experience and power. Racism, prejudice, and other sources of division in a democracy would not be overcome by a common cultural framework supplied by Western civilization so much as by a common set of spiritual experiences that replicated divine love in the human heart. The spirituality of holiness replaced the spirituality of a sacralized culture. Any scientific perspective that embodied racism or sought to exclude encounters with the divine through a materialist philosophy was to be rejected. This formed the backdrop for the initial suspicion of Darwinism as it came down in popular form. Secularization on the holiness view was an effort to remove interventionist accounts of providence so that one had history as evolution rather than revolution, process rather than the radical in-breaking of a divine crisis. Advocates of holiness were happy to claim the mantle of anti-intellectualism if that meant defending conversion as involving ongoing crises, privileging intuitionism over other forms of rationality, or engaging in populist forms of education to facilitate social reform.

4

Reimagining Christian Higher Education

Populism and the Transformation of Folk Culture in the Twentieth Century

Unlike the men and women invested in advancing liberal culture, holiness and pentecostal leaders remained deeply committed to populism. Populism was the counterpart to the non-conformity that drove revivalism. Stemming from a Wesleyan heritage of doing theology for the people through sermons and hymns, holiness and pentecostal adherents prioritized the transformation and cultivation of folk cultures across the geographical landscape. By the 1940s both groups formed part of what came to be called "lowbrow" culture, with its penchant for regional forms of music like boogie-woogie, as opposed to the middlebrow culture of mainline Protestantism and the highbrow culture of the social elite.[1]

The commitment to folk culture and populism partly accounts for the failure to recognize the way holiness and pentecostal writers drank in the common DNA that formed part of the social imaginary we have called the Romantic sensibility. By folk culture, we mean the people of a particular region (regionalism) and the familial and religious bonds that form the central threads of that region. The songs, stories, festivals, artistic expressions, and colloquialisms of the people in their particularity form the roots of any folk culture. Out of their regionalisms, both wings of the holiness movement combined social holiness with progressive populism in response to the issues of the day, from reconstruction, expansion, and immigration in the United States to colonialism in other parts of the world. They also participated in the Romantic sensibility by espousing a theology of immanence, fusing encounter and intuitive knowledge with a movement toward perfection, and privileging the role of narrative.

The emphases of the Romantic sensibility mixed with populism, charismatic encounter, and eschatology to create the ethos of the holiness and pentecostal movements and thus the choices those within the movement made concerning models of education. Populism reinforced a democratized view of the Spirit that resisted the elite education of the emerging research paradigm or liberal culture and gravitated toward educational models

---

[1]   On these distinctions, see Lawrence W. Levine, *Highbrow Lowbrow: The Emergence of Cultural Hierarchy in America* (Cambridge, Mass.: Harvard University Press, 1988); Joan Shelley Rubin, *The Making of Middlebrow Culture* (Chapel Hill: University of North Carolina Press, 1992); Matthew S. Hedstrom, *The Rise of Liberal Religion: Book Culture and American Spirituality in the Twentieth Century* (New York: Oxford University Press, 2013).

that sought to empower laity as found in the Bible school movement. Holiness and pentecostal adherents saw moral formation in terms of holiness rather than self-cultivation and the encounter with transcendence in terms of distinctive "works of grace" poured out by the Spirit. They also consciously mimicked their evangelical counterparts in cultivating models of education that maximized lay participation through vocational training.

At the same time, the embrace of premillennial eschatology tempered the emphasis on divine immanence lest Christian perfection reinforce a theory of progress. The dramatic encounter of the Second Coming became the macrocosm of the moment of crisis in the microcosm of the human heart at an altar. The crisis encounter with God meant that holiness and pentecostal thinkers resisted educational models that removed encounters with transcendence from the process of human formation. Pentecostals, in particular, yearned for an encounter-driven model of education that saw the classroom as another kind of "meetinghouse" in which the Spirit could spontaneously erupt in the context of any lecture or lesson. The path to the truth was one of deepening encounters that opened up the spiritual senses of the soul. Hence, they struggled to endorse any vocational model they perceived to exclude ongoing crises of conversion for the sake of a formative process. Liturgical formalism in worship, a sacramentalism that reinforced a slow process of spiritual formation, and Victorian Gothic architecture all smacked of conformist religiosity rather than nonconformist zeal. Education, at its best, ought to facilitate encounters with transcendence as part of the moral life, which meant that the atmosphere of the tent revival needed to be brought into school and classroom.

Nevertheless, the privileging of intuitive knowledge associated with crisis encounters of perfection and empowerment was never fully integrated in holiness and pentecostal thought. The failure of pentecostal and holiness approaches to education may be found in not integrating the various theological impulses within the movement. We take this failure to be a driving force behind Burtchaell's "pietist instability," with its temptation to divorce faith from learning.[2] Within the holiness and pentecostal movements, there was a tendency to reject discursive reasoning as inferior to the intuitive and revelatory knowledge of divine encounter, which amounted to a divorce between meditative practices and contemplative experiences. As Smith has argued, the pentecostal "I know that I know that I know" is itself a critique of modern notions of rationality that reduce the human person to a "thinking thing" rather than an embodied soul, rooted in particularity.[3] The so-called anti-intellectualism of the movement was a form of resistance to educational models and modes of rationality that were perceived to be anti-conversionist expressions of bourgeoise culture.

In light of their emphases on theologies of immanence, encounter, and perfection, all within a sacramental and symbolic understanding of the world, holiness and pentecostal adherents criticized the new emphasis on research and culture while seeking to cultivate their own model grounded upon the training institute and the multipurpose college. Although holiness and pentecostal leaders maintained the emphasis on moral formation

---

[2]   James Tunstead Burtchaell, *The Dying of the Light: The Disengagement of Colleges and Universities from Their Christian Churches* (Grand Rapids: Eerdmans, 1998).
[3]   James K. A. Smith, *Thinking in Tongues: Pentecostal Contributions to Christian Philosophy* (Grand Rapids: Eerdmans, 2010), 48–85.

and encounters with transcendence, our central claim in this chapter is that one cannot understand pentecostal and holiness approaches to education apart from situating them in the broader context of a social imaginary that focused on immanence, intuitionism, and progressivism. In drawing out these links, it will become clear how holiness and pentecostal models of education emphasized moral formation and encounters with transcendence for the purpose of mission.

Drawing on our analysis in the previous chapter, we attempt to drill down further into the holiness and pentecostal ethos to deepen the connections we have already explored. While the focus is on the emergence of radical holiness and early Pentecostalism between 1890 and 1920, we will necessarily look back to early holiness thinkers and forward to historical developments in the middle of the twentieth century. Before we can fully articulate the self-understanding of radical holiness and pentecostal adherents, we need to clear the ground by examining more closely Mark Noll's analysis of the evangelical mind.

In the first section, we dive deeply into Noll's thesis about the evangelical mind, attempting to situate it in the rise of worldview thinking and Richard Hofstadter's criticism of anti-intellectualism (§4.1). The second section begins by reexamining the debate between George Marsden and Donald Dayton in order to reveal its limitations as well as how it continues to define the historiography of late nineteenth- and twentieth-century evangelicalism in terms of the history of fundamentalism and its modernist counterpart (§4.2). The purpose is to show that holiness and pentecostal thinkers must be viewed on their own terms. Included is a discussion of mysticism and populism in light of modernity's rise to show how the Romantic sensibility better explains the emergence of the radical holiness stream and early Pentecostalism. The final section turns to models of education holiness that pentecostal adherents tried to develop in light of their emphases and concerns. (§4.3)

The burden of this chapter is to unpack this historical narrative by arguing for a misunderstanding of the holiness and pentecostal ethos on the part of historians of evangelicalism in the first two sections and then by showing how their theological emphases pointed them toward more populist models of education that privileged the humanities and vocational ends. In their own way, radical holiness and pentecostal leaders retained the emphases on education as cultivating moral formation for citizenship and an openness to transcendence in the service of mission, but they placed these emphases within their pursuit of conversion through a crisis-process dialectic and their populist approach to social transformation. The *habitus* Pentecostals were looking for in education was one in which personal holiness (moral formation) and charismatic power (encounter with transcendence) fueled social holiness through healing homes, revivals, and new forms of folk culture (mission).

4.1 EVANGELICALISM AND THE SCANDAL OF THE EVANGELICAL MIND

One of the major challenges of tracing out educational models within holiness, pentecostal, and evangelical institutions is the various ways that higher education as a whole benefitted from the post–World War II explosion of college seekers thanks to the GI Bill. Between the veterans entering higher education in the 1940s and 1950s and the baby boom generation in the 1960s, enrollments in institutions of higher education swelled to over seven million students.[4] Due to this new wave of students, many state normal institutes that had become teacher's colleges in the early twentieth century made the final transition to regional state colleges or universities.[5] The growth also meant that states began to develop more comprehensive systems that could serve all students with research universities, regional state colleges, junior colleges (which originated in California), and/or community colleges, ensuring that demands were met. Normal schools that made the transition to colleges or universities formed the heart of the regional state college.

It was also during this period that many evangelical institutions began to grow in strength and numbers as they followed larger trends. Wheaton was one such institution. The college had already produced men like Billy Graham, Edward Carnell, Paul Jewett, and Carl F. H. Henry in the 1930s. All of these men had passed through the courses of the Presbyterian philosopher Gordon Clark, who taught at Wheaton from 1937 until 1943, when he was forced to resign after a conflict over his Reformed theology with the acerbic systematics teacher Henry Thiessen.[6] Clark introduced his students to James Orr's *The Christian View of God and the World* with its development of the idea of worldview. Acknowledging his debt to Clark, Carnell framed his *An Introduction to Apologetics* (1948) around a Christian worldview, while Carl Henry would do the same in the first volume of *God, Revelation, and Authority* (1976). Alongside Francis Schaeffer, Henry and Carnell became channels through which Christianity was defended in terms of a rationally coherent system over against other systems or worldviews.

The dispute between Gordon Clark and Henry Thiessen over the former's Reformed commitments became detrimental to Wheaton for a time. After he could not get the president to dismiss Clark, Thiessen took the extreme step of disbanding the philosophy major in the hope that Clark would resign. With the hiring of Arthur F. Holmes in 1950, the discipline of philosophy began to return, which was just in time to absorb the growing student population in the wake of the GI Bill. Holmes established the Wheaton Philosophy Conference in 1955 and finally convinced the college to have a philosophy department in 1968. Recently, George Marsden has portrayed these developments at Wheaton as a conflict between fundamentalist piety and Reformed intellect, but they seem more about theological conflicts between men who were equally single-minded.[7] These moves at Wheaton kept worldview thinking within the Reformed tradition alive at the college. On the basis of worldview, Holmes discussed the integration of faith and learning in the seventies, which had become an important topic in evangelical approaches to higher education. Even with Clark's departure, the Reformed emphasis on worldview continued at Wheaton, setting the stage for its dominance in the 1970s

---

[4]   Roger L. Geiger, *American Higher Education since World War II: A History* (Princeton: Princeton University Press, 2019), 129.

[5]   Christine A. Ogren, *The American State Normal School: An Instrument of Great Good* (New York: Palgrave Macmillan, 2005), 213–35; Geiger, *American Higher Education since World War II*, 137–40.

[6]   Douglas J. Douma, *The Presbyterian Philosopher: The Authorized Biography of Gordon H. Clark* (Eugene: Wipf and Stock, 2017), Kindle ed., ch. 4.

[7]   George M. Marsden, *The Soul of the American University Revisited: From Protestant to Postsecular* (New York: Oxford University Press, 2021), 365–90. Marsden's epilogue gives a Reformed narrative of what he calls a "renaissance of Christian Academia."

and 1980s as the primary evangelical apologetic strategy and its use by Noll to offer a Reformed critique of the evangelical mind.

Noll's use of worldview as a mechanism to challenge evangelicalism requires a deeper engagement with developments in the mid-twentieth century, which is why we have framed the first section of this chapter around the evangelical mind. The section unfolds by situating Noll's work in the context of other examinations of how Christian colleges have become secular as well as the criticisms he received from scholars in the holiness and pentecostal traditions (§4.1.1), probing more deeply into worldview thinking and Richard Hofstadter's argument against populism as the two streams that form the foundation upon which Noll erects his argument (§4.1.2), and offering a critique of Noll's *Scandal* (§4.1.3). Noll's opening salvo that evangelicals had abandoned high culture, his use of anti-intellectualism, and his desire for research-driven university backed by a Christian worldview set the stage for his Reformed vision of higher education. While the new edition of Noll's *Scandal* turns more toward social issues, he still advances his concern in a critique of populism, seeing it almost as the womb of anti-intellectualism.[8] In short, Noll argues for a Christian version of the liberal culture developed by the literati of the late nineteenth century, but his vision is a new high culture set by scholars infused with the Christian system of worldview thinking. In the new preface and afterword, Noll acknowledges how successful evangelical scholarship has been while also arguing that this has not trickled down to the evangelical populist or even impacted the high culture that had united most prior to the Civil Rights era.

4.1.1 The Problem of the Evangelical Mind

In what is by now a classic across much of the North American evangelical intellectual world, historian Mark Noll challenged his compatriots near the end of the last century about the fact that there was not much of an evangelical mind. While the causes of this were varied, a few of the major culprits, in Noll's estimation, were linked to or connected directly with the holiness movement and its offspring of Pentecostalism. In particular, Noll's analysis highlighted the roles played by the revivalist tradition of the eighteenth and nineteenth centuries, the holiness movement's prioritizing of a dynamic spiritual life in the mid- to late nineteenth century, and the prophecy movement and its dispensationalist theological innovations of the late nineteenth and early twentieth centuries. For our purposes, in Noll's assessment these streams coincided in Pentecostalism. The revivalist focus on spiritual vitality was consistent with the holiness call to heart piety, and both presumed the minimal importance of the intellectual life in view of their other-worldly and dispensationalist eschatology. For Pentecostals, saving souls was much more urgent given the apocalyptic horizon within which they discerned the signs of the times unfolding. For Noll, this dynamic web of events in the history of evangelicalism was an "intellectual disaster" that generated and perpetuates the scandal of the nonexistent evangelical mind.[9]

---

[8]   Mark A. Noll, *The Scandal of the Evangelical Mind* (Grand Rapids: Eerdmans, 1994); idem, *The Scandal of the Evangelical Mind, with a New Preface and Afterword* (Grand Rapids: Eerdmans, 2022), Kindle ed., preface (2022). With the exception of the new preface and afterword, we cite from the 1994 edition.

[9]   Noll, *Scandal of the Evangelical Mind*, 108–45.

While Noll's book was working its way through to publication, Roman Catholic scholar James Burtchaell was researching and writing his *Dying of the Light*. These labors resulted, three years later, in a massive volume on the disengagement of colleges and universities from their Christian churches, and their concomitant slow spiritual death.[10] Of the seventeen institutions of higher education studied by Burtchaell, only one—Azusa Pacific University (APU)—could have been understood as having connections to the pentecostal movement, and even in that case such strands were only a minimal part of the multifaceted ecclesiastical cord woven into the original DNA of this school. And while in many respects developments at APU have bucked many secularizing trends documented in *Dying of the Light*, it also has been and remains assailed by various internal and external factors. In Burtchaell's appraisal, the fortunes of schools like APU were threatened by what he called "the pietist instability."[11]

Beyond what Noll discusses, Burtchaell explicates various aspects of such instability. First, while historical Pietism emerges oftentimes as a protest movement against an overly scholastic form of religious life, what for the protesting tradition is a simplified account of a vibrant and fervent faith in the face of a highly rationalized tradition runs the risk of devolving, for the second generation, into being merely simplistic piety. This next generation, then, is engaged at the level of the affections, but without theological substance. Faith, in this case, becomes dislodged from learning, and this in turn undermines the capacity of Pietist Christians to build strong theological institutions. In the worst-case scenario for Burtchaell's overall thesis, such pietistic instability degenerates over time into a liberal indifferentism, with the net effect being the institutional disestablishment of and disengagement from their churches.[12]

Detectable behind such analyses are a number of historical variables that are potentially confusing and that create theological mistrust on different sides. The first such variable is a lack of clarity between the diverse forces of an international Pietist movement that spanned German Lutheran Pietism, motivated Puritan forms of experimental Christianity, and generated the great Anglo-American revivalist movements. A lack of clarity among these various groups has, at times, led to bifurcated analyses in which Pietism either leads to Noll's argument against intellectual malaise or Burtchaell's assessment of incursions of nineteenth-century German liberal Protestant forces within the American college and university scene. A second variable is usually to wed a call away from Pietism to a call for a vigorous form of confessionalism, as though intellectual rigor equals confessional adherence and Pietist fervor equals personal holiness and social justice freed

---

[10] Burtchaell, *Dying of the Light*.

[11] Burtchaell, *Dying of the Light*, 838–46. Pentecostal educator Jeff Hittenberger also mentions that pentecostal-charismatic Christianity is subject to the forces of secularization due to its by and large "thin ecclesiology, idiosyncratic theology, and unstable movements"; see Jeff Hittenberger, "The Future of Pentecostal Higher Education: The Ring, the Shire, or the Redemption of Middle Earth," in *The Future of Pentecostalism in the United States*, ed. Eric Patterson and Edmund Rybarczyk (Lanham: Lexington, 2007), 83–103, at 95.

[12] Lutheran theologian Robert Benne, *Quality with Soul: How Six Premier Colleges and Universities Keep Faith with Their Religious Traditions* (Grand Rapids: Eerdmans, 2001), 36–37, although nowhere near as pessimistic as Burtchaell about the future of church-related institutions of higher education, agrees with his Catholic colleague that Pietist traditions face additional challenges to articulating institutional identity and mission in adequate theological terms.

from dogmatic norms. While such a conclusion may have some historical traction, it by no means describes the entire religious spectrum that falls under the broader description of Pietism.

A number of responses to Noll's charges emerged from the holiness side.[13] Not unexpectedly, these rejoinders emphasize that "Pietism, rightly understood, was not a movement opposed to reason, but one which sought to put reason in its proper context."[14] Rather than being a merely cognitive approach to higher education, the Pietist model is integrative, requiring engagement of the whole person in not only right thinking abut also in right worship, right behavior, and, indeed, right formation for all aspects of life. Thus, Pietism is a "head, heart and hands religion,"[15] and the Pietist tradition "promotes an education for the head, heart, and hands—one which does not reduce the educational task to the shaping of worldviews, but emphasizes formation of the whole person."[16]

Pentecostal educator and theologian Cheryl Bridges Johns, however, desists from either internalizing this oppressive narrative or offering a rebuttal.[17] Instead of buying into the dominant group's understanding of what the life of the mind consists, Johns exhorts her pentecostal colleagues to press into the scandal. Exploiting the postmodern opening to a plurality of narratives (against any hegemonic metanarrative), this approach "is a way of celebrating marginality rather than worshiping an elusive center."[18] As such, Johns insists that holiness and pentecostal Christians should embrace precisely those aspects of their tradition that Noll, in particular, criticized as fomenting evangelicalism's intellectual disaster.

[13]   See the set of responses by David Bundy, Henry H. Knight III, and William Kostlevy in the *Wesleyan Theological Journal* 32.1 (1997), and, more recently, a response from the president of Seattle Pacific University, a school in the Wesleyan tradition—Philip W. Eaton, *Engaging the Culture, Changing the World: The Christian University in a Post-Christian World* (Downers Grove: IVP Academic, 2011)—albeit the approach is less a frontal engagement with the claims of Noll and Burtchaell than a contribution to the evangelical task of higher education from a more or less Wesleyan perspective (Eaton speaks almost as much in his more generic "evangelical" voice as he does in a specific "Wesleyan" tone). However, a collection of essays from Eaton's Seattle Pacific faculty is explicitly Wesleyan in its approach: Daniel Castelo, ed., *Holiness as a Liberal Art* (Eugene: Pickwick, 2012).

[14]   Kurt W. Peterson and R. J. Snell, "'Faith Forms the Intellectual Task': The Pietist Option in Christian Higher Education," in *The Pietist Impulse in Christianity*, ed. Christian T. Collins Winn, Christopher Gehrz, G. William Carlson, and Eric Holst (Eugene: Pickwick, 2011), 215–30, at 222.

[15]   Part of the history here is the emergence into prominence of these Pietist ideas amidst wider currents, so that one of the first to develop this triadic moniker in the field of education was a Swiss pedagogue, Johann Heinrich Pestalozzi (1746–1827). Pestalozzi's educational theories entered the United States in the early 1800s and impacted primarily the formation of normal schools that we discussed in the previous chapter. See Ogren, *American State Normal School*, 35–36; Arthur Brühlmeier, *Head, Heart and Hand: Education in the Spirit of Pestalozzi* (Cambridge: Sophia, 2010).

[16]   Peterson and Snell, "'Faith Forms the Intellectual Task,'" 219 and 217, respectively. Another articulation is that Christian education shapes vocation (the mind), forms character (the heart), and nurtures competence (the hands); see Kwai Lin Stephens, "Christian Leadership Development and the Spiritual Disciplines," in *Tending the Seedbeds: Educational Perspectives on Theological Education in Asia*, ed. Allan Harkness (Quezon City, Philippines: Asia Theological Association, 2010), 193–211.

[17]   Cheryl Bridges Johns, "Partners in Scandal: Wesleyan and Pentecostal Scholarship," *Pneuma: The Journal of the Society for Pentecostal Studies* 21.1 (1999): 183–97.

[18]   Johns, "Partners in Scandal," 187.

To be sure, such responses represent the scandal not only of the evangelical mind, but of the intellectual undertaking as a whole. For Johns, this approach reflects "a knowing which is not a grasping but a letting go . . . , [a] knowing which is not grounded in its own self presence but in the presence of the source of all knowing?"[19] By drawing on Martha Nussbaum's *Love's Knowledge*, Johns assumes an inherent rationality to the emotions and the importance of the affective dimension of the human person, which returns the discussion to the patristic fusion of biblical and ancient philosophical traditions on learning and human psychology.[20] Johns has also become a contemporary channel of the intuitionism central to early pentecostal ways of knowing.

This does not mean that the tradition of reform, revivalist, and renewal Christianity—with its antecedent and constitutive revivalist, holiness, and pentecostal-charismatic tributaries—is beyond criticism. Not to recognize the suspicion of the academy that remains suffused throughout many segments of the movement is to be dishonest.[21] Yet, as we have argued in the previous chapter and continue to do in this chapter, such an anti-intellectualism stems from different forms of rationality (intuitionism vs. evidentialism), the perceived removal of encounters with transcendence from the educational process (anticonversionism), and on-the-ground activism in populism (antiembourgeoisement). In this sense, suspicion of the academy is a manifestation of a fundamentally different approach to head, heart, and hands.

Anti-intellectualism with respect to rationality may be better described as a form of antirationalism, which is to say, an implicit resistance to certain modes of rationality. If nothing else, Alasdair MacIntyre's analysis of the connection between what counts as rational and traditions of inquiry ought to create a measure of humility when historians assess movements that espouse a form of so-called anti-intellectualism. Anti-intellectualism with respect to conversion trades on the crisis-process dialectic so crucial to the holiness and pentecostal understanding of salvation with a definite preference for the crisis of encounter. Finally, anti-intellectualism with respect to embourgeoisement has to do with resistance to any capitulation to culture that results in a religious formalism in worship and a top-down approach to reform and renewal.

Despite the criticisms offered of his historical account, Noll has continued to prosecute his case in subsequent publications, as exemplified in his assertion in 2011 that "on the whole, *The Scandal of the Evangelical Mind* still seems to me correct in its descriptions and evaluations."[22] The task will necessarily involve, on the one hand, identifying the historical forces that gave rise to the prejudices inimical to loving God with our minds, yet simultaneously, on the other hand, following in the path charted out by Johns. This does not require an uncritical adoption of other forms of rationality, which will only diffuse the gifts that pentecostal-charismatic perspectives have to offer. The uncritical adoption of Reformed worldview thinking grounded in a specific kind of historical response to nineteenth-century developments, coupled with a privileging of

---

[19]   Johns, "Partners in Scandal," 197.

[20]   Martha C. Nussbaum, *Love's Knowledge: Essays on Philosophy and Literature* (New York: Oxford University Press, 1990).

[21]   A fine exposé of anti-intellectualism as aspect of pentecostal Christianity is Rick Nañez, *Full Gospel, Fractured Minds: A Call to Use God's Gift of the Intellect* (Grand Rapids: Zondervan, 2005).

[22]   Mark A. Noll, *Jesus Christ and the Life of the Mind* (Grand Rapids: Eerdmans, 2011), 152.

scholars as elite drivers of high culture over against populist transformations of folk culture, is a distinct tradition of thought that requires interrogation.

4.1.2 The Quest for an Evangelical Mind

September 13, 1980, was a heady day at Wheaton College. Over ten thousand attendees were present for the dedication of the new Billy Graham Center. Taking on such a large project had been a risk, with Wheaton pledging to raise the $15 million required to maintain the center and its impressive new building. Such an occasion represented a time to reflect and take stock of evangelicalism in order to chart a path forward. In the dedicatory address, the Lebanese ambassador and Orthodox thinker Charles Malik (1906–1987) took the opportunity to outline two critical tasks for Christianity: evangelization and the life of the mind.[23] In addition, a subtext of Malik's address was the need to ground these tasks in a recovery of Christian tradition. Malik's statements hinted at the need for an evangelical *ressourcement* akin to what had been happening in the French Catholic and Orthodox worlds as part of the *nouvelle théologie*, on the one hand, and the so-called Russian and Neopatristic schools associated with St. Sergius Orthodox Theological Institute, on the other hand. Both the French Catholics (de Lubac, Danielou, Congar, et al.) and the Russian émigrés (Bulgakov, Lossky, Florovsky, et al.) were formulating responses to modernism when Malik was on the international stage. After extolling the need for an intellectually rigorous form of Christianity, Malik identified anti-intellectualism as the besetting sin of evangelicalism. Malik's goal was to awaken the sleeping giant of evangelicalism to the need for a sustained intellectual program committed to recovering great thinkers of the past in order to take on the secularization connected to modernity.

Among those listening were Mark Noll and Arthur Holmes. Within five years, Holmes had published *Contours of a Christian World View* and edited *The Making of a Christian Mind*, which was in honor of the 125th anniversary of Wheaton.[24] His ongoing dialogue with Reformed visions of worldview had already led Holmes down that road. In the latter book, Noll contributed an essay, first delivered as a chapel talk, "Christian World Views and Some Lessons of History," in which he outlined an initial case for what would become *The Scandal of the Evangelical Mind*. Malik's address ignited a concerted effort to cultivate an evangelical intellectual tradition centered upon what James Sire had called "worldview analysis."[25] For his part, Noll drew on that tradition and added his own insights into populist revivalism, which tracked with what Richard Hofstadter had written earlier. The historiography against populism and worldview analysis were two important factors of Noll's own criticisms.

In the early 1980s, Noll and Holmes were part of a groundswell of evangelicals attempting to reappropriate worldview thinking as part of a larger project of cultural engagement. The fountainhead of this project was the work of two Reformed thinkers, James Orr and Abraham Kuyper, whose thought had been mediated in the American Reformed

---

[23] Charles H. Malik, "The Two Tasks," *Journal of the Evangelical Theological Society* 23.4 (1980): 289–96; idem, *The Two Tasks* (Wheaton: Billy Graham Center, 2000).

[24] Arthur Holmes, *Contours of a Christian World View*, Studies in a Christian World View (Grand Rapids: Eerdmans, 1983); idem, ed., *The Making of a Christian Mind: A Christian World View and the Academic Enterprise* (Downers Grove: IVP, 1985).

[25] James Sire, foreword to Holmes, *Making of a Christian Mind*, 7; see also James Sire, *The Universe Next Door: A Basic Worldview Catalog* (Downers Grove: IVP, 1976).

tradition through men like Gordon Clark and Cornelius Van Til. Orr borrowed the idea of a worldview from German scholarship, but did not concern himself with the role it had played in German thought at the end of the nineteenth century. *Weltanschauung* had become connected to the larger enterprise of *Bildung* (education as self-cultivation) within German universities. The project of self-cultivation central to *Bildung* was to result in an open, evaluative view of the world—a kind of cosmopolitan vision achieved through scholarship or science (*Wissenschaft*). As we argued in the previous chapter, this was its original intention and how it intersected with the Anglo-American intellectual enterprise. An ongoing challenge to the project of self-cultivation was the tension between cosmopolitanism and nationalism. Under the development of fascism, the tension broke in favor of a nationalism reinforced by notions of rational and racial superiority.

Rudolf Eucken, upon whom Orr partly relied for his understanding of *Weltanschauung*, utilized the term to identify the conflicts in the German system over the role of religion in the project of self and cultural creation, particularly as it related to historical inquiry into the development of human consciousness. This allowed Eucken to argue for the importance of religion in human development and bridge the transcendental and the material aspects of life, which supported his own panentheism.[26] Divine immanence in the form of a kind of natural supernaturalism had once again come to the fore as the best means to preserve some version of religion. Wilhelm Dilthey would develop the notion of *Weltanschauung* as a historiographical tool in which historical evolution as the development of human consciousness corresponded to the creation of systems. In his quest to develop a sociology of knowledge, Dilthey argued for a connection between investigation of life systems or outlooks and the interior lives of historical persons. The historian could come to terms with historical personages as products of a broader set of cultural values. *Weltanschauung* was a species of a system of culture (*Kultursystem*), embodied in the institutional structures of a society and shaping the persons inhabiting it.[27] Dilthey's analysis would have an important impact on sociology (Max Weber would react to it).

Orr's understanding of worldview resonates with Dilthey's analysis in the first decade of the twentieth century, even if the latter did not influence the former.[28] Orr's primary interest was the heuristic advantage that worldview gave him. Through the lens of worldview, he could describe the ideological conflicts of his day as a conflict of systems and apply this same method to history.[29] Because Orr's aim was primarily apologetical, he

---

26 See Rudolf Eucken, *Collected Essays*, ed. and trans. M. Booth (New York: Charles Scribner's, 1914); Fritz K. Ringer, *The Decline of the German Mandarins: The German Academic Community, 1890–1933* (Cambridge, Mass.: Harvard University Press, 1969), 81–128. It is important to note Eucken's influence on Max Scheler, who was one of his students. See Stephen F. Schneck, *Person and Polis: Max Scheler's Personalism as Political Theory* (Albany: State University of New York Press, 1987), 22–24. On the broader development of worldview, see David K. Naugle, *Worldview: The History of a Concept* (Grand Rapids: Eerdmans, 2002).

27 Wilhelm Dilthey, *Selected Writings*, ed. H. P. Rickman (Cambridge: Cambridge University Press, 1976), 133–54; Wilhelm Dilthey, *Selected Works*, vol. 3: *The Formation of the Historical World in the Human Sciences*, ed. Rudolf A. Makkreel and Frithjof Rodi (Princeton: Princeton University Press, 2002); and Herbert A. Hodges, *Wilhelm Dilthey: An Introduction* (New York: H. Fertig, 1969), 45–61.

28 Orr developed his position on worldviews in a series of lectures he gave in 1891, which were subsequently published as *The Christian View of God and the World: As Centring in the Incarnation: Being the Kerr Lectures for 1890–91* (Edinburgh: Andrew Elliot, 1893).

29 Orr, *The Christian View of God and the World*, lecture 1 and appendix, 3–48, 415–21.

focused on the ideological features of these systems, setting forth the Christian worldview in outline as a set of propositions. It also made it easier for Orr to resist the claim that Christianity was mainly a way of life and a spirituality, which he found reflected in late nineteenth-century scholarly trends. In Orr's mind, worldview was not so much a species of culture, or a part of the background understanding of a social imaginary, as a theoretical construct formulated as a kind of confessional statement about life. On the basis of such a confession, Christian thinkers could assess other systems, drawing out their strengths and identifying their weaknesses.

Abraham Kuyper's approach to the problem of secularism developed along similar lines, with Kuyper eventually assimilating Orr's thought into his own.[30] Unlike Orr, however, Kuyper recognized the relationship between worldview and culture formation. He was also more influenced by German idealism than Orr, taking as one of his starting points the formation of human consciousness in the development of the person.[31] For Kuyper, "science, in its absolute sense, is the pure and complete reflection of the cosmos in the human consciousness. As the parts of all actually existing things lie in their relations, so much the parts of our knowledge be related in our consciousness."[32] The organic relationality of the various aspects of the cosmos merged into the program of cultural engagement he outlined in his lectures on Calvinism as well as his commitment to the sovereignty of the various spheres of life, from government to the family to education. It was a restatement of the kind of cosmopolitan vision men like Humboldt had in mind for the intellectual pursuit of self-cultivation through research. While the strength of Kuyper's approach was his appropriation of the organic nature of life from German idealism, his infusion of an antithesis between the regenerate and the nonregenerate led to a seeming rejection of the unity of science as involving a denial of the new birth. Kuyper seemed to reject a common foundation of knowledge in human consciousness in light of a Reformed doctrine of election.

By employing the idea of worldview, Orr and Kuyper were attempting to update Reformed perspectives in light of the cultural clashes that were occurring in the late nineteenth century. Each struggled to move beyond Baconian induction and its connection to Reidian views of common sense in the service of an evidential Christianity. Their proposals set the agenda for many evangelicals as they were assimilated in the 1930s and 1940s by men like Cornelius Van Til and Gordon Clark and their students.[33] With their fixation on propositional truth, evangelical rationalists like Carl Henry could easily dismiss pentecostal spirituality. Worldview thinking undergirded the new field of evangelical apologetics as well as the emerging approach to the integration of faith and learning by talking

---

[30] While it is clear that Kuyper used Orr, the extent of Orr's influence with regard to Kuyper's use of "life system" or worldview is debated. See Peter Heslam, *Creating a Christian Worldview: Abraham Kuyper's Lectures on Calvinism* (Grand Rapids: Eerdmans, 1998); and James D. Bratt, *Abraham Kuyper: Modern Calvinist, Christian Democrat* (Grand Rapids: Eerdmans, 2013), 207.

[31] On the impact of German thought upon Kuyper, see Bratt, *Abraham Kuyper*, 33–35, 183.

[32] Abraham Kuyper, *Encyclopedia of Sacred Theology: Its Principles*, trans. J. Hendrik de Vries (New York: Charles Scribner's, 1898), 39.

[33] See Molly Worthen, *Apostles of Reason: The Crisis of Authority in American Evangelicalism* (New York: Oxford University Press, 2014), 24–32. Worthen sees the evangelical appropriation of worldview thinking as part of the conservative intellectual resurgence in the 1950s catalogued by George Nash in his *The Conservative Intellectual Movement in America since 1945* (New York: Basic, 1976; repr., Wilmington: Intercollegiate Studies Institute, 1996).

about presuppositions or pretheoretical commitments that inform an individual's beliefs as well as attempting to formulate a comprehensive Christian conceptual scheme. Orr's understanding of worldview as a kind of confession was coupled with Kuyper's cultural Calvinism. From the outset, this approach to cultural engagement was a Reformed enterprise, carried out mainly by Baptists, Presbyterians, and members of other Reformed denominations still shaped by the fundamentalist-modernist controversy and attempting to overcome a fundamentalist heritage. In his early essay, Noll drew upon worldview analysis, placing it in opposition to activism and experience as the path to an intellectually rigorous form of evangelicalism.[34]

A second element of Noll's critique had to do with revivalist populism. Without Malik realizing it, his call for an evangelical *ressourcement* had stumbled into a debate within American religious historiography centered on whether evangelicalism, especially in its revivalist mode, was an obstacle or not to the American experiment. As an effort to grapple with two world wars, this debate took place in the context of the consensus history of Perry Miller and others who sought to reassure Americans of their identity and place in the world. An uncomfortable adherent to consensus history who ultimately rejected it, Richard Hofstadter had answered in the affirmative, portraying revivalist forms of evangelicalism as sectarian and anti-intellectual.[35] Hofstadter's examination of anti-intellectualism in American culture was part of his long-standing effort to critique the populist mind. His *The Age of Reform* (1955) offered a reinterpretation of the populist revolts that produced the liberal radicalism of the 1930s.[36] It was a defense of Franklin Roosevelt's New Deal, which Hofstadter favored over what he considered to be the myths of Jeffersonian trust in plebeian virtue, midwestern agrarianism, and the self-made man. Hofstadter privileged a cultural and intellectual elite over against Jacksonian populist values, even if they did produce an Abraham Lincoln. The alliance between business, government, and the academy that was initially criticized by men like Charles Eliot Norton for its professionalizing of a classical education and devaluing of culture was taken for granted by Hofstadter.

It took Hofstadter several years to compose his next book on anti-intellectualism.[37] By that time, he had worked through McCarthyism and he connected it to the ongoing impact of populism in America. In a middle section Hofstadter set his sights on American revivalism as another manifestation of the populist mind gone awry. The series of awakenings within evangelical Protestantism, mixed with the rise of millenarianism, fomented an anti-intellectual ethos that prosecuted intellectuals in the name of conformity and traditionalism. In short, evangelicalism for Hofstadter was never really committed to pluralism and the creation of an American culture. In leveling this criticism, Hofstadter joined Reinhold Niebuhr's assessment of Billy Graham as offering a disastrous model for Christianity that simply regurgitated pietistic simplicity

---

[34]   Noll, "Christian World Views and Some Lessons of History," in Holmes, *Making of a Christian Mind*, 29–31, 47–54.

[35]   Richard Hofstadter, *Anti-intellectualism in American Life* (New York: Vintage, 1963).

[36]   Richard Hofstadter, *The Age of Reform: From Bryan to F.D.R.* (New York: Vintage, 1955); David S. Brown, *Richard Hofstadter: An Intellectual Biography* (Chicago: University of Chicago Press, 2006), 99–119.

[37]   Hofstadter, *Anti-intellectualism in American Life*.

in the struggle over racism and liberal Protestantism.[38] Graham's 1957 crusade in New York may have marked his turning away from fundamentalism toward the new evangelicalism of Carl Henry, but from Niebuhr's vantage point Graham sacrificed a sophisticated Reformation Christianity as an answer to modernity at the altar of naive revivalism.[39] Despite Union Seminary president Henry Van Dusen's more sympathetic view that Graham's revival fires were the catalyst that first led him down the path to Niebuhr's more dense and long-lasting embers, he could not persuade Niebuhr to change his mind.

Niebuhr, Hofstadter, Lionel Trilling, and Jacques Barzun represented a new kind of avant-garde, captured by Will Herberg's *Protestant—Catholic—Jew*.[40] It was in reality, as Trilling's *The Liberal Imagination* (1950) suggested, a reboot of Mill's and Arnold's understanding of self-cultivation and culture as interpreted through the literary realism of James and Howells.[41] Of course, this required two ways of thinking about culture, one of which was literary and artistic while the other was more sociological. Trilling recognized as much in his follow-up collections of essays, *The Opposing Self* and *Beyond Culture*.[42] The latter involves merely the beliefs, manners, customs, and practices of a people—the general culture of the whole—while the former involves certain intellectual disciplines and artistic practices. The liberal imagination moves between the two in the cultivation of the self, as Henry James' literary realism revealed. The self stands in favor of literary and artistic culture as part of its cultivation and liberation from the general culture of the masses. Trilling attempted to show how individualism and autonomy expressed themselves through the struggle and adversity against common social organization, which was nothing more than rehashing the liberal humanism of the intellectual circles that anglicized *Bildung*.

Although Hofstadter's narrative came under critique by scholars like Daniel Boorstin as a failed effort at cultural criticism that offered a distorted account of a cosmopolitanism and intellectualism at war with populism and intuition, the book remained deeply popular.[43] A student of Hofstadter, Christopher Lasch rejected his teacher because of what he saw as a kind of anti-intellectualism among the intellectuals themselves, rooted in their failure to distinguish between the intellect itself and the interests of intellectuals. He spared no words in describing the new radicalism as "unconcealed elitism" entailing "the rise of the intellectuals to the status of a privileged class, fully integrated into the social

[38] Gary Dorrien, "Niebuhr and Graham: Modernity, Complexity, White Supremacism, Justice, Ambiguity," in *The Legacy of Billy Graham: Critical Reflections on America's Greatest Evangelist*, ed. Michael G. Long (Louisville: Westminster John Knox, 2008), 141–59.

[39] Graham's legacy is still contested. See Grant Wacker, *America's Pastor: Billy Graham and the Shaping of a Nation* (Cambridge, Mass.: Harvard University Press, 2014), 90–101.

[40] Will Herberg, *Protestant—Catholic—Jew: An Essay in American Religious Sociology* (New York: Doubleday, 1955).

[41] Lionel Trilling, *The Liberal Imagination: Essays on Literature and Society* (New York: Charles Scribner's Sons, 1950).

[42] Lionel Trilling, *Beyond Culture: Essays on Literature and Learning* (New York: Vintage, 1965), ix–xx; Lionel Trilling, *The Opposing Self: Nine Essays in Criticism* (New York: Harcourt Brace Jovanovich, 1955), preface.

[43] Daniel J. Boorstin, "The Split-Level Tower," *Saturday Review of Literature*, June 1, 1963, as cited in Brown, *Richard Hofstadter*, 139–40.

organism."[44] The intellectual of the fifties and sixties thought of himself as a subversive while bearing the marks and clothing of an "Ivy League aristocrat."[45]

The small intellectual world spanning the few blocks between Columbia and Union Theological Seminary was a powerful force in the fifties and sixties. It gave rise to an intellectual program centered on advancing a new elitism that sought to transform culture as the way to shape politics. This program set its sights on populism as the enemy of the intellectual. This is the environment that shaped a young Roberts Mapes Anderson, who stayed at Columbia for much of the sixties completing a master's degree and then a doctorate. Anderson's 1969 dissertation, later published as *Vision of the Disinherited*, entailed a social history of Pentecostalism.[46] In Anderson's analysis, early Pentecostals were simply another version of the social discontent found within the populism of the Progressive Era. The movement was nothing more than ecstatic escapism for the troubled farmer or impoverished urban worker who lacked the skills to improve the world and simply rejected it instead. As a rural-agrarian, the pentecostal leader fell victim to "physical as well as cultural and economic deprivation" and managed somehow to acquire "a smattering of advanced education of relatively low quality."[47] In Anderson, Hofstadter's historiography had come of age. By the time Noll began his analysis of American evangelicalism, this was a well-established historiographical trajectory that had yet to be challenged fully.

4.1.3 The Scandal behind *The Scandal of the Evangelical Mind*

There are four criticisms of Noll's thesis that follow from our Pentecost-framework. The first two recognize and respond to how Noll's *The Scandal of the Evangelical Mind* draws upon the historiographical trajectory in Hofstadter and the worldview trajectory in Orr and Kuyper, while the other two focus on the presumptions that marginalize folk culture and that ignore how the latter are just as interested in the (trans)formation of the human person as in the pursuit of truth. As the latter two can be more summarily discussed since we have traversed some of this ground already in the foregoing, we spend more time here on how Noll's historiography is suspicious of populism and privileges an intellectual and cultural elite (highbrow culture) while also assuming the worldview frames of one evangelical tradition.

First, when Noll connects the scandal of the evangelical mind to a culture or "evangelical ethos" that "is activist, populist, pragmatic, and utilitarian," he is operating out of Hofstadter's narrative.[48] Where Hofstadter faulted a populist millenarianism, Noll referred to apocalypticism and dispensationalism. One can detect Noll's variance with George Marsden's prescriptions for evangelical scholarship, in which, following Nicholas Wolterstorff, Marsden suggests that action is the goal of the intellectual life, even as he acknowledged Noll's counter that making such a claim to evangelicals is like giving drugs to an addict.[49]

---

[44] Christopher Lasch, *The New Radicalism in America, 1889–1963: The Intellectual as a Social Type* (New York: Knopf, 1965), 316.

[45] Lasch, *New Radicalism in America*, 314.

[46] Robert Mapes Anderson, "A Social History of the Early Twentieth Century Pentecostal Movement" (PhD thesis, Columbia University, 1969); idem, *Vision of the Disinherited: The Making of American Pentecostalism* (New York: Oxford University Press, 1979).

[47] Anderson, *Vision of the Disinherited*, 113, 240.

[48] Noll, *Scandal of the Evangelical Mind*, 12.

[49] George Marsden, "The State of Evangelical Christian Scholarship," *Reformed Journal* 37.9 (1987): 15; idem, "The State of Evangelical Christian Scholarship," *Christian Scholar's Review* 17.4 (1988): 347–60.

At the outset of his critique, Noll acknowledged the challenge of defining anti-intellectualism as Hofstadter had before him. For Hofstadter, the term denoted a "complex of related propositions" reflected in a "resentment and suspicion of the life of the mind and those who represent it; and, a disposition constantly to minimize the value of that life."[50] Recognizing the ambiguity and generality of his formulation, Hofstadter offered examples he described as "impressionistic devices" that captured an atmosphere or milieu. Like Hofstadter, Noll focused on a disposition that facilitates the "sometimes vigorous prosecution of the wrong sort of intellectual life."[51] Anti-intellectualism turns out to be a "mode of intellectual activity" or a set of intellectual habits that does not fit with the shape of Christianity as Noll understands it.[52] He locates this mode in an evangelical culture, which suggests that he is also interested in offering examples that identify a milieu. Noll's new afterword trades on the distinction between a populist evangelicalism and an intellectual resurgence among evangelical scholarship to continue his indictment against the evangelical mind. In following Hofstadter so closely, Noll opens himself up to the same criticisms of pitting egalitarianism against the intellect, the embourgeoisement of the intellectual, and an elitism espousing the intellectual as expert and education as pure research in the service of a conversation among academics and cultural thinkers.

Noll's opening salvo that evangelicals have abandoned high culture sets the tone and the baseline for his understanding of evangelical culture. What became "high culture" in the twentieth century was simply an extension of the liberal culture pushed by the literati of the late nineteenth century. Whereas Hofstadter had rejected the progressivism of Woodrow Wilson's and John Dewey's commitment to facilitating a liberal culture in favor of Roosevelt's New Deal, Noll rejected the evangelical populist commitment to cultural transformation through social critique in favor of worldview analysis.[53] Noll was feeding into the late nineteenth-century proponents of the research university as facilitating a trickle-down approach that constructed and communicated high culture for the sake of soul and society. The difference is that Noll relied heavily on confessional worldview thinking as producing a set of intellectual commitments and values that supplied the boundaries for research.

When one reads Noll's analysis closely, his elastic definition of a "mode of intellectual activity" allows him to indict the rigors and cosmopolitanism of German Pietism in Kant and Schleiermacher alongside the populism of the holiness and pentecostal movements. The connection resides in viewing Christianity primarily as a way of life to the exclusion of its doctrinal commitments, which echoes Orr's appropriation of worldview. Noll objects to an extreme emphasis on experience and "feeling" in the "humanistic romanticism" of the nineteenth century.[54] Since Noll could not claim that Schleiermacher failed to represent the kind of comprehensive thinking he desired for all evangelicals, he had to shift

---

[50] Hofstadter, *Anti-intellectualism in American Life*, 7.

[51] Johns, "Partners in Scandal," 188–89 also criticizes Noll's generic definition, which she suggests allows Noll to engage in sectarian tribalism.

[52] Noll, *Scandal of the Evangelical Mind*, 12.

[53] Hofstadter's historical analysis continues to be highly disputed, even though Hofstadter's book on anti-intellectualism enjoyed a renaissance during the Reagan administration when Noll first put down his thoughts about the evangelical scandal. See John Wiener, "America, Through a Glass Darkly," *Nation*, October 23, 2006, 36–40.

[54] Noll, *Scandal of the Evangelical Mind*, 49.

the ground of criticism from anti-intellectualism to antiorthodoxy. Noll's legerdemain is already present in his earlier essay when he claims that a focus on spirituality rather than worldview usually means that "Christian faith degenerates, lapses into gross error, or simply passes out of existence."[55] This shift becomes all too clear in his use of ancient heresies as types for the problematic "modes of intellectual activity" he finds within pietistic revivalism. The habits of mind cultivated by an evangelical revivalist culture turn out to be the "intellectual heresies" of Manichaeism, Gnosticism, and docetism.[56] By utilizing ancient heresies as ideal types to ferret out unorthodox views, Noll joined a group of Reformed thinkers who were at the time indicting evangelicalism for its mysticism, Pietism, and romanticism, some of the primary ingredients of what we have called the Romantic sensibility.[57]

As a mode of intellectual activity, Gnosticism points toward a number of characteristics that reflect a preference for secret or private revelation. Initially, it means treating the Bible as an esoteric code to be deciphered, which Noll finds in the charts and speculations of dispensational writers.[58] It also points toward a traditionless Christianity that prefers sectarian interpretations to the "counterweight of Christian tradition."[59] Finally, it involves a lopsided emphasis on the supernatural that denies the public role of historical investigation, denigrates nature by appealing to scriptural texts over against the hard work of critical analysis, and constantly fixates on the end of the world to the exclusion of the present.[60] As Noll states, "evangelicals almost totally replaced respect for creation with a contemplation of redemption."[61] Taken together, these characteristics point toward a "mode of intellectual activity" that is antithetical to the kind of habits of mind commensurate with the Christian faith.

The challenge for Noll's analysis resides in the way archetypal heresies become the "impressionistic devices" needed to reconstruct the populism and folk culture he seeks to shun. There is little effort to examine the doctrines he selects in terms of their interlocking nature within a social imaginary. As we have argued, the supernaturalism espoused by holiness and pentecostal leaders remained connected to a pneumatology that followed the Romantic sensibility in viewing historical processes as enlivened by the presence of the divine. Noll never asks whether the Wesleyan notion of prevenient grace or the doctrine of divine healing alters the relationship between the natural and the supernatural.

---

[55] Noll, "Christian World Views and Some Lessons of History," in Holmes, *Making of a Christian Mind*, 40.

[56] Noll employs these basic "typologies" fairly consistently on evangelicalism and the life of the mind. See *Scandal of the Evangelical Mind*, 49–56; Mark A. Noll, "Reconsidering Christendom?" in *The Future of Christian Learning: An Evangelical and Catholic Dialogue*, ed. T. A. Howard (Grand Rapids: Brazos, 2008), 28–29.

[57] See David Wells, *No Place for Truth, or Whatever Happened to Evangelical Theology* (Grand Rapids: Eerdmans, 1993); idem, *God in the Wasteland: The Reality of Truth in a World of Fading Dreams* (Grand Rapids: Eerdmans, 1995); Michael Horton, *In the Face of God* (Dallas: Word, 1996). This was partly due to Harold Bloom's idiosyncratic assessment of American religion in general as essentially gnostic; see his *The American Religion: The Emergence of the Post Christian Nation* (New York: Simon and Schuster, 1993).

[58] Noll, *Scandal of the Evangelical Mind*, 52.

[59] Noll and Turner, *Future of Christian Learning*, 29.

[60] Noll, *Scandal of the Evangelical Mind*, 132–33.

[61] Noll, *Scandal of the Evangelical Mind*, 133.

Rooted in pneumatology, both of these doctrines form part of the way holiness and pentecostal adherents understood divine immanence.

Noll's most recent work also suggests that his own penchant is for the creedal and confessional dimension of Christian tradition over against its spiritual tradition. As we have noted, it's a preference for the Christ of the confessions over the cosmic Christ, a Thomist move over a Bonaventurian one.[62] Such a preference reflects an ecclesial location within a confessing tradition of evangelicalism, but it does not reflect the revivalist part of the movement. This suggests that Noll has imposed a particular definition of tradition on the revivalist camp, with the result that holiness and pentecostal adherents have been found wanting.

If Christian tradition is a living entity, imbued by the Spirit's ongoing revelatory work in the life of the faithful, then there are times when the *consensus fidelium* is preserved because some individuals perceive the truth more clearly than others. This was certainly the case with Maximus the Confessor, who was condemned as a heretic for his defense of two wills in Christ. Noll refers to a "hard-won wisdom" that stands the test of time without spelling out the historical processes by which theological positions were deemed to be expressions of such wisdom. In other words, one does not have a confessional tradition apart from a spiritual tradition. We tried to show in chapter 2 that the spiritual traditions have always been the heart of Christianity because theological visions emerge from spiritual encounters birthed from within the community. The archetypal use of heresies as impressionistic devices leaves out too much for Noll's analysis to be effective.

Our second critical response to Noll's thesis builds on the preceding but highlights how the worldview analysis identifies the theological dimension of the scandal. On the basis of worldview analysis, Noll seeks to promote habits of mind that cultivate comprehensive Christian thinking about "the mind, nature, society, the arts—all spheres created by God and sustained for his own glory."[63] Part of the challenge with invoking worldview analysis is the way in which Orr had connected it to confessionalism. As a system of belief, a worldview becomes a more expansive version of a confession of faith, which results in orthodoxy being defined in ever more rigid ways. While Noll finds creation science to be a product of fundamentalism, one could easily suggest that it is also a result of worldview thinking in which "right belief" came to include beliefs about Genesis because such beliefs flowed from a confession of inerrancy and the dispensational fixation with literalism in biblical exegesis.

It was the emphasis on holiness of life rather than a concern for right doctrine that prompted Ronald Numbers to conclude that holiness and pentecostal leaders generally were more relaxed about evolution than their Reformed counterparts. In his analysis of Pentecostalism and evolution, Gerald King notes that Pentecostals only gradually became attuned to fundamentalist arguments against evolution. Most of the borrowing from fundamentalist authors occurred in the 1930s on the basis of a common foe. One must keep in mind the condemnation of Pentecostals by fundamentalists in 1928 and the fact that the Assemblies of God was more open to this adoption because of the links to

---

[62]   Noll, *Jesus Christ and the Life of the Mind*, 2.
[63]   Noll, *Scandal of the Evangelical Mind*, 23.

the Christian Missionary and Alliance and Baptists within its ranks.[64] As Pentecostalism grew, pentecostal writers became more attuned to larger developments in the culture and sought to craft a way forward by borrowing at times from fundamentalist writers. Still, this borrowing was not wholesale, and it remained chastened by the way fundamentalists continued to criticize Pentecostals for their focus on spiritual experience. The same worldview lens that led fundamentalists to expand confessionalization to positions on Genesis also fueled their ongoing suspicion of Pentecostalism.

Our final two critical assessments of Noll's thesis can be summarily presented as they are derived from the more substantively articulated analyses above. The third criticism relates to Noll's seeming preference for high culture over folk culture, which sets him against the very kinds of cultural transformations holiness and pentecostal adherents made. One cannot overlook the fact that jazz musicians like Charles Mingus explicitly reference their experiences in holiness and pentecostal circles as an important influence behind songs such as "Wednesday Night Prayer Meeting," which seeks to embody pentecostal worship in a musical form. Our brief examination of the pentecostal contribution to jazz, blues, and gospel (see §4.2.3 below) reveals why Mingus looked to the Sanctified Church for the creative context of his own musicality.

Finally, Noll's prescription for education looks different from Malik's or C. S. Lewis', both of whom seem more concerned with the formation of the human person in the pursuit of truth. The abolition of humanity begins, according to Lewis, with the creation of "men without chests." It is the failure of education to help order the affections, to train individuals "to feel pleasure . . . at those things that are really pleasant" because "without the aid of trained emotions the intellect is powerless."[65] Malik seems to agree because his discussion of the sciences is more a discussion of the soul of the scientist and the fundamental integrity of the whole person. The integration of knowledge depends upon the integration of the person, which, in turn, relates to the integration of the affections in holiness or the removal of the passions.[66] Lewis' Anglicanism and Malik's Orthodoxy lead to different prescriptions that seem closer to the holiness and pentecostal emphases on sanctification as the pneumatological ordering of human love. Given his new preface and afterword, Noll wants more than a resurgence in scholarship. He catalogues the new wave of evangelical scholarship while maintaining that the evangelical mind is almost a lost cause. It is no longer that an ethos among evangelicals could not produce scholarship but that this ethos prevents the trickle-down effect of such scholarship. As long as an evangelical framework that privileges confessionalism provides the lens to interpret the holiness and pentecostal movements, their distinctive features and thus their contribution to a resurgence in education (as well as their challenges) will be misunderstood.

---

[64] Ronald Numbers, *Darwin Comes to America* (Cambridge, Mass.: Harvard University Press, 1998), 111–36; Gerald W. King, "Evolving Paradigms: Creationism as Pentecostal Variation on a Fundamentalist Theme," in *The Spirit Renews the Face of the Earth: Pentecostal Forays in Science and Theology of Creation*, ed. Amos Yong (Eugene: Wipf and Stock, 2009), 93–116; Gerald W. King, *Disfellowshiped: Pentecostal Responses to Fundamentalism in the United States, 1906–1943* (Eugene: Pickwick, 2011), 125–206.

[65] C. S. Lewis, *The Abolition of Man* (New York: Harper, 1974), 16, 24.

[66] Charles H. Malik, *A Christian Critique of the University* (Downers Grove: IVP, 1982), 35–41.

4.2   PROGRESSIVE POPULISM AND
REVIVALISTIC RESISTANCE TO MODERNITY

One of the challenges to understanding the holiness and pentecostal movements is that both have been consistently described as features of a larger evangelical world. For example, Mark Noll remarked that while David Barrett had counted 510 million for the global pentecostal movement, most of them "should also be considered evangelicals."[67] In recording such sentiments, Noll was echoing what has become standard in the historiography of evangelicalism.[68]

This approach presents three problems. The first is that such a move obscures the history of Wesleyanism as a distinctive theological tradition within Protestantism, which includes Methodism, holiness denominations (e.g., the Church of the Nazarene or the Salvation Army), and Pentecostalism.[69] Most of the significant early Pentecostals who set the tone for the movement intersected with Wesleyanism by associating with either a form of Methodism or the holiness movement. One need only consider the following leaders: Pandita Ramabai (1858–1922) and Minnie Abrams (1859–1912) had both gone through Methodism into the holiness movement when they came together at the Mukti Mission; Thomas Ball Barrett (1862–1940) was a Methodist minister when he encountered Pentecostalism; Sarah Jane Lancaster (1858–1934) was Methodist before she started Good News Hall in Melbourne, Australia; William J. Seymour first became Methodist and then holiness before leading the Azusa Street revival; Aimee Semple McPherson grew up and first worked in the Salvation Army; and the "Black Elijah" of western Africa, Prophet William Wadé Harris (1860–1929), maintained close links to the Methodism he grew up in. Situated in Europe (Barratt), India (Ramabai and Abrams), Australia (Lancaster), Africa (Harris), Canada (McPherson), and the United States (Seymour), these early leaders reveal how deep the roots of early Pentecostalism are in the Wesleyan tradition. This tradition must be analyzed on its own before it is placed under the larger umbrella of evangelicalism.

Second, the dominance of a kind of Reformed historiographical approach to American evangelicalism has led to misconceptions about radical holiness and pentecostal men and women. One can see this dominance in a recent edited volume taking stock of evangelicalism. After asserting that Pentecostals belong under the category of evangelical, there is no genuine engagement with the historiography on Wesleyanism, let alone Pentecostalism.[70] Despite Marsden's and Carpenter's arguments that fundamentalism

---

[67]   Mark A. Noll, "Introduction: One Word but Three Crises," in *Evangelicals: Who They Have Been, Are Now, and Could Be*, ed. Mark A. Noll, David W. Bebbington, and George A. Marsden (Grand Rapids: Eerdmans, 2019), 11.

[68]   See Thomas S. Kidd, *Who Is an Evangelical? The History of a Movement in Crisis* (New Haven: Yale University Press, 2019); Kristin Kobes Du Mez, *Jesus and John Wayne: How White Evangelicals Corrupted a Faith and Fractured a Nation* (New York: Liveright, 2020). Kidd recognizes that there is still debate over this question, but chooses to treat Pentecostals as evangelicals.

[69]   To see the coherence and links between Methodism, holiness denominations, and Pentecostalism, see Henry H. Knight III, ed., *From Aldersgate to Azusa Street: Wesleyan, Holiness, and Pentecostal Visions of the New Creation* (Eugene: Pickwick, 2010); Henry H. Knight III, *Anticipating Heaven Below: Optimism of Grace from Wesley to the Pentecostals* (Eugene: Cascade, 2014).

[70]   Noll, Bebbington, and Marsden, *Evangelicals*. Timothy Smith's work is mentioned as well as Dayton's, but the historians of the holiness movement such as Douglas Strong, Priscilla Pope-Levison, Kenneth

is a peculiar brand of American evangelicalism favoring ideological battles and confessionalism in its antimodernist militancy and resistance to secularity, there remains a penchant to interpret the whole evangelical movement through its Reformed and Baptist sides.[71]

The history of evangelicalism tends to flow from Puritanism to Presbyterianism to the Higher Life wing of the holiness movement to fundamentalism and conclude with modern evangelicalism. For example, Ringenberg interprets Methodist, holiness, and pentecostal educational institutions through the lens of fundamentalism, describing Henry Clay Morrison as a Methodist fundamentalist.[72] Even Molly Worthen's more sympathetic effort to include Wesleyans remains wedded to a historical framework more conducive to the fundamentalist-modernist controversy.[73] In our own analysis, this is less satisfactory as an explanation of anti-intellectualism than the three emphases we identified: intuitionism over Baconian evidential rationalism (antirationalism); populism and folk culture over liberal culture (anti-embourgeoisement); encounter-driven spirituality over liturgical formalism (anticonversionism).

Third, since the publication of David Bebbington's *Evangelicalism in Modern Britain* (1989), the four characteristics he proposed to define evangelicalism (conversionism, activism, biblicism, and crucicentrism) have been deployed as the most useful way to understand the movement. Conversionism involves the call for the heart and life to be changed and locating this change in a dramatic encounter. Flowing from personal conversion was the activist call to engage in some kind of ministry. Grounding the conversionist and activist impulses were devotion to the centrality of Scripture (biblicism) and the atoning work of Christ (crucicentrism).

One benefit of these characteristics is their elasticity.[74] At the same time, we share the criticism that these characteristics leave out pneumatology as a distinctive category, which was crucial in the holiness and pentecostal movements.[75] This is especially important to our current argument, in which holiness and pentecostal writers understood the Spirit to be the ground of divine immanence. Moreover, the elasticity of Bebbington's quadrilateral has reinforced a Reformed historiography. Consequently, the

---

Collins, Melvin Dieter, Randall Stephens, Charles White, David Bundy, William Kostlevy, and Henry Knight are not found. Nor is there reference to historians of Pentecostalism except singular references to Vinson Synan (19) and Edith Blumhofer (154).

[71] George Marsden, *Fundamentalism and American Culture*, new ed. (New York: Oxford University Press, 2006); Joel A. Carpenter, *Revive Us Again: The Reawakening of American Fundamentalism* (Oxford: Oxford University Press, 1997).

[72] William C. Ringenberg, *The Christian College: A History of Protestant Higher Education in America*, 2nd ed. (Grand Rapids: Baker Academic, 2006), 169–82.

[73] See Worthen, *Apostles of Reason*, 2, 45.

[74] See the roundtable discussion in Noll, Bebbington, and Marsden, *Evangelicals*, 123–87.

[75] See Thomas S. Kidd, "The Bebbington Quadrilateral and the Work of the Holy Spirit," in Noll, Bebbington, and Marsden, *Evangelicals*, 136–40; Timothy Larsen, "Defining and Locating Evangelicalism," in *The Cambridge Companion to Evangelical Theology*, ed. Timothy Larsen and Daniel J. Treier (Cambridge: Cambridge University Press, 2007), 1–14. Bebbington's response is that pneumatology is not distinctive, which causes one to wonder how he would describe the consistent use of baptism in the Spirit from John Fletcher to Pentecostals and the depiction of the late nineteenth century as an age of the Spirit by holiness writers. See David W. Bebbington, "The Evangelical Quadrilateral: A Response," in Noll, Bebbington, and Marsden, *Evangelicals*, 178.

Wesleyan tradition has been placed into a framework that fails to explain its theological and social concerns.

Given these problems, this second section examines the holiness and pentecostal movements on their own terms. The argument proceeds as follows: first, the Marsden-Dayton debates reveal a historiography that obscures holiness and pentecostal emphases and prevents historians from recognizing the connections to the Romantic sensibility (§4.2.1); second, the key features of Progressive Era radical holiness and Pentecostalism are an encounter-driven form of mysticism rooted in operations of the Spirit (§4.2.2); and third, radical holiness and pentecostal thinkers utilized pneumatology to drive a theology of immanence that fueled social transformation (§4.2.3). Reinforced by their theology of Spirit baptism, the eschatological impulse among Pentecostals compelled them to change the folk cultures within which they found themselves, which is one of the reasons why Pentecostalism became "a religion made to travel."[76]

4.2.1 Debating Evangelical and Holiness Identities

Central to the debate between George Marsden and Donald Dayton over evangelical identity are competing historical paradigms that attempt to understand contemporary evangelicalism from different starting points.[77] Dayton argued that evangelicalism was best viewed through the lens of Methodism and the holiness movement rather than through what he called either the "Yale" interpretation or the "Princeton" interpretation.[78] By the former, Dayton referred to Yale historian Sydney Ahlstrom's *Religious History of the American People* (1972), which in many respects was the culmination of Perry Miller's recovery of the Puritan vision in the American context.[79]

At the forefront of consensus history, Miller described the Puritan mind in terms of a single intellectual vision.[80] The strength (and weakness) of consensus history was its emphasis on overarching structures of thought to explain continuities and discontinuities over a significant period of time. The consensus view represented a quest to find a unifying narrative that could account for the whole (e.g., the Puritan mind or the evangelical heritage). Miller's work, more than any other, rehabilitated Puritanism from the previous generation of Progressive historians and launched a reexamination of American history

---

[76] Murray W. Dempster, Byron D. Klaus, and Douglas Peterson, eds., *The Globalization of Pentecostalism: A Religion Made to Travel* (Carlisle: Regnum, 1999).

[77] See Douglas A. Sweeney, "The Essential Evangelicalism Dialectic: The Historiography of the Early Neo-Evangelical Movement and the Observer-Participant Dilemma," *Church History* 60.1 (1991): 70–84.

[78] Donald Dayton, "Yet Another Layer of the Onion: Or, Opening the Ecumenical Door to Let the Riffraff In," *Ecumenical Review* 40.1 (1988): 87–110.

[79] Harry S. Stout and Robert M. Taylor Jr., "Studies of Religion in American Society: The State of the Art," in *New Directions in American Religious History*, ed. H. S. Stout and D. G. Hart (New York: Oxford University Press, 1997), 17n10. See Sydney E. Ahlstrom, *A Religious History of the American People* (New Haven: Yale University Press, 1972). Yale published a second edition posthumously in 2004, with David Hall covering the final decades of the twentieth century.

[80] Perry Miller, *The New England Mind: The Seventeenth Century* (Cambridge, Mass.: Belknap, 1939); idem, *The New England Mind: From Colony to Province* (Cambridge, Mass.: Belknap, 1953). Miller's work has been called a "classic of consensus history," although it would be better to see it as building the foundation for what would become consensus history in the 1950s. See Peter Charles Hoffer, *Past Imperfect: Facts, Fictions, Fraud—American History from Bancroft and Parkman to Ambrose, Bellesiles, Ellis, and Goodwin* (New York: Public Affairs, 2004), 55.

from this perspective, including a new stimulus to the idea of American exceptionalism after the demise of Wilsonian progressivism.[81]

Ahlstrom's *Religious History* has been called the "last great monument" of consensus historiography.[82] What Dayton rejected was Ahlstrom's use of the Puritan vision as a unifying narrative, tracing American history from its emergence to a concluding chapter on "post-Puritan America."[83] In this recovery of the Puritan contribution to the American experience, the Methodist and holiness contributions were muted at best and entirely subsumed as variants at worst.

When Dayton objected to the "Presbyterian" paradigm, he was referencing an evangelical historiography that drew on the consensus approach of the 1950s and presupposed the centrality of Princeton Theological Seminary in the nineteenth century. Dayton was building upon Timothy Smith's earlier criticism of Marsden's approach and Smith's preference to call evangelicalism a kaleidoscope.[84] Dayton's favorite exemplar of a Presbyterian paradigm was Bernard Ramm's *The Evangelical Heritage* (1973), in which Ramm argued that evangelicalism was a Western Augustinian form of Christianity stemming from the magisterial Reformation through Reformed and Lutheran Orthodoxy to the Puritans and Old Princeton, and concluding in the Neo-evangelicalism of Carl Henry and Harold Ockenga.[85] Dayton accused Marsden's *Reforming Fundamentalism* of being a more subtle version of this same paradigm.[86]

In its place, Dayton suggested a "pentecostal" paradigm, by which he meant the way in which revivalist forms of evangelicalism represented modern forms of Christianity that disrupted traditional patterns of ecclesial existence.[87] Through his "pentecostal" paradigm, Dayton proposed a lens in which the role of class and *embourgeoisement* come to the fore rather than a debate over liberal or conservative theological positions. In some publications, he has referred to his approach more in terms of viewing the Gilded Age and Progressive era as the age of Methodism.

Marsden resisted Dayton's portrayal of his work as espousing a "Presbyterian" paradigm in which Old Princeton was a central feature.[88] He countered that his work included New School Presbyterians, which Dayton had called the "Methodistic" party of Presbyterianism.

---

[81]   P. Gura, "The Puritans: Orthodoxy or Diversity?" in *Interpretations of American History: Patterns and Perspectives*, vol. 1: *Through Reconstruction*, ed. F. G. Couvares, M. Saxton, G. N. Grob, and G. A. Billias, 7th ed. (New York: Simon and Schuster, 2000), 24–30.

[82]   Catherine L. Albanese, "Understanding Christian Diversity in America," in *American Christianities: A History of Dominance and Diversity*, ed. C. A. Brekus and W. C. Gilpin (Raleigh: University of North Carolina Press, 2011), 29.

[83]   Dayton, "Yet Another Layer of the Onion," 96.

[84]   Timothy Smith, "The Evangelical Kaleidoscope and the Call to Christian Unity," *Christian Scholar's Review* 15.2 (1986): 125–40.

[85]   Following Dayton, some pentecostal scholars began to assert that Pentecostalism was more Eastern than Western in terms of early Christianity and more Arminian than Calvinist. See Steven J. Land, *Pentecostal Spirituality: A Passion for the Kingdom*, Journal of Pentecostal Theology Supplement Series 1 (Sheffield: Sheffield Academic, 1993), 29–30.

[86]   Donald Dayton, "The Search for the Historical Evangelicalism: George Marsden's History of Fuller Seminary as a Case Study," *Christian Scholar's Review* 23.1 (1993): 13–33.

[87]   Donald Dayton, "The Limits of Evangelicalism: The Pentecostal Tradition," in *The Variety of American Evangelicalism*, ed. Donald W. Dayton and Robert K. Johnston, repr. (Eugene: Wipf and Stock, 1997), 36–56.

[88]   George Marsden, "Response to Don Dayton," *Christian Scholar's Review* 23.1 (1993): 34–40; see also George Marsden, "Demythologizing Evangelicalism: A Review of Donald W. Dayton's *Discovering an Evangelical Heritage*," *Christian Scholar's Review* 7 (1977): 203–7.

Moreover, Marsden admitted that some evangelical scholars had fallen into the "Presbyterian" paradigm, but not his work on fundamentalism with its tracing out of the movement from New School Presbyterians to Higher Life adherents to fundamentalism. Finally, without explicitly spelling it out, Marsden accused Dayton of falling into the same trap of consensus history by asserting a "pentecostal" paradigm over against a "Presbyterian" one. Dayton's class analysis, so central to his "pentecostal" paradigm, was just as limiting.

The importance of the Dayton-Marsden debate for our argument is twofold. First, it illuminates the ongoing struggle to define evangelicalism as a coherent movement. The alternative of utilizing sociohistorical metaphors, such as Timothy Smith's "mosaic" or "kaleidoscope," Randall Balmer's use of a corporation like General Motors or "patchwork quilt," Robert Johnston's "extended family," or Michael Horton's "village green," does not help identify common features that unite evangelicals over against Catholics, Orthodox, or other forms of Protestantism.[89] Balmer's use of "patchwork quilt" as an extension of his claim that evangelicalism is "America's folk religion" gets closer to the important intersection of populism and folk culture, but he offered this assessment in an ethnographical portrait.[90] As the success of Bebbington's quadrilateral reveals, any theological definition of evangelicalism must be minimalist in the sense of Lewis' "mere Christianity," while historical definitions verge toward Protestant Pietism or confessionalism. Part of the ongoing debate within evangelical scholarship concerns whether to privilege pietistic forms or confessional forms of Protestantism. Invariably, one part of evangelicalism gives in to the temptation to impose its self-definition on the whole, which becomes problematic to efforts at describing an "evangelical mind."

Second, the Dayton-Marsden debate represents a transition in American historiography from the consensus history of a Daniel Boorstin and Perry Miller to the new social history that emerged in the 1970s. Dayton's "pentecostal" paradigm is a form of consensus history in the same way that Marsden's tracking with the Puritan vision of Miller and Ahlstrom is consensus history. Yet Marsden and Dayton excel at delineating the social dynamics involved in these movements. This means that Dayton's more fundamental criticism of the so-called "Yale" paradigm as an exemplar of consensus history still holds. Marsden's otherwise excellent syntheses of fundamentalism deal almost exclusively with the issues in northern Presbyterianism and Baptist life, privileging those historical collisions as defining the "evangelical heritage." His narrative in *Fundamentalism and American Culture* moves from New School Presbyterianism to D. L. Moody and Keswick / Higher Life holiness to R. A. Torrey and Billy Sunday to fundamentalism.[91] The Wesleyan side of the holiness movement and Pentecostalism remained consigned to a few scattered paragraphs. The same case holds for *Understanding Fundamentalism and Evangelicalism*, in which the dominant players are northern Baptists, Congregationalists, and

---

[89]   Robert K. Johnston, "American Evangelicalism: An Extended Family," in Dayton and Johnston, *Variety of American Evangelicalism*, 252–72; Michael Horton, "Reflection: Is Evangelicalism Reformed or Wesleyan? Reopening the Marsden-Dayton Debate," *Christian Scholar's Review* 31.2 (2001): 131–55. See also Roger E. Olson, "The Reality of Evangelicalism: A Response to Michael S. Horton," *Christian Scholar's Review* 31.2 (2001): 157–62; Randall Balmer, *Evangelicalism in America* (Waco: Baylor University Press, 2016), xii.

[90]   Randall Balmer, *Mine Eyes Have Seen the Glory: A Journey into the Evangelical Subculture in America*, 25th anniversary ed. (New York: Oxford University Press, 2014), 7.

[91]   Marsden, *Fundamentalism and American Culture*.

Presbyterians.[92] Even though the debate with Dayton led Marsden to demarcate fundamentalism more clearly from Wesleyan holiness and Pentecostalism, what remains problematic about his body of work is how he links fundamentalism, evangelicalism, holiness, and Pentecostalism on a layer of analysis that does not take into consideration differing theological emphases or the appropriation of cultural shifts.[93]

Our task here is to contribute to the Marsden-Dayton debate by returning to the underlying ethos that connected New School Presbyterians—those who entered the holiness movement and those like Henry Ward Beecher who were precursors to the social gospel movement—to Wesleyan holiness writers such as Daniel Steele and Pentecostals. Building on the previous chapter, we argue that this ethos resides in the emphases of the Romantic sensibility, and that what ultimately differentiates these groups is the way in which some New School Presbyterians bought into its high-culture manifestation, which they subsequently fused with middlebrow culture, while others bought into populism and the emerging mass culture because they saw it as a way to preserve folk culture. Nevertheless, these were not strictly separated insofar as both Woodrow Wilson and William Jennings Bryan found common cause in a progressivism centered on advancing Western civilization as Christian civilization. We have already seen how this perspective stems from the move toward a view of education as cultural literacy by Charles Eliot Norton and other liberal progressives who extended the ideas first set forth by Henry Tappan. It is no mistake that Marsden found this same emphasis on Christian civilization in fundamentalist literature.[94] Such connections suggest a common set of emphases within these movements—the Romantic sensibility.

4.2.2 Mysticism, Encountering God, and Intuitive Knowledge

As a number of historians have argued, many holiness and pentecostal writers appropriated ideas from British Romanticism.[95] The common use of poetic forms (whether hymns, religious poetry, or the use of Romantic poets), the desire to return to nature through Wesleyan-style camp meetings or Keswick meetings in the Lake District of England, the appeal to dramatic moments of crisis and encounter, the suspicion of institutions and confessional forms of Christianity, the emphasis on the perfectibility of the human person, and the use of moralizing discourse to tame optimism about technological and scientific advance all point toward shared perspectives. This attraction to British Romanticism was fueled by a deeper connection between holiness notions of encounter and Christian mysticism.

---

[92] George Marsden, *Understanding Fundamentalism and Evangelicalism* (Grand Rapids: Eerdmans, 1991).

[93] See the final chapter in Marden's *Fundamentalism and American Culture*, 231–53.

[94] Marsden, *Fundamentalism and American Culture*, 153–64.

[95] Timothy L. Smith, *Revivalism and Social Reform in Mid-Nineteenth-Century America* (Nashville: Abingdon, 1957), 141–43, 159–61; Melvin Dieter, *The Holiness Revival of the Nineteenth Century* (Metuchen: Scarecrow, 1980), 5; David Bebbington, *Evangelicalism in Modern Britain: A History from the 1730s to the 1980s* (London: Unwin Hyman, 1989), 167–68; David Bebbington, *Holiness in Nineteenth Century England* (Carlisle: Paternoster, 2000), 73–90; David Bebbington, *The Dominance of Evangelicalism: The Age of Spurgeon and Moody*, A History of Evangelicalism 3 (Downers Grove: IVP, 2005), 148–83; William K. Kay, "Modernity and the Arrival of Pentecostalism in Britain," *PentecoStudies* 10.1 (2011): 63–71.

Patricia Ward has demonstrated just how deep the vein of mysticism runs among holiness circles.[96] The primary channels were John Wesley's *Christian Library*, Thomas Upham's (1799–1872) theology and biographies of Madame Guyon and Catherine of Genoa, and the English translations of mystical writers made during the nineteenth century. As E. E. Shelhamer, a Free Methodist elder, counseled early Pentecostals in a sermon at Stone Church in Chicago, "Have you ever read Upham's interior life [*sic*]? Anything he wrote is worth reading."[97] The regular conferences and speakers at the Stone Church in Chicago played a crucial role in the dissemination of the early pentecostal message. The radical holiness preacher turned pentecostal Benjamin H. Irwin appealed to Madame Guyon's metaphorical use of fire in his description of a baptism of fire beyond initial conversion and entire sanctification.[98] Methodist, holiness, and pentecostal writers fused Catholic mystics and Protestant Pietists like Johann Arndt with ideas from Romanticism as part of describing their own spiritual experiences.

Fusing mystical writers with Wesleyan emphases, holiness and pentecostal thinkers understood "works of grace" subsequent to conversion in terms of operations of the Spirit that facilitated mystical union, ecstatic embrace, and contemplative vision. One can see this particularly in the way bridal mysticism infused language around baptism in the Spirit. Early Pentecostals resonated with the founder of the Church of God in Christ, Charles H. Mason's description of the ecstatic utterances accompanying his experience of baptism in the Spirit as "the wedlock with Christ."[99] William J. Seymour interpreted baptism in the Spirit through this prism when he stated, "We are married to Christ now in the Spirit. Not only when he comes are we married to Christ but right now, if you are sanctified and baptized with the Holy Ghost and fire, you are married to Him already."[100] Both were led to the language of bridal union in part because it fused together an eschatology of divine presence with a theology of encounter. The future had broken into the present in the form of bridal union, and tongues was the sign of such an in-breaking.

As part of his preaching tour throughout the Southeast, the evangelist G. B. Cashwell told readers, "When you receive your Pentecost, you will see that it is the Lover you receive."[101] Tongues were the inevitable ecstatic expression of being caught up by the Spirit

---

[96] Patricia Ward, *Experimental Theology in America: Madame Guyon, Fénelon, and Their Readers* (Waco: Baylor University Press, 2009).

[97] E. E. Shelhamer, "Three False Standards of Deep Spirituality," *Latter Rain Evangel* 11 (August 1915): 21. Upham's writings (especially his *Life of Madam Guyon*) are advertised or recommended in early pentecostal periodicals. He is also quoted in discussions of sanctification and faith. See Thomas C. Upham, "Appropriating Faith," *Apostolic Evangel* (June 15, 1914): 6–7, 15; *Pentecostal Evangel* 364–65 (October 30, 1920): 9; *Pentecostal Evangel* 400–401 (July 9, 1921): 13.

[98] On Irwin and his experiences, see Dale M. Coulter, "Founding Vision or Visions? The Sources of Early Church of God Ecclesiology," *Cyberjournal for Pentecostal-Charismatic Research* 21 (January 2012), http://www.pctii.org/cyberj/cyberj21/Coulter.html#_ednref27; see also Vinson Synan and Daniel Woods, *Fire Baptized: The Many Lives and Works of Benjamin Hardin Irwin: A Biography and a Reader* (Lexington: Emeth, 2017).

[99] Charles H. Mason, "Tennessee Evangelist Witnesses," *Apostolic Faith* 1.6 (1907): 7.

[100] W. J. Seymour, "The Holy Ghost and the Bride," *Apostolic Faith* 2.13 (1908): 4.4.

[101] "G. B. Cashwell's Letter," *Holiness Advocate* 7.4 (June 1, 1907): 5. On Cashwell, see Doug Beacham, *Azusa East: The Life and Times of G. B. Cashwell* (Franklin Springs: LifeSprings, 2006); Michael Thornton, *Fire in the Carolinas: The Revival Legacy of G. B. Cashwell and A. B. Crumpler* (Lake Mary: Creation House, 2014).

into the arms of the bridegroom. They were not foreign languages so much as the sign of ecstatic union. George Floyd Taylor, the first head of what would become Emmanuel College in the Pentecostal Holiness Church, developed Seymour and Cashwell's approach into his work on the Christian life as a journey through the Spirit's operations into full marital union with Christ.[102] To claim that baptism in the Spirit was a "work" of grace was to follow John Wesley in saying that grace was simply the Spirit's operations in the life of the Christian to deepen union with Christ through ecstatic encounter.[103]

The theology of bridal mysticism developed by radical holiness and pentecostal writers also involved the unfolding of a cosmopolitan vision of life. As part of his experience of Spirit baptism in 1907, A. J. Tomlinson had a vision in which the entire world came before his mind. His thoughts rapidly moved first to Central America, then South America, Africa, Asia, Russia, and Canada before returning to Cleveland, Tennessee.[104] Tomlinson also heard the people's cries for help and battled demonic forces, all while speaking in tongues. At the conclusion of the vision, he became convinced of the need for a global mission. Like Henry James' portrait of the artist, Tomlinson's vision was a kind of cosmopolitanism, made possible by the immediate association of global images and his experience of love, which, in turn, induced him to form sympathies for diverse peoples and cultures. One can see in Tomlinson's testimony the fusion of ecstatic embrace, mission, and eschatology as his vision of the diverse peoples formed a call and pointed toward the final kingdom that Christ would usher in. The sensitivity to the other birthed from this experience would be affirmed by many in the holiness and pentecostal movements.

What Pentecostals inherited in the early twentieth century was a Wesleyanism infused with insights from the Christian mystical tradition. From this fusion came the idea that love grew in the soul by ecstatic encounters with the Spirit. In short, the Christian life unfolded through a dialectic between crisis encounters and a maturation process. The mystical stream merely interpreted those encounters through the charismatic-infused language of ecstasy. Love matured and blossomed through ecstatic embrace with the bridegroom in the power of the Spirit.

Ecstatic speech became the sign for this encounter in part because of Wesley's insistence that there was a direct and immediate witness of the Spirit to the human spirit that the person was indeed a child of God. As Kenneth Collins and Randy Maddox point out, this doctrine of assurance underwent modifications in Wesley's theology as Wesley began to think in terms of degrees of assurance.[105] Corresponding to distinct moments of encounter, these degrees attested to the Spirit's direct witness to the event of the new birth and of entire sanctification, which gave the individual assurance the operation of grace was complete.

---

[102] George Floyd Taylor, *The Spirit and the Bride: A Scriptural Presentation of the Operations, Manifestation, Gifts and Fruit* (Philadelphia: Winston, 1908).

[103] See Dale M. Coulter, "The Spirit and the Bride Revisited: Pentecostalism, Renewal, and the Sense of History," *Journal of Pentecostal Theology* 21.2 (2012): 298–319.

[104] R. G. Robins, *A. J. Tomlinson: Plainfolk Modernist* (New York: Oxford University Press, 2004), 186.

[105] See Randy Maddox, *Responsible Grace: John Wesley's Practical Theology* (Nashville: Kingswood Books, 1994), 124–27; Kenneth J. Collins, *The Theology of John Wesley: Holy Love and the Shape of Grace* (Nashville: Abingdon, 2007), 129–42.

Over the course of the nineteenth century, Wesleyans described the witness of the Spirit to each work in terms of signs accompanying the encounter. These signs were both internal and external. Internal signs were the result of love's knowledge, an intuitive relational awareness that one was a child of God or that charity had increased to a level of maturation such that it governed other interior movements. External signs usually corresponded to physical manifestations like dancing, shouting, or even falling down under the power of God. The implicit idea was a correspondence between the distinctive operation of the Spirit, the ecstatic moment of encounter, and the witness of the Spirit to that encounter internally and externally. Pentecostals saw tongues as the external counter to the internal and intuitive insight they derived from the spiritual experience of an immersion into the bridegroom's loving embrace.

The appeal of mystical writers also aligned with the use of biography to engage in theology and chart the movement toward union with God. As Phoebe Palmer advised in the preface to her collection of testimonies about holiness, "you cannot illustrate Scriptural truth more instructively or more inspiringly than by your *personal* realizations" (author's emphasis).[106] In the spiritual traditions of Christianity, theology primarily concerned spiritual cartography, a fusion of one's own spiritual encounters with scriptural narratives and doctrines to map out the interior life and its path to perfection. Holiness and pentecostal writers participated in the "culture of biography" that permeated the nineteenth century, especially as a popular form of literature, choosing to access Christian tradition through an exegesis of the lives of the "saints" rather than its confessional or dogmatic dimensions.[107]

Biography created theological space for Higher Life advocates to fuse the spiritual experiences of Reformed thinkers like Jonathan Edwards, David Brainerd, and James Brainerd Taylor with mystical and Wesleyan streams, the prime example of which is William Boardman's *Higher Christian Life*.[108] Later pentecostal scholars have noted the crucial role that narrative has played in early pentecostal communities in the form of story, testimony, and biography.[109] The proliferation of testimony in holiness and pentecostal literature, coupled with numerous autobiographies like Amanda Berry Smith's, created a theological method that combined revivalist literature, the popularity of biography, and exploration of the interior life by spiritual writers.[110] Spiritual cartography fused the lives of the "saints" and a symbolic interpretation of the biblical narrative to plot out the crisis-process movement into deeper union.

While the influence of mysticism was generally positive, the connection poised challenges in relation to learning for those who did not understand its philosophical

---

[106] Phoebe Palmer, ed., *Pioneer Experiences; Or, The Gift of Power Received by Faith* (New York: W. C. Palmer, 1868), vii.

[107] On the significance of biography in the nineteenth century, see Scott E. Casper, *Constructing American Lives: Biography and Culture in Nineteenth-Century America* (Chapel Hill: University of North Carolina Press, 1999).

[108] William Boardman, *The Higher Christian Life* (Boston: Henry Hoyt, 1858). Boardman provides twenty-five biographical sketches in this volume, beginning with Martin Luther.

[109] See Land, *Pentecostal Spirituality*, 71–95; Kenneth J. Archer, *A Pentecostal Hermeneutic for the Twenty-First Century: Spirit, Scripture, and Community* (London: T&T Clark, 2004), 94–126.

[110] Amanda Berry Smith, *An Autobiography* (Chicago: Meyer and Brother, 1893). As an example of revivalist literature, see Jonathan Edwards' *Life of David Brainerd*, The Works of Jonathan Edwards, vol. 7, ed. Norman Pettit (New Haven: Yale University Press, 1985).

antecedents. In particular, quietism sharpened a distinction between meditation and contemplation that entered Western Christianity fully through Hugh and Richard of St. Victor in the twelfth century. As we saw in chapter 2, the Victorines understood meditation as focused thinking and ruminating on a subject, which prepared the soul for the contemplative flight of ecstasy. This division went back to the early Christian division between meditation as a spiritual exercise and *theoria* as the contemplative fruit of this *askesis*. French and Spanish Quietist writers exploited this distinction by seeing meditation as discursive reasoning and passive or infused contemplation as a nondiscursive mode of intuitive insight in which the mind becomes affectively aware of the other.[111] Thomas Upham channeled this distinction through his biography of Guyon, which included aphorisms from Fénelon.

Early Pentecostals utilized the language of tarrying and yielding all up to God as the way to describe the process of abandonment Quietists envisioned. In the words of one pentecostal, the final step to receiving baptism in the Spirit means that "we are to yield, to let go, to cease, to step aside, to stop trying."[112] Tarrying in verbal prayer and yielding of the entire self gave way to the Spirit's outpouring of love and glory. Rather than adopting wholesale the language of quietism, early Pentecostals received it as mediated through the holiness movement because it reinforced the language of bridal mysticism and ecstatic union. The privileging of baptism in the Spirit as a passive state akin to infused contemplation opened the door to an antirationalism while also advancing a view of knowledge as a participatory and intuitive event made possible through an expansion of the mind. The division between discursive and intuitive modes of knowing opened up a chasm that pentecostal and holiness believers sought to overcome by wedding Spirit baptism to mission through progressive populism.

4.2.3 Progressive Populism, the Spirit, and Transforming Folk Culture

Pluralism presented a challenge for everyone in North America, particularly on the frontier, where the clash between different versions of Protestantism and the growth of Catholicism required a response. The holiness movement attempted to answer pluralism by cultivating a theology of holiness and its relationship to personal and social transformation. In other words, institutional divisions were overcome by returning to a common spirituality grounded in the pursuit of sanctity of life. Whereas prominent Baptists like J. R. Graves (1820–1893), J. M. Pendleton (1811–1891), and A. C. Dayton (1811–1865) were advocating separatism and sectarianism as the best ways to preserve Baptist identity in the face of pluralism, holiness writers began advocating the common pursuit of a higher life as a means of overcoming Protestant divides. Developing a strict ecclesiology that maintained Baptist distinctives, Landmark Baptist writers reflected a creedal reentrenchment by Presbyterians, Lutherans, and Episcopalians in the face of denominational competition, especially in the

---

[111] John Wesley, *A Christian Library*, vol. 27; Thomas P. Upham, *Life, Religious Opinions, and Experiences of Madame Guyon* (London: Allenson, 1905), 389–401; James W. Metcalf, ed., *Spiritual Progress, or Instructions in the Divine Life of the Soul from the French of Fénelon and Madame Guyon* (New York: M. W. Dodd, 1853), 52, 232–39, 255; Miguel de Molinos, *The Spiritual Guide*, ed. and trans. Robert P. Baird, Classics of Western Spirituality (Mahwah: Paulist, 2010), 55–62.
[112] "The Way to Your 'Pentecost,'" *Confidence* 5 (August 15, 1908): 23–24.

South and Midwest.[113] Among Presbyterians, Princeton Seminary served as the rallying point for an aggressive adherence to the Westminster confessions, defending this position against the Mercersburg theology of John W. Nevin, Philip Schaff, and New School Presbyterianism. Princeton Seminary was at the vanguard of what Grant Wacker has described as an orthodox rationalism with its commitment to Baconian evidentialism and more ahistorical approach to Scripture as a "storehouse of facts."[114]

While the holiness and pentecostal movements were advancing their own version of social transformation, their doctrinal commitments gave them the resources to interpret nineteenth-century political upheavals and maintain a commitment to bringing the kingdom of God on earth through social holiness. As participants in the Romantic sensibility, they grounded social transformation in a strong view of divine immanence in light of their pneumatology and a doctrine of divine healing. Miracles such as bodily healing were viewed as signs of the restoration of the proper order within the natural world rather than its chaotic disruption.[115] In this sense, they pointed toward a deeper harmony between the uncreated and the created within nature, akin to the way the rhythms of the seasons attested to the well-being of the natural world. This resulted from the Spirit's presence as "that invisible divine energy which everywhere acts potentially in nature."[116] When this was coupled with Wesley's doctrine of prevenient grace, many holiness and pentecostal thinkers became comfortable with the idea that the Spirit was at work in all human beings regardless of their cultural or religious location.[117] While such a perspective probed the boundaries between a universal call and universal salvation, it rarely crossed the line because of their eschatological commitments.

Part of the logic of premillennialism in the social imaginary of the pentecostal and holiness movements was its reinforcing the divine side of consummation in the process of perfection. Premillennialism provided theological resistance to the cultural temptation of a secularized version of the kingdom of God, as was happening among the emerging liberal Protestant assimilation with its postmillennialism and propagation of the vision of a liberal culture. Among the "benefits" of holding to premillennialism, Martin Wells Knapp claimed that it secured the idea that any golden age for humanity is a result of divine intervention rather than human achievement and the pessimism that follows when individuals reduce the millennium to human processes, which are slow and subject to failure.[118]

---

[113] Stephen Stookey, "Baptists and Landmarkism and the Turn toward Provincialism: 1851," in *Turning Points in Baptist History: A Festschrift in Honor of Harry Leon McBeth*, ed. Michael E. Williams Sr. and Walter B. Shurden (Macon: Mercer University Press, 2008), 178–93.

[114] The quotation is from Charles Hodge's *Systematic Theology* (1872). See Grant Wacker, *Augustus H. Strong and the Dilemma of Historical Consciousness* (Waco: Baylor University Press, 2018), 1–42.

[115] A. J. Gordon, *The Ministry of Healing, Or, Miracles of Cure in All Ages* (Boston: Howard Gannett, 1883), 41–45.

[116] Asa Mahan, *Out of Darkness into Light; Or, The Hidden Life Made Manifest* (London: Wesleyan Conference Office, 1875), 164.

[117] As one example, see Tony Richie, "Azusa-Era Optimism: Bishop J. H. King's Pentecostal Theology of Religions as a Possible Paradigm for Today," in *The Spirit in the World: Emerging Pentecostal Theologies in Global Contexts*, ed. Veli-Matti Kärkkäinen (Grand Rapids: Eerdmans, 2009), 227–44.

[118] Martin Wells Knapp, *Lightning Bolts from Pentecostal Skies* (Cincinnati: Office of the Revivalist, Full Salvation Quarterly, and Pentecostal Holiness Library, 1898), 154–59.

Among these Wesleyan holiness writers, premillennialism reinforced an optimism about the work of God in the world because it meant that every encounter pointed toward the final encounter in which God would wipe away all tears. As the historical complement of a personal Spirit baptism, premillennialism became an interlocking eschatology that maintained a doctrine of divine in-breaking to bring about the consummation of the kingdom. While not all embraced premillennialism, those who did utilized it to maintain a tension between divine transcendence and immanence.

The early pentecostal emphasis on Jesus as coming king heightened Pentecostalism's movement into mission. The doctrine of baptism in the Spirit meant that having been caught up in love, believers now moved out in love for the other. Bridal mysticism became the means to link preparation for the coming of the bridegroom with its proleptic realization in ecstatic union that propelled mission. Such a fusion drove the early pentecostal quest for racial reconciliation as a manifestation of the love experienced in baptism in the Spirit. Before William Seymour encountered Charles Parham in Houston, he lived in Cincinnati, where he most likely attended the integrated meetings and classes Martin Wells Knapp held at Revivalist Chapel.[119] From his exposure to Knapp's ministry and his time in the Evening Light Saints, Seymour drank deeply from the radical holiness vision that the perfect love of entire sanctification would lead to racial integration. In light of this vision, he modified Parham's understanding of baptism in the Spirit so that the mission also involved the creation of a radical egalitarian community. This was social holiness in action.

When the Azusa Street revival broke out at the home of African Americans in March 1906, it quickly morphed into an integrated holiness revival atmosphere. After the fledgling group purchased the former African Methodist Episcopal Church, the integrated atmosphere of the revival spilled over, with Asians, Europeans, Africans, and Latinos praying and laying hands on one another. Seymour appointed men and women of different ethnic groups to lead, including the local leader of the Women's Christian Temperance Union, Florence Crawford.[120] This vision of a racially integrated community formed the heart of Christian mission for Seymour, and it flowed from his understanding that love was the primary effect of baptism in the Spirit.

Despite the efforts of Seymour and others to maintain a racially integrated community, the reality of Jim Crow raised its head in the figure of Charles Parham, who saw Azusa as ungodly because of the race mixing. A segregationist who had worked with the KKK, Parham could not abide Black men holding up white women who were praying. Still, the vision of racial integration became part of early Pentecostalism, with Pentecostals attempting some variety of racial mixing either in tent meetings or in local congregations. For example, in Memphis Charles H. Mason sought to make the Church of God in Christ integrated. He partnered with Leonard Adams in 1910 and held integrated meetings, with

---

[119] There is a strong oral tradition connecting Seymour to the school. See Cecil M. Robeck Jr., *The Azusa Street Mission and Revival: The Birth of the Global Pentecostal Movement* (Nashville: Nelson, 2006), 31–35; Vinson Synan and Charles Fox Jr., *William J. Seymour: Pioneer of the Azusa Street Revival* (Alachua: Bridge-Logos, 2012), 37–40; Wallace Thornton Jr., *When the Fire Fell: Martin Wells Knapp's Vision of Pentecost and the Beginnings of God's Bible School* (Lexington: Emeth, 2014), 145–46.

[120] Margaret English de Alminana, "Florence Crawford and Egalitarian Precedents in Early Pentecostalism," in *Women in Pentecostal and Charismatic Ministry: Informing a Dialogue on Gender, Church, and Ministry*, ed. Margaret English de Alminana and Lois E. Olena, Global Pentecostal and Charismatic Studies 21 (Leiden: Brill, 2016), 103–4.

A. J. Tomlinson attending at least one such meeting. Maria Woodworth-Etter attempted to integrate her tent meetings with marginal success, but eventually planted and led a multiracial congregation in Indianapolis alongside of another multiracial congregation pastored by G. T. Haywood.

None of this means that early Pentecostals escaped Jim Crow. There are plenty of examples of levels of segregation that remained within the early movement. By the end of the 1930s most pentecostal denominations were segregated along race lines or had segregated conferences and congregations. Nevertheless, the inclusion of racial integration into mission was so thoroughly part of the pentecostal vision that in the 1950s Oral Roberts and other healing evangelists integrated meetings as a recovery of that vision.

Another way Pentecostals sought to transform society was through music. Between 1910 and 1930, Pentecostals contributed to the formation of blues, jazz, and Black gospel, which is why the novelist and folklorist Zora Neale Hurston described the Sanctified Church as "a revitalizing element in Negro music and religion."[121] Pentecostal musicians like the blues guitarist Blind Willie Johnson or the pianist Arizona Dranes, who played boogie-woogie or barrelhouse, recorded their songs between 1926 and 1930.[122] Dranes influenced Sister Rosetta Tharpe, who came out of Roberts Temple Church of God in Christ in Chicago and moved to Harlem in the 1930s, where she sang in church on Sunday and at the Cotton Club during the week.[123] Dranes also influenced a young pentecostal pianist named Jerry Lee Lewis. Lewis fused barrelhouse and blues to develop a new style called rockabilly. Roberts Temple Church of God in Christ became one of the important Chicago pentecostal churches in the 1920s, helping to facilitate these new musical forms by allowing tambourines, drums, and horns into the sanctuary. Roberts Temple was one of twenty "sanctified churches" in Chicago by 1920.[124] Langston Hughes would later recall visiting holiness and pentecostal churches in Chicago as a teenager in the summer of 1918, stating that "I was entranced by their stepped-up rhythms, tambourines, hand clapping, and uninhibited dynamics, rivaled only by Ma Rainey singing the blues at the old Monogram Theater. . . . The music of these less formal Negro churches early took hold of me, moved me and thrilled me."[125]

While Pentecostals were impacting blues and jazz in the Mississippi Delta, Midwest, and Northeast, they were also contributing to southern gospel in Appalachia and Mexican and Latino *coritos* in the Southwest. Daniel Ramírez has demonstrated how Latino Pentecostals in the 1920s and 1930s were reshaping popular Mexican musical idioms as they wrote their hymns. He states, "In contrast to historic Protestantism's disdainful

---

[121] Zora Neale Hurston, *The Sanctified Church* (Berkeley: Turtle Island, 1981), 105.

[122] See Alan B. Govenar and Jay F. Brakefield, *Deep Ellum: The Other Side of Dallas* (1998; repr., College Station: Texas A&M University Press, 2013); Timothy Dodge, *The School of Arizona Dranes: Gospel Music Pioneer* (Lanham: Lexington, 2013).

[123] Gayle F. Wald, *Shout, Sister, Shout: The Untold Story of Rock-and-Rock Trailblazer Sister Rosetta Tharpe* (Boston: Beacon, 2007), 18–19.

[124] Brian Dolinar, *The Negro in Illinois: The WPA Papers* (Urbana: University of Illinois Press, 2013), 210–11.

[125] Langston Hughes, "Gospel Singing: When the Spirit Really Moves," *New York Herald-Tribune* 27 (October 27, 1963): 12–13; first quoted by Lawrence W. Levine, *Black Culture and Black Consciousness: Afro-American Folk Thought from Slavery to Freedom* (New York: Oxford University Press, 1977), 180.

distancing, Pentecostal hymnody redeemed the fiesta of Mexican and Latino culture."[126] Latino pentecostal worship infused folk culture by recreating the atmosphere of the fiesta in the context of the church in the same way that African American Pentecostals brought the blues of the juke joint into the church house. The same could be said for Appalachian folk culture. In his history of southern gospel, James Goff notes that Pentecostals "were most receptive to the music of the masses and saw little difficulty in combining the sounds of popular music with gospel lyrics," which meant Pentecostals were part of southern gospel quartets from 1910.[127] The influence of southern gospel singing became so strong that the Church of God (Cleveland, Tenn.) started Tennessee Music and Printing (1931) with a former employee of James Vaughan, the pioneer of the industry, at the helm. Vaughan had been attending a Church of the Nazarene congregation since the mid-1920s, which brought in many members of the holiness churches.[128]

Early Pentecostals were transforming folk cultures through a kind of progressive populism. With many early pentecostal women connected to the Woman's Christian Temperance Union, they supported women's rights and temperance. Following their holiness predecessors, Pentecostals saw men and women as equal partners in the proclamation of the gospel. Through their connections to the WCTU, pentecostal women like Florence Crawford participated in first-wave feminism, no doubt because as president in the 1880s, Frances Willard had bathed the movement in the hue of Pentecost with the help of holiness theologians like A. M. Hill, who described the crusade as coming "with the suddenness and the power of Pentecost."[129] Early Pentecostals also resisted Wilsonian progressivism through promoting pacifism in and through their communities in response to the First World War. During the draft, many American Pentecostals registered as conscientious objectors with the support of fledgling denominational leaders.[130] These efforts to live out their beliefs focused them on working-class people and transforming relations at that level.

Holiness and pentecostal leaders assimilated the emphases of the Romantic sensibility through the lens of populism. Their own emphasis on the Spirit's presence within the natural world fed a social program that combined personal and cultural transformation. On this point, however, an important distinction emerged. For Wesleyan holiness adherents, social justice meant spreading scriptural holiness throughout the land, whereas early Pentecostals fused the social dimension of Christianity with apostolicity. To be apostolic meant to receive the Spirit of Pentecost and recreate the mission-driven existence of the church in Acts. Behind such theological distinctions remained an emphasis on rational

---

[126] Daniel Ramírez, *Migrating Faith: Pentecostalism in the United States and Mexico in the Twentieth Century* (Chapel Hill: University of North Carolina Press, 2015), 178. See also Gastón Espinosa, *Latino Pentecostals in America: Faith and Politics in Action* (Cambridge, Mass.: Harvard University Press, 2014), 105–8.

[127] James R. Goff Jr., *Close Harmony: A History of Southern Gospel* (Chapel Hill: University of North Carolina Press, 2002), 162.

[128] Goff, *Close Harmony*, 157–66.

[129] See A. M. Hill, "Mrs. Mary A. Woodbridge," as quoted in Dale M. Coulter, "Recovering the Wesleyan Vision of Pentecostalism: 5 Theses: SPS Presidential Address 2018," *Pneuma: The Journal of the Society for Pentecostal Studies* 40.4 (2018): 478–79. See also Ian Tyrrell, *Woman's World, Woman's Empire: The Woman's Christian Temperance Union in International Perspective, 1880–1930* (Chapel Hill: University of North Carolina Press, 1991).

[130] Jay Beaman, *Pentecostal Pacifism: The Origin, Development, and Rejection of Pacific Belief among the Pentecostals* (repr.; Eugene: Wipf and Stock, 1989).

intuition and a cognitive view of the emotions that underscored an approach to knowledge as participatory and nondiscursive. This was coupled with a notion of theology as biography and a commitment to the spiritual traditions of Christianity rather than its confessional streams. The kind of culture they generated was not the liberal culture of a Tappan or a Norton, but a renewed folk culture through progressive populism.

4.3   PENTECOSTALISM AND EDUCATING FOR MISSION

Pentecostalism emerged in the first decade of the twentieth century as a distinctive form of Christianity from the radical holiness movement of the late nineteenth century. It utilized the transnational links that global holiness had cultivated through the travel and migratory patterns that the British Empire made possible. With the newer historiography stemming from Allan Anderson's work, we hold that there were multiple centers of revival in various parts of the world that contributed to the movement.[131] At the same time, Cecil Robeck's and Gaston Espinosa's claims for the primacy of the Azusa Street Mission in this global context carry weight because of the important role of Azusa as a crossroads for many early Pentecostals.[132] For this reason, it is best to think of the origins of Pentecostalism in terms of a global network of micro-Pentecostalisms that took root in Wesleyan soil and coalesced around a hub. The Azusa Street Mission was the major hub of early Pentecostalism while also being part of a larger network in which regional expressions of the movement sprang up and intersected with it. We describe the global pentecostal movement in three ways: (1) a missionary movement with a variety of institutional expressions; (2) a nonconformist tradition that privileges charismatic experience over establishment Christianity; (3) a spiritual tradition that seeks to renew existing structures rather than a confessional tradition.[133]

First, global Pentecostalism is a missionary movement with multiple institutional expressions that exist within a single historical phenomenon. During its first twenty years, early Pentecostalism gave rise to new denominations (Assemblies of God), networks like ministerial associations (Apostolic Faith), independent congregations (Stone Church), and transformed existing denominations, some of which self-identified with the movement (Church of God, Cleveland) and others of which did not (Christian Missionary and Alliance). Yet these distinct institutional expressions all remained part of a developing and highly flexible movement that prioritized mission. Persons in one institutional expression might leave and go to another expression or groups of networks might form a new denomination. Moreover, the journey of Pentecostalism into mainline Protestant

---

[131] See Allan Anderson, *An Introduction to Pentecostalism: Global Charismatic Christianity*, 2nd ed. (Cambridge: Cambridge University Press, 2014), 157; Allan Anderson, *To the Ends of the Earth: Pentecostalism and the Transformation of World Christianity* (New York: Oxford University Press, 2013), 4–10.

[132] Gastón Espinosa, *William J. Seymour and the Origins of Global Pentecostalism: A Biography and Documentary History* (Durham, N.C.: Duke University Press, 2014), 1–37; Cecil M. Robeck Jr., "The Origins of Modern Pentecostalism: Some Historiographical Issues," in *The Cambridge Companion to Pentecostalism*, ed. Cecil M. Robeck Jr. and Amos Yong (New York: Cambridge University Press, 2014), 13–30.

[133] This is to wed our phenomenological and historical approaches; see Amos Yong, *The Spirit Poured Out on All Flesh: Pentecostalism and the Possibility of Global Theology* (Grand Rapids: Baker Academic, 2005), 17–80; and compare Dale M. Coulter, "SPS Presidential Address 2018," 457–88; idem, "By Faith Alone: Pentecostals, Wesley, and the Reformation," *Journal of the European Pentecostal Theological Association* 37.2 (2017): 123–24; idem, "Spirit and the Bride Revisited."

and Catholic Christianity in the 1960s was another manifestation of what had happened when Pentecostalism entered Sunderland and the Anglican vicar Alexander Boddy embraced it. Boddy never ceased to be Anglican even though Sunderland became an important early center. The three institutional expressions of denominations, networks, and independent congregations allowed the emphasis on mission through Spirit baptism to continue to spread.

Second, Pentecostalism is a nonconformist tradition that resists establishment Christianity in favor of the charismatic experience of the people. For this reason, it inhabits folk cultures and seeks to transform them from within rather than impose reform from above. Pentecostalism also harbors a deep suspicion of institutionalization and formalism in religion. Third, global Pentecostalism is a spiritual tradition akin to mystical or pietistic streams rather than a confessional tradition in the Reformation sense. As a spiritual tradition, Pentecostalism is a form of renewal that seeks to recover and reignite older forms of Christianity. To be sure, there is a confessional core to Pentecostalism, but, like the *regula fidei* of the second century, that core functions in a narrative framework that tells a story about God and God's people. As one of us has stated elsewhere, pentecostal theology is confessionally located in that it emerges from the "matrix of the pentecostal experience of the Spirit of God."[134] In this respect, Pentecostalism is a form of Christian mysticism.[135] For this reason, it can morph into a number of different expressions of Christianity without disrupting the confessional core within other traditions.

The first two sections of this chapter tried to explain important elements of pentecostal spirituality in terms of what Pentecostals inherited from the radical holiness movement and the social imaginary of the Romantic sensibility. To do so, it was necessary to chart a new historiographical course away from evangelicalism by situating Pentecostalism in its proper historical context and by showing the presuppositions behind Noll's claims about an evangelical mind. This final section seeks to unpack more precisely what a pentecostal approach to education might look like by using the metaphors of mind, heart, and hands. We argue that rational intuitionism is key to understanding the pentecostal mind (§4.3.1), that populism and the transformation of folk cultures inform pentecostal hands (§4.3.2), and that the role of the affections in holiness and moral formation unlock the pentecostal heart (§4.3.3).

4.3.1 Spirit-Enlightened Minds: Antirationalism and Intuition

The broader context of the nineteenth century helps to situate the approach to learning and education within the holiness and pentecostal movements. As we argued in the previous chapter, educational models were constructed in light of a number of factors: (1) the focus on progressive development through a theology of immanence that tended to collapse the distinction between God and nature and removed encounter from the educational process; (2) the tension between the "utilitarian" and "liberal arts" approaches to education; (3) the bifurcation between a democratized populism that viewed the Spirit as gifting and empowering all and a cultural elitism that viewed the divinely empowered

---

[134] Yong, *Spirit Poured Out on All Flesh*, 29.
[135] See Daniel Castello, *Pentecostalism as a Christian Mystical Tradition* (Grand Rapids: Eerdmans, 2017).

heroic figure as charting the steps forward in history; (4) the correlation of evolution and social issues; (5) the tensions between colonialism and mission surrounding issues of women's rights and ongoing emancipation for African Americans. While all of these issues cannot be addressed in the space remaining, they set the stage for the holiness and pentecostal assault on certain models of higher education more so than the doctrinal divisions of the fundamentalist-modernist controversy.

The ethos of holiness and Pentecostalism flowed from the Romantic sensibility insofar as it embraced a rational intuitionism that separated discursive from nondiscursive modes of mental activity. Antirationalism, on this view, is simply a shorthand way of identifying a mode of intellectual activity outside of Baconian evidentialism. This did not mean a complete disavowal of Baconian methods, but it did situate such approaches within a broader context in which symbolic modes of interpretation and intuitive visions of God, the self, and the world were the order of the day.

First, the antirationalism prevalent in these movements translated into a critique of any view of education that separated encounters with transcendence from a participatory understanding of knowledge. Many pentecostal and holiness thinkers wished to preserve the intuitive insights generated from the experiential encounters of sanctification and Spirit baptism within the educational process and formation of the human person. Intuitive knowledge concerned the flash of revelatory insight that stemmed from the collision of ideas in the mind. William Piper, the pastor of Stone Church, spoke for many Pentecostals when he told his congregation, "About a year ago one Sunday afternoon, standing on the platform of this church, God gave me one of those intuitive flashes of knowledge and inspiration in which one learns more in ten seconds than he could learn by ordinary study in a year."[136] Piper made this statement a few months after D. Wesley Myland had opened a convention in June of 1909 by focusing on "and we know" from Romans 8:28.

For Myland, you only *know* that all things work for good "when you strike the line of both intuitive and experimental knowledge."[137] Myland went on to define intuitive knowledge as what the Spirit flashes into the soul, which must then be worked out experientially. In a brief compass, Myland put together for his audience how pentecostal interpretation functioned in relation to study. It all centered on the intuitive flash of revelatory insight, which then had to be teased out in lived experience and study. This point was the subterranean impulse behind statements about the Holy Spirit as the teacher and the Bible as the textbook.

For early Pentecostals, intuitive knowledge and encounters with transcendence could not be severed. Central to this intuitionism was a cognitive view of the emotions in which an affective movement conveyed knowledge as part of one's immediate perception. The affections supplied the bond between various ideas in the mind and the associations that comprised the simple intuitive act. A. J. Tomlinson proclaimed, "In your spirit, in your heart, far beyond all physical knowledge, far beyond all mental knowledge, you know by spiritual intuition. You know you are one and not two. . . . You are conscious of spiritual

---

[136] William Hammer Piper, "The Lord Reigneth! He Is Clothed With Majesty," *Latter Rain Evangel* 2.3 (1909): 7.

[137] D. Wesley Myland, "The Red Key: Introductory Convention Talk," *Latter Rain Evangel* 1.9 (1909): 4–5.

facts and states without education, whether you have done much thinking or not. The spirit (heart) gets its knowledge by intuition, not by reasoning powers. The witness of the Spirit is not to your reasoning faculties."[138] At the core of this insight was the affective act of wonder or awe that held together in a single vision various objects of knowledge.

One could not separate the affective movement of wonder from the insight into the truth since wonder elicited and confirmed the insight. The emotions were not mere "feelings" in the sense of physiological reactions to stimuli, as William James had asserted; they were part of the cognitive structure of the mind and thus part of the knowing process. In the language of holiness, one "feels" and "knows" that one is sanctified because the affective movements of love and joy amidst ecstatic embrace convey a relational knowledge and a kind of certainty accompanying the insight into God. Such a view did not exclude formal education as a process of perfecting the self, but it did privilege encounters as formative and consciousness raising in the educational process.

There was a continuity between an intuitive awareness of the person's identity or personal freedom, the awareness of assurance at salvation, and the awareness of deeper union in ecstasy. This continuity was set forth plainly by the Methodist theologian Olin Curtis in his *The Christian Faith*, which became a textbook in undergraduate courses for several Nazarene colleges.[139] Retiring from Drew University in 1895, Curtis focused on composing a systematic theology, which was published in 1905.[140] He saw intuitive knowledge as beginning with the Reidian awareness of personal identity, freedom, and infinity and concluding with an awareness of the Spirit's own witness to the human spirit of assurance and adoption. This awareness stems from the cognitive content of the affective movements generated by the Holy Spirit in the human spirit.[141] Knowledge was at its basis participatory and ecstatic.

It was this ethos that resided behind the early pentecostal understanding of baptism in the Spirit. The kind of cosmopolitanism these experiences generated was primarily a vision of life that flowed from ecstatic encounters with the divine. As Cheryl Bridges Johns has suggested, at its heart such a view of education promoted conscientization of the person, reflected in the ancient practice of *theoria* as a penetrating vision of the world induced by encounter.[142] Worldview was not a confession to be adopted and applied, but a unifying vision with theological emphases that unfolded in the context of transforming encounter. Theology was less a system of doctrine than a story of life teased out in terms of a way of faith.

The goal of the pursuit of perfection was similar to the advocates of high culture because ecstatic moments cultivated a sensitivity to one's environment and the other. The difference was the deep suspicion of institutions and formalism that became more

---

[138] "Advantages of the Indwelling Comforter," *Church of God Evangel* 9.41 (1918): 1.

[139] Paul M. Bassett, "The Theological Identity of the North American Holiness Movement: Its Understanding of the Nature and Role of the Bible," in Dayton and Johnston, *Variety of American Evangelicalism*, 107n95.

[140] Olin Alfred Curtis, *The Christian Faith Personally Given in a System of Doctrine* (New York: Eaton and Mains, 1905).

[141] Curtis, *Christian Faith*, 51–52, 92, 482.

[142] Cheryl Bridges Johns, *Pentecostal Formation: A Pedagogy among the Oppressed*, Journal of Pentecostal Theology Supplement Series 2 (Sheffield: Sheffield Academic, 1993), 62–110.

dominant in holiness and pentecostal circles because they drank deeply from the well of nonconformity or disestablishment Christianity. While this suspicion partly manifested as a resistance to embourgeoisement, it was also a result of a resistance to theological positions that excluded encounter from the educational process. In practice much of the time these went together. The rhetoric of dead and dry formalist religion as involving a liturgy devoid of opportunities for conscious encounters was simply applied to the sphere of educational institutions in the same manner that it had been applied to ecclesial institutions.

The focus on intuitionism did not mean that Pentecostals refrained from writing or engaging in theological discourse, but, as we noted previously, they did so through a fundamentally narrative approach. Moreover, they adopted the historical framework of dispensations from within the Wesleyan tradition as the fundamental way to understand the Old and New Testaments in relationship to one another. In this sense, they were operating within what we have called the story of God, which early Christians employed to engage in theological discourse. Historical narrative became catechetical, which was reinforced by their focus on the book of Acts.

The basic trinitarian historical framework behind narrative also meant that the work of the Spirit and the work of Christ went together. Grace was fundamentally the various operations of the Spirit at work in the person, while Christ became the pattern and purpose. Donald Dayton's historical work picked up on the way in which the phrase "full gospel" encapsulated the christological pattern of Christ as savior, sanctifier, Spirit baptizer, healer, and coming King.[143] What was lost in Dayton's scheme was the emphasis on the Spirit's multiple operations so that Christ as savior meant the Spirit's regenerating and converting grace, Christ as sanctifier and healer meant the Spirit's sanctifying operation, Christ as Spirit baptizer meant the Spirit's charismatic operation, and Christ as coming king meant the Spirit's glorifying grace.

These moves in holiness and pentecostal circles were happening at the same time that New School Presbyterians and some Methodists were following Horace Bushnell's lead in collapsing encounter into a process of growth and development. It was not that these thinkers were removing the mystical element from religion. If anything, mysticism was on the rise through its recovery by persons like Evelyn Underhill.[144] Instead, they wanted to minimize what they viewed as emotionalism in relation to religious encounters. It was a form of embourgeoisement.

At Boston University Borden Parker Bowne worked in the tradition of German idealism, calling his own version personalism. Part of his goal was to defend Christianity by asserting the presence of the divine in nature. His work *The Immanence of God* illustrates Bowne's apologetical strategy by setting forth an agenda to refute deism and "mechanical philosophy."[145] At the same time, he became deeply suspicious of the encounter-driven nature of Methodist experience, placing the emphasis instead on the moral content that flowed from experience. The slow process of transformation through Christian nurture

---

[143] Donald Dayton, *Theological Roots of Pentecostalism* (Peabody: Hendrickson, 1987).

[144] Underhill published her first significant work on mysticism in 1911. See her *Mysticism: A Study in the Nature and Development of Spiritual Consciousness* (New York: Dover, 2002).

[145] Borden Parker Bowne, *The Immanence of God* (New York: Houghton and Mifflin, 1905), preface.

had eclipsed any moment of crisis to the point that, according to Bowne's biographer, William James referred to him as a rationalist and claimed that he was more of a Methodist than Bowne.[146]

One can detect two strains of Methodism in Bowne and the holiness leader Henry Clay Morrison, both of whom see God actively at work in the world through natural processes, but who diverge in their understanding of the relationship between crisis and process with respect to the cultivation of holiness.[147] Given the trend by persons in higher education to devalue encounter in favor of historical and personal development through processes, holiness and pentecostal adherents rejected their views on education as another form of ritualism. As we have argued, this form of "anti-intellectualism" was really an anticonversionism because it resisted efforts to define conversion in a way that reduced encounter to intellectual enlightenment and faith as notional assent as part of a natural process of maturation.

Many early pentecostal educational institutions faced a challenge of how to maintain the connection between encounters with transcendence and the process of education. Instinctively, they located encounters with God as occurring during a worship service at a mourner's bench, which was confined to a worship setting. This approach also had the effect of producing a dichotomy between spirituality and learning. Pentecostals began to view the nondiscursive knowledge generated through encounter to the exclusion of discursive knowledge produced in an academic environment. Ideally, they needed to forge closer links between meditation and contemplation so that one flowed into the other. The contemplative vision of encounter could occur at any moment in the educational journey as a Coleridgean view of the whole and the interrelationships of all the parts to the whole. Instead, Pentecostals have continued to struggle with how to integrate encounter. At its most extreme, this position moved some Pentecostals into a kind of fideism. While a classroom could be interrupted with a burst of divine activity, followed by shouting, a challenge for early Pentecostals was how education could facilitate the encounter and integrate it into the formation of the self through the process of sanctification.[148]

4.3.2 Spirit-Led Hands: Populism and Training Schools

The populism so central to the holiness and pentecostal movements prompted them to gravitate toward models of education that maintained the tension between its utilitarian and classical modes. Their democratized view of the Spirit blended well with the kind of populism that had always been central to religious movements and the mystical forms of Christianity they generated. The difference was that nineteenth-century adherents of holiness utilized the mediating institutions and mass media that had become prominent in England and America. They had embraced an entrepreneurial spirit commensurate

---

[146] Frances J. McConnell, "Borden Parker Bowne," *Methodist Review* (May 1922): 347. See also William James, *The Varieties of Religious Experience* (New York: Penguin, 1982), 502, in which he asserts that the ancient spirit of Methodism evaporates under Bowne's rationalistic works.

[147] Douglas M. Strong, "Borden Parker Bowne and Henry Clay Morrison: Conflicting Conceptions of Twentieth Century Methodism," in Knight III, *From Aldersgate to Azusa Street*, 297–306.

[148] Daniel Howell explores this problem at Zion Bible College in his dissertation. See Daniel Howell, "Theological/Ministerial Education as Spiritual Formation/Transformation at Zion Bible College" (DMin diss., Fuller Theological Seminary, 2007).

with the emergence of modernity and the new economic opportunities afforded by immigration. The mass meeting (camp meeting or crusade), the conference, and the society all became important institutions that disseminated the message of holiness. Evangelicals in general had been forming societies since the eighteenth century, primarily as a platform for mission and social engagement.

While the camp meeting had been adopted by the Methodists and would be employed to great effect as a vehicle to promote divine healing and entire sanctification, the Bible conference more closely resembled the lyceum and occurred mainly in the Northeast and Midwest. Josiah Holbrook had established the lyceum in the late 1820s as a mechanism to promote learning and education among the populace at the local and state levels.[149] By the 1840s a national lyceum circuit had been established, with persons like Emerson lecturing on it. Harriet Beecher Stowe and other prominent women also became stars on the lyceum circuit. D. L. Moody had participated in lyceums both in Chicago and in Massachusetts. In addition, some Bible institutes, like the Bible Institute of Los Angeles (1908), came out of lyceums.[150] Camp meetings, societies, and lyceums were populist institutions that holiness leaders utilized as mechanisms to disseminate their message and educate and mobilize the laity within the churches.

Under the weight of their interpretation of Pentecost, Pentecostals pushed hard at the mobilization of laity that had led to the rise of religious training schools as an early vehicle of education. As we argued in the previous chapter, religious training schools were the counterpart to state normal schools and the multipurpose college. The first schools opened by the Church of God in Christ were Saints Literary and Industrial School (1917) in Lexington, Mississippi, and Page Normal and Industrial School (1927) in Hearne, Texas.[151] Although neither school survived, they reflected the desire to combine holiness and vocation around a utilitarian model of education. For many women and minorities, these were the only schools into which they could be admitted, and it is no mistake that women were prominent in early Bible institutes.[152]

When the call went out for a general convention to form what would become the Assemblies of God, one of the reasons given was to establish "a general Bible Training School with a literary department for our people."[153] To connect the establishment of a Bible school with literary training was to place education firmly in the context of the normal school. Literary training consisted of teaching grammar and rhetoric or the structure of language and the interpretation of texts.[154] The convention went on to select R. B.

[149] Josiah Holbrook, *American Lyceum, Or Society for the Improvement of Schools and Diffusion of Useful Knowledge* (Boston: Perkins and Marvin, 1829).

[150] Virginia Lieson Brereton, *Training God's Army: The American Bible School, 1880–1940* (Bloomington: Indiana University Press, 1990), 39.

[151] Anjulet Tucker, "Get the Learnin' but Don't Lose the Burnin': The Socio-Cultural and Religious Politics of Education in a Black Pentecostal College" (PhD diss., Emory University, 2009), 46–47.

[152] Brereton, *Training God's Army*, 69–70.

[153] E. N. Bell, "General Convention of Pentecostal Saints and Churches of God in Christ," *Word and Witness* 9.12 (1913): 1.

[154] See the 1885 report of the St. Louis public schools, in which literary training is part of the curriculum for the normal school. *Thirty-First Annual Report of the Board of President and Directors of the St. Louis Public Schools for the Year Ending July 31, 1885* (St. Louis: Riverside, 1885), 84–85; Ogren, *American State Normal School*, 85–103.

Chisolm's Neshoba Holiness School (Union, Miss.) and the Gospel School run by Thomas Leonard in Findlay, Ohio.[155] The former offered literary studies as part of its curriculum, which covered the basic field of normal schools, including education for elementary students in the county.

When denominational leaders established their own schools, they followed this general model. Schools like Central Bible Institute (1922) began with a basic three-year curriculum that reflected the overall trend since Moody and Simpson. Over the course of the next twenty years numerous Bible schools were established, and some expanded their curricula. North Central Bible Institute opened a business school (1938), and Southwestern Bible Institute added a junior college (1944). These moves were followed by adding seminary training to Central Bible Institute (1948). What one begins to see in Assemblies of God (AG) education during the 1940s is the move to add various training programs. These moves reflected the growth in the AG and the desire to begin to offer a more comprehensive educational program that would serve denominational youth.[156]

With the close of World War II and the emergence of the GI Bill, educational institutions in the AG began to swell with veterans. The use of federal dollars to fund education meant that the U.S. government began to examine educational programs more closely. In response to this federal scrutiny, AG leaders moved to gain accreditation for their institutions. They also began to debate whether to start a strictly liberal arts college over against a Bible school that might offer additional programs. Many rank-and-file members were afraid that a liberal arts institution might lead the denomination down the path of other Christian groups, while others pitted spirituality and revivalism against formal education. The first AG school to start a liberal arts college was Southern California Bible College (1950), now Vanguard University, due to the growing demands for degrees outside the normal curriculum of a Bible school. As secretary of education and then general superintendent, Ralph Riggs pushed hard for a liberal arts school in the denominational headquarters, eventually succeeding in establishing Evangel College, which received its first class in 1955. Within the AG, educational institutions moved from Bible institute to Bible college and then added training in other areas. These trends culminated in a debate after World War II that lasted six years over whether to establish a liberal arts school.

In the establishment of Bible Training School (1918) by the Church of God (Cleveland, Tenn.) and the Franklin Springs Institute (1919) by the Pentecostal Holiness Church, a similar evolution occurred without debate over the move into liberal arts education. In an editorial, George F. Taylor, the first head of Franklin Springs Institute, described it as a literary and Bible school for the church, by which he essentially meant a high school curriculum with a three-year course in Bible study and training in music.[157] Essentially, the

[155] Edith Blumhofer, *Restoring the Faith: The Assemblies of God, Pentecostalism, and American Culture* (Urbana: University of Illinois Press, 1993), 120.

[156] By 1941, there were 1,754 students listed in AG schools. See Barry Hugh Corey, "Pentecostalism and the Collegiate Institution: A Study in the Decision to Found Evangel College" (PhD diss., Boston College, 1992), 43.

[157] G. F. Taylor, "Franklin Springs Institute," *Pentecostal Holiness Advocate* 3.150 (April 8, 1920): 8–11. See Vinson Synan, *Emmanuel College: The First Fifty Years, 1919–1969* (Franklin Springs: Emmanuel College Library, 1968).

school had opened as a preparatory school with Taylor himself teaching French, Latin, and biblical courses. Due to financial troubles that became worse with the 1929 stock market crash, this first iteration of the institute had to close in 1931. Undeterred, denominational officials opened a new version of the school that combined a high school with a junior college (1933). Taylor returned to the faculty with a master's degree from the University of North Carolina. The new president, Thomas Aaron, had a master's degree but fell short of the coursework to complete his PhD. Under Aaron's administration (1933–1951) the school changed its name to Emmanuel College to emphasize its status as a junior college. It would take almost twenty years after Aaron retired for Emmanuel to reach full accreditation as a four-year institution (1967).

The Church of God started Bible Training School (BTS) under the leadership of Nora Chambers. The school began with a small curriculum consisting of twenty lessons that took the student through the Bible, the history of Christianity, and theology. Open to anyone, the course work was at the secondary level and remained there for the first fifteen years of its existence. During the 1930s, BTS expanded to a musical conservatory run by Otis McCoy, who had been involved in the early phases of southern gospel music with James David Vaughan and who had graduated from Vaughan's musical conservatory. The school also opened an industrial division that included secretarial training.

By 1941 then-president Zeno Tharpe signaled his intention to start a junior college alongside the high school academy. The new institution would be the Church of God Training School and College, with a college of liberal arts alongside of schools of theology, music, and secretarial science.[158] The following year, A. B. Dixon published an article defending the idea of the liberal arts, arguing that the problem was not the liberal arts themselves but their abuse in the same way that one might abuse fire or a car.[159] In 1946 the school moved to Cleveland, Tennessee, under the name Lee College, after F. J. Lee, who had served as General Overseer for the denomination. Through the 1960s it received full accreditation and became a four-year liberal arts college.

The evolution of pentecostal educational institutions follows a similar trajectory to state normal schools, with the difference that they all began as basic Bible institutes open to any student. Between 1920 and 1940 these schools moved from offering courses in Scripture, including biblical languages, to training courses that included basic studies in the liberal arts. Under the expansion of higher education after World War II, they moved to junior colleges and then four-year institutions (1940–1970). It was during this movement that Pentecostals begin to attain doctorates. The rapid increase in student populations between 1950 and 1970 opened up more opportunities for Pentecostals. Pentecostals obtained PhDs from Vanderbilt, the University of Texas, Dallas Theological Seminary, Emory University, the University of Houston, Central Baptist Theological Seminary, St. Louis University, the University of Georgia, and Bob Jones University. As they built their institutions, they remained concerned that education might become so formal that encounters with the Spirit cease to be part of the formation of the person and that education might become corrupted by secularization.

---

[158] See the advertisement in *Church of God Evangel* 32.22 (1941): 16; Zeno C. Tharp, "Superintendent Discusses Merits of B.T.S.," *Church of God Evangel* 32.23 (August 2, 1941): 14.

[159] A. B. Dixon, "Boogers," *Church of God Evangel* 33.32 (1942): 7, 14.

In keeping with their focus on mission, pentecostal educational institutions adopted models of education that emphasized vocational ends. From early on, many pentecostal institutions added not only training programs but schools of music or training in music. This was in keeping with the fundamental impulse to transform folk cultures. When one considers the contributions of Pentecostals to jazz, blues, Black gospel, Southern gospel, and even early rock, it may be that their most enduring impact in the early twentieth century on folk culture was through new musical forms.

One can also see this same thrust to mobilize laity and focus on training nontraditional students in the universities that Pentecostals have founded in Africa. For example, Central University in Ghana started as a pastoral training institute in 1988 and then quickly evolved into a full-fledged university in 2016. With schools in architecture, engineering and technology, medicine, pharmacy, law, and business alongside the arts and graduate studies, it's clear that the focus is on professional studies with the intention of transforming society. It also boasts of the William Ofori-Atta Institute of Integrity, which seeks to advance moral formation in the service of socio-economic development and leadership training. The same could be said for Pentecost University in Sowutuom, Greater Accra, which is connected to the Church of Pentecost. Its five schools are business, engineering, health sciences, law, and theology and mission. Combining an emphasis on moral formation and professional studies, the university sees its mission as empowering students to serve others with integrity.

From the beginning holiness and pentecostal leaders viewed education and learning as dimensions of a broader push to transform individuals and society at large. While they embraced the idea of education in the service of the creation of a culture, an important difference remained between their more democratized approach and Tappan's trickle-down theory. As a movement intent on renewing church and society through mobilizing a force of lay ministers, they planted educational institutions designed to maintain the tension between the utilitarian and classical approaches to education. This resulted in vocational institutions that produced professionals who could change the culture. Apart from institutional challenges, it also provides some rationale as to why the research model of education did not gain much traction.

One can see a similar approach espoused by Henry Clay Morrison during his presidency of Asbury College. In a series of commencement addresses Morrison laid out a vision for education suffused with holiness emphases. The educational enterprise remained intimately connected with the holiness pursuit of perfection. Its ground was the intrinsic worth of all human beings, which Morrison stressed by pointing his listeners away from the soul of a Moses, a Shakespeare, or a Wesley and toward the worth of "the soul of a sick and starving baby in the bony arms of a heathen mother, in the jungles of India."[160] The cultivation of holiness in the masses aimed to produce men and women of faith who had an enlarged vision and a fixed purpose stemming from their communion with God and their knowledge of their own worth.

---

[160] Henry Clay Morrison, *Commencement Sermons* (Louisville: Pentecostal Publishing, 1915); Douglas Strong, "Fighting against Worldliness and Unbelief: Henry Clay Morrison and the Transformation of the Holiness Movement within Methodism," *Wesleyan Theological Journal* 40.2 (2005): 142–56.

For Morrison, the spiritual heroes and heroines were not the scholars themselves, but the students who went forth from Asbury to wage war against the spiritual giants of their day. Whether dealing with the mysteries of religion or the mysteries of nature, the starting point for education remained investigating the unknown, and its telos was nothing less than the exportation of social holiness in the service of cultural transformation. Morrison concluded one sermon with a quotation from the New School Presbyterian Henry Van Dyke's *The Gospel for an Age of Doubt* (1896) to the effect that Christianity is a spiritual form of existence rather than a doctrinal system. Like Van Dyke, who contributed to the social gospel movement, Morrison thought that holiness of life was the primary vehicle to transform culture, and he sought to instill such a *habitus* in the students at Asbury. To investigate the mysteries of life, to promote the intrinsic worth of the human person, and to slay spiritual giants in the cause of Christ—these aspirations represented the nature of holiness as a lived reality.

4.3.3 Spirit-Infused Hearts: Cultivating Cultures and Changing Lives

The focus on holiness of life and Spirit baptism placed cultural transformation into a spirituality that accommodated pluralism. Not only did it forge a Protestant pluralism, but eventually the focus on spirituality led to connections with Catholicism and Orthodoxy as holiness and pentecostal adherents began to trace the roots of this spirituality in the broader Christian tradition. This spirituality also replaced culture formation as the ground of personal formation. The fusion of elements from Wesleyanism and Christian mysticism centered on the role of love in Christian perfection and the formation of ordered affectivity. Through the language of love that flowed through sanctification and baptism in the Spirit, Pentecostals had a way of understanding salvation as a change in the whole person, body and soul. Salvation was about ontological and ethical formation.

Talk of an ontological change related to forming right affections (orthopathy). This is because Pentecostals understood the various operations of the Spirit (regeneration, sanctification, and baptism in the Spirit) as participation in the divine nature through love. For Pentecostals, affective transformation was about being formed in Christ and conformed to Christ. As we noted earlier, the phrase "full gospel" signified a Christ-patterned and Spirit-infused existence insofar as the Spirit unleashed various operations of grace that conformed the person to Christ. As innate dispositions, the affections are movements that arise from human nature and also form it in particular ways as persons habituate themselves to this or that set of objects. Forming Christ within involves reordering affective movements that have become "de-formed," which in turn provide a new "shape" to the person. Pentecostals operated with an implicit developmental understanding of the human person whose life is reordered as the Spirit reintegrates the affections through powerful encounters that fuel a transforming journey. This process of re-*formation* occurs through the love the Spirit pours out in the Spirit's operations.

Affections are also movements of the rational soul and therefore have a cognitive dimension. Desire, joy, anger, fear, and other affective movements all relate to some object. Humans desire this or rejoice over that, which presupposes judgments of value. They take joy in what they value or learn to value what they rejoice over. To view affections in this way is to get back behind the view that emerged and then became dominant in the late eighteenth and nineteenth centuries of emotions as involuntary, irrational feel-ings.[161] As Steve Land argued, "If the heart is understood to be the integrative center of the mind, will and emotions then it is clear that affections are more than mere feelings and Christian affections are meant to characterize a person's life."[162]

At least two corollaries follow. First, since one cannot sever the connection between cognitive and affective movements, it follows that there is an intimate relationship between affections and beliefs. Affections determine beliefs and beliefs shape affective movements. Value judgments flow from the affective and cognitive dimension together. The statement "I want ice cream" has an implicit judgment about its value. This judgment springs from the connection between the desire and its object. As we noted, the holiness and pentecostal emphasis on intuitionism means that knowledge is participatory and driven by the affections. A form of rationality grounded in noetic accounts of sin and propositional truth cannot account for the crucial role of affectivity. Second, the rela-tional connections humans form through affectivity shape them in fundamental ways. Humans take on a particular character or shape as they habituate their affections toward this object or that object. To claim that humans are *Homo liturgicus*, as Smith does, is to equate worship with degrees of desiring.[163]

Transforming affective movements leads to a change in the nature of the person, not only in terms of the values held, but also in terms of the character that *forms* those values. Ontological change occurs in and through affective transformation because affectivity shapes reason and will, binding them together with value judgments based on relational connections to objects outside the self. Affective transformation alters the human being as it shapes those dispositions central to the relational nature of the person—it changes the heart and brings about a new configuration or character. It is the human person who instantiates human nature in a particular way, and affectivity is central to that unique form of instantiation. Since humans are embodied creatures of emotion and desire, per-sonhood is relational.

Pneumatology must now enter the picture because, although Christ is the form of the new creature, the Spirit brings this new form into existence. As Augustine suggests, the Spirit achieves this end as the divine love who alters human loves. The Spirit is that divine person whose movement within the heart begins to reorder affective movements and so alter a person's habits of mind. The Wesleyan insight, ultimately originating from Christian mystical traditions, was to postulate the need for crisis encounters as the fuel of Christian growth toward final perfection. Pentecostals inherited this insight and applied it.

Changing the heart does not simply relate to process of formation abstracted from concrete communal existence and the stories and narratives that transmit that existence. When Charles Eliot Norton was formulating his program of Western civilization, he saw in John Stuart Mill's adaptation of *Bildung* to England an important resource. Mill sought to preserve human liberty by creating an "atmosphere" in which individuals could carry

---

[161] Thomas Dixon, *From Passions to Emotions: The Creation of a Secular Psychological Category* (Cam-bridge: Cambridge University Press, 2003). The work of Martha Nussbaum, among others, has done much to recover the more ancient view of emotion and desire.

[162] Land, *Pentecostal Spirituality*, 132.

[163] James K. A. Smith, *Desiring the Kingdom: Worship, Worldview, and Cultural Formation* (Grand Rap-ids: Baker, 2009), 39–74.

out their quest at human development without their freedoms being violated.[164] For Norton and other high-culture liberals this translated into the creation of Western civilization as "our civilization." Through the metanarrative of Western civilization virtue could be inculcated in human lives. Western civilization would form the new story that supplied the context within which self-cultivation and human formation became possible.

Almost from the moment Western civilization became a model of cultural assimilation, however, it was being challenged by the alternative model of Ethiopianism, which had been espoused by African American writers at least since the late eighteenth century, when the slave poet Jupiter Hammond referred to himself as an "unlearned Ethiopian."[165] What was created to supply an "atmosphere" conducive to liberty and the creation of virtue had actually denigrated African forms of life by excluding them from Western civilization. The new ground of pluralism was proving to be no sure foundation.

In this context, African American writers such as W. E. B. Du Bois began utilizing Ethiopianism to recover an ancient African identity in which Africans made contributions to culture and to postulate a future for Africans in which God would raise up the continent as symbolized in Psalms 68:31 ("let Ethiopia hasten to stretch out its hands to God."). At the same time, on the African continent intellectuals were utilizing Ethiopianism as a counternarrative to European colonialism. Ethiopianism brought into focus Jim Crow and colonialism as two sides of the same coin while also revealing the exclusionary nature of Eliot's cultural liberalism and Wilsonian progressivism.

While Ethiopianism as a counterdiscourse did not impact white holiness and pentecostal preachers, it was adopted by African Americans in both movements.[166] Charles Price Jones, who split with Charles H. Mason on the issue of Spirit baptism, wrote a collection of poetry, *An Appeal to the Sons of Africa*, in which he called those "of ancient Ethiopic blood" to believe in their dignity and hope for their future in the face of Jim Crow. As Irvin's analysis of the poetry makes clear, Jones combined Ethiopianism with the holiness notion of empowerment to bring about a conscientization in the minds of his readers. The internal freedom of holiness advanced a political freedom in which one's cultural identity was not subsumed.[167]

Robert C. Lawson took Ethiopianism to the next level by constructing an understanding of the atonement in which the bloodlines of all ethnic groups were mixed in Christ's humanity so as to destroy racism by his death.[168] Lawson would employ Ethiopianism to counter racism in the south from his church in Manhattan, to the point of taking a prominent role in the early Civil Rights Movement. Mason himself embraced

---

[164] Linda Dowling, *Charles Eliot Norton: The Art of Reform in Nineteenth-Century America* (Durham: University of New Hampshire Press, 2007), 90–91.

[165] Allen Dwight Callahan, *The Talking Book: African Americans and the Bible* (New Haven: Yale University Press, 2006), 140–42.

[166] This was part of a larger program of fusing Africanisms and slave religion. See Estrelda Alexander, *Black Fire: One Hundred Years of African American Pentecostalism* (Downers Grove: IVP, 2011), 28–60, 102, 220–21.

[167] Dale T. Irvin, "Charles Price Jones: Image of Holiness," in *Portraits of a Generation: Early Pentecostal Leaders*, ed. James R. Goff and Grant Wacker (Fayetteville: University of Arkansas Press, 2002), 48–49.

[168] Robert C. Lawson, *The Anthropology of Christ Our Kinsman Redeemer*, in *Add Thou to It: The Selected Works of Robert Clarence Lawson*, ed. Alexander C. Stewart (Capitol Heights: Seymour Press, 2019), 297–352.

the central idea of a glorious African past in his own desire to retain and promote Africanisms as part of Christian worship, which fit within the ecstatic displays of holiness and pentecostal services.

Charles Price Jones and Charles H. Mason fused Ethiopianism with an effort to preserve and transmit the folk culture of African slave religion as part of a program of Black educational uplift. Both Jones and Mason had attended Arkansas Baptist College, but they rejected the emphasis on higher critical studies they found there. While they shared Du Bois' celebration of Black culture through Ethiopianism, they thought Ethiopianism was best preserved through a renewal of forms of slave religion like dancing, the ring shout, and embodied musical forms.[169] It may be that Du Bois was transmitting a fundamentally German understanding of education.[170] According to Kwame Appiah, Du Bois was adapting Johann Herder's understanding of the interrelationship between culture and the spiritual life of nations. Du Bois understood the training of men to be intimately related to human development (*Bildung*) and the development of culture. The double consciousness of his *Souls of Black Folk* was a recognition of the distance between the development of Blacks and the development of the larger culture in America.[171] Their two "souls" represented two types of cultural development in dissonance with one another. Manhood, according to Du Bois, concerned the project of integrating these two forms of cultural identity, which required the cultivation in African Americans of a form of self-development that advanced all of their faculties.[172] "Men we shall have only as we make manhood the object of the work of the schools—intelligence, broad sympathy, knowledge of the world that was and is, and of the relation of men to it."[173]

Cornel West's criticism that Du Bois did not feel Black sorrow and suffering deep enough in his bones to understand ordinary Black folk resonates with the populist critique found in the holiness and pentecostal movements.[174] Because of this populist impulse, Jones and Mason looked primarily to Booker T. Washington's model of self-help and industrial education.[175] The turn to Washington was aided by the rise of African American normal schools across the South between 1870 and 1910. There were over twenty normal schools for African Americans by the 1910s.[176] While Jones and Mason followed Washington in developing education for the masses, they did not wholesale

---

[169] See Dale M. Coulter, "Toward a Pentecostal Theology of Black Consciousness," *Journal of Pentecostal Theology* 25.1 (2016): 74–89.

[170] Kwame Anthony Appiah, *Lines of Descent: W. E. B. Du Bois and the Emergence of Identity* (Cambridge, Mass.: Harvard University Press, 2014).

[171] Appiah, *Lines of Descent*, 45–82.

[172] W. E. B. Du Bois, *The Souls of Black Folk*, in *The Oxford W. E. B. Du Bois Reader*, ed. Eric J. Sundquist (New York: Oxford University Press, 1996), 101–7.

[173] W. E. B. Du Bois, "The Talented Tenth," in *The Social Theory of W. E. B. Du Bois*, ed. Phil Zuckerman (Thousand Oaks, Calif.: Pine Forge, 2004), 185.

[174] Henry Louis Gates Jr. and Cornel West, *The Future of the Race* (New York: Vintage, 1997), 58.

[175] See David Daniels, "The Cultural Renewal of Slave Religion: C. P. Jones and the Emergence of the Holiness Movement in Mississippi" (PhD diss., Union Theological Seminary, 1992), 199–247; John Giggie, *After Redemption: Jim Crow and the Transformation of African American Religion in the Delta, 1875–1915* (Oxford: Oxford University Press, 2008), 180–81. On Washington's education program, see Virginia Lantz Denton, *Booker T. Washington and the Adult Education Movement* (Gainesville: University of Florida Press, 1993).

[176] Ogren, *American State Normal School*, 60–61.

adopt the latter's vision. Instead, they fused it to holiness and/or the ecstatic. The spirituality embedded in the holiness and pentecostal movements allowed for the kind of pluralism necessary to construct models of education that took seriously local, folk cultures and their contribution to "civilization."

The attraction of persons like Jones and Mason to Booker T. Washington's model of industrial education had to do with its focus on training the masses in the basic skills that could promote economic uplift. It should be viewed in terms of the rise of African American normal schools as well as industrial academies over the final decades of the nineteenth century. Jones had already equated holiness and humanness in *An Appeal to the Sons of Africa*, so that to become an adult meant to embrace a way of holy living. For Mason, the passage into adulthood was signaled in part through the ecstasy of slave religion, which is precisely what Du Bois wanted to exclude. The practices that emerged from Pentecostalism and slave religion promoted the kind of holy humanness Mason sought to inculcate in the saints. God's call to make Mason a man through practices such as dancing formed an alternative consciousness to the liberalizing program of Du Bois and the industrial program of Washington. Both Jones and Mason, then, sought to adapt and modify Washington's model for their own efforts at preserving a distinctive way of life centered on slave religion, holiness, and, for Mason, ecstatic forms of religiosity.

The rise of Ethiopianism as a transatlantic movement within holiness and pentecostal leaders entailed a form of resistance to the high-culture movement, which embraced Western civilization as part of the educational enterprise. It combined with the emphasis on populism and a democratized view of the Spirit to inspire the need for indigenous leadership and education even among white pentecostal groups. Although this was a slow transition from education through colonial lenses to more indigenized forms of education, it was hastened by the fusion of these three elements.[177]

From this perspective, African American and African Pentecostals and holiness leaders could not embrace Western civilization as cultivating a liberal culture and thus embodying a true humanism. Nor could they embrace, however, Du Bois' view of education as occurring through the "talented tenth," by which he meant developing exceptional men, "the Best of this race that they may guide the Mass away from the contamination and death of the Worst, in their own and other races."[178] The focus on divine love as reordering the affections central to moral formation and charismatic endowment in the holiness and pentecostal movements allowed for the kind of pluralism necessary to construct models of education that took seriously local, folk cultures and their contribution to "civilization."

The analysis of this chapter was necessary to situate how the pentecostal and holiness movements approached education. The primary thesis was to suggest that these movements were part of the Romantic sensibility in the nineteenth century as part of the background understanding to their social imaginary, but that they assimilated this sensibility through a populist lens. They embraced a rational intuitionism that espoused a participatory understanding of knowledge. This perspective offered a way of synthesizing a cognitive view of the emotions central to the understanding of sanctification as the ordering

---

[177] See Anderson, *To the Ends of the Earth*, 128–38, who traces out the slow transition from colonial models of education to indigenous ones.

[178] Du Bois, "Talented Tenth," 185.

of affectivity, the mystical view of the Christian life as a journey into deeper union punctuated by moments of ecstasy, and the philosophical resources from Coleridge and Reidian common sense. They also espoused a theology of immanence in which nature was suffused with the presence of the Spirit, whose miraculous healing of the human body pointed toward the restoration of harmony and the body's own natural rhythms. Finally, their emphasis on ecstatic encounters gave rise to symbolic modes of interpretation and a kind of cosmopolitan vision in which the transformed person glimpsed the final kingdom of God and all people in God and then went out into the world in mission. Yet the embrace of premillennialism meant that the realization of the kingdom glimpsed through personal encounter could only come about finally and fully through a cosmic in-breaking to set right the scales of justice. A close examination of these developments within the holiness and pentecostal movements reveals how they continued to view education in terms of moral formation and encounters with transcendence.

The emphases of the Romantic sensibility fueled a populist movement, a high-church movement, and a high-culture movement with most holiness and pentecostal adherents committed to the first. Mission was defined as cultural creation and transformation through personal transformation. For men like Henry Tappan, scholars were heroic individuals whose academic self-development unified a nation by forming a common culture. This same vision of the scholar or artist as Promethean hero was appropriated by a number of intellectuals, including William Dean Howells and Henry James, eventually giving rise to Charles Eliot Norton's notion of Western civilization and the creation of a liberal culture. As part of this turn toward the scholar as hero, slowly the divine was collapsed into nature and the kingdom of God equated with historical processes, which fueled Wilson's progressive liberalism as well as the social gospel.

The populism of the holiness and pentecostal movements resisted these facets of high culture by a spirituality that accommodated the emerging pluralism of modernity. In the place of the hero, they espoused a democratized view of the Spirit that unleashed the power of men and women, lay persons of all types who were formed by the Spirit's own presence. Consequently, their educational models sought to empower laity. Rather than collapsing the divine into nature, their eschatological commitments maintained a tension between transcendence and immanence that became the macrocosm to the tension between crisis and process in the microcosm of the human heart. This meant that they resisted any educational model that removed encounters with transcendence from the process of human formation. It did not mean that they produced no poetry, offered no sustained intellectual engagement with the culture, or gave rise to no transformative ethos that shaped folk cultures and influenced jazz and blues musicians. Pentecostal and holiness spirituality did all of these things. Noll's suspicion of populism as well as his focus on worldview analysis prevented him from seeing these important dimensions of both movements. The challenge that remained, however, was how to integrate discursive meditation and nondiscursive contemplation into an educational framework. Too often members of both movements have privileged the latter over the former, which has prevented them from harnessing the resources at their disposal.

Part II

What Difference Can the Holy Spirit Make?

Constructive Reenvisioning

5

Renewing the Mind

Scholarship and the Pneumatological Imagination

The preceding has covered extensive ground across the history of Christian education in a short span. We have been selective, unavoidably, with our observations culminating with developments from the holiness-pentecostal site where we concluded the previous chapter. Yet our suggestion is that this vantage point has highlighted essential aspects of the Christian educational venture that remain pertinent for our twenty-first-century efforts. In particular, we have seen that, consistently across the two millennia, a Pentecost-perspective spotlights the formative—even reformative and redemptive—character of Christian learning into the image of God in Christ by the Holy Spirit. Grounded in an integral humanism, Christian education should be Christ-patterned and Spirit-infused insofar as the structure of human rationality reveals the cosmic Christ and the full realization of human capacities points toward the eschatological Spirit. Yet this has not been an interventionist Pietism awaiting the divine Spirit to show up to achieve otherwise implausible educational results, but rather one that seeks to inculcate a *habitus* in students in which moral formation, encounters with transcendence, and investment in mission now orient them. Hence, there is a fundamental spiritual and pneumatic dimension to teaching and learning, one inseparable from but interlinked with the routines of educational formation. Our conviction is that this vision, honed over the centuries, is still central to the Christian university and can be retrieved and reappropriated now.

The remainder of this book seeks to outline what might be called a Pentecost-inspired philosophy and theology of Christian higher education that builds on the essential insights derived from the foregoing historical account.[1] In keeping with an integral humanism, education should not be a top-down enterprise but a formative one that seeks to transform regions in and through the folk cultures that inhabit them. This may be presumptive given the above narrative, which shows holiness and pentecostal groups as Johnny-come-lately-if-yet-arrived-at-all on the higher educational scene. Yet we are galvanized to methodically excavate the heretofore relatively unexplored possibilities bequeathed to us. Inevitably, our recommendations emerge from the particularity of our own pentecostal

---

[1] Jeffrey S. Hittenberger, "Toward a Pentecostal Philosophy of Education," *Pneuma: The Journal of the Society for Pentecostal Studies* 23.1 (2001): 217–44, is one of the first efforts in this direction; ours speaks beyond the modern pentecostal scholarly community that Hittenberger's article is addressing.

situatedness, yet the modern pentecostal movement from its beginnings, like other revivalist phenomena, always sought to renew the Christian life and reform the church. Our contention, then, is that a Pentecost-approach to higher education is not sectarian but ecumenical, not given only to self-designated pentecostal enterprises but premised on the promise of the Spirit of Jesus' outpouring "upon all flesh" (Acts 2:17). The Spirit of Pentecost, in other words, is not ecclesially copyrighted but belongs to all that God desires to redeem, including the world of higher education.

More precisely, Pentecost as the generative frame not only foregrounds the vital work of the Spirit in the educational effort but opens up to a more thoroughgoing trinitarian theology of Christian formation.[2] If the triune Christian confession posits God the Father as generative, one who liberates all things in Christ by the Holy Spirit, then, as intimated in the first part of this book, such a trinitarian conceptualization applied to thinking about higher education explicates the pneumatological dynamics of transformation that shares in the reconciling work of God in Christ. Chapters 5–7 unfold in a more or less systematic fashion this pneumatological and trinitarian theology of higher education—addressing the scholarship, teaching, and service central to it—vis-à-vis the redemptive mission of the triune God. Succinctly put, Christian higher education seeks the (re)formation of human persons by the same Spirit that animated the early bishops, the scholastics, humanists, and reformers after them, and the Romantics and Pietists in more recent times. Human minds (their intellect and patterns of thought), hearts (their loves and hopes), and hands (their deeds, actions, and behaviors) are to be (re)formed into the full image of Jesus Christ for participation in the divine saving of the world.

It should not be assumed that the movement and order of these chapters proceed from matters at the center of Christian higher education toward those at the periphery. Arguably, matters about the (practical) telos of the Christian university, including its being welcoming and making inclusive spaces for all people (the focus of chapter 7), or the ever-developing digitization of this enterprise (discussed at the end of chapter 6), are at the heart of many pressing debates. There is a real sense that what is dealt with in this chapter has been written already with the later themes and discussions in mind, even as any reader may proceed backwards, as it were, going from chapters 7 through 6 and then concluding here.[3] In short, we proceed always both in anticipation of what is coming even as we are mindful that what is traversed in any moment is always intertwined with and mutually informed by what is coming next.

If our pneumatological theology of Christian higher education thus involves consideration of the renewal and revitalization of human minds, hearts, and hands, we begin

---

[2] Amos Yong, *Spirit-Word-Community: Theological Hermeneutics in Trinitarian Perspective*, New Critical Thinking in Religion, Theology and Biblical Studies (Burlington: Ashgate, 2002), argues that only a vigorous and substantive pneumatology can achieve the promise of Christian theology, historically more actually binitarian than fully trinitarian. Our present efforts make this claim amidst the arena of Christian theology of higher education.

[3] In fact, while focused on theological education for seminarians rather than for the full scope of undergraduate and graduate studies, Amos' *Renewing the Church by the Spirit: Theological Education after Pentecost*, Theological Education Between the Times (Grand Rapids: Eerdmans, 2020), proceeds from the heart (the who) through the hands (the where-to) to the head (the mind), even from mission back through pedagogy to scholarship; Amos' argument is thereby complementary to that unfolded in part 2 of this volume since wherever one begins, the other moments must be engaged.

in medias res in this chapter by focusing on cognition and knowledge, given the historic emphasis of the modern university and our hopes to speak into this milieu. Thus, the three sections of this chapter unfold what could be understood as a pentecostal (in the sense of being after the day of Pentecost) and pneumatological theology of the life of the mind; reassess the multidisciplinarity that constitutes the modern university within this framework; and sketch, putatively, a charismatic theology of faith-in-relationship-with-learning and scholarship. Our goal is to reexamine the intellectual life—less in terms of Noll's understanding and more vis-à-vis the arc of the argument in part 1 above—especially as unfolded in higher education, in order to reestablish its viability within a pneumatological and trinitarian framework. As the next chapter will further argue, the Christian life of the mind cannot be ensured apart from grappling with the human heart and its loves and desires. Yet not only do we have to begin somewhere, but focusing first on the cognitional dimension of the contemporary higher educational landscape will set us up for tackling the challenging issues at the center of the late modern and even post-modern university.[4]

5.1   LOVING GOD WITH OUR MINDS: THE INTELLECTUAL LIFE AND THE PURSUIT OF THE SPIRIT

Our historical survey above makes prominent the prioritization of heart formation and missional commitment. In doing so, however, the pentecostal-charismatic quality of Christian formation may appear as without a stout intellectual dimension, at least as measured against the modern research university project (not to mention the immense economic investments that undergird such endeavors, subsidies that most Christian colleges and universities are nowhere near emulating). Yet we have already noted how the orthodox rationalism of Baconian evidentialism was only palatable as the nondiscursive and intuitive understanding of knowledge was placed alongside the discursive. Moreover, the pneumatological was found first in the intuitive grasp or the insight unfolding in the mind. Grounded in the Spirit's prevenient activity, this intuitive flash of love's knowledge became the basis for the subsequent formation of intellectual virtues that sharpened the mind and sanctified it in accordance with wisdom's pattern. Since all wisdom participates in Christ as the eternal and incarnate wisdom, we once again see how to be Christ-patterned and Spirit-infused is to link the discursive and the nondiscursive in a more holistic way. Rather than making this argument on modernist terms, we focus here first on developing the pneumatological underpinnings for a trinitarian theology of the life of the mind. Such a theological foundation will serve to sustain the intellectual division of labor that occurs across the disciplines of the modern university (§5.2) even as it also propels research and scholarship in these contexts (§5.3).

The pneumatological and trinitarian theology of the intellectual life we propose is resolutely pentecostal, not according to some contemporary denominational definition, but ecumenically in the sense of being fundamentally impelled by the Spirit of Pentecost. There will be three steps to prosecuting this thesis: first, a reconnaissance

---

[4]   We will go back and forth in part 2 between *late* modern and *post*modern, in part because periodizations are fluid in the present time and in part because it is inarguable we are all moderns, even if in varying respects.

of prior efforts in this direction, noting their achievements and unfulfilled promise (§5.1.1); second, a rereading of select New Testament pneumatological motifs in relationship to the life of the mind and in light of the Pentecost-narrative (§5.1.2); and third, a reconstruction of what we might consider as a pneumatological theology of formation primed by the biblical traditions (§5.1.3). Contrary to caricatures and stereotypes, we urge two interrelated claims in the following: first, that the vitality of the Christian life of the mind is radically dependent upon, rather than marginalizing of, life in the Spirit since it gestures toward a holistic and integrative understanding of human reason; and second, that our pneumatological theology of the intellectual life is funded by the scriptural witness on the one hand, even as our reading of sacred writ is dependent on the Spirit-infused life on the other hand.

Such a perspective is yet another way we seek to argue in support of a *habitus* made possible by the Spirit, which then opens up a pneumatological and transcendent horizon. The movement between the sacred text and the mind being sanctified and charismatically endowed initiates us into the hermeneutical spiral—of the interrelatedness between the horizon of Scripture and the contemporary horizon—which is not only unavoidable (as clarified by our present postfoundationalist intellectual landscape)[5] but also characterizes the expanding or intensifying (i.e., going outward from the mind to the heart and the hands or delving deeper from the mind to the heart, depending on which image works better for our readers) movement of our methodological approach in the remainder of this book.

5.1.1 The Holy Spirit and Higher Education: Mapping the Current Conversation

Given the Fourth Gospel's repeated references to the "Spirit of truth" (John 14:17, 15:26) who "will guide [believers] into all the truth" (16:13), it is unsurprising to find repeated efforts in the last half century or more to develop what might be called a pneumatological theology of Christian education. Rachel Henderlite's lectures at Austin Presbyterian Seminary in the early 1960s focused on education more generally, identifying the Holy Spirit as the agent of nurture who inspires faith and faithful participation in the church's mission.[6] This pneumatological motif has been picked up particularly among evangelical scholars working in the area of Christian education. Much of this has been programmatic,[7] although one scholar has written extensively about the role of the Spirit in Christian ministry, particularly that of teaching and equipping Christian believers for life and ministry.[8] To be sure, there is widespread recognition that any evangelical theology of

---

[5]   Yong, *Spirit-Word-Community*, part 2, defends a postfoundationalist epistemology that resists modernist foundationalism, which sought to base knowledge on indubitable certainties; see also J. Wentzel van Huyssteen, *Essays in Postfoundationalist Theology* (Grand Rapids: Eerdmans, 1997), and F. LeRon Shults, *The Postfoundationalist Task of Theology: Wolfhart Pannenberg and the New Theological Rationality* (Grand Rapids: Eerdmans, 1999).

[6]   Rachel Henderlite, *The Holy Spirit in Christian Education* (Philadelpha: Westminster, 1964).

[7]   E.g., Gary Newton, "The Holy Spirit in the Educational Process," in *Introducing Christian Education: Foundations for the Twenty-First Century*, ed. Michael J. Anthony (Grand Rapids: Baker Academic, 2001), 125–29; and James C. Wilhoit and Linda Rozema, "Anointed Teaching," *Christian Education Journal*, 3rd ser., 2.2 (2005): 239–55.

[8]   Roy B. Zuck, *Spirit-Filled Teaching: The Power of the Holy Spirit in Your Ministry* (Nashville: Word, 1998), expanding on his earlier article "The Role of the Holy Spirit in Christian Teaching," in *The*

Christian education ought to have some pneumatological component,[9] yet these remain ancillary reflections, begging for more comprehensive integration.

As might be expected, the emergence of pentecostal institutions of higher education during this same period of time has precipitated also the quest for a coherent theological substructure. A collection of essays appeared in the mid-1980s, spearheaded by the then editor of the American Assemblies of God's monthly *Sunday School Counselor* magazine, who had also served for two decades in the denomination's national Sunday School department.[10] The book's emphasis on the work of the Spirit in empowering teachers and illuminating learners in the educational process was not necessarily distinctive, however, within the broader evangelical world. Even as some consideration has been given to a pentecostal theology of catechesis, this has remained situated more so in the ecclesial domain—as might have been expected given the history we have sketched (see §4.3.3 above)—than carried into the higher educational arena.[11] Some of the most constructive recent work is to be found in unpublished doctoral dissertations, including one calling for a "pedagogy for renewal" focused on holistic and lifelong formation, relational and participatory knowing, and a practical orientation to teaching and learning.[12] A leading pentecostal educator primed to mine the theoretical discussion in this vein has published so far a scattering of essays and articles, although with important suggestions for engaging pentecostal and pneumatological perspectives with contemporary philosophy of higher education discussions.[13] Part of the challenge, plainly put, is the dynamic nature of this burgeoning field, which makes it difficult to keep up with what is happening in these arenas.

Yet the other part of the challenge of any trinitarian theological project is the problem of pneumatology: how do we talk about the Holy Spirit at all, much less in the context of Christian higher education. On the one side is the heir of nineteenth-century orthodox rationalism we have already discussed. This dominating logocentrism, within North American theological scholarship, generally results in a kind of Christ-centered trinitarian confession but one that otherwise marginalizes the Spirit as incidental.[14] To be Christ-patterned is more to be confessionally aligned in a way that excises orthodoxy

---

Christian Educator's Handbook on Teaching, ed. Kenneth O. Gangel and Howard G. Hendricks (Wheaton, Ill.: Victor, 1988), 32–44.

[9] For instance, Michael J. Anthony's "Pneumatology and Christian Education," ch. 7 in James R. Estep Jr., Michael J. Anthony, and Gregg R. Allison, *A Theology for Christian Education* (Nashville: B&H Academic, 2008), 147–73.

[10] Sylvia Lee, ed., *The Holy Spirit in Christian Education* (Springfield: Gospel Publishing House, 1988).

[11] Most prominent is already referred to: Cheryl Bridges Johns, *Pentecostal Formation: A Pedagogy among the Oppressed*, Journal of Pentecostal Theology Supplement Series 2 (Sheffield: Sheffield Academic Press, 1993); we return to engaging with some of the ideas promoted in this important book below (§7.2.3). See also, as applicable more in the ecclesiastical domain, James P. Bowers, "A Wesleyan-Pentecostal Approach to Christian Formation," *Journal of Pentecostal Theology* 3.6 (1995) 55–86.

[12] Vincent P. Castellani, "Revisioning Pentecostal Bible College Education: Towards a Pedagogy for Renewal" (DMin thesis, Gordon-Conwell Theological Seminary, 1999), esp. 76–80.

[13] E.g., Jeffrey S. Hittenberger, "Globalization, 'Marketization,' and the Mission of Pentecostal Higher Education in Africa," *Pneuma: The Journal of the Society for Pentecostal Studies* 26.2 (2004): 182–215, and "Global Pentecostal Renaissance? Reflections on Pentecostalism, Culture, and Higher Education," *Pneuma Review* 16.2 (2013): 20–53.

[14] In Eugene Rogers' memorial phrasing of the question and concern: "Is there nothing the Spirit can do that the Son can't do better?" See explication in Eugene F. Rogers Jr., *After the Spirit: A Constructive Pneumatology from Resources Outside the Modern West* (Grand Rapids: Eerdmans, 2005), ch. 2.

from orthopraxy and orthopathy. Worldview thinking is merely an extension of this kind of modern confessionalization, which invariably views the emotions as noncognitive and dichotomizes head and heart. While we will return repeatedly to detailing how our own construction is a deeply trinitarian and Christocentric endeavor, the other side of the precipice is the spiritualizing of the Spirit's work, a kind of pietistic mantra that waits for divine intervention in the face of insurmountable odds. In theological discourse, such approaches translate into expecting that "the Holy Spirit becomes a kind of *explanation* for the X-factor in salvation not covered by human efforts,"[15] and within the field of Christian higher education, this would be to insist that only the Spirit can bring about what humans otherwise cannot. As we already noted, one of the weaknesses of the focus on intuitive knowledge was the failure to integrate it fully into a broader framework that held together meditation and contemplation, discursive and nondiscursive modes of reasoning. The result is both a spiritualization of the higher educational enterprise in ways that pray for divine breakthroughs to rescue human creatures from their plight and what Carol Hess describes as a "Spirit of the gaps" devotionalism that discourages human participation in the outworking of the divine initiative.[16]

Along this latter route, one might also then presume that the burden rests on human beings to do all they can, and hopefully, unpredictably so, the Spirit might appear now and then to shore up our meager efforts and achieve the divinely projected outcomes. A respected evangelical philosopher whose charismatic experience has prompted fresh rethinking about the role of the Spirit in the Christian life recommends, intended or not, what seems to be such a pneumatological interventionism. His goal is to take seriously the scriptural witness to the miraculous ministry of the Spirit, manifest in Jesus' ministry for instance, but his resistance to the cessationism in his own evangelical tradition results in embracing the Spirit's work as "naturally supernatural."[17] Such formulation is beholden, as we saw in chapter 3, to Enlightenment sensibilities, especially the natural-supernatural binary, and then to the dispensing with altogether of the latter, especially in the modern university. But if the natural-supernatural binary is neither viable in our late or postmodern context nor helpful for grappling with the scriptural traditions,[18] then the way forward is not to envision the Spirit showing up, as if intermittently, to register God's mighty deeds amid otherwise hopeless creaturely conditions. Rather, it is to follow Augustine in proclaiming that the Spirit's operations are ever-present as love that infuses our loves and so opens up the possibility of the vision that leads from faith to understanding.

In sum, what has emerged are two basic paradigms for a pneumatology of Christian education, which remain in tension. The first focuses on the Spirit's cultivation

---

[15] This is a nice summary by Edward Farley, "Does Christian Education Need the Holy Spirit? Part II: The Work of the Spirit in Christian Education," *Religious Education* 60.6 (1965): 427–36, at 430 (emphasis orig.), who himself argues for a more ecclesial and also social approach that sees the Spirit enabling human participation in these spheres and processes.

[16] Carol Lakey Hess, "Educating in the Spirit" (PhD diss., Princeton Theological Seminary, 1990), 37–42; see also Carol Lakey Hess, "Educating in the Spirit," *Religious Education* 86.3 (1991): 383–98.

[17] J. P. Moreland, *Kingdom Triangle: Recover the Christian Mind, Renovate the Soul, Restore the Spirit's Power* (Grand Rapids: Zondervan, 2007), 182.

[18] As argued in Amos Yong, *The Spirit Poured Out on All Flesh: Pentecostalism and the Possibility of Global Theology* (Grand Rapids: Baker Academic, 2005), ch. 7.

of a virtue or a character that then opens the eyes to see the world in a different way. The idea is that one cannot "see" life from God's perspective without becoming like God. We have already associated this approach with the notion of a *habitus* invested in moral formation or the sanctifying operation of the Spirit. The second looks for the Spirit's ecstatically catching the person up into the divine presence. From this ecstatic experience, a new cosmopolitan vision of the world emerges. The *habitus* is not simply about moral formation but about encounters with transcendence in such a way that the charismatic life ecstatically catches individuals up to glimpse a vision of the end from which mission flows. These name the essential difference between process and crisis. Our own historical survey suggests that at their best, holiness-pentecostal practices fused both the (oftentimes ecstatic) encounter with the Spirit and the revelatory work of the same Spirit so that spiritual experiences relate to the intuitive grasp of the whole found in Christ and, as such, are part and parcel of the educational process. We see here another dimension of being Christ-formed and Spirit-infused insofar as the Spirit moves in and through the nondiscursive grasp of particularity from which discursive reasoning launches and returns the person to a more holistic vision of creation, which finds its ultimate telos in Christ the pattern for all things.

So, if the Spirit is not to be considered as if manifesting only periodically but also in the day-to-day, then are we to assume also that all things are by the Spirit, in which case, as the saying goes, *if everything is* x (of the Spirit), *then nothing is* x (of the Spirit)? Carol Hess suggests, in attempting to move beyond the "Spirit of the gaps," that education in the Spirit unfolds through the encountering of limits, the contrasting with and experiencing of otherness, not least of the living Christ in and through others.[19] Hess' pedagogy of encounter is consistent with the early Christian and medieval efforts to cultivate encounters with the divine, yet such an account needs not only to incorporate the soteriological work of the Spirit delineated in the Scriptures but to see that Christ is truly and finally found as Lord of glory in the whole to which each particular person may bear witness. Put concisely, if the work of the Spirit is to reconcile creation and creatures to God in Christ, then education in the Spirit has a "redemptive pulse" that enables participation in this strange process of theocentric and Christocentric—in other words: trinitarian—reconciliation.[20] The movement is from part to whole, from the complexity of particularity to the simplicity of that final telos and back again.

In short, a pneumatological theology of Christian higher education has to be resolutely trinitarian. But what does this mean? Robert Pazmiño has also urged a "trinitarian educational imagination," one that insists that "the Triune God being *for* us is the essential starting point for understanding the theological foundation of Christian education."[21] Pazmiño's elaboration of this trinitarian notion of education includes attention to Jesus as teacher and to the Spirit's work in Christ, in the church, and in various educational contexts. He rightly underscores that teaching in the Spirit of Jesus participates in the mission of the resurrected

---

[19]   Hess, "Educating in the Spirit," ch. 5.

[20]   Frank Rogers Jr., "Dancing with Grace: Toward a Spirit-Centered Education," *Religious Education* 89.3 (1994): 377–95, at 392.

[21]   Robert W. Pazmiño, *God Our Teacher: Theological Basics in Christian Education* (Grand Rapids: Baker Academic, 2001), 29 and 35 (emphasis orig.).

Christ.[22] Pazmiño thus presents "an educational Trinity" that understands learners engaging with content within an educational context.[23] Yet how such a trinitarian configuration is correlated theologically is ambiguous, even as the pneumatological components operate only within certain explanatory levels rather than being thoroughly interwoven with the educational vision. We have already seen how the patristic emphasis on salutary teaching pointed toward the way in which the Word was the pattern of humanity and contained all the patterns of creation. In Athanasian terms, the Word in salvation is the selfsame Word in creation, which means that the Word never ceases to teach in a multitude of ways that facilitate the full health of the human person and of humanity as a whole. This perspective resided behind Hugh of St. Victor's division of the arts into the theoretical, practical, and mechanical as corresponding to the healing of ignorance, vice, and bodily infirmity. There is a deeper trinitarian educational imagination that must be fully articulated.

If the goal of a trinitarian theology of Christian higher education is to be achieved, our claim is that such needs to proceed from a rich pneumatological foundation. The medieval schoolmen and their descendants understood that the vision of God involved encountering the living Christ through the divine Spirit. This encounter, however, was an encounter with the wisdom woven into creation all of which pointed back toward the living Wisdom of God. It was an encounter that began in particularly and ended in eschatology. Our own reconstruction of this historic insight directs our gaze back to the Pentecost-narrative. How might we reread this scriptural account toward a pentecostal, pneumatological, and trinitarian theology of Christian higher education?

5.1.2 The Spirit-Infused Life and the Life of the Mind: Performing Pentecost

Our perspective reads Acts 2 not just as one among other texts in the New Testament but as inaugurating the present dispensation between incarnation and parousia. As such, Christian theology is not only normed by the life, ministry, death, resurrection, and ascension of Jesus, but considers these events of salvation history messianically, from the standpoint of the Spirit's anointing and resting upon the Son, raising him from the dead, and baptizing others, creation itself, inevitably, into his image.[24] Christian life in the present therefore is both incarnationally understood and pentecostally impelled, overflowing through the outpouring of the Spirit, not just as a one-time event that occurred two thousand years ago but as continuously unfolded via God's promise to meet human creatures through the divine breath. This latter dynamic is thereby crucial to, rather than an optional addendum on, trinitarian faith. We have presented more extensive hermeneutical and theological justification for such a pneumatological claim elsewhere,[25] even

---

[22] Robert W. Pazmiño, *So What Makes Our Teaching Christian? Teaching in the Name, Spirit, and Power of Jesus* (Eugene: Wipf and Stock, 2008).

[23] Pazmiño, *God Our Teacher*, 141–45.

[24] See Frank D. Macchia, *Justified in the Spirit: Creation, Redemption, and the Triune God*, Pentecostal Manifestos (Grand Rapids: Eerdmans, 2010), and *Jesus the Spirit-Baptizer: Christology in Light of Pentecost* (Grand Rapids: Eerdmans, 2021).

[25] See Amos Yong, *The Hermeneutical Spirit: Theological Interpretation and Scriptural Imagination for the 21st Century* (Eugene: Cascade, 2017), and *Mission after Pentecost: The Witness of the Spirit from Genesis to Revelation*, Mission in Global Community (Grand Rapids: Baker Academic, 2019), among other works to be referred to as we go.

as we will return in the rest of this part to buttressing them for the purposes of our argument. For now, we outline a theology of the life of the mind by drawing together key pneumatological texts read in the light of Pentecost.[26]

Following the prior observation of Justin Martyr that the Messiah embodies the gifts of the divine spirit mentioned by the prophet Isaiah (see §2.2 above), we observe that Luke the theologian of Spirit-empowered witness in the book of Acts presents Jesus as the prototype of the Spirit-led life in the Third Gospel. Jesus' public ministry is pronounced as being Spirit-driven: "to bring good news to the poor . . . [,] to proclaim release to the captives and recovery of sight to the blind, to let the oppressed go free, to proclaim the year of the Lord's favour" (Luke 4:18–19).[27] It is within this depiction that Jesus as charismatic teacher is notable. Thus, when asked, within the context of a conversation in which Jesus is rejoicing in the Spirit (10:21), about how to attain eternal life (10:25), Jesus' response "substantially reproduces Deut 6:5 (LXX)"—"You shall love the Lord your God with all your heart, and with all your soul" (Luke 10:27)—but also adds "the fourth phrase 'your whole mind (*dianoia*).'"[28] On the one hand, this is not inconsistent with the synoptic witness, with Matthew (22:37) and Mark (12:30) also including reference to the mind. On the other hand, if "the primary purpose of this fourfold inventory is to stress the totality of one's love for God,"[29] then only Luke records Jesus following up the criterion with what is easily understated as a thought-provoking narrative regarding the relationship between belief and practice: that regarding the Good Samaritan.

The Good Samaritan story expands on Jesus' response to an initial question about eternal life: love your neighbor as you would love God—confirming the import of *philanthropia* as an attribute of God and a social practice toward neighbor lifted up by ancient *paideia* (§2.2.3)—as that is how one lives toward eternity.[30] Yet two additional comments are warranted here.[31] First, whereas the other gospel writers repeated the command to "love" the neighbor as oneself, Luke's version "collapses the two commandments into one,"[32] thus insisting that one's love of neighbor is no less consuming of all one's being than one's love of God. As such, the love of neighbor equally requires the mindfulness devoted to the love of

---

[26] We are unaware of other efforts to develop a theology of the life of the mind that have fronted pneumatology. One includes discussion of how the Spirit helps with understanding the Bible—e.g., J. P. Moreland, *Love Your God with All Your Mind: The Role of Reason in the Life of the Soul* (Colorado Springs: NavPress, 1997), 45–49—which is commendable. Our goal here, however, is different: to sketch a scriptural pneumatology of the intellectual life.

[27] For more on Jesus' Spirit-baptized ministry, see also Darío López Rodriguez, *The Liberating Mission of Jesus: The Message of the Gospel of Luke*, trans. Stefanie E. Israel and Richard E. Waldrop, Pentecostals, Peacemaking, and Social Justice 6 (Eugene: Wipf and Stock, 2012).

[28] Luke Timothy Johnson, *The Gospel of Luke*, Sacra Pagina 3 (Collegeville: Liturgical, 1991), 172.

[29] Joel B. Green, *The Gospel of Luke*, New International Commentary on the New Testament (Grand Rapids: Eerdmans, 1997), 428n108.

[30] While others have rightfully sought to develop a theology of the life of the mind from out of this Lukan and related synoptic parallels—e.g., John Piper, *Think: The Life of the Mind and the Love of God* (Wheaton: Crossway, 2010)—our reading takes the additional step of considering of the commandment to "love the Lord your God with . . . all your mind" in relationship to the Good Samaritan story.

[31] The following summarizes what is further explicated in Yong, "The Life in the Spirit and the Life of the Mind: Luke 10:25-29," which is ch. 12 of his *The Kerygmatic Spirit: Apostolic Preaching in the 21st Century*, ed. Josh Samuel (Eugene: Cascade, 2018), 147–61.

[32] Johnson, *Gospel of Luke*, 172.

God. Second, by way of amplification, Jesus introduces a severe case of cognitive dissonance via an unexpected reversal of roles: the exemplarity of the despised Samaritan compared with morally deficient Jews, all against the backdrop of cities on the edges of or external to the Judean world (Luke 10:13–14). It is not just that Samaritans were presumed to be outside of the covenant, but they were also impure, for all intents and purposes demon-infested (cf. John 8:48). Yet in this case, a Samaritan was the moral and spiritual superior to the Jew, and this as a servant to and on behalf of a fellow Jew no less, thereby demonstrating that eternal life might be accessible where not previously considered.[33]

Our point here is a pneumatological one regarding the life of the mind: that Jesus' Spirit-led ministry includes the call to loving God with all that we are, including the mind, so that this commitment pervades the full spectrum of our lives.[34] The Spirit that enables joy of the soul (Luke 10:21) and empowers (eternal) life-giving goodness with the hands through human creatures, regardless of their labels, is also the Spirit that invites such whole-hearted, fully activated, and thoroughly intentional discipleship forged through, as Carol Hess has indicated (above), encounter with different others. In fact, the life of the mind unfolds dynamically and formatively as the proclamation/teaching encounters the other, and in this encounter, the teaching must respond and adapt to the challenges of particularity.[35] This is essentially how discursive traditions are formed as the kernel/seed takes root in and is performed and practiced amid different soil (in this case Samaritan soil). Life in the footsteps of the Spirit-empowered Messiah is robustly intellectual, exactly what would be needed if these followers were to remain in pursuit of the Spirit that leads into all truth and enables navigation of daily life. The Spirit's leading into truth is doubly urgent in the context of competing truths, indeed when such includes falsehoods antithetical to the faith and even anti-Christic, as was the case in the community that received the Johannine letters (see 1 John 2:27). Further, the Johannine Paraclete, who is the "Spirit of truth" in the Fourth Gospel (John 15:26, 16:13), comes as a guide and an advocate to those persecuted for their messianic faith—there could be no more drastic and discordant encounter with otherness than in such cases! Yet this accentuates the role of the intellect in the most pressured of life's circumstances, even as it deepens the interrelationship between the love of God and the work of the mind (John 14:15–16), and the love of fellow human creatures by extension (13:34–35), including one's persecutors and enemies.

Reviewing the Gospels from this perspective after Pentecost highlights the life of the mind as at least parallel to, if not overlapping significantly with, life in the

---

[33] Amos Yong, *Spirit Poured Out on All Flesh*, 244–48, has heretofore considered the Good Samaritan narrative much more extensively with regard to a theology of religions and of interfaith encounter; here we revisit this account for a theology of the intellectual life.

[34] Note thus that the first section of each of the three chapters of this part of our book all begin with *loving God*—with our minds, hearts, and hands respectively.

[35] Whereas Howard Thurman considers such encounters in more general religious terms, we do so in a more pentecostal and pneumatological key; see Thurman, *The Creative Encounter: An Interpretation of Religion and the Social Witness* (New York: Harper and Brothers, 1954); see also Vasileios E. Pantazis, "The 'Encounter' as an 'Event of Truth' in Education: An Anthropological-Pedagogical Approach," *Educational Theory* 62.6 (2012): 641–57, who explicates such a pedagogy of inharmonious encounter in dialogue with continental philosophical traditions.

Spirit. The Pauline witness is complementary, including the magisterial Epistle to the Romans, which transitions from the lengthy didactic first part into the more practical implications of part 2 via a transformational pivot: "I appeal to you therefore, brothers and sisters, by the mercies of God, to present your bodies as a living sacrifice, holy and acceptable to God, which is your spiritual worship. Do not be conformed to this world, *but be transformed by the renewing of your minds*, so that you may discern what is the will of God—what is good and acceptable and perfect" (Rom 12:1–2, emphasis added). The more theoretical is assuredly distinct from the more applicational, but they are nevertheless related and interlaced in Christian discipleship. As Paul says elsewhere that our transformation is pneumatically and pneumatologically accomplished (2 Cor 3:18), so also is the renewal of the mind here, indeed the mind's redemption and empowerment, part and parcel of the spiritual life, one instigated by the divine love "poured into our hearts through the Holy Spirit" (Rom 5:5). Read pentecostally, then, the Spirit in Romans challenges, converts, and renews human minds to enable the actions of human hands.[36]

Yet the Spirit of Pentecost not only enables Christian mission but does so "in the last days" (Acts 2:17). This is the eschatological Spirit, one that both inaugurates the coming realm of God (about which we will have more to say: see §7.1.1 below) and achieves the harmony of the final reconciliation. There is therefore an aesthetic dimension of the life of the mind, one through which the intellect is drawn into contemplation of the beauty of the divine life and the glory intended for the creation.[37] As St. Paul puts it also in the Roman letter: that the Spirit resonates "with our spirit that we are children of God, and if children, then heirs, heirs of God and joint heirs with Christ—if, in fact, we suffer with him *so that we may also be glorified with him*"; and that as creatures, we are indeed yearning and reaching for the time when "creation itself will be set free from its bondage to decay and *will obtain the freedom of the glory of the children of God*," so that in the meanwhile, "we ourselves, who have the first fruits of the Spirit, groan inwardly while we wait for adoption, the redemption of our bodies" (Rom 8:16–17, 21, 23, emphases added). Creaturely life saddled with sin, suffering, and struggle is being redirected in the new covenant, "written not with ink but with the Spirit of the living God, not on tablets of stone but on tablets of human hearts" (2 Cor 3:3), toward participation in the divine glory: "And all of us, with unveiled faces, seeing the glory of the Lord as though reflected in a mirror, are being transformed into the same image from one degree of glory to another; for this comes from the Lord, the Spirit" (2 Cor 3:18).[38] Hence, the eschatological calling of the Spirit is to "Come" (Rev 22:17a), to enjoy the glory of

---

[36] For more on this pneumatological reading of Rom 12.1–2, see Stephen Mills, "Renewal of the Mind: The Cognitive Sciences and a Pneumatological Anthropology of Transformation" (PhD diss., Regent University School of Divinity, 2014). Ellen T. Charry, *By the Renewing of Your Minds: The Pastoral Function of Christian Doctrine* (New York: Oxford University Press, 1997), 46–49, also discusses Paul and the Spirit's renewal of the mind.

[37] For further discussion of the Spirit in relationship to the beautiful eschatological "transfiguration of all things," see Patrick Sherry, *Spirit and Beauty: An Introduction to Theological Aesthetics*, 2nd ed. (London: SCM Press, 2002), ch. 7.

[38] See Yong, *Spirit of Love: A Trinitarian Theology of Grace* (Waco: Baylor University Press, 2012), ch. 7, for further pneumatological readings of Paul's Corinthian and Roman letters.

the kings of the earth and the honor of all nations (Rev 21:24, 26), all now refracted through the light of the Lamb (Rev 21:22–23).[39]

Thus, pentecostally speaking, whatever else the gift of the Spirit accomplishes—and the preceding does not claim to be exhaustive in this regard—the divine wind guides (through whatever encounter of disruption) to truth through the renewal of the mind, enables the achievement of the good through the empowering of the hands, and salvages (a disharmonious) creation to its eschatological beauty through the participatory groaning of human hearts. As our predecessors in the Christian tradition (part 1) recognized that the educational path unveiled to human creatures the truth, goodness, and beauty of things through encounter with the divine, so also will we in the remainder of this book return continually to develop our pneumatological theology of the intellectual life in relationship to these transcendental ideals. In this way, the Christian gospel empowers the intellectual quest, illuminating inquiry into the fundamental concerns arising from out of the human condition and initiating us into the ideals that limn our future longings.[40]

5.1.3 Scriptural Education in the Spirit: Reappropriating Biblical Traditions

If, as the preceding suggests, the Christian life of the mind read pentecostally (i.e., starting with the day of Pentecost narrative as a kind of hermeneutical lens for approaching the Scriptures) is thoroughly pneumatological in being guided by the Spirit, then are there further biblical indications that might inform such a Pentecost-theology of the intellect? This segment of the argument suggests such a pneumatological approach to these issues, especially as they are central to the activities of the contemporary university. Our goal here is to secure further scriptural traction for thinking theologically and pneumatologically about research and scholarship later in this chapter.

We here return to comment further on Jesus the Spirit-filled teacher. Above we noted that Jesus' invitation to the life of the mind, at least in St. Luke's telling, was issued via a story, that of the Good Samaritan. Here we step back to situate Jesus' storytelling (in this case) against the broader canvas of his teaching activities and ministry.[41] We know Jesus discipled his chosen followers (the Twelve), addressed individuals (Nicodemus), interacted with smaller groups (in homes or synagogues), and addressed larger groups across the spectrum of scales (as in the Seventy or the Sermon on the Mount/Plain, which was said to be attended by thousands). It is also obvious that he used different strategies, especially striking being his ministry actions—e.g., healings, exorcisms, miraculous feeding of crowds, cleansing of the temple—that served as teaching occasions.[42] Further, as is well

---

[39]   There is much more to be said about this pneumatological invitation from a Pentecost-perspective; see Amos Yong, "Kings, Nations, and Cultures on the Way to the New Jerusalem: A Pentecostal Witness to an Apocalyptic Vision," in *The Pastor and the Kingdom: Essays Honoring Jack W. Hayford*, ed. S. David Moore and Jonathan Huntzinger (Southlake, Tex.: TKU, 2017), 231–51, and, more expansively, *Revelation*, Belief: A Theological Commentary on the Bible (Louisville: Westminster John Knox, 2021).

[40]   Bradley G. Green, *The Gospel and the Mind: Recovering and Shaping the Intellectual Life* (Wheaton: Crossway, 2010), is Christomorphic in his approach to founding the intellectual life on the *evangelion*; ours negates nothing of what he wishes to achieve, but reconstrues the whole pneumatologically and thereby in explicit trinitarian terms.

[41]   A solid overview is Pheme Perkins, *Jesus as Teacher* (Cambridge: Cambridge University Press, 1990).

[42]   See J. T. Dillon, *Jesus as a Teacher: A Multidisciplinary Case Study* (Bethesda: International Scholars, 1995), ch. 5, for more on how Jesus taught.

known, Jesus deployed various teaching forms and genres of communication: not only stories but aphorisms, proverbs, parables, questions or riddles, practical instruction, and exposition and reapplication of authoritative texts, among other means. We suggest that the plurality of methods manifest in Jesus' teaching and ministering is enabled by the anointing of the Spirit for the purposes of meeting his audiences where they were. What Luke calls "the poor" in this context (cf. Luke 4:18) includes a diverse group of individuals and gatherings, as the narrative of the Third Gospel unfolds, and our claim is that the Spirit-inspired teacher operates with a wide repertoire to effectively connect to and engage each with his or her own environmentally complicated situation.[43]

How Jesus teaches, we further contend, is intertwined with what he teaches. Jesus' Spirit-prompted message regarding the advent of "the year of the Lord's favor" (4:19) both hearkens back to the promise to ancient Israel and announces the arrival of the divine reign. In filling out the content of this eschatological message, Jesus relies most assuredly on the sacred Scriptures: "the law of Moses, the prophets, and the psalms" (24:44). These are understood first in relationship to his own life and mission, a harbinger of the impending reign of God (Acts 1:3b).

Now here is the intriguing correlation: that the scriptural traditions that are at the heart of Jesus' preaching and teaching encapsulate not just intellectual content but also affective guides and practical wisdom and counsel.[44] As Walter Brueggemann indicates, "each of these three parts of the canon (summarized in Jer 18:18 ['instruction shall not perish from the priest, nor counsel from the wise, nor the word from the prophet']) has a different *function* in Israel, proceeds with a different *epistemology*, and makes a different *claim* in Israel."[45] As Brueggemann goes on to suggest—here drawing from the Aristotelian tradition—conservatives might be drawn to Torah (*ethos*), radicals to prophets (*pathos*), and humanists to wisdom literature (*logos*). A Pentecost-perspective on this triad observes in addition not only that the different genres achieve distinct objectives but that these have epistemic implications, inviting thereby a diversity of educational modalities to challenge, interrogate, and intervene upon various learners and their challenging situations.

In effect, the New Testament parallel could be also that there are gospels, a historical text (Acts), and letters, although more pertinent for our discussion is that there are four gospels, each with its own distinctive shape, directed toward different audiences and intended to achieve diverse purposes.[46] We do not need here to adjudicate issues in the

---

[43] Dillon intriguingly concludes: "Jesus was an accomplished yet ineffective teacher. He taught well, even masterfully in some respects, yet the learning that came about did not correspond to the quality of the teaching" (*Jesus as a Teacher*, 161). This conclusion follows if the criterion of success is that Jesus' audiences "caught" what he taught and then lived out these teachings, and assuming that the evangelists' accounts were designed to communicate his effectiveness and instead recorded his failures in this regard. Our own purposes mean instead that we can still reappropriate Jesus' methods as relevant for our tasks and then judge their viability in further conversation with the biblical sources.

[44] Thus the recognition of Jesus as a sage, a teacher of spiritual and moral wisdom; see Ted Newell, *Five Paradigms for Education: Foundational Views and Key Issues* (New York: Palgrave Macmillan, 2014), ch. 5, and also Ben Witherington III, *Jesus the Sage: The Pilgrimage of Wisdom* (Minneapolis: Augsburg Fortress, 1994).

[45] Walter Brueggemann, *The Creative Word: Canon as a Model for Biblical Education* (Philadelphia: Fortress, 1982), 9 (emphasis orig.). Note that the threefold scriptural categorization of Jer 18:18 anticipates, even structures Jesus' understanding of the three-part canon of ancient Israel (see Luke 24:44—just mentioned).

[46] Francis Watson, *The Fourfold Gospel: A Theological Reading of the New Testament Portraits of Jesus* (Grand Rapids: Baker Academic, 2016).

so-called synoptic problem, as our point is a more modest one: the claim that Jesus draws from the full scope of ancient Israel's Scriptures with their plurimorphic shape is consistent both with the multivocality of his own teaching methods and with the quadratic portrayal of his bequeathed legacy.[47] More specifically, if the Spirit-empowered Jesus adopted many forms of teaching to reach his immediate audiences, then the Spirit-inspired gospel writers also wrote in stereophonic mode—in a way of saying—so that Jesus' life and message might resonate with later generations, "for [their] children, and for all who are far away" (Acts 2:39).[48] There is a congruence of form and content, in other words: the Scriptures declare one message, the creator God, his redeeming Son, and the Spirit of the divine rule to come—as was central to the early Christian understanding of human participation in the divine story (§2.2.1 above) but in different tongues that initially shock us from our complacency.

One of the letters addressed to Timothy frames the pneumatological connection between at least truth (*logos*) and goodness (*ethos*) in this way: "All scripture is inspired [literally, θεόπνευστος (*theopneustos*), or divinely in-spirated or breathed] by God and is useful for teaching, for reproof, for correction, and for training in righteousness [*pros paideian tēn en dikaiosunē*], so that everyone who belongs to God may be proficient, equipped for every good work" (2 Tim 3:16–17). There are therefore different scriptural purposes, albeit intelligible as aiming for educating in holiness and righteousness and shaping human persons for the good, and godly, life. A diversity of scriptural writings, genres, and forms—for example, story (narrative), law (which inspires trust in a God of regularity), poetry (which is affective and imaginative), wisdom (not just discursive knowledge), the prophets (which involves personal address and challenge), gospels (inculcating discipleship), epistles (written for edification, among other purposes), and apocalyptic (dealing with alienation and hope)[49]— were adapted for these disparate, even if interrelated, resolutions. The Spirit thus inspires these many types of canonical texts so that precisely through their discordance "God's deeds of power" (Acts 2:11b) are made known. There is hence cognitive content to these writings, but their informational substance is mingled with their formational and transformational— sanctifying and saving, to use the theological language of the classical Christian tradition covered in the first part of this book—aims. These latter are oftentimes goals toward which we are resistant if cognizant about at all.

Review of scholarship on education in ancient Israel can illuminate how the pastoral letter's views regarding the purposes of the sacred writings were anticipated in the wisdom literature. To be sure, it is difficult to conclude that there were any schools in the first millennium BC in any definitive sense of the word, but the ancient Hebrew sages forged a *via media* between a more mythically inclined Mesopotamian tradition and the more

---

[47] See Sylvia Wikley Collinson, *Making Disciples: The Significance of Jesus' Educational Methods for Today's Church* (Milton Keynes: Paternoster, 2004), part 2, for discussion of each of Jesus' teaching forms in the four gospels.

[48] For more on this argument, see Yong, *Renewing Christian Theology: Systematics for a Global Christianity*, images and commentary by Jonathan A. Anderson (Waco: Baylor University Press, 2014), ch. 12.

[49] Tremper Longman III, *Reading the Bible with Heart and Mind* (Colorado Springs: NavPress, 1997), part 4, discusses these various genres and their (intended) effects; note that our discussion here about many scriptural genres correlating with many biblical illocutionary effects anticipates the argument for many tongues opening up to multiple intelligences and learning aptitudes in the next chapter.

philosophically tinged Egyptian wisdom.[50] Beyond the fact that, as already indicated, the rhetorical strategies employed by Israel's sages appealed to *ethos, pathos,* and *logos*,[51] they also presumed what has turned out to be a time-honored epistemological set of intuitions and sensibilities: "The four verbs—*rā'a, sāpar, kûn,* and *hāqar*—nicely describe the cognitive analytic process as the poet understood it," denotable as that of observation, discussion, provisional hypotheses/conclusions, and analytic assessment.[52] Sagely *observation* was multimodal, reliant upon the broad spectrum of the senses, predominantly hearing and (in Qohelet or Ecclesiastes) seeing, although fed by the full range of human perceptual capacities, even as creaturely knowledge accumulated through the knowing process but, until funneled through analysis and then perspicacious application in life's circumstances, did not yet amount to true wisdom. Such existential implementation required the divine assistance: "a sage needed a gift from the deity to grasp the full meaning of information possessed by arduous intellectual effort and to put knowledge to effective use."[53] Wisdom as expression of authentic learning and formation, therefore, depends on propositions, laments, expressions of anger, songs, sayings, etc., yet is ultimately not discursively propositionalizable but manifest in life.[54] Intriguingly, the theme verse for the Septuagint version of the book of Proverbs: "The fear of the Lord is the beginning of wisdom; and good understanding to all that practise it: and piety [*eusebeia*] toward God is the beginning of discernment; but the ungodly will set at nought wisdom and instruction [*sophia kai paideia*]" (Prov. 1:7, *The Septuagint with Apocrypha*, Brenton 1885)—connects wisdom with piety and both with *paideia* (instruction, training, or even discipline).

Divinely in-spirited Scripture, therefore, seeks the sanctification of human hearts and the redemption of human actions, but this arrives, paradoxically, as from beyond us and yet in and through the creation. Thus, the sapiential tradition prompts reflection on how we

> achieve the shock of recognition when intuition arrives at insight about something wholly unfamiliar, something entirely new? . . . How can someone recognize the unheard of, the radically unfamiliar, unless through a gift of intuitive insight? Yet both types of knowledge are real, both the familiar and the effective surprise. The first type yields to self-disciplined research, the second comes upon us as if bestowed by a generous but mysterious Teacher. . . . [This] phenomenon, all the more awesome in a society that venerated the ancient *traditum* far more than any *novum*, assists in understanding

---

[50] As superbly canvassed by James L. Crenshaw, *Education in Ancient Israel: Across the Deadening Silence* (New York: Doubleday, 1998).

[51] Crenshaw, *Education in Ancient Israel*, 133–38, discusses this triad specifically in relationship to ancient Israelite wisdom (beyond the Brueggemann reference cited above).

[52] Crenshaw, *Education in Ancient Israel*, 217. Note here the parallels with the process of attention (to data), thoughtfulness (about the data), reasonableness (connecting the data to other knowledge), and responsibility (acting upon the data) proposed by contemporary epistemologist Bernard Lonergan; for an overview of the Lonerganian epistemology as applied to the Christian university, see R. J. Snell and Steven D. Cone, *Authentic Cosmopolitanism: Love, Sin, and Grace in the Christian University* (Eugene: Pickwick, 2013), ch. 3.

[53] Crenshaw, *Education in Ancient Israel*, 253.

[54] See also Walter Brueggemann, "Passion and Perspective: Two Dimensions of Education in the Bible," in *Theological Perspectives on Christian Formation: A Reader on Theology and Christian Education*, ed. Jeff Astley, Leslie J. Francis, and Colin Crowder (Grand Rapids: Eerdmans, 1996), 71–79.

the combined humility of prayer and restraints of reason in ancient discussions of the teaching enterprise.[55]

On the one hand, then, this is about the Bible's transforming power inasmuch as it mediates the unexpected encounter between creatures and Creator, even a heavenly intrusion as if from the above and beyond through the below and present. On the other hand, in terms derived from the Pentecost-imaginary, the Scripture in its diversity constitutes a myriad of conduits through which the divine spirit erupts into or through the human plane, confronting ourselves with the ultimate Other, but precisely through the various conduits of the creation. The life of the mind is then enabled by the Spirit even as the intellectual life is itself a pursuit of that same Spirit.

5.2 RECONSTITUTING THE UNIVERSITY: MANY TONGUES AND MANY DISCIPLINES

The above discussion attempted to define the Christian life of the mind in pneumatological terms, flowering from out of the day of Pentecost outpouring and thereby being part and parcel of life in the Spirit. Jesus as the paradigmatic Spirit-led teacher instructs using a plurality of methods drawing from the full scope of the tradition handed down to him but adapted to achieve multiple outcomes related to his initiation of the coming reign of God. If his own life and words provoked the learners around him with the otherness of the divine message, then his legacy is continued through his sending his messianic Spirit from the right hand of the Father to alight upon and inhabit those who would seek to embrace his mission via encounter with strangeness and unfamiliarity, beginning with that of the scriptural traditions.

We see continuity *between* this Pentecost-anticipation that wisdom comes through a pneumatic encounter with the biblical teachings *and* the medieval insistence that revelatory insight comes through an imagination fertilized with the liberal arts. The key assumption maintained by the scholastics and their heirs was that study of the arts and otherwise was both an intellectual and a spiritual task, combined rather than bifurcated. If the modern university has attempted to dissociate the one from the other, how might a Pentecost-consideration of Christian higher education today reconceive and reenact their togetherness? So while we can continue our exploration along a number of fronts, we press into this question of a Spirit-ed Christian university by attending to one question posed by the disciplines: how can these realms of knowledge and inquiry also be understood as Spirit-infused if not propelled?

Our claim in this middle section of this chapter is that a Pentecost-theology of the disciplines that constitute the contemporary university, which includes but is irreducible to the arts of the medieval university, both secures disciplinary integrity on the one hand (§5.2.1) and yet facilitates cross-disciplinary inquiry on the other hand (§5.2.2), all the while prodding the pursuit of theological truth (§5.2.3).[56] We realize that the movement

---

[55] Crenshaw, *Education in Ancient Israel*, 184–85.

[56] This section develops the nascent ideas in Yong, *The Spirit of Creation: Modern Science and Divine Action in the Pentecostal-Charismatic Imagination*, Pentecostal Manifestos 4 (Grand Rapids: Eerdmans, 2011), ch. 2.

of our argument here—from *multi*disciplinarity to *inter*disciplinarity to *trans*disciplinarity—is a bit arbitrary as there is no agreed upon technical understanding of these notions and they are used interchangeably in the literature,[57] not to mention that the last, transdisciplinarity, is explicated below in distinctively theological (read: pneumatological and trinitarian) terms absent from the broader discussion. However, this three-part dynamic of multidisciplinary juxtapositioning, interdisciplinary interacting, and transdisciplinary integrating[58] serves heuristically to connect current theorizing across the disciplines and the sciences with our theological purposes, and thus provides one domain with which to continue thinking about the Christian university according to our Pentecost-perspective. The point is not so much to reorganize the structures of higher education needed to operationalize such a vision (that would be an important next step but is beyond the scope of our argument), but to ensure that disciplinarity in its manifold and interactive aspects is theologically—pneumatologically, to be exact—envisioned. Any modicum of success in prosecuting this thesis will enable return, at the end of this chapter (§5.3), to discussion of how the intellectual life can be understood as Spirit-infused in ways that enable research across the disciplines and generate scholarship on truth, goodness, and beauty in anticipation of the triune deity's reign. And even if most Christian colleges and universities will not have funding for research that public institutions do, that does not mean we have no responsibility to attend to and nurture the disciplinary expertise that enables exploration and understanding the world in all of its interrelatedness and differentiatedness.

5.2.1 Between Berlin and Azusa: Pneumatic Multidisciplinarity

The disciplines are realms of knowledge with their own foci, concepts, methods, and practices of inquiry. We can approach variously the disciplinary pathways to human knowing, whether historically in terms of their emergence as bounded methods of inquiry focused on specific objects and bodies of knowledge in the early modern university, or analytically in terms of their fragmentation in postmodern higher education, or otherwise.[59] Our own pneumatological approach goes back to and rereads the Pentecost-narrative analogically vis-à-vis the many disciplines of the contemporary university. The shift recommended flows out from how the Acts 2 invitation to consider the Pentecost outpouring as the Spirit's way of redeeming humanity's many tongues and languages has implications for late modern human knowing, beginning with the apostolic claim "Now there

---

[57]   For instance, Margaret A. Somerville and David J. Rapport, eds., *Transdisciplinarity: Recreating Integrated Knowledge* (Oxford: EOLSS, 2000), is about *interdisciplinarity* as understood and discussed in this book (§5.2.2) rather than about the coordination of the disciplines vis-à-vis a theological horizon (what we call *transdisciplinarity* §5.2.3); while Sivakumar Alagumalai, Stephanie Burley, and John P. Keeves, eds., *Excellence in Scholarship: Transcending Transdisciplinarity in Teacher Education* (Rotterdam: Sense, 2013), are looking to overcome disciplinary fragmentation, thus describing what in our use of these terms is the movement from multidisciplinarity (§5.2.1) to interdisciplinarity (§5.2.2). We can appreciate why, within the context of teacher education, disciplinary specialization might need ameliorative cross-disciplinary fertilization (interdisciplinarity, for us), without denying the value of their distinctive methodological approaches to their variegated realms of knowing and inquiry (multidisciplinarity, for us).

[58]   See Julie Thompson Klein, "A Taxonomy of Interdisciplinarity," in *The Oxford Handbook of Interdisciplinarity*, ed. Robert Frodeman (Oxford: Oxford University Press, 2010), 15–30.

[59]   Marvin Oxenham, *Higher Education in Liquid Modernity* (New York: Routledge, 2013), esp. ch. 7, discusses the pluralization of the university, including the disintegration of disciplinary knowledge.

were devout Jews from every nation under heaven living in Jerusalem. And at this sound [of the Spirit's coming] the crowd gathered and was bewildered, because each one heard them speaking in the native language of each" (Acts 2:5–6). The narrative's explication of this phenomenon by way of enumerating a very select number of the ancient Hebrew lists of seventy nations (2:9–11) is designed first and foremost to make the point that the gospel is intended for "the ends of the earth" (1:8), overcoming linguistic, ethnic, and cultural barriers by the Spirit.[60] The point here lies not so much on the Jewishness of those gathered in Jerusalem but, as the Acts text later elaborates (Acts 6–7), on their Hellenized character, one that reflects a cosmopolitan, complex, and dynamic set of Mediterranean identities interwoven with Greco-Roman cultures and that therefore anticipates Peter's later claim: "God shows no partiality, but in every nation anyone who fears him and does what is right is acceptable to him" (10:34b–35). Not just the Jews but also Greek proselytes (2:10b; cf. Rom 1:16, 2:9–10), meaning all who are non-Jews, are also caught up in this Pentecost-outpouring.

What does the multiculturality of Acts 2 have to do with the many disciplines of the modern research university, the archetype of which is the University of Berlin?[61] If languages provide the grammars that structure human lives and relationships, and if cultures are linguistically (at least) organized social and practical environments through which interactions unfold, then we can perhaps track the following similitude: that the disciplines provide the methodological assumptions and discursive frameworks that structure human inquiry and that the sciences in their various spheres—for example, the natural, social, or human sciences—are disciplinary and institutionally organized sets of social practices through which knowledge is advanced over generations.[62] In other words, the disciplines and their various fields of inquiry are nothing less than linguistic-cultural practices, sometimes highly technical (thus getting scientific PhDs takes so many years of initiation). As the Pentecost-event signaled the possibility of the redemption of the many languages and cultures of the ancient Mediterranean world and as the early Christians were convinced the truth functioned within creation and that human rationality was patterned after the salutary teaching in the form of Christ (see §2.2.2 above), so also we can expect the Spirit to lead inquirers to all truth (about the world) through the many cultural practices (disciplines) of modern scientific and related forms of higher educational inquiry.[63]

It is within this context that pneumatic multilinguality and the modern university's multidisciplinarity might find convergent dissonance. The response of the crowd on the day of Pentecost was amazement and astonishment (Acts 2:7), indeed a perplexity and

---

[60]   For further exposition, see Yong, *Spirit Poured Out on All Flesh*, ch. 4.

[61]   On the University of Berlin, see Thomas Bender, ed., *The University and the City: From Medieval Origins to the Present* (New York: Oxford University Press, 1988), ch. 9, and Kenneth Garcia, *Academic Freedom and the Telos of the Catholic University* (New York: Palgrave Macmillan, 2012), ch. 3.

[62]   See Gavan J. McDonell, "Disciplines as Cultures: Towards Reflection and Understanding," in Somerville and Rapport, *Transdisciplinarity*, 27–33; cf. also Andrew Pickering, ed., *Science as Practice and Culture* (Chicago: University of Chicago Press, 1992), and Frederick Grinnell, *Everyday Practice of Science: Where Intuition and Passion Meet Objectivity and Logic* (Oxford: Oxford University Press, 2009).

[63]   A prior version of this argument is Yong, "Academic Glossolalia? Pentecostal Scholarship, Multidisciplinarity, and the Science-Religion Conversation," *Journal of Pentecostal Theology* 14.1 (2005): 61–80.

bewilderment that led to dismissal on the one hand ("They are filled with new wine" [2:13]) and to inquiry on the other ("What does this mean?" [2:12]). The contemporary postmodern climate has led some to see the disciplinary chasms within higher education as signaling the displacement of the *university* with a *multiversity* so that not only are there now many centers of power, constituencies, and trajectories both internal and external,[64] but also the coherent curriculum of former generations has been subverted by mere local (rather than universal) knowing.[65] Undeniably, there are disciplinary turf battles fought to secure prerogatives that result in higher educational curricular discordance, and in these cases undergraduates might come away wondering *what does this mean*, and others are bolstered in their self-perceived "anti-intellectual" inclinations to dismiss the higher educational enterprise as filled with the "wine" of human hubris.[66] Disciplinary overreach in these instances, whether of the social sciences and their reductionist anthropologies or of the natural sciences and their materialist ontologies,[67] not only sets up scholars within these disciplines as arbiters of human knowledge outside of their areas of expertise but also dispenses with the perceived "wine" of the spiritual and of the divine Spirit. The result in these cases is both the marginalization if not outright exclusion of religion, surely theology, and the pressure for Christian institutions of higher education to succumb to such presumed universal knowledge even if these claims exceed the scope of the various (secular) disciplines, at least as historically understood and developed.[68]

We will return in a moment to suggest how theology (and pneumatology) is disciplinarily relevant, but the important point here is that a Pentecost-approach to the many disciplines of the late modern and even postmodern university highlights the particularity of their distinctive perspectives amid a kind of harmonious whole. On the one hand, the

---

[64] On a historical and phenomenological perspective on the multiversity, see Clark Kerr, *The Uses of the University*, 3rd ed. (Cambridge, Mass.: Harvard University Press, 1982), ch. 1; while Kerr's model is, of course, informed by his chancellorship over the University of California's multisite system, we should also keep in mind the evolution of the multiversity idea over the last half century.

[65] The introductory chapter of Anthony Smith and Frank Webster, eds., *The Postmodern University? Contested Visions of Higher Education in Society* (Buckingham: Society for Research into Higher Education and Open University Press, 1997), discusses the challenges confronting the present *multiversity*; see also Conrad Cherry, *Hurrying toward Zion: Universities, Divinity Schools, and American Protestantism* (Bloomington: Indiana University Press, 1995), ch. 9, and Paul Wangoola, "Mpambo, the African Multiversity: A Philosophy to Rekindle the African Spirit," in *Indigenous Knowledges in Global Contexts: Multiple Readings of Our World*, ed. George J. Sefa Dei, Budd L. Hall, and Dorothy Goldin Rosenberg (Toronto: University of Toronto Press, 2000), 265–77.

[66] Such disjunction between life in the Spirit and the life of the mind is being overcome, as we are urging in this book; see also Marius Nel, "Rather Spirit-Filled than Learned! Pentecostalism's Tradition of Anti-intellectualism and Pentecostal Theological Scholarship," *Verbum et Ecclesia* 37.1 (2016): a1533, DOI: https://doi.org/10.4102/ve.v37i1.1533.

[67] More than a quarter century ago, John Milbank, *Theology and Social Theory: Beyond Secular Reason*, 2nd ed. (Malden: Blackwell, 2006), countered the social scientific hegemony; for a more recent response to how even religious educators have imbibed secular premises, see Edward J. Newell, *"Education Has Nothing to Do with Theology": James Michael Lee's Social Science Religious Instruction* (Eugene: Pickwick, 2006).

[68] Which some have thus been led to describe as the "Babylonian captivity" of theology in the modern university, e.g., Gavin D'Costa, *Theology in the Public Square: Church, Academy and Nation* (Malden: Blackwell, 2005), ch. 1. In this context, Michael L. Budde and John Wright, eds., *Conflicting Allegiances: The Church-Based University in a Liberal Democratic Society* (Grand Rapids: Brazos, 2004), labor to find a faithful way forward within a higher educational environment where church-related schools operate according to the "ground rules" established by liberal secular universities.

model of the medieval university features multiple colleges under a single umbrella; on the other hand, John Henry Newman, an Oxford student at both Trinity and Oriel Colleges, long ago both argued that theology was a branch of knowledge among other branches and admonished that each branch kept out of "the circle of knowledge" would result in other branches (or other sciences or scientific disciplines) exceeding their boundaries in order to fill in the gaps left by such omission.[69] This means at least a resistance to the possibility of any one discipline, including theology, lording it over others.[70]

The movement in the medieval model through the liberal arts was a journey into particularity and the wisdom laced throughout creation (see §2.3.1). Scholasticism also fused a discursive and dialogical (through the use of disputation) approach with the nondiscursive flight into ecstatic contemplation. The pneumatological grounded the movement into particularity to access the wisdom that took one back to Wisdom and the christological pattern that rooted the vision of the whole. If the medieval model moved from a kind of interdisciplinary dialogue around the particularity of creation to the deeper patterns evincing a divine pattern, note that our rationale is not the political correctness of postmodern knowing but a pneumatic compass of the many languages, cultures, and discursive practices each checking the other.

As Mark Noll's christological assessment of the intellectual life presumes a postmodernist perspectivalism that in turn funds "a self-consciously Christian form of chastened realism,"[71] our Pentecost-approach grounds such realistic and perspectivist humility within a broader ontology of creational diversity and plurality so that, like the two-books (of Scripture and of nature) approach prominent during the medieval period (see §2.2.3–2.3.1 above),[72] the many disciplines inquire after, uncover, and give voice to the truths of creation and its various orders. Such pneumatological multidisciplinarity thus "appears to offer the best way forward" for truth to triumph over ideology, "provided that each discipline is allowed to operate according to its own canons and without being swallowed up by its partners."[73] This is a higher educational application of the Pauline principle of charismatic manifestation and prophetic expression: "Do not despise the words of prophets, but test everything; hold fast to what is good" (1 Thess 5:20–21), and "let two or three prophets speak, and let the others weigh what is said" (1 Cor 14:29).

But there is more to the multidisciplinary matrix than the cautionary task of disciplining the abuses of knowledge; rather, the point about multidisciplinarity conceived pentecostally

---

[69] John Henry Newman, *The Idea of the University Defined and Illustrated*, ed. Martin J. Svaglic (Notre Dame: University of Notre Dame Press, 1982), ch. 4; see also Timothy Larsen, "John Henry Newman's *The Idea of a University* and Christian Colleges in the Twenty-First Century," in *The State of the Evangelical Mind: Reflections on the Past, Prospects for the Future*, ed. Todd C. Ream, Jerry A. Pattengale, and Christopher J. Devers (Downers Grove: IVP Academic, 2018), 101–23.

[70] Jaroslav Pelikan, *The Idea of the University: A Reexamination* (New Haven: Yale University Press, 1992), ch. 5.

[71] Mark A. Noll, *Jesus Christ and the Life of the Mind* (Grand Rapids: Eerdmans, 2011), 84.

[72] Also, Yong, "Reading Scripture and Nature: Pentecostal Hermeneutics and Their Implications for the Contemporary Evangelical Theology and Science Conversation," *Perspectives on Science and Christian Faith* 63.1 (2011): 1–13.

[73] As nicely asserted by pentecostal educational theorist William K. Kay, "A View from London and Bangor: Encouragement for Multi-Disciplinary Inquiry," *Pneuma: The Journal of the Society for Pentecostal Studies* 27.1 (2005): 148–55, at 154.

and pneumatologically is that together, through their divergent disciplinary practices (as pertinent to our discussion), what is enabled is speech "about God's deeds of power" (Acts 2:11b), about the creation in all of its complexity, goodness, and beauty. The many disciplines provide divergent routes of exploration, usually focused on different objects of inquiry. Thus, physics studies the laws of nature, chemistry focuses on the natural world's most basic parts, and biology looks at forms of life, combining to parallel how, as the medievals put it (§2.3.1), some of the liberal arts explored the physical and historical world and others the abstract and spiritual realms. Together, these disciplinary excursions combine to inform our knowledge of the world at these different levels and for different purposes going in different directions. The disciplines and various spheres of learning thus function, as one Christian scholar puts it, as "divergent tongues,"[74] presenting different ways of asking questions and offering provisional answers. So, if Christian scholarship walked a paradoxical tightrope between the particularity of faith and openness to other voices,[75] a Pentecost-approach would celebrate and accentuate the gifts of the latter.

Yet the multiplicity of the disciplines operates not only separately, which is important to protect the integrity of what they are each pursuing, but also, in a significant manner, together. At Pentecost "each one heard them speaking in the native language of each" (2:6) can be understood variously. Most obviously, what is emphasized is the plurality of the many other and distinct tongues, so that the Parthian (to choose one) would have surmised, intuiting initially but then confirming in the ensuing chaotic exchange, that Medean, Elamitean, and Mesopotamian, etc., dialects and languages were being spoken. In this reading, a pneumatological theology of the many disciplines observes that each does its work with its own integrity, resulting in a multiperspectival understanding—often loosely associated, and in some cases even rather disconnected, it might be said—of the world in its many parts. Yet the Pentecost-miracle could also have been one of hearing, effectively. Whatever may have been uttered by the crowd, its members heard or understood these, "each of us, in our own native language" (2:8). In this case, the work of the various disciplines is comprehended beyond their delineated boundaries.

With this we begin to move from a multidisciplinary ferment to an interdisciplinary node, one in which the former disparate trajectories of inquiry begin to intersect. There are two dimensions to this interrelationship: the diachronic and the synchronic. Diachronically, the movement is from the primary to the secondary areas of specialization. We saw this earlier among the early *paideia* (§2.1) in which the liberal arts course of study laid the groundwork at the core in order to set up studies in the major area: from the *trivium* to the *quadrivium* to rhetoric or philosophy. All disciplines are important in different ways, some because they get at foundational skills related to language and the ability to describe and organize the world, others because they ascend into the deeper/higher levels of abstract thinking, again, enabling movement from visible to invisible.

---

[74] Crystal L. Downing, "Imbricating Faith and Learning: The Architectonics of Christian Scholarship," in Douglas Jacobsen and Rhonda Hustedt Jacobsen, *Scholarship and Christian Faith: Enlarging the Conversation* (Oxford: Oxford University Press, 2004), 33–44, at 42.

[75] Richard T. Hughes, *The Vocation of the Christian Scholar: How Christian Faith Can Sustain the Life of the Mind*, rev. ed. (Grand Rapids: Eerdmans, 2005), xvii–xviii.

Synchronically, the movement is from the one to the many. Here, although the distinction between *multi-* and *inter*disciplinarity is imprecise, discussion of the *field* of neuroscience, for instance, might clarify some of the ambiguity. On the one hand, those who work in this relatively new field could be trained in any number of disciplines, from genetics to biochemistry, pharmacology, cell biology, and psychology, among others. Developments in the field as hereby understood could accrue cumulatively as advances are made within these disciplinary specializations.[76] On the other hand, there could also be calculated collaboration between geneticists, pharmacologists, and psychologists, for instance, so that there is common cause generated from mutual engagement within a shared social environment.[77] This is not to eliminate the disciplinary differences—although from a pedagogical perspective, especially in online education, the disciplinary boundaries are increasingly blurred (see §6.3)—but it is to allow for a kind of cross-disciplinary dialogue that opens up pathways for research and inquiry. Pentecostal and pneumatological multidisciplinarity, then, invites a cooperative intellectual life, an interdisciplinarity that benefits from the diversity of starting points and facilitates the emergence of new fields where previously divergent approaches come together around common questions.[78]

5.2.2 Between Athens and Jerusalem: Pentecostal Interdisciplinarity

We must now press further into the interdisciplinary space opened up in our analysis. If pneumatic multidisciplinarity pushes research and discovery forward through the diverse, and sometimes discordant, voices of the different disciplines, and if Pentecost-interdisciplinarity welcomes their distinct but mutual witnesses, what exactly is theology's role among the disciplines? More pointedly, if we are in agreement with Newman (as suggested above) that theology is but one among the many disciplines in the Christian university, then whither a *theology* of higher education? Our thesis is that it is precisely a Pentecost stance that both allows for theology to be among the disciplines on the one hand and yet for it also to speak into the disciplinary milieu on the other hand.

That in our version theology is *among* the disciplines means that we are not calling for a return to the premodern ideal of theology as queen *over* the disciplines. But this means neither that the Christian mind is unregulated by scriptural and theological commitments nor that theology as a discipline is muted from questioning conventional knowledge and

---

[76] Steven E. Hyman, "The Challenges of Multidisciplinarity: Neuroscience and the Doctorate," in *Envisioning the Future of Doctoral Education: Preparing Stewards of the Discipline*, ed. Chris M. Golde and George E. Walker (San Francisco: Jossey-Bass, 2006), 226–43, presents one understanding of multidisciplinarity. Remember though that our usage of these terms is heuristic rather than intended to be technically representative since Hyman's multidisciplinarity is, for Eunsook Hyun and her colleagues in the biomedical life sciences, transdisciplinarity; see Eunsook Hyun, Rainer Paslack, and Hilmer Stolte, eds., *Transdisciplinary Interfaces and Innovation in the Life Sciences*, Medicine, Technology and Society 5 (Frankfurt: PL Academic Research, 2014).

[77] No less than the practice of science in general, the practice of cross-disciplinarity collaboration also has to be socially, institutionally, and organizationally cultivated; see Peter Weingart and Nico Stehr, *Practising Interdisciplinarity* (Toronto: University of Toronto Press, 2000).

[78] Disciplines have never been static, now more easily granted in our information age. In fact, "Strict disciplinarity . . . is impossible in a networked world," says Carl Raschke in *The Digital Revolution and the Coming of the Postmodern University* (London: Routledge, 2003), 17. We return later (§6.3) to Raschke.

challenging the overextension of other disciplinary perspectives.[79] Rather, the Christian mind and its theological traditions are servants. Stanley Hauerwas puts it this way: that just as the church commands the loyalty of its members "because it can only rule as a servant . . . [a]ccordingly theology is only a 'queen' of the sciences if humility determines her work."[80] So, if the task of theology (broadly construed) is to provide a christologically and pneumatologically formed way of faith toward such eschatological knowing and living—to enable our participation in the story of God, as the early Christians put it (see §2.2.1 above)—then this book's argument also can be thusly framed: that a pentecostally empowered mind in the Christian university is poised to aid from its being informed by, and in its being in service to, the many other disciplines against the backdrop of the coming divine reign when we will know less dimly and more fully (see 1 Cor 13:12).

In our rendition, then, the intellectual life in the Spirit insists on a polyphonic mutuality between theology (the discipline that researches and reflects upon Christian faith) and the other disciplines. Christian scholars have long wrestled with—and rightly so given the exclusion of faith commitments from the Berlin model of the modern research university—how to bring their faith into their work. Theological perspectives can play presuppositional roles to motivate inquiry, and also inform hypothesis construction, shape scholarly agendas, interpret other disciplinary data, evaluate results of research programs, and guide the application of human knowledge.[81] All of this is true, but it has to be emphasized: interaction between Christian theology and other disciplines runs not only from the former to the latter domains; yes, Christian faith should to be brought to bear on and contribute to human research and scholarship in the disciplines, but the reverse is also true: that Christian faith can and should be informed by knowledge accumulated across the disciplines.[82] Pentecostal interdisciplinarity lifts up, rather than stymies, the many voices from across the Christian university and attempts to adjudicate, in a nonauthoritarian and neverending fashion this side of the eschaton, their different claims. Put alternatively, the disciplines feature a plurality of authorities, each in a sense speaking about divine wondrousness and power manifest in the world.

We will turn in the final part of this chapter to discuss a Pentecost-informed life of the mind in the humanities. In the rest of this middle section, however, we will essay

---

[79]   See, respectively for both claims: Al Wolters, "No Longer Queen: The Theological Disciplines and Their Sisters," in *The Bible and the University*, ed. David Lyle Jeffrey and C. Stephen Evans, Scripture and Hermeneutics Series 8 (Grand Rapids: Zondervan, 2007), 59–79, and Ian A. McFarland, "The Place of Theology in the University," in *Renewing Church and University: The Twenty-Seventh Annual Reformation Day at Emory, October 21, 2014*, ed. M. Patrick Graham, Emory Texts and Studies in Ecclesial Life 7 (Atlanta: Pitts Theology Library, 2014), 21–29.

[80]   Stanley Hauerwas, *The State of the University: Academic Knowledges and the Knowledge of God* (Malden: Blackwell, 2008), 31. Gavin D'Costa, "On Theology, the Humanities, and the University," in *Theology, University, Humanities: Initium Sapientiae Timor Domini*, ed. Christopher Craig Brittain and Francesca Aran Murphy (Eugene: Cascade, 2011), 194–212, wants to rethrone theology as queen of the sciences, but not in any dictatorial sense inconsistent with what we are proposing.

[81]   Todd C. Ream and Perry L. Glanzer, *Christian Faith and Scholarship: An Exploration of Contemporary Developments* (San Francisco: Wiley, 2007), ch. 3.

[82]   William K. Kay, "Interdisciplinary Perspectives within a Christian Context," in *The Idea of a Christian University: Essays in Theology and Higher Education*, ed. Jeff Astley, Leslie J. Francis, John Sullivan, and Andrew Walker (Milton Keynes: Paternoster, 2004), 246–62, presents five models of interface between theology and the disciplines, with the fifth emphasizing dialogical interaction.

some proposals for a Pentecost-understanding of the natural sciences. A helpful mode of mutuality between theology and the natural sciences has been developed by Robert John Russell, the founder and director of the Center for Theology and the Natural Sciences at the Graduate Theological Union in Berkeley, California. "Creative mutual interaction," Russell's proposal, identifies eight interactive pathways, three generated from theological research programs (TRP) and five deriving from scientific research programs (SRP).[83] The latter includes (1) when scientific theories provide constraints on theology (so that theological theories about divine action ought to be mindful of the parameters set by special relativity);[84] (2) when scientific theories generate data inviting theological consideration (e.g., as in $t = 0$ in standard big bang cosmology hearkens to traditional Christian teaching of creation out of nothing); (3) when philosophically interpreted scientific theories are suggestive of theological perspectives (as when quantum mechanics, indeterministically interpreted, has implications for thinking about creaturely freedom and randomness and chance in the world); (4) physical theories can be developed into a philosophical theology of nature (as in the cosmology of Alfred North Whitehead); and (5) when SRP heuristically provides conceptual inspiration and aesthetic impulse for theological imagination (as when astronomy engenders theological grandeur or biological evolution rouses a sense of divine immanence in the created world). If there is to be genuine interdisciplinarity in Christian higher education, Christian faith has to be informed by knowledge in other realms, and these are ways in which such input can be received.

But authentic reciprocity includes theology speaking into SRPs. Going in the other direction, then—and here consistent with the evangelical reflexes just overviewed about how Christian faith can inform scholarly research—Russell identifies the following: that (1) theological doctrines such as *creation ex nihilo* have fostered assumptions about philosophical contingency and rationality undergirding scientific method; (2) theological theories can inspire scientific hypotheses (Russell here provides the counterexample of how atheistic presuppositions motivated the now discredited "steady state" cosmological idea; our own suggestion would be to point to theories of intelligent design as inciting research on the so-called gaps in the sciences of evolutionary biology, even if the results are heretofore far from settled within the relevant scientific communities); and (3) theological theories can inform "selection rules" for (rival) questions within SRP (including identification of theoretical alternatives in the contested realm of quantum gravity).[85]

---

[83] Summarized in the introductory chapter in Robert John Russell, *Cosmology from Alpha to Omega: The Creative Mutual Interaction of Theology and Science* (Minneapolis: Fortress, 2008), esp. 20–24, and also in Russell, *Time in Eternity: Pannenberg, Physics, and Eschatology in Creative Mutual Interaction* (Notre Dame: University of Notre Dame Press, 2012), 72–75; cf. also Philip Clayton, "'Creative Mutual Interaction' as Manifesto, Research Program, and Regulative Ideal," in *God's Action in Nature's World: Essays in Honour of Robert John Russell*, ed. Ted Peters and Nathan Hallanger, Ashgate Science and Religion Series (Aldershot: Ashgate, 2006), 51–63. Note the examples given are largely Russell's.

[84] See Yong, "Divining 'Divine Action' in Theology-and-Science: A Review Essay," *Zygon: Journal of Religion and Science* 43.1 (2008): 191–200, and "How Does God Do What God Does? Pentecostal-Charismatic Perspectives on Divine Action in Dialogue with Modern Science," in *Science and the Spirit: A Pentecostal Engagement with the Sciences*, ed. Amos Yong and James K. A. Smith (Bloomington: Indiana University Press, 2010), 50–71, for more on a pentecostal perspective on pneumatological divine action in a scientific world.

[85] The example related to the third theological contribution to SRP is in Russell, *Time in Eternity*, 83.

Russell's proposal is not the last word about how Christian faith can inform scientific research and scholarship across the disciplines (more about this in the next section), but it is one way in which theology's role can be explicated.[86]

So how might a Pentecost-theology of the life of the mind contribute to the adjudication of disputes in Christian higher education including but not limited to the debate over evolutionary theory? A number of guidelines are recommended here. First, any major theory, that regarding evolution not exempted, will be multidisciplinary and therefore negotiated along many fronts, the theological one included; a Pentecost-perspective will support such discussion and engagement presuming a dynamic scientific "mainstream" that moves as paradigms shift. The point is to hearken to theoretical frames across the disciplines, including their disputations.[87] Human knowledge advances as arguments are mounted to and against existing hypotheses and theories. Pentecostal discrimination exists within, not external to, such controversies.[88]

But, second, Christian institutions of higher education may be well suited, perhaps uniquely so given our pneumatological and Pentecost perspectives, to develop forums— within and across institutions—to attend to the full gamut of voices sounding on any conflicted issue, even to those that are unfashionable. In the natural sciences, as another negative sample (at least from the standpoint of mainstream science), young earth creationist (YEC) ideas have also attempted to generate what Russell calls a scientific research program. Even if so far YEC proposals have not found sufficient traction in and remain unconvincing to the scientific mainstream, the Christian higher educational conversation can perhaps create space to listen to YEC concerns even if their interpretations might be argued against and rejected as scientifically illegitimate. The point is that although YEC ideas and proposals arguably do not belong in formal science courses as such, it is important to create opportunities within the Christian university to understand them as much as possible on their own terms, perhaps not in order to do science alternatively but for what YEC commitments might tell us about vast divergences across the broad spectrum of Christian faith.[89] The point is that if learning foreign languages is like having

---

[86]   For another version, again vis-à-vis the natural sciences, see J. Wentzel van Huyssteen, *The Shaping of Rationality: Toward Interdisciplinarity in Theology and Science* (Grand Rapids: Eerdmans, 1999); cf. Mikael Stenmark, *How to Relate Science and Religion: A Multidimensional Model* (Grand Rapids: Eerdmans, 2004).

[87]   As nicely done in Samuel Joeckel and Thomas Chesnes, eds., *The Christian College Phenomenon: Inside America's Fastest Growing Institutions of Higher Learning* (Abilene: Abilene Christian University Press, 2012), part 7; see also Dorothy F. Chappell and E. David Cook, eds., *Not Just Science: Questions Where Christian Faith and Natural Science Intersect* (Grand Rapids: Zondervan, 2005).

[88]   For more on how a pentecostal perspective can interact with the natural and evolutionary sciences, see Yong, "Pentecostalism and Science: Challenges and Opportunities," in *Proceedings of the Inaugural Faith and Science Conference, Springfield, Missouri, June 27–28, 2011*, ed. David R. Bundrick and Steve Badger (Springfield: Gospel Publishing House, 2012), 133–47; "The Spirit and Creation: Possibilities and Challenges for a Dialogue between Pentecostal Theology and the Sciences," in *Journal of the European Pentecostal Theological Association* 25 (2005): 81–112; idem, "The Spirit of an Evolving Creation: Surmisings of a Pentecostal Theologian," in *How I Changed My Mind about Evolution: Evangelicals Reflect on Faith and Science*, ed. Kathryn Applegate and J. B. Stump (Downers Grove: IVP, 2016), 167–72.

[89]   For more on how these matters are being negotiated within the North American pentecostal academy, whose laity includes YEC adherents, see Steve Badger and Mike Tenneson, "Does the Spirit Create through Evolutionary Processes? Pentecostals and Biological Evolution," in Yong and Smith, *Science and the Spirit*, 92–116; cf. also Michael Tenneson and Steve Badger, "Teaching Origins to Pentecostal Students,"

to be hospitable to others (strangers),[90] then scientific and interdisciplinary endeavor involves being open to perspectives on the edges of the conversation. Further, one also can never predict when and where paradigm-changing implications might be present.[91]

If research *within* the disciplines is an end in itself with respect to increasing knowledge about those disciplinary objects of inquiry, then research and scholarship *across* the disciplines are means to greater ends with respect to objects of inquiry that invite various conjoining perspectives. This means that the multiple disciplines of Berlin understood through the holiness-pentecostal lens of Azusa Street here connect with the paideiac efforts of ancient Athens viewed from the standpoint of Jerusalem. Such endeavor is regulated less by the methodological constraints operative within the various disciplines than by an interpersonal and intersubjective wisdom that facilitates associations and partnerships. This is both the wisdom that assists the many voices, sometimes hostile to one another, to speak into common space—the university, for our purposes—even as it is also the wisdom that such interdisciplinary communication cultivates.[92] The wisdom of the Spirit that is part and parcel of the life of the mind is nurtured by, rather than dispenses with, the many disciplines of the university.

5.2.3 Between Earth and Heaven: Trinitarian Transdisciplinarity

Conclusively, however, a Pentecost-theology of the disciplines cannot be content with just providing theological warrants for multidisciplinarity and then affirming a mutual interdisciplinarity, but also can, following the educational emphases of classical Christian tradition, abet encounter with the divine Spirit. Our claim here is that the many disciplines, precisely via theology's assistance, illuminate the presence and activity of the Spirit, and hence nurture encounters with the transcendent rather than undermine faith. In other words, it is not only that the disciplines enable understanding of creation (that is the claim of the Berlin academe) or that theology and wisdom can and should be in conversation with the disciplines (in the tradition of Athens), but also that the disciplines can declare the glory of God and give insight into the work of the Spirit.

The outpouring of the Spirit "upon all flesh" (Acts 2:17) on the day of Pentecost was the beginning of the promise that the divine gift would empower Christian witness "to the end of the earth [*eschatou tēs gēs*]" (1:8). *Eschatos* in the original Greek, translated as "end" in the English, connotes not only geographical scope but temporal extension.[93] It thus asserts that the gift of the Spirit both enables testimonial power from Jerusalem

---

in *The Spirit Renews the Face of the Earth: Pentecostal Forays in Science and Theology of Creation*, ed. Amos Yong (Eugene: Pickwick, 2009), 210–32.

[90] See David I. Smith and Barbara Carvill, *The Gift of the Stranger: Faith, Hospitality, and Foreign Language Learning* (Grand Rapids: Eerdmans, 2000).

[91] Such a model of exploratory inquiry across the spectrum is presented in Yong, "God and the Evangelical Laboratory: Recent Conservative Protestant Thinking about Theology and Science," *Theology and Science* 5.2 (2007): 203–21, and "Science and Religion: Introducing the Issues, Entering the Debates—A Review Essay," *Christian Scholar's Review* 40.2 (2011): 189–203.

[92] See David F. Ford, "An Interdisciplinary Wisdom: Knowledge, Formation and Collegiality in the Negotiable University," ch. 9 in *Christian Wisdom: Desiring God and Learning in Love* (Cambridge: Cambridge University Press, 2007).

[93] For further exposition of both dimensions of the eschatological ends of Acts 1:8, see Yong, *Renewing Christian Theology*, ch. 2.3.

through Judea and Samaria and beyond and anticipates that the coming of the Spirit is also the arrival of "the last days" (2:17) and that this divine promise is "for you, for your children, and for all who are far away" (2:39), thus including generations of descendants to the ends of time and the eschatological ends of the age. We suggest that such a Pentecost-imagination, applied to thinking theologically about the disciplines, hears their declaring the wonders of God along ontological and historical registers.[94]

Although we will return in the next section to discuss extant forms of faith in relationship with learning that dominates segments of the Christian university conversation, a brief look at this juncture at Augustinian-Lutheran and Roman Catholic approaches to this matter will helpfully clarify the multidimensionality of our proposed Pentecost-theology of the disciplines. Their eschatological and sacramental theologies of education are not only accommodated but secured via our Pentecost-configuration. More boldly, the full promise of such an eschatological-sacramental vision for the Christian university needs nothing less than a pneumatological theology of the disciplines and a trinitarian theology of the intellectual life.

In light of our prior discussion (see §2.2.1), it is anachronistic to think that the bishop of Hippo had a fully developed theology of the disciplines or of higher education.[95] Yet two motifs central to Augustine's theological vision are germane: that the mind finds its resting place in the divine and that the current dispensation involves two cities and two loves—those of the present world and the approaching world.[96] These combine to frame any historical undertaking against the eschatological horizon—the ends of time—so that the secular now is distinct from the coming sovereign's rule. For some, this secular-sacred distinction is antagonistic, particularly if the emphasis is placed on the former's opposing the values of the latter, so that, translated into the contemporary Christian university, there is a conflict between the naturalism, humanism, and relativism of the academy and the embrace of faith.[97] But for others, the two cities can also be understood as dialectically related.[98] The key Augustinian insight for our purposes concerns the eschatological bearing of the human heart, even if its present loves are misguided.

Over a millennium later, this Augustinian legacy can be not only discerned in Luther's protests within the church but also seen in the educational ideals derived from his theological reformation.[99] Augustine's two cities are developed into two kingdoms, that of

---

[94] We are here pentecostalizing and charismatizing the Christian pedagogical imagination, which is not surprising; on the latter, see David I. Smith and Susan M. Felch, eds., *Teaching and Christian Imagination* (Grand Rapids: Eerdmans, 2016).

[95] Karla Pollman and Mark Vessey, eds., *Augustine and the Disciplines: From Cassiciacum to Confessions* (New York: Oxford University Press, 2005), explore Augustine's theologizing about the arts in the last quarter of the fourth century, especially in relationship to how they inform biblical interpretation.

[96] On the former, see Garcia, *Academic Freedom*, 22–25; for the latter, cf. Phillip Cary, "Study as Love: Augustinian Vision and Catholic Education," in *Augustine and Liberal Education*, ed. Kim Paffenroth and Kevin L. Hughes (Aldershot: Ashgate, 2000), 55–80.

[97] As delineated by Alvin Plantinga, "Reformed Thinking: Christian Scholarship," in *Seeking Understanding: The Stob Lectures, 1986–1998* (Grand Rapids: Eerdmans, 2001), 121–38.

[98] Curtis W. Freeman, "Can the Secular Be Sanctified?" in *The Future of Baptist Higher Education*, ed. Donald D. Schmeltekopf and Dianna M. Vitanza (Waco, Tex.: Baylor University Press, 2006), 219–31, makes this argument, drawing on Augustine's two-cities model.

[99] For Luther as imbibing the Augustinian heritage, see Marilyn J. Harran, *Martin Luther: Learning for Life* (St. Louis: Concordia, 1997), ch. 3.

grace and law, the eternal "right hand" and temporal "left hand" of God, both of which persist until the parousia, so that there are "two strategies but one purpose."[100] While there is in some respects a sharp contrast between the "worldly kingdom" that is fading away and a fundamentally good creation that heralds the impending divine reign (see §2.2.3 before), there is also a paradoxical simultaneity so that the heavenly is incarnationally manifest through the creational. For a Lutheran theology of education, this christological and theological insight presents "the general or the universal in, with, under, and through the particular."[101] If in some respects the forward eschatological thrust of the Augustinian conceptualization is tempered in the Lutheran effort to think about vocation in the present world, there is acknowledgment of the dialectical tension between the historical and the approaching divine reign, and therefore also between education in the here and now and as directed toward or drawn forward by the final dispensation to come.[102]

The temporality of the Augustinian-Lutheran historical-eschatological prototype is complemented by the sacramentality of contemporary Roman Catholic theologies of higher education. If the Lutheran "in, with, and under" emphasizes incarnational descent, Thomistic thinking accents nature or the creational elements participating in and being elevated by grace. Translated into a theology of the disciplines, Catholic sensibilities propose "a sacramental view of 'the real'—a view that . . . legitimates science and art while also opening up a realm from which these worthy endeavors are methodologically barred. . . . A sacramental approach to 'the real' *requires* the legitimacy of science and art, of 'ordinary' reality. Sacramental perception deepens ordinary reality, it does not destroy it."[103] While the Catholic and the Lutheran views are both fundamentally incarnational, the latter's Reformation christocentrism slightly mutes the trinitarian mysticism at the heart of the medieval formulation wherein the universalism of the Father and the sacramental reality of the Son are traditionally (ecclesially) and rationally (via divinely aided reason) consummated by the work of the Spirit. For such a sacramental theology of higher education, the third divine person thus "represents a more communal and fully intersubjective ideal" so that the Catholic (and Christian) university "elevates love and truth and recognizes that the Holy Spirit fulfills itself in those institutions that foster community, reason, and transcendence in communion with the Church."[104] Consistent with the Augustinian pneumatology in the Middle Ages, wherein the Spirit and grace were virtually synonymous (at least until the assimilation of Aristotelian notions of *habitus*; see §2.3.1 above), another Roman Catholic theologian puts it this way:

---

[100] Russ Moulds, "One Kingdom Teaches the Other: The Two Strategies of Lutheran Education," in *Learning at the Foot of the Cross: A Lutheran Vision for Education*, ed. Joel D. Heck and Angus J. L. Menuge (Austin: Concordia University Press, 2011), 79–96, at 92.

[101] Leonard S. Smith, *Martin Luther's Two Ways of Viewing Life and the Education Foundation of a Lutheran Ethos* (Eugene: Pickwick, 2011), 70.

[102] See also Ernest L. Simmons, *Lutheran Higher Education: An Introduction for Faculty* (Minneapolis: Augsburg Fortress, 1998); cf. Brian Beckstrom, *Leading Lutheran Higher Education in a Secular Age: Religious Identity, Mission, and Vocation at ELCA Colleges and Universities* (Lanham: Lexington, 2020).

[103] George Dennis O'Brien, *The Idea of a Catholic University* (Chicago: University of Chicago Press, 2002), 183 (emphasis orig.).

[104] Mark W. Roche, *The Intellectual Appeal of Catholicism and the Idea of a Catholic University* (Notre Dame: University of Notre Dame Press, 2003), 32–33.

There must be a spirituality that catalyzes and leavens academic work, urged on by the dynamic eros of the mind for God. Spirituality implies an awareness that God dwells in us and in all created things as the Logos, not as a stagnant thing, but as a dynamic élan drawing all things toward the Godhead through the Spirit. This spirituality cannot and must not be imposed on those who do not share or experience it, but it must guide those Catholics who steer the overall direction of the curriculum.[105]

There is more to be said about such a sacramental understanding of the disciplines, but for now we observe the Spirit is both present within the immanent plane and yet transcends it.

A Pentecost-theology of higher education develops particularly the pneumatological resources within the preceding trinitarian scheme so that the many disciplines of the university witness to what in the classical (Western) tradition is understood as truth, goodness, and beauty to the ends of the earth and of time: both regarding the ontological nature of things and the historical advance of knowledge. If human hearts are searching for their final resting place in the divine, the disciplines provide intimations of the imminent unveiling of the divine wind and breath, which lures creatures toward their eschatological destination; and as the materiality of the creation in its ordinariness is approached with a sacramental posture of investigation, the disciplines become iconic portals to what may be otherwise deemed as the transcendent reality of the Spirit.[106] To be clear, this is not to say that the disciplines speak unambiguously about the divine, as their data could also be interpreted completely within the immanent zone. Yet a Pentecost-perspective posits no disjunction between the immanent and the transcendent, at least as popularly understood, as it holds the capacities of the former capable of disclosing realities of the latter. So even if there is "no direct identification of the Spirit," a Pentecost-immersion into the disciplines recognizes an "indirect witness to the Spirit's presence,"[107] one that effectively facilitates through spiritual endowment and moral formation (fruit and gifts) both encounter with the divine and realization of the pattern of the Word found within human rational structures.

Hence, the many disciplines not only might converge interdisciplinarily but also open up, through the Spirit of Pentecost, to transdisciplinary horizons. Our use of *transdisciplinary* therefore has an explicitly theological sphere, including but not limited to the transinstitutional collaboration of knowledge production that extends beyond the academy.[108] Of course, even in the latter domain, transdisciplinarity names the emerging

---

[105] Kenneth Garcia, "Academic Freedom and the Service Theologians Must Render the Academy," *Horizons* 38 (Spring 2011): 75–103 (at 94).

[106] In dialogue with Rowan Williams, *Lost Icons: Reflections on Cultural Bereavement* (New York: Bloomsbury Academic, 2002), Christopher Craig Brittain assesses how postmodern seekers can make space for "others" in order to, through such self-questioning, "find" or "establish" themselves—the "other" being thus epistemically iconic; see Brittain, "Epilogue: *Initium Sapientiae Timor Alterius* and the Constituents of the University," in Brittain and Murphy, *Theology, University, Humanities*, 213–28, esp. 224–26.

[107] Marjorie Suchocki, "John Cobb's Trinity: Implications for the University," in *Theology and the University: Essays in Honor of John B. Cobb, Jr.*, ed. David Ray Griffin and Joseph C. Hough Jr. (Albany: State University of New York Press, 1991), 147–65, at 159.

[108] Robert Frodeman, *Sustainable Knowledge: A Theory of Interdisciplinarity* (New York: Palgrave Macmillan, 2014), ch. 4; see also Juliet Willetts, Cynthia Mitchell, Kumi Abeysuriya, and Dena Fam, "Creative Tensions: Negotiating the Multiple Dimensions of a Transdisciplinary Doctorate," in *Reshaping Doctoral Education: International Approaches and Pedagogies*, ed. Alison Lee and Susan Danby (London: Routledge,

borderlessness of classical fields of inquiry even as its characterizes the cross-pollination and cross-fertilization of concepts, rhetorics, and discursive practices. Our Pentecost-imaginary, however, understands these developments as expressions of the Spirit's outpouring on all flesh, whereby the divine Spirit works within creation to redeem and renew its many orders, divisions, and kinds. Here we are reconsidering the theology of creation in a pneumatological perspective, one that recalls the fruitfulness and multiplication of its various regions from out of and through the primordial breath or "wind from God [that] swept over the face of the waters" (Gen 1:2).[109]

Our goal throughout this section has been to reenvision the multiplicity of the disciplines theologically, after Pentecost, more specifically. Yes, how to structurally facilitate and incentivize such inter- and transdisciplinary inquiry will need to be specified in order for the promise of this vision to be realized, although that takes us beyond our established parameters. The point we are making is theological: that such a Pentecost-vision of the Christian university derives from a "new unifying culture of *paideia* . . . a systemic, open, and highly interdisciplinary worldview grounded in a robust theology of creation."[110] Thus, it is that the creation itself witnesses, via the many disciplines of the university, to the same divine Spirit through which they speak.[111] And hence it also is that the multiplicity of disciplines that otherwise fragments knowledge is harmonized in pneumatically inspired faith and practical inquiry so that there is dynamically found (ebbing and flowing) coherence rather than only dissonance to the intellectual life as nurtured through the Christian higher educational process.[112]

5.3   STARTING WITH THE SPIRIT: THE SCANDAL OF THE PENTECOSTAL MIND

The foregoing section sketches a Pentecost-theology of the many disciplines as including the liberal arts, almost always at the heart of the contemporary Christian university. It is set within the larger argument of this chapter that intellectual life amidst and with the

---

2012), 128–43, and Mine Yazici, "A Tentative Research Model of Transdisciplinarity," in *Interdisciplinarity, Multidisciplinarity and Transdisciplinarity in Humanities*, ed. Banu Akçeşme, Hasan Baktir, and Eugene Steele (Newcastle upon Tyne: Cambridge Scholars, 2016), 222–32.

[109] A more extensive exposition is Yong, "*Ruach*, the Primordial Chaos, and the Breath of Life: Emergence Theory and the Creation Narratives in Pneumatological Perspective," in *The Work of the Spirit: Pneumatology and Pentecostalism*, ed. Michael Welker (Grand Rapids: Eerdmans, 2006), 183–204.

[110] Cheryl Bridges Johns, "Athens, Berlin, and Azusa: A Pentecostal Reflection on Scholarship and Christian Faith," *Pneuma: The Journal of the Society for Pentecostal Studies* 27.1 (2005): 136–47, at 145; other pentecostal higher educators are also gravitating to seeing Jerusalem and Athens as symbiotical and convergent, e.g., Denise A. Austin and David Perry, "From Jerusalem to Athens: A Journey of Pentecostal Pedagogy in Australia," *Journal of Adult Theological Education* 12.1 (2015): 43–55.

[111] See, for instance, Michael Welker, "The Spirit in Philosophical, Theological, and Interdisciplinary Perspectives," in Welker, *Work of the Spirit*, 221–32, and Wolfgang Vondey, "Introduction: The Presence of the Spirit as an Interdisciplinary Concern," in *The Holy Spirit and the Christian Life: Historical, Interdisciplinary, and Renewal Perspectives*, ed. Wolfgang Vondey, CHARIS: Christianity and Renewal—Interdisciplinary Studies (New York: Palgrave Macmillan, 2014), 1–20, for two versions of this argument.

[112] Even as such a stance provides an initial Christian response to the concerns regarding the disintegration of knowledge in the postmodern multiversity, a worry that one noted educator—first chancellor and twelfth president of the University of California—argued as ameliorated when the multiversity is also nevertheless construed and activated as an "intellectual city"; see Kerr, *Uses of the University*, ch. 3.

many disciplines is part and parcel of life in the Spirit. Thus is Christian higher education in and of faith, albeit, in our perspective, in, with, and through the divine Spirit.[113]

The following third and final part to this chapter elaborates on our Pentecost-theology of the life of the mind by focusing on the *how* and *whither* of Spirit-led research and scholarship within the Christian university. We will first develop our Pentecost-model of faith-learning interrelation not as an alternative but as complementary to existing approaches (§5.3.1), provide a more specific case analysis of what difference such makes for liberal arts scholarship (§5.3.2), and conclude with a summary of the argument so far that transitions also into the next chapter (§5.3.3). As the classical Christian educational tradition emphasized intellectual formation in a holistic manner that included the spiritual life, so will we argue that a Pentecost-form of faith and learning proceeds pneumatologically, via a renewal of the life of the mind.

One caveat before proceeding. Whereas in chapter 4 we provided a critical response to Noll's scandalous evangelical mind, here we undertake the constructive task of renewing the Christian mind after Pentecost. If earlier we spelled out the reasons for the bias against research within pentecostal and evangelical Christianity as stemming from populist reactions to elite discourses in education, preference for intuitive modes of rationality, and utilitarian models of education that focus on training for mission, our objective here is to present a more radically pentecostal and evangelical vision of the intellectual life, radical in the sense that it is rooted deep within the triune mission of creation and redemption, no less than at the heart of the incarnational and pentecostal mystery. Our goal is not apologetic in the negative sense but one of retrieval and reappropriation: to translate and redeem the many tongues of Pentecost for a robust theology of Christian higher education for the present time.

5.3.1 Faith-Interrelated-with-Learning: One Institution, Many Charisms

The challenges and opportunities for integrating Christian faith and disciplinary (secular) learning are both immense, and for that reason have generated a publishing industry of its own.[114] We have already intimated that a Pentecost-entrance into this conversation is not one that sets itself off from existing options but comes alongside, as it were, in effect to enable through the Spirit fulfillment of their promise. Here we continue on that trek, developing a Pentecost model of relating faith and learning that appreciates how the various approaches can be received and welcomed as complementary modalities of nurturing encounter with the divine.

---

[113] Randolph Crump Miller, *The Theory of Christian Education Practice: How Theology Affects Christian Education* (Birmingham, Ala.: Religious Education Press, 1980), 2, provides a book-length argument for the more general thesis: "Christian education is a theological discipline and method," with our contribution being to add "and pneumatological" before "discipline."

[114] E.g., David Claerbaut, *Faith and Learning on the Edge: A Bold New Look at Religion in Higher Education* (Grand Rapids: Zondervan, 2004); David S. Dockery, *Renewing Minds: Serving Church and Society through Christian Higher Education*, rev. and updated ed. (Nashville: B&H Academic, 2008); Todd C. Ream, Jerry Pattengale, and David L. Riggs, eds., *Beyond Integration? Inter/Disciplinary Possibilities for the Future of Christian Higher Education* (Abilene: Abilene Christian University Press, 2012), among many other offerings. For an overview of the dominant types, see Richard T. Hughes, "Christian Faith and the Life of the Mind," in *Faithful Learning and the Christian Scholarly Vocation*, ed. Douglas V. Henry and Bob R. Agee (Grand Rapids: Eerdmans, 2003), 3–25.

To be sure, there is no way we can demonstrate how comprehensively ecumenical our Pentecost theology of faith and learning is, could, and should be. The glimpses provided in the preceding subsection on interfaces with Lutheran and Roman Catholic thinking about theology of higher education certainly do not exhaust the resources arising from both traditions. Beyond these, there are a growing number of Baptist proposals emphasizing religious freedom and soul competency that could be said to include Anabaptistic or Mennonite versions—even if some within the latter trajectory would insist on a dissenting and practice-oriented posture that resists categorization within the broader contemporary Baptistic scope[115]—as there are also Reformed models that are dominant especially across the world of evangelical higher education, particularly in North America.[116] We have neither time nor space to canvas these various options, even as the rest of this book will draw from these voices as relevant to the points we wish to make. We note here, though, that as appreciative as we are of the Reformed tradition's blazing a trail in this discussion over the last half century by insisting that all truth is finally God's and thereby theological, its prevailing notion of *integration*, while comprehensible and plausible during the last quarter of the prior century when it emerged, in the current milieu both can be understood to perpetuate opposition between as much as reconcile Christian belief with "secular" scholarship and has historically been overly worldview, cognitively, and rationalistically focused.[117] Even with these reservations, we press on with at least limited use of this rhetoric of integration because we want to suggest how a Pentecost take develops a pneumatological resolution to the challenges and opportunities at hand for the Christian life of the mind. As important, we wish to show in the rest of this (and then also in the next) chapter that faith related to and with learning involves not only the mind but also the heart. Toward that end, we focus here briefly on two other models, both more closely related to the pentecostal-holiness tradition: that of Wesleyans and that of the Friends.

As already shown (§5.1 above), Wesleyans and Pentecostals are related, with the contemporary groups almost like older and younger siblings. Many members and adherents of the early modern pentecostal revival, as was indicated, came from the holiness movement, to the point that a good number of their educational efforts were conjoined, at least when that involved women at the vanguard.[118] In the last quarter century, Wesleyan colleges also have evolved into Wesleyan universities, and along the way have attempted to

---

[115] See Sara Wenger Shenk, *Anabaptist Ways of Knowing: A Conversation about Tradition-Based Critical Education* (Telford: Cascadia, 2003), and (broadly Baptistic) Roger Ward and David Gushee, eds., *The Scholarly Vocation and the Baptist Academy: Essays on the Future of Baptist Higher Education* (Macon: Mercer University Press, 2008); distinguishing between Anabaptist and Baptist definitions, respectively, is Richard T. Hughes and William B. Adrian, eds., *Models for Christian Higher Education: Strategies for Success in the Twenty-First Century* (Grand Rapids: Eerdmans, 1997), chs. 4 and 7.

[116] Classically stated (in updated version) in Arthur F. Holmes, *The Idea of a Christian College*, rev. ed. (Grand Rapids: Eerdmans, 1987).

[117] E.g., James W. Sire, *The Universe Next Door: A Basic Worldview Catalog*, 5th ed. (Downers Grove: IVP Academic, 2009), and his other books on the topic; for more on the Reformed character of this integrationist model and for the difficulties inherent in their worldview construct, see Jacobsen and Jacobsen, *Scholarship and Christian Faith*, ch. 1. See also our earlier discussion in §4.2.

[118] See Abraham Ruelas, *Women and the Landscape of American Higher Education: Wesleyan Holiness and Pentecostal Founders* (Eugene: Pickwick, 2010).

formulate a vision for Christian higher education with a distinctive stamp. We comment only briefly on their theological and operational features, building off our earlier historical discussion (§3.2.2; §4.3) but engaging with the emerging literature in theology of education.[119]

Wesley's message of Christian perfection translated first and foremost not into higher educational idiom but into pastoral training for the discipleship of the laity. Yet a number of themes related to his theology of holiness and sanctification have had normative implications for Wesleyan approaches to higher education. First, the doctrine of prevenient grace, rooted deep in the classical (patristic) synthesis of preceding grace, presumes both a synergistic anthropology that insists on the import of human responsiveness to divine initiative and a pneumatological theology of grace that makes such response possible.[120] From this, then, faithful discipleship involves the reformation of human lives toward holiness, both individual/personal and social, including the transformation of the will, so that sanctified creatures can participate in the redemptive work of the triune God. The holistic vision of Wesleyan formation, wherein minds, hearts, and behaviors are intertwined with the spiritual life, correlates with a multidimensional epistemology. The four interrelated sources of human knowing—Scripture, tradition, reason, and experience (dubbed more recently the Wesleyan quadrilateral)—understand that the full renewal of human persons in their various capacities requires redemption of these epistemic capacities. While this notion has been debated within Methodist circles because of lack of clarity about how each source relates to the others, we wish to highlight how Wesleyan approaches to the faith-learning interface have embraced the many disciplines as extensions of their pluralistic epistemology,[121] and thus wish to explicate Wesleyan theologies of higher education along these lines. Central to all of this is the sanctifying work of the Spirit in the formation of the human person and how that relates to glorification as the telos of human existence.[122]

George Fox University in the broader Wesleyan tradition also includes Quaker roots and influences.[123] We turn quickly, almost in passing, to educational philosophy in the

---

[119] The following condenses Robert W. Wall, "Review Essay: James Davison Hunter, *Evangelicalism: The Coming Generation*," *Seattle Pacific University Review* 6 (1987): 44–55, and John E. Stanley and Susie C. Stanley, "What Can the Wesleyan/Holiness Tradition Contribute to Christian Higher Education?" in Hughes and Adrian, *Models for Christian Higher Education*, 313–26. Consult also the more extended treatments in Dean G. Blevins and Mark A. Maddix, *Discovering Discipleship: Dynamics of Christian Education* (Kansas City: Beacon Hill, 2010), and John H. Aukerman, ed., *Discipleship That Transforms: An Introduction to Christian Education from a Wesleyan Holiness Perspective* (Anderson: Francis Asbury, 2011).

[120] Yong, *Spirit of Love*, part 2, explicates the details of this latter Wesleyan-pentecostal motif.

[121] See also Yong's "Reassessing the Quadrilateral: John Wesley's Epistemological Method in Philosophy, Science and Religion," in his *The Dialogical Spirit II: Contextual God and Pluralistic Selves after Pentecost*, ed. Spencer Moffatt (Eugene: Cascade, forthcoming), ch. 1.

[122] The project of Wesleyan sanctification is described in conversation with the human sciences in Amos Yong, "Sanctification, Science, and the Spirit: Salvaging Holiness in the Late Modern World," *Wesleyan Theological Journal* 47.2 (2012): 36–52.

[123] George Fox University is overviewed in Perry L. Glanzer and Todd C. Ream, *Christianity and Moral Identity in Higher Education* (New York: Palgrave Macmillan, 2009), ch. 6, and Samuel Schuman, *Seeing the Light: Religious Colleges in Twenty-First-Century America* (Baltimore: Johns Hopkins University Press, 2010), ch. 9. Full disclosure: one of us (Yong) is an alum of Western Evangelical Seminary, now Portland Seminary at George Fox University.

Friends tradition given how the pneumatic character of Quaker spirituality parallels at least some aspects of Pentecostalism.[124] As with the influence of Wesley's Holy Club on later Wesleyan thinking about formation and education, so also has the silent liturgy of the Quaker meeting informed what they have called a *friendly pedagogy*.[125] Silence, for starters, is pedagogical, inviting the inner light of the divine spirit to be made manifest amidst the circle of learners; testimony, then, is the conduit through which discernment is pronounced, and then judgment is nurtured. Memory and imagination are thus equally vital, enabling the cultivation of a democratic and conversational environment. Hence, the Friends pedagogical philosophy emphasizes "an idealism about human possibilities and a conviction that individuals grow into their best selves when supported and sustained by a healthy community."[126] All of this presumes the principal presence of the divine Spirit connecting with and encountering students and learners.

Remember that our proposed Pentecost model is neither sectarian nor ecclesially or denominationally specific since the day of Pentecost is not copyrighted by any church tradition. Thus, our proposal is ecumenical not in the ideological or political sense with which that term can be understood but in the theological sense constituted by the many tongues of the Spirit. Applied to the task of relating Christian faith and secular learning, our Pentecost proposal embraces the full spectrum of Christian approaches as charismatic vectors actualizing a plurality of integrative possibilities. These are what we might call the charisms that drive Christian higher education.[127] If "there are varieties of gifts, but the same Spirit" (1 Cor 12:4), then there are not only a diversity of churches each with distinctive witnesses by the Spirit but also a plurality of faith-learning possibilities informed by these ecclesial traditions. In the present post-denominational milieu it will be important for institutions of Christian higher education to embrace the particularity of their historical arcs even as these are rerooted in the universality of the gospel manifest at Pentecost. In that respect, faith and learning flourish as each receives the gifts of other models while clarifying their own unique contribution. Ours is a Pentecost vision that celebrates the many options—not only in terms of the intra-Christian world but also amidst the wider ecumenism of Christian higher education in a world of many faiths, to be demonstrated further later (§7.3)—as facilitating an en-Spirited life of the mind amidst the pluralism of disciplines in the Christian university.

[124] See Richard A. Baer Jr., "Quaker Silence, Catholic Liturgy and Pentecostal Glossolalia: Functional Similarities," in *Perspectives on the New Pentecostalism*, ed. Russell P. Spittler (Grand Rapids: Baker, 1976), 150–64; also, Martin William Mittelstadt and Brian K. Pipkin, eds., *Mennocostals: Pentecostal and Mennonite Stories of Convergence* (Eugene: Pickwick, 2020).

[125] See Anne Dalke and Barbara Dixson, eds., *Minding the Light: Essays in Friendly Pedagogy*, Studies in Education and Spirituality 6 (New York: Peter Lang, 2004).

[126] Paul A. Lacey, *Growing into Goodness: Essays on Quaker Education* (Wallingford: Pendle Hill and Friends Council on Education, 1998), 236.

[127] A number of chapters in section II of Ronnie Prevost, *Evangelical Protestant Gifts to Religious Education* (Macon: Smyth and Helwys, 2000), unfold educational contributions from across the Protestant spectrum. It is also wonderful for us as Pentecostals to find Roman Catholic scholars thinking charismatically, in effect, about theology of education: Charles E. Bouchard, O.P., "Preaching, Piety and Public Life: The Dominican Charism in Higher Education," *Current Issues in Catholic Higher Education* 22.1 (2001): 53–66.

5.3.2 The Hermeneutical Circle: The Spirit of the Humanities

Previously (§5.2.2) we outlined the contours of a Pentecost approach to the natural sciences and then began to shift immediately above toward thinking about a Pentecost paradigm for faith-learning interaction and Christian scholarship more broadly. Here we turn to the human sciences, the humanities in particular, to ask about what engagement might look like from this Pentecost perspective. Although we celebrate more or less recent forays of contemporary pentecostal scholars in these areas,[128] our question is asked in an explicitly ecumenical context and therefore our discussions remain at a more abstract and theoretical level. In particular, we develop the rudiments of a Pentecost-hermeneutic and historiography given the conviction that such may be viable for the full range of Christian universities regardless of ecclesial tradition.

The late- and postmodern turn in the humanities means at least that all human knowing is interpreted, at least insofar as our interpretations are informed by or confirm or are undermined by practice.[129] For study, learning, and scholarship in the humanities, then, the question regarding the science or rules of interpretation—hermeneutics—is more foundational than ever. History, literature, philosophy, and political theory, for instance, are disciplines more likely to be impacted by hermeneutical (Christian and otherwise) presuppositions.[130] Within the Christian academy the questions are more narrowly construed vis-à-vis biblical hermeneutics or theological hermeneutics.[131] Work in the humanities thus begs for methodological approaches that are no less theological, while at the same time also appropriately general.

Is it possible to articulate a pentecostal-yet-general hermeneutic? Stepping into this question stimulates the following three lines of reflection. First, the many tongues of Pentecost announce the many voices in and through any text, object, or phenomenon of interpretation. This is not to ignore the voice of an author, however that may be defined and determined, but it is to be primed for the many tongues being mediated, both within the text as embedded in its historical contexts (this is its intratextuality) and in the following reception history (this is the extratextual). Yet the side or act of reading or interpretation is no less multivocal: readers come to objects of interpretation not presuppositionless but embedded in a particular matrix and thus inculturated and fully formed over their lifetimes, however short or long, of experiences, emotions, thoughts, and desires. Beyond reading and interpreting for their own sake, readers and interpreters have reasons for

---

[128] E.g., Michael D. Palmer, ed., *Elements of a Christian Worldview*, rev. ed. (Springfield: Logion, 1998), and Paul W. Lewis and Martin William Mittelstadt, eds., *What's So Liberal about the Liberal Arts? Integrated Approaches to Christian Formation*, Frameworks: Interdisciplinary Studies for Faith and Learning 1 (Eugene: Pickwick, 2016).

[129] The by now classic text on what is now known as the hermeneutical turn is Hans-Georg Gadamer, *Truth and Method*, 2nd rev. ed. (London: Continuum, 2004); a Christian philosophical and theological argument is James K. A. Smith, *The Fall of Interpretation: Philosophical Foundations for a Creational Hermeneutic*, 2nd ed. (Downers Grove: IVP Academic, 2000), while Amos' pragmatist argument is in "The Demise of Foundationalism and the Retention of Truth: What Evangelicals Can Learn from C. S. Peirce," *Christian Scholar's Review* 29.3 (2000): 563–88, reprinted as the first chapter in Yong, *The Dialogical Spirit: Christian Reason and Theological Method for the Third Millennium* (Eugene: Cascade, 2014).

[130] Mark A. Noll and James Turner, *The Future of Christian Learning: An Evangelical and Catholic Dialogue*, ed. Thomas Albert Howard (Grand Rapids: Brazos, 2008), 98 and 117.

[131] See Yong, *The Hermeneutical Spirit*.

doing what they are doing, and such purposes have broader implications so that part of this task involves broadening the circle of conversation so that others with a stake in the matter at hand might become informed and have their say.[132] Hence, a Pentecost-hermeneutic is plurivocal with regard to the text, its history of interpretation, and its present appropriation.[133]

Pentecostal hermeneutics therefore requires a sufficiently deep form of "ethos of intellectual hospitality" that can facilitate such "practice of inclusive conversation."[134] Yet the many tongues of Pentecost are not absolutely relativistic but normed by the in-breaking of the eschatological reign and the Spirit's redemption of human creatures according to the divine image disclosed in Jesus Christ. Hence, interpretation in and after the Spirit of Pentecost operates at least at two levels: immanently in relationship to texts, etc., on their own terms, and transcendently—or better: eschatologically—with regard to the saving purposes of the triune God, which story human creatures are called to participate in (§2.2.1). So such pneumatically formed interpretation makes it possible to always not only ask about the *truth* of texts within the immanent plane but also wonder about how these texts enable, inspire, or compel performance of what is *good*, that is, whether they enable participation in the divine redemption that is here and coming. The latter does not necessarily trump the former, even as there is no route to the latter that does not go through the former. A Pentecost-hermeneutic that is constituted pneumatically through the Spirit bridges but does not collapse heaven and earth and in that respect presumes the hermeneutical circle or spiral, reading eternity within the creaturely horizon on the one hand and comprehending the latter only through the (many-faceted) divine witness on the other hand.

Yet pentecostal interpretation proceeding from and out of the Pentecost reality and crafted hermeneutically in conversation with the biblical traditions (as we saw above) is interested about *logos* (truth), *ethos* (goodness), and *pathos* (beauty). How does reading, study, conversation, or learning enable encounter with an otherwise transcendent divinity, achieve redemptive cleansing of the heart and hands, and nurture longing for reconciliation and harmony? This pathic dimension of hermeneutics thereby prompts focus on the affectivity embedded within objects of interpretation and attentiveness to the desires of our own lives as interpreting creatures. What sanctifying passions are aroused or dampened through interpretive engagement? What beatific or destructive imaginations are fired up along the hermeneutical process? What demands of justice oblige our attention and our practical agency and commitments? Scholarship can neglect these interpretive questions, but they are inevitable for the Christian life of the mind in Spirit.

---

[132] Andrew Shanks, *The Other Calling: Theology, Intellectual Vocation and Truth* (Malden: Blackwell, 2007), portrays intellectual work as a form of priesthood, indicating that intellectuals are bring together communities and their vested interests; from this, the Christian life of the mind facilitates conversation and even reconciliation between "both sides" (or however many there may be).

[133] For more, see also Yong, *Learning Theology: Tracking the Spirit of Christian Faith* (Louisville: Westminster John Knox, 2018), ch. 1.

[134] See Kim S. Phipps, "Epilogue: Campus Climate and Christian Scholarship," in Jacobsen and Jacobsen, *Scholarship and Christian Faith*, 172–83, esp. 173–79.

To illustrate the application of our hermeneutical model, we turn to historiographic method. Enlightenment historiography emphasized rank objectivity: just the facts of the past, retrievable through exact and rigorous application of research methodologies by unbiased scholars. We encountered this earlier in our discussion of the cultured scholar as the hero of the modern research university (see §3.1.2), focused on the attainment of an objective account of the past. Postmodern historiography contends, it would appear, for the opposite end of the spectrum: there is no history as such, only what biased storytellers narrate according to certain political agendas or other desired outcomes. A Pentecost historiography does not overlook interpretive subjectivity but also asks of the available data if and how the Spirit is manifest, how the interpretive evidence may have, or not, mediated sanctifying redemption, and if and how pathic qualities are discernible that anticipate the divine rest and harmony yearned for by human hearts. Retrieving or retelling history, in this case, forefronts the affective elements within texts and attends to the locutionary performances and illocutionary effects of these texts in order to divine the Spirit's repair of a broken world.[135] But again: Pentecost historiography does not seek to impose theological (or pneumatological) interpretations upon texts or other historical data or phenomena up front: history's voices, in whatever shape or form they echo in the present, have to be heeded first on their own terms. This layer of interpretation works with rather than silences or distorts the historical witnesses. More to the point: the Spirit speaks not despite history's voices but precisely in and through them.

And it is precisely by enabling the hearkening of these marginalized voices that discursive traditions are interrupted, reoriented, or even overturned. Traditions, including disciplinary discourses, are always intersecting, realigning, and reforming, yet what we are mindful about is the coming divine reign that will redeem, correct, and transform our humanly constructed cities and paradigms. The Spirit of Pentecost gives voice to the wondrous works of God in anticipation of this eschatological reign, enabling broken human witnesses to resound.

So, if a Pentecost theology of the many disciplines is derived from a pneumatological theology of creation, then a Pentecost theology of faith-learning interweaving is precipitated by a pneumatological anthropology, one that understands human beings as constituted by both the dust of the ground and the breath of life. Liberal education, then, is theologically grounded not in the Great Commission (or even in Acts 1:8) but in the *imago Dei* and the Genesis (1:26) creation narratives.[136] Hence, this is another (Pentecost) way of saying that Christian scholarship is not disinterested, but seeks the redemption of human creatures from and with their fallen condition into the glorious image of God revealed in Jesus and promised for all creation (here anticipating later discussion: §8.1.3).

---

[135] See the essays in Dale M. Coulter and Amos Yong, eds., *The Spirit, the Affections, and the Christian Tradition* (Notre Dame: University of Notre Dame Press, 2016), which depict such a pentecostal—we called it *renewal* in this book—historiography at work; Yong's concluding chapter, "The Affective Spirit: Historiographic Revitalization in the Christian Theological Tradition" (293–302), lifts up the important historiograhic implications.

[136] So argues pentecostal philosopher Michael Palmer, "Orienting Our Lives: The Importance of a Liberal Education for Pentecostals in the Twenty First Century," *Pneuma: The Journal of the Society for Pentecostal Studies* 23.1 (2001): 197–216, esp. 203–6.

5.3.3 Judgment, Creativity, Wisdom: Christian Thinking in and through the Academy

We are now almost ready to transition from this first part of our constructive argument. Hence, it is important to gather our bearings at this juncture not only because we have covered extensive ground in this chapter but because grasping its densely woven threads will be essential for thinking with the next two chapters. In brief, our focus here has been on a pentecostal and pneumatological theology of the intellectual life that drives the Christian university.

We started by developing our own Pentecost-hermeneutic, understood as the epistemic condition in, through, and after Pentecost, so that our receiving the many tongues of the canonical witness—the First and Second Testaments generally, but also more specific rereadings of the gospel testimony to Jesus as teacher and of the sapiential tradition and the learning of wisdom—was from the pluralistic site defined by meeting and experiencing the Spirit poured out on all flesh. Such a Pentecost-hermeneutic distilled the scriptural message's central salvation-redemptive thread as iconic windows to that which is otherwise deemed as transcendent, including the transcendental ideals of the mind: truth, goodness, and beauty.

This Pentecost position was the springboard, in the second and third parts of this chapter, to developing a trinitarian theology of the disciplines constituting the late modern university and to formulating a pneumatological theology of faith-learning relation through which the Christian mind pursues its vocation in higher education. The many tongues of Pentecost provide theological warrants, analogically speaking, for considering the many disciplines as redemptive witnesses to truth, both secular and theological, even as the many gifts of the Spirit deliver pneumatological perspective, metaphorically speaking, for comprehending the many models of faith informing scholarship as charisms informing varying forms of Spirit-infused research and scholarship. Our Pentecost model thus operates both ontologically to secure the plurality of disciplinary witness to the truth propounded by the higher educational enterprise and operationally to inspire the multiplicity of methodological and interpretive approaches to scholarship at the crossroads of faith and learning.

Notice that our theology of the life of the mind says nothing about modern pentecostal phenomena like miracles and healings, spiritual warfare, exorcism of and deliverance from evil spirits, or revelatory aspects of the Spirit's work classically defined as illumination, etc.[137] There is plenty of scholarship by pentecostal academics on these matters, including by us, for those who are interested. Yet our conviction is that the Christian university should not be built on such bases. So rather than suggesting that learning in these contexts occurs via pneumatic communication that can neither be predicted nor controlled (most would agree anyway that the Spirit shows up where and whence divinely willed!), we urge that the Spirit-led life is better understood as the embodiment of certain

---

[137] Intriguingly, it is evangelical scholar Andreas J. Köstenberger who notes that Christian scholars ought also to be "set apart for spiritual warfare"—see Köstenberger, *Excellence: The Character of God and the Pursuit of Scholarly Virtue* (Wheaton: Crossway, 2011), 112–14—although that is not the most effective way, in our estimation, to draw attention to the vertical or spiritual dimension of scholarly work.

dispositions and sensibilities (what we called *habitus* in chapter 2), in our case that of disciplinary practices and scholarly habits and activities.[138]

More substantively, a pneumatological theology of the Christian mind identifies the dissonant encounter with otherness—including local and even indigenous knowledges of all and various sorts (see also §§7.2–7.3) as well as with God and with the transcendental ideals—as the primary generator of the intellectual life. If human creatures have not been given "a spirit of cowardice, but rather a spirit of power and of love and of self-discipline" (2 Tim 1:7), then much Pentecost mentality is empowered toward sagacious action for the common good, is inspired toward imaginative, creative, and aesthetic ideals, and is disciplined into truthful judgments by the encounter with otherness. The Spirit-led life of the mind thus does not pull back but is drawn forward, beyond our comfortably established boundaries and toward horizons of encounter and learning that eventually touch upon and even break into that which is otherwise presumed as or to be transcendent.

We have not said much so far about critical thinking since we assume that this is what universities in the Western world—Christian and otherwise—are and have been focused on. We therefore take it for granted that higher education of whatever stripe nurtures analytical and critical capacities, thus contributing to discerning judgment. The latter, however, involves decision and action, so that the analytical and critical intellect also benefits from various other cognitive capacities: systems thinking to connect the dots between that is the focus of consideration with other contextual and broader realities; adaptive thinking to ascertain how past and present discursive habits and practices may require adjustment in view of impending developments; entrepreneurial and imaginative sensibilities in order to explore innovative ideas and their consequences for various ecclesial, public, and common endeavors; and dialogical and inter- and cross-cultural interaction nurture multiplicity of perspectives and broadened horizons of contextual assessment.[139] There are no formulas for the formation of these capacities even if there are multiple curricular pathways that provide pedagogical opportunities for their nurturing. The result is both critical and wise thinking together on the one hand, but also *scientia* as preceding *sapientia* successfully on the other.

Judgment, then, is never only ratiocinative but includes wisdom, including the prudence that derives from the latter, the combination of which emerges from out of the emotive, affective, social, and practical dimensions of cognition. Indeed, wisdom might be considered as an emergent capacity that builds on but is irreducible to the sum of a person's cultivated cognitive capacities, thus manifesting as its own form of knowledge. Wisdom to see and act therefore oftentimes proceeds by way of insight, which itself is an ecstatic event, an epiphanic unfolding of the truth, an encounter with transcendence, as we put in in the first part of this book. For this to happen, both sides of the brain, to put it colloquially, are involved, so that the critical and the creative/adaptive, the analytical and

---

[138] George Marsden's section on the Holy Spirit and the "spiritual dimensions of reality" pretty much says this, although he also emphasizes the mysteriousness of the Spirit's ways; see Marsden, *The Outrageous Idea of Christian Scholarship* (New York: Oxford University Press, 1997), 94–96.

[139] The last point I derive from Qianwen (Renee) Deng, "One Size Fits All? Postmonolingual Critical Thinking in Pentecostal Graduate Education," *Australasian Pentecostal Studies* 22.2 (2021): 234–59.

the systemic/imaginative, work together. Neither can be rushed, as they are both patiently nurtured and palpably endured.[140] A pneumatological theology of the intellectual life presumes the faithful tarrying in anticipation of such moments and a cultivation of these capacities and habits, whereby the operations of the ratiocinative intellect are nurtured through the many tongues of the many disciplines, and firing up the affective imagination amid the dissonances of life. This is the path of the many charisms, the many gifts of the Spirit even, integrating learning and faith, connecting the wisdom of the cosmos to the wisdom of the Word or Logos of the world.

If the late modern university defines the intellectual life in terms of ongoing research directed to the acquisition and expansion of knowledge, and if (as we will unpack further in §8.1.1) the postmodern university might be increasingly dominated by technical, instrumental, and utilitarian rationalities driven by the marketization of problem-solving and applicational knowing, the Pentecost rendition, informed by Jesus as Spirit-infused exemplar, suggests that knowledge forged through the Christian higher educational enterprise serves the purposes of sapiential formation.[141] Wisdom here is not opposed to knowledge in its various guises but presumes such.[142] There is no wisdom, in other words, without knowledge. Yet there can also be knowledge without wisdom. To add the latter is to include the prudential capacity to discern the consequences of and appropriately implement knowledge. Wisdom is about the capacity to gain a larger vision of the whole as opposed to the particularity of a specific discipline, and prudence is the application of this wisdom to life.

From a psychological and even neuroscientific perspective, wisdom is the practical and tacit dimension of the mind directed toward interaction with the world even as intelligence is the more formal mental realm while creativity modulates between the internal and external at the kinesthetic and behavioral level.[143] Put alternatively, wisdom is a manifestation of prudential reasoning, what we might also identify as a kind of practical intelligence, which is constituted by the analytical intelligence and the creative intelligence, a triad that Aristotle long ago called, respectively, the practical, contemplative/theoretical, and productive intelligences.[144] When the intellectual life is rationalized, as certain historic traditions have done (including that of the modern university), the result often

---

[140] Almost a century ago, Alfred North Whitehead (1861–1947), the renowned philosopher, wrote in his little book on education that the goal of the universities was the formation of the imagination of young minds under imaginative scholars (mentors) so that they are able to take up the challenging tasks of life in a complex world in a creative way; within the educational system of his time, students needed, of course, the requisite time and leisure to cultivate their minds. See Whitehead, *The Aims of Education and Other Essays* (1929; repr., New York: Macmillan, 1964), ch. 7 (95–106).

[141] Denise Lardner Carmody, *Organizing a Christian Mind: A Theology of Higher Education* (Valley Forge: Trinity Press International, 1996), ch. 5, discusses the nurturance of wisdom as central to the educational task of the Christian university.

[142] E.g., Edward P. Meadors, ed., *Where Wisdom May Be Found: The Eternal Purpose of Christian Higher Education* (Eugene: Pickwick, 2019); Melissa Smith, "Yahweh's Taxonomy of the Deeper Dimensions," in *Thinking Theologically about Language Teaching: Christian Perspectives on an Educational Calling*, ed. Cheri L. Pierson and Will Bankston (Carlisle: Langham, 2017), 239–61, has a discussion of wisdom that includes how that informs morality and spirituality (253–54).

[143] See Robert J. Sternberg, *Wisdom, Intelligence, and Creativity Synthesized* (Cambridge: Cambridge University Press, 2003), which develops Sternberg, *The Triarchic Mind: A New Theory of Human Intelligence* (New York: Viking, 1988).

[144] Robert J. Sternberg, *Beyond IQ: A Triarchic Theory of Human Intelligence* (Cambridge: Cambridge University Press, 1985).

remains at the analytical and theoretical level, which overlooks these other elements. Our pentecostalizing of the life of the mind, however, has intuitively recognized what the contemporary academy is now arguing: that the analytical and theoretical is imaginatively and intrinsically intertwined with the practical, the performative, and the productive, and human intelligence is at least tridimensional in this sense.

As our discussion has shown, remaining only at the level of heads ignores the hands and the heart. *Logos* (truth), we have already seen, is intertwined with *ethos* (goodness) and *pathos* (beauty). For our purposes, then, the formation of the Christian mind must include the wisdom of the practical and the creativity of the productive intelligence. Thus, there is no renewal of the mind (this chapter) without also the reordering of the heart (chapter 6) and the reviving of the hands (chapter 7). We therefore now turn to consideration of this central pathic and aesthetic realm of the Christian mind, what we might call the heart of knowing, learning, and education after Pentecost. We cannot insist strongly enough that the rest of part 2 is no digression from our goal of thinking pentecostally and pneumatologically about the life of the mind, higher education, and the Christian university. Rather, the scandal of the pentecostal mind might be, pointedly put, its claim that the intellectual life is both pathically motivated and practically informed.

6

Reordering the Heart

Teaching, Learning, and the School of the Holy Spirit

Although the preceding chapter focused on the cognitive, disciplinary, and scholarly dimensions of the life of the mind, all along the way we realized that these traits of the intellectual life are intertwined with the practical and productive intelligence. Human cognition includes the wisdom of the practical and the creativity of the imagination.[1] In chapter 8 we will explore the outward "fruits" and "ends," one might say, of the Christian university's practical and productive intelligence as manifest in its engagement with the world. Here, we look more deeply within, observing the practical and imaginative workings beneath the surface of Christian higher education. On the one hand, although we will seek to connect with some of the existing scholarly literature on teaching considered in pneumatological perspective,[2] ours will operate at a higher theoretical level to think systematically about how teaching in the Spirit is interconnected with a Spirit-infused life of the mind. On the other hand, whereas the foregoing elaborated on the architecture of knowledge production (via the disciplines) along with some of the mechanics (faith-learning integration) of the Christian university, the following focuses on the so-called transmission of knowledge, the teaching and learning at the heart, on the ground, and at the core of what happens therein. In short, we will be both stepping out and in, at it were, albeit in different respects, as we continue our exploration.

We will argue that exploration of the practical and productive intelligence through the lenses of teaching and learning and vice-versa enables us to further understand the pneumatic life of the mind. If the Pentecost outpouring confronts the human intellect with the otherness through which inquiry is triggered and wisdom is nurtured, then the coming of the Spirit on human flesh highlights the thoroughly embodied and aesthetic character of thought and thinking. Human embodiment requires, then, a ritual and even liturgical (in

---

[1]   Amos Yong, *Spirit-Word-Community: Theological Hermeneutics in Trinitarian Perspective*, New Critical Thinking in Religion, Theology and Biblical Studies (Burlington: Ashgate, 2002), part 2, also discusses the epistemological aspects of what he calls the pneumatological imagination; this chapter expands on these ideas with regard to the educational activities of the Christian university.

[2]   E.g., Robert L. Gallagher, "Transformational Teaching: Engaging in a Pneumatic Teaching Praxis," in *Thinking Theologically about Language Teaching: Christian Perspectives on an Educational Calling*, ed. Cheri L. Pierson and Will Bankston (Carlisle: Langham, 2017), 135–62, whose historic pentecostal perspective proposes that pneumatic pedagogy involves filling with the Spirit, prayer, vocational reliance, empowered speech.

the more popular than elitist or formalist senses) pedagogy and andragogy, teaching and learning practices that reform the habits of the heart so that the passions and affections might be properly turned toward divinely ordained hopes and loves. The three parts of this chapter will explicate a pentecostal, liturgical, and fully embodied—loving God with all that we are—approach to teaching and learning (§6.1), theorize the application of such to the curriculum of the Christian university (§6.2), and then explore its viability within the online technological platform that is already dominating higher education (§6.3). While there is much that can be said more specifically about the *how* and the *what* of Spirit-ed teaching, that is not our purpose. Instead, the goal here is to encourage at a higher level consideration of the pneumatological and trinitarian frame of the intellectual life vis-à-vis the professorial vocation of (digital) classroom instruction. If generally teachers do not realize how their theological tradition or commitments can inform their teaching,[3] then this chapter entertains the question of whether a Pentecost-infused imagination may have implications for the pedagogical dimension of Christian higher education.

The classical Christian tradition (part 1 above) understood that education needed to touch the whole person. This is in part because sin was, if we might say, a holistic problem, not just an intellectual one. Yes, sin has a rational and cognitive property, and some rightly talk about the noetic effects of sin,[4] for instance, that "sin is going against reason. The sinful action is similarly against reason, against intelligence, nonrational; and the nonrational situation will provide objective evidence for false principles."[5] But sin is also fundamentally a matter of the heart and soul of fallen human creatures, and the rescue of reason thereby has to plumb the depths of the soul as well. Hence, we need the Spirit of Pentecost not just to illuminate human minds but to purify human hearts and hands that not just influence but more often distort discursive thinking. Christian orthodoxy (right thinking and right worship), in this regard, is incomplete apart from orthopraxy (right doing) and orthopathy (right feeling).[6] The full flowering of the intellectual life cannot be achieved apart from the sanctification of the soul and the theosis of the beatific vision. How might a Pentecost approach to teaching and learning across the traditional and online curriculum facilitate such purifying transformation?

6.1 LOVING GOD WITH ALL WE ARE: EMBODIMENT AND THE LITURGIES OF THE SPIRIT

An important next step toward a Spirit-led life of the mind will be to clarify that the discursive conceptualizations of human reason and cognition are affectively shaped, performatively habituated, and kinesthetically charged. The three subsections here will spiral

---

[3] Sixty percent of faculty either do not know or do not believe that theological perspectives have pedagogical implications or applications; see table 2.2 in Perry L. Glanzer and Nathan F. Alleman, *The Outrageous Idea of Christian Teaching* (Oxford: Oxford University Press, 2019), 41.

[4] E.g., Stephen K. Moroney, *The Noetic Effects of Sin: A Historical and Contemporary Exploration of How Sin Affects Our Thinking* (Lanham: Lexington, 2000).

[5] See Robert M. Doran and Frederick E. Crowe, eds., *Collected Works of Bernard Lonergan*, vol. 10: *Topics in Education: The Cincinnati Lectures of 1959 on the Philosophy of Education* (Toronto: University of Toronto Press, 1993), 257.

[6] The orthodoxy-orthopathy-orthopraxy triad is explicated in Yong, *Spirit of Love: A Trinitarian Theology of Grace* (Waco: Baylor University Press, 2012).

around these topics, respectively. We will argue that human thinking is pathically primed, driven by our primal desires and our loves; that human learning is dispositionally angled, even if such can be practically cultivated in various directions; and that human knowing is somatically and relationally constituted and ought to be so motivated. The best practices of Christian higher education, we thus urge, will need to be both embodied and pneumatologically infused, and together they will empower tongues and interpretations to rove across these realms.

If charismatic and pneumatic knowing might seem phenomenologically to be a type of nondiscursive intuitionism, as it has been popularly imagined to be, we will suggest here that it is better understood as what James K. A. Smith calls *storied*, a narrative form of affective, palpable, and embodied experience.[7] With Smith's help (§6.1), what emerges here will be a multileveled pneumatological epistemology that will be deemed consistent with our best teaching practices but that can also continue to enrich learning in the university. Sections 6.2–6.3 will test the viability of our affective and liturgical approach as applied initially to traditional brick-and-mortar and then to online environments.

6.1.1 Pursuing Our Passions: Affectivity in the Spirit

The argument we are developing here, regarding the Christian mind as nourished by life in the Spirit, is not new. We have seen in part 1 above that the life of the mind always has been both ritual and spiritual, simultaneously liturgical and pneumatic, including the routine/mundane and the charismatic. Augustine's distinction between love for God and love for the world, we recall, was rooted in the early catechumenate where catechists "were more interested in the quality of human dispositions and affections than anything else about them."[8] Not for no reason was the later monastic *paideia* derivative from what Jean Leclercq calls a "theology of admirations," a wondrous posture of rapturous love and desire to seek after and pursue God.[9] Whereas in our discussion of the Abbey of St. Victor we expanded upon the "integral humanism" Leclercq claimed for monastic approaches to learning (§2.3.1), here we emphasize how this monastic culture of learning sprang in part off the Augustinian dictum regarding the disquiet of the heart apart from the divine rest—instinctively straining for the beatific vision—and thereby blended devotion and inquiry, piety and scholarship, spirituality and study, with the former element in each pair providing the telos that shaped and guided the latter aspects of learning.

Let us be clear: historically over the millennia, and even now, Christian education presumes both that students (and learners) have been already caught up in God's redemptive story manifest in Christ and unfolded through his Spirit, and that the journey of

---

[7] See James K. A. Smith, *Thinking in Tongues: Pentecostal Contributions to Christian Philosophy*, Pentecostal Manifestos (Grand Rapids: Eerdmans, 2010), ch. 3: "Storied Experience: A Pentecostal Epistemology"; for the record, the pentecostal instincts and sensibilities on display in this book are at the root of much of Smith's massive oeuvre, including his Cultural Liturgies project (on which more momentarily).

[8] John A. Berntsen, "Christian Affections and the Catechumenate," in *Theological Perspectives on Christian Formation: A Reader on Theology and Christian Education*, ed. Jeff Astley, Leslie J. Francis, and Colin Crowder (Grand Rapids: Eerdmans, 1996), 229–43, at 236; and also at 239: "Not *whether* you were affected but *how* you were affected was the issue" (emphasis orig.).

[9] Jean Leclercq, O.S.B., *The Love of Learning and the Desire for God: A Study of Monastic Culture*, trans. Catharine Misrahi (New York: Fordham University Press, 1961), 281–83.

redemption can be further facilitated through educational means that continue orientation to Christ by the Spirit. There is both a prior divine initiative that meets us and an invitation to continue to be open to transcendence that continues via participation in God's mission to save the world. All that we are asserting about the formative power of a disciplined course of study presumes this prior and ongoing work of the divine Spirit that enables participation in and performance of the Christian story of redemption.

From this perspective, the pursuit of the life of the mind included, rather than was segregated from, the desires and passions of the heart. French philosopher Blaise Pascal (1623–1662) had already, almost four hundred years ago, insisted that there is a logic of the heart interrelated with the rationality of the intellect and that human reason thereby presumed the impassioned life of faith, even the fullness of life in the Spirit.[10] This Pascalian perspective on rationality has not been lost in contemporary discussions about and debates over the Christian mind. Yet calls for such a *passionate intellect* have not taken a pneumatological turn.[11] What can and should be said about the pathic scope of the intellectual life for Christian higher education?

Fortunately, over the last dozen years plus, James K. A. Smith, a Reformed charismatic philosopher and scholar, has written about the Christian university as being "for lovers."[12] Building on the pentecostal spirituality into which he was immersed as a new Christian and then also on the monastic tradition and legacy, which understands learning in embodied, communal, and liturgical modes, Smith urges reconnection of church, chapel, and classroom as he argues that learning is "caught" in these various environments as much as "taught" by talking heads (professors, classically understood), even as he links classroom, dorm room, and neighborhood as presuming a holistic educational environment spanning all of real life.[13] In calling for a "new monasticism," Smith implicitly appeals to the integral humanism we have found in our discussion of scholasticism and Renaissance humanism (see §2.3.1–2.3.3).[14] While we will fill out the details in these programmatic proposals in a more concrete way as we move forward, it is important here to clarify the classically forged theological anthropology that motivates these ideas.

---

[10]   James R. Peters, *The Logic of the Heart: Augustine, Pascal, and the Rationality of Faith* (Grand Rapids: Baker Academic, 2009), is more apologetically driven than relevant for thinking about Christian higher education; for Pascal's pneumatology in relationship to his epistemology, however, see Janelle Aijian, "Baptism by Fire: The Work of the Holy Spirit in Pascal's Philosophy," in *The Holy Spirit and the Christian Life: Historical, Interdisciplinary, and Renewal Perspectives*, ed. Wolfgang Vondey, CHARIS: Christianity and Renewal—Interdisciplinary Perspectives (New York: Palgrave Macmillan, 2014), 125–41.

[11]   The title of Alister McGrath, *The Passionate Intellect: Christian Faith and the Discipleship of the Mind* (Downers Grove: IVP, 2010), is a bit misleading for our purposes since it is a popular version of his Gifford Lectures on natural theology, while Norman Klassen and Jens Zimmermann, *The Passionate Intellect: Incarnational Humanism and the Future of University Education* (Grand Rapids: Baker Academic, 2006), adopt a more Christocentric approach that is still pneumatologically thin.

[12]   James K. A. Smith, *Desiring the Kingdom: Worship, Worldview, and Cultural Formation*, Cultural Liturgies 1 (Grand Rapids: Baker Academic, 2009), 215. For Smith's own version of his pentecostal-charismatic and Calvinist commitments and their formative role in his own journey as a Reformed Christian thinker and scholar, see his essay "Teaching a Calvinist to Dance: In Pentecostal Worship, My Reformed Theology Finds Its Groove," *Christianity Today* (May 2008): 42–45.

[13]   Smith, *Desiring the Kingdom*, 223–28.

[14]   Smith, *Desiring the Kingdom*, 222n15, where Smith cites Jean Leclercq from whom we borrow the phrase "integral humanism."

Human creatures are, according to the ancients, *Homo liturgicus*, liturgical creatures in the sense that they are formed by social and cultural practices. Yet more deeply, the liturgies that undergird social life nurture human desires in particular directions: for specific reasons, experiences, and aspirations. Thus, we *Homo sapiens* are desiring and loving persons first and foremost, and it is these yearnings that precede discursive rationality and cognition.

If what Smith calls the cultural liturgies of late modern society drive human cravings along a consumeristic and narcissistic course, then Christian discipleship as a whole—which includes Christian higher education as one component of such—can reform these longings toward the coming reign of God. Ecclesial liturgies, especially those enacted in congregational worship weekly, but also those structured by the liturgical calendar and other rhythms, can restore creaturely desire toward the divine. Yet such pathic, affective, and appetitive renewal and revitalization happen not magically through the Spirit's supernaturalistic interventions but via embodied and devotional practice.[15] Thus, the need to exegete the physicality of liturgical and ritual life to see how repetitive practices figure the imagination and form desire. There is thereby both an erotic—read: embodied—facet to creaturely desire wherein innate impulses are intensified through habitual activity and the resulting perceived sense of satisfaction into intellectualized objectives and goals, as well as a social body that initiates and incorporates the individual and after which the person imitates and perpetuates.[16] Human desire, imagination, and love are hence fundamentally physical and stimulated by the senses, pretheoretically inscribed into our kinesthetic and tactile interactions with others and the world around us, which is why we need sanctifying liturgies (of the Spirit) to renew the primordial story of our having been created good (identity), reorient desire (imagination), and empower a redemptive script (our behaviors).

Smith thus urges what he calls an incarnational—following the image of God revealed in Christ—re-narration (re-birth) of the Christian story (and our personal identities) through catechetical initiation, liturgical ritual, and educational formation.[17] For these goals, the role of the arts is central, as well as the use of culturally relevant novels and films—all of which appear regularly in his writings (and to which we shall return later: §6.2.1)—for telling and retelling the Christian metastory. Beyond the diversity of media through which formation ensues, the Christian university has the opportunity to adapt traditional Christian practices of hospitality, breaking bread, pilgrimage, testimony, fixed-hour prayers according to liturgical rhythms, and the like,[18] in order to revitalize our ethos, enliven our mealtimes, enrich our service learning or study abroad, reappropriate our reflective journaling, or imbue our academic calendars with greater meaning and significance—all of which combine to form us into being more inclusive and welcoming communities. Beyond these are other communally formative practices historically proven within the Christian tradition, such as gratitude (guiding our interpersonal

---

[15] Smith, *Desiring the Kingdom*, 139–44, in which Smith resists the naturalistic-supernaturalistic binary (see also above §5.1.1).

[16] Explicated in James K. A. Smith, *Imagining the Kingdom: How Worship Works*, Cultural Liturgies 2 (Grand Rapids: Baker Academic, 2013), part 1.

[17] Smith, *Imagining the Kingdom*, 186–89.

[18] See David I. Smith and James K. A. Smith, eds., *Teaching and Christian Practices: Reshaping Faith and Learning* (Grand Rapids: Eerdmans, 2011).

relations), promise keeping (embedded within the covenants we call our syllabi), and truth telling ("no plagiarism allowed"!), that can also be arrayed in support of the higher educational enterprise.[19] Intriguingly, part of the cultivation of patristic ideas about education was its critique of "custom" because of the recognition that all education embeds itself within discourses that facilitate a communal identity (§2.2.1). The point is that our cultural liturgies presume certain narratives of the good life that we then find ourselves inserted to and even implicitly endorse, and we need countercultural or redemptive rites and practices—in the church and in Christian higher education—that can habituate us afresh into the gospel reality.[20]

If there is a sense in which Smith overplays the role of affect, embodiment, and habit in knowing and learning, he does so deliberately given his location at Calvin College, the Reformed heartland of Christian *worldview* discourse.[21] As already indicated (§5.3.1), if Christian higher education has already for the last generation developed an extensive worldview emphasis, this leaves the task of relating faith and learning at the abstract level of cognition, which remains ineffective until there are means to recognize, analyze, and redirect what happens within the interstices of the human gut. The point is not to displace the Christian mind with a type of Christian feeling but to understand that the intellectual life includes essentially, rather than can ignore or marginalize, the affective character of material creaturely reality.[22]

More directly for our purposes, a pneumatological theology of the intellectual life presumes and embraces the physicality of the Spirit poured out "upon all flesh" (Acts 2:17). This means that we are dealing not only with an epistemology of the passions and of desire, but that we are also in need of an affective pedagogy and andragogy.[23] Thus, the life of the mind must receive and develop love "as a formation strategy,"[24] a fully embodied, pathically driven, and interpersonally/communally/interrelationally nurtured

---

[19]   Christine D. Pohl, *Living into Community: Cultivating Practices That Sustain Us* (Grand Rapids: Eerdmans, 2011).

[20]   See the recent updating in James K. A. Smith, *You Are What You Love: The Spiritual Power of Habit* (Grand Rapids: Brazos, 2016).

[21]   Expectedly, then, even when Reformed theologians are sympathetic to the undercurrents of pentecostal spirituality central to Smith's epistemology, the default is to reasserting (and being apologetic about) the domain of the rational; e.g., Klaas Bom, "Heart and Reason: Using Pascal to Clarify Smith's Ambiguity," *Pneuma: The Journal of the Society for Pentecostal Studies* 34.3 (2012): 345–64.

[22]   See Barbara L. Martin and Leslie J. Briggs, *The Affective and Cognitive Domains: Integration for Instruction and Research* (Englewood Cliffs: Educational Technology, 1986); also, Marcia Baxter Magolda, "The Affective Dimension of Learning: Faculty-Student Relationships That Enhance Intellectual Development," *College Student Journal* 21.1 (1987): 46–58.

[23]   Ian W. Payne, *Wouldn't You Love to Know? Trinitarian Epistemology and Pedagogy* (Eugene: Pickwick, 2014), 238–39, has written about both an "epistemology of love" and a "pedagogy of love" in his quest for a trinitarian educational philosophy. His Barthian framework thus urges him toward a triadic epistemic stance that interlaces commitment, openness, and relationality as correlative to the triune self-revelation (revealer, revealed, and revealedness—Barthian neologians) and opens up space for understanding "Father, Son, and Spirit, respectively, being facilitator, criterion, and guide to truth." Ours can be considered a pentecostal and pneumatological assist toward such a trinitarian theology of Christian higher education; less modestly put, without a more robust version of the former (that we aim to provide), the latter (Payne's objective) will remain aspirational.

[24]   Jeannine K. Brown, Carla M Dahl, and Wyndy Corbin Reuschling, *Becoming Whole and Holy: An Integrative Conversation about Christian Formation* (Grand Rapids: Baker Academic, 2011), 34.

journey of transformation. How might such an education in orthopathic love be taught and caught in the Christian university?[25]

6.1.2 Habituating Our Dispositions: Multiple Intelligences, Sensibilities, and Capacities by the Spirit

As we turn to the question of how learners (of whatever age) learn, our pneumatological response returns to the day of Pentecost narrative. The instructing of the Spirit commences thus:

> When the day of Pentecost had come, they were all together in one place. And suddenly from heaven there came a sound like the rush of a violent wind, and it filled the entire house where they were sitting. Divided tongues, as of fire, appeared among them, and a tongue rested on each of them. All of them were filled with the Holy Spirit and began to speak in other languages, as the Spirit gave them ability (Acts 2:1–4).

Note the following "classroom" dynamics when viewing the Pentecost occasion in the Upper Room. First, there is a togetherness of learners, in this case spiritually primed for divine encounter, not only because they were instructed to wait for and expect the Spirit's manifestation (Luke 24:49) but also because their souls were behaviorally attuned— through "constantly devoting themselves to prayer" (Acts 1:14a)—to the deity's coming. Second, however, and central to the discussion at hand, the arrival of the Spirit saturates the human sensorium: the manifestation of the Spirit is heard as intensely enveloping ("like *the rush* of a violent wind"), is visibly perceived ("tongues, as of fire, *appeared* among them"), is palpably felt ("a tongue *rested* on each of them"), and then is audibly resonated (in the speaking and hearing).[26] It is an understatement to say that the experience of Pentecost is a fully embodied one; instead it is one of sensory overload, a multiply kinesthetic and pluri-sensorial event.[27]

If modern university teaching and learning in the humanities especially (but not only) has been a predominantly chirographic and literary affair dominated by assigned texts, formal manuscript-based lectures, and writing exercises, this was a shift (as we have seen through the discussion above) from the liturgical catechisms of early Christianity, the contemplative practices of monastic study, and the oral disputations of the medieval scholastics. After the arrival of the printing press and then subsequent to its domination of university culture, learning became much more textually focused (neglecting the orality more prominent during the medieval period), discursively structured (following visual operation), and individualistically undertaken (the learner on his or her own with the textbook). But in the

---

[25] These categories are also being deployed in higher educational conversations outside of the Christian sphere; e.g., Daniel Liston and Jim Garrison, eds., *Teaching, Learning, and Loving: Reclaiming Passion in Educational Practice* (New York: Routledge, 2004).

[26] For further analysis of the multitactility of the Pentecost-miracle, see the second section of ch. 2 in Amos Yong, *The Hermeneutical Spirit: Theological Interpretation and Scriptural Imagination for the 21st Century* (Eugene: Cascade, 2017), 57–61.

[27] Thus, spiritual director James Heisig urges a fully embodied spirituality (in a gnostic age that segregates religious piety from material existence), what he calls an *orthoaesthesis* that involves a recovery and full "liberation of the senses"; see James W. Heisig, *Dialogues at One Inch above the Ground: Reclamations of Belief in an Interreligious Age* (New York: Crossroad, 2003), 74.

prior age, as Walter Ong reminded us almost a half century ago, the orality that dominated human interactions was pervasive also in the social and educational spheres.[28] Whereas vision is unidirectional and dissects even as sight isolates, hearing is multidimensional and synthesizes even as sound incorporates.[29] Oral-aural humans, then, are pathic creatures precisely in and through their hearing. Whereas sight objectifies others apart from the self, sound engages the other dynamically (reverberatingly, even) through the interiority of the self. The intellectual life in a sound-filled world is in that sense alive, intersubjectively negotiated with many echoes (not to say voices). Ong intones that with the expansion of literacy in the modern world and the concomitant impairment of oral-aural capacities "a certain silencing of God may have been prepared for by the silencing of man's life-world."[30] Put in pneumatological key: perhaps modern literate humanity has not so much lost sight of God but is incapable of hearing the Spirit's address. This is a problem if deity is encountered less through reading than by hearing the divine word. As St. Paul put it: "So faith comes from what is heard, and what is heard comes through the word of Christ" (Rom 10:17).[31]

Theological educators have been at the forefront of exploring the implications of orality for effective pedagogy and andragogy, particularly and perhaps unsurprisingly in seminary environments in the majority (non-Western) world, where literacy has not displaced oral-cultural sensibilities.[32] Oral-preference learners are communal and dialogical (requiring participatory interaction rather than solitude), kinesthetic (rather than merely abstract, speculative, and theoretical), experiential (drawing from life as a whole, not just bookish), and narrative-based (inviting empathetic investment of the self rather than requiring only an objectivistic stance toward the artifacts, objects and topics of learning). While print learners generally gravitate toward distilling a general message or more abstract principle from stories, oral learners are usually comfortable with narrative ambiguity and the open-ended invitations of the text, which invite personal involvement and inhabitation.[33] Of course, since most people learn both textually and orally, it is neither that chirographic learning is inadequate (it is not in relationship to certain purposes) nor that we reverse the clock to the medieval university (we cannot and should not), but that orality perspectives foreground the many learning senses beyond the visual capacities used (predominantly, except in the case of those with visual impairments) for literacy. Human beings are feelers and hearers before they are readers, and have internalized the yearnings of the soul, the desires of the affections, and the commitments of the gut long before they open textbooks. If there is to be any hope for transformative learning that sanctifies the passions for the sake of the Spirit-led life of the mind, they will need to enter through our senses, move through our bodies, and touch our hearts.

---

[28] See the by now classic text and argument: Walter J. Ong, *The Presence of the Word: Some Prolegomena for Cultural and Religious History* (1967; repr., Minneapolis: University of Minnesota Press, 1981).

[29] Walter J. Ong, *Orality and Literacy: The Technologizing of the Word* (London: Methuen, 1982), 72–73.

[30] Ong, *Presence of the Word*, 289.

[31] For more on a pneumatological theology of orality, in this case applied to homiletical theory, see Amos Yong, "Proclamation and the Third Article: Toward a Pneumatology of Preaching," in *Third Article Theology: A Pneumatological Dogmatics*, ed. Myk Habets (Minneapolis: Fortress, 2016), 367–94.

[32] Leading the way is W. Jay Moon, "Fad or Renaissance? Misconceptions of the Orality Movement," *International Bulletin of Mission Research* 40.1 (2016): 6–21.

[33] W. Jay Moon, "Understanding Oral Learners," *Teaching Theology and Religion* 15.1 (2012): 29–39, at 32.

One way forward, we suggest, is a pneumatological theology of learning that draws from and adapts Howard Gardner's theory of multiple intelligences.[34] Our strategy depends not on any assurance that Gardner's ideas are undisputed in the field of education—they are widely if loosely applied even if there are on the one side technical questions about how intelligence is hereby understood and used, and on the other side uneasiness among psychologists that the theory is empirically warranted[35]—but because they provide a heuristic springboard to considering the various aptitudes to learning as multisensorial and corporeal activities. Gardner's proposed seven intelligences highlight the embodied character of human learning, and their dominant capacities especially as correlated with fields or disciplines:

- verbal-linguistic: reading and writing
- musical-rhythmic: composing, creating, imagining, performing
- logical-mathematical: logical and critical thinking, abstract reasoning
- visual-spatial: with artistic and aesthetic ability, imaginative, environmentally perceptive
- bodily-kinesthetic: sensory-motor agility, ability to handle objects skillfully, having a sense of timing
- personal intelligences, which includes the interpersonal and the intrapersonal: having a deeper sense of self-awareness and of other-awareness, higher social sensibilities, and emotional astuteness.

Later Gardner added *naturalistic* and *existential* intelligences, but we will stick with his original seven since our case relies not only on the technicalities of his proposal but on its fundamental insight into the many modes and forms of learning especially as these are correlated with competencies and areas of study and fields of inquiry.[36] The more important point is that human minds can be drawn forward in learning and knowing of what is true, good, and beautiful along various intellectual pathways.[37]

Our employment of Gardner's theory accentuates its exploratory character, underscores that none are superior to the other, and presumes that every person usually learns through many if not all of these means even if any single intelligence portal or medium might be stronger or weaker variously. Our takeaways at this juncture are twofold: that

---

[34] Howard Gardner, *Frames of Mind: The Theory of Multiple Intelligences*, 3rd ed. (New York: Basic, 2011).

[35] E.g., Lynn Waterhouse, "Inadequate Evidence for Multiple Intelligences, Mozart Effect, and Emotional Intelligence Theories," *Educational Psychologist* 41.4 (2006): 247–55, and Daniel T. Willingham, *Why Don't Students Like School? A Cognitive Scientist Answers Questions about How the Mind Works and What It Means for the Classroom* (San Francisco: Jossey-Bass, 2009), 158–64; Gardner engages with these and many other critical questions in Jeffrey A. Schaler, ed., *Howard Gardner under Fire: The Rebel Psychologist Faces His Critics* (Chicago: Open Court, 2006), and Branton Shearer, ed., *MI at 25: Assessing the Impact and Future of Multiple Intelligences for Teaching and Learning* (New York: Teachers College, 2009).

[36] See Gardner, *Intelligence Reframed: Multiple Intelligences for the 21st Century* (New York: Basic, 1999); cf. Katie Davis, Joanna Christodoulou, Scott Seider, and Howard Gardner, "The Theory of Multiple Intelligences," in *The Cambridge Handbook of Intelligence*, ed. Robert J. Sternberg and Scott Barry Kaufman (Cambridge: Cambridge University Press, 2011), 485–93.

[37] Howard Gardner, *Truth, Beauty, and Goodness Reframed: Educating for the Virtues in the Twenty-First Century* (New York: Basic, 2011).

effective teaching will be attentive to the distinctive areas of knowledge (disciplines) so that various intelligences are more relevantly engaged, and that learning accumulates across these intelligences so that the more of these are activated in the university, the more effective and successful higher education will be in achieving its intended outcomes. Two caveats are essential. First, our emphasis lies not on how multiple intelligences are expressed in various individual (so-called) learning styles, but in how we should attend to the many disciplines in relationship to the embodied nature of knowing and learning;[38] put otherwise, our focus here is less on the intelligences as manifest in individual learning preferences than on the spectrum of these intelligence types, especially vis-à-vis the material taught, the content presented, and the competencies intended to be nurtured or fostered. Second, our highlighting intelligence types at this juncture is not to detract from the importance of attending to the sociohistorical contexts of university environments, which also impact learning, but it is to say that skilled pedagogues will balance the personal, disciplinary, and the contextual factors in their craft.

Gardner's ideas have enabled more attentiveness to ways in which religious education engages our learning in relationship to specific content or disciplinary areas. For instance, the linguistic intelligence may follow at greater length the sermon; the musical intelligence is more engaged during the period of congregation singing; the logical intelligence intuitively follows the sequentiality of the liturgical calendar; the spatial intelligence works well with maps, models, and illustrations; the kinesthetic intelligence is invigorated by dramatic performances or ritual activities; and the interpersonal intelligence thrives amidst dialogical interaction, while the intrapersonal intelligence cherishes quiet time and journaling.[39] Our own pneumatological approach thus receives his theory in a complementary fashion. If a charismatic life of the mind embraces the many genres of Scripture for formational purposes, depends on the many disciplines for accessing the truth of the many domains of creation, and relies on the many gifts of the many ecclesial traditions for a diversity of approaches to faith-learning integration (the arguments in chapter 6 above), then our Pentecost-theology of learning welcomes the fertility of multiple intelligence theory for empowering a plurality of effective teaching practices across the various fields of study and inquiry.

At this point, then, we also need to make some brief comments about how Gardner's theory has also been fruitfully applied to the education of learners and persons with disabilities.[40] In particular, teachers have appreciated how pedagogical strategies can be adapted to engage with learners' strengths while avoiding modalities perhaps impeded or impacted by impairments; how to foreground learning objectives that correlated with student capacities and interests; how to create student-centered learning environment, activities, and hands-on learning experiences; how to develop multisensory lessons and

---

[38]   E.g., Doug Rohrer and Harold Pashler, "Learning Styles: Where's the Evidence?" *Medical Education* 46.7 (2012): 634–35, and William Furey, "The Stubborn Myth of 'Learning Styles,'" *Education Next* 20.3 (2020), https://www.educationnext.org/journal/vol-20-no-03/.

[39]   See Ronald J. Nuzzi, *Gifts of the Spirit: Multiple Intelligences in Religious Education* (Washington, DC: National Catholic Educational Association, 1996); cf. also Bob Riggert, "The How of Education," in *Learning at the Foot of the Cross: A Lutheran Vision for Education*, ed. Joel D. Heck and Angus J. L. Menuge (Austin: Concordia University Press, 2011), 169–80, for a Lutheran account of what amounts to a multisensorial pedagogy.

[40]   E.g., Judy Willis, *Brain-Friendly Strategies for the Inclusion Classroom: Insights from a Neurologist and Classroom Teacher* (Alexandria: Association for Supervision and Curriculum Development, 2007).

approaches; and how to implement various forms of assessment that can elicit and measure the range of student intelligences. The result is that multiple intelligence pedagogy fosters deeper engagement of learners with disabilities across the curriculum, promotes interaction with the learning process, and enhances learning itself.[41] Recognition that learners with impairments—whether physical or learning disabilities—nevertheless have a range of more or less dominant capacities invites expansion of the pedagogical tool kit so that each is given the best chance of learning success. Theoretical debates about the viability of multiple intelligences are thus resolved at the level of practice, not least in relationship to the most vulnerable members of any learning community.

It is well known that people with disabilities are already among the most socially marginalized, and this is historically the case also in the educational arena.[42] The higher educational endeavor is not exempt, and educators are now naming more clearly how "academia exhibits and perpetuates a form of structural ableism" in its elitism, classism, segregationism, meritocracy, individualism, etc.[43] To be sure, we are retrofitting our campuses, adopting more accessible universal design platforms and otherwise making adjustments and alterations for our learners with disabilities. Yet all of this still nevertheless presumes there is a "normal" and then an aberrational that needs to be accommodated. Why not instead shift toward a "critical multimodality" that presumes not one way of teaching and learning but many? Such "multimodal pedagogies might move forward by recognizing an expanded range of expressive possibilities,"[44] especially when activated with the various disciplines across the curriculum. Learners across the spectrum of ability can in this frame be equal citizens of the university rather than the exception. Herein we highlight the bridge between a Pentecost-vision of democratization wherein all human creatures are (potentially) caught up in the outpouring of the divine breath and a twenty-first-century ideal of rendering education as equally accessible to the masses (rather than being a relatively elitist enterprise available only to a smaller number of fortunate persons).

From a theological and pneumatological perspective, what if we recognized that whatever the perceived strengths or weaknesses of any member of the learning community, each has been given at least spiritual gifts that can build up the rest, and oftentimes these

[41]   As depicted in study after study, e.g., Victoria Proulx-Schirduan, C. Branton Shearer, and Karen I. Case, *Mindful Education for ADHD Students: Differentiating Curriculum and Instruction Using Multiple Instruction* (New York: Teachers College, 2009); Junichi Takahashi, "Multiple Intelligence Theory Can Help Promote Inclusive Education for Children with Intellectual Disabilities and Developmental Disorders: Historical Reviews of Intelligence Theory, Measurement Methods, and Suggestions for Inclusive Education," *Creative Education* 4.9 (2013): 605–10; and Nayyereh Ghaznavi, Mehry Haddad Narafshan, and Massoud Tajadini, "The Implementation of a Multiple Intelligences Teaching Approach: Classroom Engagement and Physically Disabled Learners," *Cogent Psychology* 8.1 (2021): 1–20. See also, in anticipation of our later discussion, Patricia García-Redondo, Trinidad García, Debora Areces, Pablo Garmen, and Celestino Rodríguez, "Multiple Intelligences and Videogames: Intervention Proposal for Learning Disabilities," in ch. 5 of *Learning Disabilities: An International Perspective*, ed. Carolyn S. Ryan (Rijeka, Croatia: Intech Open, 2017), 83–98.

[42]   E.g., Katie Rose Guest Pryal, *Life of the Mind Interrupted: Essays on Mental Health and Disability in Higher Education* (Chapel Hill: Blue Crow, 2017), and Stephanie L. Kerschbaum, Laura T. Eisenman, and James M. Jones, eds., *Negotiating Disability: Disclosure and Higher Education*, Corporealities: Discourses of Disability (Ann Arbor: University of Michigan Press, 2017).

[43]   Jay Timothy Dolmage, *Academic Ableism: Disability and Higher Education*, Corporealities: Discourses of Disability (Ann Arbor: University of Michigan Press, 2017), 53.

[44]   Dolmage, *Academic Ableism*, 113, 114.

gifts are also nurtured by and manifest through the expression of multiple intelligences? Here I am now connecting Gardner's intelligence theory with our pentecostal and charismatic understanding of how the many tongues and gifts of the Spirit are interrelated, including as applied to those across various registers of intellectually wise/foolish, physically strong/weak, and socially respected/despised.[45] More to the point, the Pentecost-narrative itself suggests that the miracle of the Spirit's outpouring is grasped multisensorially through bodies that the divine wind blows upon, through human speech enabled by this breath, and the hearing of others in their other strangeness. Hence, a Pentecost-epistemology is truly one of many sensorial capacities, each enabled to recognize and respond to the divine initiative so that each one, whatever the ability or impairment, can be nurtured, formed, and habituated to become a conduit for recognition of and witness to the deity's wondrous works, not least when illuminated through the disciplines.[46]

There is so much more to say about all of these matters—multiple intelligences, disability pedagogy, and a pneumatological anthropology—yet enough has been mentioned for us to resound the present point: that the life of the mind is as much embodied and affective as it is cognitive. Hence, a diversity of pedagogical approaches is needed not just to address human heads but to touch deeply human hearts and also mobilize human hands. The plenitude of human senses opens up to the multiplicity of human intelligences. What is needed then is exactly the Spirit of Pentecost who can meet us in these various sensory realms and redeem each for God's redemptive and testimonial purposes.

6.1.3 Nourishing Our Lives: Theosis through the Spirit

How then do higher educators teach not only to the intellect but to the heart? We focus here on two types of teaching that make up the two sides of the paradigmatic coin for pneumatic pedagogy introduced at the beginning of this chapter (§6.1.1): habituating practices and critical moments of encounter. Timothy Gorringe, a Reformed theologian, has proposed an educational theology of the senses and of desire that begins to address the former.[47] In an educational context, Gorringe suggests, desire can be understood as "imaginative work on appetite, including the appetite for knowledge."[48] As such, if the senses inflame the passions—of knowing, of experiencing, etc.—the appetites will need to be not only informed but disciplined. Only rehabituation can chastise the inordinate affections. Gorringe proposes a set of ascetic practices related to living in solidarity with those who are poorer not

---

[45] These three axes derive from St. Paul's first letter to the Corinthians (1 Cor 1:18–31); see Yong, "Disability and the Gifts of the Spirit: Pentecost and the Renewal of the Church," *Journal of Pentecostal Theology* 19.1 (2010): 76–93, and "One Body, Many Members: St. Paul's Charismatic Ecclesiology and the Renewal of Dis/Ability," ch. 4 in *The Bible, Disability, and the Church: A New Vision of the People of God* (Grand Rapids: Eerdmans, 2011), 82–117.

[46] See also Yong, "The Virtues and Intellectual Disability: Explorations in the (Cognitive) Sciences of Moral Formation," in *Theology and the Science of Moral Action: Virtue Ethics, Exemplarity, and Cognitive Neuroscience*, ed. James Van Slyke, Gregory R. Peterson, Kevin S. Reimer, Michael L. Spezio, and Warren S. Brown, Routledge Studies in Religion 21 (New York: Routledge, 2013), 191–208, and "Many Tongues, Many Senses: Pentecost, the Body Politic, and the Redemption of Dis/Ability," *Pneuma: The Journal of the Society for Pentecostal Studies* 31.2 (2009): 167–88, reprinted in *The Hermeneutical Spirit*, ch. 4; see also Yong, *Theology and Down Syndrome: Reimagining Disability in Late Modernity* (Waco: Baylor University Press, 2007), ch. 6 on a pneumatological anthropology informed by disability perspectives.

[47] Timothy J. Gorringe, *The Education of Desire: Towards a Theology of the Senses* (Harrisburg: Trinity Press International, 2002).

[48] Gorringe, *Education of Desire*, 91.

to denigrate human embodiment but to accentuate dissonant experiences and perceptions that draw attention to the limits of creaturely existence, to foster distinctive mindedness, and to cultivate the virtues.[49] While this seems a far cry from the pleasurable sensory experiences that contemporary plush universities, even Christian ones, construct to recruit undergraduates, it is how the earliest followers of Jesus as Messiah lived: "All who believed were together and had all things in common; they would sell their possessions and goods and distribute the proceeds to all, as any had need" (Acts 2:44–45).[50]

Yet besides arousing and even redirecting our desires, we need dissonances that stop us in our tracks. Challenging life events are occasions for learning, growth, and development, including for identifying and transforming creaturely passions. Such depth encounters with the alien and the painful (recall §5.1.2), psychologist and theologian James Loder proffers, is exactly the path of Jesus.[51] The Divine Spirit meets the human heart and soul—the human spirit, Loder prefers—in and through the suffering, pain, and even tragedy of life, as seen especially in the cross. More concretely, Loder's pneumatological logic of transformation unfolds in five steps: (1) the experience of conflict; (2) the liminal interlude of searching for resolution; (3) the flash of insight and intuition of a constructive way forward (hope); (4) a release of energy along a new pattern and trajectory; and (5) interpretation of the experience (a new narrative) and verification (healing).[52] Loder identifies this as the "renewal of life in the Spirit of Christ . . . [yielding] new ways of conceiving the life of God in our midst, so that the communion of saints may again—as at its Pentecostal inception—be ultimately defined by no other reality than the Spiritual Presence of God in Jesus Christ at work to restore an anguished creation to its Creator."[53]

There is a richness and density to Loder's pneumatological theology of transformation that precludes our taking more time with it.[54] Important for the purposes at hand is that for the pneumatological education of desire and rehabilitation of the passions to succeed, there must be both *occasions* for experiencing conflictedness and *practices* for habituation onto the path of Jesus, the Spirit-anointed one. The former points of crisis understood within a Pentecost-perspective expect the Spirit to show up, so that flashes of insight and release of energy are charismatic moments—conduits of undeserved grace—that result in the latter: disclosure of new life possibilities and opportunities.[55]

---

[49] Gorringe, *Education of Desire*, 97–99.

[50] See also Stanley Hauerwas, *The State of the University: Academic Knowledges and the Knowledge of God* (Malden: Blackwell, 2007), ch. 12, which is on Gregory of Nazianzus' "On Love for the Poor" (including the leper), and on how this relates to the Christian practices needed to shape the university and its engagement with the world; cf. F. Clark Power and Stephen M. Fallon, "Teaching and Transformation: Liberal Arts for the Homeless," in *The Preferential Option for the Poor beyond Theology*, ed. Daniel G. Groody and Gustavo Gutiérrez (Notre Dame: University of Notre Dame Press, 2014), 149–66.

[51] James E. Loder, *The Logic of the Spirit: Human Development in Theological Perspective* (San Francisco: Jossey-Bass, 1998), 339–42.

[52] James E. Loder, *The Transforming Moment*, 2nd ed. (Colorado Springs: Helmers and Howard, 1989), ch. 2.

[53] Loder, *Transforming Moment*, 219.

[54] See also a more recent collection that brings together important Loderian themes related to his pedagogical theory: James E. Loder Jr., *Educational Ministry in the Logic of the Spirit*, ed. Dana R. Wright (Eugene: Cascade, 2018).

[55] For more on Loder's views of faith development in relationship to the Spirit, see Sharon Parks, "Imagination and Spirit in Faith Development: A Way Past the Structure-Content Dichotomy," in *Faith Development and Fowler*, ed. Craig Dykstra and Sharon Parks (Birmingham: Religious Education, 1986), 137–56.

Pietist traditions have long presumed, in line with Loder's pneumatological logic of development, a view that education involves the experience of a kind of new birth, a catechetical initiation into a life of encounter that addresses the full human person, including the depths of the heart, its desires and its loves.[56] Pietist Wesleyans and their holiness cousins would say that such experiences of being born again ought to be followed by a so-called second work of grace (entire sanctification), even as some among their modern pentecostal relatives would insist on a further subsequent crisis moment: that of baptism in the Holy Spirit. In contrast to the predominantly Reformed integration model focused on the cognitive and more abstract worldview level—so that learning is intellectual even as conversion is considered as a doctrinal change of mind—what is common across these traditions of spirituality is the conviction that "education is the ongoing process of conversion whereby all involved develop as whole persons."[57] Rather than being opposed to or allegedly light on reason and the life of the mind, Pietist whole-person education thus seeks to connect the head and the heart, the intellect and the affections, cognition and the passions. For John Wesley, the "fellowship of right hearts, that supposedly can transcend most areas of doctrinal difference, also invites space for mutually beneficial and growth-producing intellectual engagement, precisely *because* Christian unity does not depend [only] on 'right thinking' but on 'right willing' and 'right loving.'"[58] Study should not be separated from worship since "truth—ultimate saving truth—can be found only in personal encounter or confrontation" with the divine.[59] Reasoning with the head thus includes palpitating the heart.

We began this section with James Smith's proposal that the Christian university is for lovers. Our construal of this claim is that Christian higher education is about the formation and transformation of the heart, of the deepest passions and desire of the human soul. Our (raw and Spirit-shaped) passions inform our perspective (the epistemic level), motivate our inquiry (the research question or hypothesis level), and move our analyses; thus "desire, or eros, guides intellectual inquiry [and there] is no such thing as disinterested scholarship unmoved by some dynamism."[60] If our loves operate in these multiple venues of research, teaching, and learning, then the Christian university is or should be nothing less than a school of love, a theater or stage in which what we want most is touched by the Spirit and aroused toward the divine rest.

We have ranged widely over disparate conceptual terrain so far in this chapter, spanning the Reformed spectrum from Smith's charismatic theology of desire to Gorringe's

---

[56] See Kurt W. Peterson and R. J. Snell, "'Faith Forms the Intellectual Task': The Pietist Option in Christian Higher Education," in *The Pietist Impulse in Christianity*, ed. Christian T. Collins Winn, Christopher Gehrz, G. William Carlson, and Eric Holst (Eugene: Pickwick, 2011), 215–30, esp. 224–26.

[57] Peterson and Snell, "Faith Forms the Intellectual Task," 215.

[58] Shirley A. Mullen, "The 'Strangely Warmed' Mind: John Wesley, Piety, and Higher Education," in Collins Winn, Gehrz, Carlson, and Holst, *Pietist Impulse*, 161–71, at 169 (emphasis orig.).

[59] Peterson and Snell, "Faith Forms the Intellectual Task," 230.

[60] Thus, Kenneth Garcia, *Academic Freedom and the Telos of the Catholic University* (New York: Palgrave Macmillan, 2012), 33; for more on love and epistemology and love and scholarship, see respectively Esther Lightcap Meek, *Longing to Know: The Philosophy of Knowledge for Ordinary People* (Grand Rapids: Brazos, 2003), and Jenell Williams Paris, "A Pietist Perspective on Love and Learning in Cultural Anthropology," in *Taking Every Thought Captive: Forty Years of the Christian Scholar's Review*, ed. Don W. King (Abilene: Abilene Christian University Press, 2011), 315–27.

ascetic education of the senses via analysis of bodily knowing in orality, multiple intel-ligence, and disability perspectives. This has brought us back to Wesleyan holiness edu-cational sensibilities, previously canvassed (§5.3.1), now refracted through a Pietist lens. These conduits of modern pentecostal instincts have charted the parameters for our inquiry: to excavate a Pentecost-epistemology of many senses, correlate such with a pneumatological theology of multiple learning modalities, aptitudes, and capabilities, and work toward a trinitarian vision for higher education and the life of the mind. The Christian intellectual life, we have urged repeatedly, involves a renewal of the mind that simultaneously sanctifies (and inspires) the imagination and purifies the soul. The goal is not just the formation of intellects but the development of material creatures into sages and, more importantly, the transformation of "human animals into saints."[61] The life of the mind in the Spirit necessarily includes the spiritual and moral domains.

In effect, our work so far in this second part of the book has consisted in connecting the classical Christian educational projects discussed in the earlier part 1 with contem-porary theological notions and Christian higher educational theories. If, for medieval theologians like Hugh of St. Victor, the ultimate objective of the arts, as handmaidens to theology, was "the restoration of the divine likeness in man" through the acquisition of wisdom that re-*formed* the cognitive, affective, and physical dimensions (*Didascalicon* 2.1; cf. §2.2.1 above also),[62] perhaps what we are doing is providing a Pietist-Wesleyan-holiness-and-pentecostal perspective on certain educational practices and values also now finding elaboration in this tradition of early medieval and Orthodox deification.[63] Following Irenaeus of Lyons, Clement of Alexandria, and Athanasius (§2.2.2), we think of deification as a process of *theopoesis*: being made, formed, or even artistically shaped into the likeness of the potter by the two hands of the Word and the Spirit.[64]

A present version of this Orthodox approach articulates an aesthetic, liturgical, and sacramental pedagogy via what is called an "iconic knowing," a "knowledge of 'the heart'" that involves cognition, imagination, memory, embodiment, and affectivity, and is directed toward sanctification or theosis.[65] This "iconic catechesis" recognizes that the divine is manifest in and through creaturely materiality and hence embraces the prac-tices and rhythms of the liturgical tradition as having educational and transformational

---

[61] Perry L. Glanzer and Todd C. Ream, *Christianity and Moral Identity in Higher Education* (New York: Palgrave Macmillan, 2009), 221. For more on the moral scope of the higher educational enterprise, see also Douglas V. Henry and Michael D. Beaty, eds., *The Schooled Heart: Moral Formation in American Higher Education*, Studies in Religion and Higher Education 4 (Waco: Baylor University Press, 2007).

[62] See Jan W. M. van Zweiten, "Scientific and Spiritual Culture in Hugh of St Victor," in *Centres of Learning: Learning and Location in Pre-Modern Europe and the Near East*, ed. Jan Willem Drijvers and Alasdair A. MacDonald, Brill's Studies in Intellectual History 61 (Leiden: E. J. Brill, 1995), 177–86, at 186.

[63] E.g., John L. Elias, *A History of Christian Education: Protestant, Catholic, and Orthodox Perspectives* (Malabar: Krieger, 2002), ch. 8; note also that Constance J. Tarasar, "Orthodox Theology and Religious Education," in *Theologies of Religious Education*, ed. Randolph Crump Miller (Birmingham: Religious Edu-cation Press, 1995), 83–120, is pneumatologically rich, much more so than any of the other paradigms of Christian education discussed in this book.

[64] See also Dale M. Coulter, "Sanctification: Becoming an Icon of the Spirit through Holy Love," in *The Routledge Handbook of Pentecostal Theology*, ed. Wolfgang Vondey (New York: Routledge, 2020), 237–46.

[65] See Anton C. Vrame, *The Educating Icon: Teaching Wisdom and Holiness in the Orthodox Way* (Brookline: Holy Cross Orthodox Press, 1999), 81–91.

scope.[66] Orthodox sensibilities culled from the long tradition of monastic practices thus situate the journey of human souls within the liturgical life of the believing community and thereby engage the full spectrum of the human senses toward an integral relationship with the world as a whole, yet ultimately human knowledge in its many domains is oriented toward union with the divine. One Orthodox scholar puts it thus: "The Orthodox understanding of *theosis* is the single greatest contribution that Orthodox scholars can offer to the academic world, no matter what the discipline is."[67]

Pentecostal and charismatically inclined Christians have much common cause to make with Orthodox scholars, themselves a group that is newly and gradually emerging on the higher educational frontier.[68] The newer pentecostal and charismatic university architects can learn from those whose roots go deep into the Christian tradition even as the Orthodox thinkers might yet also find new pneumatological perspectives helpful for their own educational projects. If the emphasis on ritual practice in Orthodox trinitarianism not just complements but empowers embodied pentecostal spirituality,[69] our own pneumatological approach includes the crisis experiences of otherness and conflict (Loder), which also facilitate ongoing learning and renovation (Gorringe). The abstractly stated goal is, to use Orthodox language, deification—holiness and sanctification of mind, body, soul, spirit, and way of life in the image of Christ—even if the process involves charismatic encounter and pneumatically mediated practices of renewal and purification.

6.2 REINVIGORATING TEACHING AND LEARNING: MANY LANGUAGES FOR COCURRICULAR MULTIMEDIATION

Of course, the Christian university is not a church, and so we cannot presume that ecclesial practices are easily transferable to or replicable in the higher educational classroom. Yet the discontinuities between the two domains are not absolute; rather, they are marked by historic continuities, as part 1 of our book shows, between the catechumenate and the Holy Club, between monastery and university, between cloister and classroom. In this next part of our argument, then, we ask how our Pentecost-pedagogy of desire and love might unfold in the more traditional, residential program of study. Our gaze will begin with the core curriculum (§6.2.1), move then to the chapel and related initiatives to explore the pedagogical implications of its central (physical and symbolic) location within the Christian university (§6.2.2),[70] and conclude with some reflections on the "curriculum" outside the classroom (§6.2.3). We will ask repeatedly what it means to nurture the pathic character of intellectual

---

[66] Vrame, *Educating Icon*, ch. 6; see also the chapter "The Higher Learning and the Metaphor of Liturgy," in James Steve Counelis, *Higher Learning and Orthodox Christianity* (London: Associated University Presses; [Scranton]: University of Scranton Press, 1990), 105–21.

[67] Aristotle Papanikolaou, "*Theosis* and Theological Literacy: Identity Formation and Teaching Theology to Undergraduates," in *Eastern Orthodox Christianity and American Higher Education: Theological, Historical, and Contemporary Reflections*, ed. Ann Mitsakos Bezzerides and Elizabeth H. Prodromou (Notre Dame: University of Notre Dame Press, 2017), 256–65, at 263.

[68] Many of the essays in Bezzerides and Prodromou (see previous footnote) document the historical reasons for the delay of Orthodoxy in higher education.

[69] See Edmund J. Rybarczyk, *Beyond Salvation: Eastern Orthodoxy and Classical Pentecostalism on Becoming Like Christ* (Milton Keynes: Paternoster, 2004), for comparative assessment.

[70] The first two sections of this chapter develop what is embryonically stated in Yong, "Whence and Whither in Evangelical Higher Education? Dispatches from a Shifting Frontier," *Christian Scholar's Review* 42.2 (2013): 179–91, esp. 185–89.

life in the Spirit, and how this might be accomplished. Doing our work well and diligently in this segment will set us up to explore the fortunes of a pneumatological pedagogy and andragogy within the online environment (§6.3).

Note that the following does not discuss the *what* of the curriculum in the Christian university. In many respects, curricular content is dictated by the shifting dynamics of the disciplines (above §6.2) as entry points into the various sectors of human knowledge. Further, while the movement starts with the formal curriculum and then moves to the cocurricular, the assumption is that we need to see these as interrelated wholes rather than as disconnected aspects.[71] Remember that our focus is on what difference the Holy Spirit makes in Christian higher education, and this goal of articulating a Pentecost-approach to teaching and learning in, through, and beyond the formal curriculum is designed to prompt consideration of how a pedagogy of many tongues facilitates encounter with otherness and difference, which forms Christians for faithful discipleship and world citizenship.[72] The following therefore unpacks further our conversation with Gardner initiated above, although what we are exploring now concerns the multiple spheres of intelligence across the Christian higher educational enterprise. Along these lines, the fundamental questions are how the Christian university nurtures orthopathic practices of transformation and sanctification and how it opens up to or makes time and space for the work of the Spirit.

6.2.1 Pedagogical Polyphony in the (Core) Curriculum: Artistic-Musical Formation

For the record, we realize that the notion of the core curriculum is under attack in the wider academy for reasons both internal to undergraduate education and external vis-à-vis the fluidity of realms of knowledge in our information age. Yet from a faith perspective, not having a core to the curriculum of the Christian university is not an option: without at least space for presentation and discussion of what *Christian* means, there would be no need to provide alternatives to publicly funded higher educational opportunities. There must be a series of courses or other learning experiences that unfold the narrative identity of Christianity through the story of God (see §2.2.1). Our discussion here therefore presumes we are all committed to having common core to some extent; the degree to which such revolves around the liberal arts tradition or includes a broader foray into the humanities needs not be adjudicated. However Christian university faculties decide, some commitment to and promotion of the faith tradition is involved. Our focus, then, is on the role of certain pedagogical modalities across the curriculum, but particularly within whatever the core is decided to be.

We noted in passing above both the role of music in pentecostal spirituality (§4.2.3) and Smith's use of literature and film as part of his narrative epistemology

---

[71] Thus, also, Todd C. Ream and Perry L. Glanzer, *The Idea of a Christian College: A Reexamination for Today's University* (Eugene: Cascade, 2013), ch. 8, esp. 100–3, urge that we resist situating learning in classrooms and playing outside of such environments and create formational experiences that encourage the latter realms as domains to live out and test what happens in the former spaces.

[72] Henry A. Giroux, "Liberal Arts Education and the Struggle for Public Life: Dreaming about Democracy," in *The Politics of Liberal Education*, ed. Darryl J. Gless and Barbara Herrnstein Smith (Durham: Duke University Press, 1992), 119–44, at 136, names explicitly the notion of a "pedagogy of difference"; Giroux's focus is on the role of a liberal education in cultivating citizenship in a pluralistic democracy, one consisting of contrasting narratives within a common, public space, but such aspirations are not extrinsic to our Pentecost-vision for Christian higher education.

(§6.1.1). As expressions of human imagination and carriers of our cultural traditions, the arts—inclusive here of literature, the visual and performative arts, and the full scope of the musical arts—are primary vehicles for bridging the secular-mundane and spiritual-moral portions of our lives, mediating awareness of truthfulness and goodness on the one hand and sparking our imaginative possibilities on the other hand.[73] The following discussion looks particularly at film and music—initially recognizable as related to Gardner's visual-spatial and musical-rhythmic intelligences—not at their disciplinary content, nor at their curricular location (we believe they should remain within the liberal arts core of Christian university curricula, even as we hope that the liberal arts are not marginalized in Christian higher education at large). Rather, our focus will be on their epistemic dimensions, aptitudinal features, and pedagogical implications. How might these filmographic and musical tongues, so to speak, serve as portals of encounter with transcendence and as conduits of personal, moral, and spiritual transformation?

Film is no doubt visual, but it is also profoundly aural and hence experienced in and through our bodies. Pedagogical use of film is powerful because we not only hear voices and words but are bathed in sound and music. Film music is thus variously affective:

> First, it elicits affect through direct physiological effects on audiences. Second, it elicits moods, which prime audiences for certain kinds of emotions. Third, it modifies the scene by suggesting its emotional valence. Music modifies, intensifies, and complicates the affective experience of a scene through polarization, affective congruence, or both simultaneously. In other words, it can move the expressive interpretation of a scene away from that inherent in the nonmusical elements, it can strengthen the scene's existing emotive qualities by adding to them, or it can elicit affect in ambiguous and complicated ways.[74]

Obviously, the content of films chosen for classroom use matter, both with regard to the issues being adjudicated within the course or discipline and with regard to Christian faith commitments. Yet pedagogically, because of its capacity to sway moods (e.g., calmness or agitation), induce emotions and passions (from joy and happiness to anxiety or disgust, among others), and intensify visceral feelings (like empathy and sympathy or sadness, etc.), film is also cathartic or therapeutic. Its narrative arc means in addition that viewers—and hearers—are invited into another storyline; the dynamic of temporality involved activates the imagination, triggers fantasy (if not fantastic alternatives), occasions creativity, stirs desire, and charts alternative life possibilities.[75] We see here, then, that film engages not only the visual-spatial intelligence, to use Gardner's nomenclature, but also the bodily-kinesthetic register. To be sure, critical engagement with film will have

---

[73] See Leland Ryken, *The Christian Imagination: Essays on Literature and the Arts* (Grand Rapids: Baker, 1981).

[74] Carl A. Plantinga, *Moving Viewers: American Film and the Spectator's Experience* (Berkeley: University of California Press, 2009), 135.

[75] Many of the chapters in Carl Plantinga and Greg M. Smith, eds., *Passionate Views: Film, Cognition, and Emotion* (Baltimore: Johns Hopkins University Press, 1999), touch on these themes.

to be attentive to the intentions of producers since their purposes may not align directly with learning objectives,[76] yet in the hands of skillful teachers, the use of film in class-rooms can enhance the educational experience.

The point is not at all to eliminate literacy but to enhance such by activating and engaging as many learner propensities and dispositions as possible. Film is a multi-sensual experience that, with appropriate pedagogical guidance, can enable us to open up alternative experiences and perspectives, confront our deep-seated prejudices, help interrogate our habituated conventions and practices, and assist in our naming and identifying the loves, passions, and desires that define our life trajectories. If the intel-lectual life is truly to be free in the Spirit, then we need learning experiences that press through the rationalizations of the discursive mind and into the heart. Seeing, hear-ing, and feeling—what we do in, with, and through film—can thereby be channels for these purposes.

There are hence multiple possibilities for use of music across the curriculum, that allied with film being only one type. Because music is, like sound, not just heard but felt (our bodies perceive percussive instruments as much as our ears hear melodies and harmonies), musical experience attunes our many senses to our practical and produc-tive intelligences. If music programs and courses involve musical composing, conduct-ing, singing, instrumentalizing, performing, etc., perhaps incorporation of a variety of embodied practices across the curriculum could provide outlets for improvisation and creativity. Now if film might include music but at least has a visual aspect, music in and on its own cannot be objectified via sight but can only be a thoroughly embodied expe-rience, and therein lies perhaps the chief prohibition against its deployment across the curriculum, that it requires attunement of whole selves, rather than can be engaged in any monodimensional manner. Comparatively, for instance, Eastern Orthodox iconography, engaged visually, is widespread across the Western academy, but not Eastern Christian song, the former involving "arguably a less invasive process" than the latter, as one Ortho-dox scholar theorizes regarding the disparity.[77] If we can begin to overcome this handicap, if in no other way than through, initially, use of music in film, then gradually we might be ready to consider this question: how might the performance side of the musical arts—which could include the visual and material arts, for instance, sculpture—invite consider-ation of learning as a process of embodied habits and expressive practices?

We will return momentarily (§6.2.2) to comment further about the role of music in worship and their conjoint pedagogical implications. For now, however, we want to press more substantively into the possibility of what we might call a musical rationality, a musi-cal way of thinking and mode of cognition, as it were. What if music were not just a noun, and what if we were to transpose it into a verb in relationship to our quest for the life of the mind? Perhaps we can call this *musicking*, referring here not only to music-making but

---

[76] This is because, among other reasons, any film's "elicited emotions and affects are characterized and differentiated by structural features, such that the film's intended affective focus can be reasonably well determined in many cases" (Plantinga, *Moving Viewers*, 11).

[77] Alexander Lingas, "Singing the Lord's Song in a Foreign Land: Teaching Orthodox Liturgical Music in Non-Orthodox Contexts," in Bezzerides and Prodromou, *Eastern Orthodox Christianity and American Higher Education*, 279–314, at 281.

also to a mode or "activity of *thinking* in or with sound."[78] This is not necessarily dependent on the ability to read, interpret, and evaluate written music—even proficient musicians may not be trained in these formal skills!—but might be a mentality that "inquires about the nature of things through music."[79] As part of his movement through liberal arts, Augustine wrote on the power of music to draw desire into the harmonies and rhythms of life itself through its elicitation of delight in the soul.[80]

Against this backdrop, and drawing specifically on Loder's transformational logic and Ong's analysis of orality (§§6.1.2–6.1.3 above), Lisa Hess considers such learning *in a musical key* as resonant with the oral habits of mind that, contextually situated, interpersonally derived, and performatively intelligible, are marked by "relational-formation, explicit embodiment, irreducible multidimensionality, and a central role for insight."[81] Such learning and knowing is both contemplative and impassioned, attuned to difference (of the subtlest or the most jarring kinds), and is celebratory, even amidst sorrow.[82] In brief, we are seeking a model of the intellectual life that embraces and includes a nonverbal and nonconceptual way of being and doing that is not just a source of knowing but also a mode of learning and life.[83]

Our claim here is not only that the arts in general, and the musical arts particularly, are conduits for the sanctifying work of the Spirit but also that the life of the mind is dependent on these tongues of the Spirit.[84] As it was said of Thomas Aquinas' prodigious and synthetic intellect, that it "owed a great deal to his participation in the Latin chant of the *Scola cantorum*," and that it was "musical education that opened his consciousness

---

[78] Mary Louise Serafine, *Music as Cognition: The Development of Thought in Sound* (New York: Columbia University Press, 1988), 69 (emphasis orig.); see also Monique Ingalls, "Introduction: Interconnection, Interface, and Identification in Pentecostal-Charismatic Music and Worship," in *The Spirit of Praise: Music and Worship in Global Pentecostal-Charismatic Christianity*, ed. Monique Ingalls and Amos Yong (University Park: Penn State University Press, 2015), 1–25, at 4. Our extended understanding here is helped also by Anne E. Streaty Wimberly, *Nurturing Faith and Hope: Black Worship as a Model for Christian Education* (Cleveland: Pilgrim, 2004), ch. 10, who discusses musicking as nurtured amidst the improvisational activity of Black church worship, thus involving the imaginative, expressive, and innovative interaction of both halves of the human brain.

[79] Joshua F. Drake, *Recovering Music Education as a Christian Liberal Art* (Mountain Home: Border-Stone, 2010), 129.

[80] See Augustine, *On Music*, in Augustine, *The Immortality of the Soul, The Magnitude of the Soul, On Music, The Advantage of Believing, and On Faith in Things Unseen*, trans. Robert Catesby Taliaferro, The Fathers of the Church: A New Translation 4 (Washington, DC: Catholic University of America Press, 1947), 153–384.

[81] Lisa M. Hess, *Learning in a Musical Key: Insight for Theology in Performative Mode* (Eugene: Pickwick, 2011), 107.

[82] Hess, *Learning in a Musical Key*, 185; see also Maeve Louise Heaney, VDMF, *Music as Theology: What Music Has to Say about the Word* (Eugene: Pickwick, 2012).

[83] We get this way of putting it from Tom Beaudoin, *Witness to Dispossession: The Vocation of a Postmodern Theologian* (Maryknoll: Orbis, 2008), ch. 2, esp. 24–25, where, in conversation with Howard Gardner's multiple intelligences ideas, musical knowing is explored as a form of theological intelligence that has the capacity to "rework other theological knowledge domains"—precisely how we are thinking about music outside the music department and across the core curriculum. See also Yong, "Improvisation, Indigenization, and Inspiration: Theological Reflections on the Sound and Spirit of Global Renewal," in Ingalls and Yong, *Spirit of Praise*, 279–88, for further discussion of how to think in and through music.

[84] See the section titled "Language and Pentecost," in which music is discussed in terms of divine communication in Drake, *Recovering Music Education*, 46–50.

to the harmonies of the spirit,"[85] so also, we suggest, do the arts represent a language of Pentecost. The artistic medium is thereby a communicative mode through which learners are formed in the school of the Spirit. If an incarnational approach to theology of music suggests a sonic theological method that hears sound as a medium through which divine and human, transcendence and immanence, are interwoven, then a pentecostal complement hears the musical arts as many voices intoned by life in the Spirit.[86] As the Spirit is the one who "gathers up and focuses the praise of creation, directing it towards the Father,"[87] then it makes sense that divine breath will also redeem the various arts to herald the impending rule and reign of God. And to the degree that the Spirit enables creaturely artistic and musical creativity, to that same degree, theologian of the arts Jeremy Begbie indicates that there is a "Pentecostal polyphony" of many distinct voices[88]—affective and cognitive, personal and social, mundane and heightened—yet in harmonious concord announcing the divine purpose. The musical arts thereby give us a window into a Pentecost-pedagogy that echoes in human ears, touches human hearts, enlivens our appreciation of and desire for the beautiful, and musters and moves human hands toward the divine rest.[89]

As music is a transcultural and international mode of communication, there is great prospect for using music and musical strategies in teaching in the multicultural classrooms that now constitute the Christian university. In this case, literature, artistic media, and music from various cultures of the world are potentially pedagogical instruments, perhaps so that learners "can be humbled by understanding others as made in the image of God and themselves as limited and sinful."[90] Precisely because music communicates from the depths of human anxieties amidst their concrete existential crises, they confront us with the passions and pains of other lives, thus possibly dividing as much as uniting fallen human creatures.[91] Yet the alienation and brokenness that comes through the soundscape can also be a source of empathic reconciliation.

Our Pentecost-approach to teaching and learning thus not only insists on the importance of keeping the arts, broadly defined, in the curriculum, within the core of the liberal

---

[85]   Stratford Caldecott, *Beauty for Truth's Sake: The Re-enchantment of Education* (Grand Rapids: Brazos, 2009), 41.

[86]   See the chapters by Malcolm Guite, "Through Literature: Christ and the Redemption of Language," and Jeremy Begbie, "Through Music: Sound Mix," both in *Beholding the Glory: Incarnation through the Arts*, ed. Jeremy Begbie (Grand Rapids: Baker, 2000), 27–46 and 138–54 respectively.

[87]   Jeremy S. Begbie, *Voicing Creation's Praise: Towards a Theology of the Arts* (Edinburgh: T&T Clark, 1991), 257.

[88]   Jeremy S. Begbie, *Resounding Truth: Christian Wisdom in the World of Music* (Grand Rapids: Baker Academic, 2007), 269–70.

[89]   For more on a specifically pentecostal aesthetic that comprehends dance, music, the visual arts, cinema, and architecture, among other expressions of human creativity, from the perspective of the Pentecost-outpouring of the Spirit, see Steven Félix-Jäger, *Spirit of the Arts: Towards a Pneumatological Aesthetics of Renewal*, Charis: Christianity and Renewal—Interdisciplinary Studies (New York: Palgrave, 2017); also his *Pentecostal Aesthetics: Theological Reflections in a Pentecostal Philosophy of Art and Aesthetics*, Global Pentecostal and Charismatic Studies 16 (Leiden: Brill, 2015).

[90]   Stephen K. Moroney, Matthew P. Phelps, and Scott T. Waalkes, "Cultivating Humility: Teaching Practices Rooted in Christian Anthropology," in Henry and Beaty, *Schooled Heart*, 171–90, at 189.

[91]   See Don Saliers and Emily Saliers, *A Song to Sing, a Life to Live: Reflections on Music as Spiritual Practice* (San Francisco: Jossey-Bass, 2005), ch. 6.

arts requirements even, but also urges that courses across the liberal arts and the curriculum deploy artistic and musical media to engage learners.[92] Artistic and musical modes of communication are effective in engaging the broad spectrum of learning aptitudes, in moving the affections, and in fostering creativity. Perhaps most importantly, a pneumatological pedagogy will inform and nurture the many sensorial wellsprings of the intellectual life, where its loves, desires, and passions may be in need of therapy, healing, and repair.

6.2.2 Chapel within a Seamless Curriculum: Spiritual and Moral Formation

We now peer beyond the curriculum, formally considered, but only in order to reconceive such in relationship to our Pentecost-vision for Christian higher education. Toward this end, we naturally shift our gaze to the chapel, obviously constitutionally central to the Christian university.[93] There are many obvious reasons to consider the role of the chapel, not only in light of the tradition's historic emphasis on the formation of spiritual and moral character (part 1 above) but also because what has emerged as a division between worship as spiritual and study as academic is now recognized as a modern dichotomy that is being overcome.[94] Our comments here both recognize the problems related to this bifurcation—for example, that chapel not only ceases to contribute to but can also undermine the learning that is the purpose of the Christian university—and seek to repair the divide. Beyond this motivation, however, learners pursuing higher education in the contemporary postmodern era, even outside but also within the Christian university context, are very introspective and spiritually interested, if not religiously active.[95] The weekly (if not more often) university chapels provide a center of gravity for the life of faith, which includes that of the mind. The mistake is to assume that the Spirit is "felt" mainly in chapel and its concomitant venues—for example, vesper meetings, Bible studies, prayer groups—while intellects are activated only in classrooms.

Yet we want to go further. It is not that we want to replicate chapel activities across the university, but that we want to ask how the chapel's focus can be instructive for spiritual and moral formation in the Christian higher educational endeavor. What if we were to shift from chapel as an event within the weekly ritual of the university to thinking about chapel-type activities and practices informing university life as a whole? This goes further than considering how the university chapel can remind academia about the crucial role of the church in the formation of the next generation of Christian disciples,[96] even as the

---

[92]   Stephen H. Webb, "Sound and Space: Making Vocation Audible," in *At This Time and in This Place: Vocation and Higher Education*, ed. David S. Cunningham (Oxford: Oxford University Press, 2016), 281–300, moves in a similar direction, albeit from his Barthian rather than our Pentecost-perspective.

[93]   See also Monte Lee Rice, "Pneumatic Experience as Teaching Methodology in Pentecostal Tradition," *Asian Journal of Pentecostal Studies* 5.2 (2002): 289–312, esp. 303–8.

[94]   There are rich essays in this direction in Siobhán Garrigan and Todd E. Johnson, eds., *Common Worship in Theological Education* (Eugene: Pickwick, 2010), that are applicable to considerations of the Christian college and university context.

[95]   See the research in Samuel Schuman, *Seeing the Light: Religious Colleges in Twenty-First-Century America* (Baltimore: Johns Hopkins University Press, 2010); cf. Alexander W. Astin, Helen S. Astin, and Jennifer A. Lindholm, *Cultivating the Spirit: How College Can Enhance Students' Inner Lives* (San Francisco: Jossey-Bass, 2010), ch. 3, which documents intensification of spiritual and religious quests during the college years.

[96]   This point is also explicated by James K. A. Smith, *The Devil Reads Derrida and Other Essays on the University, the Church, Politics, and the Arts* (Grand Rapids: Eerdmans, 2009), ch. 9.

reverse might also be true: that liturgical practice in the university could be a generative site for innovation in ecclesial worship and congregational formation.[97] Further, our query is more foundational regarding the academic venture: how might Christian higher education be revitalized by the spiritual quest symbolically enacted within the chapel experience? Put alternatively, if we are what we passionately desire and we worship what we love, then how might a life of wholehearted worship be not just forefronted during the chapel hours but extended across the full scope of the Christian university and its experiences?[98] Can, for instance, prayer and contemplative meditation be educationally and pedagogically relevant across the curriculum and not just in collective chapel or in our personal quiet or devotional time? What if, in other words, we were to think about Sabbath not only as an important day of the week (which it is), but as a way of life, especially one that provides the regularized rhythms for the life of the mind?[99]

Prayer is the obvious place to begin pursuing this question. If beginning classes with prayer has become almost perfunctory in the Christian university, how might we retrieve this practice as seamlessly characteristic of the life of faith, including the intellectual life? If prayer is the affective site through which the agonistic character of human existence is taken up with the divine,[100] then it is more rather than less relevant amidst the intellectual dissonance of grappling with alien ideas and unfamiliar realities encountered along the academic sojourn. Thus, it is in his portrayal of "the church at the heart of the Christian university proclaiming the word to the world," that Roman Catholic theologian Gavin D'Costa discusses prayer as being central to not just the spiritual and ecclesial life but to disciplinary scholarship: "by using prayer as the key to deal with the notion of 'living tradition' . . . , I have tried to emphasize the shifting relationships that constitute my tradition-specific approach. Prayer at least guards against atemporal and ahistorical notions, for it points to a living, struggling relationship that has taken on endless forms between ecclesial persons and God."[101]

So prayer belongs not only at the start of classes nor only in chapel but in both and beyond: as part of the Spirit-infused life of the mind. As one English Catholic writer put it: "The 'purpose' of the Liberal Arts is therefore to purify the soul, to discipline the attention so that it becomes capable of devotion to God; that is, prayer."[102] Prayer is thereby

---

[97] Long ago, Julian N. Hartt, *Theology and the Church in the University* (Philadelphia: Westminster, 1969), 204, wrote: "The university chapel has an unparalleled opportunity to forge and test reconstructions of the liturgical-political order" for the sake of the ongoing vitality of the church.

[98] Debra Dean Murphy, *Teaching that Transforms: Worship as the Heart of Christian Education* (Grand Rapids: Brazos, 2004), begins to take some steps in this direction, although her context is Christian education more generally than Christian higher education more exactly.

[99] We are helped here by Todd C. Ream and Brian C. Clark, "Meet George Newfellow: Sabbath Existence as a Way of Life," in *The Soul of a Christian University: A Field Guide for Educators*, ed. Stephen T. Beers (Abilene: Abilene Christian University Press, 2008), 153–67, esp. 158–59; cf. David I. Smith, *On Christian Teaching: Practicing Faith in the Classroom* (Grand Rapids: Eerdmans, 2018), 122–25, on the import of attending to the intersection of space and time in developing rhythms of learning, living, resting, worshiping, etc.

[100] See Don E. Saliers, *The Soul in Paraphrase: Prayer and the Religious Affections* (New York: Seabury, 1980), ch. 3.

[101] Gavin D'Costa, *Theology in the Public Square: Church, Academy and Nation* (Malden: Blackwell, 2005), 215 and 143 respectively.

[102] Caldecott, *Beauty for Truth's Sake*, 90.

both a means and an end, both facilitating the life of the mind and flowing forth from a fully invigorated and animated (pneumatically and charismatically charged) intellectual life. From this perspective, prayerful studying, thinking, and living enables introspective self-discernment and discovery, nurtures faith and courage (to explore, wonder, and be curious), facilitates repentance (from badly habituated and wrong ways of thinking), occasions confession (of the vices that inhibit the life of the mind), makes time for lament (of the passing of old ideas), and prompts intercession (when confronted with deeply challenging intellectual notions).[103] Even better when learners are praying with one another—here both literally and in the spirit of St. Paul's invitation for us to "pray without ceasing" (1 Thess 5:17)—and with mentors, faculty, and others along life's way.

There are of course other related practices, understood as prayer if broadly defined, but identified also by other names.[104] There is mindful reading and writing, the former with roots in *lectio divina*, and the latter including journaling, autobiographical reflection, poetry, and other forms of introspective or creative writing; listening and beholding: attentiveness here not only to form but also to sound (music), voice (the words of others), and even to silence (nonsound); movement, including walking, tai chi, yoga, drama, and related physical exercises that keep our bodies healthy and attune us to our environment;[105] and contemplative practices, including meditation, dreamwork, visualization, etc., that help us to get more in touch with ourselves even as they enable us to feel the selves of others. All of these are or can be spiritual practices relevant to a range of learning intelligences or aptitudes that could be deployed *within* classrooms, although they are also just as effective if included as assignments fulfilling course requirements. Their practice would contribute to personal well-being, health, and equanimity, problem solving, increasing presentness to self and others, discerning meaningfulness, and deepening compassion to all that is not the self. In fact, contemplative practices generate unitive experiences that are transformational.[106]

Contemplative practice also enables attentiveness to the voice and reception of the perspective of others, of the world around us, thus both confronting us with otherness and situating us in a position to grow through such encounter. As we become attuned to ourselves in relationship with others, we receive the witness of others and bear appropriate

---

[103] Anne Wimberly, *Nurturing Faith and Hope*, 165, suggests that alignment of such modes of prayer with the educational process enables formation of a "valued identity."

[104] Both John P. Miller, *Education and the Soul: Toward a Spiritual Curriculum* (Albany: State University of New York Press, 2000), part 2, and Daniel P. Barbezat and Mirabai Bush, *Contemplative Practices in Higher Education: Powerful Methods to Transform Teaching and Learning* (San Francisco: Jossey-Bass, 2014), part 2, elaborate on the following.

[105] In this regard, dance also invites consideration. Martin Blogg, *Dance and the Christian Faith* (London: Hodder and Stoughton, 1985), esp. 189–200, explicates on the body as an instrument of expression, movement as medium of such, and form as structure of such, urging that the pursuit of dance is parallel to the pursuit of Christian faith. Sara B. Savage, "Through Dance: Fully Human, Fully Alive," in Begbie, *Beholding the Glory*, 64–82, also recommends that full personal knowledge is not merely cognitive but involves movement, activity, and habituation of particular embodied forms, so that dance opens up to the perichoretic intertwining of self-other-world-God via embodied life.

[106] See Abraham Sussman and Mitchell Kossak, "The Wisdom of the Inner Life: Meeting Oneself through Meditation and Music," in *Adult Education and the Pursuit of Wisdom*, ed. Elizabeth J. Tisdell and Ann L. Swartz, New Directions for Adult and Continuing Education 131 (San Francisco: Jossey-Bass, 2011), 55–64, at 61.

witness: "The witness is that place in our consciousness that compassionately sees everything from a nonjudgmental perspective."[107] In contrast to efforts to instrumentalize contemplative practices for utilitarian purposes in the present neoliberal global marketplace, our focus is on the "inner curriculum" of the mind as learners navigate their formal disciplinary studies, albeit for the sake of not just cognitive information but also mental transformation and personal renewal.[108] We thus would agree that "contemplative practices are among the most powerful tools at our disposal for enhancing learners' spiritual development,"[109] but assert more: that Christian prayer and its related spiritual disciplines are formidable instruments for heightening learning in the Christian university. Which means this is good not just for students and learners but also for faculty: for their own spiritual practice and also for their vocational efforts.[110]

So where prior incarnational models of contemplative pedagogy have urged how mindfulness techniques and strategies can reorient learners to what is dissonant in their courses of study and education,[111] we seek additionally a more robustly trinitarian perspective. Thus, "contemplative thinking as pedagogical posture"[112] is pentecostally infused in ways that activate not just our various intelligences but the full range of our embodied senses. Our pneumatological point is that the spiritual life—prayer and worship, meditation and contemplation, fundamentally—is not extraneous but vital to Christian learning and the life of the mind (see also §2.3.1).[113] The efficaciousness of these practices, we add, derives in part from their being aesthetic forms through which our hearts are touched and our lives ordered. As we saw above (§6.2.1), the arts not only help train our attention on our embodiment, they also enable perception of the affective dynamics of knowing. Further, the arts inspire pathic reactions, and if implemented across the curriculum, could elicit affections of love, compassion, contrition, and even faith. Music's role in the spiritual life, in addition, also forges community and thereby could facilitate collaborative inquiry. Last but not least, the arts' cathartic capacities are no less therapeutic—not only in film—so their strategic use in the core curriculum could mend and repair human consciousness by building bridges to others, including other cultural and intellectual

[107] John P. Miller, *The Contemplative Practitioner: Meditation in Education and the Professions* (Westport: Bergin and Garvey, 1994), 151.

[108] For more on this idea of the "inner curriculum," see Oren Ergas, *Reconstructing "Education" through Mindful Attention: Positioning the Mind at the Center of Curriculum and Pedagogy* (London: Palgrave Macmillan, 2017), part 3; see also Oren Ergas and Sharon Todd, eds., *Philosophy East/West: Exploring Intersections between Educational and Contemplative Practices* (Malden: Wiley-Blackwell, 2016).

[109] Astin, Astin, and Lindholm, *Cultivating the Spirit*, 148.

[110] Mary Rose O'Reilley, *Radical Presence: Teaching as Contemplative Practice* (Portsmouth: Boynton/Cook and Heinemann, 1998).

[111] E.g., Robert Martin, "From Objectifying to Contemplating the Other: An Incarnational Approach to Pedagogy in Theological Education," in *Proleptic Pedagogy: Theological Education Anticipating the Future*, ed. Sondra Higgins Matthaei and Nancy R. Howell (Eugene: Cascade, 2014), 29–54.

[112] Lauren F. Winner, "Contemplative Posture and Christ-Adapted Eyes: Teaching and Thinking in Christian Seminaries," in *The State of the Evangelical Mind: Reflections on the Past, Prospects for the Future*, ed. Todd C. Ream, Jerry A. Pattengale, and Christopher J. Devers (Downers Grove: IVP Academic, 2018), 125–40, at 128.

[113] Jeff Astley, "The Role of Worship in Christian Learning," in Astley, Francis, and Crowder, *Theological Perspectives on Christian Formation*, 244–51; also Hyeran Kim-Cragg, *Story and Song: A Postcolonial Interplay between Christian Education and Worship*, American University Studies VII, Theology and Religion 323 (New York: Peter Lang, 2012).

traditions around the world.[114] In short, the aesthetic and affective qualities of spiritual practice can actually empower the life of the mind and are not merely a prelude to the rigors of formal intellectual work.

The goal here is a pentecostally infused seamless curriculum, a Christian university environment in which learning and formation occurs from the classroom to the chapel and everywhere in between.[115] Again, this is not new, although those seeking the renewal of Christian higher education can do no better than learn from colleagues like the Jesuits, whose "Ignatian pedagogy" connects intimately back to and has long been honed by premodern traditions of spirituality.[116] Our adaptation, convinced that the winds of the Spirit blow where they will (John 3:8a), expects every sector of the university—from the chapel to the dorm room to the cafeteria—to be sites of pneumatic encounter, even as it also expects the classroom to be an altar, "the place where all facets of college life were to be processed with the professors . . . , the place of divine encounter, of transformation."[117] Yet while keenly anticipating the manifestation of and encounter with the Spirit in these various venues, our Pentecost-model lifts up the many forms of practices through which eyes can see, ears can hear, desires can be reordered, habits can be reformed, loves can be redirected, and hearts can be enlivened, all so that minds can be renewed, indeed illuminated, inspired, and invigorated.

6.2.3 Co/Extracurricular Engagement and the Null-Curriculum: Lifelong Formation

Whereas this section began with a focus on the (core) curriculum and then reconsidered it from the vantage point of the spiritual life (as symbolized in the chapel and its formative practices), here we want to press all the way through the notion of a seamless curriculum both on a synchronic and a diachronic level. The question here is how a Pentecost-theology of the intellectual life cultivates sanctifying and charismatic encounter with the divine across the full scope of the university and even after graduation. Hence, we turn to develop what we might consider as a pneumatological approach to cocurricular activities and to the question of the null-curriculum.

There are at least two cocurricular realms to explicate: that within and that outside the residential university. The former includes the full spectrum of activities from residence life to athletics and everything in between: informal activities, mentoring programs, work study initiatives, etc.[118] There is neither time nor space here to comment extensively about

---

[114] See Jeff Astley, Timothy Hone, and Mark Savage, eds., *Creative Chords: Studies in Music, Theology and Christian Formation* (Herefordshire: Gracewing, 2000), esp. part 3—whose value includes but is not limited to the essay by Astley and Savage, "Music and Christian Learning" (219–38)—on the role of music in worship and education.

[115] Paul A. Lacey, *Growing into Goodness: Essays on Quaker Education* (Wallingford: Pendle Hill and Friends Council on Education, 1998), 253–54, discusses the seamless curriculum from the perspective of Friends spirituality.

[116] See especially the selections on "Ignatian/Jesuit Pedagogy" in George W. Traub, S.J., *A Jesuit Education Reader* (Chicago: Loyola, 2008), part V.

[117] These are the words of Richard Lafferty, when he was interim president of then Zion Bible College, a school affiliated with the American Assemblies of God (now Northpoint Bible College in Haverhill, Massachusetts); see Daniel W. Howell, "Theological/Ministerial Education as Spiritual Formation/Transformation at Zion Bible College" (DMin thesis, Fuller Theological Seminary, 2007), 179.

[118] V. James Mannoia Jr., *Christian Liberal Arts: An Education that Goes Beyond* (Lanham: Rowman and Littlefield, 2000), ch. 9, discusses a variety of these aspects.

cocurricular activities within the university,[119] and much of what has been said above about the seamless curriculum would be applicable. Nonetheless, what is at stake is how it either complements or contradicts the purposes of encountering the divine and nurturing a Spirited life of the mind.

Intercollegiate athletics, for instance, is a site of intense contestation, full of promise for educational formation on the one hand because of its popularity within the wider culture (thus Christian universities attempt to recruit athletes who might otherwise matriculate into secular programs because of competitive opportunities) but also distinctly challenged on the other hand because college sports is big business that can derail higher education's spiritual, religious, and moral purposes.[120] A more ominous perspective might admonish thus: "Intercollegiate athletics is an insidious threat to the Christian faith of college students . . . [as] virtually every aspect of college athletics counters the Christian narrative, its moral sensitivities, its methods, and its goals."[121] Yet the New Testament deploys athletic imagery to depict the spiritual life (see 1 Cor 9:24–27, for instance) and holistic formation in the Spirit includes the physical body.[122] Christian university athletics programs, both intercollegiate and intracollegiate, can be guided by the moral values and theological assumptions that are consistent with the mission and vision of the overall institution and implemented in ways that nurture spiritual life and shape a culture of healthy competition across the campus.[123] Athletic play can thereby occasion learning even as the innovation and creativity required could prompt imaginative consideration of divine aesthetics in relationship to the Spirit's working in a dynamic world.[124]

The point is that there is a correlation between curricular and extracurricular domains. Students learn not only from faculty but also from their peers (other learners in their various roles, including as teaching assistants), coaches, chaplains, staff, counselors, technicians, mentors, etc.[125] If the life of the mind is to be cultivated across the Christian uni-

---

[119] An excellent and quite comprehensive discussion is Perry L. Glanzer, Theodore F. Cockle, Elijah G. Jeong, and Britney N. Graber, *Christ-Enlivened Student Affairs: A Guide to Christian Thinking and Practice in the Field* (Abilene: Abilene Christian University Press, 2020).

[120] A historical sketch on the emergence of athletics programs in Christian higher education can be found in William C. Ringenberg, *The Christian College: A History of Protestant Higher Education in America*, 2nd ed. (Grand Rapids: Baker Academic, 2006), ch. 3.

[121] Dale Goldsmith, "From Surviving to Thriving: Five 2011 Survival Manuals for Christians in College—a Review Essay," *Christian Scholar's Review* 41.3 (2012): 309–30, at 329.

[122] Amos Yong, "Running the (Special) Race: New (Pauline) Perspectives on Disability and Theology of Sport," in "Theology, Disability and Sport," ed. Nick J. Watson, special issue, *Journal of Disability and Religion* 18.2 (2014): 209–25, reprinted in *Sports, Religion, and Disability*, ed. Nick J. Watson and Andrew Parker (New York: Routledge, 2014), 42–58, develops a nascent pneumatological and Pauline theology of sport in dialogue with disability perspectives. For more on the embodied and physical dimension of formation, see Diane J. Chandler, *Christian Spiritual Formation: An Integrated Approach for Personal and Relational Wholeness* (Downers Grove: IVP Academic, 2014), ch. 9; cf. also idem, ed., *The Holy Spirit and Christian Formation: Multidisciplinary Perspectives*, Christianity and Renewal: Interdisciplinary Studies (Cham, Switzerland: Palgrave Macmillan, 2016).

[123] See, e.g., Peter Schroeder and Jay Paredes Scribner, "'To Honor and Glorify God': The Role of Religion in One Intercollegiate Athletics Culture," *Sport, Education and Society* 11.1 (2006): 39–54.

[124] See Jerome W. Berryman, *Godly Play: A Way of Religious Education* (San Francisco: HarperSanFrancisco, 1991).

[125] Richard Edwards and Robin Usher, *Globalisation and Pedagogy: Space, Place and Identity*, 2nd ed. (New York: Routledge, 2008), 76.

versity, then encounter with otherness must be facilitated throughout. Dissonant voices and disputatious conversations will need to be had within classrooms and across the campus.[126] Cocurricular life in the Christian university will need to be reimagined as spaces for the Spirit to meet, challenge, and shape intellectual discourse.[127] Curricular seamlessness requires nothing less than that the Christian university in its many constitutive sites be occasions for the manifestation of the Spirit.

The cocurricular and extracurricular can also work together or in parallel outside the university. Internships, apprenticeships, service learning, cooperative-and-immersion programs, and study abroad are curricular-based usually, and mission opportunities, local and short-term in other countries are generally extracurricular, but they occur beyond university space, even if under university auspices and oversight. Service learning and mission initiatives are particularly powerful, especially if they are conducted in relationship to vulnerable populations and within impoverished communities.[128] If Christian higher education, by virtue of its prerequisites and costs, is by and large an elitist undertaking, then any occasion for learners to interact with and be confronted by poverty, injustice, and the tragic will precipitate learning.[129] Local, regional, and transnational (study abroad) partnerships can strengthen the relationships between the Christian university and its ecclesial and social communities and networks.[130]

Study abroad can and oftentimes involves missional and ministry components, and everything said above not only applies to but intensifies in this context, particularly when situated in cultural and linguistic environments somewhat removed from students' backgrounds. Herein is what one scholar calls "intellectual emigration,"[131] a journey of encounter with otherness in its many dimensions—socio-economic, political, cultural, linguistic, and perhaps even religious—that, when followed up with opportunities for discussion, reflection, and introspection, enables grappling with the discordance such experiences produce. The key is to ensure critical reflection and personal assessment about such encounters at "edge of the world"—not only in the geographic sense of where learners travel but in the epistemic sense of their horizons of knowledge—so that experiential disorientation

---

[126] Parker J. Palmer and Arthur Zajonc, with Megan Scribner, *The Heart of Higher Education: A Call to Renewal—Transforming the Academy through Collegial Conversations* (San Francisco: Jossey-Bass, 2010).

[127] Craig Dykstra, *Growing in the Life of Faith: Education and Christian Practices*, 2nd ed. (Louisville: Westminster John Knox, 2005), 63–64, calls these aspects of educational life "Habitations of the Spirit."

[128] Brian T. Johnson and Carolyn R. O'Grady, eds., *The Spirit of Service: Exploring, Faith, Service, and Social Justice in Higher Education* (Bolton: Anker, 2006).

[129] As insisted on by Timothy Gorringe (see §6.1.3 above); cf. also Jeffrey P. Bouman and Lauren Colyn, "Ways That the Pedagogy and Philosophy of Service-Learning Can Be Useful in Teaching Students in International Contexts," in *Christian Higher Education in Global Context: Implications for Curriculum, Pedagogy, and Administration—Proceedings of the International Conference of the International Association for the Promotion of Christian Higher Education 15–19 November 2006, Granada, Nicaragua*, ed. Nick Lantinga (Sioux Center: Dordt College, 2008), 295–309.

[130] Lora-Ellen McKinney, *Christian Education in the African American Church: A Guide for Teaching Truth* (Valley Forge: Judson Press, 2003), ch. 14, documents congregational education benefitting from communal service, mission, and engagement, a model that Christian higher education can benefit from.

[131] Cynthia Toms Smedley, "In Partnership with Communities: Spiritual Formation and Cross-Cultural Immersion," in *Building a Culture of Faith: University-wide Partnerships for Spiritual Formation*, ed. Cary Balzer and Ron Reed (Abilene: Abilene Christian University Press, 2012), 233–46, at 235; note: this book is billed as advocating that there is no "extra" curriculy in the Christian university (so says James K. A. Smith's endorsement on the back cover) since every aspect of this experience is educational.

occurring in these alien contexts can be generative of inquiry and transformation.[132] The manifestation of the Spirit is not limited to the four walls of traditional classrooms—not even to the virtual spaces of the online environment (on which see the next section)—but can occur through any university-facilitated (organized formally or otherwise) activity, local and abroad, especially when there is expectation for the charismatic movement of the Spirit to renew the mind. And, in anticipation of our next section discussing the digital classroom, the assumption here should not be that we are talking only about learners in Western college and university contexts going to majority world or global South locations, but, given the multidirectionality of global flows, that the point is experiential learning that provides immersion into any other context of encounter with difference and otherness.

All such opportunities that take learners into real-life contexts at home and abroad both facilitate service (the work of the hands) but provide an experiential matrix that deepens learning. Herein is a holistic model wherein hands and hearts are linked to heads. We will say more in the next chapter about the teleological horizon within which such an approach unfolds, but for the moment, the point is to emphasize that the Christian university is a central node within a broader ecosystem that shapes learners by facilitating their understanding and transformation in relationship with those they are serving, working with, and walking alongside.[133]

We wish now to briefly address the issue of the null curriculum, which concerns what any institution of higher education excludes or does not teach.[134] No curriculum is exhaustive; every program of study is and has to be selective, even within any disciplinary field, not to mention any degree program or course or study. Less charitably, some might conceptualize about the null curriculum from a social theoretic, hermeneutic-of-suspicion, or other ideologically informed (e.g., feminist or postcolonial) set of perspectives in order to attend to how knowledge is organized and communicated on the one hand or how the same is suppressed or excluded on the other hand.[135] We will return to some of these controversies later (§7.2), but at this point we wish only to observe that null curricular matters highlight what we take for granted: that since higher education can never be comprehensive in any real sense, learning should involve coming to awareness as much about what we do not know as about what we do know.

An understanding of the null curriculum can be applied both within the various disciplines or programs of study within any university and to the overarching framework

---

[132] See Lon Fendall, "Seizing the 'God Appointments' when There Is Cultural Disorientation in a Study Abroad Program," in *Transformations at the Edge of the World: Forming Global Christians through the Study Abroad Experience*, ed. Ronald J. Morgan and Cynthia Toms Smedley (Abilene: Abilene Christian University Press, 2010), 73–84; note also the title of this book woven into our sentence in the text above.

[133] See also Bertram C. Bruce, *Education's Ecosystems: Learning through Life* (Lanham: Rowman and Littlefield, 2020).

[134] See David J. Flinders, Nel Noddings, and Stephen J. Thornton, "The Null Curriculum: Its Theoretical Basis and Practical Implications," *Curriculum Inquiry* 16.1 (1986): 33–42.

[135] E.g., Maria Harris, *Women and Teaching: Themes for a Spirituality of Pedagogy* (New York: Paulist, 1988), 19, talks about the "silence in the curriculum," even as George J. Sefa Dei, preface to *Indigenous Knowledges in Global Contexts: Multiple Readings of Our World*, ed. George J. Sefa Dei, Budd L. Hall, and Dorothy Goldin Rosenberg (Toronto: University of Toronto Press, 2000), xi, clarifies from his West African educational experience: "I was deeply disappointed—not so much, however, with what colonial education taught me, as with what it did *not* teach me" (emphasis orig.).

of Christian higher education. Any course of study will be selective, limited variously by faculty expertise, funding, or other constraints, even as any university is discriminating in its choices regarding schools or faculties, organizational departments, and other parameters that confine or constrain student options. A Pentecost-perspective on the null curriculum ought to listen for the (implicit or unsounded) voices underneath the (explicit or curricularly delineated) voices, so to speak: what have we chosen to teach and why, and how does this shed light on our priorities while simultaneously spotlighting what we could focus on next, opportunity providing?

Awareness of the paradoxical presence and absence of the null curriculum also helps emphasize that Christian higher education is no more than initiatory: into a journey of lifelong learning. Why would the intellectual life in the Spirit not be otherwise? A pneumatologically infused Christian intellect might be jumpstarted within a faith-filled university replete with the lacunae in its curriculum, but its value is the capacities for a lifetime or inquiry where no subject will be off limits. Christian higher education should ignite the wonder and curiosity that perpetuates learning even as a Pentecost-theology of the intellectual life should equip learners with the tools of discovery viable long after completing their formal program of study. The many tongues of the many disciplines within the Christian university not only open up to the many partnerships and practices within and beyond the university (what happens synchronously through the seamless curriculum) but also carve out an intellectual path for the life of the mind *after* the university (what happens diachronically in the wake of formal higher education). Hence, the Christian university shapes discipleship across the life span: nurturing habits of wonder and curiosity, providing tools of inquiry and discovery, and charting pathways for Christian faith, discipleship, and citizenship in an exponentially complexifying world.[136]

6.3 DIGITIZING THE SPIRIT:
THE WORLD (WIDE WEB) FOR VIRTUE/AL FORMATION

But what happens when teaching and learning are supposed to occur not in traditional brick-and-mortar classrooms but in online environments, as is increasingly the case? It is no secret that higher education has been migrating with increasing intensity onto technologically mediated platforms, not to mention catapulted completely online with the arrival of the coronavirus pandemic in March and April of 2020. Even as we have now transitioned gradually into a post-COVID-19 world, there will be no going back to a prior "normal." There may be one handful of well-endowed universities that will be able to continue with business as usual for the foreseeable future, but all the rest of us, including all Christian universities, have online options, with programs of study which degrees can be earned fully in that mode (especially if not only for adult learners). In this new electronic world, we shift from the physical classroom as educational site to the unbounded forum of the internet; from the teacher as talking head and authority to students—better: learners—as collaborative inquirers; and from the bounded book as the

---

[136] See the work of pentecostal scholar and educational theorist Irene Alexander, *A Glimpse of the Kingdom in Academia: Academic Formation as Radical Discipleship*, New Monastic Library: Resources for Radical Discipleship 11 (Eugene: Cascade, 2013).

privileged communicative medium to the World Wide Web and its innumerable links and connections.[137] Can Christian higher education not just survive this technological (among other registers of) disruption but flourish online?[138]

More importantly, for our purposes, how, if at all, might a Pentecost-model of many tongues, many disciplines, and many teaching and learning modalities flow through the nodes of the internet? Are not disciplinary boundaries dissolving in our information age and is not the human(ities) formation and faith-learning interaction wishful thinking amidst the mass productivity and professionalized certification driving the online university? How might human passions be rightly reordered and creaturely dispositions be appropriately rehabituated in the digital world that is already deforming us by virtue of how much time we spend in front of screens? Is it possible for multiple intelligences to be engaged digitally, and is the aesthetic, moral, and spiritual formation as aspired to in the vision of the seamless curriculum of historic residential colleges and universities achievable online? If our pneumatological theology of medieval higher education presumes the interpersonal materiality of the Spirit's outpouring manifest in the cloister and humanist classroom, how can such orthopathic praxis of fleshly teaching and learning be carried over from the traditional to the digital realm?

This final section of this chapter will argue that the reordering of human hearts can occur in online environments when such are also reconstructed as e-schools that are also media of the Holy Spirit. We will attempt to make our case in three steps: first, we will overview developments in online higher education and provide a frank survey of where we are at (§6.3.1); second, we will reconsider the writings of the New Testament in light of our pneumatological model, refracted through patristic lenses, and suggest how the many modalities of spiritual, affective, and moral formation yet might ensue in the online environment (§6.3.2); finally, we will briefly consider the growing role of gamification in online teaching and learning as a case study of the possibility of orthopathic (re)habilitation in digital mode (§6.3.3). The overall movement can be considered as educational anticipations—simulations, more exactly—of the coming reign: digital modalities of virtue formation that participate in the "last days" work of the Spirit among and amid male and female, young and old, slave and free (to riff off Acts 2:17–18). If the discussion is plausible, this would buttress the trajectory of our argument toward educational orthopraxis in chapter 7.[139]

6.3.1 Constructivism in the Information Age: One Network, Many Connections

If the move from correspondence learning to distance education took almost a century (from the late 1800s to the 1960s–1970s), then the development of the computer and the emergence of the World Wide Web not too long thereafter has accelerated at exponential

---

[137] Edwards and Usher, *Globalisation and Pedagogy*, ch. 6.

[138] A disruption already anticipated long before the global pandemic, e.g., Clayton M. Christensen and Henry J. Eyring, *The Innovative University: Changing the DNA of Higher Education from the Inside Out* (San Francisco: Jossey-Bass, 2011), esp. part 3.

[139] Our discussion presumes that online education includes both asynchronous and synchronous interfaces, with videoconferencing and other online technologies enabling more of the latter in more recent iterations.

rates nontraditional and technologically mediated forms of higher education.[140] Particularly after the rise of the internet, it has since become a matter of computing power: Web 2.0 was interactive, albeit asynchronously (via discussion forums), but limited by dialup 56-kilobit bandwidth, while the bandwidth required for Web 3.0 allows for synchronous interactivity. In the next few decades, we will become increasingly intertwined with our technologies as the drive for accessibility of information, sharing of resources, remixing of ideas to forge new realities, among other forces, and draw us inevitably forward.[141]

Educational institutions have come to realize in the last two decades that they can no longer ignore the digitally mediated information age. Embrace and implementation of networked computers at the heart of the educational enterprise, however, has led to massive shifts in the twenty-first-century university. Although dated in terms of time since publication in the information age, at the turn of this century Carl Raschke's *The Digital Revolution and the Coming of the Postmodern University* anticipated much of the issues that we continue to grapple with. Already then he noted that as the nature of knowledge is now extended in multiple directions and accessible anywhere and anytime, we are now in the time of "hyperknowledge" and "hyperlearning" and have entered the era of the "hyperuniversity."[142] As his work remains remarkably prescient even after more than two decades, we unfold implications for our late or postmodern pedagogy in conversation with him along the following lines.

First, the mass mediation of knowledge through personal computers and mobile and other electronic communicative devices means that learning is now a democratic "consumer-driven process of active inquiry, exploration, and interaction" (13). "I link, therefore, I am more than I was before" (46) means that learning is now student-centered. The result is that online chat groups "can have as much educational value as, if not more than, an instructor's lecture notes" (96). In a hypertextual world, learning is "migratory" (66), without closure and "non-linear" (68), moving dynamically in as many directions as there are learners' interacting and clicking.

Second, student-centeredness then also means, from the former lecture-centric perspective, teacher marginalization. If in prior ages the teacher was the authority figure, mentor, professional, and knowledge expert, the third knowledge revolution of the internet age (following the revolutions initiated by speech and language and then by writing) may have precipitated the "end of teaching" (53). Teachers will be pressed to be ongoing researchers, as it will be precisely their skills as ongoing learners that will enable their facilitation of learning.[143]

---

[140] See Alfred Rovai, *The Internet and Higher Education: Achieving Global Reach* (Oxford: Chandos, 2009), esp. ch. 3.

[141] See Kevin Kelly, *The Inevitable: Understanding the 12 Technological Forces That Will Shape Our Future* (New York: Penguin, 2016); also idem, *What Technology Wants* (New York: Viking, 2010).

[142] Carl Raschke, *The Digital Revolution and the Coming of the Postmodern University* (New York: Routledge, 2003), viii; following paragraphs will refer to Raschke quotations parenthetically. Note that Cathy N. Davidson and David Theo Goldberg, with Zoë Marie Jones, *The Future of Learning Institutions in a Digital Age* (Cambridge, Mass.: MIT Press, 2009), say, much less provocatively, much of what Raschke says, with another decade of online developments under their belt, thus reinforcing the decision to focus on Raschke's insightful (for its time) analysis.

[143] Peter Smith, *The Quiet Crisis: How Higher Education Is Failing America* (Bolton: Anker, 2004), 138, thus predicts that "centers of learning" will replace "centers of teaching."

But if teachers are also learners alongside what were traditionally called students, then, third, the traditional university will gradually if not immutably be transformed into the "radically de-centralized" hyperuniversity (11). Institution-centeredness and structural authoritarianism will give way to consumer (student or person) centeredness and a "reversal of authority" (73). The traditional control formalized through credits, degrees, and professional memberships shifts via a "free market in culture and knowledge" (65) to a commercialization of training and a certificationization of skills. Acquisition of knowledge now serves to socialize into the global economic and political domains. Raschke puts it thus (drawing on John Dewey's educational philosophy): "Social intelligence is the ultimate aim of all public activities, and education for that reason is the most vital of public institutions. The internet is fast becoming the great reservoir of unformulated social experience. It is the job of educators to convert that experience into social intelligence" (50).

Fourth, and here taking a brief detour from Raschke's analysis, are the implications of transitioning from the book to the World Wide Web.[144] Books engage human brains more slowly with the task of focused and discursive thinking and cultivate longer-term memory, but the internet nurtures quick connections, rewards skill in efficient multitasking, and develops working memory. The former fosters more thought about less, while the latter provides the sense that one knows a little about more. Whereas printed texts allow for the possibility of communal consideration (e.g., book-discussion groups), "reading" on the net is private and effectively disembodied. If reading printed literature has the greater potential to shape us affectively, then surfing the Web initiates us into feelings associated with the thrill of the hunt. The dawn of digital technology is thus changing our intellectual ethic—leading us to prize speed and proficiency, for instance—as it is reshaping us as people and rewiring our brains. There are clearly cognitive and anthropological consequences to living in and through our connected world, not to mention social and cultural implications with huge stakes.

In sum, electronic education interweaves faculty, learners, Web developers, and network managers into the information highway, supervening upon electrical and communications systems. Raschke suggests that institutions of higher education within this grid are positioned to define the hyperuniversity of the future since "standardized 'knowledge manufacturing' installations (read 'universities') will no longer suffice in the digital climate."[145] In his words:

> Hyperlearning, and by extension the hyperuniversity, entails a culture of intellectual freedom like the familiar academy. But it is a freedom borne not of the neo-aristocratic systems of tenure and privilege . . . , but of the dynamism of a globally extensive, open architecture of client-driven questing and transactivity. The "net" is the bet for the next generation of "formal" learning, not merely because it is the worldwide information packaging system of choice, but because it is swiftly redefining the channels through which all information on its way to becoming knowledge must flow.[146]

---

[144] The following summarizes Nicholas Carr, *The Shallows: What the Internet Is Doing to Our Brains* (New York: W. W. Norton, 2010).

[145] Raschke, *Digital Revolution*, 111.

[146] Raschke, *Digital Revolution*, 112.

From a pedagogical standpoint, then, constructivist pedagogies have swept into prominence over the last generation but especially in the new century.[147] Because learners sojourning the Web are not only less reliant on assigned course texts, but also less dependent on course instructors,[148] faculties are at their best in the online environment when they possess pedagogical skills in aiding inquiry, conversation, and interaction among those in the learning community.[149] *Constructivist* pedagogical theory thereby, while oftentimes developed through focus on adult educational activities and processes, emphasizes in general student-centered initiative in learning, self-directed and autonomous inquiry, and contextually relevant learner collaboration.[150] So whereas traditional pedagogical cognitivism proceeds from the assumption of knowledge as information transfer, online constructivism recognizes knowledge as at least in part socially constructed through networks, dynamic relationships, diversity of opinions, multiplicity of sources, and decision-making connections.[151]

In the end, though, the authentication of learning depends on enabling appropriate and relevant interaction in the real world (not just in the virtual environment) so that constructivist education subordinates "instructionism" (learning-through-teaching) to a kind of "learning-by-making" and doing.[152] Hence, faculty members need support and training not only to facilitate online connections but also to inspire effective real-world behaviors and practices. Beyond that, in the big scheme of things in terms of where higher education is heading, technology needs to be seen not just in terms of enhancing traditional modes of education (even if capable of and actually so doing), but as opening up new avenues of accessibility and innovating new modes of real-world engagement. Thus is the preceding discussion regarding the seamless (co-)curriculum within the university intertwined with its relationships with the outside world. As will be discussed in the next subsection, learners are actively testing theories introduced in their courses of study within their contexts of life and work even as they bring such experiences into their classes amid the ongoing hermeneutical (or teaching-and-learning) spiral.

To what degree is a Pentecost-model and praxis of Christian higher education enhanced or challenged when digitalized? How might a pneumatological approach to the Christian life of the mind be nurtured or hindered online? It would seem that divine encounter, sanctification, and even deification (theosis) of human materiality and physicality would

---

[147] Although certainly with prior developments as well: e.g., Idit Harel and Seymour Papert, eds., *Constructionism: Research Reports and Essays, 1985–1990* (Norwood: Ablex, 1991).

[148] A. W. (Tony) Bates and Albert Sangrà, *Managing Technology in Higher Education: Strategies for Transforming Teaching and Learning* (San Francisco: Jossey-Bass, 2011), ch. 2.

[149] See Jennifer Ehrhardt, "Online Social Constructivism: Theory versus Practice," in *Distance Learning Technology, Current Instruction, and the Future of Education: Applications of Today, Practices of Tomorrow*, ed. Holim Song (Hershey, Pa.: Information Science Reference, 2010), 67–82.

[150] Alfred P. Rovai, Michael K. Ponton, and Jason D. Baker, *Distance Learning in Higher Education: A Programmatic Approach to Planning, Design, Instruction, Evaluation, and Accreditation* (New York: Teachers College Press, 2008), proceeds from a constructivist pedagogy, detailed in the first chapter.

[151] See George Siemens, "Connectivism: A Learning Theory for the Digital Age," *International Journal of Instructional Technology and Distance Learning*, January 5, 2005, http://www.itdl.org/Journal/Jan_05/article01.htm.

[152] Initially unfolded in Papert and Harel, *Constructionism*.

be virtually (pun intended) impossible. If this is the case, wouldn't any vision for the reinvigoration of the Christian university be pneumatologically handicapped and beg for a return to a christological model, perhaps an incarnational one? We will suggest, next, that the pneumatological turn for Christian teaching and learning we are here proposing goes through, but not beyond, Pentecost, even as we remember that this outpouring of the Spirit is also christologically as well as incarnationally shaped and mediated.

6.3.2 Community-Context-Character: The Mediation of the Spirit—Then and Now

John Gresham's "The Divine Pedagogy as a Model for Online Education" has been at the vanguard of theological rethinking about digital mediation.[153] Two central ideas propel this Roman Catholic educator's presentation. First, the notion of the "divine pedagogy," drawn from the church fathers, concerns God's progressive preparation for the coming of Christ through the ages, accommodating salvific and redemptive truth as recorded in the Old Testament to historical circumstances as relevant to the recipients from the patriarchal period through the monarchy and prophets to the exilic and postexilic writers and those in the intertestamental period and culminating in the incarnation. Even if, in the final case, incarnationalism refers to the Word coming in and made flesh, the more general principle is that God meets human creatures in their concrete historical contexts and according to the various levels of comprehension and understanding. In that case, the opposite of incarnationalism is not docetism or Gnosticism (even if in the context of the early christological debates it was assuredly the case) but inappropriate accommodation-ism or unengaging contextualism. Put pedagogically, incarnational pedagogy is not to be understood only in terms of the "physical bodily presence of the teacher. Rather the ped-agogy of the incarnation points to the realm of the student's life experience as the locus of divine saving action. . . . The key is the instructor's personal communication rather than the educational environment. A face-to-face classroom is not somehow inherently incar-national if the instructor adopts a detached, impersonal teaching style."[154]

The second move is to apply this understanding of the divine pedagogy to the digital domain. Gresham reasons: "It seems that virtual instruction can be incarnational if it points students toward response to the gospel in their daily lives and if the instructor communicates his or her own lived participation in the truth. . . . *Incarnational* or *embod-ied* learning involves more than physical proximity."[155] Online teachers can, like the divine revealer, adapt, accommodate, or condescend to learners in their various contexts—even via the internet, which is our contemporary Areopagus or "public forum"—in ways that allow them to be "present" to the lives of learners near and far in an engaging manner, to model that presence for these learners, and to assist them "in discovering and incarnating that truth in their own lives."[156] Indeed, online education is not just about accessibility (even if that is an important feature of the digital university), but it provides milieus that can foster virtual but no less real communities.

---

[153] John Gresham, "The Divine Pedagogy as a Model for Online Education," *Teaching Theology and Religion* 9.1 (2006): 24–28.

[154] Gresham, "Divine Pedagogy," 26.

[155] Gresham, "Divine Pedagogy," 27 (emphasis orig.).

[156] Gresham, "Divine Pedagogy," 26.

But can the kind of Pentecost-formation envisioned earlier in this chapter and even before be achieved in the digital rather than traditional classroom? Key to a more thorough consideration of this question is to ask whether online presence can generate the communal fellowship through which the Spirit shapes hearts, whether network connectedness can form historical creatures, and whether virtual interactivity can nurture the virtues in relationship to the transcendentals. Given that we are all now world citizens living in such a networked cosmopolis and learners engaged with transnationally connected learning environments, Gresham's theological considerations can be efficaciously extended for the purposes of the Christian university.[157]

For instance, online communities can be reconceived according to how some early Christian communities were formed through epistolary media.[158] The Pauline letters, among much of the New Testament writings, were communally formative mechanisms through which the apostle, while absent bodily from his audience, was nevertheless present with his parishioners through his missives (see Col 2:5 and 1 Cor 5:3–4; cf. also 1 Thess 2:17).[159] These epistles reveal an affective presence, a vulnerable and transparent author authentically and intimately interacting with his readers. There is a discernible relational dynamic that comes through these documents, reflecting bonds persisting over large distances, even in some instances between parties who had not met each other in person (as is believed to be the situation "behind" the letter to the Romans, which was written before Paul's visit to Rome).

It is by now documented that online classroom forums can generate a great deal of community vitality. Personalized instructor presence is of central import, not only for faculty-learner connectivity but in order to provide a relational ethos that both supports inquiry and also generates student-to-student interactions. It is not just that voice and videoconferencing technologies are now available to enable intersubjective presence, but discussion groups, collaborative projects, conferencing forums, debate sites, prayer-and-testimony forums, and adaptation of social media environments for classes (like wiki and Facebook pages, for instance),[160] among other pedagogical devices, can promote fraternal exchange and even *koinonia*. There is every probability that what some educational theorists call "deep learning" can occur in the interactive network nodes of a variety of online classrooms (forums) where self-discovery takes place in the back-and-forth exchange

---

[157] For more on our networked existence, see the introductory chapter to Yong, *Renewing the Church by the Spirit: Theological Education after Pentecost*, Theological Education between the Times (Grand Rapids: Eerdmans, 2020); the following also develops material outlined previously in Yong, "Incarnation, Pentecost, and Virtual Spiritual Formation: Renewing Theological Education in Global Context," in *A Theology of the Spirit in Doctrine and Demonstration: Essays in Honor of Wonsuk and Julie Ma*, ed. Teresa Chai (Baguio City: Asia Pacific Theological Seminary, 2014), 27–38.

[158] Starting with Benjamin K. Forrest and Mark A. Lamport, "Modeling Spiritual Formation from a Distance: Paul's Formation Transactions with the Roman Christians," *Christian Education Journal* 10.1 (2013): 110-24. One of our former colleagues at Regent University, Todd Marshall (then vice president of online learning), once quipped, "The New Testament is half of an email conversation" (personal conversation, August 16, 2013).

[159] Roger White, "Promoting Spiritual Formation in Distance Education," *Christian Education Journal* 3.2 (2006): 303–15.

[160] See Juha Suoranta and Tere Vadén, "Wikilearning as Radical Equality," in *Learning the Virtual Life: Public Pedagogy in a Digital World*, ed. Peter Pericles Trifonas (New York: Routledge, 2012), 98–113.

with "others."[161] This felt sense of community necessarily involves a spiritual dimension just by nature of the person-to-person engagement.[162]

To be sure, we must not minimize the challenges, not only because the individualized character of online activity means that solitariness is the default experience, but also since even if faculty work hard and purposefully to nurture digital collegiality and collaboration, true community—the Christian sense of *koinonia*—is difficult to achieve. One researcher notes: "Coexistence is high in freedom but low in relationship, task orientation, and equality. Collaboration is high in task orientation but low in relationship, freedom, and equality. Collegiality is high in relationship, task orientation, and equality, but low in freedom. Community is high in relationship, freedom, and equality, but low in task orientation. So, from this perspective, many on-line communities might be . . . better understood as instances of collegiality, or collaboration, than community."[163] The road is therefore uphill. But even in a constructivist environment, teachers can teach by facilitating interactions, exemplifying and prompting dialogical exchange, and providing helpful feedback (assessment!) to learners.[164] Hence, we believe that pneumatologically envisioning such online relationships can generate Pentecost-like moments or encounters across the semester and that it is precisely through these that formation happens.[165]

What the "net" produces, however, is not just a classroom experience but an online context that is itself constituted by multiple contexts, as many as there are learners. Physical distance translates electronically into contextual polyvocality and polyphonicity.[166] Online transactions might be explicated along at least three—namely, multi-,

---

[161] Van B. Weigel, *Deep Learning for a Digital Age: Technology's Untapped Potential to Enrich Higher Education* (San Francisco: Jossey Bass, 2002), esp. ch. 3.

[162] See Rena M. Palloff and Keith Pratt, *Building Online Learning Communities: Effective Strategies for the Virtual Classroom*, 2nd ed. (San Francisco: Jossey Bass, 2007), 128–29.

[163] Nicholas C. Burbules, "Does the Internet Constitute a Global Educational Community?" in *Globalization and Education: Critical Perspectives*, ed. Nicholas C. Burbules and Carlos Alberto Torres (New York: Routledge, 2000), 323–55, at 351.

[164] While we do not spend much time in this book on assessment, we urge not only that it be approached as required for accreditation purposes but that it be considered, with regard to teaching and learning, for its dialogical potency, particularly important in the constructivist environment that animates the digital platform. For insightful treatment of assessment from a perspective where teachers learn together with students, see E. Jayne White, "Aesthetics of the Beautiful: Ideologic Tensions in Contemporary Assessment," in *Bakhtinian Pedagogy: Opportunities and Challenges for Research, Policy and Practice in Education across the Globe*, ed. E. Jayne White and Michael A. Peters, Global Studies in Education 7 (New York: Peter Lang, 2011), 149–57, at 156. Note further that the premise of this work, the theory that language is constituted and produced by difference and variation—propounded by Mikhail Bakhtin (1895–1975), a Russian philosopher, literary critic, and scholar—is consistent with our Pentecost-vision; for discussion of Bakhtin in relationship to pentecostal studies, see Mark Jennings, *Exaltation: Ecstatic Experience in Pentecostalism and Popular Music* (New York: Peter Lang, 2014), 92–100.

[165] Heidi A. Campbell and Stephen Garner, *Networked Theology: Negotiating Faith in Digital Culture* (Grand Rapids: Baker Academic, 2016), are attentive especially to the Web's capacity to connect people.

[166] And here we have not yet even begun to take up the questions of gender, cultural, ethnic, and religious diversity. Everything we will say later (ch. 7) about these aspects of the Christian university can be inserted at this point when talking about digital contextuality. For a preliminary reference about how to not only recognize ethnic and cultural diversity in the online forum, but pedagogically engage with it in an effective and authentic manner—rather than a way in which instructors might often project themselves onto the lives of online learners—see Andrew T. Arroyo, "Diversity in Online Education," *Religious Studies News*, May 2013, http://rsnonline.org/index110b.html?option=com_content&view=article&id=1514&Itemid=1675.

inter-, and trans-, used here in ways logically consistent with their development above (§5.2)—contextuality registers. First, there are the (multi)epistemic contexts that each member, instructors included, brings into the class; this enriches even as it complicates the discussion. Yet, second, there is the actual (inter)connectivity and contact between learners, and thus the unfolding of the class as its own contextual site; such exchanges cannot be considered merely as the sum of the various contexts but generate their own contextual depth through the divergent views expressed.[167] Then third, there is the (trans) contextual outcomes related to the class, not just the formal ones identified on the course syllabus but also the ways in which the second-level class (inter)contextual dynamics then in turn prompt members to adapt thinking, performances, and practices in their own concrete socio-historic contexts. So the internet now connects not just learners in classrooms but learning communities to their variegated lives, employment environments, and other public spaces and realms of interaction.[168]

Because the net enables people situated across vast spaces and many time zones to interact, there is another point to the many tongues of Pentecost in the digital classroom. What St. Paul meant by the one body enlivened charismatically by the many gifts of the Spirit unfolds in the online classroom as one conversation of inquiry vitally carried by the many voices and perspectives of the many learners (instructors included here).[169] Where earlier we applied this Pauline metaphor to the teaching-and-learning of people with disabilities (§6.1.2), here our vision of human *koinonia* is empowered via our electronic networks and connectedness. If all learning is contextual, then, a pentecostally invigorated approach to the digital classroom will receive, telecommunicatively, the gifts of the many voices from the many contexts precisely in order to empower relevant practice—not to mention witness—in return to those contexts.

Yet the reality of interconnectedness across time zones maps onto the always-connected character of our digital interfaces in ways that urge caution. If the asynchronous aspect of online education allows for the flexibility of engaging when available, the around-the-clock networked world also prompts expectations that learning never stops, that faculty or institutional responses should be immediate if not instantaneous, etc. Here we simply need to be reminded of our earlier discussion that appropriate rhythms of learning, living, rest, worship, etc. need to be developed, consistent with what it means to be embodied creatures dependent on Sabbath rejuvenation and spiritual renewal.[170]

Assuming, then, that the Spirit of Pentecost is both always present but yet active variously in modulating our learning according to the best practices of instructional

---

[167] On how student contact and relationality lead to the peculiar dynamics of online classroom context—no two online classes thus being the same—see Mary E. Quinn, Laura S. Foote, and Michele L. Williams, "Integrating a Biblical Worldview and Developing Online Courses for the Adult Learner," *Christian Scholar's Review* 41.2 (2012): 163–73.

[168] José Antonio Bowen, *Teaching Naked: How Moving Technology Out of Your College Classroom Will Improve Student Learning* (San Francisco: Jossey-Bass, 2012).

[169] A parallel Pauline ecclesiological point also informs Stephen D. Lowe and Mary E. Lowe, "Spiritual Formation in Theological Distance Education: An Ecosystems Model," *Christian Education Journal* 7.1 (2010): 85–102, although our approach has been from divergent angles and we are headed also in different directions.

[170] See also Smith, *On Christian Teaching*, ch. 9, "Designing Space and Time."

design puts us in a better place to engage one of the important questions for online education: if the digital platform can form community and can intensify contextual engagement, can it form character, nurture holiness, and inculcate virtue?[171] Theological educators have been particularly exercised by this question, in that context wondering if digital learning enables mentoring for spiritual and moral formation. Briefly at this juncture, however, we can draw from some of the affirmative responses in this arena. Without dismissing the importance of face-to-face interaction (which can be facilitated to the degree possible via strategically organized residency opportunities and video-conferencing activities), in the hands of skillful instructors, fully online programs can promote character formation variously: through personalized (individualized or group-mediated), authentic, caring, and dialogical interaction between instructors and learners; through explicit attentiveness via assignments (e.g., involving journaling); and through facilitating a collaborative community and learner relationships and interactions, etc.[172] In the right courses and framed appropriately, programmatic practices that connect heads to hearts such as various forms of prayer, *lectio divina*, Ignatian *examen*, and other spiritual disciplines that are performable both on- and offline can be effectively deployed for pedagogical purposes.[173] In fact, much of what is done in the traditional residential university (see above, §6.2) can be recalibrated for online communal and contextual practice. Once we get over "the 'individualist' model of the purely autonomous self of Enlightenment modernity,"[174] then we realize that Christian higher education is intersubjective and interpersonal interaction that shapes persons, and this not only can be digitally facilitated but involves potentialities for formation that will continue to unfold amid technological developments.

Our point is that character is nurturable online just as community is possible in this context of multiplicity. Realistically, the formation of character and virtue is embodied in a contextual way: when hearts, minds, and practices are unfolded relationally, socially, and environmentally.[175] All we are claiming is that the online classroom can also be attentive to these dimensions of learner experiences and pathways. Extradiligent and discerning learners will find ways to correlate course content with real-life opportunities and challenges even as flexible faculty will not just allow but even encourage learners to connect assignments to contextual realities. This not only unites learners with others but allows to be woven into the mix the full range of their many intelligences with the broad panoply of online pedagogies.

[171] On the teleological centrality of character especially for Christian higher learning, see Marvin Oxenham, *Higher Education in Liquid Modernity* (New York: Routledge, 2013), ch. 13.

[172] For more on spiritual and character formation in the online classroom, see, among other works, Mark A. Maddix, James R. Estep, and Mary E. Lowe, eds., *Best Practices of Online Education: A Guide for Christian Higher Education* (Charlotte: Information Age, 2012), ch. 5, and Joanne J. Jung, *Character Formation in Online Education: A Guide for Instructors, Administrators, and Accrediting Agencies* (Grand Rapids: Zondervan, 2015).

[173] Teresa Blythe and Daniel Wolpert, *Meeting God in Virtual Reality: Using Spiritual Practices with Media* (Nashville: Abingdon, 2004).

[174] David Tracy, "Can Virtue Be Taught? Education, Character and the Soul," in Astley, Francis, and Crowder, *Theological Perspectives on Christian Formation*, 374–89, at 389.

[175] See Dallas Willard, *Renovation of the Heart: Putting on the Character of Christ* (Colorado Springs: NavPress, 2002).

The dawn of computerized intelligence in our information age worries some of us about the impending "mechanization of the mind."[176] Such anxieties ought not motivate antagonism to or alienation from digital culture but a recalibration of what digital nativity might mean for Christian faith and witness,[177] particularly, as regards our purposes, within the Christian university. Our proposal is that a pneumatological turn that is already sensitive to the many learning aptitudes, the diverse formational media, and the multiplicity of disciplines and discourses of inquiry will be better equipped to also traverse the pluralism of voices, and users,[178] in the digital world in anticipation of the coming reign of the triune God.

6.3.3 Simulating the Coming Divine Reign: Christian Formation through and beyond the Internet

But what if the internet includes waves and currents hostile to the divine blueprint? Can the Christian university nevertheless redirect the promise of digital mediation for redemptive purposes? In anticipation of the fuller response to this question in the next chapter, our answer in the following pages is to embark on a thought experiment with gaming technology. Might the "gamification of learning," as one theorist puts it,[179] spark innovative reframing of pedagogy after the Spirit in the digital domain? Three strands will inform our reflections: the formational, pentecostal, and gamificational (apologies in advance for this unattractive neologism).

We have already suggested the effectiveness of multisensorial pedagogical media such as film, music, and the arts for multiaptitudinal learning and formation (§6.2.1). The primary rationales given there were based on their greater ability to arouse the affections and to inspire meaningful, engaged, and passionate learning. Shifting now to the online platform multiplies the communicative possibilities inherent through film and music but intensifies the learning experience and encounter precisely via the much greater degree of participatory interactivity in the digital democracy.[180] What happens, then, when such interactivity is not only informative but also intensely pleasurable, purely delightful, and addictively desirable, as in the online gaming industry? What opens up when we enter into alternate and even fantastic imaginary worlds and are enabled to experience these emically (as insiders to these worlds) and existentially?[181] What if it is true, as one gam-

---

[176] This is part of the title of part 2 in Sherry Turkle, *The Second Self: Computers and the Human Spirit* (New York: Simon and Schuster, 1984).

[177] We get the notions of the *digital alien* and *digital native* from Philip R. Meadows, "Mission and Discipleship in a Digital Culture," *Mission Studies* 29.2 (2012): 163–82, who also distinguishes them from and even warns against being a *digital enthusiast* (naively accepting the digital world and all it brings).

[178] We get the correlation between *voices* and *users* from Fran Hagstrom, David Deggs, and Craig Thompson, "Clouds, Chat, and Chatter: A Philosophical Note on Technologically Enhanced Teaching and Learning," in White and Peters, *Bakhtinian Pedagogy*, 149–57, at 156.

[179] Karl M. Kapp, *The Gamification of Learning and Instruction: Game-Based Methods and Strategies for Training and Education* (San Francisco: Pfeiffer, 2012).

[180] With regard to the arts, prescient at the dawn of the computer age in the university was the claim that "digitization of the arts radically democratizes them"; and that "digitization makes all the arts fundamentally interactive"; see Richard A. Lanham, "The Extraordinary Convergence: Democracy, Technology, Theory, and the University Curriculum," in Gless and Smith, *Politics of Liberal Education*, 33–56, at 42–43.

[181] On gaming vis-à-vis alternative reality and even the otherworldly possibilities of the religious imagination, see, respectively, Curtis J. Bonk, *The World Is Open: How Web Technology is Revolutionizing*

ing scholar puts it, that "What video games do—better than any other medium in my view—is let people understand a world from the inside"—what are the implications for encountering and engaging with difference?[182] How might all of these experiential and pathic dimensions of game-playing have educational payoffs?

From a Pentecost-perspective, game-playing may be much more relevant than anticipated. There is a strand of anthropological research, built on the notion of archaic humanity as *Homo ludens*—human beings considered as playing creatures—that has been applied to analysis of pentecostal-charismatic spirituality.[183] The vibrancy of pentecostal worship, the call-and-response of pentecostal preaching, the spontaneity of pentecostal piety, the translatability of personal piety and devotion into public spaces and interactions—each of these can be understood in terms of the improvisational creativity characteristic of pentecostal-charismatic play in the Spirit.[184] More than one pentecostal theologian has thus suggested that play serves well as a fundamental metaphor for the Spirit-led life and whatever theological implications might flow out from that spiritual path.[185] Others have argued that charismatic play not only comports human creatures joyfully (thus affectively) to the world but also sparks the wonder that motivates curiosity, propels the imagination that concocts alternatives, and embraces the unpredictability that alone can thrive amidst fragility and volatility.[186] This may move us too far too fast, but pneumatic play may not just undergird faithful spirituality but also propel the digitized Christian university.

Gaming—a placeholder for the entire phenomenon of playing games and theorizing applied here to digital space—presumes a constructivist model of human sociality. There are benefits but also challenges in deploying game-based learning approaches,

---

Education (San Francisco: Jossey-Bass, 2009), ch. 9, and William Sims Bainbridge, *eGods: Faith versus Fantasy in Computer Gaming* (Oxford: Oxford University Press, 2013).

[182] James Paul Gee, *Good Video Games + Good Learning: Collected Essays on Video Games, Learning and Literacy*, New Literacies 27 (New York: Peter Lang, 2007), 16; insider role-playing has been effective in engaging learners with historical realities, here allowing encounter with the past to form who we are in the present—e.g., Mark C. Carnes, *Minds on Fire: How Role-Immersion Games Transform College* (Cambridge, Mass.: Harvard University Press, 2014).

[183] Most prominently by Dutch Reformed anthropologist of Pentecostalism in Latin America André F. Droogers; see his *Play and Power in Religion: Collected Essays*, Reason and Religion 50 (Berlin: Walter de Gruyter, 2012), chs. 12–13. In the background is a substantial religious and theological literature on play, e.g., Johan Huizinga, *Homo Ludens: A Study of the Play Element in Culture* (Boston: Beacon, 1970); David L. Miller, *God and Games: Toward a Theology of Play* (New York: World, 1970); and Jürgen Moltmann, *Theology of Play* (New York: Harper and Row, 1972).

[184] As documented by the Dutch cultural anthropologist of pentecostal movements André Droogers, *Play and Power in Religion*; see also Yong, "Observation-Participation-Subjunctivation: Methodological Play and Meaning-Making in the Study of Religion and Theology," *Religious Studies and Theology* 31.1 (2012): 17–40.

[185] Early on: Jean Jacques Suurmond, *Word and Spirit at Play: Toward a Charismatic Theology*, trans. John Bowden (Grand Rapids: Eerdmans, 1995); more recently and substantively: Wolfgang Vondey, *Beyond Pentecostalism: The Crisis of Global Christianity and the Renewal of the Theological Agenda* (Grand Rapids: Eerdmans, 2010), esp. chs. 4 and 6.

[186] Pentecostal play is central to a pneumatology of beginning again in Nimi Wariboko, *The Pentecostal Principle: Ethical Methodology in New Spirit* (Grand Rapids: Eerdmans, 2011); see also application of this principle to social ethics and economic life in Wariboko, *Economics in Spirit and in Truth: A Moral Philosophy of Finance* (New York: Palgrave Macmillan, 2014).

not least because the primary purpose of games is neither teaching nor learning.[187] Yet humans play games regularly, and increasingly online—almost 70 percent of all heads of households and 97 percent of youth, according to one study[188]—and the latter domain is progressively expansive, involving more and more of us more of the time. Further, research shows that game players coordinatively develop a wide range of sensorimotor, cognitive, imaginative, and social skills, so that games are now regularly deployed in industry, the military, and even the educational world.[189] The theoretical literature on games is now interdisciplinary and extensive, and we will not be able to do justice to its overall discussion. Within the scope of our efforts, online gaming nurtures two apparently contradictory but educationally complementary experiences: that of immersion into a virtual world and that of subjective distance to imagine and enact alternative paths.[190] Hence, we elaborate on the potential of gamification for a Pentecost-pedagogy vis-à-vis our liturgical model of learning (§7.1.3), focusing on gaming's affective potency, habituating dispositionality, social generativity, and directional orientation.

Game playing can be pedagogically effective first because it is affectively and imaginatively stimulating.[191] As previously seen, learning is deeper when it engages not only the head but also the heart and soul. Uncertainty of outcomes and risk ventures release dopamine, an organic chemical that kindles the brain and the body; interest levels spike because of investment in achieving success and avoiding failure; interactive sociality draws participants into games, effectively absorbing them within the virtual environment.[192] Games as multisensory undertakings often involve "print, speech, visuality, tactility, sound, and performance within a hybrid field that combines these forms,"[193] so they activate multiple learner intelligences. Games thus not only allow for those weaker in

---

[187] Introductory discussions of gamification in higher educational literature are Richard Andrews and Caroline Haythornthwaite, eds., *The SAGE Handbook of E-Learning Research* (Los Angeles: SAGE, 2009), ch. 4, and Steve Wheeler, ed., *Connected Minds, Emerging Cultures: Cybercultures in Online Learning* (Charlotte: Information Age, 2009), ch. 7.

[188] Mary E. Hess, "Why Games and Gaming Might Be the Best Way and Place in Which to Consider the Meaning and Purposes of Theological Education: A Reflection," *Crosscurrents* 69.1 (2019): 80–94, at 81.

[189] See Hirumi Atsusi, *Playing Games in School: Video Games and Simulations for Primary and Secondary Education* (Eugene: International Society for Technology in Education, 2010).

[190] See Peter Pericles Trifonas, "The Digital Game as a Learning Space," in Trifonas, *Learning the Virtual Life*, 198–205.

[191] The central role of simulation in the pedagogical endeavor is explicated in Wesley J. Wildman, Paul A. Fishwick, and F. LeRon Shults, "Teaching at the Intersection of Simulation and the Humanities," in *Proceedings of the 2017 Winter Simulation Conference*, ed. W. K. V. Chan et al. (Las Vegas: WSC, 2017), https://ieeexplore.ieee.org/document/8248136, DOI:10.1109/WSC.2017.8248136; cf. Manuel DeLanda, *Philosophy and Simulation: The Emergence of Synthetic Reason* (London: Continuum, 2011); also, Nigel Gilbert and Klaus G. Troitzsch, *Simulation for the Social Scientist* (Maidenhead: Open University Press, 2005); Paul A. Youngman and Mirsad Hadzikadic, *Complexity and the Human Experience: Modeling Complexity in the Humanities and Social Sciences* (Boca Raton, Fla.: CRC Press, 2014).

[192] See Kapp, *Gamification of Learning and Instruction*, ch. 3 and passim for the research in these areas.

[193] See Richard Kahn, "Technoliteracy at the Sustainability Crossroads: Posing Ecopedagogical Problems for Digital Literacy Frameworks," in Trifonas, *Learning the Virtual Life*, 43–62, at 56. Forest Woody Horton Jr. and Barbie E. Keiser, "Encouraging Global Information Literacy," *Computers in Libraries* 28.10 (2008): 6–11, 27, http://www.infotoday.com/cilmag/nov08/index.shtml, also discuss how media literacy involves, variously, visual literacy, digital literacy, and even multicultural literacy (more of this last element in the next chapter).

some aptitudes to compensate with strengths, but they are more embodied than merely cerebral and thereby more affectively engaging. If instructors are able to incorporate game-playing into their courses, absorption into game environments will touch learners at greater depths and inspire learning at deeper levels.

Relatedly, if game-playing is addictive, its repetitive simulations are also pedagogically habituating. The liturgical and even ritual character of learning, as the foregoing indicated, can easily adapt game-playing into the instructional repertoire.[194] Gamers learn by repetitive doing and adapting. To be sure, unreflective gaming tends players toward mechanization, but the power of thoughtful engagement and agency cannot be underestimated for processing feedback through the virtual process in order to improve knowledge, expand skills, and achieve objectives variously.[195] Mastery emerges via cyclical intuitive probe-hypothesize-reprobe-rethink activities even as games provide cultural worlds through which life is activated and into which players are socialized.[196] In fact, the most powerful education aspect of gaming "is their ability to scale difficulty to the player, resulting in a constant, interesting challenge."[197] So, even if games are not played in order to first learn, they are nevertheless effective teachers because they not just capture (cognitive) attention but involve (embodied) practice and inspire aspirational pursuit.

Further, if the first generation of video game-playing was a solitary endeavor, Web 3.0 and its interactivity mean that the current generation of gaming is more intensely social than ever. Massively multiplayer online games (MMOG), for instance, are nothing short of massively interactive. Quite apart from MMOGs, the industry is driven by synchronous and asynchronous interfaces between players. Even if most in the game community never meet in person, let us not underestimate its sociality.[198] If some games are devoted explicitly to developing social skills, others by virtue of their implicit frame, rules, and procedures, nurture forms of sociality.

Last but not least for our purposes, games are often multilevel affairs that deepen and intensify skill and effort. Attainment at each level draws gamers toward further investment of energy and effort. There is a built-in scaffolding of learning-and-teaching within the ever-complexifying game environment that involves gamers "*experiencing* the world

---

[194] Building here off Rachel Wagner, *Godwired: Religion, Ritual and Virtual Reality* (London: Routledge, 2012).

[195] While Kevin Schut, "They Kill Mystery: The Mechanistic Bias of Video Game Representations of Religion and Spirituality," in *Playing with Religion in Digital Games*, ed. Heidi A. Campbell and Gregory Price Grieve (Bloomington: Indiana University Press, 2014), 255–75, highlights the routinizing bias of game-playing, other chapters in this same collection—notably Shanny Luft, "Hardcore Christian Gamers: How Religion Shapes Evangelical Play" (154–69); Rachel Wagner, "The Importance of Playing in Earnest" (192–213); and Michael Waltemathe, "Bridging Multiple Realities: Religion, Play, and Alfred Schutz's Theory of the Life-World" (238–54)—illuminate the capacity of gamers to engage life realities through these simulational media.

[196] See James Paul Gee, *What Video Games Have to Teach Us about Learning and Literacy* (New York: Palgrave Macmillan, 2007), chs. 4 and 6.

[197] Kevin Schut, *Of Games and God: A Christian Exploration of Video Games* (Grand Rapids: Brazos, 2013), 114.

[198] Both Daniel White Hodge, "Role Playing: Toward a Theology for Gamers," and John W. Morehead, "Cybersociality: Connecting Fun to the Play of God," in *Halos and Avatars: Playing Video Games with God*, ed. Craig Detwiler (Louisville: Westminster John Knox, 2010), 163–75 and 176–89 respectively, develop these themes.

in new ways, forming new *affiliations*, and *preparation* [*sic*] for future learning."[199] Experienced game players also transfer the knowledge and skills gained in one forum to new gaming initiatives, thus also developing instinctive habits of applied learning pertinent beyond their virtual worlds.[200] Further, as most engaging games involve a narrative dimension, there is opportunity to expand the virtual character that simultaneously affords development of the player's self-understanding, and this is even more effective when learners are empowered within the game structure to be designers themselves.[201] Simulations, in other words, are trajectoried, aligned toward success in specific game environments but yet developing skill sets transferable across digital and even real life.

The use of games in higher education is not guaranteed. There is always the insularity of gaming communities or the violence pervasive in the gaming industry, although if deployed in the higher educational context, these are mitigated. On the other hand, simulative gaming serves a range of pedagogical functions, including modeling reality, engaging ideologies, connecting theory to practice, generating cooperation, organizing community, sparking/motivating research, inculcating history, and developing expertise.[202] Of course, appropriate games need to be found or developed within disciplinary domains, or instructors in the Christian university could also creatively deploy gaming devices in their courses. For us, the nascent gamification of learning brings with it innumerable possibilities for online instruction going forward, particularly for those who realize both that learning is as much if not more an affective and embodied as a cognitive matter and that higher education will increasingly be mediated through the digital platform. Appropriately used, games can become liturgical pedagogies through which hearts are dispositioned and lives are habituated toward learning outcomes.

More precisely, simulated learning is effective since the point of a Pentecost-approach to higher education is to enable encounter with the living God, who sanctifies our engagement with the world. The Christian university would want to embrace and deploy, very strategically, simulations—gamified or not—that form desires anticipating the coming divine government and empower learners to herald that imminent if not also immanent reality. Just as we have arrived at the end of this chapter on the rudiments, even mechanics, of pneumatic simulations in teaching and learning, both residential and online, so the next unfolds their fundamental arc and telos.

---

[199] Gee, *What Video Games Have to Teach Us*, 23 (emphasis orig.).

[200] Gee, *What Video Games Have to Teach Us*, ch. 5.

[201] See Mark Hayse, "Teaching and Learning within a Video Game Culture," *Common Ground Journal* 5.1 (2007): 21–33, at 30, http://www.commongroundjournal.org/backissues.html#v05n01.

[202] Kurt Squire, *Video Games and Learning: Teaching and Participatory Culture in the Digital Age* (New York: Teachers College, 2011).

7

Revitalizing the Hands

The Spirit's Mission in and through Christian Higher Education

The movement in this part of the book so far has been from scholarship to teaching, and this sets us up for the turn to service. If within discussions amongst evangelically affiliated universities the triad of scholarship-teaching-service is a constant refrain, the last is almost always subordinated to the other two, if not altogether neglected. Our own Pentecost-vision of Christian higher education has approached them in order, although, as we hope the discussion so far has intimated, we presume their interrelatedness so that our discursive treatment can be read as in a nested sense: either burrowing deeper into the trio (if scholarship were the outer ring and service the innermost one) or expanding outward (if scholarship were the innermost ring and service the enveloping one mediating interface with the world) on the one hand; or, on the other hand, both culminating with praxis insofar as it is directed toward or drawn forward by the anticipated divine reign *and* is normatively shaped by the redemptive mission of God heralded in Christ and inaugurated with Pentecost.[1] Put another way: practical concerns presume theoretical (theological) commitments, but theory is blind without pedagogical praxis and missional application.[2] Yet regardless of where we begin or conclude, our treatment is infused with a pneumatic dynamic that, consistent with how Christian learning was held in the patristic and medieval eras, sees scholarship-teaching-service as mutually interrelated and informing. Thus also teaching and learning (the previous chapter) have their alpha in Pentecost (chapter 5) and their omega in parousia (this chapter) even as the presence and activity of the Spirit of Pentecost in the teaching and learning arena further illuminate the meaning of Pentecost and intensify the yearning for and working toward the eschaton. So, in the following, we attempt to bring our argument, already developed in the preceding, full circle: to show how the life of the mind empowered

---

[1]   Our claim that the pedagogical and the missional are interrelated is articulated otherwise by Perry L. Glanzer, Nathan F. Alleman, and Todd C. Ream, *Restoring the Soul of the University: Unifying Christian Higher Education in a Fragmented Age* (Downers Grove: IVP Academic, 2017), ch. 15, in their call for Christian campuses to be transformed from "bubbles" to "greenhouses" so that students can be impacted by and also influence society.

[2]   Intriguingly, then, Mary E. Hess and Stephen D. Brookfield, eds., *Teaching Reflectively in Theological Contexts: Promises and Contradictions* (Malabar: Krieger, 2008), reflect this interrelationality by having each of the chapter titles in the volume being a question.

through sanctifying and charismatic encounter with the Spirit includes, rather than is disconnected from, the practices of the hands.[3]

Yet, as not all practices are equal, how might we discern which practices should govern the work of the Christian university? The previous chapter has already opened up the normative question about the teleological direction of the higher educational enterprise: what should we desire and why? Put in terms of structuring the progression of our argument from knowing to doing: if "epistemologies have ethical implications, that ways of knowing are not morally neutral but morally directive,"[4] then what is the moral fiber undergirding the Christian life of the mind? Here we see that the moral includes the teleological and that this moral-teleological arc is at least implicit within, if not explicitly thematizable from, the configuration of the many disciplines and their concomitant pedagogies. In short, a pneumatological theology of the intellectual life and its teaching and learning practices benefits from explication of their ethical and teleological arcs.

The rest of this chapter unfolds the charismatically defined mission of the university motivating our quest. We begin by unpacking correlations between loving God with our strength and our work toward the common good (§7.1), continue by exploring further the intersectional character—many tongues, many languages, understanding that aspires to be inclusive of gender, culture, and class differences—of this teleological commitment (§7.2), and conclude by pursuing its global extension vis-à-vis the many philosophical and religious traditions of the world (§7.3). Our argument will spring off from how the day of Pentecost vision of the many languages and cultures of the known (Mediterranean) world can foster a moral and educational vision of cosmic justice and enable a global citizenship attentive to intersectional particularity and interfaith/interreligious relations.

The terrain of this chapter involves much of the volatility and combustability that flames across both our society and higher educational arenas in the present time. Ours is a hyperpartisan political world of Black Lives Matter, #MeToo, and climate change on the one side of the spectrum and of conservative resurgences driven by (white) nationalism and concerns to protect religious freedom on the other side. Christian higher education, with its historic roots in European (majority and historically white) ecclesial cultures, is now grappling with the so-called "browning" of the North American landscape,[5] not to mention the shift of the Christian center of gravity to the majority world (as discussed in our introductory chapter). Thus is our Pentecost-proposal pneumatologically funded first and foremost even while attending to the biblical arc of justice and the redemptive mission of God for those from every nation, tongue, tribe, and people. If the way forward is fraught with disagreements in these interlocking domains, we proceed since our theological commitments demand a hopeful and informed accounting, not because these are politically heated topics to engage.

---

[3] Beliefs are informed by practices and vice-versa, even when thinking about the Christian university; see also Steven Garber, *The Fabric of Faithfulness: Weaving Together Belief and Behavior during the University Years* (Downers Grove: IVP, 1996).

[4] Mark R. Schwehn, *Exiles from Eden: Religion and the Academic Vocation in America* (Oxford: Oxford University Press, 1993), 94.

[5] E.g., Robert Chao Romero, *The Brown Church: Five Centuries of Latino/a Social Justice, Theology, and Identity* (Downers Grove: IVP Academic, 2020).

7.1 LOVING GOD WITH OUR STRENGTH: EMPOWERED WITNESS AND THE COMMON GOOD

We began early in part 2 of this book (§5.1.2) with the greatest commandment—"You shall love the Lord your God with all your heart, and with all your soul, and with all your strength, and with all your mind" (Luke 10:27)—and have proceeded heuristically from this text, moving from the mind (the intellect of chapter 5) to the heart (the body of chapter 6). We now arrive at the question of what it means for Christian higher education to nurture the love of God with all our strength, which invites discussion of the tasks of service, and brings with it considerations regarding the moral and ethical ends of our actions. Our moral-teleological exploration goes back to the day of Pentecost narrative, in particular its ethical and eschatological character (§7.1.1), and from there teases out implications for professional education in the Christian university (§7.1.2), before articulating a more encompassing theology of education for cosmic justice (§7.1.3). As before, our guiding question is how a pneumatological theology of the Christian university can understand the interrelationship of heads-hearts-hands in forging a faith-filled praxis for higher education in the present time.

If there is one irrepressible thread persisting through our formulation so far, it is that the many tongues of Pentecost open up to a kind of pluralistic vision for Christian higher education, one capable of and up to engaging the diversity and complexity of life in our twenty-first-century context. This fact of plurality will be exacerbated later in this chapter, especially for those who already feel threatened by too many voices. Are robustly Christian commitments possible within the higher educational sector of late modern pluralism? Our argument here is not just that only a moral commitment can bring coherence to an otherwise fragmenting postmodern multiversity,[6] but more specifically that a deeply incarnational and pentecostal telos is precisely what empowers Christian witness and engagement with pluralism,[7] including that pertaining to universities in the third millennium.

7.1.1 The Invitation of the Spirit: Heralding the Reign of God

Clearly, when thinking about the Spirit's role in education in light of the New Testament witness, there is no doubt that the "teaching activity of the primitive church is of a forthrightly charismatic nature, and furthermore is bound up with the expectation of the imminent coming of the kingdom of God."[8] But what does this mean and into what does Spirit baptism initiate messianic disciples?[9] For the early (first generation of)

---

[6] E.g., Cynthia A. Wells, "Finding the Center as Things Fly Apart: Vocation and the Common Good," in *At This Time and in This Place: Vocation and Higher Education*, ed. David S. Cunningham (Oxford: Oxford University Press, 2016), 46–71.

[7] This is an argument that Amos Yong has made in a number of his books, including but not limited to *In the Days of Caesar: Pentecostalism and Political Theology—The Cadbury Lectures 2009*, Sacra Doctrina: Christian Theology for a Postmodern Age (Grand Rapids: Eerdmans, 2010), and *The Dialogical Spirit: Christian Reason and Theological Method for the Third Millennium* (Eugene: Cascade, 2014); other references will be provided as our argument proceeds.

[8] Matías Preiswerk, *Educating in the Living Word: A Theoretical Framework for Christian Education*, trans. Robert R. Barr (Maryknoll: Orbis, 1987), 79.

[9] The best and most substantive theological response we know of is Frank D. Macchia, *Baptized in the Spirit: A Global Pentecostal Theology* (Grand Rapids: Zondervan, 2006); the following presumes what he says but takes it into higher educational venues.

modern Pentecostals, the outpouring of the Spirit that inaugurated the "last days" (Acts 2:17) meant, at least from their dispensationally informed perspective, that theirs was the time of the "latter rain" revival (their interpretation of Joel 2:23b and Matt 24:14) that would usher in Jesus' second coming.[10] Such an otherworldly predisposition was not particularly conducive to higher educational pursuits, and this has contributed to whatever "anti-intellectual"—even if more accurately described as "antirationalist," as we saw earlier (§4.3)—strains that have flowed within the tradition. However, the eschatological character of the Spirit-infused life can be unfolded in other than dispensational directions.[11] How might some of these considerations be brought to bear on the mission of Christian higher education in Pentecost-perspective?

For starters, we see that far from precipitating any "left behind" anxiety, the reception of the Spirit led instead to concrete this-worldly activities such as sharing of possessions, provision for the needy, and communal mutuality (Acts 2:44–45). Such "apostolic spirituality," a Nazarene theologian (in the tradition of Olin Curtis—see §4.3.1 above) indicates, "focuses on an active way of discipleship in which believers participate in and further their saving mission" that has spiritual but also material dimensions.[12] Thus, apostolic eschatology was not merely future-focused but included practical implications for the present world. The Spirit's apocalyptic redemption (Acts 2:17–21) involved both human souls and bodies, indeed, the socio-economic strata of our material and physical lives.

Read canonically and especially in light of Acts' prequel, the Gospel of Luke, such a partially realized eschatological vision invites further consideration and embrace. As briefly touched on earlier (§6.1.2), the outpouring of the Spirit at Pentecost on the disciples was accomplished by Jesus (Acts 2:33b), and that because his own ministry was paradigmatic for the Spirit-infused life. As announced at Nazareth, Jesus' public mission depended on the Spirit's empowerment and inspiration, as he read from a scroll from the prophet Isaiah:

> The Spirit of the Lord is upon me,
>> because he has anointed me
>>> to bring good news to the poor.
> He has sent me to proclaim release to the captives
>> and recovery of sight to the blind,
>>> to let the oppressed go free,
> to proclaim the year of the Lord's favor (Luke 4:18–19; cf. Is. 61:1–2).

---

[10] See D. William Faupel, *The Everlasting Gospel: The Significance of Eschatology in the Development of Pentecostal Thought*, Journal of Pentecostal Theology Supplement Series 10 (Sheffield: Sheffield Academic Press, 1996), ch. 6, for more on the "latter rain" motif and how it played out in early modern Pentecostalism.

[11] E.g., Peter Althouse, *Spirit of the Last Days: Pentecostal Eschatology in Conversation with Jürgen Moltmann*, Journal of Pentecostal Theology Supplement Series 25 (New York: Bloomsbury, 2003); Matthew Thompson, *Kingdom Come: Revisioning Pentecostal Eschatology*, Journal of Pentecostal Theology Supplement Series 37 (Blandford Forum: Deo, 2010); Larry R. McQueen, *Toward a Pentecostal Eschatology: Discerning the Way Forward*, Journal of Pentecostal Theology Supplement Series 39 (Blandford Forum: Deo, 2012); and Peter Althouse and Robby Waddell, *Perspectives in Pentecostal Eschatologies: World without End* (Eugene: Pickwick, 2010); cf. also Yong, *In the Days of Caesar*, ch. 8.

[12] Mark Maddix, "Spiritual Formation and Christian Formation," in *Christian Formation: Integrating Theology and Human Development*, ed. James R. Estep and Jonathan H. Kim (Nashville: B&H Academic, 2010), 237–71, at 249.

Two parts of this text are noteworthy for our purposes here. First, the reference to the "year of the Lord's favour" has eschatological overtones, related as this is to "the day of vengeance of our God" (Isa 61:2b), which was understood to fulfill the reparative promises of the ancient year of Jubilee (Lev 25:8–17). Second, this eschatological arrival of the Jubilee year involves not just spiritual but whole-person redemption, consistent with the socio-economic and political applications of the original Jubilee provisions. In other words, Jesus' Spirit-inspired mission was to herald the arrival of the divine Jubilee and to announce the availability of its assurances.[13] No wonder that upon receipt of the Spirit that empowered Jesus' mission, the earliest messianic believers themselves enacted the aspirations associated with this messianic deliverance.[14]

What then are the implications of these Lukan considerations for our task? As we argued in part 1 of this book both that patristic education educated the child for the city of God from which it engaged in a humanism grounded in "philanthropy" and civic responsibility and that Pietist, revivalist, and other retrievals of this ancient *paideia* sought to link this moral formation with broader social and mission-minded witness, so we now explicate this theme in terms of the missional dimension and the missional scope of the Christian higher educational enterprise. The emphasis here is on the overarching telos of the Christian university as guided by the impending—here-and-not-yet—administration of God.[15] If the secular university might have even a limited number of contested aims (e.g., advancement of knowledge, certification of professions, academic freedom of inquiry), our proposal is that specifically Christian commitments can be redeemed finally only according to the message of the Spirit-empowered Messiah: that related to the imminent divine reign. Secular teleology here is read according to Christian eschatology. The implications are that Christian educators empowered by the Spirit are all involved in "missionary work" in some respects, and are thereby also considered "agents of the great commission."[16]

Some might be concerned that reinsertion of teleology and morality into the Christian university confuses its task of seeking after truth. But if the modern university was founded to pursue truth in all of its objectivity untarnished by any biases, such a project is by now not just acknowledged to be bankrupt but in essence unfeasible and unnecessarily restrictive about what counted as truthful knowledge.[17] Yet we must be clear in turn that we are not proposing to turn teachers and professors into missionaries understood in classical colonial terms carried out through the early to mid-twentieth century.[18] Instead,

[13] See also Sharon H. Ringe, *Jesus, Liberation, and the Biblical Jubilee: Images for Ethics and Christology* (Minneapolis: Augsburg Fortress, 1985), and Michael Prior, CM, *Jesus the Liberator: Nazareth Liberation Theology (Luke 4:16–30)* (Sheffield: Sheffield Academic Press, 1995).

[14] As further elaborated in Yong, *In the Days of Caesar*, §7.3.1.

[15] Roger Ward, "Baptist Higher Education and the Kingdom of God," in *The Scholarly Vocation and the Baptist Academy: Essays on the Future of Baptist Higher Education*, ed. Roger Ward and David Gushee (Macon: Mercer University Press, 2008), 148–67, provides a baptistic perspective in dialogue with the North American pragmatist philosopher C. S. Peirce and the Protestant theologian H. R. Niebuhr.

[16] Joel A. Carpenter, "The Mission of Christian Scholarship in the New Millennium," in *Faithful Learning and the Christian Scholarly Vocation*, ed. Douglas V. Henry and Bob R. Agee (Grand Rapids: Eerdmans, 2003), 62–74, esp. 66–68 and 72–73.

[17] See Julie A. Reuben, *The Making of the Modern University: Intellectual Transformation and the Marginalization of Morality* (Chicago: University of Chicago Press, 1996).

[18] See Yong, *Mission after Pentecost: The Witness of the Spirit from Genesis to Revelation*, Mission in Global Community (Grand Rapids: Baker Academic, 2019), ch. 1.

we are suggesting that there is a moral and missional thrust to the work of education so that Christian scholarship, teaching, and service are normed according to the Spirit-crafted message that Jesus proclaimed and embodied in an anticipatory manner.

Yet we saw earlier (§5.2.3) that this eschatological reality can be explicated not just along temporal (diachronic) but also geographical (synchronic) axes. This means both that the mission of Christian higher education inhabits the historical dimension of the present that in each moment embraces the future arrival of God's reign and that such work also extends "to the ends of the earth" (Acts 1:8), as Luke so eloquently foresaw the reach of the Spirit's work in his day. Alignment with the divine rule in this respect means that Christian scholarship, teaching, and learning cannot but be fully public, not just by and for the church, nor only by and for any so-called Christian academia. "As kingdom-of-God theology, theology has to be public theology: the public, critical, and prophetic cry for God—the public, critical, and prophetic hope for God. Its public character is con-stitutive for theology, for the sake of the kingdom of God."[19] Hence, Christian education by the Spirit for the sake of the world must be understood in its fullest extents: geograph-ically (to and beyond Rome), politically (to and beyond Western academe), and even cosmically (to and beyond the human to include the environment, terrestrial and even extraterrestrial). If the proper *telos* of Christian higher education might be summarized otherwise as "the eschatological flourishing of all life in friendship with God,"[20] then put pentecostally and pneumatologically, the goal of the Christian university is to facilitate sanctifying and charismatic encounter with the eschatological Spirit in order to channel scholarship via the many disciplines and to propel teaching and learning through the many aptitudes and intelligences.

Thinking about Christian higher education to the ends of the earth presses upon us also considerations of its accessibility. This is a complicated question that we can only make a few brief comments about rather than resolve. The matter involves affordability (from an economic perspective), opportunity (immigrants, refugees, or others whose socio-political circumstances inhibit participation), or infrastructure (from the perspective of populations in less-developed countries and regions of the world who lack basic levels of education to begin with and/or lack basic technological resources, including access to the internet), among other variables. Responses to these issues must be at the levels of policy and economic investment, at the very least.[21] From a Pentecost-perspective, it must include a vision that both opens up a pathway for those from every nation, tribe, people, and language to higher education, and economic and other means to facilitate such access. From this perspective, Christian colleges and universities around the world

---

[19]   Jürgen Moltmann, "Theology in the Project of the Modern World," in *A Passion for God's Reign: Theology, Christian Learning and the Christian Self*, ed. Miroslav Volf (Grand Rapids: Eerdmans, 1998), 1–21, at 1–2.

[20]   John C. McDowell, "God at the End of Higher Education: Raising the *Telos* of the University Higher," *Colloquium* 47.2 (2015): 221–36, at 235.

[21]   See, e.g., Andrew P. Kelly and Kevin Carey, eds., *Stretching the Higher Education Dollar: How Inno-vation Can Improve Access, Equity, and Affordability* (Cambridge, Mass.: Harvard Education Press, 2013), Edward P. St. John, Nathan Daun-Barrett, and Karen M. Moronski-Chapman, *Public Policy and Higher Education: Reframing Strategies for Preparation, Access, and College Success*, 2nd ed. (New York: Routledge, 2018), and Or Shkoler, Edna Rabenu, Paul M. W. Hackett, and Paul M. Capobianco, *International Student Mobility and Access to Higher Education* (New York: Palgrave, 2020).

are less competitors than co-laborers in a common mission to form faithful disciples at the ends of the globe for world citizenship. Learners participate in the transformation of society through the formation of "saints" who embody all the particularities of their cultural location and yet see themselves as members of the Christian community (§2.1.1).

Framed eschatologically, then, the mission of Christian higher education is to boost heads, hearts, and hands toward the rule of God, which is both here and now but also, in a fundamental respect, yet to come. How else might our educational *hands*, especially, work in, through, and out of the Christian university? We consider one line of response to this question next vis-à-vis the scope of professional education.

7.1.2 Profess(ionaliz)ing the Spirit: Changing the World

Thinking about the moral and ethical ends of higher education should prompt questions about how such objectives might be achieved in and through the Christian university. Here aspirations about producing graduates who are equipped to make a difference in society, even to "change the world," a common refrain amongst pietistic and mission-oriented evangelical Christians and their institutions of theological education,[22] is perhaps less radically understood than was Marx's call for moving from mere abstract and speculative interpretation of the world to revolutionary action transforming it.[23] If above (§6.2.3) we touched on service learning as part of the co- and extracurricular dimensions of the university experience, in particular their roles in connecting head knowledge to the experiential and applicational phases of learning, our concern here is to develop their underpinnings: the moral scope of higher education, especially the capacity of service learning to spark, or reinforce, embodied comprehension of the axiological and theological character of knowledge.

It is not just about practicing what we as Christians might preach—although the import of this should not be minimized—but that putting theory into practice presses crucial issues related to justice, peace, and (world) citizenship.[24] What arises are opportunities for Christians to speak truth to power, to come to grips with the many-sidedness of complex sociohistorical realities and then garner the courage to in turn preach what we practice.[25] Thus do the big questions of life get adjudicated *en via*, as learners explore the relevance of theory for Christian faith and witness. In short, service-learning opportunities are essential for the Christian university not only for the learning that is provided but for the outworking of a moral vision, one that feeds back into the Christian self-understanding when demanded by adjustments and negotiations with oftentimes intractable real-world dilemmas. A pneumatological approach empowers effective transition

[22] E.g., from the president of Seattle Pacific University: Philip W. Eaton, *Engaging the Culture, Changing the World: The Christian University in a Post-Christian World* (Downers Grove: IVP Academic, 2011).

[23] On the possibility of developing a Marxist educational paradigm, see Jaroslav Pelikan, *The Idea of the University: A Reexamination* (New Haven: Yale University Press, 1992), ch. 15; we return later in this chapter (§7.2.3) to discuss one version of a post-Marxist pedagogical philosophy, that of Paolo Freire.

[24] Joseph L. DeVitis, Robert W. Johns, and Douglas J. Simpson, eds., *To Serve and Learn: The Spirit of Community in Liberal Education* (New York: Peter Lang, 1998).

[25] See Nadajaran Sethuraju, "Speaking Truth to Power," in *The Spirit of Service: Exploring, Faith, Service, and Social Justice in Higher Education*, ed. Brian T. Johnson and Carolyn R. O'Grady (Bolton: Anker, 2006), 175–90.

from theory to practice on the one side even as the many encounters with the world push back on and require reformulation of these service practices on the other side. We need to be attentive to this dynamic since otherwise, modern universities operate more or merely in the theoretical than the practical domain.[26]

If service learning is spread across the curriculum, professional education is understood to be any trade, technical, or vocation program of study related to the professions—law, medicine, business, education, etc.—beyond the liberal arts or humanities core, and it is this that also connects the university to society and the institutions, organizations, and enterprises of the wider public square, all of which will continue learning and need to do so.[27] Grounded in utilitarian models of education (see also §§3.1.3, 3.3.2, and 4.3.2), their specialized objectives are applied knowledge, often involving the development of professional competencies, the certification of vocational skills, and the authentication of promotional and advancement prerequisites. At one level, to the degree that professional courses of study in university contexts are intentional about bridging theory and practice, to that same degree they ought to be undertaken as informed by the religious/theological and moral/ethical commitments embedded within the Christian higher educational context. One Christian educator put it this way: "All honest professions are honorable," and thus deserve faithful consideration and administration amidst the Christian university.[28]

Yet there have always been nagging questions regarding professional education, even dating back to John Henry Newman's concerns in the 1850s that instruction was being increasingly limited to those subjects considered "useful."[29] These anxieties have not been allayed since, and the development of global capitalist market forces in the last few decades has confirmed these fears, instrumentalizing higher educational initiatives along the way so that it is not the cultivation of the mind but the utility of the hands that is becoming the more important goal. The question that many learners are asking is, How can I get a job?[30] But professionalization of the curriculum breeds templates in part related to accrediting associations that are responsible for the quality of such professional vocations and this in

---

[26] As academics are trained more to analyze and understand things than they are as activists equipped to make a practical difference, modern universities are generally socially conservative institutions; on this point, note the sober assessment of Nathan Glazer, "Facing Three Ways: City and University in New York since World War II," in *The University and the City: From Medieval Origins to the Present*, ed. Thomas Bender (New York: Oxford University Press, 1988), 267–89, at 287, who writes: "Conservative institutions inherently, they [universities] will continue to do what they have done in the past, educating and training those who come to them, contributing in research to the understanding of the city's problems, and adapting to change rather than guiding it."

[27] On this point, see also Michael Stevenson, "Higher Education in 2065: The Role of Universities in a Learning Society," in *Higher Education as a Bridge to the Future: Proceedings of the 50th Anniversary Meeting of the International Association of University Presidents, with Reflections on the Future of Higher Education by Dr. J. Michael Adams*, ed. Jason A. Scorza (Madison: Farleigh Dickinson University Press, 2016), 109–14, at 111.

[28] David S. Dockery, "The Role of Professional Education in Christian Higher Education," in *The Future of Christian Higher Education*, ed. David S. Dockery and David P. Gushee (Nashville: Broadman and Holman, 1999), 75–80, at 80.

[29] John Henry Newman, *The Idea of the University: Defined and Illustrated in Nine Discourses Delivered to the Catholics of Dublin in Occasional Lectures and Essays Addressed to the Members of the Catholic University*, ed. Martin J. Svaglic (Notre Dame: University of Notre Dame Press, 1982), 116.

[30] See the analysis of Roman Catholic philosopher Alasdair MacIntyre, "Catholic Universities: Dangers, Hopes, Choices," in *Higher Learning and Catholic Traditions*, ed. Robert E. Sullivan (Notre Dame: University of Notre Dame Press, 2001), 1–21.

turn erodes not just religious specificity—with the market and external agencies becoming the driving force—but also moral or other intellectual considerations.[31] Put bluntly, then, if professionalism is driving higher education, then it's the market and mammon that dictates what happens in the Christian university rather than axiological motivations.[32]

These are not merely abstract apprehensions. Christian higher education is increasingly becoming a global, international phenomenon, with hundreds of colleges or universities worldwide.[33] The documented trend distressing Christian higher educators is the pervasiveness of an extremely instrumentalist and utilitarian culture within these institutions, with the bulk of their energies devoted to the development of technical skills in learners in order to generate a competitive alumni base for the job market. There is undoubtedly high demand of specialized professional and technical education, but the question is if and how specifically *Christian* higher educational initiatives are needed for such ventures.[34] The point is that no Christian commitments are needed just to churn out professionals, if that were the goal. Yet the struggles of privatization on the one side and the competition of for-profit enterprises on the other side have generated what one scholar calls a "massification" of Christian higher learning, the multiplication of Christian colleges and universities on a global scale.[35] This massification has prioritized affordability (for middle- and lower-income classes of learners), expanded accessibility (thus the proliferation of online options), forefronted the marketization and commercialization of the higher-educated, broadened focus on social services while reducing or eliminating programs in the arts, and minimized investment into research or postgraduate inquiry. The humanities are being gradually squeezed out by this market model, even as cultural literacy is being marginalized by technical efficiency.[36] In this context, there is little room for ethical and moral formation, much less for spiritual, religious, and theological education.

C. S. Lewis himself worried a century after Newman that humanity was being displaced, even replaced, by technique.[37] If technical proficiency was urged as being a viable

---

[31]   Robert Benne, *Quality with Soul: How Six Premier Colleges and Universities Keep Faith with Their Religious Traditions* (Grand Rapids: Eerdmans, 2001), 22.

[32]   Robert W. Brimlow, "Who Invited Mammon? Professional Education in the Christian College and University," in *Conflicting Allegiances: The Church-Based University in a Liberal Democratic Society*, ed. Michael L. Budde and John Wright (Grand Rapids: Brazos, 2004), 156–70.

[33]   One of the more expansive maps of the international Christian higher educational scene is Joel Carpenter, Perry L. Glanzer and Nicholas S. Lantinga, eds., *Christian Higher Education: A Global Reconnaissance* (Grand Rapids: Eerdmans, 2014).

[34]   See Joel Carpenter, "New Evangelical Universities: Cogs in a World System or Players in a New Game?" in *Interpreting Contemporary Christianity: Global Processes and Local Identities*, ed. Ogbu U. Kalu and Alaine M. Low (Grand Rapids: Eerdmans, 2008), 151–86; cf. Janel Marie Curry, "Cultural Challenges in Hong Kong to the Implementation of Effective General Education," *Teaching in Higher Education* 17.2 (2012): 223–30.

[35]   Joel A. Carpenter, "New Christian Universities and the Conversion of Cultures," *Evangelical Review of Theology* 36.1 (2012): 14–30, at 16.

[36]   See James Engell and Anthony Dangerfield, *Saving Higher Education in the Age of Money* (Charlottesville: University of Virginia Press, 2005); cf. Martha C. Nussbaum, *Not for Profit: Why Democracy Needs the Humanities*, 2nd ed. (Princeton: Princeton University Press, 2012).

[37]   C. S. Lewis, *The Abolition of Man, or Reflections on Education with Special Reference to the Teaching of English in the Upper Form of Schools* (New York: Macmillan, 1947). A quarter century after Lewis, Roman Catholic Ivan Illich, *Deschooling Society*, World Perspectives 44 (New York: Harper and Row, 1970), also worried we were perpetuating an educational system designed to produce a modern instrumental and technical society.

educational end, this would be a deformation of teleological rationality, one that prioritized efficient productivity over moral or other considerations.[38] As professional studies, whether at the undergraduate or the graduate level, attend to social practices related to trades, vocations, and applied realms of knowledge, work toward the common good is subordinated to market forces. In today's globalized economy, then, the goals of these various professional practices—the standards of excellence, the aesthetic forms, the ethical virtues, etc.—can easily be made to serve other ends dictated by consumer preferences. In short, "know-how" is assessed neither normatively, nor ethically, but economically.

Left to market demands, Christian higher educators should be nervous that axioms of the faith will be increasingly irrelevant. If service learning and professional education involve practice, how can such outworking of the hands not be bereft of moral, spiritual, and theological guidance? How else might our teleological horizons not be obscured or shrouded by capitalist efficiencies? The Christian university's only viable counterpraxis may be pentecostal. A pneumatologically charged project of higher education can revive the hands of inquiry in accordance with the eschatological shape of the impending reign of God, and can empower transformative service and practice with the power to impact and change the world in accordance with the ethical shape of Jesus' Spirit-empowered mission and ministry. Professional education can be reoriented along a charismatic pathway wherein encounter with the Spirit of Jesus accentuates an excellence of practice normed by professional/disciplinary, moral/ethical, and theological/spiritual criteria in relationship to the coming rule of God.[39] In this way, the life of the mind may be integrated with the heart and hands.

Yet even as the professional focus is on the individual person's capacities to contribute to the craft and its vocational opportunities, the eschatological teleology of the rule of God inspires attentiveness to an ever-expanding global horizon. The good is always particularly instantiated in specific heres and nows, but even then begs for transformation of more and more of our shared commons: regional, national, transnational, terrestrial, and perhaps even beyond. How can the Christian university in pneumatological key ever have anything less than a cosmic vista commensurate with the face of the deep hovered over primordially by the divine breath (Gen 1:2)? As it is the task of the intellectual life to move dynamically from the local to the global and vice-versa, Christian higher education cannot avoid this question.

---

[38] Steven R. Loomis and Jacob P. Rodriguez, *C. S. Lewis: A Philosophy of Education* (New York: Palgrave Macmillan, 2009), ch. 4.

[39] Further unpacking of these notions is provided in two important articles by Henk Jochemsen and Johan Hegeman: "Equipping Christian Students to Connect Kingdom Citizenship to Issues in Today's Societies," in *Christian Higher Education in Global Context: Implications for Curriculum, Pedagogy, and Administration—Proceedings of the International Conference of the International Association for the Promotion of Christian Higher Education 15–19 November 2006, Granada, Nicaragua,* ed. Nick Lantinga (Sioux Center: Dordt College, 2008), 223–40, and "Connecting Christian Faith and Professional Practice in a Pluralist Society," in *Bridging the Gap: Connecting Christian Faith and Professional Practice—Proceedings of the European Conference of the European Chapter of the International Association for the Promotion of Christian Higher Education April 20–23, 2009, Biezenmortel, The Netherlands,* ed. Bram de Muynck, Johan Hegeman, and Pieter Vos (Sioux Center: Dordt College, 2011), 73–85.

7.1.3 The Groaning of the Spirit: Teaching toward (Cosmic) Justice

We have urged that there can be no life of the mind after Pentecost that does not have the ends of the earth and the ends of time at the far end of its teleological arrow. If, in the words of the Dutch Reformed philosopher, theologian, and statesmen Abraham Kuyper (1837–1920), "no single piece of our mental world is to be hermetically sealed off from the rest, and there is not a square inch in the whole domain of our human existence over which Christ, who is Sovereign over all, does not cry: 'Mine!'"[40] then a pneumatological infused vision for Christian higher education also cannot but think about the common good except in terms of the cosmic commons. The Lukan Pentecost both inaugurates and initiates "the time of universal restoration that God announced long ago through his holy prophets" (Acts 3:21), inviting us as Christian educators into this all-encompassing prospect.

St. Luke's Pentecost-perspective is complemented and reinforced by St. Paul. In the pneumatologically charged eighth chapter of his Letter to the Romans,[41] the latter puts it this way: that "the whole creation has been groaning in labour pains until now; and not only the creation, but we ourselves, who have the first fruits of the Spirit, groan inwardly while we wait for adoption, the redemption of our bodies"; that "the Spirit helps us in our weakness; for we do not know how to pray as we ought, but that very Spirit intercedes with sighs too deep for words"; and decisively that "neither death, nor life, nor angels, nor rulers, nor things present, nor things to come, nor powers, nor height, nor depth, nor anything else in all creation, will be able to separate us from the love of God in Christ Jesus our Lord" (Rom 8:22–23, 26, 38–39). The Spirit who works in and through the human passions—thus nurturing the orthopathic elements that lie also at the center of the Christian educational task—has as its eschatological goal the filling of all creation with the love of the Spirit-anointed Messiah, Jesus.[42]

Reformed philosopher Nicholas Wolterstorff has written about what might be called a *shalomic education*, which is relevant in this regard.[43] Wolterstorff's notion of shalom involves human flourishing: "people living in right relationships with God, themselves, each other, and nature."[44] The question, then, is how Christian higher education precipitates such an intellectual pursuit of well-being and enables the cultivation of the multiple moral domains through which such shalom is pursued. The curriculum cannot only inform but must transform, facilitate the maturation of, in more or less traditional college classrooms, young adults, socializing them both into the academic venture but also into right relations in these various domains. Values will need to be instilled so that

---

[40]   In James D. Bratt, ed., *Abraham Kuyper: A Centennial Reader* (Grand Rapids: Eerdmans, 1998), 488; cf. further discussion of Kuyper's ideas in relationship to political theology in Yong, *In the Days of Caesar*, §2.2.3.

[41]   For an introduction to the discussion of the Spirit in Romans 8, see A. Skevington Wood, *Paul's Pentecost: Studies in the Life of the Spirit from Romans 8* (Exeter: Paternoster, 1963).

[42]   For more on our pneumatological reading of Romans 8, see Yong, *Spirit of Love: A Trinitarian Theology of Grace* (Waco: Baylor University Press, 2012), ch. 7.

[43]   Nicholas Wolterstorff, *Educating for Shalom: Essays on Christian Higher Education*, ed. Clarence W. Joldersma and Gloria Goris Stronks (Grand Rapids: Eerdmans, 2004); see also idem, *Educating for Life: Reflections on Christian Teaching and Learning*, ed. Gloria Goris Stronks and Clarence W. Joldersma (Grand Rapids: Baker Academic, 2002), part 4, for more on this theme of education and shalom.

[44]   Wolterstorff, *Educating for Shalom*, xiii.

the moral and ethical are at least implicit within, if not explicitly articulated, through the educational program.[45]

Yet identification of right relations requires also discernment of when relations are not right, not only wrong but disfigured variously. Wolterstorff thus talks about educating for shalom as involving the naming of "the *wounds* of humanity" evincing human brokenness and a creation in need of repair.[46] More particularly, there are "the *moral* wounds" that afflict human creatures, distorting human relationships and inhibiting shalom.[47] Then there are the various traumatizations that each and every human being—and hence also every learner—brings with him or her into higher education, every one of which is an occasion when pain, tragedy, or injustice has been suffered, and these have often been internalized into the subconscious simply in order that we can survive and move forward. If educators are to be purveyors of shalom in the big scheme of things, then, we are also healers and liberators as much as we are instructors and professors.[48] Yet such healing cannot be aspired to, much less achieved, without the work of justice, and of attending to the perspective of the wounded and of the wounds that are sometimes gaping but mostly buried under the surface.[49] Wolterstoff urges: "Justice is the ground of shalom, and responsible action is its vehicle."[50] Following the Isaianic tradition, we would argue that holiness and wholeness (shalom) correspond with righteousness and justice flowing from sanctifying encounter with the divine wind. This means that the Spirit's gifts in Isaiah 11 inculcate holiness both in the Messiah and in those in union with him to facilitate renewal oriented to righteousness and justice across the earth. Christian higher education thereby provides environments through which learners can participate in just practices of socio-ethical analysis (informed here in interdisciplinary ways), concrete practices of socio-ethical advocacy and solidarity, and exploratory inquiry into social transformation, all the while developing empathetic ears for the experiences and voices of the suffering and the marginalized. Herein orthopraxy and orthopathy—the compassion that motivates action—come together with Christian orthodoxy.

Yet the quest for justice begs for ever wider realization. In a globalizing world, the work for justice effectively never ends.[51] There are various circles and spheres of publicness amidst which justice should be sought: social, economic, political, environmental, etc. Within these ever-widening horizons, justice ought to be pleaded intersectionally with

---

[45] Nicholas P. Wolterstorff, *Educating for Responsible Action* (Grand Rapids: Eerdmans and Christian Schools International Publications, 1980), was an initial foray in this direction, focused on the nurture of children.

[46] Nicholas Wolterstorff, "Teaching for Justice," in *Making Higher Education Christian: The History and Mission of Evangelical Colleges in America*, ed. Joel A. Carpenter and Kenneth W. Shipps (St. Paul: Christian University Press / Christian College Consortium, and Grand Rapids: Eerdmans, 1987), 201–16, at 209 (emphasis orig.).

[47] Wolterstorff, *Educating for Shalom*, 22 (emphasis orig.).

[48] See Laura I. Rendón, *Sentipensante (Sensing/Thinking) Pedagogy: Educating for Wholeness, Social Justice, and Liberation* (Sterling: Stylus, 2009), ch. 4, for more on how faculty are humanitarian agents of social healing.

[49] See here Mary Elizabeth Mullino Moore, "Teaching Justice and Reconciliation in a Wounding World," in *The Other Side of Sin: Woundedness from the Perspective of the Sinned-Against*, ed. Andrew Sung Park and Susan L. Nelson (Albany: State University of New York Press, 2001), 143–64.

[50] Wolterstorff, *Educating for Shalom*, xiv.

[51] Wolterstorff, *Educating for Shalom*, 87–99.

regard to gender and sexuality, with regard to racial and ethnic disparities, with regard to the pluralistic world of many different ideologies and religious commitments—all of which will occupy our attention in the rest of this chapter. The Wolterstorffian point, however, is that well-being and flourishing of shalom entreating for justice need to be enacted at all of these levels. Christian higher education therefore has a moral and teleological imperative with cosmic and eschatological reach: shalom and justice, while important if achieved in any limited sector, require ongoing extension so that the groanings of the Spirit in and through all of creation, understood as expansively as our imaginations might conceive, can be heard, soothed, and salved. From this perspective, shalom and justice cannot be anthropocentric but have to be appropriately planetary and even cosmic: with attentiveness to human relations and well-being interrelated with that of environmental, ecological, and planetary flourishing. "State of the planet" consciousness would involve alertness to world conditions, population demographics, migration trends, economic developments, environmental issues, scientific and technology advancements, and international relations, etc.[52]

If the work of the Spirit is for all of creation, then Christian higher education cannot but be fundamentally cosmic and cosmopolitan. Evangelical philosopher R. J. Snell and his theologian colleague Steven Cone put it this way: "Cosmopolitan thought attempts to go beyond the natural affections of family and clan, beyond the passions of state and nation to form a concern (and consequent institutions and policies) exhibiting solidarity for the development, dignity, justice, and flourishing of all; for the cosmopolitan, everyone is a neighbor and thus owed love. And yet bias and decline render that problematic, unlikely even, if not for self-transcendence, but the reign of sin makes transcendence unlikely."[53] For this reason, higher education cannot hope on its own to achieve such cosmic and cosmopolitan love and care, compassion and action. Rather, as Snell and Cone also recognize, such human care needs something that the Christian university must be attentive to: "The dynamic state of being-in-love is a gift of God and occurs when the love of God is poured into our hearts by the Holy Spirit, when human lives become shaped by the life of God."[54] Even secular educational philosophers recognize that the telos of education must interface with transcendence and therefore that we cannot finally dispense with "spirit" rhetoric, discourse, and categories of thought.[55] Herein is pneumatic and charismatic encounter with the divine breath called for as part and parcel of the Christian higher educational endeavor.

Our point is that the orthodoxy and orthopathy of the Christian university needs an orthopraxic thrust. Yet Christian praxis is normed by the person and work of the Spirit-led Messiah and directed toward the rule and reign of God that his life, death,

---

[52] See Robert G. Hanvey, "An Attainable Global Perspective" (1975; repr., the American Forum, 2004), https://eric.ed.gov/?id=ED116993; see also Amos Yong, ed., *The Spirit Renews the Face of the Earth: Pentecostal Forays in Science and Theology of Creation* (Eugene: Pickwick, 2009), and idem, "The *Missio Spiritus*: Towards a Pneumatological Missiology of Creation," in *Creation Care in Christian Mission*, ed. Kapya J. Kaoma, Regnum Edinburgh Centenary Series 29 (Oxford: Regnum, 2015), 121–33.

[53] R. J. Snell and Steven D. Cone, *Authentic Cosmopolitanism: Love, Sin, and Grace in the Christian University* (Eugene: Pickwick, 2013), 165–66.

[54] Snell and Cone, *Authentic Cosmopolitanism*, 172.

[55] E.g., Anthony T. Kronman, *Education's End: Why Our Colleges and Universities Have Given Up on the Meaning of Life* (New Haven: Yale University Press, 2007), ch. 5.

resurrection, ascension, and then Pentecost-outpouring inducted. Thus, the moral and teleological direction of Christian higher education is effectively eschatological in character: understood according to the ethical scope of the divine redemption that is intended for the creation as a whole. Peace is intertwined with righteousness and justice, and both are accomplishments of the shalomic Spirit, yet also achieved particularly in and through human hearts sensitive to the divine breath's groans and efforts.

7.2   REPAIRING THE (COSMO)POLIS: MANY VOICES, TRANSSECTIONAL PRACTICES

The cosmic scope of Spirit-aspired to shalom and justice related to the imminent divine rule was instated on the day of Pentecost, when those from the ends of the earth, "from every nation under heaven" (Acts 2:5b), were found gathered together on the streets of Jerusalem. In the Pentecost-moment recorded, "each one heard them speaking in the native language of each" (2:6b), so that we could argue the insights of the many disciplines (see §5.2) were pronounced in and through the many voices of the many peoples from around the known world. Moments later, St. Luke records Peter's explanation of what this means via the prophecy of Joel, one that indicated that the many languages would be carried further not just generically by their people groups but in the dialects and intonations of sons and daughters, young and old, slave and free (Acts 2:17b–18). In short, the Spirit-inspired witness to injustice and the call for reparative shalom is never only general but always encountered forcefully through the particularity of otherness, resonating in this Lukan and Pentecost-scenario from the voices of specific men and women, from the visions of youth and dreams of the elderly, from the prayers and cries of the haves and cries of the have-nots. What the scholarly literature calls *intersectionality*—wherein ethnic and racial experience is complicated by and discriminated against, more specifically, through gender, class, ability, age, sexual orientation, or other features of identity[56]—Christian moral philosophy after Pentecost calls the groanings of the Spirit through many creaturely tongues.

This section cannot even begin to aspire toward comprehensive intersectional analysis of the failed moral telos of higher education. Even limiting our focus to the opportunities and challenges for the Christian university's ethical charge viewed in gendered, ethnic, and class perspective will have to be severely narrow, ignoring important historical developments in the arguments and overlooking contestations within the literatures. In fact, we are downright uncomfortable with commenting on the topics at hand given our own privileged male, heterosexual, and elitist (both fully tenured) location.[57] Yet we have

---

[56]   See (a more succinct statement) Douglas Kellner, "Multiple Literacies and Critical Pedagogy in a Multicultural Society," *Educational Theory* 48.1 (1998): 103–22, and (a more extensive treatment) Carl A. Grant and Elisabeth Zwier, eds., *Intersectionality and Urban Education: Identities, Policies, Spaces, and Power* (Charlotte: Information Age, 2014). Further explication in dialogue with feminist perspectives is to be found in Robbin D. Crabtree, David Alan Sapp, and Adela C. Licona, eds., *Feminist Pedagogy: Looking Back to Move Forward* (Baltimore: Johns Hopkins University Press, 2009), part 3. See also Yong, *Learning Theology: Tracking the Spirit of Christian Faith* (Louisville: Westminster John Knox, 2018), ch. 4.

[57]   One of us has written about race and ethnicity—see, for instance, Yong, "Race and Racialization in a Post-Racist Evangelicalism: A View from Asian America," in *Aliens in the Promised Land: Why Minority Leadership Is Overlooked in White Christian Churches and Institutions*, ed. Anthony B. Bradley (Phillipsburg: P&R, 2013), 45–58 and 216–20, and Yong and Aizaiah G. Yong, "The Inequitable Silencing of Many Tongues: A Critical and Pastoral Response to the Economic, Political, and Racialized Dimensions of the

both been formed by and within a tradition that embraced ethnic and gender equality, even if it did not always live out its deepest commitments. This tradition reinforces our Pentecost-convictions and its promise for cosmic justice, which compel us into these arenas. Hence, we will focus sequentially on each arena, which serves the heuristic purposes of clarifying these distinctive yet interrelated domains.

In the end, Christian higher education will need to attend to these intersecting spheres of analysis all together, even if all the while also developing strategies that can confront and dismantle the injustices plaguing specific sites.[58] If the many disciplines of the university involve the many intelligences and cultures in teaching and learning, then the following presses more deeply into how the charismatic and pneumatological life of the mind can be nurtured precisely in and through confrontation with the othered voices of women (§7.2.1), racialized others and ethnic minorities (§7.2.2), and those somehow marginalized by economic, social, and political status (§7.2.3). Although the Spirit speaks not in a single voice,[59] we propose a Pentecost-transsectionality that empowers the many (intersectional and multisectional) accents and enables us to live into their witnesses— discordant as they seem—for the sake of the gospel and the just divine reign it heralds.[60] Our goal is not to resolve these highly politicized issues but to engage them from a specifically theological and Pentecost-perspective angle to chart possible paths forward.[61]

7.2.1 Male and Female: Feminist Interrogations and Constructions

On at least a couple of fronts, this subsection might seem redundant. First, given women's suffrage a century ago, we might think that women's voices in higher education are by

---

Pandemic in American Pentecostal-Charismaticism," in *Response of the Global Spirit-Empowered Church to the COVID-19 Pandemic*, ed. Wonsuk Ma and Opoku Onyinah (Tulsa: ORU Press, forthcoming)—but this is our first foray into these matters related to theology of higher education.

[58] Samuel Joeckel and Thomas Chesnes, eds., *The Christian College Phenomenon: Inside America's Fastest Growing Institutions of Higher Learning* (Abilene: Abilene Christian University Press, 2012). Parts V and VI are devoted to race/ethnicity and gender diversity in the Christian university. From a secular perspective, Stephen D. Brookfield, *The Power of Critical Theory: Liberating Adult Learning and Teaching* (San Francisco: Jossey-Bass, 2005), provides a more comprehensive assessment, with chs. 10–11 focused on racializing and gendering critical theory for higher educational purposes.

[59] The future of this complex matter rests perhaps more with the discipline of social psychology than most realize, especially since the so-called research legitimating diversity is almost more ideology- than data-driven. We will not be discussing at length affirmative action or efforts to decolonize the curriculum, etc., even if much that we have to say should motivate distinctively Christian approaches to these important matters. For an overview of some of the issues, see Stanley Rothman, April Kelly-Woessner, and Matthew Woessner, *The Still Divided Academy: How Competing Visions of Power, Politics, and Diversity Complicate the Mission of Higher Education* (Lanham: Rowman and Littlefield, 2011).

[60] Which is not to discount the call for justice as central to multicultural education already sounded by secular approaches, e.g., Christine E. Sleeter and Carl A. Grant, *Making Choices for Multicultural Education: Five Approaches to Race, Class, and Gender*, 5th ed. (Hoboken: John Wiley, 2007), chs. 6–7. We add our own theologically funded motivations.

[61] Herein agreeing with Todd C. Ream and Perry L. Glanzer, *The Idea of a Christian College: A Reexamination for Today's University* (Eugene: Cascade, 2013), that "diversity is not enough" (part of the title to their ch. 9), and with Perry L. Glanzer, Theodore F. Cockle, Elijah G. Jeong, and Britney N. Graber, *Christ-Enlivened Student Affairs: A Guide to Christian Thinking and Practice in the Field* (Abilene: Abilene Christian University Press, 2020), that it is Christ who "transforms the campus racial climate" (part of the title to ch. 10); our pneumatological approach is designed to both complement their theological and christological contributions and provide a deeper trinitarian consideration of these matters.

now a nonissue. Then, considering the central contributions women made to pentecostal-holiness movements as well as to their higher educational initiatives during the first half of the twentieth century (see above §3.3.3 and 4.3.2),[62] their efforts might be presumed to be taken for granted in any Pentecost-perspective on the current conversation, as this one is. Yet assumptions on either count would be ill-advised. The glass ceiling for women in pentecostal-charismatic Christianity is yet in place, as numerous studies have shown,[63] and this is no less the case when considering majority-world contexts, wherein Christian higher education continues to expand. Further, the concerns are not only about accessibility, as important as that is, but about the importance of gendered perspectives, and their roles in teaching and learning, as well as in research and scholarship. While there has been a line from Plato to J. S. Mill that asserted the "full equality of opportunity for women, together with social circumstances designed to minimize the impact of traditional hierarchy on women's development," there has also always been another strand, from Aristotle to and through Jean Jacques Rousseau, that has started instead with the claim regarding "innate immutable difference and derives moral imperatives from those starting points, defending asymmetrical roles for men and women."[64] If we begin with Joel's prophecy, called upon to explicate the Pentecost-event in Acts 2, we discover that the Spirit is poured out upon "*all* flesh, . . . [upon] *your sons and your daughters . . .* , [e]ven upon my slaves, *both men and women*" (Acts 2:17–18a, emphasis added). As the telos of the Christian university includes scholarship, teaching, and learning normed by the coming just reign of the divine Spirit, there is no room here for ignoring the voices and agency of one half of us in the ongoing conversation.

Consulting feminist perspectives on pedagogy and higher education unveil two recurrent themes that perhaps in some quarters have become passé but that warrant reassertion for our purposes.[65] First, feminist commitments have long alerted us to the patriarchal and hierarchical character of much of what passes for academic discussion. This is not to essentialize either patriarchalism nor feminism—both are in any case always being redefined by those with the power to do so for their own purposes—but it is to remind us that the historical discussion was carried on predominantly if not only by men and was by and large not critically reflective of their male-centered point of view, and then to ask about if and how such limited discursive self-awareness might be corrected.[66] This does

---

[62]   E.g., Abraham Ruelas, *Women and the Landscape of American Higher Education: Wesleyan Holiness and Pentecostal Founders* (Eugene: Pickwick, 2010).

[63]   See, e.g., the essays in Estrelda Alexander and Amos Yong, eds., *Philip's Daughters: Women in Pentecostal-Charismatic Leadership* (Eugene: Pickwick, 2009), and also Joy E. A. Qualls, *God Forgive Us for Being Women: Rhetoric, Theology, and the Pentecostal Tradition* (Eugene: Pickwick, 2018).

[64]   Martha C. Nussbaum, *Cultivating Humanity: A Classical Defense of Reform in Liberal Education* (Cambridge, Mass.: Harvard University Press, 1997), 212–13.

[65]   The following thematic lines can be found in any standard text, e.g., Elizabeth Kamarck Minnich, *Transforming Knowledge*, 2nd ed. (Philadelphia: Temple University Press, 2005).

[66]   The feminist concern about essentializing women's experience is that this in turn buttresses the contrasting male perspective as well, thus undermining the point of the exercise to begin with, which has in turn prompted developments recognizing all discursive speech as essentialist in one or another respect. Thus part of the task is to make appropriate, if even strategic, distinctions without absolutizing them. For an insightful analysis of such "strategic essentialism" vis-à-vis a historical case study of women in holiness ministerial traditions, see Dianne Leclerc, "Two Women Speaking 'Woman': The Strategic Essentialism of Luce Irigaray and Phoebe Palmer," *Wesleyan Theological Journal* 35.1 (2000): 182–99.

not say that perspectives from such locations are invalid, since any knowledge is situated, but it clarifies that some knowledges are proffered without any awareness of their situatedness. This is one of our major takeaways from the feminist argument: not just that women should speak from their own historical, social, and experiential site, but that all claims are also situated in some way or other.[67]

The second major theme, related to the preceding perhaps as its flipside, is the feminist argument that much of academic theory, by its abstractive and abstracting approaches from what were believed to be theoretically indubitable foundations, is projected to be universally relevant and applicable, without much if any qualification. The contributions of the many voices representing historical realities are valid only if and when they are translatable into so-called universal truths. To be sure, in the natural sciences, for instance, it would be difficult to insist that there is a feminist scientific method.[68] But especially in the humanities, feminist sensibilities are toward more democratic input, shifting the burden from the speculative one to the contextually formed many, from discursivity (at the level of thought) toward interrelationality (between thinking and reality), from theory to emancipatory practice (and back again).[69] In many of these respects, these feminist ideals have become embedded in the horizontality and interactivity of the digital age (see above, §6.3) even if they are not explicitly associated female points of view. Yet our point is not to set out women's views in contrast to men's, but to indicate how and why both belong together in any Christian account.

Yet even if perhaps already assumed in many contemporary pedagogical conversations, we should not forget such feminist commitments, if for no other reason than that we otherwise easily overlook the actual men and women enrolled across the Christian university. Here we are helped by feminist theological educators who have actually urged that their intersubjective and experiential model is incarnational at its core, based on the enfleshment of the Logos in human history.[70] From this transcendent-and-yet-immanent perspective, then, Mary Moore suggests that teaching derives "from the heart," that it involves a "loving God with all that is in us. And to this we must add loving our neighbor as ourselves"; yet this dynamic leads outward even further: "God loves every aspect of creation; thus, all creation is holy. Our love of God is linked inextricably to love of creation. Teaching from the heart is, most importantly, loving God and neighbor. A second critical

[67] For more on the positionality of all knowing, see Frances A. Maher and Mary Kay Thompson Tetreault, *The Feminist Classroom* (New York: Basic Books, 1994), ch. 6.

[68] E.g., Cassandra L. Pinnick, Noretta Koertge, and Robert F. Almeder, eds., *Scrutinizing Feminist Epistemology: An Examination of Gender in Science* (New Brunswick: Rutgers University Press, 2003).

[69] Elisabeth Schüssler Fiorenza, *Democratizing Biblical Studies: Toward an Emancipatory Educational Space* (Louisville: Westminster John Knox, 2009), proposes a vision of scholarship as radical democratic discourse that is emancipatory, postcolonial, intersectional, and conscientizing, somehow coherent despite its polyphony, indeed as a "republic of many voices" (which is in the title of her ch. 2). Note here also the educational vision of Roman Catholic philosopher Jacques Maritain (1882–1973), which aspired to theocentric (rather than individualistic) freedom and political emancipation. See Jacques Maritain, *Education at the Crossroads* (New Haven: Yale University Press, 1943); cf. Donald Gallagher and Idella Gallagher, eds., *The Education of Man: The Educational Philosophy of Jacques Maritain* (Garden City: Doubleday, 1962), esp. ch. 8, and Luz M. Ibarra, *Maritain, Religion, and Education: A Theocentric Humanism Approach*, American University Series 7: Theology and Religion 326 (New York: Peter Lang, 2013).

[70] Mary Elizabeth Mullino Moore, *Teaching from the Heart: Theology and Educational Method* (Minneapolis: Fortress, 1991), ch. 4, builds off the incarnational motif.

insight in this organic worldview is that *knowledge is energy; the heart of the matter is not matter at all, but energy.*"[71] Hence, teaching—and learning, by extension—can never be merely theoretical. Rather, the work of the Christian university always brings with it the yearning for liberation. Feminist religious educator Maria Harris insists that teaching is an activity with "healing power,"[72] and that an intentionally feminist pedagogy (usable by men as much as women) can be generative and curative, activating reparative energy to mend the brokenness of the world.[73]

For Christian colleges and universities in the evangelical tradition, of course, the issue is compounded by dogmas regarding a world created by God the Father and a church led by his male disciples. There is no space here to go into the details of how such a conflation of biblical truth and "traditional values" favors complementarian as opposed to egalitarian visions of male-and-female relations and in that respect inhibits integration of women at all levels of the higher educational undertaking. Many evangelical women and their allies seek a *via media* between secular and antireligious feminists on the left and fundamentalistic and patriarchally organized believers on the right.[74] The problem in some evangelical environments remains one of downright sexism, not only among and between learners but also among and between staff and faculty, so that this needs to be the first line of engagement, long before we can even begin thinking about research-teaching-service possibilities informed by women's perspectives.

Our hope is that a Pentecost-theology of higher education can complement Moore's incarnational feminist pedagogy so that the many voices of prophetesses registered on the day of Pentecost can continue to echo across the Christian university of the twenty-first century. And here is where Luke's Pentecost-vision two thousand years ago may be even more up to date than some contemporary evangelical Christian thinking about the role of women. Luke himself recognized that the contributions of the daughters among the sons included those categorized as "slaves" or "servants" (*tous doúlous*; Acts 2:18). This anticipates contemporary feminist concerns about inequities in the workplace and in classrooms of the present global era. As one scholar puts it: "Globalization requires feminists to rethink our conceptualization of social justice in ways that attend to difference and to fairness between differentially positioned groups in specific contexts. Feminists must develop a more powerful critique of the range of labor markets and their relationships to education and of market liberalism in general on its own terms."[75]

Beyond the intersection of gender and class registered in the use of the Joel quotation in Acts 2 and in the preceding call, the broader day of Pentecost narrative identifies women

---

[71]   Moore, *Teaching from the Heart*, 209 (emphasis orig.).

[72]   Maria Harris, *Women and Teaching: Themes for a Spirituality of Pedagogy* (New York: Paulist, 1988), 29, and ch. 3, passim.

[73]   For more on Harris' proposals considered in light of Moore's incarnational and energetic pedagogy, see Judith A. Dorney, "Maria Harris: An Aesthetic and Erotic Justice," in *Faith of Our Foremothers: Women Changing Religious Education*, ed. Barbara Anne Keely (Louisville: Westminster John Knox, 1997), 180–90.

[74]   As exemplified in this collection by evangelical feminist educators and scholars: Allyson Jule and Bettina Tate Pedersen, eds., *Facing Challenges: Feminism in Christian Higher Education and Other Places* (Newcastle upon Tyne: Cambridge Scholars, 2015).

[75]   Jill Blackmore, "Globalization: A Useful Concept for Feminists Rethinking Theory and Strategies in Education?" in *Globalization and Education: Critical Perspectives*, ed. Nicholas C. Burbules and Carlos Alberto Torres (New York: Routledge, 2000), 133–55, at 152.

not only in relationship to class but also vis-à-vis ethnicity and nationality (the latter understood according to first-century rather than modern nation-state terms). Luke refers not just to prophetess women in the abstract, but as ones derived from specific cultural and linguistic sites across the Mediterranean world. As such, there is even in Acts 2, at least theologically and pneumatologically, an "interconnectedness of racism, sexism, [and] classism," what feminists call "a matrix of domination" that requires intersectional analyses that takes each of these sites into account, both separately but also together.[76] Extrapolating from the Acts narrative, today it is not just female voices in general that need to be heard, but those of womanists, mujeristas, Asian women, etc.,[77] all in solidarity with white women and male allies. Such resonances in and out of the (digital) classroom would be the beginnings of a feminist pedagogy after Pentecost that is committed to cosmic justice.[78]

7.2.2 Race and Ethnicity: Transcultural Challenges and Opportunities

If emphasizing feminist concerns is meant not to dismiss wholesale the dominant scholarly academy but to highlight gaps and problems in its hierarchicalism and patriarchalism that need repair, then turning next to the vexed and contentious issues of race and ethnicity similarly is intended not to reject indiscriminately the Western intellectual tradition but to constructively problematize any hegemonic forms of the colonial and Eurocentric legacy in contemporary global contexts.[79] Identity politics in the present time has unfortunately become fractious, with majority-world scholars (and their Western allies) anxious about neocolonial domination on the one side, and Euro-American traditionalists (among others) worrying about multicultural relativism and the so-called multiversity fragmentation on the other side. While any way forward should heed the cautions regarding uncritical adherence to multiculturalism,[80] not least in its secular expressions, we remain convinced that earlier discussions of this

---

[76] See Anne Donadey, "Negotiating Tensions: Teaching about Race Issues in Graduate Feminist Classrooms," in Crabtree, Sapp, and Licona, *Feminist Pedagogy*, 209–29, at 203.

[77] E.g., Yong, "Yin-Yang and the Spirit Poured Out on All Flesh: An Evangelical Egalitarian East-West Dialogue on Gender and Race," *ChristianityNext* (Winter 2020): 61–77; *Priscilla Papers* 34.3 (2020): 21–26.

[78] We have focused here on the role of women rather than addressing the issue of sexual orientation in our discussion, in part because we are still a long way from achieving a fully egalitarian space for men and women in Christian higher education around the world (sad to say) and in part also because the issues regarding sexuality are complex and deserve fuller treatment. Any Pentecost-approach in the higher educational domain will need to heed the many voices chiming into this discussion and navigate the many layers of issues in an effective ethical, pastoral, and political manner. More importantly, a full response will need to work through the intersectional dynamics at all of their levels—brilliantly illuminated in Grant and Zwier, *Intersectionality and Urban Education*—which is precisely why our discussions in this section are intended to exemplify thinking through a few of the many tongues, rather than to be prescriptive about navigating any one identity marker.

[79] Note that while English education and then German served as the models for North America, as Hans de Wit, Isabel Cristina Jaramillo, Jocelyne Gacel-Ávila and Jane Knight, *Higher Education in Latin America: The International Dimension* (Washington, DC: World Bank, 2005), recount, the University of Salamanca and Spanish models served as the primary basis for the university in Central and South America; on the one hand, then, there is a diversity of European expressions, even if in the end it is also the case that medieval Europe has influenced higher education across the Americas.

[80] For instance, J. Meric Pessagno, "The Multiconfusion of Multiculturalism," in *The Common Things: Essays on Thomism and Education*, ed. Daniel McInerny (Mishawaka: American Maritain Association; Washington, DC: Catholic University Press of America, 1999), 241–46.

matter highlighted educational attentiveness to ethnocentrism, prejudice, stereotyping, culturally derived norms, cultural variation, socialization, value formation, verbal and nonverbal communication, cognitive styles, political economy and democratic forms across cultural traditions, and intercultural education, all of which remain important for Christian university engagement.[81] To proceed appropriately, our pneumatological theology of Christian higher education resources us with two key questions registered on the day of Pentecost: "How is it that we hear, each of us, in our own native language? . . . What does this mean?" (Acts 2:8, 12b). If Pentecost brought the "ends of the earth" (1:8) to Jerusalem, so also the many languages of the human family are found now in Christian universities. Can we hear each in his or her own tongue? What would it mean for Christian higher education to do so?

Preliminarily, our own earlier notion of *multidisciplinarity* (see §5.2.1) maps loosely onto the intersectional and multicultural discussions in the present context, particularly in highlighting the importance of experiential, linguistic, and cultural particularities that tend to get lost (via homogenization) in certain globalizing environments. Our point there that *multidisciplinarity* must work together with *interdisciplinarity* and *transdisciplinarity*, each with its own integrity, applies here when thinking about the many perspectives and many cultures in Christian higher education. Translated into the idiom of the present discourse, we wish to appropriate secular concerns about intersectionality and multicul-turality within our own transsectional and transcultural vision, one that welcomes the Spirit's redemptive work to transfigure, not mute, the many voices at this interface so that we can discern afresh "about God's deeds of power" (Acts 2:11b) among male and female, Jew and Greek, young and old, rich and poor (cf. Gal 3:28).[82]

---

[81]   See, for instance, Jaime S. Wurzel, ed., *Toward Multiculturalism: A Reader in Multicultural Education* (Yarmouth: Intercultural, 1988). Christian colleges and universities are also rapidly seeing how urgent it is to attend to all of these matters, not least in a time of #GeorgeFloyd, e.g., Karen A. Longman, ed., *Diversity Matters: Race, Ethnicity, and the Future of Christian Higher Education* (Abilene: Abilene Christian University Press, 2017), and Alexander Jun, Tabatha L. Jones Jolivet, Allison N. Ash, and Christopher S. Collins, *White Jesus: The Architecture of Racism in Religion and Education* (New York: Peter Lang, 2018).

[82]   Our triadic typology is not meant to be dismissive of other approaches. Robert W. Pazmiño, *Latin American Journey: Insights for Christian Education in North America* (Cleveland: United Church, 1994), 112–19, for instance, discusses his own journey beyond (a) white assimilationist (which does not dis-turb white privilege!), (b) melting pot (which leaves us each in our own, now relativized, arena), and (c) cultural-pluralist (wherein diversity of voices is subordinated to unified hegemony) models toward (d) what he calls a multicultural approach, which seeks harmony without eliminating differences, while Luis Enrique López, "Reaching the Unreached: Indigenous Intercultural Bilingual Education in Latin America," background paper prepared for the "Education for All Global Monitoring Report 2010" (United Nations Educational, Scientific and Cultural Organization, 2009), also presents a nonmutually exclusive quadruple paradigm regarding negotiating between dominant and marginal cultures: (1) submersive assimilationism that leads to a monolingual and monocultural society; (2) strategic transitionalism, which in the long run involves a bilingualism that retains the minority culture in the private sphere; (3) a maintenance devel-opmentalism, which seeks to actively preserve indigenous cultures and languages; and (4) enrichment commitment devoted to cross-cultural enrichment and cultural unity-in-diversity. We see that our trans-sectional aspirations work pentecostally along the fourth trajectory, recommended by both Pazmiño and López, albeit without wishing to be dismissive to fellow believers struggling also to make sense of the way forward in a multi- and intersectional world.

The fact of the matter is that we cannot afford to ignore the multicultural and intercultural realities in our midst.[83] Ours is a globalizing context, and even if some of us or some of our learners never leave "home" (North America for the majority of our intended readership), the information age means that we are now situated within digital currents that crisscross the globe. Further, as academics, we are no longer insulated from the global academy, and each of our own fields of expertise is relativized, epistemically at least, by the expertise of others living, working, teaching, and producing scholarship from their own locales. Our inquiry and conversation, like it or not, is inevitably international.[84] Yet if we are to be agents of the just reign of the coming Spirit, then our thinking and doing will have be both global and local—glocal in all of the complicated aspects of this neologism—attending to both majority and minority voices at work in any context. This may be paralyzing in some cases, but the groans of the Spirit in and through the many voices will not allow us to do nothing.

Our pentecostal-charismatic background and assumptions further push us into this transcultural milieu. The Azusa Street revival itself, as is well known, was led by an African American holiness preacher, William J. Seymour, and its transculturality inspired one onlooker to remark that with the mixing of races and ethnicities at the Los Angeles mission, "the 'color line' was washed away in the blood."[85] Many other scholars have elaborated on the important role of Seymour's African spirituality, mediated through the North American slave experience, in relationship to developments across the global pentecostal movement.[86] The white-Black matrix of North American Pentecostalism provides in turn a crucial lens for focused discussion of multiculturalism in Christian higher education, not least because the same binary cuts through any and all discussions about race and ethnicity in the broader evangelical world that sustains many if not most faith-based universities in this country and continent. We have noted, in particular, how holiness and pentecostal African Americans utilized Ethiopianism to challenge the hegemony of Western civilization and its devaluing of African culture, including a rich Christian heritage (§4.3.d3). If evangelical schools have been and are increasingly challenged by the increasing number of ethnic minority learners and are

---

[83] Many of the trends are documented in James A. Banks and Cherry A. McGee Banks, eds., *Handbook of Research on Multicultural Education*, 2nd ed. (San Francisco: Jossey-Bass, 2004), and these have intensified, not dissipated, in the decade since the publication of this tome; see also George Yancey, *Neither Jew nor Gentile: Exploring Issues of Racial Diversity in Protestant College Campuses* (Oxford: Oxford University Press, 2010).

[84] See the insightful analyses of Christa L. Olson, Rhodri Evans, and Robert F. Shoenberg, *At Home in the World: Bridging the Gap between Internationalization and Multicultural Education* (Washington, DC: American Council on Education, 2007).

[85] Frank Bartleman, as cited in Yong, *The Spirit Poured Out on All Flesh: Pentecostalism and the Possibility of Global Theology* (Grand Rapids: Baker Academic, 2005), 72.

[86] Starting with Walter J. Hollenweger, *Pentecostalism: Origins and Developments Worldwide* (Peabody: Hendrickson, 1997), part 1 on "The Black Oral Root"; cf. also Estrelda Y. Alexander, *Black Fire: One Hundred Years of African American Pentecostalism* (Downers Grove: IVP Academic, 2011), Gastón Espinosa, *William J. Seymour and the Origins of Global Pentecostalism: A Biography and Documentary History* (Durham, N.C.: Duke University Press, 2014), and Amos Yong and Estrelda Y. Alexander, eds., *Afro-Pentecostalism: Black Pentecostal and Charismatic Christianity in History and Culture*, Religion, Race, and Ethnicity (New York: New York University Press, 2011).

now frantically working to diversify their faculties and leadership and to promote the success of learners across the color spectrum,[87] their moral obligations, as we have seen above, are also dictated by the gospel's liberative message for the poor, the oppressed, and dispossessed. Hence, our pneumatic commitments, those informed by the revivalist pentecostal-charismatism of the present time but more importantly those inspired by the day of Pentecost narrative, urge a brief consideration of some African American voices, especially in the higher educational literature.

There is no hope here to be anywhere close to exhaustive on this issue. Our focusing on African American perspectives is not meant to dismiss Latinx or Asian American voices in this space but only to recognize both that one of the three largest Protestant denominations in the United States is the Church of God in Christ and that African American scholars are the ones who, comparatively, have already made substantial contributions to the higher educational endeavor. The literature they have produced is, not surprisingly, as vast as the higher educational challenges faced by African Americans.[88] Our sketch highlights elements of African American pedagogical reflection that interface, however tangentially (as identified by our survey of the research), with our own constructive proposal. Three themes are noteworthy in this regard.

First, just as culture is neither static nor monolithic, the African American experience is also dynamic. Yet such fluidity does not undermine calls for attending to its own cultural rootedness, so that to seek an African American Christian educational vision requires a "triple heritage" that is distinctively African yet also uniquely African American as well as Christian.[89] Within such a framework, then, there are tridimensional hybridic constructions and expressions, in effect a triune conversation between three distinct if malleable communities, each stretching diachronically over time and across many generations also, which somehow nevertheless constitute one community.[90] Simultaneously, cultural rootedness within African traditions underlines the foundational communal commitments within that indigenous matrix,[91] which is carried forward in complicated ways via the Middle Passage and within the North American experience. In other words, the African American contribution emerges in and through its twists and turns, in effect via their various disputations, and not apart from the specificities of constantly negotiated

---

[87] Long ago delineated by Alvaro L. Nieves, "Minorities in Evangelical Higher Education," in Carpenter and Shipps, *Making Higher Education Christian*, 281–93; more recently, Peter Rios, *Untold Stories: The Latinx Leadership Experience in Higher Education* (Eugene: Wipf and Stock, 2021).

[88] A helpful overview is Marybeth Gasman, Valerie Lundy-Wagner, Tafaya Ransom, and Nelson Bowman III, *Unearthing Promise and Potential: Our Nation's Historically Black Colleges and Universities* (San Francisco: Jossey-Bass, 2010).

[89] See Yolanda Y. Smith, *Reclaiming the Spirituals: New Possibilities for African American Christian Education* (Cleveland: Pilgrim, 2004), 17–20.

[90] A number of the chapters in Anne E. Streaty Wimberly and Evelyn L. Parker, eds., *In Search of Wisdom: Faith Formation in the Black Church* (Nashville: Abingdon, 2002), deal with cultural rootedness in all of its complexity and with cross-generational connectedness and formation.

[91] The communal orientation is explicit in both A. Okechukwu Ogbonnaya, *African Ways: A Christian Education Philosophy* (Chicago: Urban Ministries, 2001), and Michael Okoh, *Fostering Christian Faith in Schools and Christian Communities through Igbo Traditional Values: Towards a Holistic Approach to Christian Religious Education and Catechesis in Igboland (Nigeria)*, Tübinger Perspektiven zur Pastoraltheologie und Religionspädagogik 45 (Münster: LIT Verlag, 2012).

commitments within this triadic milieu.[92] The multiplicity and hybridity of such African American identity are consistent with the plurivocality and polyphony of pentecostal spirituality.

Second, despite such communally shaped imaginations, the African American educational journey is yet focused on the liberative formation of individuals. Learners are on a path of self-discovery and development, and education facilitates such meaning-making in relationship to those preceding (ancestors), in dialogue with those around (across the African diaspora), and in anticipation of those who will come later (the sons and daughters of future generations). One educator proposes the practice of story-linking, "a process whereby persons connect components of their everyday life stories with the Christian faith story found in Scripture," and do so via linking also with stories of the slave experience, of ancestors, and contemporary others, including teachers with learners and vice-versa.[93] Such an approach resonates with the way early Christians understood themselves through a narrative identity grounded in the story of God (§2.2.1). Within this explicitly theological frame we can also and then emphasize how individuals develop within communities, many nested within others, any and all then finding their telos in the eschatological community of the people of God. And within this overarching goal, the educational pathway is focused on the cultivation of individual heads-hearts-hands, for all that, in ways the promote well-being, hope, creativity, and wisdom.

What then are the pedagogical means? To be sure, historic African American pedagogies are normed by their cultural analysis, emancipatory historiography, embodied praxis, and liberationist experientialism, among other related approaches.[94] Even more distinctive would be the historic spirituals, not only as repositories of cultural wisdom but yet also with pedagogical potency for sparking a dialogical imagination, of engaging with personal and communal rhythms, of situating personal narratives within wider ritual and liturgical spheres, etc.[95] Earlier African American Holiness-Pentecostals like Sam Cooke, Donny Hathaway, and Marvin Gaye contributed to the formation of blues, jazz, and gospel.[96] A more contemporary application of what might be envisioned as a *spiritualized pedagogy* would be the utilization of hip-hop in the higher educational domain.[97] This genre of music brings together North American cultural styles such as harmony, movement,

---

[92] See Anthony R. Bradley, ed., *Black Scholars in White Space: New Vistas in African American Studies from the Christian Academy* (Eugene: Pickwick, 2015).

[93] Anne Streaty Wimberly, *Soul Stories: African American Christian Education* (Nashville: Abingdon, 1994), 13–14.

[94] Nancy Lynne Westfield, ed., *Being Black, Teaching Black: Politics and Pedagogy in Religious Studies* (Nashville: Abingdon Press, 2008); more theologically oriented is Maxine Howell, "Towards a Womanist Pneumatological Pedagogy: Reading and Re-reading the Bible from British Black Women's Perspectives," *Black Theology: An International Journal* 7.1 (2009): 86–99.

[95] Smith, *Reclaiming the Spirituals*, ch. 6; see also Yolanda Y. Smith, *Women's Spirituality and Education in the Black Church* (New York: Palgrave Macmillan, 2017), and, within a wider context, Elizabeth J. Tisdell, *Exploring Spirituality and Culture in Adult Higher Education* (San Francisco: Jossey-Bass, 2003).

[96] See Louis B. Gallien Jr., "Crossing Over Jordan: Navigating the Music of Heavenly Bliss and Earthly Desire in the Lives and Careers of Three 20th Century African American Holiness-Pentecostal 'Cross-over' Artists," in Yong and Alexander, *Afro-Pentecostalism*, 117–38.

[97] E.g., Emery M. Petchauer, "African American and Hip-Hop Cultural Influences," in *Closing the African American Achievement Gap in Higher Education*, ed. Alfred P. Rovai, Louis B. Gallien Jr., and Helen R. Stiff-Williams (New York: Teachers College Columbia University, 2007), 20–38.

verve, and affect, with African American cultural values such as communalism, expressive individualism, oral traditioning, socially shaped notions of temporality, self-reliance and determination, cooperation, purpose, creativity, faith, respect, honesty, responsibility, hard work, resourcefulness, courage, and integrity. The production and consumption of Black music generate literacy and literate practices, ones that include "a critical 'reading' of the world in search of ideas . . . [and] involves 'workshopping' (in the streets or in the studio) and a constant revision of texts in the studio or via public performances. . . . The reading also includes 'reading' in the sense of critically interpreting media aurally and visually."[98] In short, the important role of music in the African American repertoire can help inform our polyphonal pedagogy, which prioritizes the use of artistic and musical media for the purposes of spiritual, moral, and lifelong formation.

On the one hand, to inquire about African American approaches to higher education is important to comprehend and appreciate the opportunities and challenges confronting the communities that comprise this segment of the population. On the other hand, given the reality of white privilege and normativity in the North American context—which is not meant to homogenize the experiences of all persons of Caucasian descent—and acknowledging that all of us together face a common future,[99] African American and all other historically marginalized perspectives are of broader public concern. Against this long historical backdrop, justice for African Americans is tied in with that of all others, so that the invitation is for "us" and "others," however defined, to reach out and find fresh occasions for bonding across racial and ethnic lines.[100] The point is the welfare of North America as a continent and of the United States as a nation depends on the flourishing of African American culture (in all of its diversity), and this thriving is intertwined with the well-being of all other cultural groups, including with peoples of Caucasian descent. As James Baldwin, who was formed as a teenager in pentecostal churches, pointedly stated, "No one has pointed out yet with any force that if I am not a man here, you are not a man here. You cannot lynch me and keep me in ghettos without becoming something monstrous yourselves."[101] If institutions of higher education have decisive roles to play

---

[98] Ernest Morrell, "Rebel Musics: African Diaspora Popular Culture and Critical Literacy Pedagogies," in *Teach Freedom: Education for Liberation in the African-American Tradition*, ed. Charles M. Payne and Carol Sills Strickland (New York: Teachers College, 2008), 222–34, at 230.

[99] That Irishman John Preston, *Whiteness and Class in Education* (Dordrecht: Springer, 2009), focuses his bisectional (race and class) analysis on the United Kingdom rather than on the United States is even better—especially given his "ultimate aim . . . [to] be part of a project to abolish 'everyday' systems of white supremacy" (24)—as he provides Christian higher educators in North America a less confrontational mirror through which to view and critically assess their own context. Other approaches include responding with gratitude rather than guilt and recognizing white power and its limits, e.g., Sharon D. Welch, "Ceremonies of Gratitude, Awakening, and Accountability: The Theory and Practice of Multicultural Education," in *Disrupting White Supremacy from Within: White People on What We Need to Do*, ed. Jennifer Harvey, Karin A. Case, and Robin Hawley Gorsline (Cleveland: Pilgrim, 2004), 249–80. See also Mary E. Hess and Stephen D. Brookfield, "'How Can White Teachers Recognize and Challenge Racism?' Acknowledging Collusion and Learning an Aggressive Humility," in Hess and Brookfield, *Teaching Reflectively in Theological Contexts*, 190–201.

[100] Developed for theological education but with utmost relevance for Christian higher education is Willie James Jennings, *After Whiteness: An Education in Belonging* (Grand Rapids: Eerdmans, 2020).

[101] James Baldwin, *The Cross of Redemption: Uncollected Writings*, ed. Randall Kenan (New York: Pantheon, 2010), 14.

in fostering these discussions and relationships,[102] Christian universities also have moral and theological obligations along this front. But before outlining our contributions to this juncture, we need to complicate our quest along one more register: that of class.

7.2.3 Rich and Poor: Class Conscientization and Liberation

If justice for anyone of us is interwoven with justice for others, then considerations of male and female and young and old are interlaced with considerations of those who are free and those who are servants. The disciples recognized that Jesus' mission was directed first and foremost to the poor, the captives, and the oppressed (Luke 4:18; above §8.1.1)—in fact, Luke among the evangelists emphasized Jesus' ministry to the poor and said much more than the others about Jesus' teaching regarding wealth and poverty—and thus focused their own energies, full of the power of the Spirit, on the disenfranchised: "All who believed were together and had all things in common; they would sell their possessions and goods and distribute the proceeds to all, as any had need" (Acts 2:44–45; cf. 4:32–34).[103] For Christian higher educators committed to the eschatological teleology of Jesus' message and that of his apostolic followers, this means that questions of gender, race, and ethnicity cannot be disengaged from considerations of class, the basic social, political, and economic structures that determine educational accessibility. Historically, Christians have addressed this issue by voluntary poverty for the sake of those who struggle with involuntary poverty, which we explored in terms of Christian philanthropy (§2.2.3). Fast forward to the present: even if the work of earning advanced degrees catapults graduates from the lower classes, that does not mean that their vocation no longer has anything to do with class stratifications in society.

That early modern pentecostal believers were predominantly, albeit not exclusively, derived from the lower classes, and that such class divisions continue to characterize much of the renewal movement across the majority world in its second century ought to motivate us ethically to address these class dynamics.[104] Pentecostal scholar Cheryl Bridges Johns thus focused her early scholarship on the formative and liberative movements of pentecostal life in dialogue with Brazilian philosopher and educator Paulo Freire (1921–1997).[105] Inspired by the latter's notion of *conscientization* as the growing ability to think critically about self-oppression in relationship to the structures of power and privilege at various levels (locally, nationally, internationally, etc.), Johns pressed deeper into pentecostal spirituality to identify its conscientizing dynamic. Her theological conclusion

---

[102] Annie Howell and Frank Tuitt, eds., *Race and Higher Education: Rethinking Pedagogy in Diverse College Classrooms*, Harvard Educational Review Reprint Series 36 (Cambridge, Mass.: Harvard Educational Publishing Group, 2003), and David Gillborn, *Racism and Education: Coincidence or Conspiracy?* (New York: Routledge, 2008).

[103] See Amos Yong, *Who Is the Holy Spirit? A Walk with the Apostles* (Brewster: Paraclete, 2011), part 3, for bibliographic references to this Lukan theme and also for further discussion of the liberative economics of the apostolic way.

[104] For early Pentecostalism, see Grant Wacker, *Heaven Below: Early Pentecostals and American Culture* (Cambridge, Mass.: Harvard University Press, 2003); for the contemporary world, see, e.g., André Corten, *Pentecostalism in Brazil: Emotion of the Poor and Theological Romanticism* (New York: Macmillan, 1999), and Yong, *In the Days of Caesar*, ch. 7.

[105] Cheryl Bridges Johns, *Pentecostal Formation: A Pedagogy among the Oppressed*, Journal of Pentecostal Theology Supplement Series 2 (Sheffield: Sheffield Academic Press, 1993). Many other religious educators have drawn inspiration from Freire's emancipatory pedagogy, e.g., Daniel S. Schipani, *Religious Education Encounters Liberation Theology* (Birmingham: Religious Education Press, 1988).

was that the Holy Spirit accomplished the mobilization and liberation of believers precisely in and through their scriptural reading and other devotional, catechetical, and spiritual practices. Hence, the spirituality of the marginalized generates their dialogue, is the source of hope, and initiates their strides toward freedom.[106]

As we survey the reception of Freire's work, some of it since Johns' thesis was published, we see various overlaps with our own Pentecost-construct. Operationally, what drives Freirean conscientization is interrogation of the status quo, what he in one place calls a "pedagogy of asking questions."[107] Initially forged in classrooms constituted by students and learners from the slums of Brazil, this questioning that sustains the life of the mind presumes conversation and dialogue across challenging lines. Even if learners are autonomous, curious, conscientious, and critical thinkers capable of diagnosing unjust realities, and from that perspective are motivated to intervene in and repair the world, the heart of the Freirean classroom is mutual, critical, and interactive dialogue that has to involve many voices both inside and outside of the context. In terms of the dominant categories of liberation theology, dialogical engagement directed toward transformative liberation includes the oppressor and the oppressed—realizing here that any one of us is oppressed in some respects and oppressor considered from other perspectives—and that not facilitating, enabling, or allowing for such frank discussion is itself oppressive.[108] Pentecostal polyvocality, we are reminded here, must be all-inclusive, even of contrasting and perhaps oppositional voices. Biblically, it would involve the "enemies" believers are called to love, so how then to ensure the presence of these "others" and the ensuing interactions in the Christian university?

In terms of ethos, what shapes Freirean dialogue are pathic motivations related to love and desire. If for James K. A. Smith (§6.1.1) we worship, desire, and pursue what we love, then for Freire, we teach because we love—love of our craft and love of others—and desire the realization of our learners' full potential. Thus, Freire both proposes a "pedagogy of desire" and insists on "teaching as an act of love."[109] Love connotes, vis-à-vis the Freirean corpus, the "commitment to our [common] humanity."[110] Such an orthopathic pedagogy is orthopraxically correlated with the healing and liberating of ourselves as the human species. We yearn for and work toward "restoring our humanity,"[111] so that our hearts and our hands are always in tandem.

---

[106] See also Mary Beckman, "The Option for the Poor and Community-Based Education," in *The Preferential Option for the Poor beyond Theology*, ed. Daniel G. Groody and Gustavo Gutiérrez (Notre Dame: University of Notre Dame Press, 2014), 183–98, who emphasizes that liberative action emerges from agency *with* not just *for* those who are impoverished, an important reminder about service learning projects.

[107] Paulo Freire and Antonio Faundez, *Learning to Question: A Pedagogy of Liberation*, trans. Tony Coates (New York: Continuum, 1989), 34–43.

[108] Paulo Freire, *Pedagogy of the Oppressed*, trans. Myra Bergman Ramos (New York: Continuum, 1986), chs. 3–4, presents his classic explication of dialogue and anti-dialogical oppression.

[109] Paulo Freire, *Daring to Dream: Toward a Pedagogy of the Unfinished*, trans. Alexandre K. Oliveira, Series in Critical Narrative (Boulder: Paradigm, 2007), 5; and the title of ch. 3 in Antonia Darder, *Reinventing Paolo Freire: A Pedagogy of Love* (Boulder: Westview, 2002).

[110] Darder, *Reinventing Paolo Freire*, 35.

[111] Darder, *Reinventing Paolo Freire*, ch. 2.

Existentially, Freire's dialogical desire is also what his books call a "pedagogy of the unfinished" and a "pedagogy of hope."[112] The horizons here are lit by the vision of the empowerment of human creatures toward freedom.[113] What emerges is a moral telos that rouses the process of conversation and questioning, generates hopes and dreams, and empowers cooperation and agency.[114] In this context, education is always "a political act tied to the ideological forces of the dominant class" in order to ensure that the production of knowledge does not just remain with that class; teachers thereby also work toward a "revolutionary praxis" that is an "alliance of theory and practice."[115] While we never arrive—that is Freire's point about being *unfinished*—that never means we do not make progress. This is not a utopian pedagogy but a realistic one, an educational commitment that resists injustice in solidarity with the oppressed and fights with them for their rights and liberative possibilities.

It is time to identify paths converging into and diverging from the pentecostal out-pouring of the Spirit on all flesh—male and female, Jew and Greek, free and slave (Gal 3:28; cf. Col 3:11)—in relationship to the moral telos of Christian higher education. The charismatic life of the mind is not only animated by the affectivities, dispositions, and aptitudes of Spirit-infused learners (ch. 6) but is also guided, even lured by and toward, the just and shalomic reign inaugurated by the Pentecost-outpouring. And if the coming justice involves the many tongues from many cultures understood intersectionally, as the preceding suggests, then the multiple intelligences of learning will need to be engaged cross- and transculturally also not only because notions of intelligence vary across cultures but also because learning is always culturally situated.[116] As such, the renewal of human minds is coordinated by the reordering of hearts and the reviving of hands as worked out in the real world of inter- and transcultural exchange.

Here a bit more needs to be said about people with disabilities, who are usually poor and among the socio-economic underclass of society. Within our intersectional analysis, consider here not just people of color, but women of color more specifically, and then those with impairments or disabilities as well. Doing justice at this intersectional nexus involved enabling higher educational access at every level,[117] from that of matriculation

---

[112] Freire, *Daring to Dream*; cf. Freire, *Pedagogy of Hope: Reliving Pedagogy of the Oppressed*, trans. Robert R. Barr (New York: Continuum, 1992).

[113] See Paulo Freire, *Pedagogy of Freedom: Ethics, Democracy, and Civic Courage*, trans. Patrick Clarke (1998; repr., Lanham: Rowman and Littlefield, 2001).

[114] See also Andrew Wright, *Spirituality and Education* (New York: Routledge/Falmer, 2000), ch. 12, who weaves these Freirean insights into his own constructive articulation of an educational spirituality.

[115] Darder, *Reinventing Paolo Freire*, 56 and 81.

[116] See Judith E. Lingenfelter and Sherwood G. Lingenfelter, *Teaching Cross-Culturally: An Incarnational Model for Learning and Teaching* (Grand Rapids: Baker Academic, 2003), ch. 5. Richard Edwards and Robin Usher, *Globalisation and Pedagogy: Space, Place and Identity*, 2nd ed. (New York: Routledge, 2008), 157, note that higher education for the present time should develop learners able to negotiate cross-cultural differences, even those pertaining to the level of dialects, and also to adapt in moving between languages, however hybridized they might be; see also the New London Group, *A Pedagogy of Multiliteracies: Designing Social Futures* (Sydney: NLLIA Centre for Workplace Communication and Culture, 1995), 9, from which Edwards and Usher draw.

[117] E.g., Nancy J. Evans, Ellen M. Broido, Kirsten R. Brown, and Autumn K. Wilke, *Disability in Higher Education: A Social Justice Approach* (San Francisco: Jossey-Bass, 2017).

through that of mobility, sensory, or the learning platforms, to that of accommodations for learners with disabilities, etc. Beyond these elements would be not just decolonizing the curriculum from white or Eurocentric normative perspectives but also featuring the voices and experiences of people with disabilities. Last but not least, the teleological call toward justice and the common good involves not just the inclusion of those from every nation, culture, and language, but also the belonging of those with impairments across physical, intellectual, and sensorial dimensions of kinesthetic and mental experience. In short, the liberation of any must involve the liberation of all, not least those who have perennially been characterized as the least among us,[118] and doing so must include overcoming the ableist biases of those who are temporarily able-bodied.

Toward this end, we suggest promotion of the following reparative-healing practices and transsectional dispositions within the higher educational experience. First, we are reminded that the great cloud of witnesses is ever expanding as saints take their seats. If the purpose of Christian education is to give the child to the city of God, then it must recognize the expanding cloud to include those "saints" upon whom the Spirit has been poured out. At minimum, this requires an expansion of the received Western tradition for Christians so that it includes the full panoply of witnesses.[119] Second, listening to and dialoguing with the other across intersectional lines requires academic hospitality, authentic and heartfelt welcome of embodied, cultural, ethnic, and linguistic difference into safe spaces of engagement.[120] These differentiated voices and perspectives are to be treated in ways so that they are made to feel, even as guests, that they belong to the now differently defined "us." This involves embrace of the other as Christ himself urged (Matt 25), even while being open to learning from the other and his or her traditions, even as such a posture recognizes that the Pentecost-outpouring requires that we keep ourselves open to being surprised by the presence and activity of the Spirit in the lives of others.[121] From this, finally, the virtue of empathy can be cultivated, not in order to relativize one's convictions in the conflicted space of multivalent perspectivalism but in order to enable honest engagement with alternative views across intersectional differences.[122] The goal is not to

[118] On this point, see Yong, *The Bible, Disability, and the Church: A New Vision of the People of God* (Grand Rapids: Eerdmans, 2011), esp. 90–104.

[119] E.g., as emerging in the work of Oscar García-Johnson, *Spirit Outside the Gate: Decolonial Pneumatologies of the American Global South* (Downers Grove: IVP Academic, 2019), and Vince L. Bantu, *A Multitude of Peoples: Engaging Ancient Christianity's Global Identity* (Downers Grove: IVP Academic, 2020).

[120] David I. Smith, *On Christian Teaching: Practicing Faith in the Classroom* (Grand Rapids: Eerdmans, 2018), 21–23, attends to the affective dimension of feeling welcomed and accepted that enables attentiveness for the task of learning. See also John B. Bennett, *Academic Life: Hospitality, Ethics, and Spirituality* (Bolton: Anker, 2003); Kathleen T. Talvacchia, *Critical Minds and Discerning Hearts: A Spirituality of Multicultural Teaching* (St. Louis: Chalice, 2003), ch. 5; and Elizabeth Newman, "The Politics of Higher Education: How the Love of Hospitality Offers an Alternative," in Ward and Gushee, *Scholarly Vocation and the Baptist Academy*, 166–96, and "Hospitality and Christian Higher Education," in *Taking Every Thought Captive: Forty Years of the Christian Scholar's Review*, ed. Don W. King (Abilene: Abilene Christian University Press, 2011), 147–63.

[121] Yong, *Hospitality and the Other: Pentecost, Christian Practices, and the Neighbor*, Faith Meets Faith (Maryknoll: Orbis, 2008), 100–107, unfolds the Lukan bases for a pentecostal theology of hospitality within the broader context of interfaith relations, the subject to which we will turn momentarily.

[122] See Naomi Ludeman Smith, "(Re)Considering a Critical Ethnorelative Worldview Goal and Pedagogy for Global and Biblical Demands in Christian Higher Education," *Christian Scholar's Review* 42.4 (2013): 345–73.

diminish Christian commitments but to hold these at our deepest (heart) levels and yet work (with our hands) toward justice across the common good amid the challenges of our pluralistic public square.[123]

7.3   LIFE IN THE SPIRIT: THE WORLD AS LABORATORY

Yet the moral and teleological challenges of intersectionality for Christian higher education are additionally complicated when we consider our public space as constituted also by the plurality of religious traditions. If Christian universities can include as staff and faculty male and female, Jew and Greek, the affluent and those without much social standing, then only with difficulty, if at all, among the student body, certainly not among staff and faculty ranks, will we find the presence of religious others in Christian universities. Even if we were to organize service learning and cross-cultural semesters to engage with religious others, is this "best-we-can-do" effort sufficient to nurture the kinds of hospitable practices and empathetic virtues needed for empowering the work of our hands and participating in the mission of God among those captive within and oppressed by this world's structures? More precisely, can we talk substantively about the competencies required for our contemporary global age, important as such topic is,[124] without addressing directly the opportunities and challenges related to living in a multireligious world?

Whereas some scholars have attempted to develop a trinitarian theological rationale for Christian higher education in a religiously pluralistic world,[125] our own approach to the latter realities so far has been decidedly pneumatological, the conviction being that a robust form of the latter necessarily precedes articulation of a more fully trinitarian construct.[126] Hence, we here develop such a pneumatological approach for the specific purposes of thinking about the Christian university. We lay out the contemporary global religiously pluralistic context (§7.3.1) and then engage in a more extended dialogue with Confucian educational traditions (§7.3.2) in order to exemplify the Spirit-led habits of

---

[123] Because our approach has been fundamentally theological (and pneumatological), we have not developed policies for dealing with historic injustices in Christian higher education. On the one hand, to the degree that, especially in the West, Christian colleges and universities are historically and (remain) predominantly white, to that same degree we need to be reoriented by the multitude of tongues, peoples, and ethnicities that constitute the eschatological people of God; on the other hand, that does not mean that it will be easy to enact equitable policies and practices for whites and peoples of color, whether as a group or as pertinent to individuals. For more on the former, see Yong, "Mission after Colonialism and Whiteness: The Pentecost Witness of the 'Perpetual Foreigner' for the Third Millennium," in *Can "White" People Be Saved? Triangulating Race, Theology, and Mission*, ed. Love L. Sechrest, Johnny Ramírez-Johnson, and Amos Yong, Missiological Engagements (Downers Grove: IVP Academic, 2018), 301–17, and for a good initial discussion of the latter, see Alexander Hill, *Just Business: Christian Ethics for the Marketplace*, 3rd ed. (Downers Grove: IVP, 2018), ch. 13, "Discrimination and Affirmative Action."

[124] E.g., Ashley Shams and Camille George, "Global Competency: An Interdisciplinary Approach," *Academic Exchange* 10.4 (Winter 2006): 249–56; Sohail Inayatullah and Jennifer Gidley, eds., *The University in Transformation: Global Perspectives on the Futures of the University* (London: Bergin and Garvey, 2000); Pankaj Ghemawat, *Redefining Global Strategy: Crossing Borders in a World Where Differences Still Matter* (Boston: Harvard Business School, 2007).

[125] E.g., John M. Hull, *The Holy Trinity and Christian Education in a Pluralist World: The National Society's RE Centre Annual Lecture 1994* (London: National Society for Promoting Religious Education, 1995).

[126] Amos Yong has written many books in this area, including *Hospitality and the Other* and *Beyond the Impasse: Toward a Pneumatological Theology of Religions* (Grand Rapids: Baker Academic, 2003; repr., Eugene: Wipf and Stock, 2014).

thinking, learning, and educating we believe can sustain the quest for Christian citizenship and the common good in a multifaith world (§7.3.3). Any semblance of success in what follows secures the credentials of our proposal for providing normative moral, spiritual, and teleological guidance for Christian higher education that engages the most challenging conditions of our late modern situation, one involving many from other faiths that seek just as well to engage our heads and hearts for their own purposes.

One more comment before proceeding. This section focuses on the public situatedness of Christian higher education, albeit refracted through perspectives informed by our experience of religious plurality. There are other approaches to considerations of this public sphere of Christian teaching and learning whether in terms of contexts of globalization or trajectories of technological advance, and these are deserving of consideration.[127] However, our focus is designed to both address one specific register of Christian higher education's capacity to interface with the public square while also providing resources and examples for how intersection with other dimensions and domains might be enabled.

7.3.1 Competing Paradigms: Teaching and Learning in World Religious Contexts

There are two interrelated spheres of thinking about Christian higher education in a world of many religious traditions: that related to non-Western and predominantly non-Christian contexts and that related to what is happening on the Euro-American scene. With regard to the former, there is no doubt that Western universities will remain at the vanguard of the advance of knowledge, especially with their large scientific infrastructures, and that this advantage, built up over centuries, will continue to both privilege Western learning and attract learners from the majority world. Yet countries like India and China are poised to make substantial leaps with careful and cautious investment in a few areas of relative strength, thus earning them the description as "gigantic peripheries" of and on the knowledge frontier.[128] With the increasing growth and consolidation of higher educational capital not only within these nations but also in other sectors outside the West, Christian colleges and universities in these regions outside the West will be increasingly hard pressed to contend with and against the teaching and study of other-than-Christian cultural, philosophical, and religious systems.[129] Here we are thinking primarily of Hindu traditions in South Asia, the Buddhist, Taoist, and Confucian traditions in East Asia and its diaspora communities, and Islamic traditions across the so-called 10/40 window and the Southeast Asian straits. Yet we should also observe the resurgence of indigenous traditions around the world, even across Pacific Islander communities, and also across the Americas.[130] Higher

---

[127] On the former, see Timothy Reagan, *Non-Western Educational Traditions: Local Approaches to Thought and Practice*, 4th ed. (New York: Routledge, 2018); on the latter, see Joseph E. Aoun, *Robot-Proof: Higher Education in the Age of Artificial Intelligence* (Cambridge, Mass.: MIT Press, 2017).

[128] See Philip G. Altbach, *Comparative Higher Education: Knowledge, the University, and Development* (London: Ablex, 1998), ch. 9. Altbach has been and remains one of the leading scholars of international education.

[129] Theological educators are grappling with this phenomenon also, e.g., Eleazar S. Fernandez, ed., *Teaching for a Multifaith World* (Eugene: Pickwick, 2017).

[130] For instance, on South Pacific indigenous cultures encountering Western learning, see Leonie Rowan, Leo Bartlett, and Terry Evans, eds., *Shifting Borders: Globalisation, Localisation and Open and Distance Education* (Geelong: Deaking University Press, 1997).

educational programs worldwide are increasingly discovering and recovering indigenous cultures and value systems, including their religious heritages.

How have particularly evangelical higher educational projects engaged with this dynamic multireligious reality? A generation ago, those with explicit Christian commitments were motivated missionally and hence strategized their approaches from the perspective of advancing Christian witness.[131] Within this frame of reference, modernist (Orientalist) forms of apologetic stances were adopted toward non-Christian worldviews and ways of life.[132] An increasing number of studies on Christian higher education on the Asian front, however, have begun to recognize the need for more nuanced approaches to the extremely complex issues of having to both empower Christian witness and also educate Christians to be neighbors of and also co-laborers with people of other faiths.[133] Part of the challenge is that evangelicals operate generally with a clear distinction between *cultures*, thought to be neutral carriers of ways of life for people groups, and *religions*, which are to be opposed because their messages are antithetical to the gospel. For those assuming such a binary construct, non-Western cultural forms—for example, poetry, storytelling, proverbs, instrumental music and song, painting-drawing-calligraphy, design and crafts, drama and mime, classical-folk-tribal dance, rod-hand-string puppetry, architecture and sculpture, etc.[134]—can be redeemed so that the church in these contexts can and should embrace indigenous-traditional media in its liturgy, piety (personal and devotional), and expression.[135] But other religious teachings and practices are to be combatted. The question is whether this division is sustainable, and if not, what are the implications for Christian higher education?

In the Euro-American West the emergence of the sacred-secular dichotomy has led broadly in two directions in the higher educational matrix. Within secular universities, the approach has been mainly descriptive, involving the teaching of (but not advocating for) the religions, presumptively locating religious commitments in the private sphere and thereby communicating that there is little work religion can do in the public domain

---

[131] E.g., Rob Evans and Tosh Arai, eds., *The Church and Education in Asia* (Singapore: Christian Conference of Asia, 1980).

[132] W. Shipton, E. Coetzee, and R. Takeuchi, eds., *Worldviews and Christian Education: Appreciating the Cultural Outlook of Asia-Pacific People* (Singapore: Partridge, 2014), represent Adventist evangelical perspectives in Asia, developing apologetic responses to animism, Buddhism, Hinduism, Confucianism, Marxism, Islam, and indigenous practices (local celebrations, rituals, festivals, etc.).

[133] For example, in the editor's concluding chapter in Philip Yuen Sang Leung and Peter Tze Ming Ng, eds., *Christian Responses to Asian Challenges: A Glocalization View on Christian Higher Education in East Asia*, Anthology Series on the Study of Religion and Chinese Society 11 (Hong Kong: Chinese University of Hong Kong, 2007), 534–37, and the four papers and their responses in Track 1 (effectively part 1) of J. Dinakarlal, ed., *Christian Higher Education and Globalization in Asia/Oceania: Realities and Challenges—Proceedings of the Regional Conference of the International Association for the Promotion of Christian Higher Education 3–6 May 2008, Taipei, Taiwan* (Sioux Center: Dordt College Press, 2010).

[134] One scholar announced: "in the beginning there was sculpture"—Lynn Aldrich, "Through Sculpture: What's the Matter with Matter?" in *Beholding the Glory: Incarnation through the Arts*, ed. Jeremy Begbie (Grand Rapids: Baker, 2000), 98–117, at 103—to highlight the practical, performative, and productive potency of what might be called the sculptural imagination.

[135] Represented for instance in Kathleen D. Nicholls, *Asian Arts and Christian Hope* (New Delhi: Select, 1983).

unless it is to help human beings to get along and work together.[136] Such approaches are helpful in urban contexts that are pluralistically constituted so that citizens might become more knowledgeable about those of other traditions in order to better coexist, if not also work cooperatively toward flourishing communities. In the United States such an approach is standard in publicly funded universities, assuming that the state is not supposed to promote any one religion, much less over others.[137]

But within Christian institutions in the Western world, religious commitments are underscored so that it is at least part, if not primarily so, their aim to shape learners according to the faith. If Christian colleges and universities were to heed parental desires, they might adopt a more protective stance in order to better ensure conformity of learners with the views and values of the older generation that might be flipping part or much of the bill. But if the goal is to better equip learners to navigate the globalizing pluralism of late modernity, then the task becomes more complicated: nurturing minds and hearts in the faith in ways that they can be effective hands in a world of many cultures, faiths, and ways of life.[138] Yet the question is, how far can this take us when those in other faiths are outside the educational community, considered more as objects to be studied and understood from a distance than subjects to be interacted with?

Our own approach has been to develop a theological rationale for a Christian commitment that yet sustains an authentically dialogical approach to other faiths. We recall (§2.2.2) that the threefold teaching of the Word in the patristic witness involved the presence of the Word in the structures of human rationality by virtue of the image of God. To this we might emphasize the prevenient activity of the Spirit in the heart. Humanity is already Christ-patterned and Spirit-infused, not in the salvific sense, but in the creational sense due to the christological structure of the image and the pneumatological presence of love in the image. Augustine's depiction of humanity as fundamentally restless springs from these two dimensions. The pneumatological approach we have adopted is therefore not focused primarily on traditional evangelical concerns about the salvation of people in other faiths (which drive questions about whether religious others can be saved apart from knowing Christ).[139] Rather, our proposal proceeds along such explicitly theological lines, defining the Spirit in relationship both to Jesus Christ, thus preserving Christian specificity, and also

---

[136] E.g., Hans-Günter Heimbrock, Christoph Scheilke, and Peter Schreiner, eds., *Towards Religious Competence: Diversity as a Challenge for Education in Europe*, Schriften aus dem Comenius-Institut 3 (Münster: LIT, 2001); Gert Rüppell and Peter Schreiner, eds., *Shared Learning in a Plural World: Ecumenical Approaches to Inter-religious Education*, Schriften aus dem Comenius-Institut 8 (Münster: LIT, 2003); Farideh Salili and Rumjahn Hoosain, eds., *Religion in Multicultural Education* (Greenwich: Information Age, 2006); and Heid Leganger-Krogstad, *The Religious Dimension of Intercultural Education: Contributions to a Contextual Understanding*, International Practical Theology 14 (Münster: LIT, 2011).

[137] See here the influential text Judith A. Berling, *Understanding Other Religious Worlds: A Guide for Interreligious Education* (New York: Orbis, 2004); cf. Kevin Hovland, *Shared Future: Global Learning and Liberal Education* (Washington, DC: Association of American Colleges and Universities, 2006).

[138] See the proposal in, for instance, Jeannette L. Hsieh, Louis B. Gallien Jr. and Jillian N. Lederhouse, "Addressing Cultural Pluralism from an Evangelical Christian Perspective," *ICCTE Journal* 9.1 (2014), https://digitalcommons.georgefox.edu/icctej/vol9/iss1/.

[139] See further discussion in Amos Yong, "The Spirit, Christian Practices, and the Religions: Theology of Religions in Pentecostal and Pneumatological Perspective," *Asbury Journal* 62.2 (2007): 5–31, and "Toward a Trinitarian Theology of Religions: A Pentecostal-Evangelical and Missiological Elaboration," *International Bulletin of Mission Research* 40.4 (2016): 294–306.

to the God of Israel, who formed living human beings via the dust of the ground and the divine breath (*ruach*).[140] This means that our thinking about the religions can proceed at multiple theological levels simultaneously, vis-à-vis the doctrine of creation and theological anthropology on the one side and in relationship to the specificities of Christian incarnational and pentecostal faith on the other side.

Further, however, our pneumatological theology invites consideration of the many tongues of Pentecost as opening up to many ethnic groups but then presses more deeply into the cultural and anthropological to identify also the political, economic, social, and even religious spheres intertwined.[141] Read pentecostally, then, the redemptive potency of the outpoured Spirit on all flesh means that we should be attentive to the voices of those in other faiths as well, to discern if and how they might also be declaring "God's deeds of power" (Acts 2:11b). More pointedly, those who claim to be filled with the Spirit—Christian believers, put straightforwardly—ought to be the first ones to bear witness to others in ways that attend to the testimonies of others. Such a pneumatological approach is perhaps less a theology of religions than it is a theology of interfaith dialogue, encounter, and relations that thus invites receiving from others even as it empowers discerning interaction and witness in turn.[142]

Previously in this chapter, we considered the intersectionality of the voices of male and female, Jew and Greek, and rich and poor, and our approach was to think with and through such voices in a critical, faithful, but yet dialogical manner. Feminist, or African American, or liberationist modes of reflection mentioned above were not enemies to be expelled but resources to draw into our repertoire. Similarly, our goal is to think with and through religious others for the sake of the moral and spiritual telos of the Christian university. This means not necessarily uncritical acceptance of other faiths, but actual engagement—to the degree possible for those located mostly outside of the university orbit—with what they have to offer with regard to matters of public interest, the common good, and our terrestrial environment. In the next few pages, we propose such a thought experiment with the Confucian tradition.[143] If successful, this will not minimize its being a contrasting option within the space of global higher education, but Christian universities then will be postured a bit differently in relationship to such competing paradigms.

7.3.2 East Meets West: A Christian-Confucian Conversation on Higher Education

We must be realistic first about what we can and cannot achieve in this short space. First, there is in a sense no warrant for such a tangential foray into a tradition of teaching and learning that is as rich as Confucianism, not least because our generalizations are hopelessly incapable of communicating the internal debates and dynamics that constitute its

---

[140] Details provided in Yong, *Spirit of Love*, ch. 9; also Yong, *Dialogical Spirit*, 281–90.

[141] Fleshed out in Yong, *Spirit Poured Out on All Flesh*, chs. 4–5.

[142] Such a relational missiology toward religious others is developed in Amos Yong, *The Missiological Spirit: Christian Mission Theology for the Third Millennium Global Context* (Eugene: Cascade, 2014).

[143] The following takes off from extensive work that Yong has done with Buddhist traditions—e.g., his *Pneumatology and the Christian-Buddhist Dialogue: Does the Spirit Blow through the Middle Way?* Studies in Systematic Theology 11 (Leiden: Brill, 2012), and *The Cosmic Breath: Spirit and Nature in the Christianity-Buddhism-Science Trialogue*, Philosophical Studies in Science and Religion 4 (Leiden: Brill, 2012)—thinking with and through Buddhist interlocutors toward moral-ethical ends related to the common good.

legacy to the global community;[144] our only excuse is that to not even attempt will leave us doubly culpable, both in that we will have failed to even chart possible ways forward for a Pentecost-vision of higher education that has the ends of the earth in its sights and because our conviction about learning through encounter with otherness receives one of its most stringent tests in the faces of religious others on the global stage. Second, however, we cannot even begin to justify engaging Confucianism in this section on religious otherness against the claims that it is better understood as a moral or humanistic tradition; we can only rely on the arguments of others and will introduce in what follows only very preliminary considerations about the spirituality that drives Confucian self-cultivation.[145] Last but not least, the patriarchalism and elitism of the Confucian tradition are well known, and to that we might also add the muted sense of transcendence—the practical loss of heaven prevalent in the earliest texts, one might say—at least in contemporary iterations in global context; readers who have stayed with us until now realize that no tradition, even that going by the name "Christian," is flawless.[146] Our task at present surely cannot be redemptive of whatever Confucianism might have to offer in any comprehensive sense. Yet we can be suggestive, from our own pentecostal-charismatic site and location, of how even Confucian educational sensibilities can facilitate charismatic encounter toward moral and spiritual (trans)formation, precisely the task of this book. To engage in this task is to follow the patristic, medieval, and Renaissance engagement with Hellenism in forming its theological articulation of a Christian *paideia* (compare §2.1 with 2.2 and 2.3).

We therefore pick up *in medias res*, starting with a putatively ancient text, *Da Xue* (or *Great Learning*), albeit one that was seemingly rescued from oblivion by the Song Dynasty (960–1279) scholar Zhu Xi (1130–1200).[147] Identified as a program for moral and social development, it begins thus:

> The ancients who wished to manifest their clear character to the world would first bring order to their states. Those who wished to bring order to their states would first regulate their families. Those who wished to regulate their families would first cultivate their personal lives. Those who wished to cultivate their personal lives would first

[144] We have learned a great deal from both Frank M. Flanagan, *Confucius, the Analects and Western Education* (London: Continuum, 2011), and Barry C. Keenan, *Neo-Confucian Self-Cultivation*, Dimensions of Asian Spirituality (Honolulu: University of Hawai'i Press, 2011), about the twists and turns of Confucian education preceding twentieth-century developments. A helpful summary article is Wm. Theodore de Bary, "Confucian Education in Premodern East Asia," in *Confucian Traditions in East Asian Modernity: Moral Education and Economic Culture in Japan and the Four Mini-Dragons*, ed. Tu Wei-ming (Cambridge, Mass.: Harvard University Press, 1996), 21–37.

[145] Rodney L. Taylor, *The Religious Dimensions of Confucianism* (Albany: State University of New York Press, 1990), is as good a place to start as any other for those interested in the debate.

[146] Yong provides an initial response to the patriarchy of Confucian traditions—see his "Yin-Yang and the Spirit Poured Out on All Flesh"—even as our Pentecost-imagination broadly overcomes the binary between immanence and transcendence.

[147] The following summarizes and extends for our present purposes a previously elaborated evangelical-Confucian convergent exploration in Yong, "Evangelical *Paideia* Overlooking the Pacific Rim: On the Opportunities and Challenges of Globalization for Christian Higher Education," *Christian Scholar's Review* 42.4 (2013): 393–409, esp. 397–406; see also the pedagogical encounter with Confucianism recounted by Dale M. Coulter, "Anselm, Justice, and the Chinese," *First Things*, June 24, 2014, https://www.firstthings.com/blogs/firstthoughts/2014/06/anselm-justice-and-the-chinese.

rectify their minds. Those who wished to rectify their minds would first make their wills sincere. Those who wished to make their wills sincere would first extend their knowledge. The extension of knowledge consists in the investigation of things. When things are investigated, knowledge is extended; when knowledge is extended, the will becomes sincere; when the will is sincere, the mind is rectified; when the mind is rectified, the personal life is cultivated; when the personal life is cultivated, the family will be regulated; when the family is regulated, the state will be in order; when the state is in order, there will be peace throughout the world.[148]

There is much to unpack here that we will not be able to get to, including the long-running debate about which comes first: the nurturing of the inner human nature or getting social relations in order.[149] Yet even this debate highlights what is important for us: the interrelationship between the cultivation of the self and social and cosmic harmony.

Such harmonization involves both diachronic and synchronic dimensions. The latter is obvious in the text—rightly ordered selves presume a rightly ordered cosmos, and vice-versa—yet the former is implicit: that the rectification sought by the mind involves the extension of knowledge and this includes reaching back and bringing the past into the present. Master Kong himself linked learning from the ancients with thinking for the self in this way: "If one learns from others but does not think, one will be bewildered. If, on the other hand, one thinks but does not learn from others, one will be in peril" (*Analects* 2.14); and "There are presumably men who innovate without possessing knowledge, but that is not a fault I have. I use my ears widely and follow what is good in what I have heard" (*Analects* 7.89).[150] Hence, the right ordering of the self and of all things involves learning—through reading, hearing and imbibing, multiaptitudinal practices, we might note—from the wisdom of those preceding. This is not to kowtow unthinkingly to the tradition, but it is to be resourced by the wisdom of the elders.[151]

Such harmonization of past and present was part of the ritual process to humaneness and the peace of the world. When Westerners think about ritual, we get stuck in repetitive ceremonialism and mechanical formalism. Confucian ritual, however, refers to the cultivated aptitudes and dispositions that facilitate appropriate yet improvisational interactions with others and with the ten thousand things of the world.[152] Learning to be human is understood "as a process of ritualisation, which involves submitting to routine exercises, deferring to experienced elders, emulating

---

[148] From "The *Great Learning*," in *A Sourcebook in Chinese Philosophy*, ed. Wing-tsit Chan (Princeton: Princeton University Press, 1963), 84–94, at 86–87.

[149] One way this story is told can be found in Philip J. Ivanhoe, *Confucian Moral Self Cultivation*, 2nd ed. (Indianapolis: Hackett, 2000); another is Keenan, *Neo-Confucian Self-Cultivation*.

[150] Confucius, *The Analects (Lun yü)*, trans. D. C. Lau (New York: Penguin, 1979), 65 and 89 respectively.

[151] This is consistent with the classical medievalists who thought about creativity in terms of expanding the imagination in part through memory and memory devices. Innovation and novelty, then, are not discontinuous with the past but involved the redemption of the creational good, a refurbishing and restoring of what has been decimated by the fall. See our discussion of the Victorines (§2.2.2) and reference to the use of invention à la Mary Carruthers, *The Craft of Thought: Meditation, Rhetoric, and the Making of Images, 400–1200* (Cambridge: Cambridge University Press, 1998).

[152] For a robust cross-cultural consideration, see Robert Cummings Neville, *Ritual and Deference: Extending Chinese Philosophy in a Comparative Context* (Albany: State University of New York Press, 2008); cf. also Flanagan, *Confucius, the Analects and Western Education*, ch. 6.

well-established models, and discovering the most appropriate way of interacting with other human beings."[153] Far from being mindless, ritualized behavior is most potent when consciously refined and affectively attuned. In fact, the latter went together so that substantive intellectual engagement is best nurtured within contexts of interpersonal relations marked by "strong affective ties between the participants."[154] More philosophically put: "Since the universe consists of vital forces (or *ch'i* . . . as energy fields) rather than static matter, it never ceases to be transformative. . . . Self-cultivation . . . involves a conscientious attempt to open oneself up to the universe as a whole by extending one's horizon *of feeling* as well as knowing."[155] Ritual thus harmonizes people—filially, communally, societally, and politically—even as ritual propriety achieves coordination of the moral, intellectual, and affective dimensions of individual persons. Perhaps there is some value to understanding Confucian ritual to function similarly to Christian liturgy (discussed above: §6.1.1): the former nurtures selves in relationship to others even as the latter turns worshippers' hearts to God (firstly) and neighbors (secondarily).

The ritual character of Confucian harmonization can also be appreciated by some brief comments on the educative role of music. Our proposal earlier (§6.2.1) was long ago anticipated by Master Kong, who urged: "Be stimulated by the *Odes*, take your stand on the rites and be perfected by music" (*Analects* 8.8).[156] Music's teleological powers are activated not only interpersonally but also socially: "When the Way prevails in the Empire, the rites and music and punitive expeditions are initiated by the Emperor" (*Analects* 16.2).[157] Thus, music binds the soul and society together. It and the other arts of archery, charioteering, and calligraphy are "ways of cultivating the body" and of rightly positioning the self to the world and vice-versa.[158] Artistic, and musical, cultivation is thereby a discipline of learning in its own right, not a discipline in the sense of an academic field of inquiry.

Our goal in this exercise is neither to contrast Confucian learning with Christian education in any rigid manner nor to suggest any kind of convergence that denies their differences. If there is some benefit to identifying how difficult cultural mentalities operate in order to better appreciate human similarities across differences and vice-versa,[159] our strategic approach (developed above in dialogue with feminist and African American thinkers) discourages reifying Eastern and Western cultural mindsets even as it recommends that we explore fruitful modes of engaging the particular witnesses

---

[153] Tu Wei-ming, *Way, Learning, and Politics: Essays on the Confucian Intellectual* (Albany: State University of New York Press, 1993), 6–7.

[154] Daniel A. Bell, *China's New Confucianism: Politics and Everyday Life in a Changing Society* (Princeton: Princeton University Press, 2008), 111; this claim occurs amid Bell's discussion in ch. 7 of "A Critique of Critical Thinking."

[155] Tu, *Way, Learning, and Politics*, 53 (emphasis added). We note also that while Confucian self-cultivation is distinct from the German *Bildung* (see §3.1.2 above), we would need to write another book on comparative philosophy in order to tease out the convergences and divergences.

[156] Confucius, *Analects*, 93.

[157] Confucius, *Analects*, 139; also *Analects* 13.3.

[158] Tu, *Way, Learning, and Politics*, 33.

[159] For instance: Donald Cyr, *The Art of Global Thinking: Integrating Organizational Philosophies of East and West* (West Lafayette, Ind.: Purdue University Press, 2002), and Richard E. Nisbett, *The Geography of Thought: How Asians and Westerners Think Differently . . . and Why* (New York: Free Press, 2003).

of other traditions within the contemporary Christian university. As the Confucian tradition is now going global—there being a Boston Confucianism now, for instance[160]—then Christian higher education in the present time has to engage, rather than ignore, what this tradition, among others, offers. And if it is indeed the case, as forecasters across the disciplines are seeing, that the rest of this century will continue to see the ascension of the Chinese in East Asia and across its diasporic spread as technological, economic, and even educational leaders rivaling Europe and North America, then Christian higher education will increasingly include those who embody the Confucian worldview, so that they would be less easily ignored. Hence, this is less a matter of Christian-Confucian competition than of transcultural understanding and, as appropriate, mutual transformation.

Further, and more important for this case study, the globalization of other faiths is also prompting, gradually, the phenomenon of multiple religious belonging so that we may see more of the next generation of self-identified Christians (even in the evangelical world) who embrace aspects of other religious beliefs and/or practices, and in that case, the "presence" of other faiths on Christian university campuses might become more palpable.[161] Hence, our eastward excursion has introduced us to another dynamic and living way of "learning to be human" that involves "becoming aesthetically refined, morally excellent, and religiously profound."[162] If education since time immemorial sought somehow to form persons for the wider good,[163] then can we make common cause with our interlocutors from other traditions, despite our differences?

[160] Robert Cummings Neville, *Boston Confucianism: Portable Tradition in the Late Modern World* (Albany: State University of New York Press, 2000); see also Amos Yong, *The Future of Evangelical Theology: Soundings from the Asian American Diaspora* (Downers Grove: IVP Academic, 2014), ch. 3, for a brief discussion of this Bostonian version.

[161] See for instance Biola University philosopher Gregg A. Ten Elshof, *Confucius for Christians: What an Ancient Chinese Worldview Can Teach Us about Life in Christ* (Grand Rapids: Eerdmans, 2015). The implications of multiple or dual religious belonging for Christian higher education will need to be explored going forward; the closest discussion we could find is by a Roman Catholic theologian vis-à-vis the realm of theological education (seminaries and divinity schools): Peter C. Phan, *Being Religious Interreligiously: Asian Perspectives on Interfaith Dialogue* (Maryknoll: Orbis, 2004), ch. 4.

[162] Tu Wei-ming, *Confucian Thought: Selfhood as Creative Transformation* (Albany: State University of New York Press, 1985), 52.

[163] Nussbaum, *Cultivating Humanity*, 294, for instance, writes about the telos of education in the United States in terms of the common good and global citizenship:

> Our country has embarked on an unparalleled experiment, inspired by these ideals of self-command and cultivated humanity. Unlike all other nations, we ask a higher education to contribute a general preparation for citizenship, not just a specialized preparation for a career. To a greater degree than all other nations, we have tried to extend the benefits of this education to all citizens, whatever their class, race, sex, ethnicity, or religion. We hope to draw citizens toward one another by complex mutual understanding and individual self-scrutiny, building a democratic culture that is truly deliberative and reflective, rather than simply the collision of unexamined preferences. And we hope in this way to justify and perpetuate our nation's claim to be a valuable member of a world community of nations that must increasingly learn how to understand, respect, and communicate, if our common human problems are to be constructively addressed.

Our Confucian friends will smile at the American-centric exclusivism of this passage, but our point is that we are after all engaged in one common, global cause, and hence need one another on this planetary undertaking.

7.3.3 From Every Tongue, Tribe, and Nation: Christian Pluralism for World Citizenship

We have covered much ground in this chapter attempting to develop a higher educational theology of the hands, so to speak, one that empowers Christian learners to a moral and ethical difference in an unjust world. Our own Pentecost-approach includes both a promise and a challenge: that the Spirit's outpouring on all flesh—on male and female, across class stratifications, from "every tribe and language and people and nation" (Rev 5:9; also 7:9, 14:6)—thereby anticipates divine justice to reach to the ends of the earth (Acts 1:8); but that this means the work of the Christian university will inevitably have to engage with the difficult tasks of relating to strangers and aliens who speak other languages, are colored by other ethnicities, derive from other cultures, adhere to other faiths, and derive from socio-economic and political realities drastically divergent from our own. How, then, can a commitment to the many tongues heralding the divine reign empower learners in these directions without lapsing into an uncritical relativism? This is a particularly worrisome issue when considering intersectional voices further complicated by the plurality of other foundational religious commitments, especially when the vulnerable lives of our youth are felt to be at stake.

Our response here will address the multifaith realities that have been the focus of our attention in this final section, although extrapolations will be possible toward the intersectional concerns in the preceding one, even in some instances explicitly indicated. The overall strategy will be to suggest that the move to transsectionality briefly introduced above can inform our interventions in this arena also. Just as our Pentecost-transsectionality not just allows but requires that the many intersectional voices first be heard on their own terms, so too can our Pentecost-pluralism attend to the witness of those in other faiths first, before passing discerning judgment. The fact of *multireligious* reality requires ongoing *interreligious* engagement and dialogue that our Pentecost-pluralism funds, albeit directed morally, ethically, and in effect *transreligiously*—here again echoing the strategy delineated in this book (e.g., §5.2)—in light of the coming rule of God.[164] Such a pentecostally pluralistic transreligious trajectory can be briefly unpacked in terms of teaching, practices, and engagements.[165]

Christian higher education must teach about other faiths but cannot and should not be expected to do so except from out of considerations of and dialogue with their own theological commitments. The point about having Christian universities to begin with is to promote faith-seeking-understanding, and in this context it involves both authentic integrity and deep pluralism. So, on the one hand, this urges that the Christian university's

---

[164] Richard J. Mouw and Sander Griffioen, *Pluralisms and Horizons: An Essay in Christian Public Philosophy* (Grand Rapids: Eerdmans, 1993), use different categories in their very insightful discussion, but our Pentecost-pluralism here is consistent with their overarching argument, which recognizes that pluralism exists as a fact and that there are all kinds of ways, *associational* and *contextual*, in which such pluralisms play out in history and society, but that Christians cannot advocate any form of pluralistic commitment that includes contrasting normative commitments without lapsing into relativism.

[165] More practically oriented are Marion H. Larson and Sara L. H. Shady, *From Bubble to Bridge: Educating Christians for a Multifaith World* (Downers Grove: IVP Academic, 2017), esp. chs. 6–8, who provide very concrete practices for Christian higher educational classrooms with regard to interfaith contexts.

greatest contribution to pluralism and to a pluralistic society be different, and this happens by it being its Christian self.[166] If nothing else, the Christian university should clearly show that there are many *different* religious traditions, and Christianity is unique among the others, as each of them also are unique among the others. Yet, on the other hand, to affirm the rights and obligations of Christians to nurture such commitments for the wider conversation assumes also that other religious traditions not only have such rights—and opportunities—but are also able to shape their learners for public and interfaith interaction from their own normative perspectives.[167] The point is neither to revise core teaching nor to relativize our beliefs, but to know how to civilly engage with others and even work with others, even in some respects on their own terms, for the common good.[168] Simultaneously, as committed also to discovering and declaring truth—not to mention being led by the Spirit of truth (recall §5.1.2)—we must know what others believe about such fundamentally important matters, even engage with them and their rationales for their sake and also for our own.[169]

Yet living faith is not just about intellectual beliefs (this entire project resists such reductionism) but also about commitments and practices (hearts and hands). We know already that deep Christian formation requires affective practices, and it is from this posture that our earlier protagonist, James K. A. Smith (§6.1.1), also urges that authentic Christian engagement in and with a pluralistic world involve similarly appropriate formational practices.[170] So Christian higher education cannot just treat other religions as systems of ideas but has to engage them in practice. Evangelical colleges and universities will be drawn magnetically toward missionizing initiatives directed toward proselytism of others or, less aggressively, service-learning opportunities to bear perhaps less intrusive witness. Although in principle participation in such activities should be coordinated with local congregations and parishes, we are thinking also about other practices not just *at* but *with* those in other faiths motivated by work toward the common good. How, for instance, might people across religious traditions participate in collective action from protests, boycotts, and strikes on the one side to collaborative business, civic, and organizational endeavors on the other in the outworking of their ethical and religious

---

[166] See the seventh thesis of Richard John Neuhaus, "The Christian University: Eleven Theses," *First Things* (January 1996): 20–22.

[167] We need, as Elmer John Thiessen, *Teaching for Commitment: Liberal Education, Indoctrination, and Christian Nurture* (Montreal: McGill-Queen's University Press, 1993), 273–75, argues, an "educational pluralism" so that civil society will be enriched by multiple religious traditions; see also Thiessen's follow-up apologia for this: *In Defense of Religious Schools and Colleges* (Montreal: McGill-Queen's University Press, 2001).

[168] David F. Ford, *Shaping Theology: Engagements in a Religious and Secular World* (Malden: Blackwell, 2007), part 2, explores such interfaith engagement that interacts with the other from out of commitment rather than by avoiding differences.

[169] See Andrew Wright, *Critical Religious Education, Multiculturalism and the Pursuit of Truth* (Cardiff: University of Wales Press, 2007).

[170] See James K. A. Smith, "Reforming Public Theology: Neocalvinism and Pluralism," Herman Bavinck Lecture, Theological University Kampen, June 27, 2016; a revised and expanded version is in Smith, *Awaiting the King: Reforming Public Theology* (Grand Rapids: Brazos, 2017), ch. 4.

commitments to social and political transformation?[171] Our argument is that only a pentecostally empowered set of dispositions, aptitudes, and virtues can propel those in Christian colleges and universities out of their comfort zone far enough to forge common practices with adherents and devotees of other religions.

The most challenging of interfaith practices are certainly those normally conducted in their sacred spaces. Christians usually have no qualms about inviting nonbelievers into their houses of worship to at least observe the experience; what is to inhibit the former from entering such sites at the invitation of their friends of those in other faiths? Perhaps little, although, again, if Christians feel that their faith cannot be engaged only cerebrally but must involve in those curious an affective and empathetic willingness to "taste and see that the Lord is good" (Ps 34:8), should Jesus' followers also open up not just their minds but perhaps also their hearts in approaching experiences dear to others? We urge that although there is always a risk involved in learning—in this respect, learning about and with other faiths is no less subversive!—Christian educators need to develop multileveled pathways for engaging, crossing over, and even entering into other religious ways, albeit always anticipating return.[172] Learning that is only thought and never felt is not yet deeply traversed, and thereby the possibilities for transformation remain on the surface. Perhaps paradoxically, the surest antidote to epistemic and moral relativism is the imaginative empathy that comes with experiencing life alongside and with others.[173] Such interpersonal encounter not only allows us to walk in the shoes of others, so to speak, but enables educated persons a kind of multiple perspectival "epistemic switching" in their work (teaching, learning, researching) and lives,[174] similar to how simulated learning in virtual worlds expands our capacity to negotiate newly encountered realities. Such educational pathways develop a "compassionate imagination" that feels more personally the plight of others and thereby can envision better reparative (moral, social, or political) action.[175]

The preceding Confucian-Christian thought experiment, while remaining at the level of theory, is an invitation also to educational practice, inviting consideration of East Asian practices ordered toward the cultivation of persons nested within ever wider ritual (liturgical!) domains—of family, community, nation, cosmos, etc.—honed over millennia. Such a proposal, we recommend, is nevertheless thoroughly theological, more precisely pneumatological, as we have constructed it from the day of Pentecost

---

[171] See here the discussion of John D. Inazu, *Confident Pluralism: Surviving and Thriving through Deep Difference* (Chicago: University of Chicago Press, 2016), ch. 7.

[172] See Yong, "Francis X Clooney's 'Dual Religious Belonging' and the Comparative Theological Enterprise: Engaging Hindu Traditions," *Dharma Deepika: A South Asian Journal of Missiological Research* 16.1 (2012): 6–26, reprinted in Yong's *Dialogical Spirit*, ch. 10; cf. also idem, "Studying-Teaching-Evaluating Religions: A Comparative Theological Perspective," *Interreligious Studies and Intercultural Theology* 4.2 (2020): 155–75.

[173] As argued by Michael Ernest Sweet, "The Social Justice Imagination: A Better World as Possibility," in *Education Landscapes in the 21st Century: Cross-Cultural Challenges and Multi-Disciplinary Perspectives*, ed. Iris Guske and Bruce C. Swaffield (Newcastle: Cambridge Scholars, 2008), 375–84.

[174] See Lee S. Shulman, "The Challenges and Opportunities for Liberal Education in a Faith-Based University," in *A Higher Education: Baylor and the Vocation of a Christian University*, ed. Elizabeth Davis (Waco: Baylor University Press, 2012), 75–94, at 84.

[175] Nussbaum, *Cultivating Humanity*, 93.

outpouring of the Spirit. Herein is a mode of existing—and practicing!—in but yet not merely being of the world, a way of life and learning that hearkens to the voices of others and yet seeks, with them whenever possible, to embody redemptive practices directed toward the coming divine reign. The way forward is through shared practice—surely practice informed by theory (theology) and vice-versa—and this applies whether we are charting our future with those in other faiths or others with different identity (gender, race, ethnicity, class, etc.) backgrounds and perspectives. Whatever might be discerned to be of value in the witness—beliefs and practices—of others can inform feeling, knowing, and doing in the Spirit.

Our Pentecost-pluralism is principled, like that behind proposals inspired by the political achievements of Abraham Kuyper in leading the Dutch Reformed Church's operating within the Netherlands as a pluralistic and secular state at the turn of the twentieth century (remember above, §7.1.3). Such *principled pluralism* recognizes the diversity of religious and otherwise informed value systems but urges the development of appropriate political structures and civic practices that allow for such reasons to be registered and argued about in the public square.[176] Bluntly put: "Christians must be serious about pluralism," and so rather than being "a grudging pluralist, who settles for a weak voice since Christians can no longer control the culture . . . , the Christian is a principled pluralist."[177] Yet it is also imperative to insist that such a relational pluralism "is not relativism";[178] instead, it is a guarantee that relativism does not ensue precisely through invigorating the discussion in the public square with the many voices that have long sounded but been privatized by modern secularism, yet without escalating the culture wars.[179] Our Pentecost-pluralism thus thrusts the Christian university forward into a pluralistic world, enabling normative focus on the imminent and immanent justice of the coming rule while also inviting openness to and translation of the many intersectional and interreligious witnesses deriving from multiple directions.

Reformed philosopher Nicholas Wolterstorff, whom we met earlier in this chapter, has long argued also that public universities need to be constituted by multiple faith faculties, and that this thus requires a "responsible pluralism."[180] Christian universities operating in our charismatic and pneumatological mode will ensure that we develop future generations of faculty who are capable of existing and flourishing in such responsibly pluralist environments. Ours can be a religiously and theologically undergirded adherence to the imminent divine rule that attends to and even appropriates wherever

---

[176] Stephen V. Monsma and J. Christopher Soper, *The Challenge of Pluralism: Church and State in Five Democracies* (Lanham: Rowman and Littlefield, 2009), ch. 3, discuss Kuyper's *principled pluralism*.

[177] C. Stephen Evans, "The Calling of the Christian Scholar-Teacher," in Henry and Agee, *Faithful Learning*, 26–49, at 46.

[178] The argument here is unfolded best in James W. Skillen, *Recharging the American Experiment: Principled Pluralism for Genuine Civic Community* (Grand Rapids: Baker, 1994), 99–101.

[179] A Jesuit version, similar but not identical, is "centered pluralism"; see Bruce Douglass, "Centered Pluralism: A Report of a Faculty Seminar on the Jesuit and Catholic Identity of Georgetown University," in *Enhancing Religious Identity: Best Practices from Catholic Campuses*, ed. John R. Wilcox and Irene King (Washington, DC: Georgetown University Press, 2000), 69–90.

[180] A philosopher in the Reformed tradition, Nicholas Wolterstorff, "Public Theology or Christian Learning?" in Volf, *Passion for God's Reign*, 65–87, at 86.

possible the many voices in the "glocal" cosmopolis but yet is also committed to a global citizenship of witnessing to—with heads, hearts, and hands—the gospel of Jesus Christ for the sake of the common good.

8

Conclusion

The Spirit Says Come! Renewing the Christian University

We have in this book traveled far (over two thousand years) and wide (over the contemporary global Christian higher educational landscape). Our concluding remarks must be brief. We will summarily outline our argument, briefly address Christian higher administrators, and quickly sketch our hopes for this work.

8.1 CHARISMATIC VIRTUES FOR THE CHRISTIAN UNIVERSITY: A REVIEW

This book attempts what we might call a pentecostal intervention in the theology and philosophy of Christian higher education, especially but not only in evangelical circles. Our working premise is that if God is already to be found in the postmodern university and Christ-centeredness is presumed in evangelical schools—for instance among those related to the Council of Christian Colleges and Universities—then how might we discern and understand the role and work of the Holy Spirit in these arenas? While seeking to develop a constructive theological response, we also rooted our efforts in the history of Christian education. By placing our pneumatological intervention into a trinitarian framework, we have attempted to reframe the purpose of the Christian university as Christ-patterned and Spirit-infused.

The first part of our volume offered a selective interpretation of Christian tradition centered upon arguing for the cultivation of a *habitus* invested in moral formation, open to transcendence, and engaged in mission. We traced these ideas through Hellenism to show how it understood the cycle of studies in education as giving the child to the city by immersing the child in a program designed to heal the soul through formation in virtue. Grounded in the immortality of the soul and its connection to the divine, this program also sought to cultivate an openness to transcendence that ultimately might turn the person into a cosmic citizen. Such was the apotheosis promised in Hellenistic *paideia*. As part of this program, the student was "civilized" and "humanized," which meant that the student drank deeply from the *mythos* that embodied the cultural and historical rationale for the empire. *Humanitas* was, in fact, *Romanitas*. The cycle of studies, then, was a more or less elite enterprise designed to prepare students to contribute to the mission of Rome.

Early Christian writers recognized that education in the empire was an inculturating experience that transformed a child with a distinct ethnic and local background into a tool of Rome. It did so by offering a distinct narrative identity grounded in the *mythos* of the poets that Martianus Capella's work embodied. Over against this narrative identity, early Christians developed what we have called the story of God that redefined Christians as a distinct "race." In this way, early Christians retained the fundamental goal of education as cultivating a *habitus* centered upon moral formation and encounters with transcendence while reframing it in light of the story of God. Tertullian's famous question about Athens was in reality an incisive declaration that the mythic narrative offered by philosophers and poets could not sit with the Christian narrative of the story of God embodied in the rule of faith.

The Christian vision of education centered upon redefining moral formation as formation into the Word (*theopoesis*) through the sanctifying and charismatic activity of the Spirit. Because encountering the Word was a return to the one who created all things out of nothing, they redefined encounters with transcendence as eschatological interventions that prepared the person for the next life. Moral formation became conversion centered in the cultivation of piety and salutary teaching, and encounters with transcendence became ecstatic and charismatic ascent into the presence of the Word through the Spirit. Central to this program was the view that the Son was the Wisdom who governed the cosmos and the soul and who became flesh. The Spirit's graces saturated believers with gifts of wisdom, knowledge, and power so that they might recover the structure of rationality that, in its full realization, opened up a vision of Christ at the center of all. The eschatological vision of Christ was proleptically realized in ecstatic encounter. The liberal arts and philosophy served as a kind of propaedeutic to prepare the person for conversion and also as ongoing tools for those who knew how to use them for the sake of wisdom. Early Christians reclaimed the idea of education as inculcating a *habitus*, but this new disposition was nothing less than full formation into Christ so that they embodied Christ's piety and prophetic power, which was then used to engage in mission. This basic reworking of Hellenistic *paideia* established the parameters upon which scholasticism and Renaissance humanism built.

The Middle Ages and Renaissance built on early Christian commitments by constructing a program of learning designed to promote an integral humanism. In this program, the liberal arts became part of the ascent to God by helping humanity extract wisdom from creation in the service of moving from being to beautiful being. Meditation was the primary practice for reading and studying the two great books of creation and Scripture in the hope that the soul might take contemplative flight. The liberal arts helped the individual combat ignorance of the mind and vice in the will, while the mechanical arts helped the body deal with the curse of fallen existence. By the time of the Reformation, this program of ascent became wedded to a biblical humanism in which the flight to God came through the interpretation of the Scriptures as the place of faith. The liberal arts returned to the status of propaedeutic in the cultivation of a civic righteousness and as aids to the interpretation of Scripture. The question was whether they facilitated the ascent to God and internal righteousness or served as aids to facilitate the understanding of creation in the context of building a culture that advanced justice in the city.

At the dawn of the modern era, enlightenment thinkers in Germany were developing a new approach to the liberal arts grounded in self-cultivation (*Bildung*) and science (*Wissenschaft*). Stripping self-cultivation of its ground in Christian discourse, men like Goethe and Humboldt utilized it to refer to the process of self-discovery and realization through the pursuit of knowledge. As the hero, the scholar required the autonomy of academic freedom to engage in research and self-cultivation in the service of knowledge and its relationship to culture. The modern university must privilege academic freedom in terms of self-formation and pure research in its production of knowledge. The religious dimension was retained in the form of a spirituality whereby the soul tapped into the mysterious presence of the divine either as creation itself or within creation. For some thinkers this transcendent presence became the presence of the other. Through self-cultivation the individual engaged in moral formation and encountered transcendence, although the latter was slowly evacuated of doctrinal content and then religious content over the course of the nineteenth century.

What we have called the Romantic sensibility, then, was the fusion of divine immanence, intuitionism, and a progressivism that developed a liberal high culture in relationship to self-cultivation. It retained the basic paradigm of constructing a *habitus* invested in moral formation and open to encounter through making culture the primary mission. Self-cultivation and culture reinforced one another through the emphasis on the aesthetic dimension as the person encountered transcendence and formed the self through art and literature. This was the ground for the turn to Western civilization as advancing a recovery of great minds in the service of human development. Aesthetics became the new spirituality as various forms of pantheism, panentheism, and naturalism allowed for some version of the ecstatic embrace of the transcendent in wonder and awe.

The holiness and pentecostal movements participated in the Romantic sensibility through their emphasis on pneumatology as the expression of divine immanence, their focus on holiness as the best form of self-cultivation, their use of intuitionism to understand the encounter with transcendence, and their progressive populism in the service of transforming folk cultures. Nevertheless, it was the focus on progressive populism that prompted them to move toward the multipurpose college or the normal school as the best models of education. Training the laity and training the citizen were fused together so that education was not so much an elite enterprise of scholarly minds who pursued research to build a new culture as a utilitarian program that formed persons who transformed local cultures. Still, within this approach the basic paradigm of constructing a *habitus* invested in moral formation and open to transcendence for the sake of mission remained in place.

The secularization of education by elites in favor of the sacralization of a liberal culture prevented holiness and early pentecostal thinkers from fully recognizing the common elements in the Romantic sensibility. This led to an anti-intellectual impulse that was less a movement away from education or the use of the liberal arts and more a movement away from a specific approach to education deemed to be secular or worldly. Any educational model that evacuated the encounter with transcendence (anticonversionism) from the process of formation, advanced a rationalism connected to empiricism that denied rational intuitionism (antirationalism), or privileged high culture over populism and folk culture (antiembourgeoisement) was seen as advancing a formalism and institutionalism in line with secularizing trends.

Due to the push against forms of populism in the 1950s, anti-intellectualism became more about being against the interests of the elite and high culture than against the intellect. Intellect and interests were fused together in the 1950s and 1960s, which, according to men like Christopher Lasch, simply reinforced the elitism of the academy. This elitism had its own version in evangelicalism as the bias against populism and folk culture formed one side of the indictment of the evangelical mind while worldview formed the other side. Worldview replaced the self-cultivation of *Bildung* in the context of a research program that sought to advance knowledge and transform culture from the top down. This is how Reformed worldview thinking became part of confessionalism, with the new form of confession being the system of life that any particular worldview articulated. Rational intuitionism was viewed as a form of irrationality along the lines of Schleiermacher's emphasis on experience without even seeing how it functioned as a fusion of Common Sense philosophy and German idealism in men like Samuel Taylor Coleridge. For this reason, holiness and pentecostal adherents were part of the problem of the evangelical mind rather than its solution; and yet, as we have seen, there was a holiness and pentecostal approach to education that centered on head (rational intuitionism), heart (affective transformation), and hands (populist engagement with folk culture). This approach was a return to education as Christ-patterned and Spirit-infused in line with the emphasis on the cosmic Christ rather than the Christ of the confessions. It was a robust trinitarian vision of education.

Part 2 of this book thus built on these ecclesial and historical foundations, exploring the life of the mind in pneumatological perspective, teaching and learning in light of the sanctifying work of the Spirit, and higher educational service in light of Pentecost's eschatological dynamic. Encounter with others in the Spirit confronts us with truth, beauty, and goodness beyond ourselves. "Others"—not just persons but also texts, objects of study, fields of inquiry, etc.—both provide new perspectives and also challenge our sense of what is. "Others" invite curiosity, prompt wonder, and inspire imagination to experience the world and all there is afresh. "Others," in all their differences and particularities, urge us—sometimes obligate us: for instance, climate change!—to develop new ways to behave in and relate to the world. If Henry Tappan was a modernist who located the transcendentals in the innate ideas of the mind (§4.2), our claim is that "others" encountered via the Spirit both resonates with the ideals of our hearts but yet also extends before us as if limning the horizons at the edges of our known and continually-being-discovered world.

Yet charismatic encounter not only introduces us to otherness but through this also transforms our lives. As learners open themselves to the redemptive work of the triune God in the world, the Spirit renews our minds through the witness of others, continually leading us into the truth and conforming us to the mind of Christ. The media of life—we discussed film, music, and the gaming industry, but there are many others—become conduits for the Spirit to reorder our hearts, in the process purifying our loves, redirecting our affections, and beautifying our hopes. Finally, the Spirit revives the work of our hands, enabling us to love our neighbor as we love ourselves, and to care for the world that God has given to us. Hence, we have argued that the Christian university can be an environment for the sanctifying work of the Spirit wherein orthodoxy (right thinking and right worship), orthopathy (right feeling and desire), and orthopraxy (right behavior and actions) are nurtured simultaneously and together.

Last but not least, however, the many tongues of others achieve the sanctifying of our many lives but all in accordance with and oriented toward the coming rule of God inaugurated in the life and ministry of Jesus and in the outpouring of his Spirit upon all flesh. Our insistence throughout, however, is that the imminent reign of God does not cancel out the many voices—disciplinary, pedagogical, intersectional, intercultural, interreligious, etc.—but redeems them for divine purposes. Our faith is enriched through the many witnesses; our hope is inspired through the many visions of the beautiful; and our love is inflamed through the work of many others—within and outside the Christian university—for the common (terrestrial and cosmic) good. The mission of the Spirit invites all who are willing to "come" (Rev 22:17a), and Christian higher education's task is at least in part to equip believers to co-labor with others in response to the Spirit's invitation and anticipation of the divine rule to come.

The second part of this volume thus demonstrates the interrelationship between scholarship involving the mind, teaching and learning informed by the reordering of the heart, and service empowered by the reviving of the hands. Charismatic encounter, pneumatic sanctification, and Pentecost-teleology are interwoven with each domain. This means that the work of the Spirit pertains to the life of the mind as much as it does to the loves of the heart and the work of the hands.[1]

8.2 PENTECOSTALIZING CHRISTIAN HIGHER ADMINISTRATION: AN EXHORTATION

Although one of us has served decanally at both a decent-sized university-situated divinity school and a separate stand-alone theological seminary, we are not presumptive in this section and do not want to appear to be making (uninformed) demands of administrators at Christian universities. There are many things to think about at this level, and we certainly do not have the formal expertise, much less the space, to be comprehensive.[2] Yet our thesis throughout this book is about the many tongues of the Spirit and their capacities to renew minds, mold hearts, and inspire hands for the purposes of Christian higher education, and this itself begs for additional consideration for administrators who already feel pulled in so many directions (students-and-parents, other adult learners, alumni, donors, churches, the market at large, etc.). Hence, what might we now say not just to faculty colleagues but also to administrators and trustees so that the Christian university—rather than the multiversity—can live into the promise of Pentecost? We make three remarks regarding academic freedom (of course!), mission, and sustainability.

---

[1] Norma Cook Everist, *The Church as Learning Community: A Comprehensive Guide to Christian Education* (Nashville: Abingdon, 2002), argues using different but complementary categories: we learn through growing and serving.

[2] Mary Landon Darden, *Beyond 2020: Envisioning the Future of Universities in America* (Lanham: Rowman and Littlefield Education / American Council on Education, 2009), identifies many of the important issues, for those who want to read more widely.

We start (no surprise here!) with the many tongues of Pentecost and hereby reiterate that they cannot do their work on Christian university campuses unless their voices are allowed to resound. The Christian university ought to be a place where exploratory inquiry can proceed and where ideas can be freely discussed and processed. Christian university administrators hence should cultivate such spaces, perhaps via what Anthony Diekema, who served for two decades as president of Calvin College, calls a "socratic covenant" that promotes critical conversation and dialogue.[3] On the one hand, Christian scholars "need to protect both their discipline and their faith-based identity; and university administrations need to help them do it,"[4] so that student learners in these environments can learn by example about what it means to steer a *via media* between dogmatic indoctrination and relativistic secularism. As one scholar put it, "The church's role is primarily priestly; the college's role is primarily prophetic. The priests emphasize loving God with your heart; the prophets emphasize loving God with your mind."[5] Our contribution is the reminder that even if the notion of academic freedom has long been secularized by and within the modern university, there is an underlying theological (and pneumatological) principle related to the divine desire to redeem creation's many voices. In other words, academic freedom is to be prized and protected not just by secularists who wish to fend off (putatively) dogmatic religionists.

On the other hand, to be sure, there is no such thing as academic freedom in any absolute sense, since inquiry and conversation are situated and hence contested rather than existing only as ideal types.[6] So within the Christian context, freedom serves mission, in this case, to work toward the coming reign of God revealed in Jesus of Nazareth and heralded by the outpouring of his Spirit. Hence, all activities of the Christian university are to be so guided, including that related to considerations of academic freedom.[7] Leadership in Christian higher education thus must clearly understand institutional mission in relationship to the mission of God as without this connection, there is no point to self-identifying as *Christian* in any real sense. Yet a commitment to the *Christian* vision of the true, the good, and the beautiful itself frees up agency—of faculty, of learners, of staff, and of other constituencies within this broad domain—to discern how what they do works toward the shalomic justice of the coming divine rule.[8]

---

[3]   See Anthony J. Diekema, *Academic Freedom and Christian Scholarship* (Grand Rapids: Eerdmans, 2000), ch. 5.

[4]   Mark Hutchinson, "Third Race and Third Culture: Academic Freedom in Pentecostal Colleges; The View from Australia," *Asian Journal of Pentecostal Studies* 11.1–2 (2008): 45–68, at 59–60; originally published as "The Battle Hymn of the Republic of Learning," *Australasian Pentecostal Studies* 9 (2006), https://aps-journal.com/index.php/APS/article/view/84.

[5]   William C. Ringenberg, *The Christian College and the Meaning of Academic Freedom: Truth-Seeking in Community* (New York: Palgrave Macmillan, 2016), 173.

[6]   Alan Charles Kors and Harvey A. Silverglate, *The Shadow University: The Betrayal of Liberty on America's Campuses* (New York: Free Press, 1998), ch. 5, show that even political correctness, as important as that is in various contexts, is in liberal and secular university campuses a circumscription of certain freedoms of speech (e.g., those that contravene PC rhetoric).

[7]   See also Yong, *Renewing the Church by the Spirit: Theological Education after Pentecost*, Theological Education between the Times (Grand Rapids: Eerdmans, 2020), ch. 9.

[8]   The conclusion of Harry R. Lewis, *Excellence without a Soul: How a Great University Forgot Education* (New York: Perseus, 2006), 253–68, urges that educational success be missionally defined and forged.

Missional commitments guide not just exploratory inquiry but also every segment of the Christian university. In a time when institutions of higher learning are discovering that their operational models were based on structures developed and affordable two or more generations ago but are no longer sustainable today, the question is if and how Christian higher education can survive and be healthy in the late modern context. If none of us can do all that we might want to do (that is the recipe for financial failure),[9] then we must focus on what we should and must do, and this brings us back to the telos of the divine reign. Obviously, financial best practices must be adopted across the board. Our Pentecost-perspectives, however, prioritize the fostering of many voices within the Christian university. This relates therefore not as much to the expansion of programs and disciplines (which are fine if missionally funded) as to the multiplication of personnel to represent the full scope of the coming divine reign, and the diversification of funding sources for the myriad enterprises of research, teaching, and learning.[10]

But if the addition of faculty and staff from diverse backgrounds will contribute to the ethos and practice of the Christian university, the other side to this question involves the student body. The goal here cannot be to accept only those who can afford such an experience. Higher educational endeavors are already extremely elitist, so the Spirit's blowing to the ends of the earth means that the egalitarianism of the day of Pentecost must be embraced, that we have to find ways to welcome learners from as diverse a set of backgrounds as possible, since it is through connectivity—learner-to-learner—that iron sharpens iron, to use the biblical phrase (Prov 27:17a).[11] Some institutions devoted to maintaining a fairly exclusive residential model or constrained by topographic or zoning considerations may opt or be required to cap student enrollment, but our point is that expansion and growth of the student body should not to be driven by economics but by mission and philosophical and theological warrants, in this case related to enabling many voices to reverberate.[12]

Can a Pentecost-axiology galvanize support to make such an egalitarian and mission-ally driven intellectual life affordable? It is natural to worry that too many voices in any institution of higher education leads to fragmented (and fragmenting) incoherence (the multiversity keeps rearing its head). Our hope, however, is that to welcome the Spirit of Jesus is to empower men and women, young and old, the haves and the have nots, in pursuit of the life of the mind, the passions of the heart, and the resulting works of informed and impassioned hands. These many voices will check whatever sinful proclivities exist within our institutions (and they are there!) even as they will enhance the Christian witness to the *missio Dei*. Of course, none of this will happen overnight. Rome was not built

---

[9] See Jonathan A. Knee, *Class Clowns: How the Smartest Investors Lost Billions in Education* (New York: Columbia Business School, 2017), ch. 6.

[10] On the last point, see Clark Kerr, *The Uses of the University*, 3rd ed. (Cambridge, Mass.: Harvard University Press, 1982), 155.

[11] See Heinz-Dieter Meyer, Edward P. St. John, Maia Chankseliani, and Lina Uribe, eds., *Fairness in Access to Higher Education in a Global Perspective: Reconciling Excellence, Efficiency, and Justice* (Rotterdam: Sense, 2013).

[12] The outlier would be the for-profit Christian university, which we here do not address; for-profit models are discussed in Sheila Slaughter and Gary Rhoades, *Academic Capitalism and the New Economy: Markets, State, and Higher Education* (Baltimore: Johns Hopkins University Press, 2004).

in a day, and Christian universities also do not come down from out of heaven (only the New Jerusalem does that). Hence, Christian higher administrators are better off committed to the longer haul, consulting the many voices, drawing them into the mix, and empowering their speech (and acts), while discerning all along their faithfulness according to the norm of shalomic justice in the here and now.

8.3 PNEUMATIC ANTICIPATIONS— WHITHER CHRISTIAN HIGHER EDUCATION? A WAGER

Our desire is that Christian universities, starting with those in North America, can see the importance of asking about where the Holy Spirit might be present and active in the higher educational task. Our proposal has sought to be ecumenically informed— plumbing the depths of historic Christian tradition as well as being informed by the full scope of contemporary Christianity as a world religion—and as such intends not to displace other theocentric perspectives or even christological and incarnational models of higher learning, but to come alongside and, where possible, enable the further success of others inspired by the coming reign of God. If the basic thrust of the preceding were to be adopted and implemented, what difference would this pneumatological approach make? We chart three lines of responses to this question: academic, ecclesial, and political.[13]

First, our Pentecost-proposal is meant to renew the Christian university and, relatedly, to revitalize its role in the wider academy. Higher education is already convulsing through a multitude of disruptions amid and through which the modern university is being transformed.[14] And although Christian colleges and universities more often than not follow what is happening in the wider higher educational environment, might we also be able to innovate on our own terms in response to the present challenges? Fundamentally, this begins with facilitating a more robustly trinitarian vision for Christian higher education via development of the pneumatological and charismatic dimension. Our hope is that attentiveness to the person and work of the Spirit will spark imaginative scholarship, expand innovative teaching and learning, and empower creative witness and service within Christian initiatives of higher learning. In many respects, we believe that much of what we are advocating for is already to be found within Christian educational environments. We desire to make explicit the theological and pneumatological underpinnings for these educational activities and, by so doing, deepen the Christian character of what we might be doing anyway with other warrants.[15] More importantly, we do not want to forget this important truth: that whatever we might be doing vocationally in the higher educational sector can succeed only as aided by the Spirit. Yet this recognition means not

---

[13] These three Christian theological publics of society, church, and academy have become classic since formulated by David Tracy, *The Analogical Imagination: Christian Theology and the Culture of Pluralism* (New York: Crossroad, 1981), ch. 1.

[14] There are many models and accounts; one that holds together commitments to knowledge production and accessibility is Michael M. Crow and William B. Dabars, *The Fifth Wave: The Evolution of American Higher Education* (Baltimore: Johns Hopkins University Press, 2020).

[15] For instance, what Stanley Hauerwas and John H. Westerhoff, eds., *Schooling Christians: "Holy Experiments" in American Education* (Grand Rapids: Eerdmans, 1992), call "holy experiments" in Christian education even at the primary and secondary level anticipate what in our proposal goes by the *pentecostal* nomenclature.

that our work as scholars, researchers, and teachers is unimportant but that in all of these we are co-laborers with the Holy Spirit. In short, if successful, perhaps what we are doing here will enable greater perceptivity of the Spirit's presence and openness to how the one who raised Jesus from the dead might yet dynamically enliven our efforts across the many fronts at which we might be at work in the domain of academia.

Second, we believe that what we do as Spirit-led educators will be gifts to the people of God. What the church usually calls the *body of Christ*, our pneumatological imagination describes as the *fellowship of the Holy Spirit* (cf. 2 Cor 13:13). In today's postdenominational climate wherein our distinctive Christian traditions seem less and less important, our point is certainly not to promote any narrowly construed pentecostal or charismatic ecclesial identity in the current global landscape. At the same time, however, our goal very much is to ensure that what we are doing as Christian higher educators is consistent with and empowered by the work of the Holy Spirit. Only as such, we are convinced, will the potential of our contribution to the common good be achievable. So in effect we agree with this way of putting it, that the "church-related college can justify its distinctive educational mission by stressing its role in ensuring that its denomination's particular mode of discourse remain part of the wider cultural conversation. . . . [This] is a form of authority available to any institution that takes upon itself the purpose of articulating a distinctive and traditional voice in a pluralistic society"[16]—with one exception: that what is important is how to do not *denominational* but *Christian* higher education in the contemporary global and digital context. For this task, the empowering work of the Spirit is mandatory. To be filled with the Spirit, however, requires not just educational degrees and imprimaturs (although these are necessary) but also participation in the body of Christ and the fellowship of the Spirit. The Christian university can only be as strong as the church, effectively feeding off the vitality of the church. Yet the work of the Christian university also contributes to the church's renewal and revival. There is, in short, mutual and reciprocal relationship between the Christian church and the Christian university. They are not to be conflated but they are also not to be segregated. The former can go on without institutional forms of the latter but not without the work of inquiry, critical reflection, and discipleship that happens within its ranks.

Last but not least, we believe that what we do as Spirit-led educators has implications not only for the academy and the church but also for the polis. This assumes, assuredly, the moral, missional, and teleological frame that inspires the Christian contribution to the formation of global citizens.[17] But beyond this, it also believes that the Christian witness to the world is to be deeply informed by renewed minds and cultivated hearts, and vice-versa. Hence, the *vita activa* and the *vita contemplativa* are interrelated, neither subordinated to the other. The life of the mind is interconnected with the transformation of the heart and the activity of the hands. Christian mission and world-impacting and transforming witness emerge from out of the commitment to nurture the intellectual

---

[16]   Richard Kyte, "Conversation and Authority: A Tension in the Inheritance of the Church-Related College," in *Professing in the Postmodern Academy: Faculty and the Future of Church-Related Colleges*, ed. Stephen R. Haynes (Waco: Baylor University Press, 2002), 115–29, at 117–18.

[17]   Justin D. Cooper, "The Christian College Has a Public Mission," *Comment Magazine*, Fall 2011, 79–84, discusses preparing graduates for participation in the academy, but argues especially for leadership as citizens and for service in the community.

life, rather than on merely activistic dispositions. Put otherwise, without setting aside the time, energy, and effort to cultivate the life of the mind, the promise of the Christian ministry of the hands will remain unfulfilled. Our wager is that Christian mission, empowered by the Holy Spirit, presumes rather than bypasses scholarship, inquiry, and learning. This is not to mention that we will be able to provide further (theological) articulation for the witness we bear and embody in a broken world.

The Holy Spirit is the giver of many gifts. This book attempts to explicate some of these donations in and across Christian higher education. There is nothing spooky about invoking the presence and activity of the Spirit, as the preceding hopes to have shown. Yet at the same time, our wager is that by attending more purposefully to the Spirit poured out abundantly on the world, according to the day of Pentecost narrative, we will be caught up in the work of the triune God to redeem the many tongues of creation for divinely intended purposes. Come Holy Spirit, baptize the Christian college and university with a fresh Pentecost!

Index of Subjects and Authors

Index of Scripture

CPSIA information can be obtained
at www.ICGtesting.com
Printed in the USA
LVHW071133260423
745052LV00001B/1